MARX, DURKHEIM, WEBER

Formations of
Modern Social Thought

Second edition

Ken Morrison

Los Angeles • London • New Delhi • Singapore

First edition published 1995. Reprinted 1996, 1997, 1998, 2000, 2001
(twice), 2002, 2003 (twice), 2004, 2005
Second edition published 2006
Reprinted 2008

 SAGE Publications Ltd
1 Oliver's Yard
55 City Road
London EC1Y 1SP

SAGE Publications Inc.
2455 Teller Road
Thousand Oaks, California 91320

SAGE Publications India Pvt Ltd
B 1/I 1 Mohan Cooperative Industrial Area
Mathura Road
New Delhi 110 044

SAGE Publications Asia-Pacific Pte Ltd
33 Pekin Street #02-01
Far East Square
Singapore 048763

British Library Cataloguing in Publication data

A catalogue record for this book is available from the British Library

ISBN 978 0 7619 7055 2
ISBN 978 0 7619 7056 9 (pbk)

Library of Congress Control Number: 2005938439

Typeset by C&M Digitals (P) Ltd., Chennai, India
Printed in Great Britain by the Cromwell Press, Trowbridge, Wiltshire.
Printed on paper from sustainable resources

To the memory of my mother
Gertrude Morrison

Contents

Preface to the Second Edition

This edition of Marx, Durkheim, Weber differs from the first in several respects. I have given special consideration to extending the coverage of concepts and theoretical discussion that have generally been omitted or abbreviated by other commentators and traditions of commentary. In this case, many more concepts and more extended theoretical discussion have been provided that have not been treated by previous commentaries on classical theory. Also, attention has been given to expanding the story line of classical social theory beyond what was covered in the first edition.

This was necessary in the first place because of the overall retreat from classical knowledge that has taken place in social theory as a result of the opposition to classical thought that followed upon the postmodern movement. In the second place, it was necessary to extend the scope of theoretical discussion because of the overall development in the last two decades of the interdisciplinary movement in the University, which in many ways has blurred the lines of distinction between classical knowledge and postmodern theories of knowledge and has led, in some cases, to the disappearance of classical forms of knowledge altogether. In this edition, my intention was to bring back as much of the archive of classical knowledge as is possible in a global world, with its altered tolerances and its many dislocations. Third, much consideration was given to the overall choices related to how far to expand the discussion beyond what was covered in the first addition.

In the Marx chapter, for example, I have extended the coverage of concepts and added more theoretical discussion related to the history of social classes and the formation of society, and I have provided extended definitions of concepts such as social class, means of production, the materialist theory of history, relations of subordination and the concept of ideology. In addition to this, more context has been provided as a way of situating classical social theory and theoretical argument in its period. This has been done in the Marx chapter by providing more history on the shifting duration of the work day, the structure of the wage form, and the extended supervision of the worker as the means of production fell into private hands during the transition to the industrial period. Also, the sections on the theory of value, the commodity and commodity fetishism have all been expanded. This way, it is possible to see Marx as providing a theory of economic class formation and a theory of history over and against advocating revolution or communism, as some commentators have suggested. Also, issues and debates have been included where useful in the discussions related to controversies between structural theory and postmodernism in the Marx chapter, the intersections between rationalist philosophies and Durkheim's argument on the categories of understanding in *The Elementary Forms*, and the controversies generated by Weber's study of capitalism in *The Protestant Ethic*.

In the Durkheim chapter, several sections have been re-written and expanded. These include the sections on *The Division of Labor*, *The Rules of Sociological Method*, the study of suicide, and *The Elementary Forms of Religious Life*. The presentation of Durkheim has been much improved by providing a more extended account of the reception of Durkheim's work in France and in America, with an outline of the theoretical battles he had to wage against Gabriel Tarde to defend his view that social realities exist outside the individual, and the resistance he encountered to the study of suicide in America.

In the Weber chapter, much has been added by way of expanding Weber's discussion of the world religions and the relationship of religion to the rationalization process. In this respect many sections in the Weber chapter have been re-written, including the introductory section on religion and rationalization, the section on *The Protestant Ethic and The Spirit of Capitalism* and the section on social action and on rationality.

Acknowledgments

During the four years in which this book was written I have built up considerable debt and owe gratitude to many. I am indebted to Chris Rojek at Sage for encouraging me that a second edition of Marx, Durkheim, Weber would be worth writing. His advice on which direction to pursue in writing the second edition was invaluable and much appreciated. I would also like to thank Richard Christy and Garry Potter, both colleagues in the Department of Sociology at Wilfrid Laurier University, for their support and for the use they have found for this book in their own teaching. Among those I would also like to thank are Samuel Jedwab and Martin Fischer who gave me positive encouragement and much support; and Dorothy Smith whose work over these many years has been a positive influence. In addition, I would like to thank my wife Susan for her unconditional support during the years over which this book was written and for her tireless and good natured assistance with the editing process, not only on this book but on many other projects. To my son Frank, as always, thanks for encouraging me that a book of this sort was possible to write.

1

Introduction

The Origins and Foundations of Modern Social Theory: 1750–1920

Modern social theory first emerged during the period of the 'great transformation,' a term used by Karl Polanyi to describe the massive social change which took place in Europe between 1750 and 1920.[1] In practical terms, it is possible to outline some of the steps leading to these developments by looking at three geographical centers in European society: France, Germany and England. Generally, the story begins in France in the decade of the 1780s as France approaches the revolution. The French revolution of 1789 was one of the most decisive determinants leading to the development of a theory of society that was officially separate from philosophy. By the time the revolution had ended, it had delivered three distinct blows against society, history and politics. First, in asserting the reality of individual rights and freedoms, the revolution shook individuals in their political and social foundations. Second, the economic and political consequences of the revolution rocked the foundations of feudal society in its social and economic existence. Third, the political and social changes of the revolution shook the framework of philosophy in its inward looking and introspective existence. These blows to society, history, philosophy and politics set the stage for the development of an autonomous social theory by creating a division in philosophy along two distinct lines of development. In the first place, it necessitated a break with the philosophic tendency to look inward in favor of a direct encounter with reality and history. As Herbert Marcuse points out, this tended to bring philosophy into the sphere of history.[2] In the second place, all of the philosophical concepts which had been preoccupied with abstraction began to pattern themselves after social and historical content. By 1800, social and historical concepts had been brought more fully into the sphere of philosophy and these came fundamentally to rest in the subject matter of society and history. This had a profound effect on the development of social theory since all of the economic and political theorizing which had been packed into the philosophic mind since Plato and Aristotle had become externally manifest in the social and historical world as a consequence of the revolution in France.

---

1 Karl Polanyi, *The Great Transformation: The Political and Economic Origins of our Time*, Boston: Beacon Press, 1944.

2 Herbert Marcuse, *Reason and Revolution*, New York: Humanities Press, 1954, p. 253.

By 1810, the impact of historical development on philosophy was fully realized in the work of Georg Hegel. It was Hegel who, in 1806, responded to the events of the French Revolution in his writings and, despite its philosophic language, his works were extremely forward looking in their focus on society and history. Hegel's response to the revolution not only changed philosophy and history, it also led to the development of an autonomous social theory distinct from philosophy itself.[3] Hegel brought this about in several ways. First, he took the view that the French revolution fundamentally changed the way thought understood reality and history. Previously, history had been seen as fixed in its political and social existence. The rapid decline of French society after the revolution led Hegel to observe that one form of social and political existence was replacing another and this led to the view that society itself changes from one form to another. This made it clear that economy and politics were obviously linked to society and history, a point which had not been stated in precisely this way before. It was Hegel, therefore, who was the first to understand that historical change took a social form and that this manifested itself in terms of a set of distinct stages of development from ancient, feudal and industrial societies.[4] Second, in showing a direct line of political development from slavery to the modern state, Hegel was able to make political functions the focus of social and historical development. This step made it clear that philosophy could only understand history by adopting social concepts and that history was, in fact, social in nature. Third, Hegel's philosophy was forward looking in its focus on individual freedom and self realization. In making the individual part of historical development, Hegel was one of the first to make individual experience the subject matter of historical and social analysis, a step which became more fully developed in the writings of Marx.[5] Fourth, to the extent that Hegel believed that history was marked by distinct stages of development, he was the first to conceptualize the different stages of society as distinct social forms which followed a pattern of social and historical development. In addition, all these social forms, according to Hegel, represented actual ways of thinking and being which could be separately studied by looking at the social and political characteristics of a given society.[6]

By 1844–45, many of the developments in Hegel's philosophy began to be consolidated in the writings of Marx and Engels and, as a result, the philosophical and historical concepts changed once again. With Marx and Engels, the critical elements of Hegel's philosophy began to turn more distinctly into social theory. But, where Hegel

---

3 Hegel, in this regard, was the first to identify social subject matter as distinct from the subject matter of history and philosophy. See *The Philosophy of History*, New York: Dover, [1830] 1956, chapters 1–5.

4 Until this time, the concept of 'society' did not exist in classical knowledge. Durkheim confirms this in his inaugural lecture of 1888 when he states that, while there was no absence of discussion of 'society' in the ancient world, 'the greater part of the works of ancient philosophy were dominated by ideas that prevented the social sciences from being formed'. See E. Durkheim, 'Inaugural Lecture at Bordeaux' (1887–8) *Sociological Inquiry*, 44, 1974, 189–204.

5 J.N. Findlay, *Hegel: A Re-Examination*, London: George Allen & Unwin, 1968.

6 For a discussion of the steps which Hegel took to conceptualize society beyond the enlightenment thinkers see *The Philosophy of History*, New York: Dover, [1830] 1956.

had used philosophic concepts, Marx used economic and social concepts to explain historical development.[7] Where the French revolution had shaped Hegel's historical perspective, it was the economic and industrial changes in England which shaped Marx's and Engels' thinking. Where Hegel had absorbed society and history into philosophy, Marx was absorbing philosophy into history and economy and this led to the use of distinct economic concepts to understand society and social existence. This shift from philosophy to economy necessitated the second critical transition of philosophic concepts to the sphere of political economy and the study of industrial capitalism.

Parallel to these developments, large scale social changes were taking place in Europe and in England, and these occurred on several different fronts. First, by 1830 industrial capitalism had replaced the old feudal economies of the preceding period and Adam Smith had laid the foundations for the first study of capitalism, making him the founder of modern political economy. Second, the mechanical discoveries necessary for industrial production had made England the 'workshop of the world' and therefore an industrial center. This began to dissolve the old agrarian economy of the countryside and led to rapid developments in commerce, science and industry. As a result, agricultural land began to be used for commercial purposes and land-holders began to evict tenant cultivators from their agricultural holdings, leaving them without the means of economic livelihood. This not only set in motion a period where property in land began to be privatized, but it also began an extensive transfer of the rural population from the countryside to the industrial centers, where they became an impoverished class and a problem population. Third, economic changes occurring in land and labor necessitated the rise of a new working class of wage laborers who were forcibly separated from the land as a primary means of economic survival.[8] At this stage, the migration of philosophic concepts into history and social theory had become more complete and, by the time Marx had published *Capital* in 1867, social and historical concepts were more fully incorporated into social thought and began to form the first theories of society.

In France, there were similar developments. At the time, French social thought was being shaped by thinkers such as Saint-Simon (1760–1825), Auguste Comte (1798–1857) and Emile Durkheim (1858–1917) who were grappling with the themes of revolution, social progress and industrial change. Comte and Durkheim, for their part, founded a school of social theory which was largely shaped by the themes of science, by a conservative response to the French revolution and by a rejection of philosophy as a basis of social inquiry. By 1830, an important step was taken with the appearance of Comte's *Positive Philosophy*.[9] For his part, Comte had described the age primarily in terms of the development of the scientific method which he wanted

---

7 Marcuse, *Reason and Revolution,* pp. 251–257.

8 For an account of this period see Maurice Dobb, *Studies in the Development of Capitalism,* New York: Basic Books, 1947.

9 Auguste Comte, *Cours de Philosophie Positive*, Paris: Bachelier, 1830–1842.

to extend to the study of society.[10] In France, this began a period of reaction against speculative philosophy, culminating in the work of Durkheim who wanted to found a scientific theory of society. With the publication of such works as *The Division of Labor* in 1893 and *Suicide* in 1897, Durkheim began to differentiate himself from Comte's theory of society, essentially by conceiving of society as a structure of social elements existing outside the individual. This led Durkheim to turn his attention to the study of what he called 'the two great currents of social life' which he thought had formed 'two distinct types of structure'.[11] This made Durkheim the first to identify the study of 'structure' as the single solitary subject matter of social theory, and as a result structural concepts began to be more formally incorporated into the study of society.

By 1905, with the publication of works such as Marx's *German Ideology* and *Capital*, Emile Durkheim's *The Division of Labor* and *Suicide,* and Max Weber's *The Protestant Ethic and the Spirit of Capitalism*, a body of knowledge was formed and a common perspective emerged which began to define social thought separately from historical thought, leading to a perspective referred to as structural theory. Based on the works of Marx, Durkheim and Weber, structural theory is the name used to describe a family of perspectives in social thought which use specific techniques of interpretation for studying history, human nature and society and, in the main, it gets its name from the tendency to conceptualize society as a structure of social fields which exist outside the individual. The central idea is that these structures first constitute themselves as diverse social fields, which include the economy, the political structure, the family system and the field of law and religion. These social fields were thought to structure social activity, impose external limits on action and compel individuals to act in ways which often override their personal considerations and their private will. The tendency to conceive of society as a structure of social fields existing outside the individual and as having the power to structure social interchanges, led to a third transition in the development of social thought which changed the concepts once again. With Durkheim's assertion that social thought was separable from philosophy, and that the structure of society was separable from the structure of history, it meant that all the philosophic and critical language of Hegel and Marx was to be converted into investigative concepts and into an investigative language for identifying elements of structure which were thought to exist outside the individual.

It was therefore Durkheim who had discovered a distinct subject matter which owed nothing to the already constituted disciplines of philosophy, psychology or history. Durkheim, in fact, was the first to identify the external structure of society by outlining a system of duties and obligations lying outside the individual that

---

10 D.G. Charlton, *Positive Thought in France*, London: Verso, 1979; W.M. Simon, *European Positivism in the Nineteenth Century*, New York: Cornell, 1963.

11 See Durkheim, *The Division of Labor in Society*, p. 229. Some commentators take the view that Durkheim conceived of society as a unified organic whole whose parts function in organic-like interrelationships. However, by the time Durkheim had written *The Division of Labor*, he had broken with this view after criticizing Spencer's contention that social differentiation was related to the organic traits of society.

constituted a new subject matter 'to which the term social was to be applied'.[12] Durkheim's structuralist language had for the first time asserted the existence of a field of social activity lying beyond the individual, and this led to a more systematic study of the structure of society as a field of investigation. As a result, observation, description and classification replaced the search for historical laws and the underlying themes of economic development that had been established by Marx.

In Germany, the work of Max Weber (1864–1920) represented a fourth shift in the direction of modern social theory. Though he was born in 1864, Weber did not write his first theoretical work until 1903 when he published his first formal theory of capitalism. By this time, Weber's overall theory of economic organization had established the study of capitalism as a central focus of modern social theory.[13] In contrast to Marx, who focused on the economic changes of the early nineteenth century, Weber's theoretical work was largely in response to the themes of late modern society which focused on the direction of historical change and civilization processes taking place in the West. Later, this led to a series of broad historical works on ancient economies, feudalism, bureaucracy, household organization, the formation of rational law and the history of world religions.

In looking at society from the perspective of what he called the overlapping social spheres of religion, economy, politics and law, Weber was among the first to assert that a theory of society could be obtained only by looking at the causal influences of various social spheres, which he conceived of as forming different 'departments of life'. Rather than restricting his analysis to the economic sphere, as Marx had done, Weber focused on the affects of the religious sphere on the economic and political spheres. Weber, in fact, develops the concept of the 'social sphere' into a methodological tool, which he used to study the legal and political influences leading to the formation of modern social classes and the specific influences of the religious sphere on the development of capitalism and the formation of the modern economy. This made Weber one of the first to challenge Marx's theory of capitalism and to question his claim about the role played by economic forces in social and historical development.[14]

The fundamental insight by Weber that society could not be understood without looking at the role played by the overlapping social and institutional spheres cannot be overestimated. He thought the political, economic, religious and legal spheres of society defined the nature of social life in the changes occurring after the period described by Marx in the nineteenth century. This led him to look at the underlying conditions leading to the formation of the modern household as it became separate from the sphere of

---

12 Durkheim, *The Rules of Sociological Method*, pp. 1–2.

13 Weber put forward two theories of capitalism. First was *The Protestant Ethic and Spirit of Capitalism*, New York: Scribner, 1958; second was his *General Economic History*, New York: Collier, 1961.

14 Weber's analysis of religion and its effects on the formation of an economic ethic can be contrasted with Marx's theory of society as a succession of economic epochs. Weber's opposition to Marx's theory of history can be found in the first three chapters of *The Protestant Ethic*, where he outlines the effect of a religious ethic on an economic ethic.

work, and to examine the changes taking place in the modern class system, the formation of status groups, the function of statute law and the overall formation of modern economies.[15] Subsequently, Weber's comparison of modern economies with ancient and feudal economies led him to identify patterns of development as diverse as the social activity resulting from the adoption of Roman law in the West, to the technical utilization of scientific knowledge for purposes of the rational mastery over reality.

In addition to this was Weber's methodological innovations and the role they played in the development of the social sciences. In contrast to Marx or Durkheim, Weber challenged the validity of adopting a straightforward scientific view of society that was modeled on the methods of the natural sciences. It was within this framework that Weber put forward a general theory of social action, which he outlined in a work entitled *Economy and Society*, and it was this that established his difference from Durkheim. Whereas Durkheim had explicitly focused on trying to found a method of investigation which broke with speculative philosophy by adopting scientific positivism, Weber questioned the necessity of adopting the methods of the natural sciences in the context of the social sciences. In his methodological essays, Weber drew on what he thought was the necessary distinction between the subject matter of the social sciences and the subject matter of the natural sciences, and this led him to focus on human 'social acts' which he thought were fundamentally distinct from physical 'acts' in nature. This led Weber to believe that 'evaluation' and 'judgment' underlie human social acts and this led him to pursue the dimension of human 'inner states' by propounding a theory of interpretive social action.

To the extent that Weber's theory of social action called Durkheim's focus on external social facts and restraint into question, the concepts changed once again. Weber's stress on the role played by 'judgment' and 'evaluation' in human social action shifted the investigative focus from the external social rules and 'outer states' described by Durkheim to the 'inner states' of actors and the necessity of integrating human inner states into a theory of society.

Modern Social Theory Defined

The term modern social theory grew out of the framework of European social thought beginning in the nineteenth century, and began to take shape in a more definitive form with the transition to modern times, the growth of industrialized economies, modern political systems and the development of social thought proper.[16] Modern social theory therefore formed as a discipline by undertaking the study of the changes that were taking place in the structure of social institutions during the transition from

---

15 Weber's discussion of these themes is evident in his writings on economic organization, where he describes developmemnts in modern economies after Marx.

16 It was these themes that formed the distinct subject matter of social theory and identified a domain whose field of activity was distinct from 'historical' subject matter.

feudal to industrial society.[17] As a formal response to the changes of modernism, the writings of Marx, Durkheim and Weber led to the development of large-scale explanatory perspectives on society and history and to the formation of theories of society and its objective structure. Social theory, therefore, came into being on the basis of three broad areas of investigation. First was the focus on the description of societies past and present and their historical development. In itself, this took the form of a historical comparison between different kinds of societies, including the forms of political authority, the means of economic production, the development of legal rules, the forms of religious belief, the role played by large-scale social institutions, the growth of individualism and the development of modern capitalism. This focus took the form of accumulating factual knowledge of different societies and endeavored to understand their social, political and economic organization by a comparison of the system of social relations, the patterns of historical formation, the form of the class structure and the mode of collective and economic organization.[18] With the general focus on structure, it was possible to classify different societies along the lines of their different structural characteristics as well as looking at which institutions were dominant during a given period of history. It was this interest which led Marx, Durkheim and Weber to pursue a comparison of the different economies, the different forms of household organization, the different forms of administration, the different manifestations of the class structure, the different religious doctrines and the differences existing in the suicide characteristics of diverse societies.

A second broad area of investigation to emerge in social theory relates to the way of looking at society and history. This focus deals primarily with the explanatory framework of social theory and its underlying foundation in the history of social thought. It was this latter focus that established the formal connection between theory and society and, for all practical purposes, it was based on three interrelated assumptions about society. First, was the belief that underlying the factual world of everyday experience is a system of values, standards, ethics and politics which derive from societies in the past and which act as common conditions of action in the present. These social and political values, so to speak, form the underlying basis of society and act as common conditions of human social action. Second, was the belief that, since values and standards often manifest themselves in a system of politics and ethics, the formal assumption was that they may be employed to describe societies past and present, and to look for underlying patterns of development and the effects of this development on human social groups. Third, was the view which held that, since all human experience was in some way related to the social world, a theory of

---

17 By 1890, the study of the transition from feudal society to industrial society appeared in two central sociological works: Marx's study of the transition from feudal to industrial society in *The German Ideology*, and in Weber's discussion of the different forms of political domination in *Economy and Society*.

18 Marx's *German Ideology* and Durkheim's *The Division of Labor* were among the first nineteenth century works to form bodies of knowledge about the organization of different economies, the different systems of social relations and the different structural characteristics of society.

society could not be divorced from a theory of politics, economics, ethics and religion. Under these circumstances, these 'social things' formed a class of events which were distinct from 'physical things' and these things were to be studied in their own right, forming a body of knowledge separate from the knowledge of the physical or natural world. At this point, the central purpose of social theory was to separate 'social things' from 'physical things', and to form a theory about how these social things form themselves into patterns of social action and into the total structure of society.

A third broad area of investigation to emerge in social theory relates to describing the way in which the values and standards which have existed in the social and historical past come to act on us in the present.[19] That is, to the extent that the social practices, duties, obligations and system of social relations imply an existence outside ourselves in the form of a social framework, one of the interests Marx, Durkheim and Weber had was to show how the network of these practices and social obligations form themselves into total societies and patterns of action which often come to override our own personal choices and private discretions.

This takes us directly to the question of the central subject matter of social theory. Generally, the subject matter of social theory encompasses three broad dimensions of social change and development: first are the political changes brought about by the French Revolution and the shift taking place in the feudal dynamic; second are the economic changes leading to the growth of modern industrial economies and the emergence of capitalism in England; third is the development of industrialization and individualism.

The Central Subject Matter of Social Theory

1 Political Change, the Feudal Dynamic and the Revolution in France

The events leading to the French revolution began to be shaped in the decade of the 1780s and came to a turbulent conclusion in July and August of 1789. By 1791, a whole way of political and economic life had been replaced by new social and political conditions. In order to understand these developments, it will be necessary to look more closely at the social and political changes which took place in France in the context of the feudal dynamic in the last half of the eighteenth century.

In the eighteenth century, France was largely a feudal society. Feudal societies originated in the countryside with settled agriculture and landholding, and it was this overall structure which gave the unmistakable stamp to feudal societies as distinct from the societies of antiquity. In order to understand why the feudal dynamic was

---

19 Sheldon Wolin, *Politics and Vision: Continuity and Innovation in Western Political Thought*, Boston: Little Brown, 1960.

so important to the social and political changes taking place at the time, it will be worthwhile to outline the structure of feudal society more generally.

The history of feudal societies began in the countryside with agriculture and landholding and the absence of towns and cities. Feudalism and feudal economies may be defined as a system of land holding that was entirely rural and, in the main, had two key structural characteristics: an agricultural economy geared to the production of a food supply, and a system of social relations centering on class distinctions between the landholder and the serf cultivator. Historically, feudal societies have appeared in diverse forms with different patterns of social and historical development and are found in Asia and India and in other regions of the East. In fact, the main characteristics of feudal societies – agricultural economies, rigid class or caste structure and relations of subordination centering on the landholder and the peasant cultivator – have appeared in various forms throughout history.[20] In England and France, the feudal way of life began during the ninth century and comprised a total way of economic and political life by the end of the tenth century. The feudal economy was entirely rural, land was used solely for agricultural purposes, and there was a complete absence of towns and town life.[21] Based principally on the allotment of large parcels of land to a political aristocracy, feudal estates were made up of autonomous political and legal jurisdictions and were managed by an aristocratic class who used land as a source of economic livelihood. The principle activity of the feudal estate was thus confined to agricultural production, and in this sense feudal estates were politically and legally autonomous and comprised a total way of life, including parish, village and various branches of rural economy.[22]

At the center of feudal society was the production of a food supply, a production highlighted by a system of land holding based on social relations of subordination between the landholder and the serf. Serfs occupied agricultural holdings comprised of small undertakings in which they cultivated land and produced their economic livelihoods. While the landholder was the legal and political head of the feudal estate, a complex system of obligations and customary rights linked the peasant to the lord.[23] Among these, five distinct social characteristics stand out. First, was a series of economic obligations imposed upon the serf by the lord, and chief among these were the corvée system of labor rights.[24] The corvée right, which was so central to the feudal

---

20 On the history of Indian agricultural economies see Irfan Habib, 'Economic History of the Delhi Sultanate: An Essay in Interpretation,' *Indian Historical Review*, 4, 2, 1978, 287–303; and R. S. Sharma, *Indian Feudalism*: c 300–1200, Calcutta: University of Calcutta, 1965.

21 Georges Duby, *Rural Economy and Country Life in the Medieval West*. Columbia, S.C.: University of South Carolina Press, 1968, pp. 5–11.

22 Perry Anderson, *Passages From Antiquity to Feudalism*. London: Verso, 1978.

23 Ibid., pp. 182–196.

24 Georges Duby, *Rural Economy and Country Life*, pp. 39–42.

economy, goes back as far as Roman law and can be defined as a legal privilege of the landholder to compel or requisition work from a serf or a slave and to specify the form and the amount of labor to be provided. Corvée rights allowed landholders to compel forced unpaid labor service from the serf, either in the form of work on the lord's agricultural holdings or labor within the manor. On average, labor service could amount to one week in four. Under these circumstances, serfs were the direct producers of physical labor, and while serfs produced for the landholder, the landholder did not produce for the serf.[25]

Second, serfs were legitimately subordinated to the lord through a system of legal and social distinctions derived from the class divisions of feudal society. While resting formally on physical coercion, the subordination of the serf was mediated by a complex system of prerogatives and obligations supported by political, legal and religious distinctions based on the social position of the landholder. In many respects, the social relation between the lord and serf duplicated the coercive mechanism of slavery, even though the social fabric of feudal society was such as to link individuals by obligation and customary right.[26]

A third characteristic of feudal society was the right of the landholder to obtain control over the agricultural production of the serf. In this case, landholders were able to take as much as half of the serf's agricultural production, which was surrendered to the lord on a regular basis and which appeared in the form of economic levies imposed on the serf by the lord. The social and economic advantage given to the landholder meant that, while the serf provided agricultural production for the lord, the lord did not provide agricultural production for the serf. A fourth characteristic of feudal society was the right of the landholder to impose a system of economic exactions on the serf.[27] In many instances the exactions took the form of taxes, dues and fees levied on the peasant population. In some cases, they manifested themselves in the form of levies imposed upon the serf for the use of the lord's milling facilities, or for purposes of grinding corn and for the use of presses related to wine production.[28] In other cases a system of exactions, usually rendered in the form of labor service, existed in the form of rent, dues and taxes payable by the serf to the lord. In still other instances economic

---

25 While the landlord system seems to be duplicated in the East in the Indian village communities, the exact formation of the system of subordination and the class of intermediaries and their political and economic powers is a matter of debate. See Irfan Habib, 'Classifying Pre-Colonial India,' *Journal of Peasant Studies*, 12, 1985, 44–53; Marx, 'British Rule In India,' in R. Tucker, *The Marx-Engels Reader*, Second Ed., pp. 653–58; and H. Fukazawa 'A Note on the Corvée System in the Eighteenth Century Maratha Kingdom,' *Science and Human Progress*, Bombay, 1974, pp. 117–30.

26 Alexis De Tocqueville, *The Old Regime and the French Revolution,* New York: Anchor Books, [1856] 1955.

27 Anderson, *Passages from Antiquity to Feudalism*, p.193; and Albert Soboul, The French Revolution 1787–1799. Vol. 1. London: NLB, 1974, pp. 33–67.

28 This is discussed by Stephen Marglin, in 'What Do Bosses Do? The Origins and Functions of Hierarchy in Capitalist Production,' *Review of Radical Political Economy*, 6, 2, 1974, 33–60.

exactions took the form of the right of the lord to control the agricultural production of the serf.

A fifth characteristic of feudal society was the tendency to develop a fixed social hierarchy and a system of social and class distinctions which were backed up by legal and religious sanctions. While wide variations existed within the social structure of the manor and between the lord and the serf, the social distinctions existing in the class structure of feudal society defined not only the relations of dominance and subordination between the classes, but they also defined a complex system of obligations existing between the lord's household and the serf's. These obligations were often defined outside the specific duties of the corvée right and assigned to individual serfs who were responsible for specific tasks performed on the lord's holdings during certain times of the year. Still other obligations and restrictions existed when serfs performed corvée labor at remote locations for extended periods of time. Other duties were imposed on serfs who owed a fixed number of corvée labor days to the lord during certain seasons and who were required to carry out corvée labor on the lord's holdings.[30] In addition, other serfs were obligated to work smaller holdings and pay ground rent by surrendering part of their agricultural production, while others were required to take fire wood and food stuff directly to the manor.

In the years preceding the revolution, France retained the political and economic characteristics of a feudal society: rigid social hierarchy, social and economic inequality, a system of economic exactions and mandatory unpaid corvée labor. By 1780, France had begun to show signs of economic distress and, in the years preceding the revolution, tenant cultivators found it difficult to maintain their livelihoods while paying excessive dues and taxes. Eventually, poor crops, rising prices and economic mismanagement led to a crisis, calling for economic and political reform. As the crisis deepened, demands for reform became more urgent and antagonism between the peasants and the aristocracy grew. By 1787, members of the middle classes began to form a revolutionary committee, which drew up a set of demands which were submitted to the central authority of the French state called the Estates General, a three hundred year old political body comprised of the three main orders of society, the aristocracy, clergy and the peasants.[31] The demands, or grievances as they were called, became the central political focus of reform and received extraordinary philosophical sanction by upholding human rights, equality and liberty.

The Fall of Feudalism and the Elimination of Social Distinctions   By May of 1789, the Revolutionary Committee challenged the authority of the king and, in

---

29 See Duby, *Rural Economy and Country Life*, pp. 56–8.

30 Ibid, p. 40.

31 Georges Lefebvre, *The French Revolution From its Origins to 1793*, London: Routledge, 1962.

response, the king called a meeting of the Estates General, hoping that the aristocracy and clergy would outvote the peasants and avoid a crisis. But, by the time the Estates General had assembled, the loyalties of the clergy had shifted in support of the peasants and, shortly after, a turbulent debate broke out over voting procedure. On June 17, 1789, the Third Estate split off from the Estates General, proclaiming a new political body called the National Assembly.[32] On June 27 the king backed down from the confrontation, leaving the National Assembly as the dominant party of social and political reform. Between June and July of 1789, riots swept France and troops appeared in Paris. By the time an armed mob had stormed a military garrison at the outskirts of the city called the Bastille in July of 1789, the revolution had become a political reality.

Shortly after these events, the National Assembly drafted the 'Declaration of the Rights of Man,' which was a central political document defining human rights and setting out demands for reform. The political rights and freedoms proclaimed by the 'Declaration' were so wide-ranging in their human emancipation that it set the standard for social and political thinking, and formed the central rallying point of the revolution. The 'Declaration' stated at the outset that all human beings were born free and equal in their political rights, regardless of their class position, and this proceeded to set up a system of constitutional principles based on liberty, security and resistance to oppression. With philosophical authority, the 'Declaration' proclaimed that all individuals had the prerogative to exercise their 'natural right' and that the law rather than the monarch was the expression of the common interest.[33] This led to the elimination of all social distinctions on the one hand, and the right to resist oppression on the other.

By August the National Assembly began to deal directly with political and legal reforms, first by eliminating feudal dues and corvée privileges and then by abolishing serfdom. Second, by compelling the church to give up the right to tithes, the National Assembly altered the authority and class position of the clergy. Third, in declaring that 'all citizens, without distinction, can be admitted to ecclesiastical, civil and military posts and dignities,' it proclaimed an end to all feudal social distinctions.

As the criticism of social and political inequalities spread throughout society, there was a widespread critique of economic inequality altogether and this led to putting into question all other forms of subordination. With this came the idea that human beings, without distinctions, were the bearers of natural rights – a concept which had a corrosive effect on all other forms of inequality. Finally, from the assertions inherent in the 'Declarations of Rights,' a new category of social person came into being which came fundamentally to rest in the concept of the 'citizen,' whose social and political rights were brought within the framework of the state.

As the political changes began to take effect, there were abrupt social changes in the form of altered politics and in the form of the political reorganization of the feudal way of life. This brought with it two central historical shifts. First, it

32 Soboul, *The French Revolution 1787–1799.*
33 Lefebvre, *The French Revolution from its Origins to 1793.*

transformed the existing class structure of feudal society and led to the decline of class privilege and a change in the relations of subordination which had existed up until that time. Second, it set loose political and legal reforms which brought about a change from a political aristocracy based on sovereign authority to a democratic republic based on the rights of the citizen.[34]

2 Economic Changes and the Development of Capitalism

Another dimension of change was the wide-sweeping economic development of the eighteenth and nineteenth centuries. Though largely confined to England and the rural economy in the early stages, economic change eventually spread throughout Europe and transformed the economic and political structure of society. As a result, there was large scale social disruption, leading to a total transformation in the way people lived, how they earned their livelihoods and in the way they had labored. At first, the economic changes came in the form of wide-sweeping social transformations. Then they began to manifest themselves in the form of the introduction of an industrial economy, the centering of economic life in cities and the growth of industrial capitalism. This was a period of the most far reaching political, social and economic upheaval and, taken collectively, it fragmented social life, segmented social institutions, accelerated social crises and differentiated peoples and collectivities. While change was occurring at all levels of society, the center of this change was in the economic system, and this eventually led to the transition from feudalism to capitalism. In order to understand the impact of these changes, it is important that we look more closely at the structure of the feudal economy in England in the period before these changes took place.

Earlier, we used the term feudalism to refer to a period of social and economic organization defined by the formation of self sufficient feudal estates which were economically and political autonomous. Landholders drew their social and political powers from links to an aristocratic class, whose rights centered on land holding and economic prerogatives in which landholders had powers over tenant serfs. Based on landholding, the feudal way of life involved large bodies of land used primarily for purposes of agricultural production and these formed independent economies, with class distinctions and relations of subordination between landholders and serfs based largely on the corvée right.[35]

In the early stages of feudal society the rural way of life was universal, there was an absence of towns and the production of a food supply dominated everyday life.[36] Serf cultivators labored on their own agricultural holdings to satisfy their economic needs and performed unpaid labor service on the lord's estate in accordance with the

---

34 For the changes taking place in the class system after the revolution see Perry Anderson, *Lineages of the Absolute State*, pp. 85–112.

35 Georges Duby, *Rural Economy and Country Life*, pp. 28–54; Anderson, *Passages from Antiquity to Feudalism*, pp. 16–22.

36 R.H. Hilton, *The English Peasantry in the Later Middle Ages*, Oxford: Clarendon, 1975; and *The Transition from Feudalism to Capitalism*, London: NLB Humanities Press, 1976, pp. 9–30.

corvée right. While landholders held jurisdiction over the land and assumed entitlements, it is important to note that they did not own land outright as private property. In the place of private property was an elaborate system of customary obligations linking individuals to each other and to the land. Within the scope of these rights existed distinctions in the kinds and uses of land. First were estate lands, which included the lord's agricultural holdings.[37] Second were the distinctions in arable land called 'open fields,' which were directly used by serfs for agricultural purposes to produce crops and provide economic livelihood. Third was the distinction in land referred to as 'common fields', which was a term used to refer to lands on which no tenant claim existed, but which were generally used for purposes of grazing domestic animals. In exchange for the use of land, serfs were obligated to pay 'labor rent,' which existed as an entitlement of the lord to place a claim upon the serf payable in the form of labor service on the lord's holdings.

By the middle of sixteenth century, however, economic changes began to have an impact on the feudal economy as a whole, and these manifested themselves in the form of four broad dimensions of change. First was the transformation created by the enclosure movement and the demographic transfer of the agricultural population from the rural economy to the economies of industry. Second was the shift to the town economies which began to replace the feudal economies of the countryside and to facilitate capitalist development. Third was the transformation which followed upon the decline of the power of the trade guilds, which up until that time had contained capitalist expansion. Fourth was the change which occurred at the level of the management of the 'dangerous classes' and the problem population who began to form in the industrial centers as cities became the center of economic life and as the conditions of labor and the structure of the workday began to harden. Since no complete understanding of the scale of this change is possible without further examination, let us look more closely.

Depopulation, the Enclosure Movement and the Demographic Transfer of the Population   The first sign of industrial change manifested itself in England in the form of land enclosures which began to occur in the rural economy as early as 1560, when landholders began to assert rights of private property over feudal land. Essentially, the enclosure movement can be described as a system whereby tenant holdings in feudal land and agriculture became enclosed and made available for the private use of the landholder.[38] As a result, peasant families were evicted from their holdings and in many cases thrown off the land. While many of the first enclosures were initiated by landlords in order to appropriate tenant holdings, in the latter stages of change they were used to make way for sheep pastures. However, by 1710 the first Enclosure

---

37 Eric Kerridge, *The Agricultural Revolution,* New York: Augustus Kelly, 1968.

38 See A.E. Bland, P.A. Brown, and R.H. Tawney (eds.), *English Economic History: Select Documents*, London: Bell & Sons, 1925; William Lazonick, 'Karl Marx and Enclosures in England,' *Review of Radical Political Economics,* Vol. 6, 2, 1974, 1–32. Kerridge, *The Agricultural Revolution,* pp. 19–24; Chambers and Mingay, *The Agricultural Revolution 1750–1880.*

Bill appeared which legalized the enclosure of tenant holdings by Parliamentary Acts.[39] With parliamentary approval, enclosures could proceed at a more advanced rate and eventually became commonplace by mid century as conversions became more rapid. By 1800, 4000 Parliamentary Acts had been passed and in excess of six million acres of land had been enclosed.[40]

As the pace of economic change began to intensify, the rate of enclosures accelerated to the point where the displaced population of agricultural workers began to increase dramatically and this began to mobilize a transfer of the population to the centers of industry. As this occurred, commissioners of enclosures were appointed to report to the courts classifying the number of tenants to be foreclosed and the amount of land, fuel and pasture which were to be re-allotted. While commissioners were initially responsible for the enclosing of estate lands as such, they eventually began to mobilize the necessary legal force for evictions and foreclosures to proceed on a mass scale.[41] As statutory enactments gave the power of eviction to landlords, legal proceedings multiplied the rate of local evictions and at the same time restricted the use of pastures from domestic animals, prohibited the use of arable land from tenant agriculture, and displaced agricultural workers and hereditary tenants.[42] In the case of the enclosures at the Chancery at Durham, for instance, all lands and common fields were to be 'measured, divided and respectively hedged, fenced and enclosed at the lord's advantage.'[43] At this stage there was a more formal clearing away of the remaining serf population of agricultural workers.

In practice, enclosures became a society-wide depopulation movement fueled by mass evictions and foreclosures which coercively separated peasants from their means of livelihood by removing them from their own agricultural holdings. As serfs were forced off the land, landlords were able to assert rights of modern private property over land to which they previously held only feudal title. This hastened the transformation of land into a commercial commodity, first by subjecting it to buying and selling, and second by extending its capacity to produce money rent.[44] Under these circumstances, customary rights and obligations in land began to be forcibly dissolved, and with this went the bonds connecting peasants to the land through hereditary tenure and leasehold. As soon as money rents replaced labor rent, peasants were forced to

---

39 R. H. Tawney, *The Agrarian Problem in the Sixteenth Century*, p. 62.

40 Lazonick, 'Karl Marx and Enclosures in England,' p. 10.

41 Rates for evictions of persons and families are listed in *The Doomsday of Enclosures: 1517–1518*, London: Kennikat Press, 1971. Data of this kind are useful in determining the extent to which the structure of British society was totally redrawn during this period. See also *English Economic History: Selected Documents*, A.E. Bland, P.A. Brown, and R.H. Tawney (eds.), London: Bell and Sons, 1925, p. 525.

42 Statutory enactments fueling evictions flooded the legislative agenda of parliament and fortified the law and corrective institutions. For evidence of this, see A.E. Bland et al., *English Economic History: Select Documents*, London: G. Bell and Sons, 1925.

43 Ibid., pp. 525–6.

44 See J.D. Chambers, 'Enclosure and the Labor Supply in The Industrial Revolution,' *Economic History Review 2nd Series*, Vol. V, 1953, 319–343; Eric Kerridge, 'The Movement of Rent, 1540–1640,' *Economic History Review 2nd Series*, Vol. VI, 1953, pp. 17–34.

focus their attention on their own holdings, making money rent a precondition to economic survival. Those who were unable to pay were eventually ruined or evicted.[45] At this point it became possible to express the value of land in money, and this led to the transformation of land into private property and eventually a commercial commodity. As land became subject to buying and selling, the economic balance between serfs and landlords was upset and feudal obligations in land and livelihood began to deteriorate.

As the breakdown of feudal obligations in land continued, it began to place the serf population under new forces of social differentiation and fragmentation. This put the serf population at the disposal of the new forces of production, which put into play a massive demographic transfer of the agricultural population into the industrial centers, bringing about a more complete transition to a new category of labor based on wages. At this stage, the flow of population from the old feudal economies to the new economies of industry became a more urgent fact of economic change, and this began to complete the process of transforming the agricultural worker of previous centuries into the wage laborer of the industrial economy.

By 1840 the transition to an industrial economy was more or less complete. Agricultural labor was forcibly cleared from the land, feudal obligations in land were dissolved, pastures were enclosed, and the rights of modern private property were asserted.[46] As a result, peasant cultivators were wrenched from their roles as agriculture producers and formed a class of detached landless laborers who were forced to seek their livelihoods in the new industrial centers.[47] At this stage the separation of the agricultural worker from the means of production was more or less complete and the loss of control over their own livelihoods was more or less formalized.

Several consequences ensued as a result of the displacement of the serf population from the rural economies. First, the eviction rates and rates of displacement became part of the political arithmetic of the regional restructuring of ownership and population, leading ultimately to the reorganization of life, land and livelihood. Second, as the transfer of the population proceeded, it brought about a massive social displacement which dispersed families, uprooted local economies and undermined regional modes of life and livelihood.[48] In and of itself, this created several broad shifts in relation to the economy of the city as compared with the economy of rural agriculture. First, it dissolved the serf's relationship to the land and altered the system of economic livelihood, forcing serfs to sell their labor for a wage, and severing the serf's feudal relation to the agricultural means of production. Second, the shift to an industrial economy meant that wage laborers were

---

45 Rodney Hilton develops this line of argument in his 'Capitalism: What's in a Name?', *Past and Present,* 1, 1952, 32–43.

46 Paul Mantoux, *The Industrial Revolution in the Eighteenth Century,* London: Methuen, 1907.

47 E. P. Thompson, *The Making of the English Working Class,* Harmondsworth: Penguin, 1968.

48 William Chambliss' analysis of vagrancy law and the statutory regulation of the period related to vagrancy shows how the legal definition of vagrancy coincided with the identification of a 'class of persons' who fell within the statute, even though 'idleness' was not a criminal offense. After the statute, however, idleness became a criminal offence. See W. Chambliss, 'A Sociological Analysis of the Law of Vagrancy,' *Social Problems,* 12, 1964, pp. 67–77.

unable to employ the means of production on their own as they once did in a feudal economy, and as a result they lost control over the ability to put the means of production to work. Third, as the shift to an industrial economy became finalized, the old class structure of feudal society was replaced by the formation of a new commercial class who were at the center of power and industry. This began to bring about the transfer of the ownership of the means of production to the commercial classes and, consequently, as the means of production fell into private hands, it became the property of one class.

The Growth of Town Economies   A second dimension of change was the growth of town economies. In the early stages of the feudal economy there were no towns as such. Economic production was confined to rural agriculture and the production of a food supply. Gradually, towns began to develop and by the fourteenth century the town was put into economic competition with the rural economy of the countryside.[49] This had the effect of gradually dissolving the economic boundaries of the feudal estates and promoting more open economies. By the seventeenth century, towns began to gain an economic foothold over the rural economy due to the growth of concentrated skills and crafts and, as towns gained the upper hand, small scale production in textiles and weaving in towns began to operate independently of the feudal economy. Though they were not capitalist enterprises by any means, the development of new production techniques, the level and intensity of commodity production, and the division of labor, were sufficient to add to the productive push to establish manufacturing in towns, making them the center of economic life over rural economies. This led to the centering of the economy in towns and to a decline of the feudal economy. In addition, it changed forever the way livelihoods were earned.

   As the formal shift in the economic center of gravity from agriculture to industry took place, towns became economic centers over the economy of rural agriculture. As a result, new class interests began to be mobilized in the industrial cities, and this led to changes in the way livelihoods were earned and to changes in the way the means of production were utilized. As a result of cities becoming the center of economic life, a new social axis was formed on the old axis of land, agriculture and feudal title.[50] This constituted the formation of new institutional alignments centering on work, family and schooling, as opposed to the old alignments of the monarch, the church and the aristocracy which had been characteristic of the feudal way of life up until that time.

Decline of the Guild System and the Beginning of Capitalist Development
A third dimension of change was the transformation of the role played by the handicraft guilds and the guild system in economic life. The guild system may be defined as a professional association of craftsmen whose basic function was to protect and regulate

---

49 For discussion on the development of towns and the competition between rural and town economies, see A.B. Hibbert, 'The Origins of the Medieval Town Patriciate,' *Past and Present*, 3, 1953, pp. 15–27.

50 At this point the institutions of work, family and schooling became the central axial points of society over the old social axis of monarchy, estate and guild.

work relating to trades.[51] Trades included all goods and services produced by persons who were skilled and who had served a period of training under a master. During the sixteenth and seventeenth centuries, guilds played a predominant role in economic life by restricting capitalist development. Chief among the function of guilds was the practice of restricting access into trades and occupations by the system of apprenticeship and by controlling entry to trades through restrictive practices such as licensing. In addition, guilds regulated the prices of goods and restricted competition among workshops by controlling rival markets.[52] Of all the restrictive functions performed by guilds, the regulation of the expansion of workshops was the most significant. Guilds, in effect, were opposed to the development of large scale enterprises and capitalist expansion. By restricting the number of employees and the kinds of labor used in shops, guilds prevented existing workshops from turning into large scale capitalist enterprises. Also, by discouraging the intermingling of trades, guilds were able to thwart the development of a complex division of labor, thereby blocking the development of the specialization necessary for full scale capitalist production and manufacture.

By 1800, guild regulations began to lose their influence over selected workshops, giving way to concentrations of capital, industrial production and free wage labor. As mechanical production in England began to focus almost wholly on cloth and woolen goods, it began to bring about an overall expansion in industry to the point that there was growth in commercial markets and in world trade. This put the pressure of expansion on the centers of production and, as the demand for woolen goods increased, some workshops began to be infiltrated by non-guild labor and gradually guild regulation broke down altogether.[53]

Management of the Problem Population: Unemployed Idle Laborers and the Dangerous Classes   A fourth dimension of economic change occurred at the level of the management of the unemployed classes as cities became the center of economic life. In the main, this came about as feudal economies were replaced by industrial economies and the old conditions of labor were replaced by new conditions of wage labor. As the new centers of industrial production began to emerge, it led to a centralized authority and a new class system which began to be mobilized on the decline of the old economic classes and class structure. Consequently, there was a formal transfer of power from feudal landlords to the commercial classes and, soon after, there was a central market economy and a system of exchange for the buying and selling of labor and the buying and selling of commodities. At this point, new class interests began to form which created the need for state administration and the basis for a state political apparatus. This acted to accelerate the growth of cities, mobilize the demographic transfer of

---

51 See Antony Black, *Guilds and Civil Society in European Political Thought from the Twelfth Century to the Present*, London: Methuen and Co., 1984.

52 See Maurice Dobb, *Studies in the Development of Capitalism*, p. 90,

53 Antony Black, *Guilds and Civil Society in European Political Thought from the Twelfth Century to the Present*, London: Methuen and Co., 1984.

the remaining agricultural population, and formally complete the process of separating the agricultural worker from the land where they had lived as hereditary tenants.

However, as the pace of economic change brought about a more effective clearing away of the old feudal society, the industrial cities became populated with a large class of unattached workers who sought their livelihoods in the newly emerging industrial economies.[54] All this put pressure on the population of unemployed workers in cities such as Manchester, Stoke-on-Trent, London and other centers. Eventually, unattached workers began to be perceived as a problem population who, as a result of being outside the economy, became subject to Poor Law enactments, workhouse confinement and statutory regulation such as the anatomy act.[55] As the unemployed populations increased, statutory regulation began to mount and new procedures were put in place to manage the problem population by a classification of their social needs on the one hand, and a classification of their deviance on the other. This included a classification of the degree of their poverty, the state of their hygiene, the content of their skills, the characteristics of their living quarters and the condition of 'the child' as it related to family, life and labor. This led to a whole new class of statutory acts which were imposed in the form of vagrancy laws and Poor Law administration on the one hand, and labor regulations regarding the codification of the laborer and the length and duration of the workday on the other. All this set into motion the machinery for managing the problem population who were becoming part of a growing army of unattached vagrants and idle laborers.

Several consequences ensued as a result. First, the existing rates of unemployed workers became part of the political arithmetic of the regional restructuring of the urban population. Second, with the new institutional axis forming in relation to the family, work and schooling, the urban population began to be patterned in relation to their social position within the family and work. This led to the identification of those who were outside of work as posing a social danger, and this became extended to other 'dangers,' such as the danger of poverty, the danger of the absence of employment, the danger of crime, and the danger of the criminal population.[56] This acted to shore up the gap which had existed between the formation of the new institutions of politics, law and government, and the conditions under which these institutions could become corrective. This led to the definition of more distinctly defined social functions which began

---

54 During this period the rural population had formed into what Marx called the 'hospital' of the reserve army of unemployed workers. For more on the confinement of this class, see Michel Foucault, *Madness and Civilization*, New York: Vintage Books, 1988, pp. 38–64.

55 The 'Anatomy Act' of 1832 required that unattached vagrants who died in the houses of correction were to be given over to medical hospitals as cadavers to be dissected. Some argue that this was a form of postmortem punishment of whosoever was deviant and whosoever was poor. Like the vagrancy act before it, the anatomy act marked the point at which poverty was recast as a criminal act at precisely the time that economic categories became dominant. For further discussion of the anatomy act, the anatomy inspectorate and a comparison with the factory inspectorate, see Ruth Richardson, *Death, Dissection and the Destitute*, London: Routledge & Kegan Paul, 1987.

56 It is at this point that the 'dangerous individual' became a subject of psychiatry and law. See Michel Foucault, 'About the Concept of the 'Dangerous Individual' in Nineteenth Century Legal Psychiatry,' *International Journal of Law and Psychiatry*, 1, 1978, pp. 1–18.

the process of containing and correcting the new social dangers of idleness, vagrancy, poverty, crime, contagion and disease, etc.[57]

In the nineteenth century, this led to formation of new social policy and the study of the urban population that was directed to the problem of the industrial laborer and the working poor. This, in turn, led to a more precise identification of the different dimensions of the problem population, including their living conditions, their nutrition, their poverty, their birth rates, their mortality rates, their idleness and the degree to which their living conditions affected the health of the child. The intervention by statutory acts into public and private spaces led to a further classification of different kinds of workers and different kinds of work; of the distinction between the places of work and schooling, and to the new powers of segregation which began to emerge between these spaces and other more dangerous spaces and their possible application to the social and political spaces of the city.[58] Then there arose all kinds of statutory regulations and public ordinances in relation to these spaces, so that for each of the possible elements of the population – the idle laborer, the working poor, the able-bodied pauper, the child, the commercial classes, the destitute working-poor, etc. – there emerged classifications and statutory regulations whose function it was to segregate the vagabond from the idle laborer, the unemployed worker from the vagrant, the working poor from the wealthy classes. All this served to identify poverty, idleness, indigence, illness and unemployment as dangers, and as a form of existence that was outside the norm and subject to the law and to state power.[59]

Eventually, this led to the acquisition of new forms of knowledge that were related to the prevention of the problem population by enactments restricting their movement. In 1835, the statutes of Edward were enacted with respect to vagrancy and the idle laborer, declaring that 'no laborer at the end of their work term could depart from the place where they dwell.' In addition, legal restrictions prevented unemployed laborers from traveling to localities where there was an accumulation of unemployed indigent workers. Then in 1837 came the distinction between persons who were unemployed because they could not get work, and persons unemployed because they did not want to work. This led to enactments which forcibly set the 'unemployed to work and committed those who did not want to work to the houses of correction.'[60]

Then there were the statutes which required the prevention of poverty by the containment of the poor within the work houses. As a result, statutory regulation began to classify the poor into several groupings comprised of able bodied idle paupers and able bodied workers. This formed a point of separation between those who worked, and

---

57 Discussion of the history of vagrancy law can be found in William Chambliss 'A Sociological Analysis of the Law of Vagrancy,' *Social Problems*, 12, 1964, pp. 67–77. He shows that the legal definition of vagrancy coincided with the criminal identification of a 'class of persons' who fell within the statute even though their 'idleness' was not a *de facto* criminal offense.

58 Ibid., pp. 6–7.

59 Michel Foucault's study of the birth of the confinement movement, the process of social separation and the emergence of the houses of confinement is relevant here. See *Madness and Civilization*, New York: Vintage, 1988.

60 A.E. Bland, *English Economic History: Select Documents*, London: G.Bell and Sons, 1925, p. 364.

those who did not, and from this arose a set of restrictions against begging by those who were idle in certain localities within the city.[61] Then came the acts that assigned the poor to places where they were permitted to beg and receive aid, and those places where the poor and the impoverished were prohibited from gathering. This had the effect of confining the poor to one place where they could be observed and classified. In addition, it brought public attention to the large agenda of statutory regulation enacted between the eighteenth and nineteenth centuries, showing a distinct turn in the law toward a great 'setting to work' of those who were among the idle population on the one hand, and those who would be committed to 'the houses of correction in accordance with the act' on the other.[62]

As the effects of this became more pervasive, it enlarged the space of public regulation in three distinct ways. First, by defining those spaces which were to be subject to public regulation, it became possible to enact public infractions on the basis of statutory requirements in relation to poverty, begging, hygiene, sickness, contagion, disease, unemployment and criminality.[63] Second, by increasing the space of public regulation and defining what was normative, it turned the industrial city into the sphere of civil society so that its commerce, its living quarters, its places of labor and public leisure, became the space of social classes, of families, of workshops and of public civility. This necessitated the appearance of legality in relation to the disruption of these spaces, particularly in relation to crimes of property such as loitering, drunkenness, false occupancy, fraud, illegal access and trespass.[64] Third, as the city became the center of commence, there was the necessity for constant policing that arose in relation to the protection of property, and this led to concentrations within the city proper of municipal authorities whose concern was to maintain levels of decorum and the appearance of public order. In turn, this gave rise to a whole network of statutory regulation which governed the new illegalities and the new departures from legality.

As soon as the class of social dangers began to be linked to knowledge about possible forms of their correction, they began to be related to other branches of public hygiene, to the formation of schooling institutions, to the living conditions of workers and other classes, and to the problem of over population and the condition of the 'child.'[65] This led to further coercive measures by social institutions. For one thing, it extended the power of social institutions related to family life, work and schooling by extending their laws and their regulatory reach to other institutional domains. In and of itself, this gave rise to new forms of statutory regulation of public social spaces – the space of the poor, the space of the alcoholic, the space of commerce, the

---

61 Ibid., pp. 366–7.

62 Ibid., p. 364.

63 On the question of the new classification of the vagrant population and the corrective endeavors of the vagrancy act, see W. Chambliss, 'A Sociological Analysis of the Law of Vagrancy,' *Social Problems*, 12, 1964, pp. 68–71.

64 Foucault, *Discipline and Punish*, especially the 'Gentle way in punishment,' pp. 104–13.

65 Michel Foucault, 'The Politics of Health in the Eighteenth Century,' in *Power/Knowledge*, New York: Pantheon Books, 1972.

space of crime. This was made manifest by the new statutory classification of the illegal vagrant, the unattached idle worker, the able-bodied pauper and the destitute, whose poverty was made the subject of enactments in respect to the workhouse and the workhouse test.[66] As a result of the definition of these spaces, a new category of criminal misdemeanor emerged along with a new classification of public space and civil society.[67] This, in turn, created the category of the possible disruption of public spaces and the concept of the menace of public space by misdemeanor, worker strikes, the unemployed idle laborer and the presence of criminality.

3 The Dual Movement of Individualism and Industrialization

Following the large-scale changes in the political and economic foundations of society there emerged a third significant development. This concerned the individual's relation to society as a whole and to its collective unity. This theme, so central to the development of modern social theory, is called the process of individualism.[68] The term 'individualism' grew out of the framework of European social thought that first emerged during the Enlightenment and the French Revolution. Thinkers such as Joseph de Maistre and Henri Saint-Simon were the first to use the term to criticize the glorification of the individual over the dominance of social and political institutions which began to occur after the French Revolution.[69]

Historically, the theme of individualism refers to the process in modern economies and in modern politics that create privatizations in the form of the detached isolated individual, whose relation to society took on a new form in the modern industrial economies. Gone were the old unities of society that once existed in the form of the social attachments to groups and political bodies outside the individual. Gone were the cooperative forms of work which existed in the old agrarian economies. These had been replaced by the new unities of the modern state which brought about the dual movement of industrialization and individualism and which created unprecedented social conformity at the same time that it created unprecedented modes of isolation, separation and privatization.

But beyond this, the process of individualism defines the point in the development of society where individuals began to be separated from the roles they once played

---

66 The workhouse test was an extension of the vagrancy statutes in that its aim was to penalize those who refused to labor. For the exact functioning of the workhouse test and the use of the test as a 'trick' on the unemployed worker by the official institutions see A.E. Bland et al., *English Economic History: Selected Documents*, London: Bell and Sons, 1925.

67 On this see Michel Foucault, *Discipline and Punish: The Birth of the Prison*, New York: Vintage Books, 1979.

68 Steven Lukes, *Individualism*, Oxford: Basil Blackwell, 1973; C.D. Macpherson, *The Political Theory of Possessive Individualism*, London: Oxford University, 1962; K.W. Swart, 'Individualism in the Mid-Nineteenth Century (1826–1860),' *Journal of the History of Ideas*, 23, 1962, 77–90.; A.D. Lindsay, 'Individualism,' *Encyclopedia of the Social Sciences*, 7, 1930–33, 674–80.

69 See R.R. Palmer, 'Man and Citizen: Applications of Individualism in the French Revolution,' in Milton R. Konvitz and Arthur E. Murphy (eds.), *Essays in Political Theory*, New York: Kennikat Press, 1972, pp. 130–152; W. Swart, 'Individualism in the Mid-Nineteenth Century (1826–1860),' *Journal of the History of Ideas*, 23, 1962, 77–90.

in previous societies and in previous economies. Individualism in this sense refers to the process of setting up society into what is called 'individuals'; that is, into autonomous, juridical political persons who are the subjects of certain legal rights and political freedoms and whose unity to society is represented in the form of the modern political state.[70] In the main, individualism refers to the process of isolation that occurs between the individual and the wider society which ensues during the dual movement of industrialization and privatization. Since no complete understanding of nineteenth century social theory is possible without looking at this process and at the relationship between the individual and society, let us look more closely.

Within the context of European social thought, the collective maintenance of society was thought to depend on the preservation of large scale institutional powers consisting of the church, the monarchy and the state. Within this social framework, individuals were thought to participate in society and social life only as members of much larger social groups, such as the estates and guilds with whom they cooperated and formed attachments. These groups asserted collective rights over individuals, acted as corporate bodies which exercised proprietary powers over them and, to a large extent, determined their place in society.

In addition to this, the social bonds linking groups to larger corporate bodies and dominant social institutions often determined individual legal rights and social obligations, and this acted to define the individual's place within society as a whole and determine the extent of their social attachments to the group. Large collective bodies, such as the guilds, churches and feudal estates, functioned as corporate entities whose authority, prerogative and proprietary powers over individuals were spelled out by state government. Generally, these large political bodies dominated social life, controlled trades and regulated occupations. Here, individuals participated in society only as members of larger groups.[71] Many were unable to participate in occupations or trades except as members of these corporate bodies, and only as members of these bodies did individuals participate in the wider society. Under these circumstances, the rights and purposes of collective bodies seemed always to exceed the rights and purposes of individuals.

Thus, predominantly, in earlier historical periods the 'individual appears as dependent, and as belonging to a greater social whole defined by the family, then by the family extended to the clan and then later to the various forms of collective society arising from the clan formations.' Only in the eighteenth century, 'does the individual appear as detached and isolated from the wider collectivity.'[72] Individualism, then, is the name given to the overall process leading to the political, social, and economic separation of individuals from the wider ties they once had to larger social groups and dominant institutions. Historically, three immediate forces were at work to bring these changes about. First, after the French Revolution, the legal rights that

---

70 See N. Poulantzas' *State, Power, Socialism*, London: NLB, 1978, pp. 50–71.

71 Lukes, *Individualism*, p. 21; and Louis Dumont, 'The Modern Conception of the Individual,' *Contributions to Indian Sociology*, 8, 1965, 13–61.

72 Marx, *Grundrisse: Foundations of the Critique of Political Economy*, Middlesex: Penguin Books, 1973, pp. 83–4.

were assigned to individuals began to dissolve the old proprietary powers inherent in corporate bodies.[73] Second, as a result of the political changes following the French Revolution, all the estates and guilds were abolished and their powers, rights and prerogatives assigned as legal entitlements to individuals. What had thus been corporate and collective in nature was suddenly centered on the individual. Third, as a result of the development of modern economies, the old collective participation in economic life suddenly shifted to the detached isolated individual whose economic livelihood was their own private responsibility. In a 'society of free competition, the isolated individual thus appears detached from their natural bonds which in an earlier historical period makes them the accessory of a definite and limited human conglomerate.'[74] This period 'produces isolated individuals' who confront each other 'as a means towards their private purposes;' and in this the individual emerges on the stage of history at the expense of the larger institutions of society.[75]

By 1890, the term 'individualism' began to be used by Durkheim in *The Division of Labor* and in *Suicide* to designate the themes of egoism and autonomy which were thought to have been brought about as a result of the disappearance of the social links and bonds that once connected individuals to larger groups. But beyond this, Durkheim found that the level of individual attachment to the wider society largely depended on the structure of the pervasive network of social inks and bonds that tied individuals directly to society as a whole. From this came the idea that the process of individualism was itself social in origin, and Durkheim set out to find how changes in the economic structure of society and the social division of labor would have led to the breakdown of the broader system of social attachments. Other thinkers took the view that the progressive focus on the individual evident in the expanded rights and freedoms that occurred after the French revolution, automatically jeopardized the greater collective interests of society and, for some, this meant the collapse of social unity and the dissolution of society.

In French social thought proper, individualism was seen as a threat to aggregate social maintenance and many believed that it would undermine the political and economic order of society.[76] In France, where the concept of society had been premised on individual self interest and autonomy, the process of individualism was looked upon as the social and political equivalent of a crisis. It threatened to dissolve society and destroy collective unity, and at every level of society it was thought to signify autonomy, freedom, and lack of restraint from collective social rules.

---

73 See, R.R. Palmer, 'Man and Citizen: Applications of Individualism in the French Revolution,' in Milton R. Konvitz and Arthur E. Murphy (eds.), *Essays in Political Theory*, New York: Kennikat Press, 1972, pp. 130–152.

74 See Marx's discussion of isolated 'independent individuals' in *The Grundrisse*, pp. 83–4; and N. Poulantzas' discussion of the 'isolation effect' in his *Political Power and Social Classes*, London: Sheed and Ward, 1973, pp. 130–291.

75 Marx, *Grundrisse*, Middlesex, England: Penguin Books, 1973, p. 84.

76 Durkheim's reaction to the problem of advancing individualism is evident in his study of *Suicide* and his discussion of the problem in 'Individualism and the Intellectuals', *Political Studies*, 17, [1898], 1969, 14–30. Also, see Gregory Claeys, 'Individualism, Socialism and Social Science: Further Notes on a Process of Conceptual Formation 1800–1850,' *Journal of the History of Ideas,* 33, 1986, 81–93.

By 1895, the process of individualism found support in an economic doctrine called laissez-faire competition, and then it found support in a political doctrine known as utilitarianism. This had claimed that the only right actions and the only right laws were those which maximize individual utility and private interest. In this view, individuals were thought to share common motives of individual utility and personal gain which impelled them to pursue their private interest through economic attainment, but beyond this the individual owed nothing to society in its own right. In this context, society was nothing more than the spontaneous actions and interests of individuals acting in the world on the basis of their utility, and as such the concept of society was reduced to the spontaneous actions and attitudes of individuals.[77]

As an economic doctrine, individualism found its basis in Adam Smith's defense of the system of private interest and private enterprise, which he developed in a work called *The Wealth of Nations*, published in 1776.[78] In it, Smith justified the conception of individual competition by setting out the fundamental principle of private enterprise, stating that each individual was free to compete among their fellows and pursue their self interest in the form of private economic gain. While this may not seem extraordinary in itself, the effects of universal competition based on the private acts of individuals cut deeply into the social fabric and into the form of the social attachments. Where individuals had once been linked by a system of common obligations, cooperative work and economic bonds, these were suddenly replaced by the independent pursuit of self interest, free enterprise and private gain. Seen from this perspective, society was little more than an association of autonomous, isolated individuals acting on the basis of private utility and economic self interest. Smith's conception of society as the pursuit of individual competition thus reduced society and the collective restraint to the spontaneous interests and competitive acts of individuals, and to this extent society had no purpose in itself. Instead of conceiving of individual competition as a stage in social and historical development, Smith thought that individual competition and private gain were the natural outcomes of economic progress.

What was extraordinary about Smith's proposal concerning the pursuit of private interest was its conception of the collective whole and the community of individuals. It was Smith's view that the individual was a 'natural' member of the social order only by their individual pursuit of private gain, and only through this gain did individuals contribute to the common prosperity of society.[79] According to this view, individuals were 'free agents,' able to make contracts and enter into economic interchanges without obligation to the wider society. Conceived of in this way, social relations between individuals were reduced to a set of commercial transactions and economic exchanges, and the idea of the common authority of society was reduced to straightforward economic utility and self interest.

---

77 A.D. Lindsay, 'Individualism', *Encyclopedia of the Social Sciences*, 7, 1930–33, 674–80.

78 Adam Smith, *The Wealth of Nations,* London: Dent & Sons, [1776] 1910.

79 See Jacob Viner, 'Adam Smith and Laissez Faire,' in J.M. Clark and P.H. Douglas et al., *Adam Smith 1776–1926*, New York: Augustus Kelly, 1966.

Smith's economic justification of private enterprise and individual competition was thus ingenious. Though based on a crude appeal to the collective good conceived of in terms of 'fiscal well being' and the duty to accumulate wealth, Smith pronounced his rationale for individual competition by stating that 'in pursuing their self interest, the individual promotes the greater good of society by contributing to its national wealth and this they do more effectively than when they really intend to promote it.'[80] By conceiving of the unity of society as a 'common economic prosperity,' Smith was able to reduce the maintenance of society to collective forces of self interest and economic competition. Accordingly, all the collective social functions of society shrank to the role of protecting private rights of individuals so that they could engage in the pursuit of private interest and economic gain.

Modern Social Thought and the Nineteenth Century Theories of Knowledge

No complete understanding of the history of social thought or of the theoretical works of Marx, Durkheim and Weber is possible without some discussion of the theories of knowledge which were dominant during the latter part of the nineteenth century. In fact, by the end of the century, three dominant philosophies had come to the forefront during the development of classical social theory. These were the philosophies of idealism, empiricism, and positivism, and what is important to note is that each of these philosophies influenced the development of social thought and had an enormous impact on nineteenth century social theory as a whole. Let us begin by looking at the first body of knowledge called idealism.

Classical Idealism   Philosophical idealism originated in 480 B.C. with the work of Socrates and Plato, who were among the first to set out principles of thought which acted as guidelines for investigating the existence of a realm of concepts thought to be beyond the physical world.[81] As a philosophic perspective, idealism got its name from a branch of knowledge which believed that the most important task of philosophy was to inquire into a realm whose existence could only be grasped by theoretical activity, rather than by straightforward observation or straightforward logical reasoning. The growth of idealist philosophy is best understood in opposition to a type of philosophical thought which existed in Greece during the fifth century B.C., and which focused on the origins of the natural world.[82] Among the first philosophers to put forward a rudimentary theory of nature and physics were those who believed only in the ultimate reality of the physical world. Among the claims put forward by these philosophers was the idea that the natural world was primarily made up of

---

80 Adam Smith, *The Wealth of Nations,* p. 423.
81 This practice was common in the dialogues of Plato.
82 Ernest Barker, *Greek Political Theory*, London: Methuen, 1918.

physical matter and that, according to this view, the object of philosophy was to explain how change took place in reality and in the physical world itself.

The tradition of philosophic idealism can best be understood therefore as a direct response to the very straightforward philosophic view which insisted that reality was to be regarded as nothing more than what can be determined with the senses and by sense perception in relation to physical reality. By 430 B.C., however, Socrates began to advance an idealist doctrine which argued that, beneath the basic physical structure of reality, was some greater fundamental reality giving purpose and meaning to existence, and that, without this, individual existence made little sense. It was Socrates, therefore, who was the first to put forward the view that a more enduring pattern or purpose must underlie the apparent physical reality of experience and that this pattern was not itself subject to change, but was eternal and unchanging.[83]

This disagreement in philosophy over the appropriate subject matter of investigation, between 'physical matter' on the one hand, and the 'values' and 'ideals' related to universals such as equality, freedom and social justice on the other, led to the formation of two distinct schools of thought; in fact, two distinct tendencies in knowledge. The first of these perspectives took the view that only the world of physical reality exists and that knowledge of physical reality can be apprehended and brought to light only by the senses and by sense perception. The second perspective, by contrast, took the view that the proper object of philosophical investigation were the 'realities' and 'concepts' which involve the well-being and equality of the social and political community, since it was these realities that bear on human and political things in contrast to physical or material things. Furthermore, because these concepts and realities were above physical things, it was thought that they could only be brought to light through theory and theoretical activity.

The distinction between 'physical or natural' things and 'human' things, was thus the central starting place of idealist political philosophy and the focus on human political and social questions. In contrast to physical reality, therefore, those things studied by the branch of knowledge concerned with the human political community could not be known by sense perception, since they involve principles, standards, ideals and ethics not directly graspable by the senses. According to this view, social and political things form a class of objects by themselves and, therefore, should be studied separately from physical things.

The absolute starting place for social and political thought is therefore Plato's *Republic*. The central discussion in this work relates to the importance of social and political ideals and standards for collective life and for society. While many believe that Plato's *Republic* is a political fantasy, others take the view that Plato had a more serious purpose in mind. In fact, the *Republic* is one of the first sustained philosophic conversations about the 'ideal' social community, and in it Socrates puts forward the view that the state is founded on two primary functions. The first of these concerned

---

83 A. E. Taylor, *Elements of Metaphysics*, London: Methuen, 1956.

practical matters and physical things such as the division of labor, the production of a food supply, a system of education, and the conditions of safety and security.[84] These physical functions of society serve practical ends and relate to securing the material well being of individuals and the community. But Socrates believed that the second group of things – formally defined as 'ideal' functions – involves principles, practices and standards of society which relate to the system of human conduct and thus involves the social and political good of society.[85] In contrast to the practical functions, these functions are organized in reference to human and political things. In these terms, the 'ideal,' then, can be described simply as anything relating to the human political community which strives for what is beyond the functional or practical level of activity and which promotes the well-being of the human political community.

As far as idealist philosophy was concerned, practical things had a utilitarian sanction, while those things relating to larger purposes or standards of society and the political community were given an extraordinary ethical sanction.[86] Plato believed that the leap from the practical to the ideal was, in fact, ethical in nature and it was this that formed the basis of Greek political philosophy and its focus on political functions and institutions. Social and political theory, therefore, was an instrument first used to make the central social and ethical questions about society and human necessity seem compelling and important, and as a necessary social and political good. Since everything depends on the system of ethics and values of the society we live in, the first social and political thinkers believed that a special branch of philosophic thought should be dedicated to things political and human, and this branch of thinking got its name in direct contrast to the body of thought which studied material reality and physical things.

It was Plato, then, who was among the first to make the ideal realm an object of discussion in his dialogues, and to assume that knowledge was attainable only by making the distinction between the 'ideal' and the 'material' realms. The first of these realms, Plato thought, is the sense world, which is the world of everyday material existence. This, according to Plato, is the most immediate and first level of experience. But here the objects of the material world are in a constant state of change and, therefore, cannot be known absolutely since, when in a constant state of change, no object maintains its form over time. Plato reasoned, therefore, that since the world of immediate experience was constantly changing, any absolute knowledge of it was impossible.

The second realm recognized by Plato is made up of what he called 'universals', or more simply 'forms' or 'concepts.' Basically, this dimension gets its name from a set of ideas and concepts such as justice and equality, which the Greek philosophers believed were essentially unchanging because they were related to human things and applied universally to all social and historical circumstances.[87] These 'absolutes' get

---

84 Richard Nettleship, *Lectures on the Republic of Plato*, London: Macmillan, 1958.

85 Taylor, *Elements of Metaphysics*, pp. 18–22.

86 The distinction between utilitarian and ethical sanctions is developed by Laszlo Versenyi, *Socratic Humanism*, New Haven: Yale, 1963, pp. 79–98.

87 Ernest Barker, *Greek Political Theory,* pp. 282–283.

their name from a set of ideas which were thought to supersede time and place, and accordingly surpass all social and historical situations since they apply to all societies. So far as they applied universally to all societies and were believed to be unchanging, the ideals and concepts were thought to be applicable to all human social and political communities.

In this context, three distinct characteristics of classical idealism can be outlined. First is the reliance on a conception of philosophy as a body of thought aimed at understanding existence by means of universal concepts, such as history, human necessity and equality, which cannot be known by sense perception or by experience alone. Second is the implied philosophic relation between knowledge of universal concepts, and the knowledge of the structure of human societies as associations whose line of development reflects the essential concepts and standards held to be universally valid. Third is the reliance on a form of knowledge which attempts to develop theories of society, history and existence, in contrast to scientific knowledge which attempts to develop factual knowledge of the natural empirical world and the human body.[88]

Hegelian Idealism and the Theory of Historical Development

A second current of philosophical idealism emerged in Germany with the writings of Georg Hegel (1770–1831). Hegel is best known for developing a complete system of idealist philosophy, which by the nineteenth century had become the dominant philosophic framework in Western Europe. By 1830 he had pioneered theoretical investigations into history, existence, politics and social thought and was the first to introduce the concept of society into classical knowledge. But to understand the impact of his work on the development of idealism and social theory, we must look more closely.

Hegel was born in 1770 in Stuttgart and studied theology and philosophy at Tubingen University. In 1806, when at the University of Jena, Hegel wrote his first major philosophical work, entitled *Phenomenology of Spirit*. Hegel's writings were central to the social and political thought of the time in several respects. First, he forced philosophy to confront historical and social questions, thus transforming philosophic concepts into social and historical ones.[89] Second, Hegel's writings acted as a theoretical background to Marx's and Engels' economic and political works because Hegel had identified society as a field of activity outside of history. Third, it was Hegel's philosophical idealism which later shaped Comte's critique of philosophy known as 'positivism,' leading eventually to a widespread opposition to idealism and to its eventual decline.

In order to put Hegel's work into perspective, it will be useful to look at his main theoretical writings by placing them in the context of classical idealism. As we noted earlier, classical idealism had taken the view that the physical world could not be known with any direct certainty because its material existence was always changing. This ultimately forced classical idealism to abandon the material world in order to

---

88 Nettleship, *Lectures on the Republic of Plato*, p. 61.

89 Herbert Marcuse, *Reason and Revolution;* J.N. Findlay, *Hegel: A Re-Examination*; Sidney Hook, *From Hegel to Marx.*

focus on the realm of absolute truths whose existence could be relied upon as objects of theoretical investigation. Hegel, however, thought that the tendency in classical idealism to draw sharp distinctions between the material world and the ideal world ultimately split human experience into two separate spheres and this, he thought, canceled out the study of the material world of experience. Hegel's most important contribution to the development of social theory, therefore, was his re-introduction of the material world back into thought. This immediately rescued the material world from the philosophic extremities where it had been placed since antiquity, mainly by bringing it back into a theory of knowledge.

Hegel's main theoretical influence was Aristotle.[90] What interested Hegel in Aristotle's work was his rejection of Plato's doctrine of the transcendent realm of absolutes which tended to stand above the material world of experience. Aristotle maintained that Plato's separation of the material and ideal realms was unnecessary, and he took the view that both the ideal and the material worlds were in fact immanent in human experience, and thus fundamentally belonged together and should be treated as a philosophic unity.[91]

For Hegel, this was a key philosophic step, since it took the view that the principles of human and social development worked implicitly toward ultimate ends and that the process of development was itself implicit in social and historical subject matter. As a result of Hegel's incorporation of the principles of material and social development within history, the focal point of philosophical and theoretical activity shifted from an investigation of the realm of Platonic absolutes to one of studying and explaining the material processes of social and historical development itself. This brought with it several important things. First, it led to the introduction of the concept of society as an independent reality and as a field of activity. Second, it separated the space of society from the space of history in a way that had not been done previously up until that time. Third, it led to the assertion that historical development itself took a social form represented by distinct societies, whose system of politics, forms of class distinction, religion, and inward social divisions obeyed principles of their own. These steps made it clear that philosophy could only understand history by adopting social concepts and that history was, in fact, social in nature.

This led Hegel to introduce what he called the four social realms, or historical kingdoms, which constituted one of the first expressions of the distinct social forms in societies past and present.[92] According to Hegel, there was the Asiatic form where the individual was part of the social mass, religion was dominant, the ruler was a dynastic lord, law was undifferentiated from custom and morality and 'class differences became crystallized into hereditary castes.'[93] Then there were the societies of

---

90 J.N. Findlay, *Hegel: A Re-Examination,* London: George Allen & Unwin, 1958.

91 Ibid.

92 The four social realms or historical kingdoms are outlined by Hegel in *The Philosophy of History* and *The Philosophy of Right.*

93 Hegel, *Philosophy of Right*, Oxford: Clarendon, 1958, p. 220.

antiquity where, according to Hegel, individuals were separated from the social mass, decision-making was based on oracles, ruling was in the form of shared politics, and existence was divided into classes of slaves and of free individuals. Then came the feudal period, where the community was structured in relation to an economy of agriculture, and there emerged a trading class of guilds where ruling was in the form of sovereignty and existence was divided into classes of landholders and serf cultivators. What was unprecedented about Hegel's characterization of the four political realms of society was the expression, perhaps for the first time in social thought, of the fact that societies differ in their structures in terms of their class systems, their institutions, the form of their politics, and the degree to which the individual is or is not submerged into the social mass.

At the basis of all this was Aristotle's assertion that the natural and social world acted according to ultimate purposes or ends which, in his view, were actualized in the principle of development. The name Aristotle gave to this process was 'teleology,' a concept which took the view that the ideal and material realm were fused together in a process of development. In this view, human and material things ultimately act according to ends or purposes in the process of social development, and the function of theory in this regard is to explain these processes as they appear in the formation of distinct societies. Drawing from Aristotle, Hegel attempted to pioneer a system of thinking that endeavored to explain human existence as a process of development. Simply stated, Hegel believed that the 'ideal' and 'material' realms belonged together and were fundamentally rooted in the structure of reality and history.[94] This step was of central philosophic significance because it tied the universal concepts of history and necessity into existence, rather than placing them above experience as classical idealism had done. In this sense, Hegel's idealism was thus founded upon a theory of history and society.

Empiricism and the Growth of the Scientific Outlook   It was clear that by the second half of the nineteenth century idealist philosophy was in decline and that by 1850 a serious critical attack against idealism began to be mounted. In order to understand these developments it will be useful to look briefly at the history of empiricism in relation to the development of a theory of knowledge in the social sciences. Essentially, the term empiricism originates from the Greek word 'empereiria', meaning experience. It can be defined as the general name given to the doctrine in philosophy which holds that knowledge of the material world must be based on straightforward observation and sense perception.

It was Aristotle who is historically believed to be the founder of empiricism by his attempt to integrate experience into a theory of knowledge. In contrast to idealism, therefore, the fundamental tenet of empiricism is the belief that knowledge is the product of a straightforward perceptual encounter with the natural world. Eventually, empiricism attained its place in Western thought because of its relation to modern

---

94 Sidney Hook, *From Hegel to Marx*; Findlay, *Hegel: A Re-Examination.*

science and its emphasis on substantiating knowledge statements by recourse to observation and the accumulation of facts.[95] As successes in the natural sciences began to mount in the nineteenth and twentieth centuries, there was universal acceptance of empirical methods in the social sciences and these became standardized in disciplines such as history, social science, psychology and anthropology.

One of the principle qualities of empiricism is its reliance on sense perception. This is expressed in a number of key assumptions which characterize the empirical standpoint. The first of these assumes that things in the material world remain the same over time and are subject to observation and description. Second, empiricism asserts that, while a division exists between the 'outer world' of things and the 'inner world' of the mind, knowledge is the straightforward grasping or apprehension of the object in the material world. Third, empirical methods assume that accounts concerning the validity of observation must be given about the operations and procedures used to obtain knowledge of things in the outer world. Where no account can be given, claims may not be validated. Fourth, empirical methodologies assume that certainty lies in the methods of measurement used to obtain reliable knowledge from the physical world and believes that these methods are an indispensable means of representing the factual consistency of the natural world itself. Fifth, empiricism assumes that the tendency to commit error in the formation of knowledge can only be reduced when we increase our reliance on observation and measurement.[96] Historically, it was this reliance on measurement, and the belief that the outer world could be measured, that eventually gave birth to the scientific outlook and the scientific method and its utilization in the social sciences. But, as we shall see later, there were problems in the social sciences when it became time to derive knowledge from the material world based on an uncritical reliance on empirical and scientific techniques.

The Development of Positivism   This takes us directly to the development of positivism as a theory of knowledge which emerged in the nineteenth century. Primarily a philosophic doctrine associated with the work of Auguste Comte, positivism may be defined as a scientific movement which began to create reforms in the way knowledge was acquired. While Comte published his work on positive philosophy in 1830, positivism did not become a world wide movement until the latter part of the nineteenth century, when it announced that the age of 'speculation' and 'intuition' in philosophy was at an end.[97] Historically, positivism came fully into prominence only when it mounted a critical attack on idealist philosophy.

In a work entitled *A Course on Positive Philosophy*, Comte put forward two basic premises. First, he asserted that all the speculative philosophies of knowledge would be replaced by the methods of the natural sciences and, second, he took the view that

---

95 Paul K. Feyerabend, *Problems of Empiricism*, London: Cambridge University Press, 1981.
96 Ibid.
97 Auguste Comte, *A General View of Positivism*, London: Routledge, 1908.

positivism was the highest possible stage in the development of knowledge. Comte, therefore, tended to equate positivism with scientific progress and social reform. As a scientific doctrine positivism emphasized two key points of departure from idealist philosophies which had been dominant up until that time. It stressed the reliability of observation as a basis for a theory of knowledge; and it placed an extraordinary emphasis on the search for factual regularities which Comte believed would lead to the formation of general laws. Positivism thus constituted a key shift in the philosophy of knowledge, to the extent that it insisted that the old idealist search for underlying meaning and ultimate causes or truths be abandoned and replaced with the ultimate stress on observation and description.

The influence of positivism on the development of the social sciences was therefore dramatic.[98] Generally, there were two pivotal assertions which made positivism so influential. First, Comte's 'law of three stages' had the effect of essentially equating the use of the scientific method with historical development and social progress. Second, Comte developed a system for classifying the sciences by arranging them in terms of a definite order, and by hierarchically organizing the sciences in relation to their complexity and utilization of the scientific method.[99] This left no doubt that, in contrast to the social and historical sciences, the methods of the natural sciences had obtained greater precision and thus had attained the highest rank. Though Comte's law of three stages was basically straightforward, its social impact was considerable. It had taken the view that the human mind develops in three distinct and unalterable phases: the theological stage, in which human beings explain causes in terms of the will of anthropomorphic gods; the metaphysical stage, in which causes are explained in terms of abstract speculative ideas; and the positive stage, in which causes are explained in terms of scientific laws. What proved to be so controversial about Comte's assertion that positivism constituted the highest stage in knowledge was its immediate claim that the speculative stage of knowledge was to be replaced by the positivistic stage and that the development toward this stage was necessary if social thought was to become a credible science. In essence, this meant that positivism became associated in the minds of many with progress and social reform. Under these circumstances, it became a matter of historical urgency for the social sciences to develop from the speculative to the positive stage, thereby marking their scientific stature. In this respect, positive philosophy did nothing less than mark the end of speculative thought going back as far as the philosophy of antiquity.

In addition to differentiating itself from idealism, positivism made itself distinct from empiricism. Whereas empiricism advocated the general philosophical view that reality was to be equated with the physical world and sense perception, positivism was a social movement which pronounced the demise of speculative philosophy by promising to resolve the 'intellectual anarchy' that was thought to exist in the

---

98 Simon, *European Positivism in the Nineteenth Century,* pp. 4–18.
99 Ibid.

philosophical sciences.[100] While positivism had adopted the empirical principles of observation and sense perception, it gained its historical significance by proclaiming that the age of speculative philosophy was at an end.

By 1890 positivism had become a dominant social force advocating scientific change and social reforms and had adopted methods premised on the natural sciences.[101] The key characteristics of positivistic method can best be outlined as follows. First, positivism was premised on the assumption that a search for universal truths or ideals be abandoned in favor of a search for law-like regularities. Second, it took the view that the only legitimate objects of scientific investigation were those which were subject to observation, since observation had become the central criterion of verification. Since verification was preparatory to the formulation of general laws, laws themselves were to be subject to the test of facts. Third, with its stress on observation, positivism equated knowledge with the experience of factual regularity and this greatly reduced the role reason had played in theory formation. Eventually, these distinctions in knowledge brought about a split in social theory between the study of human necessity, politics and social inequality on the one hand, and the study of facts and laws on the other. By the twentieth century, the study of politics and human economic necessity was abandoned for the study of facts, and the search for knowledge was itself reduced to a search for facts in the observable world. Fourth, positivism's straightforward acceptance of the physical sciences as a model of certainty and exactness put other disciplines on notice that the methods of the natural sciences were to be the ultimate goal of all disciplines in their search for knowledge. Fifth, positivism upheld the view that progress and social reform depended on an orientation to facts and factual knowledge.

It is important to remember that, in advocating the adoption of positive methods in the social sciences, Comte was responding to two particular challenges which he felt represented a threat to the threshold of a new scientific age. The first of these was the social and political anarchy which had been caused by the revolution in France. Second, was the perceived anarchy of philosophical speculation which had prevailed since the dominance of Hegel's idealism in European thought. Comte took the view that the new science of positive philosophy would in fact serve two specific purposes. It would make French society whole again by examining the problems of society scientifically, and it would pronounce the end of speculative philosophy and its mystical view of nature, society and history.[102] Viewed from this perspective, positivism may be defined as a scientific outlook on the world which departed from speculative philosophy by abandoning the search for ultimate, final, or first causes or truths.

---

100 See Marcuse, *Reason and Revolution*, pp. 323–360.

101 For discussion of the social and political reforms of positivism, see, D.G. Charlton, *Positive Thought in France During the Second Empire:1852–70*, Oxford; Clarendon Press, 1959.

102 See D.G. Chartton, *Secular Religions in France 1815–1870*, Oxford: Clarendon, 1963.

2

Karl Marx

The Historical Context of Karl Marx's Work

Karl Marx was born on May 5, 1818 in Trier, a small city situated in the southern part of the German Rhineland. He grew up in a middle class Jewish household which had converted to Protestantism to escape the social difficulty suffered by Jews in German society. Marx's father, a lawyer, played a major role in his life, acting as both his advisor and friend, and Marx corresponded with him regularly until he died. In contrast with his father, little is known about Marx's mother or the role she played in his life. In 1835, at the age of 17, Marx entered the University of Bonn as a law student and shortly thereafter left Bonn for the University of Berlin. It was in Berlin that Marx first read the works of Georg Hegel whose theoretical writings influenced him throughout his life.

In April of 1841, Marx received his doctorate and headed back to Bonn to search for work at the university. Unable to find academic employment, he tried to earn a living as a journalist, and during this period met Arnold Ruge who was the editor of a popular periodical called the *Deutsche Jahrbucher*. Ruge invited Marx to contribute and, in 1842, Marx published his first work in the *Jahrbucher*. Thereafter, Ruge helped Marx publish a series of critical articles and eventually helped him obtain the editorship of the *Jahrbucher*. In 1843 Marx moved to Cologne where he studied the works of Ludwig Feuerbach, and during this period his writings were shaped by his criticism of Hegel and Hegel's dominance in German philosophy. In the same year, Marx produced two major writings related to the criticism of Hegel's conception of the state, entitled *A Critique of Hegel's Philosophy of Right* and 'On the Jewish Question.'[1] Immediately following these critiques, he began to develop an outline of a theory of history and economic life, which later became one of his most important theoretical contributions.

In October of 1843, Marx moved to Paris where he took up the study of political economy by reading the works of Adam Smith and David Ricardo. While he was in Paris, social and political questions began to become more pressing and he became involved in the socialist movement. By May of 1844, Marx drafted some notes

---

1 Karl Marx, *Critique of Hegel's Philosophy of Right,* J.J. O'Malley (ed.), Cambridge, University Press, [1843] 1970; R.C. Tucker, *Marx-Engels Reader,* New York: W.W. Norton, 1978.

related to classical economics and alienated labor entitled *The Economic and Philosophic Manuscripts*, which became one of his most famous writings. Later, this led him to the formal study of political economy and economic history. Parallel to these developments, European societies were coming to grips with the effects of industrialization which had brought poverty and social distress to the working classes. Low wages, long hours and poor working conditions led to growing social unrest and worker protest, and eventually in 1848 to social revolution in France and throughout Europe. During this period, Marx became more involved in economic questions and this began an open criticism of society and eventually a more intense focus on economic problems. While working on these questions, Marx read Frederick Engels' *The Conditions of the Working Class* in 1845, and as a consequence became aware of the scale of misery of the industrial worker. In the same year, Engels went to Paris to visit Marx and, as a result, they struck up a friendship and a collaboration which was to last a lifetime.

In 1845, after Marx left Paris for Brussels, his collaboration with Engels grew more frequent. One of the first collaborations was a work entitled *The Holy Family*, a polemical writing attacking the Young Hegelians for their philosophic view of society and history. As a result, they consolidated their common theoretical interest in social issues and economic questions.[2] Later, they collaborated on a work entitled *The German Ideology,* which laid out the conditions for the break with German philosophy and outlined what later became the materialist theory of history, one of Marx's most important contributions.[3]

Near the end of his stay in Brussels, Marx became more involved in the workers' movement which took him further into economic questions. It was against this background that in 1848, the Communist League asked Marx and Engels to draw up a workers' charter. This led to *The Communist Manifesto* of 1848, which had an enormous impact on the workers' movement throughout Europe. In 1850, Marx left Brussels to settle in London where he pursued economic questions and began work on a detailed analysis of capitalism. It was here that he saw first hand the collapse of the rural economy, the development of industrial capitalism and the migration of the agricultural worker to the cities of industry. By 1850, the average work day was in excess of 16 hours in duration, extending in some cases from 5:00 am to 9:00 pm, seven days a week.[4] In addition to this, wages were extremely low and on average tended to sink below the rate of subsistence. Workers often lived in conditions of extreme poverty with sixteen hour workdays and had to contend with the prevalence

---

2 Marx and Engels, *The Holy Family, or Critique of Critical Criticism*, Moscow: Progress Publishers, 1956 [1845].

3 Marx and Engels, *The German Ideology*, New York: International pub., 1947, [1845–7].

4 Marx's discussion of the history of the workday is interesting for showing how the workday fluctuated between many different lengths from eighteen, sixteen, fourteen, twelve, ten and to the present eight hour workday. For more on this see, *Capital,* Vol. 1, pp. 341–416. Also, for the conditions of the worker and the structure of the workday in the nineteenth century, see S. Pollard, 'Factory Discipline in the Industrial Revolution,' *Economic History Review*, 16, 1963–4, 254–271; Frederich Engels, *The Condition of the Working Class in England* in 1844, Oxford, 1968.

of women and child labor. In some cases, children as young as ten were pressed into factory labor. In others, women and children often worked through the night and slept in the factory in order to meet the next shift. In some factories where the workday exceeded eighteen hours, many of the machines and furnaces were never shut off. Under these circumstances, the workday dominated the life of the worker and, in the absence of any legal limit on the workday, many employers often extended it beyond the point to which it could be humanly tolerated.[5] It was at this point that Marx formed his lifelong interest in the social conditions of the industrial worker, and by 1859 he had sketched an outline of a work called *A Contribution to a Critique of Political Economy,* whose famous preface is one of the most frequently quoted passages from his writings.[6] Over the next ten years, Marx devoted himself to writing and preparing his most famous work entitled *Capital*, which was published in 1867. In the following years, Marx wrote two more volumes of *Capital* and, eighteen years later, he died in London at the age of 65 in 1883.

Theoretical Influences on Marx's view of Society and History: The Shift to Materialism

In addition to observing first hand the emergence of the industrial worker and the development of capitalism in Europe and England, there were a number of key influences shaping Marx's conception of society and history at the time. These influences led to several theoretical developments which were key to the formation of Marx's overall view of society and history, and of these at least two stand out. First, was Marx's break with Hegel's idealist philosophy which helped him devise a method that was suitable to the study of society and history which was formally outside philosophy. Second, was the introduction of materialism and the materialist outlook as a theoretical perspective for looking at the formation of historical societies. Having introduced the materialist perspective, Marx then was able to show that the very first act of all societies was always economic because human beings had to satisfy their everyday material needs before anything else. This later became a major theoretical perspective for looking at the social and historical development of societies from the point of view of their economic production and the division into social classes. To begin with, let us look at Marx's break with Hegel.

Rejection of Hegel and Idealist Philosophy   No complete understanding of Marx's work is possible without some discussion of his life long fascination with the work of Georg Hegel. Philosophically, Hegel was by far the most dominant thinker in Europe. By 1815, he had written several powerful books which advanced a broad

---

5 For differences in the length of the workday between different industries see E.P. Thompson, 'Time, Work-Discipline, and Industrial Capitalism,' *Past and Present*, 38, 1967, 56–97.

6 Marx, *A Contribution to the Critique of Political Economy,* Moscow: Progress Publishers, [1859] 1977.

theory of existence which was both philosophical and historical in its orientation. Without question, Hegel was the dominant philosopher during the time in which Marx worked and, even though he had died in 1831, the legacy of his writings were extremely important to the intellectual and social background in which Marx lived. In fact, a great deal of Marx's early writings can only be understood in relation to Hegel's thinking. Hegel was the originator of one of the most far-reaching philosophical doctrines of the nineteenth century called philosophical idealism. Idealism can be defined as a philosophic perspective which put forward the idea that the ultimate conditions of human existence and development can be arrived at only through the examination of abstract philosophic categories. As a philosophical perspective, idealism had claimed that the fundamental task of philosophy and social thought was to understand human existence by an examination of abstract categories such as reason, history, and existence. The importance of Hegel's observation was that it viewed the world, history and existence in terms of interrelated processes rather than seeing individuals and history as separate, free-standing entities. The terms Hegel used to denote the interconnectedness between the human and historical realms were reason, history and existence.

While a student at the University of Berlin, Marx had read Hegel and this marked a turning point in his intellectual career, as it had for many other students. Hegel was intoxicating for a generation of thinkers because of the radical form of his philosophy and the method he used to explain broad aspects of historical and individual development. The turning point came for Marx when he realized that, while Hegel's system constantly referred to 'history' and 'existence' as its subject matter, the everyday world of human experience was not an object of philosophic contemplation. As a result, Marx began to call into question the whole basis of Hegel's philosophy and the role it played in explaining human existence. This criticism of Hegel is evident in an early work called *The Holy Family* where, speaking of Hegel's system, he wrote:

> The whole destructive work results in the most conservative philosophy because it thinks it has overcome the real world merely by transforming it into a 'thing of thought.' [Hegel thus] stands the world on its head and can therefore dissolve in the head all the limitations which naturally remain in existence. If, from real apples, pears and strawberries, I form the general idea 'Fruit,' if I go further and imagine that my abstract idea 'Fruit,' derived from real fruit, is an entity existing outside me, is indeed the true essence of the pear, the apple, etc., then, in the language of [Hegelian] philosophy I am declaring that 'Fruit' is the 'Substance' of the pear, the apple, etc. I am saying, therefore, that to be a pear is not essential to the pear, that to be an apple is not essential to the apple; that what is essential to these things is not their real being, perceptible to the senses, but the essence that I have extracted from them and then foisted on them, the essence of my idea – 'Fruit.'[7]

From the quotation above it is evident that in his own work Marx was moving more in the direction of developing an understanding of reality and history and ultimately

---

7 K. Marx and F. Engels, *The Holy Family,* or *A Critique of Critical Criticism*, Progress Publishers, p. 72.

the material world of experience. This led him to focus his attention on the questions of social existence and economic necessity, and in order to develop a body of thought consistent with it, Marx went on to outline what he thought were the conditions of the break with philosophical idealism by resting his rejection of Hegel on four central theoretical premises.

First, Marx objected to the role Hegel had assigned to philosophy. Hegel had asserted that the fundamental task of philosophy was to examine the role played by the abstract categories of history, reason and existence in human development. As far as Marx was concerned, this led to the view that only philosophic categories were real, whereas the real problems of living individuals were overlooked or ignored. If, as Hegel had reasoned, only the categories were real and individuals were abstract, then the philosopher's duty is to concentrate on abstract processes rather than on real individuals. Marx felt that this was a fundamental distortion, since to understand history as a series of philosophic categories was equivalent to reducing human experience to abstract processes. In fact, Marx took the view that the categories put forward by Hegel referred neither to concrete human activity nor physical reality, but only to abstract processes grasped as ideas. This ultimate distortion, Marx thought, consisted in raising the categories to the level of existence, as if they had 'natures', 'processes' and ultimately, 'needs' of their own. Marx believed that Hegel's stress on the abstract conception of history made the real questions of human existence seem abstract and unimportant. Marx believed that when the existence of human beings is understood only as 'ideas and thoughts,' the more real and practical problems of individual lives are overlooked.

Second, Marx disagreed with Hegel over the role of ideas in history.[8] Hegel had stated that ideas were paramount in understanding social and historical development because they acted as causes. Marx, by contrast, took the view that Hegel's ultimate stress on the reality of ideas led him to misrepresent the essential nature of human social life. Whereas Hegel had believed that human reason was the highest good, Marx thought that individuals have physical needs and requirements which sustain their life and well being, and these needs come before intellectual needs and can only be satisfied by direct productive activity in the world. Marx, then, took the view that, in and of themselves, 'ideas' do not live or act, nor do they have needs, only human beings do. In this respect, Marx reasoned that the most significant fact about human beings is that they must satisfy their material needs in order to live and that these needs must be met on a daily and hourly basis, otherwise there is no life and no material existence. Thus, where Hegel had stressed the role played by reason in human history, and had placed the theoretical emphasis on 'ideas in history' and raised them to the level of an abstraction, Marx thought that the single most important aspect of human life was the fact of material well being which he thought could only be brought about by the satisfaction of human material needs. Thus, for Marx, materialism was placed in opposition to idealism.

---

8 See Marx and Engels, *The German Ideology*, and Lucio Colletti, *Marxism and Hegel,* London: Verso, 1979.

A third basis of disagreement relates to Hegel's view of the ultimate role of society and the state. Hegel's philosophical perspective took a politically conservative view of history and society. Hegel thought that society and the state developed out of what he had called the forces of the spirit in history and 'the actualization of the ethical.'[9] This meant that the state was synonymous with a process of development based on ethical and moral categories which were realized through historical processes rather than individual acts. This led to the view that the state was, in essence, a theological embodiment of the spirit of human beings. In this way, Hegel had empowered the state with a kind of 'eternal' quality which meant that its activities were unalterable. Marx rejected this view by stating that Hegel had created the illusion that inequality and human hardship were in fact natural outcomes or actualities of history rather than resulting from social disadvantages and historical social inequalities of society.

A fourth point of disagreement concerns Hegel's understanding of human hardship and social inequality itself. Hegel had claimed that human hardship and suffering originate from conscious thought existing in the minds of individuals rather than from material obstacles existing in reality which act to hinder individual freedom. The classic statement on this was Hegel's discussion of the master-slave relation in *The Phenomenology of Mind*. In it, Hegel understands the slave's subjection to the master as an inner dialogue which takes place in the slave's consciousness. Hegel therefore believed that the condition of slavery and subjection originated in the capacity of slaves to see themselves as subjects of others. Thus, for Hegel freedom can only take place when slaves see themselves in another light and change their consciousness. He therefore reasoned that, in relation with others and society, the primary form of subjection is thus self imposed.[10]

While Hegel's classic example of the relation between the master and slave was the philosophic prototype of the class struggle, Marx could not disagree more. For Marx, the origin of class inequality and human hardship was not to be found in the abstract forces of the development of consciousness, but rather in the concrete material conditions that made it necessary for one class of persons to be dominant over others. In Marx's view, it was economic necessity, not abstract conscious relations, that binds the slave to the master. While Hegel believed that freedom from oppression exists when individuals change their consciousness, Marx asserted that individual subjection stems from the economic and class inequalities that arise when one class owns the means of production and the other class is compelled to sell their labor in exchange for a wage. Marx therefore believed that Hegel had mistakenly assumed that individual hardship is a product of consciousness, when in fact it derives from the material conditions which emerge from economic and class inequalities. While Hegel had asserted that individual freedom ultimately comes when individuals change their consciousness,

9 G.W. F. Hegel, *The Philosophy of Right,* Oxford: Clarendon Press, 1942, p. 218.

10 For this discussion, see *The Phenomenology of Mind,* New York: Harper & Row, [1807] 1967, pp. 229–240. The passage on ' Lordship and Bondage' should be read by modern readers for its social configuration of the relation between the master and the slave.

Marx thought that such a view amounts to asking individuals to interpret reality in a different way, when in fact they can only eliminate their hardship and social inequality by altering their social and economic conditions.

Materialism as a Theoretical Perspective In addition to the break with German philosophy, a second development that was key to Marx's view of society and history was his introduction of a new interpretive framework for understanding history called the materialist perspective. This was introduced by Marx in order to overcome the problems posed by idealist philosophy and its abstraction of society and history. But what did Marx mean by materialism in this context? Simply stated, materialism is a theoretical perspective which looks at human problems by studying the real conditions of human existence, especially those related to the satisfaction of simple economic and material needs. It is the most basic premise of materialism that the very first thing human beings must do is satisfy their material needs by obtaining food, shelter and clothing. It goes on to assume that society and history are created from a sequence of productive acts which are designed to fulfill these needs. Materialism, therefore, may be defined as a theoretical perspective which takes as its starting place the view that, before anything else, human beings must satisfy their everyday economic needs through their physical labor and practical productive activity.[11] In this view, history and society are historical outcomes of the simple economic acts of production in which people produce simply in order to satisfy their immediate material needs. The theory goes on to explain that history begins in a series of economic acts, leading to different economic epochs in which the structure of society takes the form of the productive relations. What was so important about this perspective was its attempt to devise a theory of society and social existence from the starting point of human practical needs and economic production.

The distinction Marx made between 'materialism' and 'idealism' in this case was therefore central to his thinking in several respects. First, by anchoring theoretical activity in material reality, Marx put social theory in the service of human experience and made this a formal requirement for theoretical work. Up until that time, all philosophy had merely interpreted history in various ways, whereas Marx believed it was the aim of theory to change history.[12] Second, by beginning with human experience and practical productive activity rather than its representative philosophic categories, Marx separated the aims of philosophy from materialist social theory by outlining the conditions of the break with speculative philosophy. What made this position so unique was that it marked a turning point in the history of social thought itself. Whereas all philosophy up until that time had taken as its starting place the idea that the subject matter of philosophic investigation was to be found lying above the realm

---

11 *The German Ideology,* p. 16.

12 The assertion by Marx that philosophy only ever interprets history rather than changing it can be found in the eleventh thesis on Feuerbach, where he states that 'the philosophers have only interpreted the world differently, the point is to change it.' See *The German Ideology*, International Edition, 1947, p. 199.

of everyday experience, materialism had taken as its starting place the most basic human act, the production of material necessities of food, shelter and clothing, making these the subject of history and society.

The German Ideology

Fundamental Aims of the Work and The Materialist Theory of History

Written essentially as a collaborative work between 1845–6, *The German Ideology* was Marx's and Engels' first major theoretical writing. While it tends to be a difficult work, *The German Ideology* had two principle and basic aims. First, was to outline the conditions of the break with German speculative philosophy and to 'settle accounts' with Hegel.[13] Second, was to develop and expound the materialist conception of history by setting out the views of materialism in opposition to Hegelian philosophy. This was largely undertaken in the second section of the work which begins with an outline of the framework for developing the materialist theory of history and which goes on to form the central subject matter of the work. Because of its broad historical outlook and far reaching interpretation of history, this section of the work has had a much greater theoretical impact. In order, then, to understand the materialist theory of history put forward by Marx and Engels, it will be useful to examine their argument more closely.

After criticizing Hegelian philosophy, Marx and Engels turned their attention to developing a framework for the materialist theory of history. Perhaps the single most important element in Marx's social thought, the materialist theory of history is the cornerstone of his social and political thinking and remains one of the most thoroughgoing perspectives on historical and economic development ever devised. Marx outlined the rudiments of the materialist theory of history by considering what he called the three main premises which shaped his understanding of society and economic history, and these are as follows.

First, Marx believed that before anything else, human beings must be in a position to obtain food, shelter and clothing in order to live.[14] Thus, the first and most important historical act is the act of production of the means to satisfy human material needs such as food, shelter and clothing.[15] A second assumption, according to Marx, is that human beings actually distinguish themselves from the animal world to the extent that they must produce the means to satisfy their primary material needs.[16]

---

13 Marx and Engels, *The German Ideology*, pp. 3–6.

14 Ibid, pp. 7–9.

15 *The German Ideology*, p. 16. Marx states: 'The first premise of all human existence, and therefore of all history, is that human beings must be in a position to live in order to be able to make history. But, life involves before everything eating, drinking, a habitation, clothing and many other things. The first act is thus the production of the means to satisfy these needs, the production of material life itself.'

16 *The German Ideology*, p. 7.

Thus, while animals find what they need in nature, human beings must produce their material needs of food, shelter and clothing on their own, and to this extent they enter into a conscious relation with the natural world in order to survive. A third premise of the materialist theory of history, according to Marx, is that the way in which human beings produce depends on what they find in nature and what they must produce to survive. How they exist and how they live, thus tends to 'coincide with what they produce and how they produce, and the nature of individuals depends on the material conditions determining their production.'[17] On the basis of these premises, the materialist theory of history took up the task of understanding historical and social development from the perspective of human economic activity.

As we said earlier, historical materialism is a term used in social thought to describe Marx's main theoretical perspective for understanding society and history and, in order to look more closely at the premises and scope of his theory, it will be useful to quote from the 1859 preface of a work by Marx entitled *A Contribution to the Critique of Political Economy*, since it is one of the most incisive summaries of his theory of society ever written. Marx writes:

> In the social production which men carry on they enter into definite relations that are indispensable and independent of their will. These relations of production correspond to a definite stage of the development of their material forces of production. The totality of these relations of production constitute the economic structure of society, which is the real foundation, on top of which arises a legal and political superstructure to which correspond definite forms of social consciousness. It is not the consciousness of men, therefore, that determines their existence, but instead their social existence determines their consciousness. At a certain stage of their development, the material forces of production in society come into conflict with the existing relations of production, or – what is but a legal expression of the same thing – with the property relations within which they had been at work before. From forms of development of the forces of production these relations turn into their fetters. Then occurs a period of social revolution. With the change of the economic foundation the entire immense superstructure is more or less rapidly transformed.'[18]

From this passage we can derive four fundamental concepts that are central to the materialist theory of history. These are: (i) the means of production; (ii) the relations of production; (iii) the mode of production; and (iv) the forces of production. Taken together, these concepts make up the core of the materialist theory of history and, in order to see how they relate theoretically, let us look at the concept of the means of production.

---

17 Ibid.

18 Marx, *A Contribution to the Critique of Political Economy*, Moscow: Progress Publishers, [1859] 1970, pp. 20–21. H.B. Acton's article on historical materialism interprets Marx's 1859 preface by giving weight to the 'forces of production' at the expense of the means and relations of production. This tends to reduce Marxism to the 1859 preface at the exclusion of the other writings of Marx. For Acton's emphasis see 'The Materialist Conception of History,' *Proceedings of the Aristotelian Society*, 1951–2, pp. 205–224.

Means of Production   Marx begins by asserting that, in every stage of history, human beings have had at their disposal certain productive forces of land, animals, tools and machinery, etc., which are necessary to produce the means of their survival. These are called the means of production. According to Marx, the means of production refers to anything in the external world which is used to obtain livelihoods, produce incomes and acquire material needs. The means of production can therefore be defined as anything in the outside world which is utilized to produce food, shelter and clothing so as to satisfy human material needs and maintain existence.[19] For instance, the way jobs are used to produce wages, and land is used to produce food and fuel, constitute the means of production. It is important to note, however, that material needs and economic necessities cannot be produced privately on one's own, but rather only when we employ the means of production. But, said Marx, what we observe historically is that only one class of persons has always owned or monopolized the means of production throughout history. This condition of ownership over the means of production is the single most fundamental fact of the materialist theory of history since it is this that leads to the division of society into economic classes.[20]

The key division, Marx reasoned, is between owners and non-owners of the means of production. This is a central distinction since the existence of these classes denotes that only one class is the owner of the means of production, while the other is subordinated to those who have control over it.[21] Marx went on to refer to the class of non-owners as the direct producers of physical labor, and he argued that the most distinctive characteristic of this class is its inability to obtain unobstructed access to the means of production for purposes of satisfying their material needs. Because the ownership of the means of production tends to reside in only one class, Marx thought that the economic acts of individuals throughout history always seem to encounter social and historical restrictions which act as obstacles in the path of their access to the means of production.[22] As far as Marx was concerned, two fundamental consequences occur as soon as the means of production become the property of one class. First, the means of production are concentrated in a class who come to monopolize it as their private property, and in doing so they obtain control over it. Second, as soon as the means of production become the private property of one class, 'a momentous switch' takes place in how the means of production come to be used by the worker. Marx reasoned that when the means of production fall into private hands, workers no longer employ the means of production freely on their own as they once did in

---

19 Marx thought that all human beings must employ the means of production in order to meet their basic material needs and that, before anything else, human beings must of necessity satisfy their material needs. This means that the daily and hourly pursuit of material needs consequently structures the rest of their acts and activities in history. Consequently, economic acts become the most important historical acts.

20 *The German Ideology*, pp. 8–13.

21 *The German Ideology*, p. 9. The various stages in the development of history, said Marx, 'are just so many different forms of ownership,' and that the history of society is the history of classes.

22 In some societies, this path is so obstructed that some classes may be shut out of the means of production altogether. Certain caste categories in India and slaves in the societies of antiquity belong to this class.

previous societies, but rather the means of production employ them. As far as Marx is concerned, this constitutes a reversal of what existed in the past, since instead of the worker employing the means of production on their own free will, the means of production now employ the worker.[23]

Marx went on to argue that as soon as one class in society possesses a monopoly of the means of production, certain restrictions come into play that relate to how the means of production are to be used by the worker. These restrictions emerge essentially at two different levels. First are the restrictions which appear in the form of hiring policies, the imposition of work schedules, and the limits imposed on wages and wage levels as far as workers are concerned.[24] Second are the restrictions which penalize the worker in terms of infractions related to the hours of labor, the conditions of work and the rules regulating the conduct of the worker during the workday. The first class of restrictions form a clear set of obstructions to the means of production because, given restrictive hiring policies, some workers may never be hired, while other workers may be excluded on the basis of class, gender, race or age characteristics. Other restrictions may exist for untrained workers who may have limits imposed on their wages, or who may be required to work without wages until they are trained, or who may be required to work shifts with extended hours of labor.

Among the second class of restrictions are the practices that exist for regulating the conduct of the worker during the workday. This may involve penalizing workers by reducing their wages for faults or mistakes created in the production process. Also it may include the punishment of the worker for slackness in the labor process or for conduct that slows the process down or delays it. Similar to these are the penalties imposed on workers for lateness, infractions during hours of work and for slackness in work routine. Often, these penalties reduced the wages of the worker and in some cases simply led to dismissal.[25] In other cases, they may push the level of wages below the means of subsistence for certain categories of work and in others they may simply diminish wages by introducing penalties on workers for infractions during hours of work.[26]

While the first set of restrictions functions simply by excluding workers from access to the means of production on the basis of their physical characteristics, the second set of restrictions involve the regulation of the worker's conduct during the

---

23 Marx, *Capital*, Vol. I, p. 798.

24 For a discussion of these restrictions in feudal economies see Marglin, 'What do bosses do'? The Origins and functions of Hierarchy in Capitalist Production,' *Review of Radical Political Economy*, 6, 2, 1974, 33–60. For how these restrictions manifest themselves in industrial societies in the form of punishments, fines and the dismissal of the worker see S. Pollard, 'Factory Discipline in the Industrial Revolution,' *Economic History Review*, 16, 1963–4, pp. 260–3.

25 See Marx, *Capital,* Vol. 1, p. 551.

26 For the system of penalties introduced against the worker during this period see S. Pollard, 'Factory Discipline in the Industrial Revolution,' pp. 254–271. In industry, the control over wages and limits on wage levels were extended by the 'minimum wage' laws that appeared in North America and Europe. While the history of the minimum wage restrictions shows that it first protected the worker by setting a limit above what bosses wished to pay to workers, it has since acted as a limit on wages by keeping them below the level of subsistence. Wages under these laws, therefore, are not a living wage.

hours of labor. In contrast to the first set of restrictions these function by reducing the actual wages which the worker earns during the span of the workday. In the main, these are enforced by the imposition of fines for mistakes, lateness, waste and absence from the work place. As soon as these restrictions began to be formalized in the nineteenth century, they introduced a more rigorous regulation of the workplace that appeared in the form of the control over how the production process was to be carried out and the rules regarding workshop order. This not only governed how the worker used the means of production and subjected the worker to constant supervision, but it also tended to reduce by fines and penalties the actual material benefit which the worker derived from the production process. In some cases, the restrictions imposed on how the means of production were to be used provided a direct advantage to the employer and a direct disadvantage to the worker.[27] These included restrictions imposed on the wages of women and children, or the restrictions imposed on workers in terms of their movement at the work site which existed in cases where a full workday was carried out.[28]

Relations of Production   A second concept in the materialist theory of history is the existence of the relations of production. These are of central importance to the materialist theory of history because it is the relations of production which economically bind one class to another in the production process. Accordingly, one of the clearest ways of understanding what Marx meant by the relations of production is to remember that he used the term 'relations' repeatedly in his writings to indicate the connection between the way a society produces and the social roles allotted to individuals in the production process. Marx believed that the roles individuals assume in production are directly related to the wider system of social relations which arise from the fact that ownership tends always to be concentrated only in one class of society. Marx thought that the tendency for ownership to reside in one class created two distinct roles in production: producers and non-producers of physical labor. These different productive roles formally separate the two classes in terms of production since, while one class engages in productive labor during the workday, the other presides over the worker and the means of production itself.

The role played by the relations of production therefore becomes clear when we look at the result of class relations in historical terms. Marx thought that these could be outlined by noting essentially two characteristics. First, non-owners are compelled to enter into relations of production in order to satisfy their material and economic

---

27 An example of this is the restriction imposed on the payment of wages at the end of the work cycle rather than the beginning of the work cycle. Payment at the end of the work cycle ignores the immediate need of the worker for food, shelter and clothing for each day that they labor and each day that their need arises. In effect, it requires the worker to advance a loan to their employer in the form of the worker's wages and it imposes controls on the payout of wages.

28 Examples of unlawful restrictions existing in certain commercial operations are those where employers routinely require workers to work for 'free' during training shifts, where they falsely claim that they are not by law required to pay workers during training, thus extracting free labor.

needs, and as a result they are subordinated to the class who are dominant over them. Second, since workers tend historically to be subordinate to their bosses, they are compelled to labor both for themselves in terms of their own livelihoods and for their bosses in terms of the economic value that is derived from the production process by the very fact of their labor. This subordination in productive roles gives rise to several key consequences outlined by G. A. Cohen in his useful book on Marx.[29] First, non-owners produce for others who do not produce for them; second, the livelihoods of the non-owners depend on their relations with their superiors; third, the owners of the means of production have direct rights over the economic product of the producer; fourth, the owners of the means of production always receive more from the production process than the direct producer; and fifth, non-owners are subject to the authority of their superiors.[30]

Marx, then, used the concept of the 'relations of production' to indicate how the productive roles were actually structured, and to look at what happened when the worker put the means of production to work. Marx noted that every time the worker put the means of production to work in order to earn a livelihood, they were compelled to enter into a relation with their bosses which gave their bosses rights over how the means of production were to be used. In addition to this, Marx noted that the relations of production were always entered into against the will of the worker and this tended to add a level of compulsion that did not exist for other classes. Marx, therefore, thought that the relations of production arose from the necessity to produce in society, and as a result of this necessity coercive relations between bosses and workers were created, to the extent that bosses seem always to have greater authority over workers within the production process.[31] We can therefore outline the historical features of the relations of production as follows: first, are the different productive roles which arise directly from the class relationships and which are patterned after them; second are the relations of dependency which arise as soon as workers enter into relations of production to satisfy their material needs, since as soon as they do so they become personally dependent on their superiors for their livelihoods; third are the relationships of dominance and subordination which emerge from the productive relationships themselves and which are a direct reflection of the class relationships.

Feudal societies expressed this relation very clearly when it came time for the serf to use the means of production in order to produce their livelihood. At the moment that production took place, the serf enters into a relation of production with the landholder so that relations of subordination come into play at the moment that the landholder extracted unpaid forced labor service from the serf during the corvée days, and then again when the landholder exercised their right over the agricultural product of

---

29 G. A. Cohen, *Karl Marx's Theory of History*, New Jersey: Princeton University, 1978.
30 Ibid., pp. 69–70.
31 Marx believed that as soon as the worker uses the means of production the relations of dominance and subordination come into play. See his discussion in *The German Ideology* and in *Capital*.

the serf. In a feudal society, therefore, every time the serf employs the means of production, the relations of subordination existing in the form of the corvée right came into play and constituted the social relations in which production took place.

A second major feature of the relations of production is their tendency to govern the way the worker uses the means of production to satisfy their material needs and create a livelihood. In this case, non-owners are unable freely to produce the means of their own existence since they do not have unobstructed access to the means of production. This can be made clear if we look at feudal society once again. In a feudal society, the relations of production are between lord and serf who are respectively owners and non-owners of the means of production. Marx reasoned that in order for serfs to put the means of production to work, they are compelled to enter into a relation with the landholder, giving the landholder the right over the labor of the serf and the right over the serf's agricultural production as provided by the corvée right. Marx thought that this right actually structured the system of social relations between the landholder and the serf and that it reflected the underlying class relations of dominance and subordination which were a part of the relations of production.[32]

Marx went on to argue that the relations of production create three central elements which make them conceptually key to the materialist theory of history. First is their ability to be transformed into relations of dominance and subordination. Second is the ability of the relations of production to become a physical and economic disadvantage for one class, and an economic advantage for another.[33] Third is the ability of the relations of production to be backed up by coercive sanctions legitimated by the political and legal institutions of society.[34]

A third feature related to the relations of production is their tendency to appear in all societies. Marx maintained that the relations of production manifest themselves historically at different stages of economic development and these always seem to coincide with the way societies produce. The names given to these different relations of production correspond to the stages of economic development. For instance, the relations of production in ancient society are between patricians and slaves, while lord and serf are the names given to the relations of production in feudal society, where a landholding class rely on an ensurfed peasantry to perform necessary labor. In industrial societies, on the other hand, relations of production are between bosses and workers where a large class of wage laborers produce for a class which is dominant over them.

It is important to note at this point how the differences existing in the class system actually structure the way individuals are positioned within the relations of production themselves. These class positions, Marx thought, create differences in the way individuals come to perceive their own relation to the means of production as well as

---

32 *German Ideology*, pp. 11–13.

33 Marx, *Contribution to the Critique of Political Economy*. He states: 'these relations turn into their coercive bonds,' p. 21.

34 Marx, *Contribution to the Critique*, p. 192–93.

their relation to the wider society. In this respect, workers and bosses tend to relate to the means of production in fundamentally different ways, and this seems to actually shape the different perceptual standpoints of the individuals involved. For example, workers tend to relate to the means of production mainly in terms of economic necessity such that it turns the workplace into a means to obtain only wages. It stands to reason that the relation which the worker has to the means of production leads them to view the conditions of work as a limitation not of their own making. Workers thus see the world from the set of limitations and standpoints which they inherit from their positions within the means of production.

In contrast to this, owners of the means of production tend to relate to the means of production in a way that confirms their self-identity in society and history beyond what their actual incomes provide in terms of material wealth and well-being. The essential difference between these two types of identification – one negative, the other positive – is a function of how one's class position tends to shape the outlook of the individuals involved, both to themselves and to the outside world, and how this outlook is a function of their class standpoint that arises from how they are situated in the relations of production.[35]

Mode of Production, Forces of Production   A third concept in the materialist theory of history is the mode of production. While Marx never completely elucidated the term, he did leave various references to it throughout his writings. In one of these he points out that 'social relations are closely bound up with productive forces. In acquiring new productive forces, human beings change their mode of production; and in changing their mode of production they change their way of earning their living and all their social relations. The handmill thus gives you a society with the feudal lord; the steam mill, a society with the industrial capitalist.'[36] In 'broad outline', said Marx, 'we can designate the Asiatic, ancient, feudal and the modern industrial modes of production as so many epochs in the process of the economic formation of society.'[37]

Initially, then, the term mode of production is used by Marx to identify the primary elements of a given historical stage of production by showing how its economic base shapes its social relations. In this sense, the way people actually produce and enter into social relations with one another is called a mode of production and this comprises the total way of life of society, its social activities and its social institutions. But, in and of itself, this does not give us a clear understanding of the term and so we must look more closely.

In order to have a clear understanding of what Marx meant by the mode of production, we have to distinguish between 'forces of production' and 'relations of

---

35 For a discussion of how an individual's class relation to the means of production structures their personal relation to society and the differences created in the mode of identification see Marx, 'Wage Labor and Capital.' In R.C. Tucker (ed.), The Marx-Engels Reader, 2nd Ed., New York: W.W. Norton & Company, [1849] 1978, pp. 203–17.

36 Marx, *Poverty of Philosophy*, p. 109.

37 Marx, *A Contribution to the Critique of Political Economy*, p. 21.

production' since together these define the mode of production.[38] As we noted earlier, the forces of production may be taken to mean the instruments, equipment, land, tools, etc., which are put to work for purposes of producing a livelihood. As such, forces of production only have capacities to be put to work; but, in and of themselves, these forces can only be put into operation, so to speak, when people in society enter into the relations of production. The relations of production, therefore, are always about how the forces of production are to be used in order to produce, and one key idea stemming from the relations of production is that one class are always the proprietors over these forces, while the other class is subordinate to them.

This being the case, two key conditions of the relations of production can be highlighted: first, the right by one class to control the labor of the producer; and second, the right by the owners of the means of production to control the products of labor. This can be shown directly when we look at the different modes of production. For instance, in the ancient mode of production, the patrician class presided over the forces of production in such a way that the relations of production entered into by the producer transformed them into slaves and, as far Marx was concerned, this was as a result of the existing relations of production which derived from the way ancient societies engaged in the production process.[39] In feudal society, on the other hand, the landholder directly presided over the forces of production and had rights to control both the labor of the serf and the serf's agricultural production. In an industrial society, by contrast, bosses have direct control over the means of production as well as the terms of employment, and this gives them rights over the disposition of the product of labor, and control over the laborer and the production process.[40]

A second major characteristic of the mode of production is its ability to determine the system of social relations arising from it. For instance, in feudal society the primary way of producing economic necessities was by cultivation. This produced food crops, domestic animals, shelter and clothing, which is already clear enough. But in addition to producing material needs, a system of social relations emerged between the lord and serf which tended to govern how the means of production were put to work, and how they were used to derive livelihoods. Since the landholder and the serf constitute the central social relation of production in feudal society, Marx argued that the unequal relations arising from the fact that one class of persons tends to be dominant and preside over the forces of production is a function of a mode of production. The concept of mode of production, therefore, allowed Marx to identify the

---

38 For a discussion of the distinction between 'forces' and 'relations' see Maurice Cornforth, *Historical Materialism*, London: Lawrence and Wishart, 1962, p. 36.

39 Marx pointed out that the 'fact' of slavery was to be considered as a product of social relations rather than as an accident of nature. 'Society', says Marx, 'is not merely an aggregate of individuals, but rather is the sum of the relations in which these individuals stand to one another.' Outside of society, a slave is but a human being; whereas inside society a slave is the result of a socially determined relation, and thus only a slave in and through society. See Marx, *Grundrisse*, 175–6.

40 The control over the level of wages paid to labor is evident when wages are set below the rate of subsistence, which was the case in industrial societies of the nineteenth and twentieth centuries.

primary economic elements which tend to confer an advantage to one class over another in any given historical period by showing directly how the productive system shapes the system of social and class relations.

It is important at this point to keep in mind that the materialist theory of history was designed to explain the key process of historical development in which all societies seem to divide themselves into unequal social classes. Marx thought that the division of society into distinct and separate classes was a law of social and historical development, and to provide historical evidence for this he divided history into three main economic stages or epochs, which he characterized in the form of ancient, feudal and capitalist societies. Each of these stages in economic history, according to Marx, has four central tendencies. First, they perpetuate the division of society into classes, in which one class is dominant over another. Second, they confer prerogatives and privileges to the dominant classes, but not to the subordinate classes. Third, they perpetuate economic, political and social inequality between classes; and fourth, at each stage of economic development, unequal class relations are supported by religious, legal and political institutions.

Laws of Historical Development *Different Forms of Ownership Over the Means of Production* Up till now we have seen that the materialist theory of history is above all a theory of historical development that explains human existence in terms of a series of economic stages in which individuals are compelled to produce in order to live, and where society divides itself into a system of unequal social classes and unequal productive relations. After laying out the basic framework for the materialist theory of history, Marx turned his attention to obtaining evidence that would confirm his thesis that the historical development of society tends to be economic in nature. To do this, Marx conceived of history in the form of different types of ownership over the means of production which he thought could be expressed in terms of four separate stages or epochs of social and historical development: tribal, ancient, feudal and capitalist.[41] This broad conceptualization of history in terms of stages of economic development was central in two key respects. First, it constituted what some scholars believe to be a 're-periodization' of linear history, in that it substituted the then dominant views of historical time marked by religious epochs for a form of development marked by economic stages.[42] Second, in focusing on the sequence of economic stages, it reconceptualized historical development by concentrating on the 'system of production' which was characteristic of all societies. In addition to this, Marx went on to point out that each of the stages of historical development had three characteristics: a system of production and division of labor; different forms of

---

41 Marx and Engels, *The German Ideology*, pp. 9–13; and in Karl Marx, *Pre-Capitalist Economic Formations*, New York: International Publishers, 1965 [1857–58], pp. 67–120; and Marx, *A Contribution to the Critique of Political Economy*, p. 21

42 On Marx and the re-periodization of history see L. Althusser and E. Balibar, *Reading Capital*, London: Verso, 1979, pp. 102–3.

property ownership; and a system of class relations that emerge from the ownership over the means of production, giving rise to the productive relationships.

As we noted earlier, Marx saw world history in terms of different forms of ownership over the means of production, and essentially he thought there were four distinct economic stages in which this ownership was expressed. The first type of ownership Marx calls tribal. This encompasses a society with a rudimentary economy in which people produce principally by hunting and gathering. In this case, the division of labor is rudimentary, there is no development of private property, and the social structure is derived from the family and kinship system. Because property is communal, there is no developed system of class relations, although there is some incipient exploitation within the family system. The tribal form of association originated from a productive system which was largely based on kinship and on a collective and cooperative orientation to production. This led to a society where there was no division into classes and a system of production where there was greater social equality and cooperation in the production of material needs and economic necessities. As a result, no dominant class owned or monopolized the means of production, since these tended to be shared in common, and little or no exploitation develops between groups.

The second form of ownership discussed by Marx is found in ancient society. This is a form of social organization which developed from an association of tribes who formed a group of city states, giving rise to a political and civil organization. Ancient societies were mainly situated in cities with an outlying rural economy that was largely agrarian with rudimentary industry and a system of trade and commerce.[43] Societies of this type are found in classical antiquity in Greece and Rome where a patrician class monopolize the means of production, and class relations were hardened into a dominant and subordinate class of patrician and slave. In contrast to tribal society, there was private property and a system of class relations developed from property ownership. The relation between owners of property and producers of physical labor formed itself into a class system of citizen and slave. Unlike tribal society, the division into classes had crystallized and the primary form of labor was slave labor. Societies of this type occupied vast territories and the productive system had an extensive division of labor. In addition, a civil, political and military authority emerged as an adjunct to the productive system. The ancient Graeco-Roman world is an historical example of economies where productive labor is in the form of slavery.[44] In this case, ownership of the means of production is concentrated in the hands of a patrician class who are a military elite, who live by conquering territories whose lands were seized and whose population was turned into slaves.[45]

Patrician classes maintain their economic existence by searching for ever widening means of production, resulting in a political organization combining conquered lands in order to form new political territories. Rome's march into Brittany in the

---

43 Marx and Engels, *German Ideology*, p. 9.
44 Ibid., p. 10.
45 Marx and Engels, *The German Ideology*, p. 9; Marx, *Pre-Capitalist Social Formations*, p. 72.

fourth century is an example of development of this type. The division of society into a class of patrician and slave grew directly from the structure of the economy and the social relations of production. As the population of slaves died off, they were replaced by newly acquired slaves from other territories. The prevailing relations of production are between patricians and slave laborers, and the patrician class draw their wealth from the class of slaves who act as the direct producers.

A third form of ownership identified by Marx is feudal society. In this type of society, agriculture is the main source of economic production and the ownership over the means of production is concentrated in the hands of a land-owning class made up of a landed nobility. The focal point of the economy was the countryside, agriculture was widespread, there was little or no industry and town life was not developed.[46] Unlike tribal or ancient societies, ownership was concentrated in a class of landholders who acted as the sole proprietors over the land as the principle means of economic production. The chief form of property was landed property, with a developed class system emerging between a peasant class who perform necessary physical labor, and a class of landholders who had social and political prerogatives, giving them rights to control both the labor of the serf and the serf's economic production.[47] Feudal societies existed largely in Europe and England between the ninth and the seventeenth centuries, but are not unknown in the East in India and China. The social and political power of the landholder was backed up by legal and political institutions which provided landholders with the powers of coercion over the class of serfs.

The fourth stage of ownership over the means of production arises in industrial capitalism. With the development of industrial society, said Marx, comes the destruction of the feudal mode of production and a transition from the economy of the countryside to the economy of the city. During the decline of feudal society, the class of peasant serfs are coercively divorced from the land as a means of livelihood and, as a result, are transformed into a class of wage laborers who had to sell their labor to meet their economic needs. In a society of this type, the economy is industrial with an advanced division of labor which develops trade and commercial activity. As the rural economy declines, city life becomes the center of economic activity and there is a fully developed political and civil life, and the productive system shifts from agriculture to industry. There is the widespread emergence of private property and a developed class system of industrial capitalists who are the owners of the means of production and wage laborers who are producers of physical labor.[48] In contrast to feudal society, the means of production have become diversified and largely consist of machinery, technology and the industrial means of production, which in this case have become the monopoly of one class. Ownership of the means of production is therefore in private hands and this ownership is over economic resources, factories,

46 *German Ideology,* p. 11–13.
47 *German Ideology,* p. 12.
48 *The German Ideology,* pp. 43–78.

tools, technologies and other productive materials. Owners of the means of production draw their wealth from the class of wage laborers who function as the primary producers, and wage labor is the prevailing form of productive labor.

The Concept of Class and Class Structure   Having looked at the main concepts of the materialist theory of history, I now want to turn my attention to the concept of social class as it was first used in classical Marxism. It is important to note at this point that by the time Marx had written *The German Ideology* and *Capital*, he had neither defined the concept of class, nor had he worked out how the concept was to be explained, despite the fact that he had isolated the principle of class formation at different stages of historical and social development and had identified at least three distinct periods where classes had formed.[49]

The conceptualization of social classes by Marx thus goes back as far as his early writings and can be found in works such as *The German Ideology*, *The Communist Manifesto*, *The 1844 Manuscripts* and *The Poverty of Philosophy*. But because the concept is key to social thought and because it has recently been the subject of criticism and debate by commentators such as Gramsci, Sorel, Laclau and Mouffe, E. O. Wright, Poulantzas, Lukacs, Michelle Barrett, Ellen Wood and others, it will be useful to briefly outline the history of the concept from the point where it was first used in the nineteenth century by Marx and Engels to designate class formation in history.[50]

Marx's observations about class and class structure began in several of his early writings, but explicitly it becomes a subject of historical discussion in the *Communist Manifesto*, published in 1848. Here, Marx identifies the concept of class, class formations and the class struggle in the following way:

> The history of all hitherto existing societies is the history of class struggles. Freeman and slave, patrician and plebeian, lord and serf, guild-master and journeyman, in a word, oppressor and oppressed, stood in constant opposition to one another, carried on an uninterrupted, now hidden fight, a fight that each time ended either in a revolutionary reconstitution of society at large, or in the common ruin of the contending classes. In the earlier epochs of history, we find almost everywhere a complicated arrangement of society into various orders, a manifold gradation of social rank. In ancient Rome we have patricians, knights, plebeians, slaves; in the Middle Ages, feudal lords, vassals, guild-masters, journeymen, apprentices, serfs; in almost all of these classes, again, subordinate gradations.'[51]

In this quotation, Marx sets out several key characteristics for describing the concept of class. First, he identified the historical tendency in all societies to divide themselves into

---

49 Marx attempted a systematic definition of class in the 1860s when he was planning his chapter outline for volume three of *Capital*. This discussion appears in chapter 52 of Vol. 3 of *Capital* which Marx's titles simply 'classes.' However, the manuscript breaks off after only a page and a half.

50 For discussions of these works and the concept of class see N. Poulantzas, *Political Power and Social Classes* London: Sheed and Ward, 1973.

51 Marx, *The Communist Manifesto*, F.L. Bender (ed.), New York: Norton, 1988, pp. 55–6.

two unequal social classes: patrician and slave; lord and serf, capitalist and wage laborer. Second, he pointed out that classes are always structured according to what he called 'manifold and subordinate gradations of social rank,' which identified that classes are structured in a hierarchy and that these gradations of rank seem always to form in relation to social and economic privileges which tend to concentrate themselves at the top of the class hierarchy, with little if any privileges or power at the bottom of the class hierarchy.[52]

Third, according to Marx, classes are always engaged in what he calls a 'historical struggle' which is carried out as an 'uninterrupted fight between the contending classes which often ends in the ruins of the these classes.'[53] Fourth, in each economic epoch a given population is transformed into a class when the prevailing economic conditions of existence act to transform this group into a relatively homogenous population. For example, when agricultural workers were transformed into a mass of wage laborers in the nineteenth century during the transition from feudalism to capitalism, one class was transformed into another. While this was a process which Marx referred to as the proletarianization of labor, it had definite class consequences. Fifth, Marx believed that the transformation of a 'mass of people' into a class created what he called a common set of interests that define a class situation and that, over time, this class becomes a mass mobilized in a struggle or a conflict which opposes itself to the interests of the dominant classes in a political struggle.[54]

Class Structure and the System of Social Relations   In order to define the concept of class more explicitly, it will be useful to look at a concept Marx used frequently in his work which he referred to as the 'system of social relations.' Initially, the term social relations is used in social theory to refer to the set of social connections which arise between individuals when they engage in structured interchanges with society, but in the main these types of social relations arise within the production process carried on within the economy when we produce our livelihoods.[55] The concept of social relations therefore identifies two immediate principles referring to society and social history. First, it refers to the system of social relations individuals enter into principally for purposes of production, which are always the immediate

---

52 For example, in ancient societies such as Greece and Rome, the difference between the dominant and dominated positions of patrician and slave is greater than that found in feudal society, where class relations exist between the dominant and dominated positions of lord and the serf.

53 Note that the term 'class struggle' is not restricted to the subordinate class since all classes are engaged in the struggle to realize their interests historically.

54 Most of the characteristics of social classes stated here can be found in *The Communist Manifesto* and *The Poverty of Philosophy*. An additional definition of class can be found in *The Eighteenth Brumaire of Louis Bonaparte* which states: 'In so far as millions of families live under economic conditions of existence that divide their mode of life, their interests and their culture from those of the other classes, and put them into hostile contrast with the latter, they form a class.'

55 For a discussion of the interconnections in social relations between bosses and workers see Marx, 'Wage Labor and Capital,' in R.C. Tucker, *The Marx-Engels Reader*, New York: W.W. Norton, 1978, pp. 203–17.

result of the social and economic necessity which acts on them. These social relations always reflect a set of definite connections with other individuals with whom they must relate, and it is always within the system of social relations that social activity takes place. Second, the concept refers to the way in which the system of social relations entered into by individuals always structure the conditions under which the various social interchanges with society take place, and this structure often manifests itself in the form of dominant and subordinate class relations which are exemplified in the relations between bosses and workers, landlords and tenants and producers and consumers. Sometimes, these relation are called 'structured oppositions' in that the individuals who occupy the class positions within these relations are opposed to each other. In this case, the 'opposition' is a structured or constitutive part of the social relations.[56]

It is important to note at this point that Marx thought that individuals were situated in society and history by the positions they occupied in the relations of production, and that without this he believed that their social activity could neither take place or be understood. Marx went on to elaborate on this point in a writing entitled 'Wage Labor and Capital' where he asked a series of questions which were stated in the most obvious way: 'what is labor,' 'what are wages,' 'what is a slave,' what is a capital' and, lastly, 'what is a worker as distinct from a boss'?[57] Marx believed that these questions could not be answered without referring to the social framework that constituted the system of social relations within which these class relations exist. Thus the question what is a worker as opposed to a boss, takes on meaning, Marx thought only within a certain system of social relations and he compared this to how physical objects take on certain identities within a given system of productive relations. For example, a 'spinning jenny,' said Marx, only becomes 'capital' in relation to a certain historical context as opposed to being a simple machine for spinning cotton. When torn from these relations and relationships, and when taken out of its context as a tool of industrial production, it 'is no more capital than gold is in itself money, or sugar the price of sugar,' or an Afro-American a plantation slave.[58]

Marx's answer to the question 'what is a worker' as distinct from a boss, is that workers only becomes workers when they enter into specific and definite social relations with one another and only then do their social connections and relations as workers take place. Thus, the fact that they are workers, bosses and slaves, etc., is a result of entering into social relations after which they become subjects of a social framework. Thus, their social relations are always a product of the specific internal organization and relationships arising from the definite connections with one another

---

56 I draw on Pierre Bourdieu's use of the term 'structured oppositions' because it clarifies what Marx meant by the concept of class and because it draws on a definition of class as an aggregate that exists in a social field only in relation to other aggregates. Classes are, in effect, structured oppositions. See his *Practical Reason: On the Theory of Social Action*, London: Polity Press, 1998, pp. 1–34.

57 Marx, 'Wage Labor and Capital,' pp. 204–209.

58 see Marx, 'Wage Labor and Capital,' pp. 203–217.

in society and without these, workers, bosses and slaves would not exist.[59] While Marx tried to systematize class relations by noting that each of the individuals within the class relationships had different ranks, different powers and different privileges and gradations, he tended to conceive of class relations in the form of structured oppositions where the individuals within the class relations had different and opposing interests. While Marx commented mostly on structured oppositions within the economy, he thought that class relations were largely structured and even defined by the roles individuals played in economic production, and to this extent he looked at how different societies tend to structure the way in which individuals enter into class relations and the different degrees of coercion and force that existed within these relations.

Initially, then, we can define class and class relations as the name for a certain type of structured social relation that is formed within the field of the economy and the relations of subordination that arise from it. In feudal societies, for instance, class relations were formed when the landholder and the serf entered into relations of production that were clearly marked out in law and custom, as well as in time and space. What we learn here is that feudal societies gave rise to a whole system of social positions which form structured oppositions that define, in economic and political terms, the entire system of social relations entered into by the landholder and the serf.

The Concept of Class and the Relations of Subordination   Since the concept of class is closely linked to what we have called the relations of subordination, it will be useful to trace the history of the term in relation to the concept of class. Traditionally, the relations of subordination have been the subject of special study in the context of social class and class inequality, the structure of the caste system, the history of racism, and the study of gender relations within social and political thought proper. But before these terms were used in contemporary social theory, or in Women's Studies, the term 'relations of subordination' was used by Hegel, Marx and Weber in the nineteenth century to pinpoint a system of structured relations between individuals in which different forms of dominance and subordination manifest themselves at different stages in history.[60]

For all practical purposes, it was Hegel who first identified the existing relations of subordination by outlining the forms of dominance and dependency existing between the master and the slave in societies of antiquity. It is here, in fact, that we find the prototype for the social relations of authority and power, and the prototype for the class distinctions and oppositions which were so much a part of early feudal

---

59 Marx is saying that social idenity in this case is determined by the existing social relations between individuals in society. For example, a human being is a 'slave' only in and through society, whereas outside of society they are only human beings. See Marx, *The Grundrisse*, pp. 175–6.

60 One of the first discussions of the relations of subordination in the context of nineteenth century economies is found in Marx's preface in *A Contribution to the Critique of Political Economy*, Progress Publishers, 1970, pp. 19–22.

societies of the West, and previously ancient societies of Greece and Rome, whose economies presupposed the existence of slave labor.[61] It is here, too, that we find the prototype for the form of dependency of an individual upon a superior who, through the power of their class position, or the force of legal sanction, assumed a position in a social relation which was dominant over the subordinate position. The relations of subordination thus refer to a whole series of structured relations and oppositions which have existed historically between classes and castes, between bosses and workers, between landlords and tenants, and these relations have existed in the past and continue to exist in the present. The relations of subordination existing in societies of the past thus pinpoint the different degrees of subjection and dependency that exist in society and the use of force over an individual that may exist when a system of social relations assigns powers of rank and privilege to classes or castes in positions of dominance.

Relations of subordination have thus existed in societies since classical antiquity and are evident historically up to the modern period. For instance, in ancient Greece there was the Athenian aristocrat and the slave laborer; in ancient Rome there was the *Civis Romanus* and the slave; in Russia there was the boyar and the peasants; and in India, there were landlords (jagirdars) and peasant cultivators.[62] Much later in history, of course, there was the American slave owner and then eventually the modern landlord and employer in industrial capitalism. All these relations of subordination have their historical roots in social formations going back as far as classical antiquity.

In the West, the prototype of the relations of subordination can be found in societies of antiquity, where social relations tended to exhibit forms of dominance and subordination whose most extreme expression is found in the institution of slavery and in slave economies.[63] Societies of this type existed in Greece and Rome from the fifth century B.C. to the third and fourth centuries A.D. In Rome, for instance, economic life was centered on a type of economy referred to as an 'Ergastula,' a villa-like system of landed enterprises, sometimes rented, sometimes owned, in which production focused on the extensive ranching of sheep, the cultivation of cereal crops and the production of military supplies.[64] In some cases, a semi-industrial annex was attached to the villa for purposes of industrial production involving supplies and military armaments. While economies of this type were centered mostly on the periphery of the Roman cities, what we find historically is that economic and material production was by slave laborers who were political captives forced into labor

---

61 M.I. Finley, *Slavery in Classical Antiquity*, Cambridge: Heffer, 1968; *The Ancient Economy*, London: Ghatto & Windus, 1973; Maurice Godelier, 'Politics as 'Infrastructure': An Anthropologist's thoughts on the Example of Classical Greece and the Notions of Relations of Production and Economic Determination,' in J. Freidman and M.J. Rowlands (eds.), *The Evolution of Social Systems*, London: Duckworth, 1977, pp. 13–28.

62 On these relations of subordination see Marx, *Capital*. Vol. I, p. 344.

63 While little is known about the structural characteristics of slave economies, D.W. Rathbone provides interesting information that has not been discussed previously in 'The Slave Mode of Production in Italy,' *The Journal of Roman Studies*, Vol. 73, 1983, 160–68.

64 D.W. Rathbone, 'The Slave Mode of Production in Italy,' pp., 160–68

service against their will and who often labored until death without the provision of subsistence. In the period of the Roman empire, wealthy Romans secured large plots of public land which were worked by squads of slaves, who were either recruited by the Roman elite or by contractors who recruited slaves for the Ergastulas when they lacked a pre-existing labor force.[65]

The early Roman slave economies were thus simple and brutal: they enslaved large populations, supervised forced labor service until death and appropriated all production. In Rome, slaves were utilized extensively in large squads or gangs primarily for purposes of agricultural and military production. In addition, slaves were used in public projects for the purpose of constructing Roman buildings and for the rebuilding of the Roman infrastructure.[66] As a social category, slaves were excluded from society, had their rights curtailed, were prohibited from taking part in political life and were not permitted to acquire things for themselves. In Rome, slaves were utilized in the fifth century A.D. for purposes of forced labor, the economic provisioning of cities and the construction of public monuments and buildings. It is therefore in the economies of the ancient world that we find individuals who are set apart from the rest of society and enslaved for purposes of forced compulsory labor, and it is in this context that the relations of subordination first emerge in their classical form.

Historically, the term 'relations of subordination' grows out of the tradition of European social thought, beginning in the nineteenth century with Hegel's famous description of the relations of subordination and dependency existing between the master and the slave and with his description of the four types of political society and the relations of subordination resulting from them.[67] In this context, Hegel recounts a system of social relations existing between individuals and the political structure which he defines as a form of dependency by an individual upon a superior who assumes control over the existence of another for purposes of economic advantage. Throughout history, therefore, various dependencies thus emerge in all societies in relation to economic, political and class differences between people. These vary in the degree of restrictiveness, use of force, the extent of control over labor and the degree of control over the product of the labor of others. Slavery is the most extreme expression of the relations of subordination and, as we said earlier, it was introduced for purposes of economic production in Greece and Rome due to the fact that the dominant classes did not engage in physical labor themselves.[68] Under such circumstances, the

---

65 Ibid., pp. 160–63.

66 For a more detailed description of the 'slave forces' at the disposal of the Romans and the various distinctions in Roman society concerning the slave classes see P.A. Brunt, 'Free Labor and Public Works at Rome,' *Journal of Roman Studies*, 70, 1980, 81–99.

67 Hegel's framing of the relations of subordination is important for the history of social theory because it constitutes the prototype for all class and caste relations where different forms of dominance and subordination prevail. For his discussion of the master-slave relation see Hegel, *The Phenomenology of the Mind*, New York: Harper, 1967 [1807], pp. 234–40. For the discussion of the four types of political society and the resulting relations of subordination see *The Philosophy of Right*, London: Oxford University Press, 1958 [1820], pp. 220–222.

68 M.I. Finely refers to slavery as 'the economic miracle' of the ancient world.

relations of subordination always involve compulsion of some kind, whether this is directly through force or indirectly through economic coercion.[69] While relations of subordination appear most frequently in economic circumstances in the form of class relations between bosses and workers and between landlords and tenants, they also appear in families, in gender relations, in politics, in schooling and in the existing relations between race and class.

Since the concept of class was used in Marxism to refer to a historical principle evident in the process of economic development where unwanted or unwilled class relations re-occur throughout history, the concept of class and class formation has been historically important in classical Marxism in the last century. In this context, the concept of class is often defined as a historical social relation in which the principle of production manifests itself in the form of the separation of people into class categories which reflect dominant and subordinate economic and political relationships. However, in the 1970s and 1980s the ability to isolate fixed groups in the outside material world that conformed to the conception of social classes occupying fixed locations within the economy was called into question by postmodern theories found in the writings of Ernesto Laclau, Chantal Mouffe and Michele Barrett, who argued that in the context of a theory of discourse the term class does not signify a unique identity outside of the linguistic system and, in and of itself, this put the material existence of social classes and class relations into question. In addition to this, Marxism itself was called into question.[70]

Opposing himself to the theoretical obstacles introduced by poststructuralist conceptions of society as either 'impossible' or 'non-existent,' Pierre Bourdieu has recently reclaimed the concept of class in classical structuralism and classical Marxism essentially by working around the obstacles of a straightforward objectivist or structuralist view of society that was subject to attack by postmodernist thinkers such as Foucault and Derrida.[71] As a way of elucidating what Bourdieu referred to as social fields of deployment, in which classes are located within a variety of social spaces, Bourdieu argued that each individual is assigned a position in a class of neighboring positions which are constituted by an individual's position within a particular region in social space itself. Since the properties and features constituting this space are always active, Bourdieu believed that a social space can be looked upon as a field of forces or a field of obligations and practices which activate agents and which are imposed on the individuals within the social field in question. Bourdieu's

---

69 Thomas Weidemann, *Greek and Roman Slavery,* London: John Hopkins, 1981.

70 In the 1970s and 1980s poststructuralist theories of discourse found in the writings of Foucault, Derrida, Laclau and Mouffe and Michele Barrett called the existence of social classes into question essentially by disputing their material existence. This led to a theoretical debate about structuralist theories of society and class unities which brought about a crisis in Marxism that is still unresolved. The crisis has come to be known as postMarxism.

71 Pierre Bourdieu's writings on the space of social classes and the practices the classes use to make their social distinctions and choices appear in a work entitled *Distinctions: A Social Critique of the Judgment of Taste,* Cambridge, Mass.: Harvard, 1984. In the 1990s Bourdieu's writings constituted the first serious opposition to the PostMarxist writers who argued that the concept of class as a category of Marxist thought no longer exists.

concept of 'social fields,' 'habitus,' 'class dispositions' and the 'space of social classes' re-defined the theory of social class found in classical Marxism and the criticism of the concept of class put forward by poststructuralist theories.[72]

Marx's Theory of Ideology

The History of the Term in Hegel and Marx

Marx and Engels first introduced the concept of ideology in 1845–46 in *The German Ideology* as a way of pursuing the discussion of the conception of society first put forward in the materialist theory of history. The general theory of ideology outlined by Marx and Engels was developed as a criticism against a group of thinkers who had followed Hegel and who accepted his principle argument that ideas were forces and agents in history.[73] As we said earlier, the title of the work was initially intended as a critical attack against the Young Hegelians who Marx and Engels thought were the central 'ideologists' of German society. During the 1840s, they espoused philosophical views about German history and society that involved a critique of Christianity, and then eventually a criticism of the state political authorities. As followers of Hegel, the Young Hegelians put forward a critical view of history and religion which argued that all reality was nothing more than the outward manifestation of internal human ideas actualized historically in concrete social and historical events. This led to the view that world history was merely the external expression of internal thought actualized as ideas in the outer world, in the same way that Hegel believed that the French revolution was the outward manifestation of the internal 'freedom idea' in history.

It was against this background that Marx and Engels wrote *The German Ideology*, directing their critical comments to what they saw as the distorted philosophical views of Hegel's conception of world historical progress. At the root of Hegel's philosophy was the belief that historical forces were put in motion by ideas like Hegel's 'freedom idea,' and that social and historical problems could be analyzed by looking at the role these ideas played in social and political life. By 1845, Marx and Engels began to criticize this approach in a number of ways. First, they objected to the role Hegel had assigned to ideas, since for Hegel ideas were seen as active agents in history and as real historical causes. Marx and Engels believed that this was a fundamental error since it concluded that ideas were real forces and thus had material existence. Second, Marx and Engels took the view that every time philosophy represented reality it tended to 'turn it upside down' in order to force it to conform to the picture of the philosophical world. In this case, they believed that Hegel's philosophy simply distorted external

---

72 For how Bourdieu has redefined classical theory itself, see Rogers Brubaker, 'Rethinking Classical Theory: The Sociological Vision of Pierre Bourdieu,' *Theory & Society*, 14, 745–75; 1985.

73 See Marx *The German Ideology*, International edition pp. 13–14; 39–43; and Marx and Engels, *Collected Works*, Vol. 5, pp. 35–37; 59–62.

reality because Hegel thought that reality was a manifestation of internal ideas. In this view, philosophy itself can only be a distortion of reality because it always misrepresents reality by forcing it to conform to the philosophical picture of the world.[74]

In direct opposition to this, Marx and Engels took the view that a theory of ideology was possible only if it showed that the actual ideas and conceptions people had of the outside world and of society originated from material activity and from material production. Accordingly, they put forward the theory of ideology in relation to the view that philosophy was a system of thought which tended to 'invert' the real world by turning it upside down in reality and by forcing it to conform to the philosophic picture of the world. As Paul Ricour points out, Marx and Engels wanted to reverse philosophy's 'inversion' of reality by 'putting things back in their real order.'[75] As a result, they took the view that philosophy must be the ultimate distortion of reality since it tended to elevate ideas to the level of existence in a way that pictured the world in terms of another reality.

Since Marx and Engels first outlined the theory of ideology in 1846, contemporary discussion of the term by Georg Lukacs in the 1960s and 1970s took the direction of pursuing a theory of ideology by treating it as a form of 'false consciousness.' In a work entitled *History and Class Consciousness* Lukacs took the view that ideology could be described as a type of false consciousness, which is a term he used to define a situation in which workers were unable to grasp the 'true' nature of their interests or their historical role as a subordinate class because their view of reality was filtered through their class position.[76] While this term was never used by Marx, it was used by Engels in a letter to Franz Mehring in 1893 to describe how workers attribute false motives to the causes of their hardship and suffering. Subsequently Lukacs took the view that the worker's consciousness became 'false' as a result of the contradictions arising from industrial capitalism.[77] While Lukacs's overall conception of ideology was influential during the 1960s and early 1970s, it eventually fell out of favor by the late 1970s when Louis Althusser's conception of ideology as a form of material practice replaced the older conception of ideology as a distortion, inversion or false consciousness. From Althusser's perspective, ideology was to be defined as 'materialized in practices and rituals' that involved a relation to the world which 'transformed individuals into subjects'; for example, when they participate in practices such as 'baptism or confession' which, in Althusser's view, defined them as religious subjects'. At bottom, Althusser defined ideology as 'the imaginary relationship of individuals to their real conditions of existence.'[78]

---

74 *German Ideology*, p. 14.

75 On the inversion by philosophy of the real world and its relation to a theory of ideology see Paul Ricoeur, *Lectures on Ideology and Utopia*, New York: Columbia University Press, 1986, pp. 1–59.

76 G. Lukacs, *History and Class Consciousness*, London: Merlin, 1971.

77 Eventually, the term 'false consciousness' became so misleading and theoretically imprecise that it was eventually abandoned as a way of describing ideology.

78 Loius Althusser, 'Ideology and Ideological State Apparatuses,' in *Lenin and Philosophy*, New York: Monthly Review Press, pp. 127–186.

After Althusser, Norman Geras defined ideology as a distortion of reality that takes place when we come to believe that our social relations with others are based on the capacity of the things we own to signify our place in a class system in a way that elevates our social prestige.[79] Geras thought that this was an ideological relation to reality because, in conferring powers to the things we possess, it led to imaginary perceptions about how others see us in relation to the things we own. Dorothy Smith, on the other hand, conceptualized ideology 'as the ordinary form in which the features of everyday life become observable', and much later Slavoj Zizek defined it as 'materialized in rituals and apparatuses which include the operations of a free press, the process of democratic elections and the belief in universal freedom.'[80] By this time, the conception of ideology as an inversion of reality was being redefined in the form of material practices as these were described by Louis Althusser in terms of a process he called 'interpellation.' What Althusser had shown was that ideology had the capacity to affect our own imaginary relation to reality.

By the 1980s, with the advent of poststructuralism, the criticism of Marxism and of structural theories of society began to appear in the writings of Michel Foucault, Ernesto Laclau, Paul Hirst and Michele Barrett. At this point the concept of ideology began to fall out of favor because of the misleading distinctions between reality and appearances, and the underlying assumption that a dominant reality existed beneath the 'real social relations.'[81] Today, commentators such as Terry Eagleton and John Keane argue that ideology is a form of 'discourse' or 'language' used by specific individuals to make statements which have a particular 'effect,' and that ideology 'is essentially a figure of speech.' In this case, Eagleton defined ideology as the set of 'ideas and beliefs which symbolize the conditions and life experiences of a specific group or class.'[82] In still other circumstances, commentators such as Giddens and Hirst criticize the concept of ideology in relation to what they feel were the central weaknesses of classical Marxism, evident in the inability to reconcile a theory of ideology with what they call the 'level of the real relations' on the one hand, and

---

79 Norman Geras, 'Fetishism in Marx's Capital,' *New Left Review*, 65, 1971.

80 See Dorothy Smith, 'The Ideological Practice of Sociology,' *Catalyst*, 8, 1974, p. 54; and S. Zizek, *Mapping Ideology*, New York: Verso, 1994, p. 9; and S. Zizek,' The Sublime Object of Ideology,' London: Verso, 1992.

81 See Ernesto Laclau's critical opposition to classical Marxism and the concept of 'society' and 'ideology' in 'The impossibility of Society,' in *The Canadian Journal of Political and Social Theory*, 7, 1 & 2, 1983, pp. 21–24; and in Michele Barrett's, 'Ideology, Politics, Hegemony: From Gramsci to Laclau and Mouffe,' in Slavoj Zizek, *Mapping Ideology*, London: Verso, 1994, pp. 235–264. Barrett's approach is based on the critique of structural Marxism that aligns with the theory of discourse proposed by Laclau and Mouffe. The theory of discourse proposed by them takes the view that material relations are never given in reality outside of language, but are rather only constituted by discourse. This, however, is a radical theory of discourse because even Foucault agreed that beyond discursive statements institutional complexes always have a 'material element' that exists outside of language. Laclau's and Mouffe's theory of discourse is therefore grounded in a Cartesian theorization of the outside world so far as it situates all materiality in the space of 'extension' where no objects exist.

82 See Terry Eagleton, 'Ideology and its Vicissitudes in Western Marxism,' in S. Zizek (ed.), *Mapping Ideology*, London: Verso, 1994, pp. 179–226; and in Eagleton, entitled *Ideology: An Introduction*, London, Verso, 1991, pp. 1–31.

the processes of signification and symbolically mediated signifying practices on the other.[83]

Definition of Ideology and its Material Origins

Despite these criticisms, Marx's and Engels' theory of ideology can be defined by elucidating several of its key characteristics. To begin with, we can define the concept of ideology by pursuing a line of discussion in an early statement by Marx and Engels having to do with what they referred to as the 'system of ideas,' and here two key points are noteworthy. First is that in focusing on the system of ideas, Marx and Engels wanted to establish the basic principle that all our ideas and conceptions are derived from material activity and are always related to material production and material social relationships in society. In doing so, Marx and Engels wanted to differentiate themselves from Hegel who believed that ideas emerge fully formed from the sphere of thought and proliferate in material reality. In this respect, Marx and Engels simply wished to invert Hegel by asserting that ideas have a material origin rather than having an origin in thought or in universal principles that are above the material world. This led to an initial definition of ideology as simply a system of ideas, attitudes, standpoints, conceptions and beliefs which arise in relation to material activity, and which are capable of affecting the perception of reality. This put material relations first, and ideas second, thus making ideas dependent on material reality itself.

The theoretical basis for asserting that our beliefs and conceptions are related to our material relationships and to material production originates in the first place from Marx's own assertion that our ideas and conceptions of the outer world always have their origin in material activity. In addition to this, Marx used two particular definitions to show how our ideas and conceptions tended to reflect material activity and material processes. In the first, he stated that 'if in all ideology human beings and their relations appear upside down, this phenomenon arises just as much from their historical life processes as the inversion of objects on the retina does from their physical life processes.'[84] In the second, he points out that 'if in their imagination human beings turn reality upside down, then this is the result of their limited material mode of activity and their limited social relations arising from it.'[85] Since for Marx and Engels material production was uppermost in that it kept people alive by forming a material relation to the world and to life processes through economic production, he felt that all our ideas, conceptions and standpoints arise out of our material activity and they come to reflect this activity in our relation with others and the world.

---

83 For the line of discussion pursued by this criticism see John Keane, 'Democracy and the Theory of Ideology,' in *The Canadian Journal of Political and Social Theory*, 7, 1 & 2, 1983, pp. 5–17; and A. Giddens, 'Four Theses on Ideology,' *The Canadian Journal of Political and Social Theory*, 7, 1 & 2, 1983, pp. 18–21.

84 Karl Marx and Frederick Engels, *Collected Works*, Vol. 5, p. 36; International ed., p. 14.

85 Ibid., p. 36.

Marx and Engels, however, went beyond showing the material origins of ideas by arguing that our ideas and conceptions in fact come to represent our material relations with others, and that these ideas and conceptions ultimately function as lenses through which we come to see the world and have material relations with it. In this respect, ideology is a set of beliefs and standpoints through which we come to see the world, and as such it draws attention to one of the most fundamental ideas in Marx's and Engels' theory of ideology. This has to do with the fact that in society we do not ever encounter the material world directly but rather through prevailing conceptions, ideas and beliefs, and that these beliefs always act on our material relations with reality and with others. In short, these beliefs come to function as lenses through which we see the world and form relations to it. This can be seen in the view of the world that many have in terms of the way they conceive of how things happen and what happens to them. Many, if not most, believe that luck plays a key role in coming to understand how the world works and what happens to them in it. When, however, we form a relation to the world based on luck, we not only enact an imaginary view of the way the world works, but we also tend to enact an imaginary relation to reality since we assume that an external agency determines the outcome of things regarding our own providence before they actually occur. Marx would say that this is an ideological relation to reality and to the material world because it conceives of the way the world works as being beyond our control, lying instead within the control of providence or fate, or some other powerful agency beyond us. Marx would go on to say that these beliefs are products of a distinct social framework rather than arising from the individual alone, and that they tend to show the extraordinary value we place on future determinations and outcomes.

It follows from this that a second definition of ideology has to do with the relation between the common ideas and conceptions, and our own conception of the way the world works and our relation to it. That is, if all our ideas about the way the world works arise from material activity, then all our encounters with reality must always be reflected through these ideas and conceptions that originate from material production. This can only mean that there are no direct encounters with reality itself, since these encounters are always mediated through the ideas and conceptions that spring from material life. An example of this can be seen in our perceptions toward the material objects we possess, and the belief that these objects often confer powers which enact our imaginary relation to reality because we imagine how others see and rank us in the light of the material things we own. If we can accept this view, it takes us in the direction of acknowledging that our relation to reality is thus always a product of an already constituted social and historical framework related to the society in which we live.

This emphasizes the simple principle that we live in a social world rather than a natural one, and that our social relation to reality is always constituted by the specific practices and ideas in terms of which we relate to reality. Marx, then, believed that our relation to reality was always filtered through the material ideas and conceptions we have of the world, as well as our class position.[86] This meant that our perceptions of reality and the outside world are always filtered through economic and material lenses, and that through these lenses we always see things in terms of the judgments of value that are related to dominant economic and material relationships and productive relations in society.

Under these circumstances, the prevailing ideas and beliefs always seem to turn on and tend to symbolize our economic and class relations and the experiences we have with others in society. Since no encounter with reality is directly through our sense perception alone but rather through the filters of our ideas and conceptions that arise from our social location in a class system, Marx wanted to know how these ideas, conceptions and standpoints tended to affect our perception of social relations, and whether they have the power to modify our perceptions of reality and the outer world and our perception of our class relations to others.

A third way of defining the concept of ideology originates from observations made by Marx when he pointed out that ideology is always enacted in activities that take place in relation to the world rather than being divorced from it.[87] Marx believed that ideology is an activity that takes place in relation to the world and is enacted through our lived relations with it, which is always ongoing in everyday life.[88] When ideology is conceived of as an activity, our ideological practices can be made observable simply by looking at our perception of the world in relation to the activities that arise in family life, schooling, and work experience, and in our views about others. Marx and Engels thought that ideological relations are found not so much in objective relations between things, but in our specific social connections with others, since it is usually these direct social connections that structure the activity of living. For example, our perception that luck operates in mysterious ways that we cannot control reflects an ideological conception of the way the world works, because it points not only to what we believe about the world, but our relation to it. This often means that we picture ourselves and our lives in terms of the luck that happens or does not happen.

The assertion by Marx that our ideological practices always occur in relation to activity in the world is explained by him when he describes how Feuerbach saw the world and others through the distorting lenses of philosophical ideas and activity. Marx writes that through these lenses:

> Feuerbach conceives of human beings as an object not as an activity since he still remains in the realm of philosophy and conceives of human beings not in their given social connection, nor their existing conditions of life which have made them what they are. Accordingly, he never arrives at the really existing active human beings, but stops at the abstraction 'man' and

---

86 In this, Marx took the view that thought's relation to reality and existence was not identical and was not governed by an unobstructed subject-object identity.

87 On this point, see Dorothy Smith, 'The Ideological Practice of Sociology,' *Catalyst*, 8, 1974, pp. 39–54.

88 Ibid., p. 50.

knows no other human relationships. Thus, he never manages to conceive the world as the total living activity of the individuals composing it and when, for example, he sees a [homeless] over-worked and consumptive starvelings, he takes refuge in the philosophic perceptions and ideal compensations of the species. In this respect, he does not see the necessity of the transformation created both by industry and of the social structure.'[89]

If, as Marx said, we come to view the world in a way that transforms our perceptions of others in the material activity of living, then this is as much a product of our economic ideas and perceptions as Feuerbach's lenses are products of his philosophical ideas. Marx shows this clearly by drawing our attention to how Feuerbach sees the homeless through the philosophic and economic lenses which are products of the ideas of the social framework that was immediate to the nineteenth century. Marx illustrates this when he draws attention to Feuerbach's lack of awareness of the transformation that took place in the way he perceived the homeless and the unemployed who had less value than others because he saw them through the distorting lenses of labor, industry and commerce. In this case, they had less value because they were outside the sphere of work, and outside the sphere of the economy.[90]

Since, in general, Marx took the view that ideology was diffused throughout society, was embodied in social institutions and was put to work as soon as the existing class relations were enacted during material production, he wished to secure a link between the specific beliefs and conceptions people had and the inversion of our perception in relation to reality. This active turning of reality upside down was apparent in the quotation above where Feuerbach conceived of the unemployed wretches of the nineteenth century through the ideas and filters of his own 'higher class perceptions' and categories. Marx notes that he did this outside the self awareness of precisely how the category of 'industry' and 'work' transformed his ideas and perceptions of the value of others in a dramatically active way. But what does this mean?

Simply, it means that in a society where work, industry and productive activity are of paramount importance and are, in fact, the dominant ideological categories, we tend to see the outside world and others through the economic filters and lenses where we believe that work 'elevates,' and 'idleness' and the absence of work degrades or devalues. Consequently those who do not work or who are outside of work or schooling are seen through the economic lenses of 'lower perceptions,' and are believed to have less value. It is at this point, said Marx, that we see them 'upside down' in relation to reality, since in reality all human beings have value. From the perceptual standpoint of our economic lenses, therefore, we can see that in a society where the economy and social class are the major categories of experience, we tend to believe that those who are outside of work, such as the homeless, are valueless and without human worth since they are outside of the value creating perceptual

---

89 Marx and Engels, *The German Ideology*, p. 37.
90 For the relationship between material activity and ideas, see *The German Ideology*, pp. 1–37.

categories of work and labor, in addition to being outside the dominant material relationships and perceptual standpoints concerning the way the world works.[91]

It is in this sense that Marx thought that through our material activity in the world, we are led to see things through economic lenses as if they were upside down and this, in his view, is where the inversion takes place. Thus, in the case of the example used by Marx to refer to the homeless population of the urban centers in the nineteenth century, he said that their value and their humanity were turned upside down, to the extent that we see them as valueless in the light of prevailing ideas of 'industry and work' which constitutes the dominant perceptual lenses and economic categories. In short, it is through these economic and class lenses that they appear to us to be stripped of their 'human value' since, in being outside of work and labor, they appear to have no value. The inversion takes place Marx reasoned because this is the way we see them, when in reality they remain human beings, and all human beings have value despite the fact that our ideas of industry and work tend to strip them of this value. This constitutes the 'double vision,' or the two views of the ideological relation – the real and the imaginary.

The Five Building Blocks of Marx's Theory of Ideology

In order to look more closely at the theory of ideology and to understand how Marx developed the concept, five broad building blocks will be discussed. First, is the relation between ideas and material activity in society; second, is the relation between the concept of ideology and a theory of perception; third, is the relationship between ideology and the dominant classes; fourth, are the main social functions of ideology; and fifth, is the relation between ideology and the relations of production where we look at how one's position in the relations of production affect how others see us.

The first building block related to a theory of ideology is the link that exists between ideas and material activity in society. There are two issues here: first, since every society has different ways of producing, it means that their material relation to reality will always reflect the way they produce. For example, in societies of antiquity, Romans believed that slaves were valueless because Romans elevated themselves in the world by refusing to labor, and as a result believed that all labor was degrading. This only came to pass, however, because of the economic categories with which they saw the world. Second, as we said earlier, Marx thought that ideas have their origin in material and productive activity and that 'the production of ideas is directly interwoven with material activity itself.'[92] Marx reasoned therefore that the very first thing human beings do is produce the material means of their existence, and that this production is so central to their material well-being that the subsequent shape of society always seems to coincide with the way they produce. Furthermore, the manner in which this production is

---

91 For more examples about the way the world works in terms of the specific transformations that occur in our lived relation to material activities see D. Smith, 'The Ideological Practice of Sociology,' *Catalyst*, 8, 1974, pp. 39–54.

92 Ibid.

carried out determines the system of social relations which tends to arise from it, so much so that it creates the division of society into classes; one of which is dominant over the material means of production, the other subordinate to the extent that they are subject to the will of those who rule over them.

From this simple starting place, we can see that the system of social relations always reflects the prevailing material social relations of production, and as such two important points can be drawn from this: first, the act of economic production necessitates the formation of classes which shapes social relations and the structure of society; second, the production carried on between the classes gives rise to a system of conceptions, ideas and beliefs which come to represent the productive relations that stand as 'conscious images in mental life.'[93] Marx therefore reasoned that the ideas individuals have are always related to the way they produce and the class relations they form in the system of production.

A second broad building block of the theory of ideology concerns the way ideology is related to a theory of perception, and to how individuals come to perceive the outer world from the standpoint of their positions in the relations of production. There are two issues here: first, as we said earlier, Marx believed that we do not ever encounter the material world directly but rather only indirectly through the lenses and filters of our ideas, which are always related to material activity. Second, not only do we see the outside world through the filters and lenses of our positions in the relations of production and the class structure, but also we tend to form a conception of the way the world works, and, in this sense, our ideological practices function to explain what takes place in the world in relation to our lived material connection to the existing productive and class relations in society.

If we then define ideology as a system of attitudes, conceptions, ideas, standpoints and beliefs which are capable of inverting our perception of reality, we have to show how these ideas have the power to alter our perception of the outer world as such. But, the question then is, what does Marx mean by this, and how is it possible for the outer world to appear upside down or in an inverted form in our imaginations?[94] Marx wishes here to illustrate the most general mechanism in society where reality takes on appearances which constitute distortions in the real conditions of existence, and it is essentially at this point that Marx's theory of ideology becomes a theory of perception.

Recalling for the moment that, according to Marx, we do not perceive the outside world directly through our senses, but rather through our ideas and conceptions of the way the world works, then the question is: how do our ideas act to distort our perception of reality by making social relations distorted in perception; and second, in

---

93 Marx and Engels, *The German Ideology,* p. 14–16.

94 For discussion on the relationship between philosophy, ideology and the inversion of the real succession of the perceptual order see Paul Ricoeur, *Lectures on Ideology and Utopia*, New York: Columbia University Press, 1986, pp. 1–102.

what way does society deceive individuals into thinking that these perceptions are acceptable substitutes for reality?[95]

An example of this can be found in the class system of feudal society. In feudalism, the prevailing economic and religious conceptions of those at the top and those at the bottom of the class structure acted as a material justification for the serf's economic inequality in relation to the landholder. Marx and Engels thought that in the period where religious ideas were dominant, conceptions about the way the world works and what happens to us in life, as well as what becomes of us after we are gone, somehow got inverted by a religious conception of the way the world works. In fact, it was from certain religious ideas and standpoints that specific relations to the world and to God were born and among these was the idea that we should not expect too much from the world; and that we should look to the next world for compensation for our suffering and hardship.

Marx and Engels therefore believed that certain ways of looking at the world turned things upside down, that is to say, it constituted an inversion because it conceived of reality as full of suffering, and the next world as a substitute for the real world, and a compensation from suffering. As a result of the conception about the way the world works, the serf carries out economic tasks and material activities within society which advantaged the landholder and disadvantaged the serf, and the serf accepts these conditions as the necessary social and material connection to their livelihood. The question then is how does the world appear to the serf through ideological lenses?

Marx reasoned that for the social inequality and hardship of the serf to 'appear' to be an acceptable substitute for reality, meant that the dominant religious beliefs distorted reality in favor of one class to the extent that dominant religious beliefs explained away the serf's suffering. It was for this reason that Marx believed that ideology had the ability to take on an independent existence having the power to affect perceptions about material life and class relations. This active turning of reality upside down in perception through the distorting lenses had directly to do with the fact that the dominant material conceptions always reflect the dominant material relationships, and this happens, Marx thought, when the ideas and beliefs reflected the wills, intentions and interests of only the dominant classes.[96]

So far, we have been able to show in the first place that 'ideas' have a material base so far as they reflect the wills and interests of the dominant classes; and second, that ideas stem from the dominant material relationships in society, since 'the class which has the means of material production at its disposal has control over the means of mental production, so that, generally speaking, the ideas of those who lack the means of mental production are subject to it.'[97] Another way to understand how ideas can distort reality is to look at the distinction which Marx employed often enough in his own work,

95 J. Larrain, *Marxism and Ideology*, London: Macmillan Press, 1983; and Dorothy Smith, 'The Ideological Practice of Sociology ,' *Catalyst,* 8, 1974, 39–54.

96 *German Ideology,* pp. 39–40.

97 Ibid.

which is that between appearance and reality. Historically, the distinction between reality and appearance goes back to the earliest times of social and political thought and was used by Plato to draw attention to the differences between the way things 'appear' on the surface, and the way they appear in reality. As we have already said, one of the first and most basic precepts of ideology is that we do not perceive the world directly but rather we see it through the distorting lenses of our conceptions, attitudes and ideas which arise from material relationships. This is already clear enough. But Marx believed that these ideas had the power to transform the real empirical conditions of reality into what he called their 'appearance forms'.[98] In this manner, reality presents itself in a distorted way and appears to be other than it really is.

The distinction between reality and appearance stressed the idea that the perceptible world is often contradictory to some underlying pattern, and this signifies a split between what something appears to be and that which it is in reality. While Marx believed that appearance and reality never really coincide, he stressed the view that reality is not distorted by itself, but rather is distorted because our ideas and beliefs grow out of our social relations which in turn arise from economic production. It is these material relations that act as distorting lenses through which we come to perceive the world and our relation to it.[99] Immanuel Kant's view on how we come to know the external world is useful in illustrating Marx's point. In the eighteenth century, Kant wrote a philosophical treatise called *The Critique of Pure Reason* which was important for putting forward a theory of how the human mind is capable of grasping external reality. Kant maintained that we can never know the external world as it is in reality because the knower always contributes something to the perception of reality. In Kant's view, what the knower contributes are the main perceptual categories of space and time, and this subjectively alters reality.

According to Kant, we are always forced to alter reality in the act of apprehending it and Kant's position was that we mis-perceive reality because we alter it through the categories of space and time. Marx, however, went one step further by showing that our economic production, in fact, shapes the way we come to understand reality itself and our material relation to it. But, how is this possible? The short answer to this question is that we see the world through a position allotted to us within a social class. According to this reasoning, our apprehension of the world is always shaped by our position within a social class and how, through our class position in society, we come to use the means of production. While this point seems obscure, the process it refers to is simple. Marx believed that our perception of the world is always conditioned by the terms under which we produce and the roles we play in economic production. This much has been said so far. More specifically, the terms under which we work for our livelihoods condition our perception of the world, and this means that our apprehension of reality is conditioned

---

98 *German Ideology,* p. 30.

99 Norman Geras, 'Essence and Appearance: Aspects of Fetishism in Marx's *Capital*,' *New Left Review*, 65, 1971, 69–85.

by our location in a social class and the perception of others in relation to this class location. For example, in Arthur Miller's play *The Death of a Salesman*, Willy Loman's perception of himself as 'desperate' and his other family members as 'liked but not well liked,' depended entirely on his imagination about how he thought others saw him and his brother in terms of his place in society as defined by their social class. This lived relation to reality through our class position makes our apprehension of life always concrete and consequential and important to how we see ourselves in the eyes of others in relation to our own perception about our class position. The important thing to note is that while these relations should reflect human qualities, they often don't and instead appear as relations between the things we own as this relates to our class position. But precisely why? In order to answer this question we need to look at Marx's third building block of his theory of ideology which has its basis in class relations.

The third building block in the theory of ideology is the relation between ideology and the interests of the dominant classes. Marx said:

> The ideas of the ruling class are in every epoch the ruling ideas: i.e., the class, which is the ruling material force of society, is at the same time its ruling intellectual force. The class which has the means of material production at its disposal, has control at the same time over the means of mental production, so that thereby generally speaking, the ideas of those who lack the means of mental production are subject to it. The ruling ideas are nothing more than the ideal expression of the dominant material relationships, the dominant material relationships grasped as ideas; hence of the relationship which makes the one class the ruling one, therefore the ideas of its dominance.[100]

This capacity of ideas to invert reality originates, according to Marx, from the fact that ideas represent the economic interests and dominant material relations of one class of persons over another. Two specific questions remain: first, what is the specific link between the dominant classes and the ruling ideas; and second, how do ideas come to turn reality upside down and rule over our perception? There are many clues in the above quotation. The class which presides over the means of material production 'controls the means of mental production.'[101] This means that with each period of history, the dominance of one class leads to a group of persons who act as 'ideologists,' that is, persons or agents who disseminate ideas and beliefs which represent the dominant material interests of the ruling classes.

For example, during the time when an aristocracy was dominant, the conceptions of honour, fealty and allegiance were dominant, as were the categories of subordination that went with it. By contrast, in industrial societies where material production is monopolized by one class, conceptions of 'freedom' and 'equality' are prevalent.[102] What happens during this period of dominance, Marx argued, is that the conceptions

---

100 Marx and Engels, *The German Ideology*, p. 39.
101 Ibid.
102 Ibid.

and the ideas 'take on the form of universality,' meaning that they are disseminated throughout the wider society and take on a life of their own.[103] The dominant classes then represent their interests as the dominant interests and this interest takes on the character of an 'ideal', and comes to be represented in society and history 'as the only universally valid ideas.'[104] The final step, said Marx, takes place when the ideological relations turn everything upside down. Simply stated, this means that the real relations are represented upside down or in an inverted form by conceptions which 'assume an independent existence over and against' individuals and appear to them to be the legitimate system of ideas and social relations. This happens, said Marx, when the ideas and beliefs reflect only the will and interests of a dominant class, specifically the economic and legal ideas of the dominant social class as determined by the economy. In realizing the interests of only one class, these social relations stand in a contradictory relation to the class of workers. In this sense, ideology legitimates and justifies the reality of one class. The theory of ideology, therefore, is about how reality comes to be set up in opposition to individuals who are economically outside the dominant ideas.

The fourth building block of a theory of ideology has to do with the role played by the relations of production and the prevailing social conceptions about how we come to see those who are outside the legitimizing sphere of the economy. So far, we have shown that Marx believed that ideology grew out of the economic structure of society and our material relations and relationships with the system of production. As we noted, it was from our material production in society that a system of ideas arise which comes to represent the productive relations and that these stand as 'conscious images in mental life.' In addition to this, Marx thought that the system of ideas arises from the way people produce and that these ideas always seem to reflect the dominant material and class relationships in society. In this respect, Marx thought that the dominant economic material relationships and ideas always reflect the existing class relations, and that ideology is always class based.

But, in order to make this clear we have to define the relations of production. First, the relations of production may be defined as the roles individuals play in the system of production in the economy where the productive relations that emerge are between bosses and workers. The most important characteristic of the relations of production is that they constitute the workers' social connection to society and to the material means of production necessary for them to produce their livelihoods.[105] Second, the relations of production can be defined as the coercive relations that exist within the roles played in the relations of production themselves. As we said earlier, in the economy these relations are between bosses and workers and what is important to

---

103 Ibid.

104 *German Ideology*, pp. 40–41.

105 This characteristic of the relations of production is discussed in *The German Ideology*, where Marx points out that the relations of production are always entered into by reason of some 'compulsion' that is imposed on a population by virtue of economic necessity.

note is that the relations of production are structured along the lines of class relations in which one person is dominant and the other subordinate.

In addition to this, it is important to point out that the relations of production are transformed into material activity as soon as we enter into production to earn our livelihoods. It is important therefore to note that in order to live in society we are compelled to always enter into the relations of production and to comply with their requirements and coercive expectations. Thus, everyone in society is compelled to enter into the relations of production in order to satisfy their material needs and, as a result, they enter into structured relations with others that are often based on dominance and subordination.

Since dominant ideological conceptions are put into play wherever and whenever we engage the means of production, and whenever we enter into the dominant material relationships, Marx took the view that ideology was therefore diffused throughout society, was embodied in social institutions and reflected within the dominant material relationships of the relations of production. Therefore, in an industrial society where everything revolves around employment, commerce and labor, it stands to reason that those who are officially outside the confines of commerce and labor are viewed as a problem population because their acts and behaviors are viewed through the filters and lenses of an economic ideology that tends to see them as tending to call into question the existing relations of production in society.[106]

In 1975 Steven Spitzer studied the relations of production that existed in industrial societies and he looked at the specific populations that were outside commerce and labor. Spitzer found that these populations tended to be more policed and targeted as criminal, in contrast to the population who were legitimated by the fact of being inside commerce and labor.[107] He pointed out that the relations of production were so important to the economic structure of society that deviance was often created or produced when problem populations, such as the unemployed, single mothers, welfare recipients or juveniles, either refused or failed to participate in the relations of production and assume productive roles in society.

In fact, Spitzer found that the rate at which problem populations were converted into deviant populations reflected the importance of the productive roles beings refused.[108] One example of this would be those who systematically challenge the validity of the family system, such as gays, who become part of the problem population when they refuse to enter into the productive roles of the family system and its sphere of values. Also, another population which tends to be subject to deviant labels are juveniles who refuse to be schooled, and who refuse to enter into the relations of production existing within schooling institutions. Spitzer found that deviant populations are thus produced in society not because of how people act or the laws they

106 Steven Spitzer, 'The Production of Deviance in Capitalist Society,' *Social Problems*, 22, 5, 1975, 641–646.
107 Ibid., p. 642.
108 Ibid.

break, but rather by the extent to which they refuse or are unable to enter into the relations of production. Thus, those outside schooling or work tend to challenge or threaten the prevailing relations of production and thus come to occupy positions in society that are defined as deviant or criminal. Spitzer said that these 'populations become generally eligible for deviant labels when they disturb, hinder or call into question' any of the prevailing material relations of production.[109] These threats to the relations of production, said Spitzer, may take various forms as they disturb, hinder or otherwise call into question any of the relations of production in society.

Having outlined Marx's and Engels' theory of ideology, I now want to turn my attention to looking briefly at some of the functions of ideology in society. Generally speaking, Marx argued that ideology performed three basic functions: it legitimates the existing class system in which one class monopolizes the material means of production; it makes the subordinate classes politically passive and accepting of the ideas of the dominant classes; and it tends to conceal the class divisions and class conflict resulting from the inequality in society and the coercive nature of the class system by making this inequality appear to be acceptable.

Explaining Contradictions

No discussion of ideology would be complete without providing a clear understanding of the concept of contradictions.[110] A contraction may be thought of as a way of denoting the social, economic and political distinctions existing between individuals in a society which politically proclaims equality of opportunity on the one hand, and at the same time promotes the legal principle that 'all human beings are created equal' on the other. Marx believed that in contrast to these principles society somehow always develops within the framework of a contradiction where, for instance, in the period of antiquity there were 'free men and slaves'; and in the middle ages there were landholders and serfs. These contradictions, Marx believed, were carried forward to the modern period where there are distinctions between bosses and the workers.[111] For Marx, then, it is clear that the first contradictions emerged in class distinctions and therefore classes are the original site of contradictions that appear when individuals and groups wish to be included in economic activity and be protected by a form of law which is intended to ensure equality.

To this extent, one of the primary functions of ideology is to make class distinctions and the existing material differences between classes disappear altogether, so that they appear to be legitimate distinctions rather than contradictory ones. A contradiction, in this sense, is a concept used by Marx to understand how social distinctions come about due to the existence of a class structure and how these

---

109 Ibid.

110 See J. Larrain, *The Concept of Ideology*, Athens: University of Georgia Press, 1979, Chapters 1 and 2; and *Marxism and Ideology,* London: Macmillian Press, 1983, chapter 4.

111 Marx and Engels, *The German Ideology*, p. 42.

distinction come to exist side by side in society. Contradictions therefore have their roots in class inequalities and therefore always reflect the fact that social relations are based on unequal class divisions. The job of ideology therefore is to manage the contradictions; first, by making them appear as legitimate and, second, by explaining them away essentially by assigning their causes to sources other than social inequalities and class differences.

Marx's Economic Works: 1850–1867

Following *The German Ideology*, Marx turned his attention to writing economic works after arriving in London in 1850. On the whole, Marx's economic writings make up one of the most comprehensive contributions he made to the history of social and economic thought. Beginning first with a series of notebooks compiled between 1857–8, and then a work entitled *A Contribution to the Critique of Political Economy,* written in 1859, Marx began to draft a sketch for an economic theory related to the material development of society and this served as an outline for his study of capitalism. Later, a three volume work on the origin and history of capitalism entitled *Capital*, written between 1859 and 1867, constituted the central core of his economic writings.[112]

While Marx had tackled many of the major economic elements of capitalist development in *The German Ideology,* there were several issues which he wanted to outline in his formal study of capitalism. First, he wanted to look at how the transition from feudalism to capitalism brought about distinct economic changes in the dominant way of life and livelihood, and how these changes led to a transformation from the labor of agriculture to the labor of wages at the same time that it transformed the agricultural economy into the economy of industry. Second, he wanted to outline the framework of historical changes taking place in the conditions of ownership over the means of production that accompanied capitalism, leading to what he thought were new forms of private ownership over property. Third, Marx wanted to lay out the substance of what he thought were the new economic categories that began to form as result of the development of capitalism, and these included relations such as the money price for commodities, production by manufacture, wage labor, exchange value, industrial production, the price for labor based on units of time and the formal separation between commerce and industry. Marx's interest in the history and origin of the new economic forms coming into being at the time led him to critically evaluate the economic theories of Adam Smith and David Ricardo whose views on the origins of capitalism and capitalist economies had come into prominence by the early nineteenth century, and it is to this that we now turn.

---

112 Marx, *A Contribution to the Critique of Political Economy,* Progress, [1856] 1977.

Marx, Capital and the Critique of Political Economy

It is almost impossible to deal substantively with Marx's economic writings without looking at the history of classical political economy and the criticism Marx leveled at the political economists and the methods they used to describe capitalist society. First and foremost, the term political economy is used by Marx to refer to a body of writings by two prominent thinkers, Adam Smith and David Ricardo whose economic writings had become well known by the nineteenth century. More explicitly, political economy is the name given to a branch of economic theory which attempted to explain the economic laws and structural characteristics of capitalist economies. Since economics was not yet an established science, political economy was the name given to early nineteenth century economic theory.

Historically, classical political economy had developed on the basis of two central theoretical works: Adam Smith's *The Wealth of Nations*, published in 1776, and David Ricardo's *Principles of Political Economy*, published in 1817. By the early nineteenth century, these works had become among the most important economic documents of the period in which Marx worked.[113] Between 1850–1859, Marx sketched an outline for a criticism of political economy focusing on Smith's and Ricardo's conception of the main economic categories leading to the development of capitalism. Essential to their view were the economic categories of capital, money, commodities, labor, production, exchange, wages, etc., and it was in this context that Marx's criticism of Smith and Ricardo is to be understood. In fact, just as Marx's philosophic side can be understood in relation to his criticism of Hegel, so his economic side can be understood in relation to his criticism of classical political economy.

Marx criticized Smith and Ricardo on at least four distinct fronts: first, he disagreed with their assertion that capitalist society was governed by fixed economic laws which were universal for all societies. Second, he criticized their tendency to conceive of the common good of society as consisting of the private pursuit of economic gain, while at the same time being totally indifferent to the economic inequalities and class considerations inherent in the acts of exchange. Third, he rejected the claim by Smith and Ricardo that 'value' was a substance inherent in commodities; and fourth, he criticized the political economists for their theoretical methods and their use of abstract categories, which tended to view economic activity as existing above the practical acts of individuals. Let us look more closely at what Marx has to say on these central points.

First was his criticism of Smith's and Ricardo's conception of society as a fixed set of economic laws which were universal for all societies.[114] Smith, for his part, had thought that the development of all societies was premised on universal economic

---

113 A. Smith, *The Wealth of Nations,* Volume 1, London: Dent, 1910 [1776]; and D. Ricardo, *Principles of Political Economy and Taxation,* London: Dent, 1973 [1817].

114 Marx, *Grundrisse: Foundations of the Critique of Political Economy,* Middlesex, England: Penguin, [1953] 1973, pp. 100–111.

categories that included production, consumption, money, competition and exchange and that these were governed by unchangeable laws of economic activity that paralleled the laws of nature. While Smith had used the categories of production, consumption, competition and exchange as general economic categories for all societies, Marx thought that production and consumption were always particular in that they varied in relation to a given social and historical stage of development. This meant that what Marx had found in contrast to Smith, was that rather than the form of production and consumption being the same for all societies, it varied from society to society. In Marx's view, therefore, there is no production and consumption in general. Rather, production and consumption always manifest themselves in relation to a particular social and historical stage of development and therefore always express themselves in a particular form, e.g., agricultural production, production by cattle rearing, production by manufacture, etc. This meant that as far as Marx was concerned, production was not a general economic category that remained the same for all societies but rather was something that depended on a given social and historical stage of development.[115]

In thus using economic categories such as production, profit, money, commodities and wages as economic categories in general, Smith had assumed that the relationship between the price of commodities, wages and profit paralleled economic laws which were self-regulating like the laws of nature. On this basis Smith and Ricardo assumed that the wages paid to workers reflected calculable laws of capital and profit, and reflected fair payment in wages to the worker on the basis of the labor expended. Marx, however, reasoned that if economic laws paralleled the laws of nature as Smith had suggested, it meant that the low wages and the poverty of the working classes were expressions of natural laws rather than specific manifestations of political and class relations of inequality. Marx thus criticized Smith for not seeing that money, commodities and profit alone do not make capitalism. Rather, Marx believed that money and commodities had to be transformed into a system of class relations based on a division between classes, in which individuals enter into economic and political relationships where one group is dominant and the other is subordinate. As far as Marx was concerned, this meant that the economic categories of capital, labor, wages, profit and the money price for commodities derived from historical social relations which made their appearance only in certain stages of economic development rather than existing as fixed attributes of all societies.[116]

A second front on which Marx criticized Smith and Ricardo was for their tendency to conceive of the common good of society as consisting of competition and the pursuit of private economic gain, and for their conception of individuals as free merchants engaged in separate acts of buying and selling. Smith, in fact, had argued

---

115 Ibid., pp. 85–91.
116 For Marx's discussion of the methods of political economy see *Grundrisse: Foundations of the Critique of Political Economy,* pp. 100–108.

that in pursuing their self interest individuals contribute to the overall good of society by increasing the wider national prosperity. 'It is not,' said Smith, 'through the benevolence of the butcher, the brewer or the baker that we expect our dinner, but rather from their regard for their own self interest.'[117] In Smith's view, each individual is obligated to pursue private monetary gain since it is their self interest and competition which contributes to the common prosperity of society. Smith went on to reason that, in and of itself, this makes each individual a 'merchant' to the extent that they live by exchange and meet in the market as buyers and sellers of labor and commodities.[118]

In response to Smith's and Ricardo's assertion that individuals were 'merchants' engaged in acts of exchange, Marx believed that Smith and Ricardo were totally indifferent to the economic and class inequalities inherent in acts of exchange. Marx believed that Smith's assertion that capital and labor meet in the market as equal merchants who freely exchange different commodities – one labor, the other wages – showed that Smith failed to recognize that the economic exchange between capital and labor was in fact conditioned by their social class. Looked at from this standpoint, the drama between these 'free agents' who are buyers and sellers of labor takes on an entirely different light. Said Marx, 'he who is the money-owner strides out in front as a capitalist; the possessor of labor power follows as his worker. The one smirks self-importantly and is intent on business; the other is timid and holds back, like someone who has brought his own hide to market and now has nothing else to expect but a tanning.'[119]

A third front on which Marx criticized Smith and Ricardo was for the way they tended to conceive of the concept of value. In their writings, Smith and Ricardo had assumed that value was a substance inherent in a commodity and argued that labor adds value to the commodity in the act of production. Accordingly, they went on to reason that the value added to the commodity by labor forms a part of the substance of the commodity itself. In this case, Smith had taken the view that value increases the wealth of society and emerges as commodities exchange for a price on the market and, in this case, value is an attribute of a commodity and inheres in it as a 'substance' that is exchanged for a price.[120] This position has come to be known as the labor theory of value, since it takes the view that the value a commodity has has been added to it by labor during the process of production. In response to Smith's claim that value emerges from the production process and from the interaction of commodities on the market, Marx believed that Smith had failed to see that value was part of a social framework and therefore was a historical phenomenon and thus a product of society. Marx thus rejected their view by stating, in the first place, that value is not an independent economic phenomenon that can be found in a commodity, but is in fact related to a whole sequence of social relations which come into being

---

117 Smith, *Wealth of Nations*, p. 13.
118 Smith, *Wealth of Nations*, p. 24.
119 Marx, *Capital*, Vol. 1, p. 280.
120 R. Meek, *Studies in the Labor Theory of Value*, London: Lawrence & Wishart, 1956, p. 62.

only in a capitalist society. In demonstrating that value is a historical creation rather than an independent economic phenomenon, Marx was able to shift the dispute from a quantitative argument focusing on price related to the value of a commodity, to a qualitative argument focusing on social relations.[121]

One way Marx had of showing this was to demonstrate that the concept of value as a thing inherent in a commodity was to point out that exchange value arises only in societies whose system of production is based on exchange and whose commodities are produced for exchange. In this way, Marx was able to show that exchange value was historical and that in less developed societies no exchange value exists and that value is in the form of use or utility. In thus demonstrating that an active system of commodity production and exchange only comes into being in industrial capitalism, Marx showed that the concept of value was linked to a given stage of social and historical development rather than being a fixed law of economic progress. In natural economies, for instance, there is no exchange and no money price for commodities. Under these circumstances value exists only in the form of use rather than something that inheres in the commodity as a value in exchange.

Fourth, Marx criticized Smith and Ricardo for their claim that the economic activities of production, consumption and exchange could be studied as if they were independent economic categories operating above social and political life. He argued that political economy had failed to consider the fundamental connection between human social life and economic categories and that this was illustrated in Smith's straightforward assumption that production and consumption were independent economic acts. Marx, on the other hand, thought they were fundamentally related to each other and felt they could only be understood as a system of social relations in which production presupposed consumption. This is nowhere more evident than in his discussion of production and consumption as forms that condition each other. Marx stated that we cannot think of a product as a vague indeterminate object without the concept of consumption, and consumption cannot be thought of without visualizing the active subject. 'A dress,' said Marx, 'becomes really a dress only by being worn' and thus, 'a product is a product, not because it is materialized activity, but only in so far as it is an object for the active subject.'[122]

Marx went on to say that the economic categories of Smith and Ricardo were therefore products of a one-sided theoretical perspective. The fact that their methods looked at only one side in the relation of economic categories was fundamental for Marx, since he looked at these categories from the vantage point of their interconnectedness. Drawing upon the concept of social relations, Marx argued that the economic categories discussed by Smith and Ricardo were not separate but interconnected, and as such he believed that there are always two sides in any social relation. He thought that when the political economists considered economic concepts, they

---

121 Ibid., pp. 63–4.
122 Marx, *A Contribution to a Critique of Political Economy*, p. 196.

did so only from what Marx called the 'non-active side' in the relation; that is, from the side of capital rather than labor. To illustrate, Marx used the example of wealth. He believed that wealth was not something independently produced outside of a mode of production, but was inherent in the activity of human labor. By showing that wealth was not some abstract product of economic laws, Marx drew attention to the existing social relation between human labor and capital. Under these circumstances, Marx thought that political economy was incomplete in two major respects: first, because it did not look beneath appearances to underlying social and historical relations and, second, because it mistook production, consumption and exchange as the reality of economic life when, as far as Marx was concerned, the essence of capitalism was the system of social relations in which capital and labor are interconnected in the production wealth.[123]

Marx's Study of Capitalism: A Social and Historical Definition of Capitalism

Marx wrote the first volume of *Capital* between 1855 and 1866 and published it in the winter of 1867. While it is a wide ranging study comprising 33 chapters, *Capital* is a scholarly work grounded in the history of the nineteenth century. Apart from its economic, political and social analyses, it is a vivid picture of nineteenth century England that conveys, step by step, the economic and historical development of industrial capitalism. While Marx's study of capitalism is unrivaled as a work of social theory, it is also an enormously complicated work because of its immense historical coverage and its theoretical scope.

As a historical and theoretical study, *Capital,* Vol. 1, can be divided into three main sections: (i) the economic analysis of capitalism; (ii) the historical analysis of capitalism; and (iii) the social consequences of capitalism. The first nine chapters constitute the core of the economic analysis and these tend to be difficult. When read in context with the historical chapters on 'cooperation', 'the working day,' 'division of labor,' and 'primitive accumulation,' Marx's overall argument becomes clearer in terms of the way it fits into the overall plan of the work as a whole. While it goes beyond the scope of this study to cover the entire text of *Capital*, it is possible to cover the two main substantive sections: (i) the chapters which relate to the economic theory in particular, such as those on commodities, theory of value, process of exchange, labor process and surplus value; and (ii) those chapters which trace the historical origins of capitalism, such as those on the working day, the division of labor, machinery and large scale industry, wages, and primitive accumulation.

Before we look further into Marx's study, it will be useful to define the term capitalism. First and foremost, capitalism can be defined as a name for a type of economy which emerged during the period of social and industrial development in the eighteenth and nineteenth centuries. It employs industry, commerce, labor and

---

123 Marx, *Grundrisse,* pp. 100–105.

capital to produce commodities for purposes of consumption, the creation of wealth and the advancement of society. Its main aim is to employ workers for purposes of earning their livelihood and for creating wealth and prosperity in society. Capitalist economies emerged in the West during the eighteenth and nineteenth century from the ruins of feudal society whose economies were agrarian, and where agricultural production was a dominant way of life. Essential to the development of capitalism, therefore, is the transition from feudal to industrial society that began with the growing conflict between the rural economy of the countryside and the economy of the city leading to a separation between production and commerce.[124]

The development of capitalism is thus rooted in a number of key social transformations beginning in Britain between 1475 and 1850, during the period of massive economic change that took place in property relations as feudal land was transformed into private property. With the creation of private property, serfs and agricultural workers became detached from the land as a means of economic livelihood. As land began to be enclosed and the seizure of property became commonplace, serf laborers were unable to meet their basic economic needs and were placed at the disposal of the new forces of production, making them a detached landless class who began to move to the emerging industrial centers to sell their labor in search of a livelihood. By this time, town economies had become dominant over the rural economies.

In the light of these historical conditions, Marx defined capitalism as a system of social relations set in motion historically during the transition from feudal economies to the economies of industry. While the political economists of the eighteenth century defined capitalism as a market system utilizing land, labor and capital to produce wealth, Marx believed that neither money, labor or commodities alone were sufficient to define capitalism. Instead, he took the view that for a society to be capitalistic, money and commodities had to be transformed into a system of social relations which he thought took place only when the following four historical conditions were met.[125]

The first condition that needs to be met, according to Marx, is the forcible separation of the serf laborer from the means of production where they once earned their livelihoods in feudal agriculture. This process largely took place during the seventeenth and eighteenth centuries, when the class contentions of feudal society made capitalist production possible by expelling the worker from the land and by divorcing the worker from the ownership of the means of production. This led to the detached laborer who had 'nothing to sell but their own skins' in the form of industrial wage labor.[126] As feudal land fell into private hands and was transformed into private property, 'a laboring class appears which had to bear all the burdens of society without enjoying any of the advantages and, as the separation of the worker from the means

---

124 Marx emphasizes this conflict between rural agriculture and town economies in *The German Ideology*, pp. 48–68.

125 Marx, *Capital*, Vol. 1, p. 163.

126 Ibid., p. 873.

of production became more complete, it became a formal expression of the industrial mode of production itself.'[127]

A second condition of capitalist development had to do with the process by which one part of society came to possess a monopoly over the means of production. Generally speaking, this process largely took place when there was a division of society into two unequal classes which then entered into the production process. Marx believed that the ownership of the means of production by one class thus created a 'momentous switch' in how the worker employed the means of production, since as soon as the means of production fell into private hands, the worker was unable to freely employ the means of production on their own say so, as they once did in feudal society.[128] Historically, this switch took place during the transfer of ownership of the means of production to a commercial class in the eighteenth and nineteenth centuries when the means of production became the private property of a dominant class.

A third condition necessary for the development of capitalist production was the emergence of a system of exchange governing the buying and selling of commodities. A system of exchange can be defined as a sphere in society where commodities enter into the process of circulation in order to be exchanged for a money price. Marx observed that as soon as a system of exchange emerges there is a formal separation between production and commerce, and between production and consumption. What is important to note in this respect, is that the system of exchange does not exist in natural economies where production takes place cooperatively and where all production is consumed directly without entering into the medium of exchange. In isolated natural economies such as the village system of India or the ancient Inca economies of Peru, exchange relations did not exist since all production was consumed directly to meet the needs of the community.[129] In such circumstances, use value predominates over exchange value, use is the only form of value and commodities do not enter into the system of exchange. Marx thought that as soon as the system of exchange began to stand on its feet, it shaped all social relations in the form of exchange which in turn replaced all natural and feudal relationships with class relationships, and all social interchanges with economic interchanges.

Fourth, Marx identified the advent of capitalism with a process he called 'primitive accumulation.'[130] This is a process in which feudal land was coercively transformed into private property in which the agricultural laborer was coercively divorced from

127 Marx and Engels, *The German Ideology*, p. 57.

128 Marx, *Capital*, Vol. 1, p. 60.

129 For more discussion of the characteristics of natural economies see Rosa Luxemburg, *The Accumulation of Capital*, London: Routledge, 1951, pp. 368–94. According to Luxemburg, natural economies are to be understood as system of production in which land is owned in common, production is not for exchange and all that is produced is for immediate use and for the immediate personal needs of the community. In natural economies the class system does not develop, economic production is for the maintenance of life, and there is no separation between industry and commerce or between production and consumption. Examples of natural economies are to be found in the village system of India, the peasant communities of central and south America and the ancient agricultural economies of Peru and China.

130 For a discussion of this see Marx, *Capital*, vol. 1. p. 873.

the means of production by the outright appropriation of land based on parliamentary approval. The process began, according to Marx, in the seventeenth and eighteenth centuries as capitalist production became established and it altered the labor process in feudal society where the laborer had direct access to the means of production, owned the product of their labor and directly produced their livelihoods. In capitalism, by contrast, this process is reversed since workers find themselves divorced from the means of production, directly under the control of the industrial capitalist, and unable to control either their own laboring activity or the product of their labor.

Capital, Vol. 1, Part A: Economic and Social Elements of Capitalism

Commodities: Use Value and Exchange Value

Marx began his analysis of capitalism by looking at the commodity. A commodity, said Marx, is a thing whose qualities are capable of satisfying human needs.[131] Examples of commodities are bread, shoes, clothing, gasoline, heating oil, etc. In addition to this, he said, a commodity can be looked at from two very different points of view: its use value and its exchange value. Since the distinction between 'use' and 'exchange' is central to Marx's theory of capitalism, let us look more closely at the meaning of these terms.

First and foremost, the use value of a commodity may be defined as the particular quality a commodity has to satisfy human material needs. The use value of a commodity, therefore, has several characteristics. First, it refers to the specific social functions a commodity performs in meeting human needs, and so, understood in this sense, use value is the ability of a commodity to render a particular service to an individual. For example, a coat provides warmth, bread diminishes hunger and gasoline facilitates transportation. A second characteristic of the use value of a commodity is its ability to satisfy only one particular human need or function. For instance, the ability of a coat to render warmth cannot be rendered by another commodity such as bread or coal. Understood in this sense, the use value of a commodity fills only one particular need, a need which is not transferable to another commodity. The capacity of a commodity to meet only one particular need is explained by Marx when he talks about the relationship between the physical characteristics of the commodity and the specific function it serves. For instance, bread and coal are commodities whose use value is tied up with the physical properties of the commodity itself, and these are not transferable to other commodities.[132] For instance, coal cannot diminish hunger, and bread cannot provide heat. A third characteristic of use value therefore is that it

---

131 *Capital* , Vol. 1, p. 125.
132 *Capital*, Vol. 1, p. 126.

'serves directly as a means of existence,' as something that sustains life.[133] Marx thought that because use values satisfy particular human needs and sustain life, their meaning is always concrete and particular since it serves a direct human purpose.[134]

Having defined use value as the particular quality a commodity has to satisfy a human need and to render a service to an individual, it becomes possible to describe feudal economies as societies where use value was largely predominant, and where use value was the major form of value. The clearest example of this is to be found in the way commodities are used in feudal societies. Here everything that was produced was consumed directly, there was no separation between consumption and production, and what was produced did not enter into the medium of exchange since it served only as a means of existence to sustain life. What is important to note at this point is that in a feudal economy there was no buying and selling, no markets, and no system of exchange. Since production in feudal economies was always predominantly for use, the prevailing form of value was therefore use value, or value in use.

Marx next turned his attention to the concept of exchange value. While the discussion of exchange is more obscure and difficult to grasp, a first step in understanding Marx's meaning is to note that exchange value only arises in developed economies, and therefore is found only in capitalism. Earlier, we had pointed out that one of the key characteristics of capitalism is that commodities are bought and sold and thus enter into a medium of exchange. It is important, therefore, to note that the system of exchange is historical and does not develop until capitalist society.

Now that the question of exchange can be linked to capitalistic economies we can look more closely at the issue of exchange value itself. Simply stated, exchange value refers to the ability of specific quantities of one commodity, such as one ton of rice, to be expressed in the value of a specific quantity of another commodity, say a quarter ton of coffee. This expression of value takes the form: the value of a quarter ton of coffee is equivalent to one ton of rice, and vice-versa. For one ton of rice to have the equivalent value of a quarter ton of coffee, the value of the rice must be expressed in the form of the value of the coffee. What looks to be a trade off of use values is in reality a new form of value, one Marx called 'value in exchange.' Exchange value, then, is not one commodity exchanging for another, nor one commodity being traded for other, but it is rather quantities of one commodity being *expressed* in terms of the value of quantities of another commodity, any commodity.[135] In exchange, therefore, value comes to consist in the exchange relation between one commodity and another, as opposed to use value where the value consists in the human service rendered by the commodity.

---

133 *A Contribution to a Critique of Political Economy,* p. 28

134 To illustrate the difference between use and exchange, Marx cites Aristotle's example of the use value of shoes. Shoes, he says, are made for wear and the person who needs them indeed uses the shoe as a shoe. The person who uses the shoe in exchange for money or food does not use the shoe for its true purpose, for a shoe is not made to be an object of exchange. See Marx, *A Contribution to a Critique,* p. 27.

135 Marx, *Capital,* Vol. 1, p. 128.

While this may be difficult to follow, the meaning of exchange value is fundamental to understanding capitalist social relations and Marx's entire theory of value. What is of interest to Marx here is the capacity of quantities of one commodity to have their values *expressed* in the form of quantities of another commodity: one ton of rice has the exchange value of a quarter ton of coffee, etc. What rivets Marx's attention is that as soon as this comparison is made, a 'common element' is found between the two different commodities making their values commensurable in exchange.[136] Two things happen as a result. First, all commodities become comparable in terms of their value in exchange and as such use value drops out of the equation. Second, in capitalism exchange value becomes predominant to an unprecedented degree, so much so that it shapes all other social relations.

As soon as this takes place, Marx believed a new relation of value emerges which has never been seen before. This is called 'value in exchange' or 'exchange value.' There are three reasons why Marx thought exchange value was so central to the development of capitalism. First, in reality commodities are not comparable as exchange values, since each commodity has a different use value which serves a unique human function and satisfies a different human need. Second, Marx thought that 'value in exchange' is historical and found only in capitalist society and not in other modes of production. Third, since in exchange use value disappears because commodities are mutually replaceable with one another, all value in capitalist society is expressed abstractly in terms of a quantitative relation between one commodity and another.[137] The importance of this will become apparent in a moment.

To illustrate the problem, Marx compares two different commodities: corn and iron. He explained that whatever their exchange value may be in the market, both of these commodities have the capacity to be represented by an equation in which a given quantity of one commodity is equated in value with a given quantity of another – two tons of corn with one ton of iron. The crucial importance of this observation is that as soon as the value of one commodity is equated with the value of another, a common ground is established between two essentially different use values, corn and iron.[138] This common ground, Marx believed, does not exist in reality, since each commodity has a unique use value, and *only* a use value. Therefore, in use value commodities differ in quality – the quality of bread to diminish hunger, the quality of a coat to provide warmth, the quality of gasoline to provide transportation, etc. In exchange value, however, commodities differ in terms of quantities – 'a quarter of wheat, a hundred weight of coffee,' a bolt of linen, a dozen knives. In all these cases, the unit is the quantity or measure, not the use or the human service rendered by the commodity to the individual.[139] As use values, then, commodities differ in quality,

---

136 *Capital,* Vol. 1, p. 127.

137 Marx meant that use drops out only within the context of exchange and within the medium of the market. See *Capital*, Vol. 1, pp. 126–128.

138 *Capital,* Vol. 1, p. 127–28.

139 Capital, Vol. 1, pp. 128, 955.

whereas as exchange values they can only differ in quantity. Exchange value, therefore, manifests itself as something totally independent of use value and is a value form existing outside of use.[140]

The Commensurability of Use with Exchange

After discussing the distinction between use and exchange, Marx turned his attention to looking at the origins of exchange value and its historical derivatives. In this respect, Marx believed that exchange value arises as a result of a social process having to do with changes in the system of social relations occurring in the transition from feudalism to capitalism. Since in a feudal society there was no system of exchange, and value was not determined by exchange but rather by use, how then does exchange value arise?

In part, Marx's answer to this question was that as capitalist society became established, what happened was the means of production became the exclusive property of one class. Marx reasoned that this had the effect of making production private and subsequently a market formed so that what was produced entered into the medium of exchange created by the market. As commodities became subject to buying and selling, Marx believed that exchange value emerged as soon as commodities entered into the system of circulation where they were subject to buying and selling. This can only occur, however, when a comparable basis was found between two commodities so that their values could be expressed in relation to each other. Marx referred to this process as establishing what he calls a 'commensurable magnitude' between two commodities.[141] For example, if one ton of rice is to have an exchange value equivalent to a quarter ton of coffee, a commensurable quantity of each commodity is arrived at which determines their value in exchange. This takes place, Marx thought, when a quantitative measure is used to arrive at the value of one commodity in the act of exchange with the value of another commodity.[142] Marx thought that when commodities are compared in terms of exchange, their values are determined by identifying comparable quantities of each commodity which makes them commensurable in the act of exchange. More to the point, 'commensurable magnitude' refers to a process in capitalist society whereby a quantitative measure is established between different quantities of two commodities. If one ton of rice is to have the equivalent exchange value of a quarter ton of coffee, Marx is saying that specific quantities of each commodity have to be arrived at to make rice and coffee commensurable in the act of exchange. This exchange value is now expressed by stating that one ton of rice has the same value as a quarter ton of coffee, and vice versa. Looked at in another way, if a quarter of wheat is exchanged for one ounce of gold, a hundred weight of coffee, or three bolts of linen, then in the exchange

---

140 Marx's point here is that as soon as exchange value stands on its feet during capitalist develoment, the two 'values' – use and exchange – were forever severed from each other.

141 *Capital*, Vol. 1, p. 141.

142 *Capital*, Vol. 1, p. 129.

relation the wheat comes to have many exchange values instead of just one use value. When commodities enter into exchange with one another, said Marx, 'one use value is worth just as much as another so long as it is represented in appropriate quantity.'[143]

How, then, is exchange value arrived at? Basically, Marx outlines five distinct steps. First, the exchange value between two commodities is arrived at when one kind of use value (rice) is represented by another use value (coffee).[144] Second, exchange value is determined when a given quantity of one commodity (one ton of rice) comes to represent the exchange value of a given quantity of another commodity (a quarter ton of coffee). For this to occur, the use value itself has to be immaterial to the act of exchange, since in exchange commodities are 'mere clumps' represented only by the common magnitudes of weights and measures. Third, a universal ground is then established between all commodities in exchange and this ground is represented by quantitative measures only. This, said Marx, reduces all use values to an identical element which they share in common.[145] Fourth, as far as Marx is concerned this common element cannot be based on the size, shape or intrinsic utility of the commodity, since this relates to its use value. Rather, exchange value must itself be based on something else and he reasoned that this something constitutes the common ground which is found in their quantitative relation to each other.[146] Fifth, 'when commodities are in relations of exchange, their exchange value manifests itself as something totally independent of their use value.'[147]

Consequences of Exchange on Social Relations

After defining the concept of exchange value, Marx went on to look at the effects of the system of exchange on social relations and, in the process, isolated three separate consequences. First, whenever commodity exchange takes place, Marx believed it is abstracted from use value because only the common element of 'quantity' determines the value of a commodity in exchange. Marx believed that in reality, however, commodities are not comparable in terms of quantity because each commodity serves a unique function, has a specific use value and satisfies a particular human need. The importance of this criticism centers on the fact that in order for commodities to be commensurable in exchange, all the useful distinctions between different kinds of commodities must be eliminated.

A second consequence of exchange outlined by Marx is that it tends to eliminate the qualitative distinctions between the different kinds of human labor which produce

---

143 *Capital*, Vol. 1, p. 127.

144 *Capital*, Vol. 1, p. 126.

145 *Capital*, Vol. 1, p. 127.

146 *Capital*, Vol. 1, p. 141.

147 *Capital*, Vol. 1, p. 128. An example of the distinction between 'exchange value and use value' and the social circuitry in which 'exchange is independent of use value' is found in Alfred Sohn-Rethel's *Intellectual and Manual Labor*, where in reference to the state of exchange in respect to commodities he says that 'there in the shop windows, things stand still. They are under the spell of one activity only; to change owners. They stand there waiting to be sold. While they are there for exchange they are not there for use,' p. 25.

commodities. Marx thought that all labor was distinct and that this distinctiveness is expressed by the different skills and abilities of labor – skills and abilities which allow different use values to be produced. This individual quality of labor can be illustrated by comparing two different types of commodities: shoes and coats. As far as Marx is concerned, the labor which makes shoes and coats is qualitatively different because each has different kinds of skills and abilities which is reflected in the different use values of shoes and coats. In capitalist social relations, however, the shoemaker and coatmaker are paid a wage according to the labor time required to produce the shoes and the coats, and the value of these commodities is set according to the price paid to labor. Shoes and coats are thus compared using a quantitative measure of labor time as a way of arriving at the value of the labor of the shoemaker and the coatmaker. Marx believed that it is precisely in the 'act of equating' the labor of the shoemaker with the labor of the coatmaker that reduces both of their different kinds of labor to characteristics they have in common.[148]

What Marx wishes us to consider here is that the labor which produces shoes and coats is qualitatively different, so much so that they do not lend themselves to comparison. Their difference exists on two accounts: first, as use values shoes and coats serve two distinct social functions and satisfy two different human needs. Second, since shoes and coats are produced by different kinds of labor and different qualitative skills, neither are comparable and thus share no common ground. This can be shown by the fact that the labor which produces shoes and coats are products of the activity of different individuals and therefore the result of individually different kinds of labor and skill manifested again in the different use values of shoes and coats.[149]

A third effect of exchange value is its impact on social relations. Marx stated that the dominance of exchange value became so great in capitalist society that it shaped all other social relations in its image, so much so that it acts as the sole determinant of value. In this state, Marx believed that all social relations between persons take the form of economic transactions in which all social relations are reduced to exchange since everything they do becomes subject to buying and selling. This is only possible, Marx reasoned, in a society where all value is determined by the ability of people and things to enter into the medium of exchange, to circulate with other articles of value and to be subject to buying and selling. What this meant, however, was that if the worker was unable to sell their labor in exchange for a wage, it was thought that they had no value and that they were not valuable. Marx reasoned that this was only possible in a society in which exchange had become the dominant form of value. He thought that this constituted a major reversal of earlier forms of social relations that existed in natural economies which had no exchange relations, and in other societies

---

148 *Capital*, Vol. 1, p. 129.

149 How the different forms of labor create different use values is illustrated again by Marx's use of Aristotle's example of the use value of shoes. Shoes, he says, are made for wear and the person who needs them indeed uses the shoe as a shoe. The person who uses the shoe in exchange for money or food does not use the shoe for its proper purpose, for a shoe is not made to be an object of exchange. See Marx, *A Contribution to a Critique*, p. 27.

where human beings were valuable in themselves independent of the medium of exchange.[150]

Fourth, Marx argued that when exchange value becomes dominant two things happen: first, all social relations between persons take the form of economic transactions in which their social relations are reduced to the utility of exchange alone. Second, Marx thought that when exchange value becomes the only determinant of value and comes to shape all social relations, it alters the way value is determined and what is considered to be valuable. Problems arise, Marx thought, when human beings are considered to be 'valuable' only when they can sell their labor in exchange for a wage, and 'valueless' when they are unable to enter into the medium of exchange and sell their labor on the market for a wage. This is only possible, Marx reasoned, in a society where all value is determined by the ability of things to enter into circulation with other articles of value. In this case, human beings come to be valuable only when they can enter into exchange relations. Marx believed that this was a major reversal of earlier systems of social relations in which human beings were valuable in themselves independent of the value conferred by the medium of exchange.[151]

Labor Theory of Value and The Dual Character of Labor: Useful vs Abstract Labor

Following the discussion of exchange value, Marx turned his attention to the question of what makes a commodity valuable and this takes us directly into the labor theory of value. At this juncture, it will be useful to look at Marx's predecessors. Both Adam Smith and David Ricardo had put forward a theory of value which took the position that commodities are valuable because of the labor that goes into them. For the most part, Smith and Ricardo focused their arguments on the idea that labor was the sole source of all value, stating that 'it was the real measure of the exchange value of all commodities.'[152] Ricardo, for his part, refined the theory by stating that the measurable quantities of labor time that went into the production of the commodity created all value, and went on to say that these 'quantities' could be calculated in units of labor time. Thus, where Smith tended to locate value in labor generally, Ricardo focused on specific 'units of labor time' that produced amounts or quantities of value. This view is called the labor theory of value and essentially it holds that the value of a commodity is created by labor and that value inheres in a commodity as a thing or substance by virtue of the labor applied to it.

While Marx adopted the rudiments of the labor theory of value from Smith and Ricardo, he took two additional steps beyond their work. First, he disagreed with the claim that labor only imparts exchange value to the commodity and thought that classical political economy had completely overlooked the question of how 'value is

---

150 *Capital*, Vol. 1, pp. 133–136.
151 Ibid.
152 Adam Smith, *Wealth of Nations*, p. 44.

transformed into exchange value.'[153] Second, he rejected the view put forward by Smith that only one kind of labor is embodied in the commodity and insisted that there are two elements that labor puts into the commodity. Marx referred to these elements as the 'dual character of labor' and it is precisely in this that his revision of the labor theory of value went beyond the political economy of Smith and Ricardo. Because he thought that the concept of the 'dual character of labor' was one of his most important discoveries, it will be useful to look more closely at this concept.

Useful Labor   Marx began by putting forward two characteristics of labor: useful labor and abstract labor.[154] In order to illustrate the distinction between useful and abstract labor he compared two distinct types of commodities, ten yards of linen and one coat. The coat, he observed, sells for twice what the linen sells for and, therefore, has twice the exchange value as the linen. What, said Marx, makes the coat have twice the value of the linen? This, he said, is a mystery that no political economist has ever solved. He thus begins to unravel the mystery of the value of the linen by essentially pointing out that both the linen and the coat have a use value, in that they satisfy distinct human needs, and that both the linen and the coat require a certain kind of productive activity to bring this utility into existence.[155] This productive activity, said Marx, is determined by a distinct human aim, using a particular means and aiming for a particular result.[156] This he calls 'useful labor' and it may be defined as the capacity of human labor to bring about 'usefulness' or 'utility' in a commodity and produce simple use values.

Then, said Marx, it is important to note that the capacity of labor to produce these use values in commodities is, in fact, qualitatively different in each of the different kinds of labor, as this is evident in the different skills and craft that it takes to produce linen and coats, evident again by the specialized trades existing for weaving and tailoring. It is, Marx said, absolutely essential to understand that 'useful labor' is qualitatively distinct, since if it were not, linen and coats could not meet in the market as commodities with different exchange values; they could not, in short, confront each other as commodities. Marx reasons that since all commodities contain useful labor, use value cannot exist in commodities unless 'the useful labor contained in them is qualitatively different.'[157] What is important to note here is that useful labor, not labor generally, creates use values.

Then, Marx turned his attention to the question of how individual acts of useful labor are transformed into commodities. The short answer to this question is that useful labor is transformed into commodities only in a society which has the products of labor take the form of the commodity. While this seems obvious, the observation

---

153 Ibid.
154 *Capital,* Vol. 1, p. 132.
155 Ibid.
156 Ibid.
157 *Capital,* Vol.1, p. 133.

is epochal because Marx is saying that only in capitalist society do the products of useful labor take the form of commodities. In order to illustrate the point, he compares useful labor in different societies. In feudal society, for instance, the products produced by labor never took the form of commodities since there was no system of exchange. Again, neither did the products produced in tribal society assume the form of commodities because their labor was the product of cooperation rather than isolated acts of labor. Looked at from a historical point of view, useful labor has been going on for thousands of years since it is nothing more than the simple creation of utility or use value.[158] Human beings, in fact, have produced 'coats for thousands of years under the compulsion of the need for clothing' without the coats becoming a commodity or their producers becoming tailors.[159] Labor in its useful form is thus a condition of human existence since it serves a specific material purpose which is to sustain life. Labor in its useful form is therefore independent of society and is thus a simple condition of human life.

Here is the point: while the products of useful labor have always been objects of utility, they have not always been commodities subject to exchange. This indicates that the products of useful labor made under different historical circumstances and different productive arrangements, did not assume the form of commodities. Only in capitalist societies, said Marx, do the products of labor assume the form of commodities and only in this case are they subject to buying and selling in the system of exchange.

Abstract labor   After focusing on the commodity in relation to useful labor, Marx turns his attention to abstract labor. The question at hand is what makes the value of the coat worth twice that of the linen? To this point we have two distinct types of useful labors (weaving and tailoring), two distinct trades (the weaver and the tailor), and two kinds of value (the value of the linen and the value of the coat). Marx went on to reason that if we set aside what useful labor is in its ability to produce different types of utility and different use values, what remains is that weaving and tailoring are both 'expenditures of human energy, products of human brains, muscles, nerves, hands, etc.'[160] Seen from this perspective, all useful labor shares in common the fact that it is a physiological expenditure of energy which can be measured in units of labor time.[161] It is therefore Marx's argument that from the perspective of capital it is possible to leave aside useful labor in all its qualitative distinctions, and focus on nothing more than the expenditure of energy. The central shift from a qualitative framework in which labor is useful in that it creates use value or utility, to a quantitative framework in which labor is measured by an expenditure of energy quantified by time, yields what Marx called abstract labor. From this point of view, tailoring and weaving are now but the quantitative expressions of what was a qualitative distinction in different kinds of useful labor.

---

158 *Capital*, Vol. 1, p. 134.
159 Ibid.
160 Ibid.
161 *Capital*, Vol. 1, p. 135.

This is to say, weaving and tailoring are now considered quantitatively as an expenditure of labor time and human energy, rather than qualitatively as the creation of specific use values. In order then to make the transition from useful to abstract labor, an abstraction is made from all the specific qualities, skills and aims of useful labor. The abstraction focuses only on what is comparable in all productive labor which is nothing but an expenditure of energy – labor time.

What makes the value of the coat twice as much as the linen can now be looked at with some clarity. Marx believed that in a capitalist system of production the useful labor contained in the coat is measured in quantitative terms, and only in this sense is it the same as the labor contained in the linen. When labor is conceived in this way, said Marx, it is abstract labor and this is arrived at only in capitalist society when useful labor is measured in terms of 'a temporal duration of labor time.'[162] Here then is the key point: in actuality the linen and the coat have the same use value in so far as they both have useful labor in them. In this sense, the values of the coat and the linen are the same, at least when considered in the light of qualitative criteria of useful labor. But when measured quantitatively in terms of the duration of labor time, the coat contains *twice* as much labor time as the linen. While from the standpoint of useful labor, the amount of labor contained in the linen and the coat are the same; from the standpoint of capitalist production, the coat is worth twice as much as the linen precisely because it has quantitatively more labor time in it.

While this may be difficult to grasp, the point is central for understanding how Marx went beyond Smith and Ricardo in his revision of the labor theory of value. From the perspective of capital, all labor is conceived of quantitatively as a physiological expenditure of energy and this reduced all useful labor to a certain amount of movement, nerve, muscle, etc. Labor conceived of in this general rather than differentiated sense is abstracted from useful labor, and Marx calls this 'abstract labor.'[163] He writes:

> [T]o measure the exchange value of commodities by the labor time they contain, different kinds of labor have to be reduced to uniform, homogenous, simple labor; in short to labor of uniform quality, whose only difference, therefore, is quantity. This reduction appears to be an abstraction, but an abstraction which is made every day in the social process of production. The conversion of all commodities into labor time is no greater an abstraction, and is no less real, than the resolution of all organic bodies into air. Labor, thus measured by time, does not seem, indeed, to be the labor of different persons, but on the contrary the different working individuals seem to be mere organs of this labor. In other words, the labor embodied in exchange values could be called human labor in general. But this abstraction, human labor in general, exists in the form of average labor which, in a given society, the average person can perform, and is the productive expenditure of a certain amount of human muscles, nerves, brain, etc.'[164]

---

162 *Capital*, Vol. 1, p. 136.
163 *Capital*, Vol.1, p. 137.
164 *A Contribution to the Critique of Political Economy*, pp. 30–1

It is this abstract labor which has the characteristic of being equal in an expenditure of energy according to the capitalist, and it is abstract labor which forms the exchange value of commodities.

A proof of Marx's reasoning exists in the example of modern industrial production. In industrial societies with an advanced division of labor, two coats can be produced in the time it takes to produce one coat in previous societies. From the side of useful labor, this means twice the use value has been created. But from the perspective of capital, the same amount of labor quantitatively conceived has been expended and is paid at the rate of one hour of labor. While this increase in the production of use values – two coats for one – means an increase in material wealth for the capitalist, this wealth is not shared by the worker. No matter how productive, the same labor carried on for a specified amount of time produces value only by units of time.

Capital, Vol. 1, Part B: The Theory of Value

The Origin of Value and the Value Form

After the discussion of useful and abstract labor, Marx turned his attention to putting forward an overall theory of value, focusing specifically on the history and origin of value itself. Essentially, he begins with two kinds of facts in hand. The commodity has a dual nature in that it is both an object of utility and, at the same time, a bearer of value in exchange. But, asked Marx, in what form does this value exist? While his response is confusing and even controversial, it is absolutely fundamental to understanding Marx's theory of value. He begins by asserting that the value that a commodity has does not exist in the body of the commodity as a substance. As far as Marx is concerned, value is not a substance found in a commodity, for this, he said, is impossible. He stated: 'not one atom of matter enters into the objectivity of commodities as values.' In fact, if we take the linen or the coat 'we may twist and turn a simple commodity as we wish, it is impossible to find the substance which represents its value. No chemist has ever found this substance reposing in the commodity as such.'[165]

It is clear that almost all of Marx's theoretical rigor is brought to bear on this single point of analysis; namely, in what form does value exist? In his response to the question he rejects out of hand the claim put forward by political economists which asserted that the commodity is a bearer of value. Marx maintains that the exchange value of a commodity does not lie in it as a substance, but is rather a product of a social framework and thus lies hidden in what he calls the 'value form.'[166] He believed that for the answer to this question we have to look behind the value form itself. According to Marx, the origin of value lies not in the laws existing for the exchange

---

165 *Capital*, Vol. 1, p. 138.

166 For an expanded discussion of this question see I.I. Rubin, *Essays on Marx's Theory of Value*, Montreal: Black Rose, 1973, pp. 63–75.

of commodities or in the money price obtained for them in the market, but rather in the system of social relations. In order therefore to arrive at the secret of value, said Marx, 'we have to perform a task never attempted by political economy.'[167]

Marx went on to reason that since the value a commodity has is not a substance which lies in it, then value must be an expression of something else! This form of value Marx called the 'relative form of value,' and it is this that is key to his theory of value.[168] Once this crucial step is understood, the commodity can be taken out of the shadows as a thing possessing value in its own right and seen in reality as a thing in relation to other things.

Relative and Equivalent Forms of Value

Our starting place is the idea that value does not inhere in the commodity itself. Therefore the value that a commodity has, according to Marx, arises from what he calls its 'relative form.' By the term 'relative,' Marx means that the value of a commodity can only be arrived at in 'relation to' other commodities which are seen to have value. In this view, no commodity can have value in isolation, by itself. Rather, the value of any commodity must be expressed relatively; or, to put it another way, in relation to some other commodity. The example used by Marx is the value of linen. He stated, the value of twenty yards of linen cannot be expressed in terms of the linen itself. We can't say 'twenty yards of linen is worth twenty yards of linen.'[169] For linen to have value, the value must be expressed in relation to some other commodity. Hence, no value as such lies hidden in the commodity as a solitary independent object. But, when linen is set into comparison with other commodities the picture changes and exchange value emerges as soon as this comparison is made.[170] For this to take place some other commodity such as a coat must confront linen in an equivalent form of value.

The mystery of value can now be resolved with some clarity. Stated simply, 'value' emerges at the moment when one commodity is compared with another commodity and is brought into relation with it. Marx reasoned that if no commodity has value by itself, then value does not belong to a commodity naturally by itself, but is rather a product of social relations which exist within the ongoing framework of society. Hence 'exchange value' emerges only at a historically given epoch, precisely at the moment when, in capitalist production, the value of one commodity is brought into a relation of exchange with another commodity.[171]

To this point the value of a commodity is determined by its relation to some other commodity, and this Marx calls 'relative value.' But in order to complete the analysis, we have to get behind the question of value itself and to do this Marx introduces

---

167 Ibid.
168 *Capital*, Vol. 1, pp. 139–40.
169 *Capital*, Vol. 1, p. 139.
170 Ibid.
171 *Capital*, Vol. 1, p. 142.

the term 'equivalent value.' While theoretical debate on the concept of equivalent value is unclear and contentious, it will be sufficient to state only some rudiments of the concept of equivalent value. Marx stated that value occurs when the relative and equivalent form of value confront each other. In these terms, the relative and equivalent form of value constitute 'two poles of the expression of value' and, therefore, in order for value to occur commodities must confront each other in these two forms.[172] Value emerges, according to this view, only when two commodities enter into a comparison with respect to their relative and equivalent forms.[173] For example, as stated previously, the value of linen could not be determined until it is brought into comparison with the value of the coat. In this view, linen does not know its own value until it is reflected in the mirror provided by the value of the coat.[174] The valuing moment, Marx reasoned, occurs when the relative and equivalent forms of value swap meanings so to speak, so that the value comes to rest temporarily in the commodity and, in this case, assumes the form of the coat.' The 'whole mystery of value,' wrote Marx, 'lies hidden in this simple form.'[175]

On the concept of relative value Marx thus writes the following:

> We see that all our analysis of the value of the commodities is already told by the [story of] the linen itself so soon as it comes into communication with another commodity, the coat. Hence in the value equation in which the coat is the equivalent of the linen, the coat officiates as the form of value. The value of the commodity linen is expressed by the bodily form of the commodity coat, the value of one by the use value of the other. As use value, the linen is something palpably different from the coat; as value, it is the same as the coat, and now has the appearance of the coat. By means, therefore, of the value relation in our equation, the bodily form of commodity B becomes the value form of commodity A, or the body of commodity B acts as a mirror to the value of commodity A. By putting itself in relation with commodity B, commodity A converts the value in use, B, into the substance in which to express its, A's own value. The value of A, thus expressed in the use value of B, has taken the form of relative value.[176]

The distinction between relative and equivalent forms of value can therefore be made clear by drawing on Marx's example of linen and coats once again. We can say that, as far as Marx is concerned, the linen has value only in relation to the coat since it is in relation to the coat that the exchange value of linen emerges. Within the confines of this logic, 'the first commodity plays an active role, the second a passive one. The value of the first commodity is represented as relative value. The second commodity fulfils the function of equivalent value, in other words it is in the equivalent form.'[177]

---

172 *Capital*, Vol. 1, p. 139.
173 *Capital*, Vol. 1, p. 148.
174 Alan Carling, 'Forms of Value and the Logic of Capital,' *Science and Society*, 50, 1986, 52–80.
175 Ibid.
176 Ibid.
177 Ibid.

The coat serves in the role of equivalent value for two reasons: its state is more 'worked up' than the linen since as a coat it has a greater use value; and second, it is the standard against which the value of linen is established. Marx stated: 'the relative form of value and the equivalent form are inseparable moments which belong to and mutually condition each other, but at the same time they are mutually exclusive or opposite extremes, i.e., poles of the expression of value.'[178] A good example of this problem is provided by Alan Carling who compares the two forms of value discussed by Marx to Lacan's mirror stage of development. He said, the linen 'does not know its own value until it is reflected in the mirror of the coat; until it sees itself as the coats sees it. Like the infant, linen exists only in the eyes of another.'[179] Or as Marx would say: 'the value only comes to look like the coat,' that is, it takes the form of the coat, or the coat form.

Fetishism of Commodities

To this point we have shown that Marx's criticism of capitalism centers on the question of the commodity and the dominance of exchange value over use value. Marx's discussion of these questions raised two fundamental theoretical issues: a commodity only has value in relation to some other commodity; and that exchange value is a product of a social framework at a certain stage of social and historical development rather than a substance which exists in a commodity. We now turn to the final extension of Marx's theory of value by looking at his discussion of commodity fetishism.

Marx began *Capital* by tracing the origin of value to what he called the set of 'inner connections' that existed between a society and its relations of production in which value derives from the social framework rather than from a substance which inheres in a commodity. This line of investigation was unique because the underlying claim by Marx was that commodities only had use value and that exchange value was not a substance inherent in a commodity. The claim by Marx that value cannot exist or function outside of a social framework is thus key to understanding his overall theory of value, since he is saying that value is predominantly a product of a social framework. If the source of value is not to be found in commodities, then where is it to be found?

To this point Marx had asserted that, since 'not one atom' of exchange value lies in the commodity, then for the commodity to become valuable the origin of value must lie somewhere else.[180] In order to trace the origin of the concept of value down to its social interconnections, Marx introduced the concept of 'commodity fetishism,' and it is here that the exchange value of a commodity takes on new meaning. Simply stated, a fetish can be defined as the display of unusual devotion toward a material thing or object in the belief that it has extraordinary abilities and powers. Historically, the term fetish was first

---

178 Ibid.
179 Alan Carling, 'Forms of Value and the Logic of Capital,' *Science and Society,* 50, 1986, 52–80.
180 *Capital*, Vol. 1, p. 138.

used to refer to any object which excites intense feelings of attachment and desire, and which focuses or rivets attention to a single thing or object by assuming that the object has powers. The term first emerged in the nineteenth century in the description of totemic religions where certain practices were involved in setting objects apart from other objects because they were thought to have greater religious powers.

These objects then became the focus of religious worship in the form of a fetish that was manifested by the degree of desire shown toward it and the tendency of the object to elicit religious worship and devotion because of the assumed powers that it had. In totemic religions such as the tribes of Central and Northern Australia, for example, the totem was an object of great desire and subject to religious worship because it was thought to contain powers which the worshipers themselves did not have. Instead, the worshiper's came to believe that they obtained their power from the object and that, because of this, the power of the totem flowed to them, but not the other way around.

Initially, then, the concept of commodity fetishism was used by Marx to indicate the process whereby individuals assign extraordinary value and power to commodities which circulate in the system of exchange, and they come to believe that these commodities have powers to the extent that their relations with them resemble a tribal fetish. But why the fetishism of commodities? If commodities have only simple use values and not one atom of value is to be found in the commodity as a substance, then how do commodities obtain their powers?[181] Marx used the term fetishism, then, to describe the tendency in capitalism for it to be possible that value appears to be a substance inherent in commodities, and to mark the point historically when we are inclined to assign extraordinary value and power to the things we produce and to find greater value in the relations we have with these objects, making them objects of extreme desire.

In this respect, Marx's theory of value thus stands in dramatic contrast to the theory of value put forward by Smith and Ricardo. Marx thought that Smith and Ricardo had overlooked the question of value on two specific counts: first, on economic grounds, political economists believed that commodities were bearers of value as this was evident in their set money price; and second, on theoretical grounds they refused to look further into the 'nature of commodities' after dealing with price and exchange value, and thus decided to terminate their investigation. Marx stated that in this respect they came to the question of value *post festum;* that is, at the end of the process.[182] As a result, Smith and Ricardo tended to overlook the actual social process by which value came to reside in commodities and the extent to which this value

---

181 Marx states: 'Not one atom of matter enters into the objectivity of commodities as values. We may twist and turn a simple commodity as we wish, it is impossible to find the substance which represents its value. No chemist has ever found this substance reposing in the commodity as such.' *Capital,* Vol. 1, p. 138.

182 Literally, 'after the feast.' Marx uses the term to point out that there must have been a process by which value was formed and that, historically, this formation has been overlooked by political economy because they examined only the product of this process.

becomes an object of desire and religious worship. Let us look more closely into Marx's theory of commodity fetishism.

Marx began his discussion of commodity fetishism by pointing out that while commodities appear to be trivial things, they have a mysterious nature in that they manifest powers which are believed to be part of their nature.[183] This mysterious power however arises not from the use value of a commodity itself since, at the level of use, commodities satisfy only human material needs and thus there is nothing mysterious about them. But as soon as a system of exchange arises, commodities acquire a mysterious nature when they circulate in a system of exchange with other articles of value. Only in societies whose social relations are at this stage, Marx argued, are individuals compelled to believe that 'value' is a substance which inheres in the commodity, and only at this stage does the commodity begin to take on an extraordinary power which is manifested in the desire we have for these objects and our wish to own or possess them.

While this may be difficult to grasp, the point is central to Marx's theory of value. Marx believed that the mysterious nature of commodities occurs only in societies whose social relations mistakenly compel people to believe that the value of a commodity is, in fact, part of its nature. When this happens, said Marx, we form relations with the objects we possess – computers, jewelry, watches, cars, shoes, etc – that often surpass in intensity the relations we form with other human beings. Eventually, the social relations we form with things becomes so great that they begin to act as substitutes for social relations with others. Marx believed that once this had become established, all social relations in society are shaped by our social relations to things.

Marx then went on to state that when commodities are believed to have value in and of themselves, we mistakenly assign powers to them which they do not have in reality and the powers we assign to them seem to excite powerful desires and passions in us. To understand this process, Marx looked at religion in tribal societies.[184] In tribal societies, individuals assigned magical powers to objects because they believed these powers grew out of the object themselves, and as such became fetish objects of religious devotion and desire. Marx argued that it was their beliefs, in fact, that led them to think that the power resided in the object. Marx would say that, by themselves, objects have no powers, and he thought that the hidden source of this power was, in fact, the individual's active relation to the object. This relation was shaped by none other than the system of social relations in which their beliefs were imbedded and with which they thus tend to form religious relations with objects. Marx thought that the same process takes place in capitalist societies in which individuals confer extraordinary powers and capacities to commodities, and the name he gives to this process is commodity fetishism. How, then, do commodities obtain these

---

183 *Capital*, Vol. 1, p. 163.
184 *Capital*, Vol. 1, p. 165.

powers and how do we come to desire these objects in believing that their value is part of their nature?

The first thing that Marx looked at was the system of exchange. In capitalism, commodities are produced for exchange and so capitalism is an economic order whose system of commodity production is based on exchange where commodities circulate in the market with other objects of value. Marx believed that it is only at this stage in the history of social development that, as articles of exchange, 'the products of labor acquire a socially uniform objectivity as values.'[185] From this perspective, commodity fetishism is historically determined in that it arises only in societies whose commodities enter into the medium of exchange, where they acquire powers to the extent that they create the desire to be owned and confer prestige on those who possess them. Marx then pointed out that the objectivity that commodities have in exchange is different from the 'objectivity they have as articles of use.'[186] The defining moment, for Marx, is when commodities appear to be bearers of value only when production is for exchange rather than use.

Having been produced for exchange, commodities thus appear to enter into social relations with one another and their values appear to be part of their nature. It is at this point, said Marx, that the objects we accumulate take on the fetish form. That is, in a society such as ours where the acquisition of commodities such as cell phones, computers, leather jackets, Manolo Blahnik shoes and BMW automobiles are dominant, we tend to desire these objects with the intensity of religious worship, and as a result of this our social relations tend to be based on confronting each other in social life as possessors of these commodities, rather than as human beings. This, Marx believed, is the point at which the social relations between people are converted into object relations between things, and it marks the point at which the commodity 'assumes a fantastic form different from its reality' as mere use value.[187] Marx wanted to get at the process of transformation that takes place in human social relations when the possession of commodities becomes the sole aim and object of social life, and when individuals feel valuable only so long as their social relations are based on the possession of these commodities.

To make this point clear, it will be useful to employ a distinction which Marx has used often enough in his own work between feudal and capitalist societies. In feudal societies the relation of the individual to the society was predominantly governed by use value, since production was primarily for immediate use and no system of exchange existed.[188] In this case, the serf laborer was directly connected to the means of production and labor itself was for purposes of creating use values which served immediate economic purposes such as the direct maintenance of life. The important fact about feudal society is that production is not separate from consumption, since

---

185 *Capital*, Vol. 1, p. 166.
186 Ibid.
187 *Capital*, Vol. 1, p. 170.
188 Barbalet, *Marx's Construction of Social Theory*, p. 89–90.

everything produced is used to sustain the maintenance of life. Thus, what was produced did not assume the form of a commodity because it did not enter into the medium of exchange to acquire exchange value. To reiterate Marx's point: what was produced in feudal society never assumed a form different from its reality as a use value. Therefore, the system of social relations between people in feudal society did not take the form of exchange since there was no fetishism of commodities. In other words, they did not engage in social relations based on confronting each other with what they owned.

Contrast this with capitalist society. Here, the laborers' direct relation to the land has been dissolved and, as workers, they are compelled to sell their labor in exchange for a wage. Under these circumstances, what is produced by labor in manufacturing is not consumed directly, since the product of labor must enter into the medium of exchange where it circulates in a medium that is subject to buying and selling. In this case, and only in this case, do the products of labor assume the form of commodities having exchange value.[189] But, why is this the case? To get to the bottom of the problem of fetishism we need to take a few more steps. So far, we have shown that in a feudal society the products of labor did not acquire a form different from their reality as use values and their direct function of fulfilling human needs. The question, then, is: in a system of social relations governed by exchange, how do commodities obtain powers and desires beyond their simple use value?

The answer to this question is two fold. First the existence of a system of exchange is created by the emergence of the market. In this sense, capitalism is distinct from feudalism because only in capitalism is it the case that commodity production is based on a system of exchange in which everything produced is compelled to enter into the medium of exchange where it sells for a money price. In all societies up to the development of capitalism, production was primarily for use and recognized as a social process. Second, a transformation in social relations takes place in capitalism. In all societies up until then, social relations have been between individuals rather than between the products and commodities they possess. Only in the stage of commodity fetishism, according to Marx, does it appear that social relations are between things and articles of value rather than between individuals.[190] Fetishism in this sense can only be described as the stage in commodity production in which human beings are dominated by the products they possess, and are compelled by the powers these products have over them.

A further characteristic of commodity fetishism is the tendency to eliminate what Marx called the 'two-fold social character' of production.[191] In this case, Marx believed that production served two basic and primary purposes: first, it provides use value which serves directly as a means of existence; and second, the production of use value is inherently a social activity in that it plays a role in collective social processes and is fundamental to the extension of social life. This situation existed in feudal

---

189 *Capital*, Vol. 1, p. 166
190 I.I. Rubin's discussion of fetishism is among the best. See his *Essays on Marx's Theory of Value*, pp. 5–60.
191 *Capital*, Vol. 1, p. 166.

society so far as production filled the needs of others and was inherently useful and, therefore, part and parcel of collective life. Under these circumstances, everyone is dependent – serfs, landholders, laymen and clergy.[192] This dependence characterized their social relations of production as much as it did other spheres of social life. Precisely because these relations of dependence formed the basis of their social framework, 'there was no need for labor and its products to assume a fantastic form different from their reality.'[193] In fact, their social relations took the form of their transactions and appeared in the form of services and obligations in kind. Here, 'the natural form of labor was its immediate social form and the form that their labor takes in fact parallels the form of their social relations.' In this case, social relations between individuals appears in the form of their personal relations, and are not 'disguised as social relations between things and articles of value.'[194] Their labor, said Marx, is labor in common and what is produced does not confront them as commodities with independent value that has power over them, since all their value is in the form of use. As far as Marx was concerned, the labor which creates these products is in their natural form, since their socially useful character is manifested in their direct use value to others.

In capitalism, by contrast, social relations take the form of exchange and this begins to shape the system of social relations in two significant ways. First, people are only valuable if they can sell their labor in exchange for a wage and second, they are valuable only to the extent that the commodities they accumulate have the power to signify their value, giving rise to social relations between objects. Here, the relations of dependency which once existed in feudal society between lord, caste and guild are replaced by what Marx called the detached isolated individual who, in being without dependent social relations, creates relations of dependency with objects and things.[195] In this case, all the characteristics of labor are individual rather than social. Essential to capitalism, therefore, is the isolated individual who performs common social functions only for the purpose of private economic gain and the accumulation of commodities that are strictly outside the sphere of use value. All the activities of buying and selling, of producing and consuming are for private gain and private interest. All the relations connecting the individual producer to the rest of society are in fact mediated by relations of exchange. Thus, all their social relations can be looked upon as taking exactly the same form as their transactions in society, namely ones of exchange.[196]

It is Marx's view that only when social relations are dominated by exchange do individuals confront each other as possessors of commodities which establishes their

---

192 *Capital*, Vol. 1, p. 170.

193 Ibid.

194 Ibid.

195 Sometimes Marx refers to the private producer as 'private laborer,' and in some cases the 'isolated individual.' Whatever the usage, it is key to understanding the system of social relations in capitalism. See *Capital*, Vol. 1, p. 172.

196 *Capital*, Vol. 1, p. 170. Marx's discussion of the connection between the shape of society and the system of transactions is significant.

value by conferring prestige in the form of their class standing. This, said Marx, leaves human beings in a narrow, shrunken individuality, the individuality of exchange relations where human beings are valuable only on the basis of the commodities they accumulate. In capitalism, in contrast to feudalism, social relations between individuals appear as relations between material objects.[197] This means that social relations between individuals become obscure since they assume the form of social relations between individuals only as possessors of things.

It is at this point in the development of commodity capitalism, Marx believed, that the transactions between material things becomes like a fetish. Commodities appear to be sensuous objects of desire and have a life of their own only when they enter into social relations with one another in the system of exchange, and as such appear to have sensuous qualities and powers as they appear frozen in the store windows. Fetishism 'is nothing but the definite social relation between human beings which assumes the fantastic form of the relation between things.'[198] As a direct consequence, human social relations become 'thing-like' in two related respects: first, we relate to the objects we possess – BMWs, leather jackets, a Burberry scarf, an Armani suit, an ipod – in a more 'sensuous' way than we do with other human beings. Second, in so far as individuals confront each other as the possessors of objects and commodities, objects appear to have a value which they do not have in reality, and this may mean that they are more valuable to us than the individuals with whom we relate.

The value that these commodities appear to have, Marx believed, does not exist in reality since it is a product of our imaginary relation to commodities and the self-defining powers we come to believe that these commodities have when others see us possessing them. In addition to this, it means that the commodity appears to us in a form which is in direct contrast to the use value of the commodity in its ordinary relations of sustaining human existence. This establishes a new relation to material objects since, whereas in the past commodities had use values and performed services for individuals by sustaining their existence, they now supplement their social relation in the world and to others by the 'feeling' that is created when we imagine the affects that the possession of these commodities have on others who see us as owners of these commodities.[199]

Marx thought that so long as we come to believe that the commodity confers value rather than the other way around, people come to believe that value resides in the commodity rather than in themselves. In this way, the commodities seem to have powers which individuals themselves do not possess. It is in this respect that

---

197 *Capital*, Vol. 1, p. 167.

198 *Capital*, Vol. 1, p. 165.

199 A recent news item stated that while crossing a street in a third world country, a man using a cell phone was hit by a car and subsequently died. When someone picked up the cell phone at the place were it came to rest after the accident, it was discovered to be made of wood. Here is an example of the 'fetish value' conferred to the object and reflected back to the subject who imagines that, when others see them, the value that is produced flows back to the subject in the form of a socially important person. CNN, June, 1998.

fetishism constitutes a fantastic reversal of value in that things appear here to be more valuable only in so far as they have the power to confer value, whereas human beings come to believe that they do not have value by themselves. This constitutes a reversal, according to Marx, because in this light commodities and material objects appear to have a human form only so far as they enter into social relations of exchange; while human beings appear to take the form of things because they are themselves subject to acts of exchange and dependent on the powers of commodities, and to this extent lose their human qualities. Since their social relations reflect their economic transactions, all their social relations are not direct relations between individuals but rather 'material relations between persons and social relations between things.'[200]

Fetishism in this sense brings about what Marx called a 'fantastic reversal' of the value form. That is, to the extent that social relations between individuals is governed by the interaction of the things and objects they possess, the interaction of things assumes human qualities so far as they have: (i) social relations among one another because they enter into exchange and become objects of desire which focus our attention and channels our activity; and (ii) because they are believed to be exclusive determinants of value in that they confer value to those who own or possess them. In this, individuals are presumed to have no value in themselves, but obtain this value only through the commodities they accumulate. Like objects of religious worship, commodities are 'endowed with a life of their own which enters into relations both with other commodities and with the human race.'[201]

Marx believed that the social effects of the process of fetishism can be outlined in several ways. First, under commodity fetishism relations among people take the form of the relation among things. At this stage, social life is mediated by what Marx calls the exchange of matter. In this 'fantastic relation,' human beings confront one another as economic subjects; as agents of economic categories and as possessors of commodities. As owners of these commodities, human beings are simply carriers of economic processes, since they enter into acts of exchange with one another and as long as this is the case, it obscures both their human form and the human form of society.

Reification of the Economy and Society

After the discussion of the concept of commodity fetishism, Marx looked at the overall effects of exchange on the system of social relations, and in one instance he refers to this as the process of 'reification.'[202] The discussion of reification begins by assuming at the outset that human beings make society. In fact, Marx believed that the individual and society are unitary things, since human beings create society by their labor. Taking into account the fact that human beings make society, reification

200 Ibid.
201 *Capital*, Vol. 1, p. 165.
202 *Capital*, Vol. 1, pp. 1045–1055

reverses this process by making it appear as if society gives birth to human beings. To the extent that economic functions make it appear as if society creates human beings, rather than the other way around, reification is the experience of society in the form of objects and processes which are independent of human beings and which dominate over them. In the process of reification, said Marx, the forces of society confront the individual as something objective or ready made, existing as if it were without their intervention.[203]

Marx believed that reification originates from the fact that economic categories in capitalism are so predominant that they lead to the belief that society and human behavior stem from the categories of production, when, in fact, it is the other way around. While in reality economic categories originate from human labor and are produced by human beings, reification reverses this process by assigning human purposes to economic forces – for example, the 'needs' of capital and the 'drives' of production – and this makes them appear as if they were human. When this takes place economic processes are 'personified' and take on human qualities, consequently reifying human activity by making it thing-like. In this case, individuals become outcomes of economic processes and appear to enter into economic activity as if it were their nature. From this standpoint human beings appear as if 'they arose' from economic processes and 'belonged to them,' rather than giving birth to economic processes in the first place.[204] Reification can be conceived of as the historical moment in the process of commodity capitalism when the characteristics of thinghood become the standard of objective reality.

Capital Vol. 1, Part C: Theory of Surplus Value

To this point we have looked at some of the central arguments in the development of capitalism focusing on the commodity, the emergence of a system of exchange and the dominance of exchange value. This has taken us from the discussion of commodities to the theory of value, and then to the stage of the fetishism of commodities, the abstraction of human labor and to the reification of the economy and society. In all this, the commodity occupied the center of discussion.

In the next section of *Capital* , Marx focused his attention to a discussion of what he calls the concept of surplus value. In order to adequately understand what Marx meant by surplus value we have to go through four separate independent steps: first is to describe the emergence of what Marx called 'free labor' and labor power; second is to make the distinction between necessary and surplus labor; third is to describe the importance of the working day and its relation to the history of surplus labor; and fourth is to describe the development of the wage form in relation to unpaid labor. In addition to these steps, there are two conceptual problems remaining

203 Ibid.
204 *Capital*, Vol. 1, p. 1055.

which will make our discussion more complete. These are the concepts of labor power and the wage form. Let me begin with free labor and labor power.

Free Labor and the Emergence of Labor Power

The central starting place for the theory of surplus value begins with the concept of free labor. Marx's discussion of the development of 'free labor' and 'labor power' is to be found in chapter six of *Capital*.[205] While it is only a short chapter, the concepts in this section are key to understanding Marx's theoretical position. We can begin by pointing out two fundamental historical facts: first, capitalism has replaced feudalism, and as a result the serf's relation to the land as source of livelihood has been dissolved, forcing the serf to sell their labor in exchange for a wage. Second, in capitalism the essential aim is to purchase labor at sufficiently low rates to make a profit. For the capitalist to make a profit, they must be able to find a commodity on the market which has the property of creating more value than it costs to purchase. The only commodity, said Marx, which answers to this demand is human labor. Marx then went on to say that human labor has two essential attributes which fit this demand: (i) it is found on the market and can be purchased as if it were a commodity; (ii) it produces more value in the production process than the price it is purchased at. The name Marx gives to the commodity which the capitalist buys is 'labor power.' But, why not just labor?

The answer to this question is reasonably straightforward. The term 'labor power' enabled Marx to make a central distinction between 'labor' as a human activity and 'labor power' as the capacity to add use values to commodities, a distinction not made by the political economists. Both Smith and Ricardo believed that it was simply 'labor' that was exchanged and purchased by the capitalist. Marx thought, however, that political economists had erred in their understanding of the term and went on to make a distinction between 'human labor' and 'labor power' in order to show that there existed an intervening category of labor.[206] Human labor, in contrast to labor power, according to Marx, is the actual work and physical activity incorporated in the body of the laborer. Labor power, on the other hand, refers to the capacity of labor to add use values to commodities and is the name Marx gives to the commodity sold to the capitalist at a value less than the value it creates. Here is the point: in purchasing the worker's capacity to labor and add use values to commodities the capitalist is able to profit while at the same time pay less to the worker in wages than the value created by his or her labor.

This distinction between 'labor' and 'labor power' allowed Marx to pinpoint the precise mechanism which creates profit in capitalist society since, in order to profit, capitalists must find a commodity on the market which has the property of creating more value than it cost to purchase. What Marx pointed out in his distinction was that

205 *Capital*, Vol. 1, pp. 270–280.
206 Raya Dunayevskaya, *Marxism and Freedom*, London: Pluto Press, 1971, p. 34.

what the capitalist actually buys is not 'labor' outright, since if it were, slavery would be reintroduced. Rather, the capitalist buys 'labor power.' Labor power has two essential attributes: (i) it is found on the market and can be purchased as if it were a commodity; and (ii) it produces more value than the price at which it is purchased. In this respect, Marx had taken a leap beyond political economy. That is, in splitting labor into two categories – human labor and labor power – Marx found that the second category, labor power, was what the worker sold to the capitalist.[207]

In order, then, for the capitalist to find labor power on the market as a commodity, two essential conditions must be met. First, the possessor of labor power – the worker – must be in a position to sell his or her labor as a commodity, and second, the laborer must seem to be the 'free proprietor' of his or her own 'labor capacity' in the sense of being able to dispose of it as they see fit.[208] This very precise condition of being 'free' to dispose of one's own labor capacity on the market is called 'free labor' and it is fundamental to capitalism since it makes the buying and selling of labor power possible.

As Marx stated earlier, for capitalism to exist the owner of labor power must be in a position to sell his or her labor to a buyer. Under these circumstances, one would tend to assume that in a free market both the buyer and the seller of labor meet on an equal basis and that both are governed by the laws of exchange, a premise Smith and Ricardo believed to be true. They took the view that in capitalist societies laborers are free to sell their labor power in the market and, because of this, they were thought to be the sole proprietors of their own commodity. This position led Ricardo to take the view that so far as the worker is able to sell their labor power for a price, they may be thought of as existing on the same economic footing as the capitalist since both enter into free economic exchange.

Marx disagreed with this on several grounds. First, the laborer is without the means to sell products of his or her own labor since, by definition, a laborer is in the condition of being without the means of production. Second, since laborers cannot sell commodities produced by their own labor, they must sell as a commodity the labor power existing in their own bodies.[209] Marx reasoned that when we look again at the drama between the buyer and seller of labor, it is obvious that the advantage is conferred to the buyer of labor power since 'the buyer of labor power strides out in front as a capitalist, while the possessor of labor power follows as the worker. The one smirks self importantly and is intent on business; the other is timid and holds back, like someone who has brought their own hide to market and now has nothing to expect but a tanning.'[210]

'Free labor' thus constitutes only the 'appearance of freedom' since in all cases the worker is compelled to offer their labor for sale and cannot exist without doing so. If we look carefully at the conditions which make it appear as if the worker is a 'free'

---

207 Ibid.
208 *Capital*, Vol. 1, p. 270.
209 *Capital*, Vol. 1, p. 272.
210 *Capital*, Vol. 1, p. 280.

agent who enters into contractual relations to sell their labor power, in reality the 'period of time for which he is free to sell his labor power is the period of time for which he is forced to sell it.'[211]

Surplus Labor, Surplus Value and the Maintenance of the Worker

Following the discussion of labor power, Marx turned his attention to the concept of necessary and surplus labor. We can define these concepts initially by reviewing the process which Marx described as the 'reproduction of the worker.'[212] Generally speaking, this refers to the process by which the worker must use part of their wage to maintain their actual physical existence as workers. Since labor power exists in the living body of the individual, it makes sense to reason that the physical energy the worker expends during labor must be replaced. As labor power expends itself it must be replaced each day in order for the laborer to repeat the process. In this regard, the physical needs of the worker such as food, shelter and clothing have to be satisfied each day in order for workers to maintain themselves and continue to sell their labor power. Thus, laborers have to be supplied on a daily basis with the necessary food and fuel in order to 'renew their life processes.'[213]

Drawing on the discussion of the maintenance of the worker, Marx makes a conceptual distinction which triggers the first key observation regarding surplus value. This consists of essentially two concepts: necessary labor and surplus labor. Necessary labor refers to the time in the work day it takes for the worker to produce in wages the cost of his or her own maintenance. Marx reasoned that if the workday is eight hours, it takes approximately four hours of labor to produce the cost of maintaining the worker in food, fuel, rent and clothing. Surplus labor, on the other hand, refers to the part of the working day in which the laborer expends labor power, but creates no value for him or herself.[214] In this part of the workday the laborer adds value to the products worked on, and the value the worker creates during this part of the day belongs to the capitalist alone, not to the laborer.

Marx took this reasoning one step further. He stated that the laborer is paid only for one part of the workday – four hours rather than eight hours. According to Marx, the first four hours is the cost of their wages since it is clear that with these wages workers are only able to maintain themselves in food, rent and clothing and never get beyond the point of making ends meet. Marx then reasoned that if workers are only paid for the first four hours of the workday, what about the next four hours? Marx argued that the next four hours is the 'unpaid part' of the workday, and that this part constitutes the 'surplus' labor which produces the value for the capitalist but not the

---

211 *Capital*, Vol. 1, p. 415.
212 *Capital*, Vol. 1, p. 275.
213 *Capital*, Vol. 1, p. 276.
214 *Capital*, Vol. 1, p. 325.

worker. In the concept of surplus labor, Marx identified the portion of the working day in which the labor of the worker is over and above the labor workers need to reproduce themselves in food, rent and clothing. Marx called this added labor, 'surplus labor.' In surplus labor 'workers expend their labor, but this creates no value for them. Instead, they create surplus value which, for the capitalist 'has all the charms of something created out of nothing'. This part of the working day Marx called 'surplus labor time,' and to the labor expended during this time, he gave the name 'surplus labor.' [215] As Marx had already stated, the labor expended by the worker during this time provides no benefit for them, but instead adds value to the product and the value the worker creates during this part of the workday benefits the capitalist alone. Surplus value, therefore, can be defined as the value created by surplus labor. Surplus value has four central attributes: (i) it is the value created by the surplus labor of the worker; (ii) it is unpaid and therefore creates value for the capitalist but not the worker; (iii) it presents a deception since it claims to be paid labor; (iv) it is the recognized form of overwork and thus goes to the heart of the exploitation of the worker in that the worker is not paid for the value that is created by their surplus labor.

The History of Surplus Labor: The Working Day

The third step in resolving the theory of surplus value is to be found in Marx's discussion of the workday and the history of surplus labor. In chapter ten of *Capital*, Marx pointed out that 'surplus labor' is not new and, in fact, has a historical basis that reaches its highest stage of development in capitalist societies.[216] This can be made clear if we contrast industrial society with feudal society. In a feudal society, the surplus labor carried out by the serf for the landholder 'is demarcated very clearly both in space and time' by the corvée requirement.[217] In the corvée right, the lord is able to extract unpaid forced labor – surplus labor – from the serf during the corvée labor days; and then again by the corvée right which required the serf to expend surplus labor by producing agricultural products for the lord. Both instances of surplus labor performed by the serf are clearly marked off in space and time, and both these instances are clearly unpaid labor as required by the corvée which, in this case, appears in the form of a distinct advantage to the landholder. In addition, the labor which the serf expended for the purpose of his own maintenance was marked off clearly from the surplus labor which the serf performed for the maintenance of the landholder. In the first instance, the serf carried out the labor for his own maintenance on his own field, whereas in the second instance, the surplus labor carried out during the corvée days for the landholder was performed on the lords' estate, and was unpaid.[218]

---

215 Ibid.
216 *Capital*, Vol.1, pp. 344–353.
217 *Capital*, Vol. 1, p. 680.
218 For more discussion on this see *Capital*, pp. 346–7.

Marx went on to say that 'both parts of the labor time thus exist independently, side by side with each other, so that in the corvée 'the surplus labor is accurately marked off from the necessary labor.'[219] Also in societies of antiquity, the distinction between necessary and surplus labor is clearly demarcated since all the labor performed by the slave appears as labor for the master. In these two instances – feudalism and slavery – unpaid labor appears as 'unpaid.' Only in capitalism, however, does unpaid labor appear as 'paid.' Marx stated that the unpaid portion of the worker's labor disguised itself as paid labor and therefore the capitalist system of wages and the means of their calculation is deliberately deceptive. In all other systems of production, including feudal and slave societies, unpaid labor is clearly demarcated. Only in capitalism is surplus labor 'extorted from the immediate producer' since it presents itself as paid and thus enters into a deception.[220]

To get to the bottom of this question, Marx believed that surplus labor had its recognized form in all societies and that it had obvious roots in the social inequalities created by the system of ownership and the class structure. We can therefore define the concept of surplus labor simply as the form of overwork that is extracted from the worker in the production process that is of a direct advantage to the owners of the means of production. The concept helps explain why workers seem always to struggle to make ends meet, while owners of the means of production become wealthier and more affluent. In feudal society, we saw that the recognized form of overwork existed in the form of the corvée system, while in Greece and Rome it was slavery, and in capitalism it is wage labor.[221] Marx stated that industrial capitalism 'did not invent surplus labor, since whenever a part of society possesses the monopoly of the means of production, workers, free or unfree, must add to the labor time necessary for their own maintenance an extra quantity of labor time in order to produce the means of subsistence for the owner of the means of production, whether this proprietor is an Athenian, an Etruscan theocrat, a Wallachian boyar, a modern landlord or a capitalist.'[222]

It stands to reason that since surplus labor benefits the owner of the means of production, then the appetite for surplus labor would be unlimited. In order to demonstrate this Marx examined the history of overwork in different societies. A dramatic example, used by Marx, occurs in Roman history when, in the Roman gold mines, workers were compelled to work until they died. Their labor was labor until death and all their labor was surplus labor with nothing for their own maintenance. In feudal societies, by contrast, surplus labor appeared in the form of a debt obligation in which the serf owed the lord twelve corvée days of labor.[223] Only in capitalist society does this surplus labor take the form of surplus value, and its form of overwork is wage labor.

219 Ibid.
220 *Capital*, Vol. 1, p. 325.
221 *Capital*, Vol. 1, pp. 344–48.
222 *Capital*, Vol. 1, pp. 344–45.
223 *Capital*, Vol. 1, p. 347.

The Wage Form: Unpaid Labor

Finally, we come to the fourth step. In chapter nineteen of *Capital*, Marx examined the history of wages and looked closely at the development of the 'wage form.'[224] Marx believed that the industrial wage form was a deceptive method of compensating the worker, and argued that it makes unpaid labor appear as if it were paid labor. By making surplus labor appear as paid labor, the worker is deceived into believing that, by their labor, they only maintain themselves, when in reality the unpaid portion increases the wealth of the capitalist. As far as Marx was concerned, this was the most powerful expression of appearances distorting reality. This is stated very clearly when he wrote:

> We see that the value of 3 shillings, which represents the paid portion of the working day, i.e., 6 hours of labor, appears as the value or price of the whole working day of 12 hour which thus includes 6 hours which have not been paid for. The wage-form thus extinguishes every trace of the division of the working day into necessary labor and surplus labor, into paid labor and unpaid labor. All labor appears as paid labor. In feudal society, it is different. There the labor of the serf is for himself, and his compulsory labor for the lord of the land is demarcated very clearly both in space and time. In slave labor, even the part of the working day in which the slave is only replacing the value of his own means of subsistence, in which he therefore actually works for himself alone, appears as labor for the master. All his labor appears as unpaid labor. In wage labor, on the contrary, every surplus labor or unpaid labor appears as paid. In the one case, the property relation conceals the slave's labor for himself; in the other case the money-relation conceals the uncompensated labor of the wage-laborer.[225]

Capital Vol. 1, Part D: The Genesis of Capitalism

Primitive Accumulation

Technically speaking, all the major economic and theoretical steps taken by Marx in *Capital* are more or less complete, and we can now turn our attention to the historical steps. In line with this, Marx focused on several key historical changes leading to the development of capitalism and one of the first issues he looked at was the process he called 'primitive accumulation.' Since this is one of the key concepts discussed by Marx in the context of the historical development of capitalism, it will be worthwhile to look more closely at the origins and genesis of the term.

Generally speaking, Marx's discussion of primitive accumulation begins relatively late in relation to his overall treatment of capitalism, almost near the end of the work.

---

224 *Capital*, Vol. 1, pp. 675–682.
225 *Capital*, Vol. 1, p. 680.

Nevertheless, Marx used the concept in this context to understand the coercive forces being played out between landlords and serf laborers during the transfer of feudal land into private property. In this case, Marx wanted to outline what he thought were the historical forces leading to the transition from feudalism to capitalism, and in order to do this he had to look at the mechanisms of social and historical change taking place during the transfer of the means of production.

Primitive accumulation in this context is a concept used by Marx to understand the coercive forces that were at work during the period of accumulation when capitalism came into being. He thought that this accumulation was the 'original' event leading to the moment when capitalism stands on its feet, and he thought that the form of accumulation was therefore 'primitive' because it pinpointed the early crude stages by which capitalist production accumulates masses of capital and masses of labor in order to produce. Whereas Smith and Ricardo had largely thought that this was a peaceful process, Marx argued that in fact it took the form of violent expropriation, conquest and private enrichment.

To show how this drama was played out, Marx referred to the process of primitive accumulation as though it were the 'economic equivalent of original sin.'[226] He thought this was the case because the process revealed a pattern of forced accumulation that had divorced the peasant serf from the means of subsistence and had separated them from the conditions of ownership over their own labor. The history of what Marx called the 'economic equivalent of original sin' thus traced the process whereby the serf laborer was forcibly expelled from the means of production in a way that was equivalent to Adam's and Eve's expulsion from paradise, thereby marking the point at which the means of production had become capital, and the serf laborer had become a wage laborer.[227]

To make the process clear, Marx drew on the popular legend explaining the existence of two groups in society: the rich and the poor.[228] Most people, stated Marx, believe that the rich are industrious, well-disciplined and frugal; while the poor are lazy, spendthrift and undisciplined. This myth, said Marx, explains how some people came to be blessed with wealth, whereas others are condemned to poverty. 'And it came to pass,' said Marx, 'that the first group accumulated wealth and riches, while the latter group had nothing to sell but their labor.'[229] But in actual fact, said Marx, the truth is otherwise, since the poverty of the great majority is a tale of 'coercion, expropriation and robbery.'[230] Primitive accumulation, then, is a concept used by Marx to understand the coercive forces leading to the loss of the use of the means of production by the worker and the process of accumulation which had transformed

---

226 *Capital*, Vol. 1, p. 873.
227 Ibid.
228 Ibid.
229 Ibid.
230 Ibid.

it into property. In order to see how this drama was played out, let us look a little further.

Marx thought that historically the drama of capitalism could best be understood as the coming together of two very different kinds of commodity owners. First were the owners of money and the means of subsistence who were eager to buy labor power in order to put it to work; and second were 'free laborers who were sellers of their labor power.'[231] Marx believed that the key to understanding how these two groups came together at this point in history had everything to do with the process of intense accumulation of capital on the one hand, and the process by which the 'free labor' was created, on the other.

According to Marx, the point at which the free laborer is created is thus essential to the development of capitalism, and he believed that the precise focal point for the emergence of the free laborer was the battle of accumulation taking place between landholders on the one hand, and agricultural laborers on the other. This, said Marx, is a 'process which operates two transformations at the same time': first, the means of subsistence is transformed into private property which is subsequently turned into capital; and second, the serf laborer is divorced from the means of production and transformed into a wage laborer.

It was therefore Marx's contention that in order for capitalism to be possible, labor must be 'free' in the sense of being subject to buying and selling so that it can be purchased as a commodity on the market. But, said Marx, in order for this to take place two essential conditions must be met. First, the possessor of labor power must be in the condition of being divorced from the means of production, and as a result must necessarily be compelled to sell their labor on the market in order to live. Second, at the same time that the laborer is 'free' to dispose of their labor for a wage, they must also be 'forced' or compelled to sell their labor in order to live. This very precise condition of being able to freely dispose of their own labor on the market, and also be forced to sell it, is called 'free labor' and is fundamental to capitalism.

The concept of original accumulation thus identifies the precise historical moment when capitalist production stands on its feet by the accumulation of masses of capital on the one hand, and masses of labor power on the other. This accumulation, Marx thought, appears as primitive because it forms the pre-history of capital and the mode of production corresponding to it. Marx notes that as soon as capitalist production becomes possible, it not only maintains this separation between the worker and the means of production but reproduces it on a constantly extending scale. The process which creates capitalist social relations is therefore nothing other than the process which divorces the worker from the ownership over the conditions of their own labor.[232]

---

231 Ibid.
232 Ibid.

The Stages of Primitive Accumulation

Marx believed that primitive accumulation took place in two distinct historical periods. The first stage, according to Marx, takes place with the expropriation of the agricultural laborer from the land. This stage began during the seventeenth century when large populations of agricultural workers were 'forcibly' thrown off the land by eviction and foreclosure leading to the dissolution of a whole way of life. The second stage was marked by the legal transfer of feudal lands into private hands by direct seizure and expropriation leading to the loss of the means of production. This took place by means of the bills of enclosure, which by the middle of the nineteenth century had created the industrial worker, the wage laborer, the factory system and private ownership of the means of production. This was a process which took place, according to Marx 'without the slightest observance of legal etiquette.'[233]

Cooperation and Division of Labor

After discussing the conditions leading to surplus labor, surplus value and primitive accumulation, Marx turned his attention to discussing the development of industrial manufacturing and the creation of the factory system that stands at the center of capitalist production. Marx conceived of the impact of industrial manufacture on the worker as taking place essentially along three broad planes of activity. Each of these involves substantial shifts in the way human labor was carried out and is discussed under three separate categories: (i) cooperation and large scale industry; (ii) division of labor and manufacture; (iii) machinery and large scale industry. Let us begin by looking at cooperation.

The starting place of 'cooperation and large scale industry,' said Marx, is the assembly of a large number of workers in a factory. For this to occur, a large number of workers have to be brought together in one place for purposes of production. This step, said Marx, presupposes the decline of the trade guilds which formerly restricted the unification of crafts and trades under one roof to protect their hold over professions. On this basis, capitalist production could proceed by unifying many workers and many trades under one roof and at the same time bring them under the control of one capitalist. Marx's interest here was to focus on what he called 'the combined effect of labor.'[234]

He began by observing three broad effects of combined cooperation. First, he pointed out that the effect of combined labor could not have been produced by the isolated worker working on their own, and so he reasoned that the combined effect of factory labor created a form of cooperation which increased the productive power of the individual. The fact of bringing a number of workers together in one place thus produced a combined effect so that a quantitative gain resulted from a qualitative act. But,

---

233 *Capital*, Vol. 1, p. 884.
234 *Capital*, Vol. 1, p. 443.

what exactly was this? Marx believed that the combined cooperation of many workers creates a qualitative effect in that it concentrated the means of production in one place.[235] In this case, the advantage is to the capitalist since the total value of labor power is greater than the total sum of wages the capitalist pays to the worker.

Marx then points out that the cooperation created between workers with the advent of the factory system gives rise to what he called a 'system of interconnections' which emerges between the individual laborers.[236] This system, said Marx, is neither the plan of the workers as a group or the plan of one individual worker, but rather it is something created by the capitalist. In this respect, the interconnections existing between the workers, according to Marx, confronts the workers collectively in two ways: first, it neither serves the workers as individuals, since their activity is for the most part for the capitalist that brings them together; second, what they do collectively is not the result of their own plans, since their unification into a single body is something they do not understand in that it 'lies outside of their competence.'[237]

Division of Labor: Simple and Complex Cooperation

After looking at the combined effect of cooperation, Marx looked at the process of the division of labor. He believed that the division of labor and the social form of cooperation which it presupposes are found first and foremost in classical manufacture. The division of labor, he stated, developed throughout the period of the nineteenth century with the development and progress of manufacturing and industry. According to Marx, the division of labor led to a 'particular sort of cooperation' which he called 'complex cooperation.'[238] As soon as the division of labor takes place, he reasoned, there is an important change from manufacturing based on simple cooperation to complex cooperation. But, what exactly does Marx mean by the term complex cooperation?

According to Marx, complex cooperation occurred when the skills formerly embedded in the worker become a function of the process of the division of labor itself. Previously, guilds had restricted the division of labor in order to preserve the integrity of distinct trades and crafts. But, as soon as these trades were combined under one roof, the qualitative skill formerly belonging to the worker became the property of the combined division of labor and this robbed workers of their skill. As an example, Marx drew on the carriage trade. He said that formerly this trade involved various handicrafts and skills; coach work, enamel work, carriage work, upholstery and wheel right. Before capitalist production, each of these operations were specialized trades regulated by guilds in order to maintain their separation from

---

235 *Capital*, Vol. 1, p. 447.
236 *Capital*, Vol. 1, p. 449–50.
237 *Capital*, Vol. 1, p. 450.
238 *Capital*, Vol. 1, pp. 455–58.

each other. As soon as the division of labor is established, however, the carriage maker becomes 'exclusively occupied with making carriages.'[239] As a result, individual trades immediately lost their specialized skills which concentrated their combined activity exclusively in making carriages. Marx pointed out that 'at first, the manufacture of carriages appears as a combination of various independent handicrafts and trades. But it gradually began to involve the splitting up of carriage production into various and detailed operations and each single operation crystallized into the exclusive function of a particular worker, the manufacturing as a whole being performed by these partial workers in conjunction.'[240]

Marx then went on to make the distinction between simple and complex cooperation more explicit. Simple cooperation may be defined as a situation of production in which one capitalist employs a number of craftsman who all perform the same work, e.g., making carriages. This, said Marx, is simple cooperation. Each craftsman makes the entire commodity from beginning to end and performs the series of operations necessary to produce the entire commodity. Complex cooperation, on the other hand, occurs when each individual performs operations which are disconnected and isolated from one another and carried on side by side. Each operation is assigned a separate craftsmen and the commodity is produced by the combined action of the cooperators, but no single craftsmen produces the commodity themselves. In this case, according to Marx, the commodity has gone from being a product of the individual craftsman to becoming the social product of the union of craftsmen, each of whom performs only one operation. The development of the division of labor, said Marx, presides over the breakdown of handicraft skills and the 'decomposition of handicrafts into different and partial operations.'[241] Labor as such becomes transformed into a 'life long partial function.'[242]

Theory of Alienation

History of the Concept in Hegel

The term alienation first came into general use during the nineteenth and twentieth centuries to describe a state of disruption and change taking place in the human labor process and system of social relations as a result of the development of modern society. It was first used as a philosophic concept in the nineteenth century by Georg Hegel who employed the term to describe the struggle for self-realization that took place in the wider historical world. Following Hegel, Ludwig Feuerbach and Marx were among the first to give systematic expression to the concept of alienation, and it is their work which constitutes the starting place for a full-blown theory of alienation.

---

239 *Capital*, Vol. 1, p. 454.
240 *Capital*, Vol. 1, p. 455–6.
241 *Capital*, Vol. 1, p. 458.
242 Ibid.

In 1807, Hegel used the term 'estrangement' in a work called *The Phenomenology of Mind* to outline a framework for a theory of human development. In his theory, Hegel argued that human beings strive to realize themselves in history though a process he referred to as 'self actualization.' Hegel, however, believed that individuals do not realize themselves in the world directly but, in fact, always encounter obstacles and limitations which act against them to block their self-realization. Hegel called these obstacles 'oppositions' in which the external world acts to work against the individual by 'shutting out their existence' and by preventing them from obtaining self-realization.[243] These oppositions and negations, Hegel reasoned, occur in the world when people are forced into servitude, experience poverty, have a sudden illness or suffer setbacks and losses that threaten to cancel out their existence.

Using the concept of opposition and negation, Hegel was perhaps the first to understand that human beings can experience their own activity as something external to them, something that is 'not self,' and he described this moment in human experience as alienation. In fact, Hegel was one of the first thinkers to capture the idea that individuals can experience themselves as not fully human, and that human beings can live their lives without ever being completely or fully developed. The idea that human beings could experience themselves as incomplete or not fully developed was altogether new and fit the experience of modernism simply by giving expression to the fragmentation of human experience and the loss of control associated with modern society.

Feuerbach's Theory of Religious Alienation

After Hegel, Ludwig Feuerbach, a contemporary of Marx, developed a theory alienation in a work entitled *The Essence of Christianity* where he outlined a theory of religious alienation based on a criticism of Christianity.[244] Feuerbach's critical views on Christianity served as a central theoretical focus for Marx in several respects. First, Feuerbach provided a stunning criticism of Hegel stating that his philosophical views duplicated religion because, like religion, they promoted the idea that the abstract spiritual world rules over the real world, and in this sense was nothing more than religion. Second, Feuerbach established a link between philosophy and religion by claiming that both constituted human alienation to the extent that they misrepresented reality and human experience. This criticism had a considerable impact on philosophy, since Feuerbach showed that philosophy, in being based on belief rather than reason, was a mythology similar to religion itself. Third, by moving away from Hegelian idealism, Feuerbach was moving in the direction of materialism, and this served as a basis for Marx to crystallize his thinking on the economic origins of alienation.

---

243 See Hegel, *The Phenomenology of Mind*. Hegel believed that some people oppose others by deliberately shutting out their existence and he referred to this process as 'negation' so far as it denied the existence of others. Hegel believed, however, that human beings often act to cancel out these negations by a process he called 'as negation of the negation' in which they reassert their right to exist.

244 Ludwig Feuerbach, *The Essence of Christianity,* Buffalo, N.Y.: Prometheus, 1989.

Feuerbach's main argument focused on religious alienation. He had argued that in making religion, human beings unwittingly project their human essence onto an image and in making this image into God, they assign qualities to it that are distinctly non-human. According to Feuerbach, they do this to the point that the image of God eventually meets the criteria of perfection to the extent that human beings in comparison appear to be imperfect. This image, argued Feuerbach, becomes the birth place of rules and prescriptions which, in turn, are re-imposed on the life of human beings in the form of unwanted regulation and self denial to the point of being alienated from what defines them as human beings. Feuerbach maintained that the self imposition of restraint and imperfection constituted the height of alienation because, in making religion, human beings simply experience their own human qualities acting back upon them in the form of alien rules which reproach them for their natures and forcibly narrow their lives to an image of perfection that can never be attained. 'Religion,' said Feuerbach, 'is thus the disuniting of human beings from themselves,' and in this sense it is non-human or anti-human.[245]

Two immediate philosophical consequences emerged as a result of Feuerbach's criticism of religion. First, in asserting that physical and material being was true being, Feuerbach turned Hegel right side up by placing the emphasis on the material origin of religious life. In stating that religion had a material base, therefore, Feuerbach was one of the first to point out that religion itself was an 'anthropology' to the extent that it showed that religion derived from human material development, and was a product of human material activity rather than a product of a spiritual realm. In this view, religion was no longer the exclusive domain of theology but rather was seen as an activity that belonged to human anthropology.[246] Second, the criticism of Hegel's philosophy by Feuerbach was viewed by some as an attempt to found religion on materialist premises, and this eventually led Marx to Feuerbach's work.

Marx's Rejection of Feuerbach

After reading Feuerbach's *Essence of Christianity*, Marx thought that while Feuerbach had taken a step in the right direction by assuming that religious alienation had its origin in the material activity, Marx eventually criticized Feuerbach for not going far enough. His criticism of Feuerbach was thus both social and historical, and he began by pointing out that Feuerbach had mistakenly confused the human 'religious essence with the abstract human individual' and that for Feuerbach the 'human individual' was nothing more than 'an inward mute generality'. According to Marx, Feuerbach did not see that 'the religious mental disposition was a social product and that the abstract individual whom he analyzed belonged to a particular form of society.'[247]

---

245 Feuerbach, *The Essence of Christianity*, p. 33.

246 For a discussion of the connection between Feuerbach, Hegel and Marx, see Nathan Rotenstreich, *Basic Problems in Marx's Philosophy*, Indianapolis: Bobbs-Merrill, 1965.

247 Marx and Engels, *The German Ideology*, New York: International Publishers, 1947, Sixth Thesis, pp. 198–9.

Marx therefore criticized Feuerbach's abstract conception of religious alienation on the basis that it had no particular material origin in social or economic activity and that, according to Marx, Feuerbach had believed that humanity was nothing more than a 'dumb generality.' Marx thought that this was a serious error because, in looking for the material origin of religion, Feuerbach had failed to relate religious activity to material economic activity, and in so doing failed to see that the class struggle for existence was a material struggle rather than a religious struggle. As far as Marx was concerned, human existence could only be understood in terms of material production and material activity, and this meant that the very first act of all human beings was always economic in that human beings must satisfy their material needs of food, shelter and clothing before they satisfy their religious needs. Marx therefore thought that Feuerbach had reverted back to Hegel's idealist outlook by asserting that religion was the origin of human alienation. In opposition to this, Marx argued that alienation was a consequence of material life, and that as such it had social and economic origins. As a result, Marx began to pursue an analysis of the origin of alienation by looking outside Feuerbach's religious realm of experience to the material realm of economic experience and then eventually to the class struggle for material existence.

Marx's Theory of Alienation and the 1844 Manuscripts

Historically, Marx first outlined his theory of alienation in a worked entitled *The Economic and Philosophic Manuscripts,* which were written in 1844.[248] In order to completely understand his theory, it will be useful to briefly compare it with Hegel's view of estrangement along the lines of two broad distinctions. First, Hegel had argued that the concept of estrangement required an investigation into abstract philosophical concepts such as history, consciousness and human reason. While Hegel believed that the struggle for human self-identity and emancipation took place between the individual and abstract forces in the external world, Marx thought that this struggle was primarily acted out on the economic front, and was therefore material in nature. Thus, as far as Marx was concerned, Hegel had mistakenly conceived of the struggle between the individual and the external world in terms of abstract forces he called 'oppositions' and 'negations.'

Second, while Hegel had looked at the historical 'oppositions' existing in different forms of servitude and slavery, Marx thought that these 'oppositions' and 'negations' were entirely material, so far as they were economic realities materialized in the form of the struggle for economic existence rather than existence generally speaking, as Hegel had thought.[249] For Marx, then, the struggle for self realization against opposition in the external world was a material struggle played out on the economic front,

---

248 Marx, *The Economic and Philosophic Manuscripts of 1844*, New York: International Publishers, [1932] 1964. See also Bertell Ollman, *Alienation: Marx's Conception of Man in Capitalist Society*. London: Cambridge University Press, 1971.

249 The classic example of this is Hegel's discussion of the different forms of servitude and the master slave relations that emerge throughout history. Hegel's view of alienation in this context exists when the master obtains self recognition through the slave's servitude and the slave's existence is 'canceled out' or 'negated.' See Hegel, *The Phenomenology of Mind*, pp. 229–40.

and this shift from the abstract to the material realm by Marx replaced Hegel's abstract struggle for self-realization in thought.

Marx, then, developed his theory of alienation to convey two central and dominant ideas. First, he wanted to convey the idea that human beings begin their existence by making society and that at some point feel that society is a natural extension of their nature and their being, in that it reflects them and they feel at home in it. Second, Marx wished to convey the idea that, as modern society develops, human beings begin to feel that society is not of their own making and that it no longer reflects their being or their nature, but instead appears to be alien and thus stands over and against them. The idea that society starts out as an extension of human beings that reflect their nature, and then ends up as something apart and external, is precisely what the theory of alienation attempts to explain.[250]

Marx's Theory of Human Nature

To completely understand Marx's theory of alienation, it is necessary to look at his theory of human nature. In many of his writings, Marx stressed the idea that human beings define themselves in nature and history primarily through their laboring activity, and that through this they form relations with the material world outside themselves. Marx, in fact, believed that laboring was so central to human existence that it formed part of their essential nature in that it defined them as human beings. In this respect, he argued that labor defined human beings in at least three specific senses. First, through it individuals exert control over nature and natural obstacles in the world, and thus feel themselves to be active rather than passive in history. Second, labor is the source of human existence in that it produces material necessities of food, shelter and clothing without which the individual could not survive and would not exist. Third, labor is part of human self-definition since through it individuals sustain their life, control their circumstances and actively feel confirmed in their existence through their laboring activity.

In addition to this, Marx went on to argue that laboring activity performs connective functions which link human beings to existence by forming social relations with the external world in three important ways.[251] First, it connects them to nature in so far as they are reliant on the means of production to satisfy their material needs by producing food, shelter and clothing. In this sense they form relations with the means of production since from it they derive economic subsistence and survival by their livelihoods. Second, labor connects them to the means of self-affirmation because it helps them gain control over obstacles in nature, in that by exerting themselves through their labor they facilitate well-being and existence and create an objective world outside themselves. Third, it connects them to the product of their labor to the extent that the product has a use value which is directly used as a means of subsistence.

---

250 Ibid.

251 For a discussion of the concept of 'social relation' in the light of Marx's theory of alienation see Bertell Ollman, *Alienation: Marx's Conception of Man in Capitalist Society*, Cambridge: The University Press, 1971, pp. 12–42.

The fact that Marx had outlined a theory of human nature based on the social relations individuals form outside themselves, showed that by the time he had written the essays on alienated labor and estrangement, he had abandoned Hegel's theory of the doctrine of relations by replacing it with a theory of relations based on social relationships. This is nowhere more evident than in his view of labor in which all the relations formed between individuals and their external realities were defined in the form of definite social relations and definite social relationships. Thus, for example, the term capitalism for Marx was not simply the name for a type of economy, but was rather a term he used to define a network of social relations formed between individuals and the means of production, between individuals and their laboring activity, between individuals and their relations of production with their superiors, and between individuals and the relations they form with the pre-existing social framework. In every case, Marx's theory of alienation refers to a definite set of social relationships which were first formed in feudal societies and then became disrupted in modern industrial society. In this respect, every type of alienation referred to by Marx points to a specific disruption or break that occurs in the social relations individuals form in the external world outside themselves.

Marx went on to present his theory of alienation by looking at what he believed were the four broad relations that are formed within the context of human laboring activity.[252] These relations are conceived by Marx as relations (i) with the product of labor; (ii) with laboring activity; (iii) with the human species; and (iv) relations with other human beings. Since he thought that alienation breaks the fundamental link human beings have to their self defining qualities, he went on to identify four distinct types of alienation: (i) alienation from the product of labor; (ii) alienation from productive activity; (iii) alienation from the human species; and (iv) alienation from fellow human beings.[253]

Alienation from the Product   The first type of alienation discussed by Marx is product alienation. This takes place, said Marx, when human beings become estranged from the things they produce and lose control over their product. But how can the worker lose control over what they produce? To answer this question, we can briefly look at production in feudal society. In a feudal society, production is carried on for purposes of existence so that what is produced is consumed directly to satisfy material needs without the product entering into circulation for purposes of buying and selling. By the very fact of their material labor, workers thus form relations with what they produce since what they produce has immediate use value, belongs to them directly, and they consume it to satisfy their economic needs. In this case, the product of labor directly satisfies their material needs and this sustains their life and existence. In addition, what the laborer produces in feudal society not only has immediate

---

252 For a different conception of these relations see Bertell Ollman, *Alienation: Marx's Conception of Man*, p. 137.
253 Marx, *Economic and Philosophic Manuscripts*, p. 106

use value, but it affirms their relationship to themselves in their own productive powers because it sustains their life and existence.

In modern society, by contrast, this situation is reversed. To begin with, production is for exchange rather than immediate use, and what is produced by the worker must enter into the medium of exchange called the market. In this sense, the worker loses control over the product of their labor since the product belongs to the owner of the means of production where it is put into circulation for purposes of purchase and sale. Product alienation thus occurs when the product no longer belongs to the worker and circulates in the medium of exchange where it appears to be detached from the laborer who creates it. In thus circulating in the system of exchange, the product now confronts the worker as something alien and unrelated to the worker's existence. At this point in the production process the worker no longer has control over what they produce and, since the ownership over the means of production is concentrated in another class, both the product of labor and the labor itself confront the worker externally as a thing not of their own making.[254]

Marx went on to argue that product alienation alters the individual's social relation to what they produce and to the natural world. Whereas in feudal society workers receive subsistence and self definition from the product, in industrial society the worker is alienated from what they produce because both the product and the means of production no longer belongs to them but are owned privately by the capitalist. To this extent, alienation appears in the form of the worker's separation from both the product and the means of production. Under such circumstances, the product of labor may be said to stand over and against the worker because the worker never engages the means of production directly since it is mediated both by the ownership of another class, and by the necessity for purchase and sale of the product in the system of exchange.

As the means of production become the property of only one class in society, human labor and the product of labor stand over and against the worker as an alien thing. This happens, Marx thought, in two distinct ways. First, since human labor is mediated by a system of ownership in which the worker is forced to sell their labor to the capitalist in exchange for a wage, they no longer own or have control over their labor as they once did in feudal society. Second, as result of the fact that the product enters into the system of exchange, the product creates no use value for the worker either in the form of direct subsistence of self definition.[255]

In addition to this, Marx thought that product alienation breaks the connection workers form in identifying with the product they produce. In feudal society, according to Marx, what the laborer produced affirmed the relationship they had to their own productive powers because 'labor is realized in its object or product.'[256] To this extent, the product of labor is always the 'summary of the activity of production' so that the product constitutes a source of self-identification.[257] As exchange becomes

254 Marx, *Economic and Philosophic Manuscripts*, p. 110
255 Ibid., p. 111.
256 Ibid., p. 108.

the dominant social relation, however, product alienation becomes greatest when the worker cannot use the product they produce.

Alienation from Productive Activity   The second form of alienation discussed by Marx is alienation from productive activity. In this type of alienation human beings lose control over the capacity of their laboring activity to affirm their being and define their self-existence. But in order to understand what Marx meant by this term, it will be useful to look at a concept he used frequently throughout his work called a 'social relation.' Historically, the term social relation is primarily used by Marx by to describe the relationship that is formed between the individual and the outer world in the labor process, and to pinpoint the way in which human beings are essentially connected to existence and to the external world through their laboring activity. Understood in this sense, individuals are connected to existence by their labor in two broad ways: first, it connects them to themselves to the extent that they receive self affirmation from it in the form of material satisfactions; second, it connects them to others and to the social world in that by their laboring activity they form relations with history and society. Looked at from this point of view, every relation created by human labor can be viewed from two distinct vantage points: from its relation to itself, and from relations external to itself.[258] Marx went on to describe alienation from productive activity in the following way:

> First, the fact that labor is external to the worker, i.e., it does not belong to his essential being; that in his work, therefore, he does not affirm himself but denies himself, does not feel content but unhappy, does not develop freely his physical and mental energy but mortifies his body and ruins his mind. The worker only feels himself outside his work, and in his work feels outside himself. He is at home when he is not working, and when he is working he is not home. His labor is therefore not voluntary, but coerced; it is forced labor.

> Its alien character emerges clearly in the fact that as soon as no physical compulsion exists, labor is shunned like the plague. External labor, labor in which man alienates himself, is a labor of self-sacrifice, of mortification. Lastly, the external character of labor for the worker appears in the fact that it is not his own, but someone else's, that it does not belong to him, that in it he belongs, not to himself, but to another. As a result, the worker no longer feels himself to be freely active in any but his animal functions – eating, drinking, procreating, or at most in his dwelling and in dressing up, etc.; and in his human functions he no longer feels himself to be anything but an animal. What is animal becomes human and what is human becomes animal. Certainly eating, drinking and procreating, etc., are also genuinely human functions.

But abstractly taken, separated from the sphere of all other human activity and turned into sole and ultimate ends, they are animal functions.[259]

257 Ibid., p. 110.
258 S. Hook, *From Hegel to Marx*, London: Victor Gollancz, 1936, p. 23.
259 Marx, *The Economic and Philosophic Manuscripts*, pp. 110–11.

In the above quotation Marx stated that alienation from productive activity breaks the connection the worker has to the self affirming and self defining aspects of their laboring activity, and it does this in three broad ways. First, to the extent that the worker sells their labor in exchange for a wage, their labor is external to them in that it belongs to another during the course of the workday. The external character of labor exists, according to Marx, when the worker cannot dispose of their labor as they see fit, and when they are compelled to sell it to the capitalist in exchange for a wage. Because the worker loses control over their laboring activity in this case, their labor does not 'affirm' them because the labor no longer belongs to them. This type of alienation takes place in industrial society when the worker's movements are not their own, but are directly controlled by a superior who clocks and tabulates their movements for purposes of measuring their efficiency and controlling the outcome of their labor. When workers lose control over their laboring activity and cannot control their own body movements while being told 'how to work,' Marx argued that they only feel 'at home when they are not working,' and when 'they are working they are not at home.'[260] In this respect, labor is external in that it confronts the worker in a alien form that they do not recognize. This has a double impact. While the labor of the worker belongs to someone else, workers 'only feel human outside their work, and in their work they feel outside themselves.'[261] This is labor which has as its end the loss of the worker, since the worker's labor operates on them independently of their will, purpose and desire.

Second, alienation from productive activity reverses the individual's relationship to themselves and their own productive powers. Under these circumstances, the labor of the worker does not hold out the direct satisfaction of their material needs as it once did in feudal society since what is produced enters into the medium of exchange. This, said Marx, converts the worker's activity into nothing more than a means to satisfy their human need, so that the sole purpose of life becomes that of fulfilling needs. This alienates individuals from the capacity of their labor to define their essential being since, in capitalism, labor is performed only to fulfill immediate economic needs. Under these circumstances, the laborer can only understand work as springing from internal needs and thus labors only to satisfy their physical necessities. This type of alienation is experienced when the worker simply lives from pay check to pay check and is never able to catch up, but rather always falls behind. In this condition, the worker comes to believe that the maintenance of their individual existence is the single and solitary aim of their life activity. On this basis, the worker thus lives solely to acquire the means of living.[262]

Third, alienation from productive activity reverses the individual's relation to their own physical body. While in feudal societies productive activity defined the sphere

---

260 Ibid.
261 Ibid, p. 111.
262 Ibid.

of free actions in all functions, in capitalism productive activity is free only in those functions which workers share with animals such as eating, sleeping, drinking and procreating, since only these functions are free and unsupervised. In their human laboring functions, therefore, workers feel themselves to be like animals, since 'what is animal becomes human and what is human becomes animal.'[263] In this case, individuals are alienated from their physical bodies because they are no longer able to dispose of their labor as freely as if it were their private property. Under these circumstances, those functions they share with animals such as eating, drinking, sleeping and procreating constitute a 'reversal of human and animal functions' because the 'activities which human beings share with animals appears more human than those activities which mark them off as human beings.'[264]

Since their productive activity no longer belongs to the worker, their defining relation to themselves and their powers are reversed: 'activity becomes suffering; strength becomes weakness; action becomes emasculation' and in this state the worker can no longer depend on their own activity for their life.[265] Marx believed that alienation from productive activity thus breaks the most important social relation of all, the active connection human beings have to themselves.

Alienation from Species Activity   A third type of alienation discussed by Marx is alienation from the human species. In species alienation, Marx believed that human beings are alienated from their own species-being and from their own species activity. But, in order to be clear on Marx's meaning here, this category of alienation requires further explanation. Marx thought that human beings live in an active relation to the outside world and because of this he believed that they have human qualities which mark them off from other species. In the main, he thought that the chief qualities separating human beings from the animal world was a characteristic he referred to as 'conscious mental being,' and he thought this had to do with the ability human beings had to take themselves into account, reflect on their circumstances and be conscious of themselves in history.[266]

In contrast to this, Marx thought that animals have only physical being, but not conscious being. Because animals do not have conscious being, he thought that their life activity was qualitatively different from human life activity. Accordingly, Marx took the view that species alienation breaks the connection which human beings have to their conscious mental being in two fundamental respects: first, because it turned laboring into a physical act, it revoked the advantage nature had given to human beings over animal life by converting conscious being into physical being during the act of labor.

---

263 Ibid.

264 Ollman, *Alienation*, p. 140.

265 Ibid.

266 Marx, *The Economic and Philosophic Manuscripts*, pp. 113–14. Marx says that 'conscious life activity distinguishes human beings immediately from animal life activity … to the extent that human beings contemplate themselves in a world that they create.'

Second, by converting conscious being into physical being, it made human labor like the labor of animals by reducing labor to physical being over mental being. In this type of alienation, human nature is turned against itself in that human beings become creatures of their physical activity and their physical existence.

Marx reasoned that the relations individuals form with the external world thus differs from animals in several respects. First, animals live directly off nature and thus do not produce and do not have to create use values by their labor. Human beings, on the other hand, 'prepare nature to make it palatable and digestible' and in this sense they must labor upon it to work it up.[267] Second, human beings are a species distinct from animals because they have conscious being with which they reflect upon themselves and their purposes in relation to their own powers and to their own future in the world. Third, animals find what they need in nature and need only to satisfy their direct physical needs, whereas human beings must produce and in doing so create an objective world in the form of history, society and civilization. In this, they work up inorganic nature by producing social institutions of various kinds and through this they create social history which survives them as a species. In producing in this way, human beings proclaim themselves to be a species since the object of their labor is the 'objectification' of the human species, 'for they duplicate themselves not only in consciousness, but actually in reality.'[268] Since species life was meant to be with others in society and experienced in a collective way, Marx thought that species alienation breaks the existing connection with the species by making all experience individual experience, isolated and separate from the species. In this respect, species alienation reverses the advantage which nature gives to the species because it transforms human consciousness and mental being into solitary physical being. In this type of alienation, human beings find themselves alone in the midst of society as private individuals, and in this case society itself is no longer experienced in its human form.

Alienation from Fellow Humans   A fourth type of alienation discussed by Marx is alienation from fellow human beings and from the human social community. This comes about, Marx reasoned, when the sole aim of life is competition and all social relationships are transformed into economic relationships and economic transactions. There are two specific senses in which alienation from fellow human beings takes place: first, so far as industrial capitalism compels individuals to be isolated and separate from one another in order to pursue their private interests for economic gain, they enter into competition with each other as private individuals alone and separate. While at one time individuals were essentially collective beings and worked cooperatively, they are now detached individual beings who work separately and live privately. Second, alienation from fellow human beings occurs as society makes only one class the sole benefactor of the product of the labor. Marx argued that during earlier

---

267 Ibid.
268 Marx, *Economic and Philosophic Manuscripts*, p. 114.

periods of history, the product of individual labor was once used directly to provide material needs and sustain life, whereas now it is used to benefit only one class who are able to realize themselves in history.[269] This type of alienation takes place, Marx thought, when the product of labor produces 'wealth and beauty' for one class, and poverty and deprivation for the worker.[270]

As human beings are estranged from their product, their productive activity and their own species, so also are they estranged from their relationship to their fellow human beings. In Marx's view, this category of alienation breaks the social relation which human beings have to each other as part of the human social community.[271] There are two important senses in which this has occurred. First, so far as individuals are isolated from one another by private competition, they are made into isolated individual beings where they were once collective beings. As universal competition becomes the norm, individuals thus find themselves alone in society. Second, alienation from fellow human beings occurs as only one class in society becomes the sole recipient of the product of the labor. This, said Marx, parallels an earlier period in history when the product of individual labor was only for the 'gods,' and the main aim of production was in the service of gods, e.g., temples, pyramids, etc.[272] Since in capitalist societies the products of labor do not belong to the worker, only one class are able to realize themselves in history to the extent that they have become the sole benefactors of the products of labor.

Marx's Political Writings

History of Marx's View of the State

I now want to turn my attention to Marx's political writings. Historically, Marx became interested in political theory after moving to Dresden in 1842. During his stay there, he began studying the historical conditions leading to the political revolutions in France and England, and this led him in the direction of political philosophy. As a result, he began reading the works of political thinkers such as Rousseau, Tocqueville, Machiavelli and Hegel and, as a consequence, developed an interest in democracy and state functions. In an early writing entitled Critique of Hegel's *Philosophy of Right* published in 1843, Marx undertook a critical revision of Hegel's political philosophy, which led to one of Marx's first systematic discussions of the state.[273] Then, in a work entitled 'On the Jewish Question' published later in the same year, Marx looked at the relationship between civil society

---

269 Ibid., p. 115.
270 Ibid., p. 110.
271 Ibid., p. 114.
272 Ibid., p. 115.
273 Marx, *Critique of Hegel's Philosophy of Right*, J. O'Malley (ed.), Cambridge: Cambridge University Press, 1970.

and the development of the modern state.[274] Ten years later in 1851, Marx undertook a historical study of the state in a work called *The Eighteenth Brumaire of Louis Bonaparte*, focusing on the 1848 rebellion in France and the rise of Louis Bonaparte. Finally, in a work called *The Civil War in France*, written in 1871, Marx focused on the development of the French political state.[275]

Though Marx's political writings do not form a single line of argument or develop a coherent theory of the political state, they do constitute a set of fundamental principles which frame discussion about the formation of the state and the nature of state political activities. Consistent with this view, there are at least four central propositions which form the basis of Marx's theory of the state. The first of these is the assertion that the state has a material origin and is therefore not independent of the economic structure of society. In this regard, Marx thought that the state arose out of the productive relations of society and therefore had its origins in economic activity. Second, Marx asserted that the modern state develops only under certain historical conditions arising in the productive forces of society, and under these circumstances he thought that the state was historical and social in nature. Third, is Marx's assertion that the state reflects the prevailing class structure of society and thus acts as an instrument of the dominant classes. In this regard, Marx believed that the political function of the state derives from the underlying economic base and productive relations, meaning that the interests of the state always seems to coincide with the interests of the dominant classes. Fourth, is the assertion by Marx that the appearance of the state in society is historically dependent upon the development of what he called 'civil society.'

Hegel's View of the State

Like so much of Marx's early writing, his theory of the state can best be understood by looking at Hegel's discussion of the political institutions of society. Hegel, in fact, had written a key work on the historical development of the state entitled *The Philosophy of Right*, published in 1821.[276] The view Hegel took up formed almost a complete philosophical sketch of the political structure of society, and he founded these views on an idealist conception of the origins, functions and activities of the state.

Hegel's perspective can best be set out in a series of five assumptions. First and foremost, Hegel assumed that the state was the embodiment of what he called 'right action.' By the term 'right,' Hegel meant the whole sphere of rules and ethical norms which guide human action toward what is ethically good in the human spirit. Hegel therefore thought that the expression of 'right action' was nothing more than the manifestation of human 'ethical will' in history. This ethical will, insisted Hegel, reached its highest point of development in the political sphere of society which concerned itself with ethical functions and rules of conduct that guide human action along the path of what is politically good. In this view, all the conventions of the state could be seen to be nothing more

---

274 R. T. Tucker, *The Marx-Engels Reader* (2nd Ed.), New York: Norton, pp. 26–52.
275 Marx, *The Civil War in France*, Moscow: Progress, 1977; Peking: Foreign Languages Press, 1970.
276 Hegel, *The Philosophy of Right*, Oxford: Clarendon Press, [1821] 1952.

than the manifestations of human 'ethical will' embodied in the state itself. This tendency to view the state as a form of ethical will led Hegel to take the position that the state was involved in maintaining ethical relationships between the various institutional spheres of society that included the sphere of the family and the law.

Second, Hegel assumed that while state functions serve the purpose of mediating the various social spheres of society, the political realm of the state was completely separate from the civil realm of the economy and economic exchange, which he tended to refer to as the arena of individual interests. In this way the state serves what Hegel called 'mediating' functions in maintaining ethical harmony between the sphere of public interest on the one hand, and the sphere of private interest on the other. Third, Hegel had assumed that since the state is an expression of human 'ethical will,' it must represent the common good of society and, through historical processes, ensure that the 'universal interest' always prevails over the particular interest of any one individual or group. Fourth, Hegel thought that the activities of the state were separate from the activities of civil society.[277] The activities of the political sphere of society, according to Hegel, pursued ends reflecting the 'general' interests of the whole political community and were thus universal in nature. Actions in the civil sphere, on the other hand, pursued ends which reflected the 'particular' interests and private rights of individuals and groups, and in these terms were thus 'particularistic' in nature. In this view, ethical actions reach their highest stage of development in the political sphere of society when office holders exercise the common good in the name of the political community and the universal interest. Thus the political sphere for Hegel is synonymous with the ethical life of society. Fifth, Hegel asserted that since the state emerges from human ethical will and is a manifestation of it, the state does not have a social or historical character but is rather the expression of the 'ethical idea' deified in the political structure of society and, in this sense, it is historically eternal.

Marx and the Materialist Origins of the State: Base and Superstructure

By 1843, Marx had undertaken a critical revision of Hegel's theory of the state in two early works entitled *Critique of Hegel's Philosophy of Right* and 'On the Jewish Question.' But, it was not until Marx wrote *The German Ideology* that he began to set out some of the historical and materialist principles of state development. Marx began to establish a historical focus on the state by rejecting Hegel's view that the state was an embodiment of ethical ideas. He thought that the central abstraction in Hegel's work made it appear as if political institutions were 'determined by a third party, rather than being self determined.'[278]

Marx countered Hegel's idealist conception of the state in two broad ways. First, while Hegel had tended to deny the social and historical character of the state, Marx

---

277 Hegel, *Philosophy of Right*, pp. 155–56.
278 Marx, *Critique of Hegel's Philosophy of Right*, p. 22.

was able to show that the state, in fact, had a historical origin by linking its development to economic production and productive relations. In this way, Marx was able to
demonstrate the economic and material origins of the political structure of society.
Second, in contrast to Hegel, who believed that the state was eternal and existed for all
time, Marx showed that the state only came into existence at a certain stage of historical development in the productive forces of society. In this way, Marx was able to
demonstrate that the state emerged at certain stages in productive relations rather than
being a philosophical abstraction that was eternally given. This consolidation by Marx
of the material and historical origin of the state made his theory of political society distinct from previous political thinking and distinct from Hegel's political philosophy.

The assertion by Marx that the state has a historical origin is explicitly discussed
in the 1859 preface to *A Critique of Political Economy*, when he stated:

> In the social production which men carry on they enter into definite relations that are indis-
> pensable and independent of their will; these relations of production correspond to a defi-
> nite stage of the development of their material forces of production. The totality of these
> relations of production constitutes the economic structure of society, which is the real foun-
> dation on top of which arises a legal and political superstructure to which correspond defi-
> nite forms of social consciousness. It is not the consciousness of men, therefore, that
> determines their existence, but instead their social existence determines their conscious-
> ness. With the change of the economic foundation the entire immense superstructure is
> more or less rapidly transformed.[279]

In this passage, two important ideas regarding the state are put forward. First, is the
idea that the productive relations constitute the economic structure of society which,
said Marx, is the 'real foundation' and economic base of society constituting the
material foundations of the state. Second, is the idea that on top of the economic
foundation of society arises a legal and political superstructure which corresponds
directly to the productive relations in the economy. What Marx is saying explicitly
here is that the central features of the state grow out of the economic base of society
and that the state is not independent of the economic foundations of society. Within
the scope of this reasoning, not only does the economic base give rise to the superstructure of society and its institutional configuration, but as the productive system
changes so does the political and legal superstructure of the state.

In arriving at a connection between the economic base and the state, Marx was
able to show that the state had a material and historical origin. This assertion was key
to Marx's thinking in that the state could be seen to be no more than the political
expression of the class structure of society and, at the same time, a derivative of the
relations of production. The material link between the political and economic structure of society can be shown directly by looking at the main premises of the materialist theory of history. In the act of producing the material means of existence, said

---

279 Marx, *A Preface to a Critique of Political Economy*, pp. 22–24.

Marx, individuals produce the subsequent form of their social relations, and in doing so shape the form of society. In this view, the form or shape of society always seems to coincide with the way people produce, since the manner in which this production is carried out determines the system of social relations which tend to arise from it, so much so that it creates the division of society into two distinct classes, one of which is dominant because it presides over the means of production; the other subordinate, because it is subject to the will of those who rule over them.[280]

Marx's assertion that the form of society and its system of social relations always seems to coincide with the way individuals produce and the form of their class relations, derives its force from the simple fact that the very first act of all societies is always economic production. From this simple starting place, we can see that the system of social relations always reflects the social relations of production. Marx, however, was able to go further than this by showing that the political structure of society seems to take the form of the productive relations and that on top of these relations 'arises a legal and political superstructure.'[281] Two concepts used by Marx to describe the social process of state formation are relevant at this point. First is the concept of economic base and second is the term superstructure. Marx used both these terms to demonstrate how the system of social relations form themselves into a political state and how the state itself is derived from economic production. Marx reasoned that since human beings must produce to satisfy their material needs, the first act of all societies is economic production, and this leads to the formation of all subsequent social relations. Since the very first act of all societies is always economic, Marx's concept of the economic base is a term used by him to define the underlying historical principle propelling human beings to produce the means of their survival and satisfy their material needs. Marx argued that since all societies are founded on the necessity to produce and to engage in economic production, society itself tends to take the 'form' of the social forces of production. Marx believed that the evidence for this exists in the class structure of society which always reflect economic relations of production.

In direct contrast to the economic base is the term superstructure. This is used by Marx to refer to the social institutions and institutional structure which arises on top of the economic base as a function of the historical principle propelling individuals to produce. Chief among these are the legal and political institutions which, in Marx's view, are not separate from the economy and in this sense are determined by it. Marx thought this was the case because the state places itself on the side of the economy by legally and politically protecting the class relations that arise from in its defense of the principle of private property. Using the concepts of economic base and institutional superstructure, Marx was able to show (i) that economic production shapes social relations and hence the structure of society; (ii) that economic

---

280 Marx and Engels, *The German Ideology*, pp. 4–16.
281 Marx, *A Preface to a Critique of Political Economy*, pp. 22–24.

production shapes the formation of the class structure and the corresponding ideas related to the roles which people play in production when society forms class and property relations.

Two broad conclusions can be drawn from Marx's perspective on state formation. First, economic production shapes social and class relations and hence the political structure of society. Second, economic production gives rise to a legal and political superstructure which comes to represent the productive relations. Taking Marx's materialist theory into account, the political structure of society and later the state, always reflect the prevailing class interests and is never independent of them.

The Historical Origins of the Modern State: the Period of State Formation

Having shown that political institutions have a material origin, Marx turns his attention to the historical formation of the state. This is first outlined in a writing called *The Eighteenth Brumaire of Louis Bonaparte*, in which Marx recounted the story of the historical stages leading to the formation of the French political state.[282] These stages can be enumerated in broad outline by looking at the central features of the state which develop from the dissolution of feudal society and the productive forces of the new class interests which were emerging during the development of industrial society. The process begins, said Marx, with a clearing away of the old localized powers of feudal estates with their separate economic and political jurisdictions. With the break up of the separate feudal economies and political jurisdictions, the possibility of a centralized political authority was formed and, with the shift to the new industrial economy, a transfer of power from landlords to the new political and economic classes was created and came into being at the end of the eighteenth century. Once this had occurred, the centralized state political machinery was in a position to be 'perfected' by the material interests being mobilized by the ruling political and economic classes.[283] These new interests created the need for a state administration and bureaucratic apparatus.

After tracing the development of the modern French state, Marx turned his attention to a discussion of some of the key political developments taking place in France between the rebellions of 1789 and 1851 in a writing entitled in the *Eighteenth Brumaire of Louis Bonaparte*. The historical context of the rebellion began, Marx pointed out, in 1848 – a period of unprecedented industrial production. At the time, increased industrial activity had led to prosperity for a small commercial class and greater poverty and social distress for the workers. Low wages, poor working conditions and unemployment led many to criticize capitalism for its social inequality and restriction of economic advantage only to one class in society. This began a period where there was widespread rebellion throughout Europe and workers began to protest

---

282 Marx, *Eighteenth Brumaire*, pp. 50–9.
283 Marx, *The Civil War in France*, Peking: Foreign Language Press, [1870] 1970, p. 11.

their limited social opportunities. In France, this led to an open rebellion by the working class to claim the French republic on behalf of the worker, and during this period France oscillated between a political monarchy and a democratic republic.

At this point, historically, there were three distinct periods of state formation which Marx dealt with. First were the February days marking the beginning of the rebellion by the workers. Second was the period of the constitution of the French Republic which occurred between May of 1848 and May of 1849. Third was the period of the formation of a Constitutional Republic and the formal elimination of the French monarchy from May 1849 to December 1851. In looking at these periods or stages, Marx explicitly focused on the political play between what he called the political manipulation by the leaders of the particular and general interest which, in his view, led to the formation of the modern French state. The actual formation of the state apparatus arises, said Marx, from the new class interests emerging at the time which involved what he called 'the severing' of the 'common interest' from the 'general interest' of society.[284]

Marx went on to trace the steps of state development emerging from the three periods that follow the rebellion of 1848. The first period, the February period, is described by Marx as the prologue to the revolution. During February of 1848, the workers mounted an open rebellion against the authorities and breached the barricades which had been put up by the national Guard. The French troops responded without much resistance and many believed that it was a victory for the workers against the monarchy and the commercial classes. The workers, Marx points out, had 'proclaimed France to be a social republic.'[285] In the second period, formally called the period of the constitution, the commercial classes acted to block the advances of the workers by parliamentary devices and reduced the revolution at this stage to a victory by the dominant political classes. In the third period, headed by Louis Bonaparte, there was the formation of the Constitutional Republic in which the commercial classes ruled in the name of the people and the demands of the workers were suppressed by the emerging 'general interest' that was mobilized at the time by Louis Bonaparte.

Marx's discussion in *The Eighteenth Brumaire* focused on how the French state was formed as its political power began to mobilize so that a more exclusive interest could be maintained against a wider, more general interest. Marx showed that at that moment the state 'severs the common interest from the general interest of society.' Two central passages illustrate this key process in Marx's theory of the state.[286] The first of these is from *The Civil War in France*, the second from the *Eighteenth Brumaire*.

The centralized state machinery which, with its ubiquitous and complicated military, bureaucratic, clerical and judiciary organs, encoils the living civil society like a boa constrictor, was first forged in the days of absolute monarchy as a weapon of nascent modern

---

284 Marx, *Eighteenth Brumaire*, pp. 104–51.

285 Marx, *Eighteenth Brumaire*, p. 16

286 In his *State, Power and Socialism*, Nicos Poulantzas argued that 'no general theory of the state is to be found in the Marxist classics,' p. 20.

society in its struggle of emancipation from feudalism. The seignorial privileges of the mediaeval lords and cities and clergy were transformed into the attributes of a unitary state power, displacing the feudal dignitaries by salaried state functionaries, transferring the arms from medieval retainers of the landlords and the corporations of townish citizens to a standing army; substituting for the checkered anarchy of conflicting medieval powers the regulated plan of a state power, with a systematic and hierarchic division of labor. The first French revolution, with its task to found national unity (to create a nation) had to break down all local, territorial, townish and provincial independence (and their localized powers). It was, therefore, forced to develop, what absolute monarchy had commenced, the centralization and organization of state power, and to expand the circumference and the attributes of the state power, the number of its tools, its independence (from the people), and its supernaturalist sway over real society which in fact took the place of the medieval surpernaturalist (theological concept of heaven) heaven, with its saints. Every minor solitary interest engendered by the relations of social groups was separated from society itself, fixed and made independent of it and opposed to it in the form of state interest, administered by state priests with exactly determined hierarchical functions.[287]

The legitimate monarchy and the July monarchy added nothing but a great division of labor within bourgeois society creating new groups of interests, and, therefore, new material for state administration. Every common interest was straightway severed from society, counterposed to it as a higher, general interest, snatched from the activity of society's members themselves and made an object of government activity, from the bridge, a schoolhouse and the communal property of a village community to the railways, the national wealth and the national university of France.[288]

In this passage, Marx showed that as the new material interests become consolidated, the agents of these interests, whether political, economic or military, 'sever' themselves from the common interest and begin 'counterposing' it to a 'higher general interest.'[289] This 'general interest' said Marx, is thus 'snatched from the self-activity of society's members and made an object of state machinery and governmental activity from the bridge, the school house, the judiciary and the church which act as its representatives.'[290] As a result of the political play between Bonaparte's maneuvers of proclaiming to create the French republic on the one hand, while at the same time suspending constitutional powers on the other, Marx stated that the modern state apparatus comes into being at the point that Bonaparte was able to detach the controlling offices of the state apparatus from the parliament by converting them into organs of the state executive power. At that moment, said Marx, the state is separate from society and its powers are independent and autonomous of the interests of all the classes. Marx thus used the term 'Bonapartism' to identify the actual creation of the modern political state and the powers used to relieve the commercial classes of their claim to political dominance.

---

287 Marx, *The Civil War in France*, Peking: Foreign Languages Press, 1970, 162–3.
288 Marx, *Eighteenth Brumaire of Louis Bonaparte*, p. 104.
289 Ibid., pp. 104–105.
290 Ibid.

These maneuvers, Marx pointed out, had the following effects: first, it weakened the political power of all the classes while at the same time claiming to represent all classes equally; and second, it rendered the commercial classes incapable of realizing their own political interests. While Marx thought that Bonaparte himself was unimportant historically, he believed that the period was significant in that it marked the development of the modern state by pointing to the political vacuum that was created at the moment when all classes lay 'prostrate' before the state machine.[291]

The State and Civil Society in Smith, Hegel and Marx

After tracing the stages of state formation, Marx turned his attention to the development of civil society. No discussion of Marx's theory of the state would be complete without looking at the relationship between political and civil society. The term 'civil society' first made its appearance in the works of Adam Smith and later in the work of Hegel.[292] Initially, Smith used the term civil society to refer to a sphere in which competition and self interest were played out in the market, but he believed it was separate from the political realm as such. Smith thought that the confrontation of many individuals engaged in separate acts of buying and selling in the market is what gave civil society its particular character of competition and motivated self interest. Smith believed, however, that the separate economic acts of self interested individuals contributed to the common good of society by promoting national wealth and economic well being.

While Hegel had read Smith, his conception of civil society was completely different. In contrast to Smith, Hegel saw civil society as a separate sphere existing outside the political realm of the state. In *The Philosophy of Right*, Hegel had argued that while civil society and the political state were separate spheres, he thought that the political state itself acted to 'mediate the particular interest through the universal interest.'[293] Hegel reasoned that 'individual self seeking turns into a contribution to the satisfaction of the needs of everyone and, by a dialectical advance, self seeking turns into the mediation of the particular through the universal, with the result that each individual's earning, producing and enjoying is at the same time producing and earning for the enjoyment of everyone else.'[294] While, for Hegel, civil society is associated with the sphere of self interest and individual acquisition, it is opposed to political society and is separate from it. Thus, unlike Smith, Hegel thought that the state was above self interest and overcame the contradiction between the self interest of the individual and the public obligation of the citizen by upholding the universal interest or common good.

In two early writings, *A Critique of Hegel's Philosophy of Right* and 'On the Jewish Question,' Marx rejected as absurd Hegel's assertion that the state 'mediates' the

---

291 For Marx's discussion of Bonaparte's political strategies and how the French political state was born during this period see Marx, *Eighteenth Brumaire of Louis Bonaparte*, pp. 101–114.
292 Hegel, *The Philosophy of Right*, pp. 129–30.
293 Ibid.
294 Ibid.

private interest by upholding the common good of society. Instead, Marx took the position that the state was complicit in the split between the political and civil realm and in fact actively supported self interest in its defense of private property. Marx went on to reason that, in its defense of private property, the state was the instrument of the ruling classes since it supports the outright ownership of the means of production by only one class in society. Marx thus equates the state with the economically powerful classes who act through state coercion and power. From this viewpoint, the state is equated with the ruling classes, since only these classes are able to use the state as an 'instrument' to realize their own economic ends and interests.

The remaining question, then, is how does civil society arise and how has it come to be defended by the state? In order to answer this question we have to look more closely at Marx's concept of civil society. Marx borrowed the term from Hegel's writing. In the *Philosophy of Right*, Hegel had asserted that the state rises above self interest by mediating it through the universal interest.[295] Marx fundamentally rejected this view by asserting that it was not possible for the state to rise above 'self interest,' since the state promoted it through its defense of private property and its ultimate alignment with the ruling classes. Marx thought that only when the state renounces property relations can it stand above the particular interest, and only then can the state constitute itself universally.

Subsequently Marx turned his attention to the historical development of civil society. He pointed out that during the feudal period, all of society had a political character and there was no formal separation between the civil and political realm. In this sense, all aspects of civil life such as property, occupation and family had been subsumed under the political realm in the form of lordship, caste and guild.[296] While in earlier periods individuals were commonly a part of larger political bodies, and the state encompassed the political and the civil realm at the same time, there was no independent private or civil sphere defined by the economy as such. The modern state, therefore, comes into existence only with the institutionalization of the capitalist economy and the effect of this economy on the political structure.

The term civil society, then, is intended to point to the precise historical moment when there is the development of an independent economic realm that emerges as a consequence of individuals pursuing private interest through economic gain. With the emergence of civil society, therefore, there is a shift in the center of political gravity from the state to the economy and this shift comes about in the modern state when the civil sphere becomes separate from the political sphere of society as such. Historically, this change is thought to have come about as a consequence of the Industrial Revolution, and the term civil society is thus intended to designate the split that occurs in society between the political and civil spheres which is unique to modern times. Specifically, civil society does not develop in previous periods of state

---

295 Ibid., p. 134.
296 Marx, 'On the Jewish Question,' p. 44.

formation and only comes into being in modern industrial societies, where it creates a situation in which the state political and governmental apparatus retreats into the background so to speak, and gives up its old position of intervention and incursion into the overall social and civil arena of society more generally. In this case, the structure of civil society is formed in direct relation to the retreat elements of the state political machinery, in which case civil society becomes a more autonomous field of action resistant to intervention.

At the center of civil society stands the 'free individual' stripped of all ties to communal bodies who begin to pursue their private interest for purposes of personal gain. These individuals, said Marx, are the 'citizens whose political rights and freedoms are simply the rights of the egoistic individual, the individual separated from community, isolated and withdrawn into themselves.'[297] According to Marx, the development of civil society presupposes three distinct but interrelated elements: (i) the satisfaction of all wants through the pursuit of private economic gain; (ii) the protection of private property; and (iii) the replacement of direct ties with society by abstract political and legal links to the state.

These developments were key to the formation of the modern state in several respects: first, as the break up of the old political bodies of estate, caste and guild took place, civil society became an autonomous sphere of social and economic action separate from the political institutions of the state. Prior to the emergence of civil society as a separate sphere, all of society was political. Second, all action became the 'private affair' of the individual rather than the subject of the political state or the wider community. Third, as the separation between civil society and the political state came into existence after the decentralization and setting aside of the political monarchy, the economy became the absolute center of social activity. Fourth, state affairs became the public affair of the people rather than the private affair of the monarch. Fifth, political links between members of society began to be abstractly conceived in the form of laws, rights and political freedoms, leading to the disappearance of all concrete ties to the state. Sixth, with the advent of economic society and the market, there was a shift in the center of political gravity from the state to the economy, and as a result this led to a split between the political and civil sphere which made the civil realm the main arena of social action and economic activity.

Marx believed that civil society brought about the breakdown of the individual's relation to the wider society by fragmenting the whole of society into political and civil parts. At the end of this process, said Marx, is the isolated individual whose private autonomy is a political and social absurdity. In his view, modern civil society sets individuals into conflict with each other in two specific respects: first, so far as it encourages individuals to pursue their private interests, they are thrown into competition with one another since each seeks to maximize their private economic gain. Second, so far as the state confers upon them common political rights, the individual's relation to society

297 Marx, 'On the Jewish Question,' p. 42.

appears to be cooperative, when in reality it is coercive. Where Hegel saw civil society and the political state as separate, Marx saw them as one and the same. 'At certain periods,' said Marx, 'the political state comes violently to birth in civil society.'[298]

Marx's Dialectical View of History: The Theory of Development

By the time Marx had completed his study of the class struggle in *The Eighteenth Brumaire of Louis Bonaparte* in 1869, and by the time he traced the path of development from feudalism to capitalism in *Capital* in 1867, he had discovered what Engels called the 'great law of historical motion' according to which one social form passes into another.[299] This law of development, according to which one society is transformed into another and a new class is constituted, was first proposed by Marx in his theory of history outlined in *The German Ideology*. In the main, Marx's theory of development hinges on the historical periods during which the two great economic classes collide with each other, and create what he called the historical conditions of transformation and change. It was this 'collision' of the classes, Marx believed, which put history in motion so to speak, and this made it apparent to Marx that it was 'the class principle that made the history, and not the history that made the principle.'[300]

While Marx had pinpointed a theory of development in some of his early works, he had not explicitly outlined the theory of development after completing *The German Ideology,* even though some fragments of it were accessible in works such as *Capital,* and others such as the *Poverty of Philosophy*. In these works, Marx referred again and again to the historical 'emancipation' of the worker, stating that while human beings are essentially free, they are everywhere subordinated to economic conditions of existence in which one class is subject to another. What was important about this observation was that, for the first time, it had shown that class relations were not permanently fixed for all time but, in fact, were subject to change and transformation. Key to his thinking along this line was his reference to the historical principle, by means of which individuals were gradually freed from the social and historical conditions which transform them into economic subjects. These changes, he thought, would mark the period of transition from class history into what he called human history, and he traced this type of development in a famous passage in *The Poverty of Philosophy* where he writes:

> Economic conditions had first transformed the mass of people of the country-side into workers. The combination of capital has created for this mass a common situation, common interests. This mass [of people] is thus already a class against capital, but not yet for itself. In the struggle, of which we have noted only a few phases, this mass becomes united, and

298 Marx, 'On the Jewish Question,' p. 36.
299 See Engels's preface to the Third German Edition of Marx's *The Eighteenth Brumaire of Louis Bonaparte*, p. 9.
300 Slightly modified, see Marx, *The Poverty of Philosophy*, New York: International Publishers, [1847] 1963, p. 115.

constitutes itself as a class for itself: The interests it defends become class interests. But it is a question of making a precise study of [the] forms in which the workers carry out before our eyes their organization as a class.[301]

The language of development used by Marx in this passage – 'class-in-itself,' 'class-for-itself,' 'opposition,' 'antagonism,' 'already a class against capital,' etc. – is distinctly Hegelian in its use of the dialectical method of treating history as so many stages of development in which one class constitutes itself in the form of another. It is here, then, that Marx refers specifically to the theory of development, and it will be useful to briefly trace the origins of this theory by looking at the history of the dialectic, and then at Hegel's dialectical thinking.

History of the Term 'Dialectic'

The term dialectic can be traced to early Greek philosophy beginning with the work of Socrates and Aristotle, who essentially used it as a method to get at underlying truths which could not be obtained using techniques of observation and sense perception. Later, in the eighteenth and nineteenth centuries, dialectics reached its highest stage of development in the work of Hegel, who had employed the method in showing the interconnections between categories of existence such as history and human consciousness. In the twentieth century, dialectics fell into disuse after British philosophers claimed that it was unreliable as a method due to its speculative nature.

Though Marx never completely outlined his dialectical theory of history, Engels elaborated on the principle of the dialectic in a work entitled *Anti-Duhring*. According to Engels, the central principle of dialectical thinking is to be found in the concept of 'relation' and 'interconnection.'[302] According to this view, the natural world and the human world appear as a vast set of interrelations in which everything is related in terms of the past, present and further.[303] Under these circumstances, said Engels, it is possible to visualize these interconnections when we picture ourselves, the world, and others in terms of 'relational' concepts such as humanity, history, experience, existence, etc. 'When we reflect on nature and human history,' said Engels 'we see the picture of an endless maze of connections and interconnections in which nothing remains as it was, but everything moves, changes and comes into being and passes away. This primitive, naive, but intrinsically correct conception of the world is that of ancient Greek philosophy, and it was first clearly formulated by Heraclitus: everything is and also is not, for everything is in flux, is constantly changing, constantly coming into being and passing away.'[304]

Given this broad outline, it is possible to isolate three interrelated features of the dialectical method which makes it distinct as a theoretical tool. First is the tendency

---

301 Marx, *The Poverty of Philosophy,* pp. 170, 173–4.
302 Frederich Engels, *Anti-Duhring,* Peking: Foreign Languages Press, 1976, p. 24.
303 Ibid.
304 Ibid.

to view all human beings as linked to the world and to others through a series of interconnected social and historical relations which confer unity and difference at the same time. For example, we are individuals, yet we are also members of nations which unify our social and political purposes. These similarities we share with other human beings in other nations may be understood in terms of collective concepts called 'totalities.' These include concepts such as humanity, history, reality, existence, etc. In this case, the conception of our interconnections with society refers here to the fact that while we are distinct individuals, we are at the same time connected in fundamental ways to larger social totalities such as the world, humanity, history, existence, etc. A second concept related to the dialectic is the tendency to believe that these totalities and our links to them form an interconnected web of relations which defines our humanity in some fundamental way. Third, is the assumption that all history and all historical progress is in a state of constant change, movement and transformation in which things are coming into being, existing and passing away. Under these circumstances, no individual thing, no part or segment, is entirely separate from any other, but is always a part of a larger whole or unity to which it is essentially connected.

Hegel's Dialectic

In 1812, Hegel had referred explicitly to the interconnections and relations existing between human beings and history in a theory of dialectical development he put forward in a writing called *The Science of Logic*.[305] In it, he advocated a theory of historical development by stating that all human beings and things in the world are in a continuous state of motion and change, and that the general laws of motion are intrinsic to the development of individuals, history and thought. In these terms, Hegel viewed the world, existence and being in terms of processes in which all things were interconnected and related to one another as opposed to being separate by themselves. Viewed in this way, everything is subject to change and development since nothing remains unchanged over time. The existence of any one thing, Hegel thought, can only be understood 'in relation to' another, and this relational view led to an understanding of the integration of separate things into larger totalities of being which Hegel essentially conceptualized in terms of the categories of history, human consciousness and reason.[306]

The doctrine that all things are interconnected into larger wholes later became the theoretical basis for the dialectical view of reality and history. According to this perspective, no individual is independent or separate by themselves since each is connected to a time and place, and to larger historical wholes which define their relation to history. Hegel's concept of 'being in relation to' not only established the

---

305 G. Hegel, *The Science of Logic*, Vol. 2, London: Allen & Unwin, 1929 [1812].
306 For discussion of Hegel's dialectic see J. N. Findlay, *Hegel: A Re-Examination*.

interconnectedness between what appeared to be disconnected, but it also challenged the view of the world which had asserted that each thing is separate in itself. The concept of a thing existing in itself as well as the belief that there are sharp distinctions between stages of existence such as being and non-being, freedom and slavery, self realization and estrangement, were being rethought in the light of the dialectical perspective proposed by Hegel.

In the light of this, Hegel went on to reason that one of the key features of historical development was the process he called 'contradiction.' Stated simply, the principle of contradiction refers to the existence of opposites or conflicting elements in reality. Hegel believed that there can be no development without contradiction and that, in fact, contradiction was rooted in reality and history. Simply stated, contradiction, according to Hegel, refers to the presence of the principles of 'affirmation' and 'negation' existing at the same time. Hegel believed that contradiction is always present in history and reality and is reflected in the existence of opposing elements which bring about the process of change and development. In religion, for instance, contradiction exists in the struggle between two opposing tendencies in human experience, such as good and evil. In theological reasoning, neither of these exist independently of each other but only in relation to some other principle from which it derives its existence. Hegel's theory of contradictions amounts to nothing more than the belief that existence and being reflect the principle of tension through which there is development and change. In everyday life, for example, the essential contradictory nature of conflicting elements express themselves in the wider struggle of existence and in the struggle against overt obstacles which tend to oppose us by setting up fundamental resistance, including sudden illness, personal setbacks, poverty, etc.

In his philosophic works, Hegel went on to develop the principle of contradiction into a full blown theory of development. He believed that there were three main stages in the process: first, is the stage he called 'affirmation,' sometimes referred to as the thesis or the coming into being of thing or state. Hegel, then, used the term affirmation to refer to any thing which has being or existence. Understood in this sense, affirmation is the capacity of any existing thing to affirm itself and to be in the world, actively rather than passively. This means that in its being, it 'affirms' itself, and this affirmation is a principle of its own being or existence. Moreover, as it affirms itself it expresses inherent 'potential' for development and propagation, for this is its positive element and positive state.

The second stage of the dialectic is referred to as the 'negation,' sometimes called antithesis or simply the negative. In Hegel's view, this refers to the principle in the world which acts to impose a limit on human development by thwarting or blocking existence outright. For Hegel, the concept of negation was key to the dialectical process since it refers to any limitation which acts to thwart or restrict the capacity of an existing thing to develop its own being and its own existence. In this sense, the principle of negation not only stands as the opposite of affirmation but it also implies the stronger connotation of that which shuts out existence as well as denoting limit or boundary.[307] Hegel used the term primarily to understand the tendency of individuals to encounter limitations which act to 'negate' their further development by imposing boundaries or shutting out their existence altogether. While Hegel believed that all things had their characteristic way of being negated, he thought that negation itself gives rise to further development and 'therefore is an act in a sequence of development' within the struggle for existence.[308] According to Engels, the negation 'does not simply mean no, or declaring that something does not exist, or destroying it in any way one likes.'[309] Rather, negation can be looked upon as a principle of development in that it sets up the tendency to resist, and resistance as such, acts as a means of affirmation.

A third principle of the dialectic is the concept of 'negation of the negation' or synthesis.[310] While Hegel had used the term to express what he saw as the completion of a cycle of development, its primary reference is to the capacity of the negation to be reconstituted or fundamentally altered in its nature. Since negation itself stands for limit or boundary, then simply stated 'negation of the negation' is that principle of development which reconstitutes the limits by surpassing or bringing an end to the boundaries and limitations. Hegel went on to reason that both terms expressed laws of development because the negation of the negation altered the state of the individual's limitation, and in this sense was transformative. This can be seen in Hegel's example of the master-slave relation. Hegel believed that the severe limitations imposed upon the slave by the master can be transformed at the point that the slave re-appropriates his or her self activity through a conscious 'negation of the negation,' in a process Hegel referred to as 'formative activity.'[311] In this formative activity, he reasoned, the slave 'destroys the negative elements which stand over and against the slave as an individual, and thereby the slave becomes someone existing 'freely' on their own account.'[312] What is important here to note is that the categories of 'freedom' and 'emancipation' are implicit within Hegel's theory of human development.

Marx's View of the Dialectic and his Theory of Development

While many of the concepts used by Hegel to develop a theory of existence and development were used by Marx, he took the dialectic in a completely different direction. In order to outline Marx's use of the term, it will be useful to look again at the distinction Marx made between materialism and idealism. Idealism had asserted that, before

---

307 Hegel often used the term 'shutting out existence' to describe negation. Simply stated, a negation is an external thing or principle which acts to negate that which exists. Hegel, *Phenomenology of Mind,* New York: Harper Tourchbooks, 1967, p. 510.

308 Engels, *Anti-Duhring,* p. 181.

309 Engels, *Anti-Duhring,* p. 180.

310 See Z.A. Jordan, *The Evolution of Dialectical Materialism,* New York: St. Martins Press, 1967.

311 Hegel, *Phenomenology of Mind,* pp. 229–240.

312 G. Hegel, *The Phenomenology of the Spirit,* p. 118.

anything else, thought had primacy over matter in the development of history. Hegel believed that the 'idea' came before reality and therefore was the fundamental focus of philosophy. Marx, by contrast, believed that the material world preceded the world of ideas and this laid the foundation for a theory of historical development based on human economic needs. The doctrine of materialism, therefore, held that since the material world comes first, then the development of the mind must be derived from material existence.[313] The problem with Hegel's thinking, as Marx saw it, was that Hegel believed that ideas were ultimate realities, so much so that relations between human beings were seen as consequences of the relations between ideas. So much did Hegel view ideas as dominant forces in history that he believed that ideas rather than individuals were the ultimate causal agents in historical development. This meant that, for Hegel, ideas were always the focal point of historical process and change.

Marx rejected this view and went on to criticize Hegel in a number of ways. First, he thought that Hegel's dialectic was mystical because of its extraordinary emphasis on vague ideas rather than on historical processes. Second, he thought that Hegel's understanding of the principles of motion in the theory of development offered little opportunity to explain detailed historical mechanisms. Third, Marx claimed that Hegel's system provided no clues on how to establish an empirical basis of development founded upon historical reality.

One of the key assumptions of materialism was its presumption of the existence of motion and change as the key principles of development. Both Marx and Engels believed that motion was the primary existence form of matter. But in order to distinguish this view from Hegel, Marx and Engels had to develop the principle of motion more explicitly, and this meant that it had to be explained and classified. In order to do this, they had to adopt, at least in part, the laws of development which had been worked out by Hegel. Borrowing primarily from Hegel's *Logic*, Engels took the view that motion was the central principle of historical change and believed it accounted for the changing nature of the society, experience and matter.[314] From this position, Engels argued that historical motion was the principle determinant of change and as a theory of change he believed it explained the conditions under which matter forms links with larger wholes and transforms itself from one state into another. This doctrine, later described as the first law of the dialectic, was referred to as the doctrine of leaps, and it maintained that matter undergoes qualitative change as it moves from one form to another and changes from one substance into another, such as water to ice, liquid to gas, etc.[315]

Marx and Engels believed that the doctrine of the dialectic was a central explanatory principle and therefore regarded it as a formal theory of development.

---

313 This was made evident in Marx's statement in the 1859 preface to *A Critique of Political Economy,* where he states 'It is not the consciousness of men that determines their existence, but their social existence that determines their consciousness,' p. 21.

314 Engels, *Anti-Duhring*, pp. 24–25.

315 Engels, *Anti-Duhring,* pp. 69–94.

Understood in this way, the dialectic explained two key principles of social and historical change: first, it put forward the view that change was inherent in all matter; second, it implied that in the process of change and development certain relations exist between the historical, political and social spheres. On these two assumptions, Marx and Engels were able to put forward a theory of change which explained the process of transformation from one state of being to another and, at the same time, were able to describe the decisive moment of change itself.

Difference Between Marx and Hegel in the Dialectical View of History

Having outlined Hegel's and Marx's view on the dialectic, it is possible to discern several differences between them. First, while Hegel believed that social development occurs as a result of the change taking place in ideas, Marx took the view that social change takes place on the basis of material conditions of existence and only these changes, he thought, affect historical processes. In contrast to Hegel's dialectic, therefore, Marx's theory of development and social change is called the materialist dialectic in order to indicate the shift Marx brought about from the stress on the role of ideas to the historical role played by material and economic processes in society. Whereas Hegel had believed that the principles of development found in concepts such as contradiction, opposition, affirmation and negation were represented by ideas acting in history, Marx took the view that the central principles of change were manifested at the level of class formations and in the concrete historical development of economic production in society. Marx defined his difference from Hegel, therefore, by placing a decisive materialist emphasis on what Hegel had seen as the effects of ideas in history.[316]

Second, on the question of contradictions, Hegel's doctrine stated that any existing thing encounters opposition without which there can be no development. Marx, by contrast, believed that Hegel's concept of contradiction was too abstract since it referred to processes and forms of development only in mystical terms. In direct contrast to this, Marx thought that the law of contradiction was manifested historically in the form of the coercive class structure of society, in which the law of contradiction was expressed at the material level of the class struggle which took the form of economic relations. Third is the question of the stages of development themselves. While Hegel believed that the stages of development progressed from inexplicit and undifferentiated stages to more explicit and differentiated levels, he never went beyond the speculative dimension in conceiving of this development. Marx, by contrast, saw the stages of development taking place in historical societies, and he thought that their historical progression was related to economic production and the system of class relations. In this sense, Marx's historical conception of the successive

---

316 On this point see Engels, *Anti-Duhring*, pp. 12–15.

form of societies – ancient, feudal and capitalistic – and their class struggles made the dialectic historically real.

A fourth difference between Marx and Hegel exists at the level of the 'doctrine of relations.' Earlier, we said that this concept of 'relations' is important in the thinking of both Hegel and Marx, to say nothing of how systematically Marx used the concept as a major analytical tool in *Capital* and other works.[317] While the concept of relations embodies complex philosophical precepts, its basic underlying principle is simple and goes to the heart of dialectical thinking. Simply stated, one of the key assertions of the doctrine of dialectics is the web of interconnections existing in human relations and in the conditions of existence. The term relation, then, is a philosophic concept used to describe the connection between two different wholes or realities which act in respect to each other. Looked at from this perspective, what Marx and Engels had learned from Hegel was that every relation can be viewed from two distinct vantage points: (i) from the relation a person has to themselves; and (ii) from relations which a person has to others and to the world.[318] Both Hegel and Marx spoke of these relations in terms of what they called 'subject-object relations.'

Hegel, for his part, believed in the reality of opposites – subject-object, general-particular, unity-difference – and he took the view that only when taken together could these opposites be understood. Hegel used the concept of relation, therefore, as a way of indicating that in looking at oppositions such as master and slave, subject and object, one must comprehend two sides of the relation, for without both sides there is no unity. Since, in this view, the essence of reality has two sides – a subject and an object, a part and a whole – all analysis must capture the experience and reality of either side in the relation to form a complete representation of the whole. Taking the principle of development into account, Hegel believed that no process could be understood completely by itself since all development must form a relation with other things in the movement from one stage into another. The term relation, therefore, is a way of getting at the intermediate causal connection implied in the movement between stages.

When applied by Marx, the concept of relation became an extraordinary analytical tool. For Marx, each relation had two sides which were fundamentally connected, and it is only the totality of these relations which form reality in his view. Like Hegel, Marx examined the connection between both sides of the relation since he believed that either side represents a dimension of experience and reality which is necessarily excluded when only one side is examined.[319] This is nowhere more evident that in Marx's criticism of Smith and Ricardo. He believed that they failed to see the fundamental connection between economic categories such as capital, labor, production and consumption. He thought that these central concepts could not, in fact, be used to define independent economic activities, such as capital and labor, production and

---

317 Sidney Hook, *From Hegel to Marx,* London: Victor Gollancz , 1936, p. 70.
318 Ibid.
319 Ibid.

consumption, but in every case made reference to fundamental interconnections which existed of necessity. His critique of theories which lose sight of these interconnections is therefore fundamental to his procedure.

Application of the Dialectic to History

So far, two precepts characterize the materialist dialectic. First, the view that there is a tendency for a social form to pass into another due to the economic contradictions inherent within it. Second, the belief that there is a capacity of a given social form to be replaced by a new one in which the preceding social relation forms part of the new society, giving rise to a class struggle from which a new formation emerges. Both Marx and Engels believed that the principle of development put forward by Hegel expressed itself directly in the form of social and historical development. While Hegel had believed that history demonstrated the process of coming into being, passing away, etc., Marx's and Engels' point of departure was to show how this pattern of development operated at the historical level.

According to Marx, historical events tend to confirm the existence of such a pattern, since when we look at the development of capitalist society and its class formation, it tends to rise from the ruins of feudal society. The events of 1789 and 1848, both of which were revolutionary expressions of change and development, confirmed the tendency of the pre-existing social order to pass from one social form into another and that, as the old order gave way to the new one, old productive forces were gradually replaced by new productive forces and the laboring classes were less subjugated. At the same level of historical reality, other events such as the workers uprising of 1831 and the agitation by factory workers during the Chartist rebellion of 1842, pinpointed the pattern of the class struggle that existed between two kinds of groups in society, between the sellers and buyers of wage labor; between bosses and workers, between the class of property owners and the class of laborers. This pattern of development, Marx thought, made possible the economic interpretation of history in a way not seen before. Engels stated this clearly when he pointed out that now 'all past history, was the history of class struggle; that these social classes warring with each other are always the product of the relations of production and exchange; in a word, of the economic relations of their epoch.'[320] As Engels stated, a way had been found for a materialist treatment of history in which human consciousness could be explained by economic being.[321] This view of history is expressed clearly in Engels' comment on Marx's method where he stated:

> It was Marx who first discovered the great law of motion of history, the law according to which all historical struggles, whether they proceed in the political, religious, philosophical

---

320 Engels, *Anti-Duhring*, p. 33.
321 Ibid.

or some other ideological domain, are in fact only the more or less clear expression of struggles of social classes, and that the existence and thereby the collisions, too, between these classes are in turn conditioned by the degree of development of their economic position, by the mode of their production and of their exchange determined by it. This law, which has the same significance for history as the law of the transformation of energy has for natural science – this law gave him the key to an understanding of the history of the second French Republic.[322]

Having concluded our discussion of Marx's and Engels theoretical perspective, I want now to turn my attention to the next chapter and to the work of Emile Durkheim.

---

322 See Engels's preface to *The Eighteenth Brumaire of Louis Bonaparte*, Moscow: Progress Publishers, 1977.

3

Emile Durkheim

The Historical Context of Emile Durkheim's Work

Emile Durkheim was born on April 15, 1858 in Epinal, a small town in rural France. He grew up in a traditional Jewish family which lived on a modest income and provided a conservative upbringing. Durkheim's father was a rabbi who served the community in the surrounding province while his mother added to the family income by working outside the home.[1] At an early age, Durkheim was a successful student and acquired the personal discipline that enabled him to focus on academic pursuits early in his life. In 1879, he obtained entrance to the École Normale Supérieure in Paris where he began to work on his doctorate. While at the École Normale, Durkheim was influenced by Charles Renouvier (1815–1903) and Emile Boutroux (1845–1921) who were his teachers at the time, and who encouraged him to study philosophy, history and religion. By 1885, Durkheim received a fellowship to study at the University of Berlin for one year and, after returning from Germany, he obtained a university position at Bordeaux at the age of 29. While he was at Bordeaux, Durkheim completed three major sociological works including *The Division of Labor*, *The Rules of Sociological Method* and *Suicide*. In 1902, after obtaining a position at the Sorbonne, Durkheim moved to Paris where he began work on one of his most ambitious studies entitled *The Elementary Forms of Religious Life,* published in 1912. At the Sorbonne, Durkheim established himself as a major figure in French social thought and turned his attention to the study of religion and to publishing the first sociological periodical called the *L' Année Sociologique,* whose first issue appeared in 1898. During this period, Durkheim focused his efforts on advancing knowledge related to the study of society as a domain of research, and as a result of his many publications he attracted scholars who wished to work with him by pursuing studies related to society and social development. By the time of his death in 1917 at the age of 59, he had produced a large body of scholarly work and founded one of the most coherent theoretical perspectives of the nineteenth century. He is best known for founding sociology as a discipline and for defining the boundaries of its subject matter.

Historically, the circumstances shaping Durkheim's theoretical interests were rooted in the political climate that existed in France between 1870 and 1895. By 1871, France was in a deep political crisis which had led to a decline in its national unity. The

---

1 S. Lukes, *Emile Durkheim: His Life and Works,* Stanford: Stanford University Press, 1973.

ensuing social and political changes taking place in France during this period shaped the intellectual and social climate in which Durkheim worked. By 1880, France began to pursue a policy of political consolidation to rebuild its national identity and this led to a stress on two broad social themes. First was the national stress on science and social progress that had developed with the discoveries of the natural sciences. This had increased the prestige of the scientific method to such an extent that one historian referred to it as the 'cult of the sciences' in France.[2] This led many thinkers to take the view that the direction of the nation would be best served by promoting scientific development and by studying the problems of society scientifically.[3] The national emphasis on science unified the French educational system and brought about changes to the French institutional structure by promoting political and educational reforms. As French nationalism began to grow, new intellectual currents such as positivism developed and this led to the use of the science to solve social problems.

The second theme which emerged in France during the period was the problem of individualism and the increasing autonomy of the individual's relation to society. While this theme had its roots in the social upheaval of the French Revolution, a political crisis, known as the Dreyfus Affair, in 1894 accelerated the controversy and threatened to divide France by drawing attention to the individual and by putting the national unity into question. The controversy in France over individualism centered primarily on the question of the autonomy of the individual from the collective unity of society. Many believed that since the revolution, the individual was separate from society and entered into relations with it only out of economic necessity and self interest. Durkheim, by contrast, believed that this tended to place the individual ahead of the national unity of society and threatened the cohesion of social institutions by obscuring the unifying nature of the collective order. The social upheaval and lack of national direction arising from the Dreyfus affair led Durkheim to take a strong anti-individualist stance in favour of the greater social cohesion, and this was reflected in his tendency to criticize the growing autonomy of the individual.[4] As a result, Durkheim's central investigative focus was based on the view that individual autonomy grows only at the expense of the collective unity of society.

Theoretical Influences On Durkheim's View of Society

Auguste Comte's Influence on Durkheim

In addition to the political changes taking place in France at the time, there were a number of key theoretical influences which shaped Durkheim's conception of

2 Charlton, *Secular Religions in France 1815–1870,* London: Oxford University Press, 1963.

3 For a description of the social and historical context in France see D. G. Charlton, *Positive Thought in France During the Second Empire, 1852–70*, Oxford: Clarendon Press, 1959.

4 Durkheim's anti-individualist stance is clearly outlined in his 'Individualism and the Intellectuals,' *Political Studies,* 17, [1898] 1969, 14–30.

society. Of these, at least four separate influences were significant. First was Auguste Comte's perspective on scientific methodology called positivism which helped Durkheim devise a scientific approach to the study of society. Second was the adoption of a philosophical perspective called social realism which Durkheim used to study society as an external reality existing outside the individual. Third were the debates related to the problem of individualism that were common in France up to the period of the 1890s. Fourth were the influences derived from the political writings of Thomas Hobbes and Jean-Jacques Rousseau whose individualist doctrines tended to trace the origins of society to individual human nature. Beginning with Comte, let us look at some of the influences affecting Durkheim's view of society.[5]

Though Comte did not obtain the academic stature which Durkheim had, the impact of his writings on Durkheim was significant. Historically, Comte is best known for developing a philosophical perspective called positivism which had an influence on Durkheim's work as a whole and on the development of the social sciences throughout Europe.[6] Comte had outlined his views on positivism in a work called *A Course in Positive Philosophy* which was published in 1834. Mostly developed in response to what he perceived as the anarchy of speculative philosophy that had prevailed since Hegel, Comte defined positivism as a scientific movement which sought to extend the scope of scientific investigation to the study of society. Central to Comte's positivism were two points of departure which it took beyond the dominant philosophy of the eighteenth and nineteenth centuries. First, it proclaimed the end of speculative thought and the mystical view of nature and history and second, it established the authority of observation in developing a theory of knowledge.[7]

Generally, there are two interlocking assertions which made Comte's positive philosophy so influential. First was the view Comte put forward in respect to the 'law of three stages' which tended to equate science with historical development. Second was his classification of the sciences by arranging them in terms of a definite order and by hierarchically organizing the sciences in relation to their complexity.[8] Both these steps had a significant impact on the social sciences in France which had been governed by speculative thought up until that time. Comte's law had asserted that the human mind develops in three distinct and unalterable stages: the theological stage, in which human beings explain causes in nature in terms of the will of anthropomorphic gods; the metaphysical stage, in which causes are explained in terms of abstract concepts and speculative truths; and the positive stage, in which causes are explained in terms of scientific laws relying on observation and fact.

While Comte's understanding of scientific development was clear enough, what proved to be so controversial was his straightforward claim that the replacement of

5 Philippe Besnard (ed.),*The Sociological Domain: The Durkheimians and the Founding of French Sociology*, Cambridge: Cambridge University Press, 1983.

6 W. Simon, *European Positivism in the Nineteenth Century*, New York: Cornell University Press, 1963.

7 On this point see D.G. Charlton, *Secular Religions in France 1815–1870,* London: Oxford University Press, 1963.

8 Simon, *European Positivism*, pp. 4–18.

the speculative stage by the positive stage of knowledge was inevitable and therefore a fact of historical progress. In essence, this meant that for many positivism became associated with progress and social reform, and that suddenly it became a matter of historical urgency that all disciplines develop from the speculative to the positive stage, thereby marking their scientific stature.

In addition to this, Comte developed a system for classifying the sciences and for drawing comparisons between the sciences in terms of their rank.[9] He had shown that the most developed sciences were positivistic, and that the sciences of mathematics, physics and biology were successful precisely because they used positivistic methods. This had the effect of drawing into comparison positivistic and non-positivistic disciplines such as history, economics and philosophy. This proved to be devastating for the social sciences because their non-positivistic stance was associated with an outright lack of development. By 1880, there was widespread diffusion of positivism in France and England, and Durkheim, who was the direct heir of Comte's positivism in France, began to establish the study of society as a scientific discipline at Bordeaux.[10]

Having looked at the impact of positivism on the social sciences, we can now define some of its central characteristics. First and foremost, positivism may be defined as a scientific outlook whose aim was to place all the speculative sciences including history, philosophy, and political economy on the same footing as the natural sciences. It did this by stressing three central criteria. First, it put forward the view that the search for ultimate or abstract truths be abandoned in favor of a search for law-like regularities. Second, it asserted that all statements about the outside world were to be based on observation and that observation alone should be the basis of a theory of knowledge. Third, positivism stressed a search for facts and believed that relationships among facts would lead to the discovery of general laws. From this perspective, positivism was nothing less than the 'extension of the scientific method to the study of society.'[11] Comte's ultimate stress on the scientific study of society influenced Durkheim in several respects. First, he accepted the positivistic thesis that the study of society was to be founded on an examination of facts, and that facts were to be subject to observation. Second, like Comte, Durkheim upheld the view that the only valid guide to objective knowledge of society was the scientific method and the reliance on factual observation. Third, Durkheim agreed with Comte that the social sciences could become scientific only when they were stripped of their metaphysical abstractions and philosophical speculation.[12]

---

9 Ibid.

10 For Durkheim's own view of the social sciences in the 1880's see 'Emile Durkheim's Inaugural Lecture at Bordeaux,' in *Sociological Inquiry*, 44(3), 1974, pp. 189–204.

11 D. G. Charlton, *Positivist Thought in France During the Second Empire: 1812–1870*, Oxford: Clarendon, 1959, p. 29.

12 For Durkheim's discussion of how sociology must free itself from philosophy, see *The Rules of Sociological Method*, pp. 141–46.

The Realist Perspective and the Study of Society

A second influence on Durkheim's view of society beyond Comte's positivism was the philosophical outlook called social realism. Historically, Durkheim adopted the realist perspective in order to demonstrate the existence of social realities outside the individual and to show that these realities existed in the form of the objective relations of society. Since the realist perspective is generally not well understood or explicitly described by Durkheim, a definition will be useful in understanding the overall role which realism played in Durkheim's approach to the study of society.

First and foremost, realism can be defined as a perspective which takes as its central point of departure the view that external social realities exist in the outer world and that these realities are independent of the individual's perception of them. In this context, the realist perspective takes the view that our awareness of and knowledge about the outside world is a straightforward encounter with the visual perception of reality. However, while this may seem obvious and even straightforward, a philosophical perspective known as empiricism, put forward by David Hume, opposed this view by holding that all realities in the outside world were only products of human sense perception, and did not exist independently of these perceptions. Added to this was the view by empiricists that material things and substances in the outside world had no causal powers in themselves and did not therefore directly affect people's actions. Since according to this view external reality is nothing more than a product of sense perception which does not exist on its own and cannot be confirmed by observation, Durkheim had to wage theoretical battles against the empiricist view in order to defend his realist argument that social realities exist outside the individual and that they have causal powers that affect individual acts.

Second, realists believed that the external framework of society can be treated as if it were made up of structures and mechanisms that constitute 'realities as substantial and definite as those of the psychologist or biologist'.[13] For example, in some societies the 'marriage mechanism' fixes by custom the type of social relationships which will exist between the father's subsection and the mother's subsection, and in other societies the 'class structure' will determine the rank and position of individuals in the social hierarchy.[14] On this view, realists argue that the structures and mechanisms in the outer world have powers and dispositions which affect people's actions by the limitations and restrictions they place on them, and that these powers and constraints are intrinsic to the structures and mechanisms of society.[15] Third, in direct contrast to the empiricists, realists accept the view that the external realities of society have powers that are capable of

---

13 Ibid., p. 13.

14 On the 'marriage mechanism' see Claude Levi-Strauss, *The Elementary Structures of Kinship*, pp. 168–75.

15 Roy Bhaskar, 'Philosophy and Scientific Realism,' in M. Archer et al. (eds.), *Critical Realism*, London: Routledge, 1998, pp, 16–47. In the seventeeth century, Hume argued that objects in the world have no power to affect actions and that these 'powers' are simply products of our perceptions. Later, this became an issue for Durkheim in *The Elementary Forms of Religious Life,* where he argued that religious interdicts have material powers that are evident in direct material practices which reflect the power of society.

exerting restraint, and that these restraints create effects that are visible in people's actions when external social realities impose limits on action in the form of duties and obligations that override their private choices. To this extent, realists therefore assert that social realities act as direct causes that are defined 'externally to the individual' and are made manifest by the effects that social practices and obligations have on individuals.[16] While realists believe that external social realities are the ultimate cause of our perceptions, empiricists assert that individual sense data are part of the perception of the object which they believe is ultimately assembled by the mind. Since, according to this view, objects and material realities do not exist independently of individual perceptions and have no necessary powers to cause individual acts, external reality is thought to be 'inert' and have no power.[17] In contrast to this view, however, realists treat the external world as structures not perceptions, and in contrast to empiricists, realists see the outer world as arrangements of things that have necessary powers rather than as products of the mind that have no powers.[18]

Historically, Durkheim began using the realist perspective as early as 1888 and later adapted it in works such as *The Rules of Sociological Method* and *Suicide* in order to isolate the external framework of society as a material reality that existed outside the individual.[19] He outlined the substance of this method by stating that:

> The sociological method as we practice it rests wholly on the basic principle that social facts must be studied as things, that is, as realities external to the individual. There is no principle for which we have received more criticism, but none is more fundamental. For sociology to be possible, it must above all have an object of its own. On the pretext of giving [sociology] a more solid foundation by establishing it upon the psychological constitution of the individual, it is thus robbed of the only object proper to it. It is not realized that there can be no sociology unless societies exist, and that societies cannot exist if there are only individuals.[20]

The Problem of Individualism and Utilitarian Theories of Society

A third major influence affecting Durkheim's conception of society were the views on individualism predominant in the last quarter of the nineteenth century. In fact,

---

16 Durkheim, *The Rules of Sociological Method*, pp. 1–13.

17 For this assertion see David Hume, *Enquiries Concerning Human Understanding and Concerning the Principles of Morals*, Oxford: Clarendon Press, [1751] 1975, p. 63.

18 Roy Bhaskar, *A Realist Theory of Science*, London: Leeds Books, 1975, p. 25.

19 Durkheim's realist method of treating social realities as things having powers was used by him in 1888 when, in an early paper entitled 'Suicide and the Birth Rate,' he argued that 'birth rates constitute social facts and were thus a living reality.' See David Lester (ed.), *Emile Durkheim Le Suicide: One Hundred Years Later*, Philadelphia: Charles Press, [1888] 1994, pp. 115–132. A recent discussion by Robert Alun Johns dates Durkheim's realist language to a later period. See his *The Development of Durkheim's Social Realism*, Cambridge: The University Press, 1999. For a critical review of Jones' discussion see Ken Morrison, *The Canadian Journal of Sociology*, www.cjsonline.ca/reviews, March–April 2000.

20 Durkheim, *Suicide*, 1951, p. 37–8.

many of Durkheim's views on society cannot be completely understood without providing some historical background on his thinking about the relationship between the individual and society. In France, for instance, the concept of individualism had become a full-blown problem by the time of the French revolution.[21] Following the 'Declaration of the Rights of Man,' the individual had become the absolute center of society and for many this signified unheard of constitutional and legal reform. At the center of these reforms were individual political and legal rights and for many this not only served to place the individual at the political center of society, but it also jeopardized the collective authority of the state. While French society endorsed the concept of the individual at the political level, at another level many believed that the focus on the individual tended to undermine the authority of collective concepts of society and the state.[22]

By 1870, many began to concern themselves with the excesses of individualism and it came under attack as some thinkers of the period began to adopt an 'anti-individualist' stance in their political and social views.[23] This led to key debates among thinkers who began to take up positions on the relationship between society and the individual and between collective obligations and individual rights. Durkheim set out to pursue these questions by showing that 'social life would not be possible unless there were interests that were superior to the interests of individuals.'[24]

In order to make these views as explicit as possible, Durkheim had to wage theoretical battles to defend his claim that society was an objective reality existing outside the individual. Chief among these was his opposition to utilitarian social theory which had become an influential doctrine by the second half of the nineteenth century. Primarily advocated by John Stuart Mill and Jeremy Bentham, utilitarianism put forward two principle views which placed the individual at the center of social life. First, utilitarians asserted that individuals act on their own free will and are completely autonomous and self determined. Second, utilitarians put forward a theory of human motivation which held that individuals share common motives of utility which impel them to realize their self interest by the pursuit of private economic gain. In this view, individual social action is based on economic interchanges of utility with society, but beyond this the individual owes nothing to society in its own right. To the extent that individuals were autonomous, owed nothing to society, and entered into exchanges with it only on the basis of rational self interest and private utility, the larger context of social rules outside the individual were historically and socially

21 See R.R. Palmer, 'Man and Citizen: Applications of Individualism in the French Revolution,' in M.R. Konvitz and A.E. Murphy (eds.), *Essays in Political Theory*, New York: Kennikat Press, 1972; K. W. Swart, 'Individualism in the Mid-Nineteenth Century (1826–1860), *Journal of the History of Ideas*, 23, 1962, 77–90. For Durkheim's contribution to problem of individualism his 'Individualism and the Intellectuals' (trans. S. and J. Lukes), *Political Studies*, 17, [1898] 1969, 14–30.

22 On these issues see, Swart 'Individualism in the Mid-Nineteenth Century'; and Palmer, 'Man and Citizen: Applications of Individualism in the French Revolution.'

23 S. Lukes, *Individualism,* Oxford: Basil Blackwell, 1973, pp. 3–16.

24 Durkheim, 'Individualism and the Intellectuals,' *Political Studies,* 17, 1969, 20.

irrelevant. In this light, utilitarians maintained that the laws of society were nothing more than the actions and passions of individuals acting in the world on the basis of their private utility, and to this extent it reduced society and its collective existence to the spontaneous actions, decisions and attitudes of individuals.[25]

In direct opposition to this, Durkheim asserted that the tendency of utilitarians to reduce society to the spontaneous acts of individuals led them to ignore the larger system of social rules which acted as restraints on individual action. He therefore went on to attack utilitarian doctrine on several distinct fronts. First, in focusing on individual autonomy and self interest, Durkheim argued that utilitarian theory had completely overlooked the existence of the larger framework of social rules and the immediate social obligations that acted as restraints on individuals.[26] Second, he reasoned that since society is always prior to the individual historically and made up of a system of social rules and probitions, then it must therefore have the power to impose an external limit on individuals that is fixed by custom. Third, since society comes first, individuals are not analytically separable from it, and in this sense society and the individual constitute a total social and collective whole. In this view, individuals are neither separable from society nor are they to be studied independently of it since they are a part of the total social unity that exists outside the individual in the form of the social framework. Fourth, so far as society precedes the individual historically and exists as an objective structure, it would be theoretically defensible to focus on society without taking into account the individual's separate attitudes and dispositions.

Individualist Theories of Society: Hobbes and Rousseau

A fourth influence on Durkheim's view of society was the individualist theories of Thomas Hobbes and Jean-Jacques Rousseau.[27] In works such as *The Rules of Sociological Method*, Durkheim set out to separate his own views of society from the individualist theories put forward by Hobbes and Rousseau who generally looked for the origins of society by focusing on individual human nature. In order to see how Durkheim dealt with these views, let us look at the main assertions of their arguments.

In a work called *Leviathan*, Hobbes began by tracing the origins of society to what he called the 'original state of nature.' Hobbes thought that the state of nature existed when individuals live in a condition in which law and government are absent. What Hobbes tried to do was describe what life would be like in a condition in which there were no laws or restraints on individuals. Hobbes, then, went on to reason that

---

25 The reduction of society to the spontaneous actions and decisions of individuals is characteristic of the utilitarian view of society. Some of these views are expressed in C.B. Macpherson's, *The Political Theory of Possessive Individualism*, Oxford: Oxford University Press, 1962, p. 231.

26 Durkheim's criticism of utilitarian social theory can be found in *The Rules of Sociological Method*, p. 4, and in *The Division of Labor*, pp. 278–9.

27 Durkheim's discussion of Hobbes' and Rousseau's individualist theories can be found in *The Rules of Sociological Method*, New York: The Free Press, 1938, pp. 121–24; and *The Division of Labor in Society*.

without law or government to restrain them, individuals would be free to use violent means to satisfy their immediate needs and wants and would continually subdue others in order to maintain dominance over them. From this starting place, Hobbes deduced two central social and political premises which he thought were inherent in the formation of society: first, he argued that the absence of law and government would lead to an uninterrupted struggle for dominance and power in which no one could secure peace or safety; and second, he thought that in a state of nature individuals would be subject to violent attacks from others because everyone would be free to use physical force to satisfy their needs and obtain their ends. Hobbes reasoned that the struggle for dominance would lead to what he called a war against all, in which everyone would be in constant fear of violent death.[28]

Hobbes went on to assert that society thus comes into existence only when individuals contract out of nature and into society in order to secure peace and safety.[29] According to Hobbes, as individuals contract out of nature they form society by placing common rules at the disposal of a ruler who is capable of restraining them all. The formation of society is complete, according to Hobbes, when individuals renounce violent means to pursue their own ends in exchange for the peace and safety of common social rules.

While Hobbes' theory of the political state was one of the first to highlight the restraining capacity of society, Durkheim disagreed with the emphasis Hobbes had placed on the individual in stating that society and social restraint originates from individuals when they contract out of nature. According to Durkheim, this view accepts the idea that individuals are naturally resistant to society and comply with it only when they are compelled by the force of an external ruler and the restraint inherent in law. Taken one step further, if society is only an association serving ends dictated by individuals, then individuals must create society.[30] For society to exist in this framework, the individual has to be persuaded to comply with social rules by an appeal to their interest in self preservation.

Durkheim, however, disagreed with Hobbes' individualist doctrine on several fronts. First, he pointed out that according to Hobbes, individuals impose restraint on themselves by agreeing to contract out of nature and by agreeing to the rules which the sovereign imposes in the form of law. In this view, Durkheim argued that restraint is nothing more than a by product of individual will which is added incrementally to social reality. Durkheim, by contrast, believed that restraint was imposed externally

---

28 Hobbes' wording is: 'In such condition, there is no knowledge, no account of time, no arts, no society; and what is worst of all, continual fear and danger of violent death. In this case, the life of man is solitary, poor, nasty, brutish and short.' Thomas Hobbes, *Leviathan*, Middlesex, England: Penguin, 1968 [1651], p.186.

29 The problem has been referred to by Talcott Parsons as the 'problem of social order' which is discussed in *The Structure of Social Action*. Parsons' claim that Durkheim posed the Hobbesian problem of order is not supported by the textual evidence. This is the case because Durkheim criticized Hobbes for assuming that, so far as individuals impose restraint on themselves, society comes from individuals. In Durkheim's view, this overlooked the social origin of the system of restraint. See Durkheim's discussion of Hobbes in *The Rules of Sociological Method*, pp. 121–4.

30 Durkheim, *The Rules of Sociological Method*, pp. 121–124.

by society independent of the individual and this made restraint the center of Durkheim's view of the structure of society. By arguing that restraint springs from collective life rather than from the individual, Durkheim thought that restraint could be studied in its own right as an independent social reality.[31]

A second individualist theory of society was Jean-Jacques Rousseau's conception of the 'social contract' outlined in a work entitled *The Social Contract and Discourse on the Origin of Inequality*.[32] In contrast to Hobbes, who focused on restraint, Rousseau concentrated on the question of the creation of common social rules in society. Like Hobbes, Rousseau gave priority to human nature in the formation of society, and he reasoned that as soon as society begins to develop, it tends to create private property and self interest. This, said Rousseau, leads to disputes between individuals as they compete in a world in which jealousy and envy prevail. Rousseau thus focused his attention on society by looking at how a 'common interest' arises to replace individual self interest. He reasoned that a common interest arises only when human beings subordinate their individual will to what he termed the 'general will' of society. When this takes place, he thought, the conditions of society come into play as the common interest replaces the self interest of individuals. Rousseau's description of the formation of the 'general will' is significant in two respects. First, he asserted that the general will is formed by individuals pooling their own distinct separate wills. Second, Rousseau thought that when this occurs, a transformation takes place in the nature of individual will to the extent that the individuals involved become subject to the totality formed by their common union. In other words, it is by the common act of individuals that the general will takes its shape and 'receives its unity.'[33] Rousseau went on to argue that the act of pooling all the separate individual wills would produce the collective will of society. In these terms, society takes the form of an association whose moral and collective authority is made up of many members, and accordingly Rousseau believed that in the last instance society was the corporate reflection of individual wills.

While Durkheim's view of society parallels Rousseau's in many respects, he rejected Rousseau's individualist doctrine in a number of ways. First, he thought Rousseau's tendency to ultimately derive society from the individual was mistaken. Durkheim believed that Rousseau had used a method which started from individual disposition in order to arrive at social subject matter, and in this sense Rousseau's individual was complete organically and morally, and thus owed nothing to society.[34] Durkheim, by contrast, believed that the collective structure of society was separate

---

31 Ibid.

32 Jean-Jacques Rousseau, *The Social Contract and Discourse on the Origin of Inequality*, New York: Simon & Schuster, 1967.

33 Ibid., pp. 18–19.

34 S. Lukes, *Emile Durkheim: His Life and Work,* p. 285. Durkheim states that 'neither Hobbes nor Rousseau seems to have realized how contradictory it is to state that the individual is the author of a machine which has for its essential role his domination and constraint.' See *The Rules of Sociological Method,* pp. 121–124.

from the individual and thought that it could be studied as a reality in its own right, and in this way he thought it was independent of the individual. Second, Durkheim reasoned that Rousseau's account of the emergence of society was unsatisfactory because it was overtly reliant on philosophical and idealist concepts of individualist natures and in this sense failed to take the realist step of treating society as an independent reality existing outside the individual. Third, Durkheim criticized Rousseau's explanation of the individual's obligation to adhere to the collective authority of society. According to Rousseau, society could always be reduced to individual wills, and this called into question the obligatory nature of social duties and obligations which Durkheim saw as an independent source of investigation since they originated from society. We now turn our attention to Durkheim's central sociological works, beginning with *The Division of Labor in Society*.

The Division of Labor in Society

Central Thesis and Definition of The Division of Labor

The Division of Labor in Society was Durkheim's first major theoretical work. It was written during the 1880s as part of his doctoral requirement and later published as a complete study in 1893 while Durkheim was at the University of Bordeaux. *The Division of Labor* is first and foremost a study that developed a way of thinking about society that was completely new and, as such, it had several key aims. First, Durkheim wanted to make a distinction between what he called the 'social division of labor' in contrast to the 'economic division of labor.' Second, he wanted to make inquiries into the nature of the social links connecting individuals to society and the social bonds which connect individuals to each other. Third, he wanted to examine the specific origin of the social links and bonds in order to see in what way they were related to the overall system of social cohesion in society, and the extent to which this cohesion was formed within the different social groups he studied. Fourth, Durkheim wanted to look at the extent to which the system of social links change as the structure of society became more complex and subject to changes in the division of labor. He stated this aim of the study when he asked 'why do individuals, while becoming more autonomous, depend more upon society? How can they be at once more individual and yet more cohesive?'[35] In order to look at Durkheim's answer to this question we begin by defining the concept of the social division of labor.

The term ' the division of labor' is used in social theory to refer to the process of dividing up labor among individuals in a group so that the main economic and domestic tasks are performed by different people for the purposes of the collective maintenance of society. The process of the division of labor therefore begins as soon as individuals form themselves into groups where, instead of living isolated or alone,

---

35 Durkheim, *The Division of Labor in Society*, New York: The Free Press, 1968, p. 37.

they cooperate collectively by dividing their labor and by coordinating their economic and domestic activities for purposes of survival. Durkheim believed that the division of labor was therefore the result of a social process taking place within the structure of society rather than the result of the private choices of individuals or the result of organic traits that emerged during evolution.[36]

In looking at the division of labor in different societies, Durkheim began by making a distinction between what he called the 'social division of labor' and what Adam Smith had called the 'economic division of labor.'[37] In the eighteenth century, Smith used the term economic division of labor to describe what happens in the production process when labor is divided during manufacturing. Smith had used the term initially to pinpoint the increase in productivity that takes place when production tasks are divided between workers during the manufacturing process.[38] Smith noted that as soon as people divide their labor to perform various tasks and operations, the quantity of what they produce increases dramatically and that the process of dividing labor tends to accelerate the rate of production.

Durkheim looked at the process he called the 'social division of labor' in comparison with Smith's somewhat more narrow focus on the economic division of labor. The term social division of labor was thus used by Durkheim to describe the social links and bonds which develop during the process that takes place in societies when many individuals enter into cooperation for purposes of carrying out joint economic and domestic tasks. Under these circumstances, Durkheim thought that the social division of labor was distinct from the economic division of labor.[39] When used by Smith, the division of labor referred only to the process of dividing up labor for purposes of increasing the rate of production; whereas when used by Durkheim, it referred to the principle of social cohesion that develops in societies whose social links and bonds result from the way individuals relate to one another when their labor is divided along economic and domestic tasks.

What Durkheim observed beyond Smith was that the social division of labor led to the formation of what he called social 'links and bonds' that attach individuals to the wider society and to each other by linking actual 'cooperators together.'[40] These links and bonds, he went on to reason, formed a system of attachments to society which Durkheim referred to as social solidarity, and it was from these links that whole societies were formed and a whole set of social relations were created.[41]

---

36 See Durkheim, *The Division of labor*, pp. 201–27. Durkheim makes this point in his criticism of Herbert Spencer who asserted that the division of labor is the result of individual selection and biological traits.'

37 *Division of Labor*, pp. 39–40; 275.

38 Adam Smith was the first to introduce the term 'division of labor' into social thought and to discuss the role it played in the manufacturing process. Since then the term has been adopted in social theory in the nineteenth century by Herbert Spencer, Karl Marx and Emile Durkheim. For Smith's discussion of the economic division of labor and the process of the division of tasks into various operations, see *The Wealth of Nations,* London: Dent & Sons, [1776] 1910.

39 *Division of Labor,* pp. 39–40; 275.

40 Ibid., p. 63.

41 For more information on the different forms which the attachment take see *The Division of Labor*, Chapter 1.

Durkheim believed that two kinds of links and bonds existed during the social division of labor. The first of these involves links of dependency which determine social relations between individuals who carry out economic and domestic tasks jointly and collectively. Second are the bonds of obligation which regulate expectations and interchanges between individuals from the same society. While links of dependency often emerge between those who perform tasks related to economic and domestic production, bonds of obligation between members of the same society arise from the network of duties and obligations that form in relation to religious and family institutions. Durkheim's central point, then, was that within the system of activities which the social division of labor coordinates, links and bonds arise which affect the various attachments between individuals and that these attachments generate obligations and dependencies which would never have developed if individuals lived separately or in isolation.[42] What Durkheim found beyond Smith, then, was that the social division of labor leads to specific social links and bonds between individuals in the same society, and that these links and bonds actually formed a structured network of activities which shaped their social attachments and structure their overall social cohesion.

The Concept of Social Solidarity and Social Cohesion

Beyond focusing explicitly on the social division of labor, Durkheim looked at the question of the overall unity of society. Generally speaking, he referred to this unity as social solidarity and initially he used the term in several distinct ways. First, he used it to refer to the system of social bonds which link individuals directly to the wider society. 'Without these social links,' said Durkheim, 'individuals would be independent and develop separately, but instead they pool their efforts' and live collectively.[43] Second, Durkheim used the term 'solidarity' to identify a system of social relations linking individuals to each other and to society as a whole. Without these 'social links,' he pointed out, individuals would be separate and unrelated. Third, he used the term solidarity to refer to the system of social interchanges which go beyond the brief transactions that occur during economic exchange in society. He stated:

> Consequently, even where society relies most completely upon the division of labor, it does not become a jumble of juxtaposed atoms, between which it can establish only external, transient contacts. Rather the members are united by ties, which extend deeper and far beyond the short moments during which the exchange is made. Each of the functions that they exercise is, in a fixed way, dependent upon others, and with them forms a solidary system.'[44]

In this passage, Durkheim isolates a system of social interchanges that forms a vast network of cohesion extending to the whole range of social relations which link

---

42 For Durkheim's discussion of 'links and bonds' see *The Division of Labor*, pp. 59–61.
43 *The Division of Labor*, p. 61.
44 Ibid., p. 227.

individuals together in the form of a total social unity. This solidarity, he pointed out, 'extends far beyond' the brief moments in which the 'exchange takes place,' and it expands further to form a community of beliefs and social practices. Fourth, Durkheim used the term solidarity and cohesion to describe the level of intensity that exists in the social attachments linking individuals to the collective structure of society. In this respect, he thought that social cohesion acts as a 'social cement' which creates attachments between individuals in society, and he thought that these attachments not only link individuals to society but also exercise an emotional hold over them by making their attachment more intense and cohesive.

Characteristics of Mechanical and Organic Solidarity

After outlining the concepts of the social division of labor and social solidarity, Durkheim turned his attention to the question of how social cohesion and social solidarity manifest themselves in different societies. This cohesion, he thought, can be expressed in two very broad and distinct ways, and the terms he used to designate these two broads system of social solidarity are 'mechanical' and 'organic.'[45] There are, he said:

> [T]wo great currents of social life to which two types of structure correspond. Of these currents, that which has its origins in social similarities first runs on alone and without a rival. At this moment, it confounds itself with the very life of society; then, little by little, it channels itself and rarefies while the second is always growing. Indeed the segmental structure is more and more covered over by the other, but without ever completely disappearing ... and we shall find the cause for it in a moment.[46]

In this passage, Durkheim stated that in societies whose solidarity is mechanical, social cohesion is based on common roots of identity and similarity. In societies of this type, the individual is linked directly to society through various points of attachment which act to bind all the members of the group together collectively.[47] The force of these social links are such as to discourage individual autonomy and the entire society envelops the individual so completely that there is no distinction between the individual conscience and the collective conscience.[48] Collective rules and social practices are predominantly religious in nature and tend to define and encompass all aspects of social life and social activity. Under these circumstances, religion is the dominant social institution and religious ceremonies and periodic rites form the basis of their common social attachments. The division of labor is rudimentary and divided up so that individuals perform economic and domestic tasks for common social

---

45 Durkheim, *The Division of Labor*, p. 229.

46 *Division of Labor*, p. 229.

47 *Division of Labor* pp. 129–132; 116; 147–173; 174–181. For characteristics of organic solidarity see *Division of Labor*, pp. 181–229.

48 *Division of Labor*, p. 152.

purposes in which they cooperate together collectively. Under these circumstances, links of dependency emerge between individuals and bonds of obligation exist between the members of the group who carry out collective economic and domestic tasks. This leads to a common system of beliefs and practices rooted in religious life, and on the basis of this they form a community of beliefs and attachments that tie them together collectively. Because their system of beliefs is primarily religious in nature, the common conscience is rooted in religious law. As a result, offenses against common beliefs and social practices are punished by repressive sanctions which act to re-affirm their beliefs and associated social rules by deliberate and direct physical punishment based on penal law. The individual's relation to society is such that the individual does not emerge as separate from the group, and any individual differences are subordinated to the solidarity of the group. In this case, individuality is at its lowest point of development, there is no private life and no individual autonomy. All social attachments governing relations between individuals are based on bonds of obligation, in contrast to bonds of contract or contractual relations. A fundamental criterion of mechanical solidarity is the ability to mobilize the entire social mass of society due to the immense leverage that religion has over the common beliefs and associated social practices of the group. Because the degree of proliferation of common beliefs and social practices extends throughout the entire society, the social cohesion of the group is intense and the links binding the individual to the society as a whole are strong and unified. The greater the unification of common beliefs, the greater is their individual similarity and the ties attaching the individual to the wider society form an almost perfect social consensus.[49]

Beyond emphasizing the social characteristics of mechanical and organic solidarity, Durkheim went on to elaborate on the structure of these groups. He pointed out that societies of this type are made up of groups he called 'segments' consisting of many homogeneous clans who band together to form a confederated tribe. These groups, said Durkheim, are disposed over a confined territory, live in close proximity and are united together in a confederation of people similar to the native tribes of North America. Durkheim used the term 'segmental societies' to describe a type of social structure made up of small groups linked together in a defined social territory.[50] Segmental societies have a structural organization, according to Durkheim, that is like the 'rings of an earthworm,' an image he used to signify the separate segments or rings which form the structure of the group into one integrated social body.[51] In some cases

---

49 *Division of Labor,* p. 129–132; 147–154. Durkheim states that their consensus is so great that their 'their consciences vibrate in unison.'

50 Durkheim refers to the Iroquois tribes of North America as an example of a people who are constituted as an association of clans or segments. He points out that these are a people whose social structure is made up of small groups or segments which are dispersed over a territory and who live in close proximity. Their social unity comes at the point where they view themselves as a confederated people who share a central religion, have a coordinated division of labor and perform collective family, political and religious functions. See *The Division of Labor,* pp. 174–199.

51 *Division of Labor,* p. 175.

the separate segments of clans form a linear series of groups, as in the case of the North American Indian tribes. In other cases, they form unions of several clans, 'each with a special name' descended from one tradition and from the same ancestor.'[52] Whatever their structure, these societies constitute typical examples of mechanical solidarity because their structural characteristics derive from the form of their social solidarity. These societies have a simple division of labor which patterns their activity, so that links of cooperation develop between the segments along religious and political lines where they coordinate their activities and cooperate together. Distinct social bonds develop between the segments and between individuals, forming a system of social obligations that are based on common religious beliefs which have their roots in religious law and which acts to consecrate the group as a sacred people.

Segmental societies take their basic form from the family and political unit. All members of the group are considered to be unified by a family name, creating affinities and bonds which unite them. In some cases, these societies are made up of several thousand people who share domestic and economic relations with members from each segment acting as the central religious and political authorities.[53] While each of the segments are distinguishable from the others and each has different features and often different tribal names, they resemble one another in several fundamental respects. In the first place, their similarities emerge from their system of religious beliefs and common social practices that identify them as a sacred people. Because their religious system is the most active social component, it forms a community of common beliefs which 'pervades the entire social group and which is made up of common collective practices deriving from the unanimous adhesion of a very particular intensity.'[54] In the second place, similarities emerge from their common structural characteristics which forms various points of attachments between the clans and the joint family and religious system.[55] These groups live collectively within the confines of the camp and form multiple families which live commonly in dwellings that are the site of their domestic activities. There is little private life, no separation between individuals and families, and they have a rudimentary economy based on hunting and gathering with some agriculture. This, said Durkheim, leads to a simple division of labor around economic, domestic and religious functions in which their tasks are performed cooperatively, rather than being carried out by separate individuals. Their social division of labor thus acts to pattern their activity in ways that coordinate their tasks for common collective purposes, where there are no private possessions and the maintenance of life through economic and domestic functions is carried out and shared by everyone.

While the social division of labor divides tasks among separate individuals in economic and domestic functions, it acts to coordinate their activities so that their

---

52 *Division of Labor*, p. 178.
53 Ibid, p. 176.
54 Ibid., p.178.
55 Ibid., p. 177.

tasks are carried out cooperatively. To this extent, their labor is cooperative rather than individual, and what is produced is shared commonly. From the division of labor around economic and domestic functions, flows links which attach individuals to society directly, and these links in turn create a system of social bonds and social obligations between individuals with whom they are connected and related. These links and attachments arise from two distinct types of activities. First, they arise from the dependences and reliances that emerge from the social division of labor that is created when individuals carry out common economic and domestic tasks with others. Often these are expressed in the form of links arising from obligations and social duties. Second, are the attachments that arise as a result of coming together for purposes of common religious ceremonies where their social relations are intensified to the point of exaltation. By the very fact of coming together for the performance of a religious ritual, their social relations and attachments are intensified and consecrated in a collective form when they participate in a religious rite together. At this point, said Durkheim, they come to see themselves as a 'sacred people.'[56]

The fact that their social division of labor coordinates their economic and domestic activities collectively cannot be overemphasized. Those who carry out economic and domestic tasks do not act alone or for themselves, but rather act for the entire group. This creates social bonds and unities between individuals which express themselves in the form of social duties that are imposed on individuals by force of their collective obligations. Social bonds, in turn, exert an emotional hold over individuals which are expressed by the force that their social obligations exert over them, and by the hold that is manifested over them in the performance of their collective religious ceremonies. These social bonds in turn act to link individuals directly to society through various points of attachment which bind all the member of the group together collectively. Of these attachments, family and religious institutions form the most intense relations.

Because their religious practices are the most active element in their society, religion proliferates throughout the entire social life of the tribe. This serves to produce a system of social practices which creates common customs and social rules that provide almost total social cohesion. Their solidarity in this sense is mechanical because they share underlying beliefs and practices which unify them as a common people, and because they act in unison and have their social personality defined by their religious personality. In this case, their social links and bonds tie the individual directly to society without private life or other forms of social separation.[57] In such circumstances, individuals are more dependent on society as a whole and the collective personality is invested with unusually strong powers. This reduces their individuality to a minimum since the social similarities absorb the individual so completely within the confines of the group that individual differences disappear completely. Durkheim thought that the direct links individuals have to society are observable in

---

56 *Division of Labor*, p. 182.
57 *Division of Labor*, p. 180.

their religious enactments which he believed strengthen their attachments to each other and to the collective whole in two distinct ways. First, their ritual observances and common celebrations increase their attachments to society by consecrating their acts and activities as a sacred people, giving them a common identity that is enacted and re-enacted in the form of rituals and periodic ceremonies held during religious rites. Second, it increases their attachments to each other by providing a form of social representation in which they see themselves as a group which shares common origins traced to a single sacred ancestor.[58] The social bonds which emerge during these collective religious enactments bind them together as if they were blood relations even though they are not, and it serves to identify them as if they were members of the same family, even though they are not. In addition, their social bonds compel them to recognize social duties toward each other which are equivalent to blood obligations. These include duties of reciprocal aid, vengeance, mourning, and the obligation not to marry among themselves. It is this special cohesion, said Durkheim, 'which absorbs the individual' into the social mass to the point that the individual becomes almost indistinct.[59]

To summarize, societies whose solidarity is mechanical are characterized by: (i) a homogeneous population which is small and isolated; (ii) a division of labor based on social cooperation that coordinates economic, political and religious activities so that people live commonly and cooperate collectively; (iii) a system of social institutions in which religion and the family system are dominant and function as the major source of social cohesion in that they link individuals to each other by obligation; (iv) a system of religious beliefs which are uniformly diffused throughout the society, creating uniformity in attitudes and actions that act on them by unifying their minds and by exerting an emotional hold over them; (v) a low degree of individual autonomy in which private life never develops and the individual is not a distinct social unit; (vi) a system of penal law based on repressive sanctions which punish individual transgressions swiftly and violently, serving the function of reaffirming core beliefs and values when sacred social rules have been violated; (vii) a social organization in which the individual's place in society is determined by kinship and family organization; (viii) a system of social cohesion which produces a high degree of consistency in social practices and beliefs and in individual attitudes and actions; (ix) a state in which individualism is at its lowest point of development and where the individual does not appear as distinct from the group; and (x) a system of social links and bonds between individuals based on custom, obligation and social duties that reflect a dependency on society.[60]

---

58 For discussions of these ceremonies see *The Division of Labor*, pp. 129–32; and *The Elementary Forms of Religious life* on effervescent assemblies and the intensity of public shared enactments, pp. 214–220; 344–50.

59 Ibid., 179. In *The Elementary Forms of Religious Life*, Durkheim referred to these ceremonies as 'effervescent assemblies.'

60 For the clearest discussion of the characteristics of mechanical solidarity see *The Division of Labor*, pp. 176–218.

Characteristics of Organic Solidarity

In contrast to mechanical solidarity is the type of solidarity Durkheim called organic. The principles of organization on which this society rests are completely different from societies whose solidarity is mechanical. In effect, individuals are grouped according to the role they play in the occupational structure rather than being grouped by the social activity they carry out in the tribal segment or in relation to the lineage of clans. Due to the development in the division of labor, the occupational environment in which their economic roles are carried out is distinct from the existing family environment and the overall structure of the population. As a result of being 'grouped according to occupations, people begin to lead their own lives' separate from others and this leads to private life and separation from the family and religious system.[61] Under these circumstances, the occupational environment does not coincide with the territorial distribution of the population, any more than it does with the family environment. In this respect, the new framework of occupations is thus substituted for the old framework of segments.[62]

Societies whose solidarity is organic therefore have larger populations spread out over a broader geographic territory encompassing a large land mass. The economy is industrial and a complex division of labor begins to pattern social activity so that people perform separate and specialized occupational and economic functions, and work separately from each other rather than cooperating collectively. In this case, organic solidarity is characterized by an increase in the density of society due to the expansion of the population, the growth of cities and the development of means of transportation and communication. A network of occupational and economic functions is thus created, where individuals no longer cooperate directly, but rather their cooperation is indirect and patterned through the division of labor as this compels them to satisfy their economic needs by performing separate occupational tasks.

Consequently, societies of this type have an institutional structure that expands beyond the focal point of the family and tribal segment, and as the economy develops it replaces religion as the dominant social institution. As a result, the community of beliefs begins to disappear and the links and bonds to society created by religious solidarity begin to deteriorate and re-emerge in the form of separate institutional organs and specialized occupational functions that individuals perform within the division of labor. As the division of labor expands to encompass the entire social territory, occupations and occupational roles become uppermost. Consequently, specialized economic functions and occupational roles are needed, private life emerges, and cooperation and social obligation begin to decline. At the same time, the social hold that collective beliefs and social practices have over individuals is reduced and, in such circumstances, the social division of labor begins to link individuals to society only indirectly through the specialized occupational roles they perform. These new

---

61 Ibid., p. 188.
62 *Division of Labor*, pp. 189–90.

links to society begin to increase the mutual dependency that each individual has on others to perform their occupational functions since they are unable to perform other occupational functions while performing their own. In this respect, their social cohesion thus takes place through the division of labor rather than directly through the immediate social cooperation of the tribal segment.

As the division of labor advances to encompass the entire population, a new system of links emerge which create different points of institutional contact and different forms of social cohesion. As the density of the population increases, 'personal bonds become rare and weak, and individuals more easily lose sight of one another.'[63] Consequently, the social links which once attached individuals directly to society and to each other through obligation begin to disappear. As the division of labor becomes more specialized, the social reliance between individuals in their performance of occupational roles increases their dependency on each other since they are unable to produce products that others produce while they are engaging in their own occupations. In this sense, their solidarity is 'organic' in that their links develop from the dependency individuals have on others performing occupational functions that they are unable to perform themselves. As their social links change, bonds of obligation are replaced by bonds of contract and contractual obligation. Since bonds of contract are different from bonds of obligation, Durkheim thought that the changes occurring at the level of social obligations altered social life and social cohesion. As the social division of labor became more widespread, the process of social differentiation separate individuals from the group structure to which they once belonged, and as this process accelerated individuals became more autonomous and acquired a fully developed private life.

Organic solidarity is thus characterized by an increase in the density of society due to the expansion of the population, the growth of cities and the development of a means of transportation and communication. As cities form, individuals live separately, private life emerges and individuals are differentiated into isolated nuclear families who cooperate only indirectly rather than living fully absorbed in tribal life. This accelerates private experience and creates the pursuit of private interest, altering the nature of social links and bonds. As the social mass increases, the population is disposed over a broader territory and the division of labor becomes more complete. The bonds of obligation once governing relations between individuals in mechanical solidarity are expressed in the form of contracts and contractual relations. The force of these bonds integrates individuals in their occupational functions and the direct ties which they once had to the collective order of society are replaced by indirect links that operate through the division of labor. This, said Durkheim, alters social relations that were once based on bonds of obligation since, in societies where bonds of obligations exist, no one can refuse to be useful to others because the obligation operates in a direct and immediate way. In this case, said Durkheim, social

---

63 Ibid., p. 299.

obligations are the normal form for regulating social relations and maintaining social links, since the law need not intervene.[64]

As a result of individuals being grouped according to occupations instead of by tribal segment, the individual's place in society is determined by their occupation rather than by clan affiliation or tribal lineage. Workers grouped by occupation thus lead their own lives separately from others rather than working commonly within the tribal organization. Then, as the system of law begins to reflect the new division of labor, restitutive sanctions emerge in which judicial rules redress social wrongs by restoring things to their original state, rather than by repressive sanctions. At this stage, individualism is at its highest point of development and the individual has more autonomy and becomes the object of legal rights and freedoms. In addition, social bonds are formed on the basis of interdependencies created by increased reliance on each other's occupational functions. Autonomous social organs develop in which political, economic and legal functions become specialized and there is a minimum of shared understandings between members of the group.[65] In this case, the collective conscience is less resistant to change and becomes weaker as its content becomes more secular and economic and, as a result, it loses its religious content. Instead of individuals resembling each other, their weaker solidarity presupposes individual differences leading to a new form of social cohesion.

As organic solidarity develops, the form of social obligation reappears in an entirely different light. Contracts develop to regulate the exchange between individuals and, as such, the contract becomes the normal form for regulating relations between individuals. Consequently, the hold which social duties and obligations once had over individuals begins to decline and is replaced by legal regulation. Durkheim believed that when social relations between individuals are governed by contract, what happens is that individuals can 'refuse to be useful' to others, and as the law protects them from being useful, the ties linking them by social obligation disappear.[66]

To summarize, the main characteristics of organic solidarity are: (i) large populations spread over broader geographic areas; (ii) an increased complexity of division of labor leading to specialized economic function in which individuals are more reliant on others to perform economic functions which they cannot perform themselves; (iii) a system of social relations in which individuals are linked to each other by contract rather than by sentiment, obligation or explicit social duties; (iv) a system in which individuals obtain their place in society by occupation rather than by kinship affiliation within the tribal segment; (v) an increased individual autonomy based on a system of laws recognizing rights and individual freedoms; (vi) the development of contract law based on restitutive rather than repressive sanctions in which judicial rules redress social wrongs by restoring things to their original state.[67]

---

64 Durkheim, *The Division of Labor*, p. 216.

65 *Division of Labor*, p. 183–9.

66 Ibid., p. 217.

67 For further discussion of the characteristics of organic solidarity see *Division of Labor*, pp. 185–190.

The Common Conscience and the Division of Labor

After having completed the discussion of mechanical and organic solidarity and after having looked at the different social links and bonds and the distinct forms of social cohesion and social division of labor, Durkheim turned his attention to the question of the social mechanism that holds the groups together and the name he gave to this is the collective conscience, a central concept used by Durkheim in *The Division of Labor*. Essentially, Durkheim uses the term to refer to a body of beliefs, practices and customary enactments which are held in common by all members of a society.[68] These beliefs, he argued, are diffused throughout the society, define social purposes, give action meaning and generally structure the pattern of social life. Durkheim believed that the common conscience develops according to its own laws and is not an expression of individual consciousness and, in this sense, is analytically separable from it. It may be thought of as a determinate system of beliefs and social practices which create social likenesses and similarities among all members of society. To this extent, the common conscience may be thought of as deriving from the total structure of beliefs that are formed as a result of society.

In addition to providing a broad definition of the common conscience, Durkheim went on to elaborate a number of elements related to the substance of the common conscience itself. Among these, he thought that the common conscience was a 'determinate system' which acts as the main 'organ' of society, extending throughout the entire collective space of society and was diffused throughout its physical or geographic boundaries.[69] It creates common conditions of existence, functions to connect successive generations to each other and acts to define individual relations to each other and to society in the form of binding obligations and social ties.[70] Durkheim went on to distinguish four interrelated characteristics of the common conscience including its volume, intensity, determination and content. First is the volume of the collective conscience which refers to the pervasiveness of collective beliefs and the degree to which they extend throughout society as a whole. The volume of the common conscience denotes the capacity of the collective beliefs to 'envelop' the individual by extending its reach throughout the entire society.[71] In addition, the volume of the common conscience refers to the degree of intrusiveness of beliefs and practices into the lives and attitudes of the individuals. The greater the volume of the common conscience, the greater is the individual's attachment to prevailing collective beliefs. In this respect, the extent of the social attachments is therefore greatest when society completely 'envelops' the individual and imposes an emotional hold on them. Examples of this are be found in the special class of rules Durkheim called

---

68 *Division of Labor,* pp. 79–80. For an extended discussion of Durkheim's concept of the Common Conscience see S. Lukes, 'Prolegomena to the Interpretation of Durkheim,' *European Journal of Sociology,* 1971, 183–209.

69 *Division of Labor,* p. 79.

70 Ibid.

71 *Division of Labor,* p. 152.

religious interdicts, which are used in society to enforce necessary adherence to what is forbidden in regard to religious ceremonies or what is forbidden during religious days where certain dietary restrictions operate. Not only do these rules and practices designate what is forbidden across the entire range of society, but they regulate individual acts and activities by laying out precise material consequences that may ensue if interdictive restrictions are not adhered to.

A second characteristic of the common conscience is its intensity. Durkheim uses this term to refer to the degree of leverage collective beliefs exert over individuals. The greater the intensity of the common conscience, the more leverage is exerted by the collective beliefs and social practices. Consequently, the more intense the common conscience, the greater the social cohesion and the more developed is the social uniformity. In addition, the intensity of the common conscience refers to the extent to which the collective beliefs and practices exert an emotional claim on the individual. The more intense the collective beliefs, the greater is the similarity between individuals and the more encompassing is the common conscience.[72] Third is the characteristic of determinateness. This refers to the amount of resistance offered by collective beliefs and how willingly they give way to change, transgression or violation. The more uniform and well defined the collective beliefs, the greater the consensus and, therefore, the greater the resistance to change in the prevailing social rules and beliefs. When collective beliefs and practices lack determinateness, however, they become less resistant to change and to individual transgression.[73] In this case, the more general and vague the rules become, the more they encourage individual transgression. In such circumstances, the common conscience has little determinateness and collective social rules are subject to individual interpretation.

Since the determinateness of the collective conscience refers explicitly to the degree of definition of collective social rules and the social hold they have over individuals, the less resistance these rules have the greater is the likelihood that individual will take recourse to private judgment. By direct contrast, the more defined and strict the collective social rules, the less inclination there is for individuals to vary in their understanding of common social expectations. Hence, the greater the determinateness of the common conscience, the more perfect the consensus and, as Durkheim pointed out, this constitutes a state where 'all individual consciences vibrate in unison.'[74]

The fourth characteristic of the common conscience discussed by Durkheim is content.[75] Though he did not explicitly elaborate on the question of content, some substantive points can be drawn from his discussion. Essentially, the content of the common conscience refers to the dominant characteristic of the society and to its

---

72 Ibid.
73 *Division of Labor,* p. 153.
74 Ibid., p. 152.
75 Ibid, pp. 167–169

collective disposition. In this sense there are two prevailing forms of content. First is religious content in which the primary form of collective beliefs and practices originate from religious law and exert a hold over individuals through religious expiation and the power to consecrate social acts and common social rules. Examples of this exist in the power of religious interdicts which mark the beginning of feasts and celebrations that are important to the collective identity of the group. Second is secular content which entails a process whereby the collective sentiments are divested of their religious content and 'little by little, political, economic and scientific functions free themselves from religion and constitute themselves apart by taking on a different character.'[76] In this case, the overall content of society and its social relationships are mediated by practical and economic necessities of life.

System of Laws and Social Solidarity: Repressive and Restitutive Sanctions

After looking at the common conscience and the role it plays in social cohesion and the division of labor, Durkheim turned his attention to a discussion of the different forms of law and the different judicial rules. In fact, Durkheim believed that there was a fundamental relationship between judicial rules and social solidarity. But what exactly did he mean by this? Simply stated, Durkheim thought that the legal rules a society has and the way it punishes offenses and criminal transgressions is a clue to its system of solidarity and social cohesion. He stated that 'since law reproduces the principal forms of social solidarity, we have only to classify the different types of law in order to discover the different corresponding types of social solidarity.'[77] Durkheim believed that the best way to establish the relationship between judicial rules and solidarity is to examine the way societies punish offenses against the collective beliefs.

Penal Law and Repressive Sanctions   Durkheim began his discussion of the institutions of law and punishment by asserting that there are essentially two distinct systems of law that are found in societies, penal law and contractual law.[78] Penal law can be distinguished from other forms of law by its straightforward intention of imposing harm and suffering upon the offender. It does this in one of two distinct ways: (i) by reducing the social honor of the offender and thus 'inflicting' some form of 'loss' or damage; or (ii) by depriving the offender of either their freedom or their life. In the system of penal law found in segmental societies, for instance, punishment is severe, often bringing physical harm to the offender and applying sanctions against offenders which are 'repressive.' It is the essential function of repressive sanctions to maintain social cohesion by setting examples by means of punishment which act to preserve and reinforce the collective rules and sacred beliefs, and by repairing the

---

76 Ibid, p. 169.
77 *Division of Labor,* p. 68.
78 Ibid., p. 69.

damage done to the collective conscience as a whole as a result of the offense. Penal law is evident in many tribal societies where social cohesion is highly developed and where crimes that offend important social practices often offend religious law as well. In such circumstances, offenses are punished directly on the body of the offender, often without mediation by law.

In direct contrast to penal law is contract or written law. In this system of judicial rules, the intention of the social sanctions is not to inflict suffering upon the body of the offender, but only 'to restore things to their previous state' before the offense took place, and to 're-establish what had been disturbed by putting it back into its normal state'.[79] In this form of judicial sanction, the aim of the law is not to punish the wrongdoer so much as to cancel out the damaging act by annulling it and by divesting it of its social significance. Such a system of law, according to Durkheim, employs 'restitutive' rather than repressive sanctions. The overall effect of restitutive sanctions on the social cohesion of society is, however, minimal.

In order to understand Durkheim's theory of penal and contractual law more fully, it will be useful to examine the characteristics of repressive and restitutive sanctions. At the basis of Durkheim's argument is the idea that each form of solidarity that a group has can be expressed by different types of judicial rules and a system of laws and punishments corresponding to it.[80] To make this as explicit as possible, we need to keep two things in mind when discussing Durkheim's theory of law. First is that the body of social rules and prohibitions established by a society are called judicial rules by Durkheim. Judicial rules, moreover, can be of two sorts: those which are unwritten and part of customary tradition originating from religious laws; and those which are written and part of a system of law and a tradition of legal reasoning. A second thing to keep in mind is that the system of punishment related to offenses against social rules is called sanctions by Durkheim, and these refer to acts which a society considers appropriate in punishing offenses. This gives us two systems of laws and sanctions: penal law, giving rise to repressive sanctions and contract law leading to restitutive sanctions.

The key observation here is the connection Durkheim makes between different types of judicial rules and sanctions on the one hand, and the distinct types of solidarity on the other. Penal law, as we saw, corresponds to societies whose solidarity is mechanical and whose social cohesion is intense. In practice, the acts which this system of judicial rules prohibit and label crimes, are of two kinds: (i) acts which are particularly violent in nature and manifest too much of a violent contrast between the act of an offender and the accepted practices and rules of the group; and (ii) those acts which directly offend, attack or in some way diminish the common conscience.[81] In the first case, acts of this type offend the common rules and customary practices

---

79 Ibid.
80 *Division of Labor,* p. 68
81 *Division of Labor,* p.106.

of the group, whereas in the second, they offend the sacred customs of the group by defiling core religious beliefs and practices. Both of these acts thus threaten the social cohesion of the group by undermining the fact that as a whole they see themselves as a sacred people. In either of these cases, the distinguishing characteristic of penal law is that its repressive force is always proportionate to the damage caused by the offense. Thus, in repressive sanctions 'the punishment matches the severity of the crime as exactly as possible,' since the crime is against the collective beliefs of the group.[82] Under these circumstances, punishment is always severe, swift and based on passionate emotions, in which the main function of the sanction is to maintain as much social cohesion as possible by reinforcing the collective beliefs and the power of the common conscience. Severe punishment and repressive sanctions have the effect of re-affirming core beliefs by acting swiftly against the individual and, in such circumstances, the aim of repressive sanctions is total 'public vindication.'[83] In circumstances where acts offend the religious beliefs of the group, the aim of the repressive sanction is to obliterate the offender and their acts altogether through religious expiation.

A second characteristic of penal law is its tendency to enlist the collective force of society as a means of carrying out punishment for acts it designates as criminal. The spectacle of 'moral outrage' of the group tends to be so severe and intense that it mobilizes the entire force of society and marshals social disapproval to the focal point of the offender. The mobilization of the collective force of society stands as a measure of the social cohesion and degree of outrage which the group expresses toward the offender. This observation extends to all types of traditional societies where religious law is common and where it was commonplace for punishment to signify the collective outrage of the group. The form which punishment takes in a system of penal law is therefore always severe in its affects and 'neat and precise' in its punishment.[84] Also it is evident that in societies where penal law prevails, it is not the intention of the law to provide justice through a measured response to an offense, but rather to 'strike back' with the greatest possible force.[85] In this respect Durkheim thought that penal law always seeks public vindication and therefore acts without fully weighing the circumstances of the offense.

A third characteristic of penal law and repressive sanctions is its origin in religion and religious beliefs. Durkheim maintains that the rules which these wrongdoings offend are so central to the well being of the group that they possess a sacred authority. Understood in this light, the purpose of repressive sanctions is to 'expiate' or expunge the offense and offender from the collective experience and to eliminate it entirely from collective memory. In this view, the main function of penal law and repressive sanctions is to preserve the vitality of the collective rules and regulate

---

82 *Division of Labor*, p. 88.
83 Ibid.
84 Ibid., p. 79.
85 Ibid., p. 86.

offenses against them by ensuring that individuals who violate collective rules and practices are discouraged from committing offenses. The protective function provided by religious law and repressive social sanctions in this case serves to maintain the unity and social cohesion of the group by preserving and reinforcing the vitality of the common conscience.[86]

Contract Law and Restitutive Sanctions   The second system of law is called contract law and its sanctions, according to Durkheim, are restitutive in nature. In contrast to penal law and repressive sanctions, the system of contract law arises only in industrial societies whose social cohesion is organic. By the term contract law, therefore, Durkheim is referring to the system of modern law in advanced societies. Under this system of judicial rules, sanctions are restitutive rather than repressive. To be completely clear on the distinction between contract law and restitutive sanctions, we must look more closely. Contract law is a derivative of industrial society. This is evident if we remember that one of the most important characteristics of industrial society is its system of autonomous social institutions and its complex division of labor. It was on this understanding that Durkheim put forward the idea that the development of specialized social institutions was a consequence of an advanced division of labor that encouraged the emergence of separate and interdependent social organs which included the development of independent legal and political spheres. Only in this sense did Durkheim believe that the emergence of separate legal institutions with a system of written laws came to reflect the development in the division of labor. But this was not all. Clearly, one major way in which the system of judicial rules came to reflect changes in the division of labor was through its sanctions and punishments; hence, restitutive sanctions.

First and foremost, Durkheim thought the system of legal rules and judicial sanctions found in industrial societies was distinct from penal law in several major ways. First, he thought that industrial society leads to the development of various social institutions which become increasingly specialized as they replace the institutions of the tribal segment.[87] Second, these social institutions begin to function through specialized agencies such as the courts, arbitration councils, tribunals and administrative bodies.[88] Third, Durkheim maintained that the authority of the legal rules is exercised through specific functionaries such as judges, magistrates and lawyers who possess specialized credentials.[89] Fourth, he thought that sanctions and punishments themselves ultimately reflect changes in the division of labor and these he called restitutive sanctions.

One of the central characteristics of restitutive sanctions is their direct concern to establish a criterion of justice by ensuring that the punishment adequately fits the

---

86 *Division of Labor,* p. 106.
87 *Division of Labor,* p. 113.
88 Ibid.
89 Ibid.

offense. In contrast to repressive sanctions, therefore, restitutive sanctions have the job of restoring things to the way they were before the offense took place. The intention of restitutive sanctions, therefore, is to undertake compensation and restore the damage created by the offense rather than to inflict suffering on the offender. A second characteristic of restitutive sanctions is the sphere of their social functions in relation to cohesion. Specifically, they function to regulate relations between particular individuals or parties rather than acting in the name of the collective cohesion of the group. To this extent, Durkheim maintained that the rules which restitutive sanctions protect do not directly emanate from the common conscience, but bypass it in some fundamental way.[90] Thus, while restitutive sanctions tend to reconcile conflicts and disputes between individuals, they often do not affect collective social cohesion.

Essentially, the job of contract law is to develop rules which bind individuals to each other by regulating contractual obligations. Durkheim took the view that this system of law did little for social solidarity since it does not regulate the bond between the individual and society but rather restricts itself to regulating contractual links between individuals. This is evident when we realize that restitutive sanctions 'are established not between the individual and society, but between restricted special parties in society which they bind.'[91] In addition, because restitutive sanctions are more specialized in the sense that they only reconcile interests between contracting parties, they tend not to arouse collective social sentiments and thus do not contribute directly to the overall cohesion of society.

The characteristics of restitutive sanctions become clear when we look at the nature of written law itself. Written law has essentially two specific functions. First, to prescribe obligations and expectations by binding contracting parties; and second, to define sanctions as they relate to offenses and breaches against contracts. When we look at civil law, for instance, these two tasks are treated separately as independent procedural functions. While this tends to achieve a better fit between the offense and its punishment, the decision making regarding sanctions is always procedural in nature and reflects specialized functions and specialized institutions. To the extent that rules and sanctions are separate in written law, the purpose of defining sanctions is precisely that of determining, as practically as possible, the most appropriate sanction. This is in direct contrast to the motives of penal law which are repressive in their sanctions and unconcerned with arriving at a balance between the offense and the appropriate just punishment.

Transition From Penal Law to Contract Law   After outlining the distinction between repressive and restitutive sanctions, Durkheim turned his attention to identifying the points of transition from penal law to contract law. Predominantly, he believed that contract law develops only in societies in which the division of labor is advanced,

---

90 *Division of Labor,* p. 115.
91 Ibid.

and that only through the division of labor could specific changes in the sanctioning mechanism of society take place. Of these, Durkheim maintained that three central changes were significant. First, restitutive sanctions are mediated by specialized social institutions in which the actual sanction no longer stems from the collective conscience itself. In this case it is only a 'feeble expression of its state.'[92]

Second, because society steps in to determine what the restitutive sanction will be by appointing intermediaries and specialized agencies such as the courts and tribunals, the actual linkages assumed to exist between the commission of an offense and its actual punishment may become indistinct and ambiguous.[93] Consequently, in this case society loosens the grip which it once had over individuals by direct repressive punishment and, as far as Durkheim was concerned, this reduced social cohesion. In societies where penal law exists, the exact opposite is the case. Since repressive sanctions stem directly from the common conscience, they function entirely without mediation by courts or tribunals. Punishment, therefore, is swift, cohesion is intense and regulation of the individual is immediate and direct.

Third, Durkheim thought that the shift from repressive to restitutive sanctions creates changes which alter the perception of the damage that is perceived to be caused by the offense. For instance, in cases where sanctions are repressive, damage is perceived to occur to society and the collective unity of the group and its associated social rules. Where sanctions are restitutive, however, the primary binding agent is the contract and damage is perceived to be between 'contracting individuals rather than to the unity of society.' On the whole, this alters the social understanding of damage from that of a collective concept to an individual one. Damage occurs not to the society as such or to its collective interests, but to restricted individuals.

The Transition From Segmental to Advanced Societies

After developing a theory of law and punishment, Durkheim turned his attention to the transition taking place from segmental to advanced societies. Up until this point in the argument, three things are evident about the social division of labor. First is that societies which group individuals by tribal segment have different social links and bonds and form more intense attachments in comparison with societies that group individuals by occupation, where they live separately and develop privately. Second, as different forms of social cohesion develop in relation to these groups, we can see that the group would not have existed had individuals lived separately, but only under circumstances where they pool their efforts and live collectively. Third, their social cohesion is not something that merely exists for a short period of time during which their collective tasks are performed, but rather it extends further into the society as a whole to form links of dependency and bonds of obligation between individuals and society. In this case, the question then is how do these different

---

92 Ibid.
93 *Division of Labor,* p. 113.

principles for grouping individuals come about? In the main, Durkheim thought that it was the social division of labor that gave birth to the two types of groups and the different system of attachments which linked and grouped individuals together in the form of the tribal segment, and then to groups whose partitions emerged in the occupational environment.

Durkheim thought that the process of development can take different directions. For instance, in the case of the tribal segment the social links and attachments derived from a single tradition and from one community of beliefs in which religious and family attachments have the most intense relations. In contrast to this was industrial society, which developed from the new occupational framework that was substituted for the older framework of segments, and the new principle of grouping individuals formed by the specialized organs and institutions. As the old attachments existing within the family and religious systems of the segments were replaced by links of contract that formed in the occupational groups, new institutional organs emerged as a result of the increased social density of the population and the development of the division of labor in the economic, political, legal spheres ensued.

Durkheim argued that this process took place in several ways. For one thing, the central social mass became coordinated around a central political institution which exercised a moderating influence on other institutions, rather than organizing around similar tribal segments or around the same ancestral group.[94] Second, the central economic, political and legal institutions were formed from different social material from that found in the segment. As Durkheim pointed out, 'the social material must enter into entirely new combinations in order to organize itself upon completely different foundations.'[95] Third, as the population spreads out over a broader geographical territory, a change comes about in the existing proximity between individuals which forces social life into new activity and from this a new organization with divided functions begins to form. This propels individuals into specialized occupations, which in turn alters the nature of their social links so that the connection to society is through occupation and the social division of labor is based on contracts. As a result of the connection to society through occupation, private life emerges and individualism is at its highest point of development. As a result, individuals are generally grouped by occupation rather than by tribal segment and occupation, not family ties, mark their place within society. As industrial societies begin to appear, they utilize the social elements of the tribal segment, causing the segments to alter the principle according to which individuals are grouped. As these changes occur, said Durkheim, one of the first steps is that segments become 'permeable' and thereby lose their resistance to change.[96] Fourth, when individuals are grouped by occupation, segments transform into organs which occur due to the pressure of occupational

---

94 *Division of Labor*, p. 181.
95 *Division of Labor*, p. 183.
96 *Division of Labor*, p. 187.

functions. These changes can be so complete that, as their development takes place, the new social framework that is created bears little resemblance to the group structure of the previous segments.

Since the differences between mechanical and organic solidarity grow out of the way society connects individuals to the larger social whole, Durkheim thought that there were two key changes which could be observed: first, he thought that as segments are transformed into organs, their functions become more and more specialized; second, as organs develop they produce new aptitudes which tend to efface their former segmental structure.[97] As a result, the social material forms into new combinations and proceeds by organizing itself on completely new foundations. Dissimilarities begin to emerge and the system linking individuals to society based on similarities is replaced by ties which link individuals indirectly through the division of labor. As these changes take place, all resemblances formerly based on common beliefs and social practices begin to disappear and the old system of attachments comes to an end.

Durkheim thought that the development of institutions had the effect of setting segments into new relations with one another so that the functions performed between them became coordinated. Under these circumstances, the segments no longer functioned as separate family aggregates, but rather as interrelated territories.[98] As a result, the social similarities between segments began to diminish and this changed the form of the social bonds derived from common similarities and social affinities. Boundaries separating segments became less resistant to change and, as a result, the social layers became more 'permeable' and began to lose their cohesion.[99] As the new segments began to re-organize, they took the form of an occupational structure which carried with it the tendency to specialize. Durkheim believed that occupational specialization brought about a new form of society and a new type of group formation. While, formerly, individuals were grouped according to the tribal segment in which the family and religious attachments were the most intense, as the division of labor advanced the group came to be divided according to occupation. As the new social framework developed, it replaced the organization of the segment and found its solidarity operating organically through the occupational system.

Main Causes of the Division of Labor

After looking at the transition from mechanical to organic solidarity, Durkheim turned his attention to the causes of the division of labor itself. He believed that one of the primary causes leading to the growth in the division of labor comes about as the boundaries separating groups form distinct gaps between the tribal segments.[100] In order to understand this process, we have to look once again at segmental societies.

---

97 *Division of Labor,* p. 182.
98 *Division of Labor,* p. 187.
99 Ibid.
100 *Division of Labor,* pp. 187, 256.

Durkheim described segmental societies as unions of several clans each with a special name descended from one tradition and the same ancestor. These societies encompassed thousands of people who formed themselves into a linear series of groups with a distinct tribal structure whose social cohesion was based on common religious practices.[101] In this sense, segments were distinct aggregates integrated into a single social body. As soon as the division of labor began to expand, however, new social, economic and political boundaries dividing segments began to form and the divisions between segments broke down and they began to come together. As the segments became more and more 'permeable,' they became less resistant to change which created movement between the parts of the social mass.[102] Instead of social life being arranged over separate segments, it became more consolidated and localized, which tended to increase the moral density of society.

Durkheim thought that there were three primary causes leading to the changes in the division of labor. First, were the transformations which occurred in the geographic proximity of individuals as the population began to concentrate itself in more confined areas instead of being spread out over larger territories. This led to 'a certain tightening' in the social fabric as the human elements come closer together and became more geographically proximate.[103] Second, was the 'formation of cities' which occurred as the social density was increased.[104] This created an intensification of interaction between individuals leading to an increase in the overall social mass. As the social mass increased, it tended to accelerate the mixing of segments into more consolidated social organs. Third, was the increase in social volume. This came about, Durkheim reasoned, when the growing social mass created more frequent communications and the need for transportation, leading to new forms of social interchange. As interchanges between the population increased, it 'suppressed gaps' between segments, thus leading to an increase in moral density, intra-social relations and the frequency of contact between individuals.[105]

Seen in this light, the stages in the development of the division of labor are as follows. First, the division of labor grows as the intensification of the struggle for existence increases due to the additional density in population.[106] Second, individuals living in close proximity find that they must live cooperatively and in this sense their social cooperation takes the form of the division of labor, because it provides the most efficient means of material survival to the greatest number of individuals. Third, lines of demarcation emerge between tasks and functions in order that material needs can be met, and as these arise it leads to the specialization of occupations in which labor is separated or specialized to meet the various material needs. Fourth, a system of mutual

---

101 For a concise elaboration of segmental societies see *Division of Labor,* pp. 174–199.
102 *Division of Labor,* pp. 256–282, 174.
103 *Division of Labor,* p. 258.
104 Ibid.
105 *Division of Labor,* pp. 259–260.
106 *Division of Labor,* p. 278.

social relations arises from the form of interdependence produced by the division of labor and these are expressed in rights, contracts, laws and social rules that form an overall normative order. The relations that these arrangements govern derive from a framework that serves as a basis of social cohesion and as a result their immediate social links and attachments formed by the tribal segment decline and are replaced by contractual links and attachments. At this stage, the struggle for existence becomes more acute. Fifth, a system of social links ensues from the material links which make up the new system of social cohesion based on the functional division of labor.[107]

As the division of labor develops, major social functions within society are broken down into smaller more localized segments which have specialized functions. The fact that social functions are divided up into distinct social categories and allotted to individuals who may be separated in time and space goes to the heart of the system of social cohesion. Individuals are functionally interconnected through the division of labor since they are reliant upon others to produce what they cannot produce on their own. This mutual dependence is key to the new system of social cohesion, since individuals are more dependent upon society while at the same time being more autonomous.[108] The essence of the division of labor, therefore, is that it alters the system of social cohesion by compelling individuals to form social bonds based on their occupational interconnections. In this way, their links to society are based on their performance in specialized economic roles and in contributing to society by their specialized occupations.

In addition to labor being divided into specialized functions, production and consumption grow narrow as well. Since individuals can no longer produce all the goods and service which correspond to their needs as they did in earlier societies, they must rely on occupational links to others who produce what they are unable to produce. In effect, the division of labor dictates that individuals are more reliant on other productive sectors of society for goods and services which they need to maintain their own existence. These new social links produce spheres of competence and work whose allocation is no longer determined by custom. Social experience, in this case, is reduced to the occupational sphere and to performance within productive roles. This results not only in social differentiation, but in a less cohesive society and ultimately in what Durkheim referred to as the 'cult' of the individual.[109]

The Process of Individualism and the Division of Labor

The autonomy of the individual that is created in industrial societies is referred to by Durkheim as 'advanced individualism.' He believed that individualism tends to be more developed in industrial societies than in segmental societies which existed in

---

107 For a discussion of how cooperation and the division of labor are social rather than economic in nature see *Division of Labor*, pp. 278–279.

108 *Division of Labor*, p. 279.

109 This argument is developed in *Division of Labor*, p. 172.

earlier times. But, what exactly does this mean? Generally, Durkheim believed that one of the outcomes of the division of labor was an overall weakening of the links and attachments tying individuals to society, leading to an increase in individual auto-nomy. While this may be difficult to completely understand, Durkheim was not alone in holding the view that the transition from mechanical to organic solidarity increased the autonomy of the individual. At an earlier period, French social thought had focused on the problem of advancing individualism, which many believed came about as a result of the breakup of the collective authority of society and the loss of social cohesion. In *The Division of Labor*, however, Durkheim went a step further by show-ing that in fact 'individualism' had a social origin and could therefore be explained sociologically.[110] Durkheim's reasoning took several different directions. First, he believed that the individual was not a conspicuous social unit in societies integrated by mechanical solidarity.[111] According to this view, individuality must have been at its lowest point of development because the 'toll' exerted upon the individual by the com-mon religious practices was so great as to absorb all individual differences and pur-poses into collective purposes. If mechanical solidarity is the stage at which the individual is 'subordinated' to the collective forces of society, then organic solidarity must mark the beginning of individual separateness and autonomy. This can take place only when the 'toll' exerted by the common beliefs and practices are diminished.

A second direction taken by Durkheim was to look at the 'individual' from the point of view of social development in different societies. He argued that in the his-torical sense, 'individuals' must have first made their appearance in society in the form of the chief or leader of the tribe, and that chiefs must have been the first autonomous individuals to become 'distinct from the social mass.'[112] Chiefs, he main-tained, must have been the first to differentiate themselves and step out as individu-als who were separate from the undifferentiated tribal mass. Chiefs were separate because their authority puts them beyond others and because the distinctness of their experience and responsibilities confers individuality upon them, making them distinct from others. The 'power of chiefs makes them autonomous and capable of activity beyond the collective norm' and this opens up the possibility of personal initiative, and constitutes the 'first moment when the individual steps forth from the group as someone distinct from its usage.'[113]

On this basis Durkheim thought that 'individualism' was a direct product of industrial society. This comes about, he suggested, as the change in social cohesion reduces the intensity of the social attachments existing between society and the individual. In segmental societies the individual tended to be absorbed in collective life, and links to society were direct and social control repressive. As the force of

---

110 Ibid.

111 He states clearly that individuals *per se* do not appear in mechanical solidarity, since 'individuality is some-thing the society possesses.' *Division of Labor*, p. 130.

112 *Division of Labor,* p. 195.

113 Ibid.

social links began to weaken the bond between the individual and society, individuals became the recipients of rights and freedoms in which their ties to society were expressed indirectly. As industrial societies developed, adjustments in social solidarity changed the overall nature of the social mass, and this encouraged the development of individual autonomy in a number of ways. First, individuals were generally freed from the claims which society placed upon them in the form of social allegiances. As a result, beliefs and customs which were not directly part of social life began to develop.[114] Second, as the social density of society grew, individual ideas began to dominate over collective ones. This stretched social life beyond the limits set by previous beliefs and moral rules. Third, as the division of labor accelerated, individuals were placed within a framework of causes which connected them to their own needs and wants rather than to the needs of society or the needs of others. This encouraged individual appetites and created the need for exploration and initiative. Fourth, as the population increased, social activity, grew more varied and created a more differentiated social life. Fifth, changes occurring in the dependence of the individual on society as a whole brought about new activity, giving rise to 'traits of psychic life' which became developed to an extent 'never before seen in human society.'[115] Sixth, as societies developed in their division of labor they became more condensed and this caused one form of 'psychic life' to disappear and be replaced by another. Initially, individual differences started out by being subordinated to collective forces, but as societies developed a psychic life appeared, and this in turn transformed the psychic life of society. As a result, society itself became freer and more extensive.

As the social density of the population increased, 'personal bonds become rare and weak' and, in this case, individuals lose sight of one another other and thus lose interest.[116] As this 'mutual indifference grows it results in a loss of collective surveillance and the sphere of free autonomous action of each individual is extended in scope and, in fact, becomes a right.'[117] As a result, the collective conscience begins to lose its hold over the individual and becomes more vague, ambiguous and indeterminate. As such, collective social rules lose their clarity and due to the increasing density of the population, the center of social life changes. Individuals no longer live at the center of social life since it is spread over a larger territory. Under these circumstances, public opinion has less of an effect on the individual and exerts less constraint. As the collective grasp of society over the individual loosens, there is more individual divergence and society is divided into smaller compartments enclosing the individual.[118]

---

114 *Division of Labor,* p. 345.
115 *Division of Labor,* p. 346.
116 Ibid.
117 Ibid.
118 *Division of Labor,* p. 300.

Abnormal Developments in the Division of Labor:
Anomie and the Forced Division of Labor

In the concluding section of *The Division of Labor,* Durkheim turned his attention to problems in the division of labor which were inconsistent with what he called its 'normal' development. He stated that, up to now, we have looked at the division of labor only in terms of its normal development, but like all other social facts it can lead to problems and difficulties which have the capacity to disrupt whole societies. In this context, Durkheim thought that the overall social cohesion of society has the capacity to exhibit what he called 'abnormal forms.'[119]

Book three of *The Division of Labor* focuses on three distinct types of abnormal forms which occur in advanced societies. These are (i) the anomic division of labor; (ii) the forced division of labor and (iii) the poor coordination of functions resulting from the division of labor itself.[120] Durkheim's examination of abnormal forms takes two important directions. First is its focus on what deregulates individuals from the social cohesion of society; and second, is the stress it places on what deregulates the main social functions of society from one another. The first abnormal form referred to by Durkheim is called the 'anomic' division of labor. Generally, he believed that the anomic division of labor arises during an economic crisis when there is widespread commercial failure. This crisis, he suggested, tends to undermine the social cohesion existing between specialized functions and creates a decline in overall social solidarity.[121] There are, according to Durkheim, two distinct senses in which the anomic division of labor takes place. First is when there is a breakdown in social solidarity and social integration; and second, is when individuals are unable to comprehend or grasp all of the separate elements of society as a whole, and as a result do not feel that they belong to it or are part of it. This takes place, Durkheim believed, as soon as the totality of society and its overall social mass increase to the point that individuals are unable to visualize social processes and boundaries and thus cannot comprehend the social whole at a glance.

Industrial and commercial crises constitute examples of the anomic division of labor. This can occur when 'social functions are not adjusted to each other' and lead to a decline in overall social cohesion.[122] In such circumstances, the social separations and divisions between social functions grow rigid due to the intervention of special interest groups who attempt to gain control over it to the point that their different interests create conflict, resulting in rigidity. Attempting to reconcile the different interests between capital and labor, for instance, constitutes an example of this kind of conflict. Consequently, the social cohesion previously existing in social groups is no longer mediated by traditional social processes, but rather by individuals whose

---

119 Ibid.
120.*Division of Labor,* p. 389.
121 *Division of Labor,* p. 354.
122 Ibid.

private interests are channeled for purposes of protecting their specialized roles. In this case, social groups previously mediated by links of social cohesion grow rigid and social solidarity is jeopardized. This contrasts with the situation in segmental societies where the interchanges between individuals and groups are maintained by customary practices which reinforce their social links to common social purposes. In such circumstances, individuals work side by side in the same work environment and in a tighter framework of solidarity. In modern industrial societies, by contrast, social functions and operations are more specialized and individuals are not necessarily linked by common social ties or bonds.[123] Durkheim thought that in circumstances where the anomic division of labor is allowed to develop, specialization is often taken so far that social disintegration may result. In addition, social functions become so specialized that the common principle which makes these functions reciprocal within the division of labor itself are lost between the participants occupying the functions. In such circumstances, a common authority no longer links individuals to each other, but only to their private interests. As a result, the social institutions 'grow opaque' and lose their ability to maintain social linkage between individuals and groups.

A second form of social deregulation is the process Durkheim referred to as the 'forced division of labor.'[124] This occurs when the existing specializations within the division of labor become instruments placed at the disposal of certain social classes and their interests. As a consequence, the division of labor no longer meets the social needs of cohesion, but rather serves the specialized interests of certain social groups.[125] As a result, specific class interests function at the exclusion of others which leads to what Durkheim called the 'forced division' between social functions.[126] This may occur in a society when certain institutional elements become too specialized or over developed, such as when legal institutions over regulate economic or schooling institutions through litigation. Since the division of labor only produces solidarity when its divisions are spontaneous, the forced division of labor replaces spontaneous functions with forced functions. Durkheim thought that this leads to a loss of social cohesion, since when restricted social classes manipulate functions in order to satisfy their own interests, it disrupts the process of social solidarity. In addition, the forced division of labor prevents individuals from occupying their social positions within the framework of society since it allocates occupations and functions based on birth or class.[127]

In Durkheim's view, the forced division of labor undermines social attachments between individuals and between individuals and social institutions. He maintained that when inequalities are imposed in society by special interests, it tends to undermine social bonds by mis-attaching individuals to their social functions in society either through force or coercion. In addition, the forced division of labor creates

---

123 *Division of Labor,* p. 368.
124 *Division of Labor,* p. 374.
125 *Division of Labor,* p. 374–84.
126 *Division of Labor,* p. 356.
127 *Division of Labor,* p. 375.

conflicts not only by imposing social inequalities, but by creating irregular and unjust forms of exchange. Under normal conditions of exchange, what is exchanged is usually equivalent in value and this functions to maintain equilibrium between exchanging parties. But when one group takes unfair advantage of another without equally imposing restraint on itself or imposes checks on other groups without checking itself, the system of exchange is no longer balanced.[128] When the division of labor is forced, restraint does not come from a centralized authority and social cohesion diminishes.

The Rules of Sociological Method

The Central Aims of the Rules

I now want to turn my attention to Durkheim's second work entitled *The Rules of Sociological Method*, published in 1895 while he was at the University of Bordeaux.[129] Largely a methodological study, the primary aim of *The Rules* was to outline the nature of sociological subject matter and to set out the steps of sociological investigation. By and large, the text of *The Rules* has four broad aims. First is to establish the existence of social realities outside the individual and to elaborate on the features and characteristics of this reality by showing how external limits imposed by society on the individual become general rules of conduct. Second is to identify the nature of social subject matter by putting forward a definition of 'social facts' and by identifying the 'power of external coercion' which they exercise over individuals. Third is to outline the rules to be used in observing social subject matter by making distinctions between psychology and sociology in order to establish the study of society as a domain in its own right independent of the individual. Fourth is to outline a system for classifying societies according to their structure and complexity, a process Durkheim referred to as 'social morphology.'

   Durkheim wrote *The Rules of Sociological Method* during the 1890s and, at that time, there were several considerations which were uppermost in his mind. In the first place, he wanted to establish the existence of social realities outside the individual and to begin the investigation of these realities by the technique of observation and description. In order to accomplish this he had to do several things. First, he had to make a distinction between psychology and sociology in order to identify the realities of society existing outside the individual, as opposed to looking at the mental life of individuals. Second, he had to make sociology independent of philosophy by replacing speculative thought with factual observation and a search for the existing similarities in the structure of society.[130] Under these circumstances, factual observation was used by

---

128 *Division of Labor,* p. 383.

129 Durkheim, *The Rules of Sociological Method,* New York: The Free Press, [1895] 1938.

130 Durkheim, like Comte before him, wanted to change sociology from a science of 'existence' to a science of things and thereby establish a factual basis for the existence of society, thus eliminating any further need to 'speculate into its reason for being.' See *The Rules,* p. xxxvii.

Durkheim to gather knowledge of society by providing an inventory of the numerous social facts that existed in different societies. Third, Durkheim had to set out what he thought was the specific subject matter of sociological investigation, and in order to do this he had to demarcate sociological subject matter from the subject matter of psychology. This involved Durkheim in considerable theoretical opposition to the prevailing psychological view which had existed during that time and which had asserted that the individual was at the center of society.

Establishing the Existence of Social Realities Outside the Individual

Having outlined some of the central objectives of *The Rules,* it is important to keep in mind the primary focus of the work. This, above all, is to establish the existence of social realities outside the individual. Historically, there were several reasons which led Durkheim to believe that he alone had to establish the independent nature of sociological subject matter. First, by 1890 Durkheim saw himself as the leader of a school of thought with well established followers, and this led him to believe that certain guidelines were necessary if sociology was to develop into a separate discipline of its own. Second, Durkheim frequently concerned himself with the issue of consistency in sociological work and wanted to set out rules of investigation that would promote a coherent approach to the study of sociological subject matter. Third, Durkheim was concerned by the existing reluctance of some scholars to make adequate distinctions between psychology and sociology and, more than anything else, this prompted him to take serious steps to outline the differences between the two disciplines and the importance of undertaking to treat society as a subject matter in its own right.[131] Fourth, by the 1890s many believed that the 'individual' was at the center of society, and some took the view that the individual, therefore, was the preeminent focus of a theory of society. For this reason, one of the central problems forcing Durkheim to emphasize the importance of social subject matter was the individualistic doctrine being put forward by two major schools of thought, utilitarian social theory advocated by Jeremy Bentham and John Stuart Mill, and the theory of society put forward by Gabriel Tarde (1843–1904), a contemporary of Durkheim who had argued that society was the result of 'imitative acts' transmitted from one individual to another. Since both of these schools of thought had a pervasive hold over the role played by the individual in social life, no complete understanding of Durkheim's concept of social facts and social subject matter is possible without first examining some of the views of these schools.

By the second half of the nineteenth century, utilitarian social theory had become one of the most influential perspectives of the period, exerting a pervasive hold over social thought itself. Principally espoused by John Stuart Mill and Jeremy Bentham, utilitarian social thought was based on two fundamental assumptions that led to its virtual dominance

---

131 *Rules,* p. li.

as a theory of society. First, utilitarians put forward a doctrine of social action which asserted that all human acts were completely autonomous and self determined, and as a result they tended to believe that private intention was the springboard of all human action.[132] Second, utilitarians put forward a theory of human motivation which held that all human behavior had common motives of private utility that impelled individuals to pursue self interest and economic gain. On this assumption, individual satisfaction consisted of private interchanges of utility with society, but beyond this the individual owed nothing to society in its own right. To the extent that each individual was autonomous, owed nothing to society, and entered into exchanges with it only on the basis of rational self interest and free will, utilitarians had completely overlooked the existence of the larger framework of social rules and customary requirements which acted as external restraints on individuals. Durkheim had argued that utilitarians had therefore overlooked the fact that societies were associations which tended to create what he had called 'groups of cooperators,' and this showed that society was a framework of customary rules and practices capable of overriding the private will and personal discretion of individuals. Durkheim stated:

> This important truth has been disregarded by utilitarians and is an error rooted in the way they conceive of society. They suppose isolated individuals who consequently enter into relationships only to cooperate, for they have no other reason to clear the space separating them and to associate. This theory deduces society from the individual. With autonomous individualities, nothing can emerge save what is individual and consequently cooperation itself, which is a social fact submissive to social rules, cannot arise.'[133]

Almost immediately after the utilitarians had taken the view that there were only individuals acting on their free will irrespective of society, Gabriel Tarde, a contemporary of Durkheim's, argued that the 'laws of imitation and imitative acts were responsible for social facts.' In Tarde's view, society was nothing more than the transmission of imitated acts from one individual to anther.[134] Tarde, therefore, saw himself as putting forward a theory of 'social facts' based on the study of the individual and, in 1895, Tarde published a work on the theory of imitation in the same year Durkheim had published *The Rules of Sociological Method*. Tarde had argued that 'anything social, whether a religious rite, a legal statute or a moral maxim was transmitted and passed on from one individual to another by imitation,' and that society was simply the sum total of imitated acts transmitted from one individual to another.[135] In Durkheim's view, this had the effect of reducing society to nothing more than individual acts of imitation since, according to Tarde, each 'act is a product of the imitation of gestures

---

132 Elie Halevy, *The Growth of Philosophic Radicalism,* Boston: Beacon Press, 1955.
133 Durkheim, *The Division of Labor,* pp. 278–79
134 Gabriel de Tarde, *The Laws of Imitation,* 2nd Ed., Gloucester, Mass.: Peter Smith, [1895] 1962.
135 Terry Clark, *Gabriel Tarde on Communication and Social Influence* Chicago: University Press, 1969, pp. 7–69; 136–140.

between minds in which social facts were thought to be the result of imitation.' After defining imitation as 'actions at a distance of one mind upon another,' Tarde believed that he had discovered the origin of society stating that society itself was based on the imitation of the acts of other individuals and nothing more. This led him to assert that 'if the individual is subtracted from society nothing remains, and thus nothing really exists in society but individuals.'[136]

While Tarde and Durkheim had many sharp exchanges during the period, it was not until 1895 when Tarde began to put forward a rival theory of social facts that a full blown debate broke out between them. By 1897, after Durkheim had published *The Rules of Sociological Method* and *Suicide*, Tarde followed with an attack on Durkheim's central argument that social realities existed outside the individual. Tarde stated that 'it is difficult to understand how, after excluding individuals, Durkheim can have a society as a remnant' since 'society is nothing other than individuals and individual acts' and that 'individual minds' are the central sociological subject matter.'[137] While the debate continued until 1901, when Tarde published an article criticizing Durkheim's theory of society, Durkheim responded to Tarde in chapter two of *Suicide* by stating that if we accept Tarde's view that 'there can be nothing external to the individual' then, under such circumstances, sociology has no distinct subject matter of its own. It is therefore against this background that Durkheim's *Rules of Sociological Method* had to defend what Tarde and others had disputed, namely the objective reality of social facts.

The Existence of Social Facts and their Differences from Individual Facts

Given the difficulty Durkheim had in arguing for the existence of social realities outside the individual, we can begin to look more closely at some of the assertions he made about the existence of social facts. In chapter one of *The Rules*, Durkheim began by stating that 'it is important to know which facts are commonly called social.'[138] If we look at the things individuals do such as eating, sleeping and reasoning, he said, none of these activities may be called social, since these acts only identify a set of individual facts in so far as individuals regularly do these things.[139] In addition, if all these individuals facts were to be viewed as social, then 'sociology would have no subject matter exclusively its own, and its domain of investigation would be confused with that of biology and psychology.'[140] All these individual acts, he went on to say, cannot be counted as social facts and, if they were, sociology would have no distinctive subject matter of its own and no social reality to identify since there would only be individual reality. But, said Durkheim, in every society

---

136 Ibid.
137 Ibid., p. 69.
138 *Rules*, p. 1.
139 Ibid.

there exists a group of facts which may be studied independently of these individual facts. He stated:

> When I fulfill my obligations as a brother or citizen, I perform duties which are defined externally to myself and my acts, in law and in custom … I feel their reality objectively, for I did not create them. [We find these] beliefs and practices … ready made at birth; their existence is prior to our own and implies an existence outside of ourselves. Here, then, are ways of acting, thinking and feeling that present the noteworthy property of existing outside the individual consciousness.[141]

Durkheim went on to reason that when these 'duties and obligations' are differentiated from other things, and are 'defined externally to myself in law and custom,' they have two distinct properties which qualify them as 'social facts' as distinct from individual facts. First, they present the noteworthy property of existing outside the individual, and second, their existence is prior to the individual and as such they therefore precede individuals in the historical sense. Here, said Durkheim, 'are a class of externally independent rules and customs which are clearly withdrawn from individual discretion' and personal will. 'A rule of conduct,' he went on to say, only becomes a rule to the extent that 'the group consecrates it with its authority,' and above all, it is a rule because it has a means of exerting an obligation upon the individual which is 'withdrawn from individual discretion.'[142] These rules and obligations, he said, 'constitute a new subject matter' that is external to the individual 'and it is to these things exclusively that the term 'social' ought to be applied.'[143] Durkheim went on to define social facts in the following way:

> We thus arrive at a point where we can formulate and limit in a precise way the domain of sociology. A social fact is to be recognized by the power of external coercion which it exercises over individuals, and the presence of this power may be recognized by the existence of some specific sanction or by the resistance offered against every individual effort that tends to violate it. The essential characteristic is that it is independent of the individual forms it assumes in its diffusion.[144]

The observation by Durkheim that social facts are to be 'recognized by the power of external coercion which they exercise over individuals,' and by the 'presence of some specific sanction against the individual's effort to violate it' was pivotal in setting out the characteristics of social subject matter. It was pivotal in the main because it

---

140 Ibid.

141 *Rules*, pp. 1–2. Slightly modified.

142 Durkheim, *The Division of Labor*, p. 4.

143 *Rules*, p. 3–4.

144 Ibid., p. 10. After defining social facts as 'the power of external coercion exercised over the individual,' Durkheim stated in a footnote that his definition 'diverged' from the definition 'which formed the basis of the system' put forward by Tarde, who stated that social facts could be attributed to imitation.

challenged utilitarian thinking and imitation theory on at least three separate and distinct fronts. First, in stating that social facts were 'recognized by the power of external coercion which it exercised over the individual,' it shifted the focus from individual motives and intentions to the external social rules existing in the framework of society. This opposed the utilitarian view that individual actions were completely self determined by showing that social facts not only had authority over the mental disposition of individual acts and were thus independent of them, but also by showing that social rules had the power to fix by custom an external limit imposed on individual behavior. Second, in asserting that society has the power of coercion over individuals in the form of external social rules and obligations, it showed that individual action in fact derives from society, thus placing the individual within the larger framework of social rules and customary restraints. Third, in response to Tarde's claim that 'nothing exists in society but individuals, and that when we subtract individuals from society nothing is left,' Durkheim stated that 'if there is nothing in society except individuals, how can there be anything external to them' and how does this reality external to individuals exercise itself? In showing that society exists, said Durkheim, we show that 'the material form which a social fact has is nothing but the active expression of the reality that exists external to the individual.'[145]

On the one hand, this opposed the utilitarian view that individuals only enter into interchanges with society on the basis of their free will by asserting that social facts place external limitations and restrictions on individuals that are fixed by law and custom. On the other, it opposed the view put forward by Tarde that 'laws of imitation were responsible for social facts' by showing that customary rules and social practices constituted a reality that existed independently of the individual. Durkheim went on to point out that when the term 'social constraint' is used in this way to indicate the existence of an external reality 'we risk shocking the partisans of absolute individualism who profess the complete autonomy of the individual.' Those who take this view believe mistakenly that the individual's 'dignity is diminished whenever they are made to feel that they are not completely self-determined.'[146]

In order, then, to make a distinction between the study of the individual and the study of society, Durkheim simply divided sociology from psychology by distinguishing social facts from individual facts. Consequently, the study of social facts became the central domain of sociological research. In addition to this, he argued that, in contrast to individual facts, the domain of social facts were identified by 'the power of external coercion it exercises over individuals, and the presence of this power may be recognized by the existence of some specific sanction or by the resistance offered against every individual effort to violate it.'[147] While this may seem difficult to follow, Durkheim's point is simple and straightforward. To illustrate, take

---

145 Durkheim, *Suicide*, pp. 310–14.
146 *Rules*, p. 4.
147 Ibid., p. 10.

for instance the powers associated with the totem object in tribal societies. On certain days it is forbidden to eat the totem plant or animal during the days that mark the beginning of a religious feast. In light of the definition of social facts stated above, Durkheim would say that their 'beliefs' thus have the power of external coercion to prohibit individuals from eating the totem on feast days, and that this power to impose an external limit on individuals is fixed by custom, and does not come from within.[148]

An additional example of the power of external coercion existing in social facts can be found in the system of 'obligations' related to the generalized systems of exchange in all societies. In a study of the systems of exchange in tribal society, Marcel Mauss found that initially a system of exchange brings two things together. First, it brings together persons who carry out the exchange, who may be members of groups, clans, tribes or families. Second, it brings together the things to be exchanged, such as food, feasts, enduring objects, services, aid or simply gifts.[149] Mauss noted at the outset that a generalized system of exchange in society constitutes what he called a 'total social fact' because it is so widespread in its occurrence, and because it is universal across societies.[150] Mauss's aim was to show that exchange in primitive societies was a total social fact because, apart from the simple form of the transaction, generalized exchange touched on many social mechanisms including the religious, economic, judicial, and moral mechanism. A total social fact, according to Mauss, therefore always concerns the whole of society and its institutions: economic, political, religious, legal, etc. Focusing specifically on gift exchange, Mauss showed that within the context of the social life of groups 'the circulation of objects occurred side by side with the circulation of persons and rights.'[151] Mauss wanted therefore to show that a set of social obligations existed in the form of social facts that take effect during 'gift exchange' in the societies he studied. He pointed out that in the societies he looked at, the social obligations governing gift exchange operate like a logic in so far as the giving of a gift created the obligation on the part of the recipient to return a gift. Mauss referred to this as a total social fact because it assumed a form in which an external obligation was fixed by custom and he referred to this as a rule he called 'gift and return gift.'[152] Mauss not only argued that the rule 'gift return gift' had existed for long periods of time and was fixed by custom in many societies, but also that the social fact related to generalized systems of exchange isolated a powerful social mechanism which 'obligates' an individual externally in a way that originates from society, rather than from within the individual.

---

148 Durkheim noted that the social facts related to dietary restrictions imposed during religious days have the power of the religious order and thus constitute what he called a special case of religious interdicts. The religious restriction on Catholics regarding the consumption of meat during Lent is an example of the interdictive powers of religious social facts.

149 Marcel Mauss, *The Gift: Forms and Functions of Exchange in Archaic Societies*, London: Routledge, 1970, pp. 1–21.

150 Mauss, *The Gift*, pp. 1–21.

151 Ibid., p. 45.

As far as Mauss was concerned, the universal social logic which emerged during gift exchange was the social fact of the 'obligation' that was put in motion during the act of exchange itself. He thought that the obligation, in fact, seems to be something independent of individual psychology and was therefore part of the objective framework of society. Seen in this light, the recipient of a gift receives the obligation that attaches to the gift and this, said Mauss, is not only part of what is exchanged but it is a way that society has for matching 'persons to things' independent of individual inclinations.[153] This means that everything that happens in the course of the exchange has to do with the fact that the 'obligation' seems to circulate independently of the actual mechanics of the interchange of things and people, since it extends beyond the personal wishes or discretions of the individuals involved. In this case, the total social fact to be observed is the obligation that has been created during the exchange, and this obligation is over and above the material exchange of the gift itself.[154] Furthermore, there is nothing to indicate that the 'obligation' comes from within.

An additional example of how social facts structure individual acts can be found in the system of social separation that exists in all societies. In *The Elementary Forms of Religious Life*, Durkheim noted that all societies tend to make spatial separations according to certain categories, and that these divide themselves into regions corresponding to the religious separation of the world into sacred and profane spaces.[155] These spatial separations, he argued, operate like social facts to the extent that they divide the social world of things, persons and spaces into restricted zones or areas which have the power to restrict or limit contact between persons and things. Thus, for instance, in the space of food preparation, clean things are separated from things that are dirty or defiled, and things that are dirty or defiled are treated as objects to be separated from things that are clean. In the space where food is prepared, in addition, raw food is kept separate from cooked food according to the rules of hygiene and food preparation, and when an eating utensil falls from the table to the floor, it is separated from the space where the food is to be eaten.

In addition to the separation of things and persons are the rules that apply to the separation of spaces. For instance, in certain spaces in the household separation rules are observed between the bathroom and the kitchen in so far as they are often kept separate from one another. In such circumstances, separation rules have the power to fix by custom an external limit imposed on individuals to 'wash one's hands' before leaving the washroom for the kitchen or before entering other more controlled spaces or restricted zones, such as the space where food is prepared or eaten.[156] In addition to this,

---

152 Ibid.

153 Mauss states that 'the mechanism of obligation is thus resident in the gifts themselves.' See ibid., p. 21.

154 In a total social fact, said Mauss, 'the whole of society is involved, including all the institutions in which exchange is the concern of individuals.' See Ibid., p. 76.

155 Durkheim said that the system of separation in society 'separates all that is sacred from all that is profane.' See Durkheim, *The Elementary Forms*, p. 302.

156 Ibid., pp. 17–40.

other rules govern spatial separations which mark off certain spaces as inaccessible or off limits, and which take recourse to spatial markers such as barriers, closed doors or simple refusals of access to the public. Admittance to these areas may be subject to authorization or to some form of monitoring or surveillance by those who wish to restrict these spaces from access by unauthorized personnel. These are only some examples of the realm of social facts which govern our experience of society, and which illustrate the set of social restrictions and prohibitions that are imposed on us as a matter of social necessity.

The Characteristics of Social Facts and Their Observation

After having established that the objective reality of social facts is external to the individual and that social facts have the power to fix by custom an external limit imposed upon the individual, Durkheim turned his attention to outlining the characteristics of social facts themselves. Let us look at what he had to say about social facts:

> A social fact is every way of acting, fixed or not, capable of exercising on the individual an external constraint; or again, every way of acting which is general throughout a given society, while at the same time existing in its own right independent of its individual manifestations.[157]

and

> Thus apart from the individual acts to which they give rise, collective habits find expression in definite forms: legal rules, moral obligations, popular proverbs, social conventions, etc. As these forms have a permanent existence and do not change with the diverse application made of them, they constitute a fixed object, a constant standard within the observer's reach, exclusive of subjective impressions and purely personal observations.[158]

Three distinct characteristics of social facts stand out from others. First, they are 'general throughout society' and 'diffused within the group'; second, they are 'external to individuals,' exist independently of individual will and constitute the objective structure of society in the form of social rules and customary practices; and third, 'they exercise external constraint over individuals which is recognized by the power of external coercion, and by the existence of some sanction or by the resistance offered against individual efforts to violate them.'[159] This category of facts, said Durkheim, 'consists of all the ways of acting, thinking and feeling, external to the individual and are endowed with the power of coercion by reason of which they exert control.'[160] 'These ways of thinking,' Durkheim went on, 'should not be confused

---

157 *Rules*, p. 13.
158 *Rules*, p. 45.
159 *Rules*, pp. 2, 10, 13.
160 *Rules*, p. 3

with biological givens, and thus constitute a new subject matter to which the term 'social' ought to be applied.'[161] This can be illustrated if we take the activity of 'eating' as an example. While eating is a biological given, we can look at some of the ways in which 'eating' is structured by society, even though it satisfies elementary biological needs. For instance, when we look at the customary practices in different societies, we can see that while eating itself is not a social fact, the act of eating is structured like a social fact in several ways. For instance, in France the practice for consuming one's food during a meal is to cut the food with the knife in the right hand, and move the food to the mouth with the fork in the left hand. In North America, by contrast, the custom is to cut the food with the knife in the right hand, put the knife down on the plate, move the fork to the right hand and then move the food to the mouth.

While in North America the customary rule involves an extra step, both these social practices constitute 'social facts' developed over long periods of time in the sense that they act as customary rules which govern how individuals consume their food in different societies. In addition to this, each of the different social practices for consuming food employs the use of eating utensils as 'necessary constraints' within which eating as an individual act is structured externally by society. Since in this example social facts operate to regulate individual acts within a given social framework, it makes the existence of society and the role it plays in the structuring of acts more apparent.

After setting out the characteristics of social facts, Durkheim turned his attention to outlining the rules for the observation of social facts and put forward several general principles. The first of these is that social facts are to be considered as things.[162] To understand this somewhat controversial assertion, we have to remember that, for Durkheim, what separates the observation of social facts from the speculative doctrines of the past is the direct focus on 'social realities' as opposed to insubstantial 'ideas.' In stating that social facts are 'things,' Durkheim is asserting that, for purposes of observation, social facts are to be treated as if they were 'material things,' as opposed to simple 'ideas' which are not things. The crucial difference between 'ideas and things,' according to Durkheim, is that 'ideas have no reality' in themselves, whereas things have material existence and are subject to observation.[163] According to this view, therefore, to treat legal rules, customs and moral or religious regulations as material things having the power of external coercion means that they can be treated as objects or realities in the material sense of the term. In this way, Durkheim thought that they are subject to observation because they exist outside the individual. Second, Durkheim maintained that for social facts to be observed, they must be considered as distinct in themselves and separate from 'consciously formed impressions' in the mind.[164]

---

161 Ibid.
162 *Rules*, p. 14.
163 *Rules*, p. 23.
164 *Rules*, p. 28.

This requires that social facts be considered apart from any conscious or individual representations in the mind of the observer. In Durkheim's view, therefore, social facts are not synonymous with mental images or constructs, but are rather distinct things – rules, social practices, duties, obligations, customs and sanctions – which have a distinct existence in their own right, and as a result have a social rather than an individual nature. Third, social facts, according to Durkheim, must never be looked upon as if they are products of individual will, but rather should be looked upon as things external to the individual, having the capacity to structure social activity by means of external coercion which has the power to override personal and private considerations.[165] Fourth, Durkheim believed that social facts must be viewed as having independent existence. All social facts, he maintained, must be treated independently of individuals, and thus be considered as part of a system of rules and practices whose regularity and patterning exists independently of the mental states of individuals.[166]

In addition to looking for the origins of social facts, Durkheim wanted to outline what he thought were the distinct characteristics of the society being investigated. Durkheim discussed two distinct factual considerations in this case. First were the facts relating to the overall density and size of the population of the society and the complexity of its social and institutional structure. Second were the facts related to the proximity of individuals to each other and the extent and frequency of their interchanges, interactions and social relations. The term Durkheim used to describe this later characteristic was 'dynamic density.' In these circumstances, he used the term to denote the degree of the 'concentration of aggregates' or masses of the population and the conditions under which concentrations of individuals would lead to certain kinds of economic, social or political activity in society. Durkheim thought that measurement of the 'dynamic density' of a society would determine the degree of intensity of social life and the threshold of individual 'thought and action' in a society.[167] The concept of social milieu on the other hand, helps establish relations of causality among different types of social facts and prevents recourse to individual explanation.

Problems in Observing Social Facts

After defining the characteristics of social facts and outlining the rules for observing them, Durkheim turned his attention to the problems encountered in the observation of social facts. The importance of this discussion rests on one of the key aims of the *Rules* which is to establish the existence of social facts independent of abstract philosophical speculation. For this to be possible, the primary criterion of social facts is that they be treated as 'things' external to the individual existing within the framework of

---

165 *Rules*, p. 29.
166 *Rules*, p. 45.
167 *Rules*, pp. 113–14.

society. Durkheim, however, encountered a number of problems in achieving this aim. First, in claiming that external social duties and obligations are capable of exerting constraint and external coercion, Durkheim was unable to grasp these 'forces' conceptually or make their 'causal nature' subject to direct observation. Second, any causal connection between the coercive power of social facts and their effects on the conduct of individuals had to be assumed rather than observed directly. In this light, the causal capacity inherent in social facts to bring about certain effects and to exercise the power of coercion, had to be inferred simply as implicit forces inherent in the social framework. This meant that the coercive power of social facts to bring about effects in individuals was only 'indirectly' expressed in the various duties, customs, social rules and legal regulations of society.[168]

Collective Representations

After discussing the nature of social facts and the methods for observing them, Durkheim turned his attention to a discussion of facts which he thought were socially given, and the general name he gave to this group of social practices he calls 'collective representations.'[169] Simply stated, collective representations may be defined as any social subject matter into which the customary structure of society has been condensed so that they come to 'represent' the sum total of collective practices of society. Examples of collective representations into which social subject matter is concentrated are religious doctrines, legal rules, statutory regulations, social rules, obligations, and customary arrangements that have existed for long periods of time. Durkheim maintained that collective representations reflect social subject matter in four distinct ways. First, they reflect a reality different from that of the individual, in that they are imposed externally by the objective structure of society. Second, they have characteristics of their own which take the form of general rules or prohibitions that are external to the individual and thus constitute the objective structure of society. Third, they can be observed in their own right without being brought under psychological or biological laws; and fourth, they arise from group life and are part of the structural framework of society. What collective representations convey, according to Durkheim, is the sum total of collective social rules and practices related to the 'way the group conceives of itself.'[170]

In addition to these characteristics, collective representations are distinguished by the fact that they exercise a coercive power over the individual which originates from the authority of the collective social rules and obligatory ways of acting, rather than from individual or personal disposition. These rules, said Durkheim, impose habitual ways of acting that have been 'consecrated by the authority of the group' and carry with them the 'prestige with which these representations are invested.'[171] He pointed out that 'they

---

168 *Rules,* p. 45.
169 *Rules*, pp. xli–lviii.
170 *Rules,* p. xlix
171 Durkheim, *The Division of labor*, p. 4.

dominate us and impose rules and practices upon us, and these practices act on us from without.'[172] Fundamentally, the essential characteristic of 'collective representations' is their ability to exercise social constraint and this, Durkheim reasoned, marks the reality of collective ways of thinking and acting which cannot be avoided.

Social Morphology and the Classification of Social Types

After having discussed the nature of social facts, Durkheim turned his attention to describing societies by the nature and type of their organization. In this case, he was concerned with setting out the study of the material 'structure' of society and its institutions as a valid subject matter of the sociological description. He began by stating that if there were only individuals, as the psychologists believed, then societies would be nothing more than the sum total of their population. Under these circumstances, there would be nothing to observe since social life would be reduced to the interaction of individuals. If, on the other hand, societies were made up of a complex of structures and distinct social institutions that existed outside the individual, then we should set out to enumerate all the characteristics of these different social fields by showing how they constituted themselves in the form of the economy, the political structure, the family system, the field of religion and law. If we are to study society, said Durkheim, a criterion must be found which extends beyond the individual to the distinct objective characteristics of societies.[173]

The very first thing we should look for, he said, is what he calls the 'social elements' of these societies. Using the concept of 'elements,' Durkheim put forward the idea that societies are organized in relation to a series of social elements in two basic ways. First, by the nature and number of institutional elements which are to be found in societies; and second, by the extent to which the elements form combinations leading to more complex elements and structures. The name Durkheim gave to the study of these elements is 'social morphology.'[174] Simply stated, social morphology is a term Durkheim used to refer to the study of the form and structure of societies and how these structures may be classified according to their various social and institutional attributes. Durkheim believed that social morphology was the first principle of social classification since, in the main, it conceived of society as a composite of institutional elements as opposed to a simple composite of individuals in the population. In order to completely understand what Durkheim means by social morphology, we must look a little more closely.

There are, according to Durkheim, two broad morphological classifications. First, there are societies whose organization is simple due to the arrangement of a limited number of institutional elements. These societies have few institutions and the relationship

---

172 *Rules*, p. lv.
173 *Rules*, pp. 79–80.
174 *Rules*, p. 81.

between them often leads to an uncomplicated simple form of social structure. Second, there are societies whose organization is complex in that the institutional elements are more numerous. These societies, he pointed out, have multiple sets of institutional elements which form more complex structures leading to a more complex social life. Durkheim maintained that the procedures for classifying societies should begin with the step of understanding the morphology of simple societies. Once this has been accomplished, observers can examine the principle of internal change taking place in the elements of these societies and the conditions leading to the point at which they become more complex. In beginning with simple societies and progressing to complex ones, said Durkheim, we are able to understand the principle of morphological change.

To begin developing this system of classification, Durkheim looked at the characteristics of simple societies. These have two basic structural attributes: first, they form a whole whose institutional elements are in general not interdependent in terms of social functions, and second, societies of this type have no regulating center, according to Durkheim. The first example of a society of this type, Durkheim suggested, is a society he called a 'horde.'[175] A 'horde' is the most elementary social form and is characterized by the fact that it 'contains a single segment.'[176] What riveted Durkheim's attention to the organization of the horde is the fact that there are no special groups within its structure, unlike other simple societies.' The horde, he said, is a social aggregate that does not include any other more elementary aggregate or group but is directly composed of individuals.'[177] From this, he pointed out, we can conclude that the 'horde' is the most basic social form, the simplest of societies and the sociological correlate of the biological world of protoplasm.[178] The next morphological type referred to by Durkheim is a social structure he calls a 'clan.' Clans may be formed by the combination of various hordes or groups whose union forms a more complex group structure. In contrast to the horde, clans are aggregates which have formed segments, and while Durkheim thought these societies were once hordes morphologically, their parts have re-organized and consequently their morphology has changed.

Another type of classification of the structure of society Durkheim referred to is 'polysegmentals.' These societies are made up of the combination of many groups which form a total social structure. An example of this type would include the Iroquois nation, whose social structure is formed around aggregates of confederated groups which form a common tribe. Structures of this kind are synonymous with the early organization of tribes whose institutional structure later gave rise to the Roman city state.[179] After these came polysegmental societies, which are doubly

---

175 *Rules*, pp. 82–3.
176 *Rules*, p. 82.
177 *Rules*, p. 83.
178 Ibid.
179 *Rules*, p. 84.

compounded, according to Durkheim. These social groups are the outcome of the juxtaposition of polysegmented societies such as the city states of Greece and aggregated tribes.

Durkheim's Study of Suicide

Historical Background and Central Thesis

I now want to turn my attention to Durkheim's study of suicide, and in order to begin I think it is worthwhile to look at the history of Durkheim's interest in the problem. Essentially, Durkheim first began to study the problem of suicide in 1888 while he was working on an article related to suicide and the birth rate.[180] After completing this work, Durkheim gave a series of public lectures on the topic between 1889 and 1890. Seven years later, in 1897, he published his formal study entitled *Suicide*, and this constituted his third major sociological work.

In broad historical terms, there are several reasons why Durkheim took up the theme of suicide when he did. First, suicide was a growing social problem in Europe by 1850 and many felt that it was associated with the development of industrial society. Industrialization had advanced individualism, accelerated social fragmentation, and weakened the social bonds tying individuals to society. Second, industrial society had made economic institutions dominant over other social institutions and this served to place individual self-interest and economic gain over the collective forces of society. As individual autonomy and political freedoms increased, the individual became the center of social life and this served to reduce the level of social restraint and to call into question the nature of collective social purposes. Third, the political crisis of the Dreyfus affair in 1894 was a serious blow to French national unity and drew attention to how much social fragmentation and egoistic forces had replaced the collective authority of society. This led Durkheim to believe that the theme of social dissolution brought about by industrial society could be examined sociologically by looking at the mechanisms in society which link individuals to social purposes outside themselves. Fourth, factual evidence made available by comparative mortality data from different societies linked suicide to social factors such as industrial change, occupation, family life and religion, and this served to focus attention on society and social institutions rather than on complex psychological factors. Durkheim found that the statistical data contained in the records of suicidal deaths for the period could be categorized according to age, religion, sex, occupation, military service and marital status, and this led directly to a search for the role played by social factors in the cause of suicide. Overall, Durkheim studied the records of 26,000 suicides, and his colleague, Marcel Mauss,

---

180 Durkheim, 'Suicide and the Birth Rate,' in D. Lester (ed), *Emile Durkheim Le Suicide: One Hundred Years Later*, Philadelphia: Charles Press, [1888] 1994, pp. 115–132.

helped assemble the maps contained in the study and aided in compiling the statistical tables on suicidal deaths relating to age and marital status.[181]

The Shift From a Psychological to a Social Theory of Suicide

One of the primary aims Durkheim had in pursuing a social theory of suicide was to look for the social causes of suicide within the existing framework of society rather than looking at the psychological states of individuals who take their own lives. This shift in perspective from a psychological to a sociological theory of suicide was disconcerting for many, and perhaps the best way to understand this shift is to look at the problem of suicide prior to Durkheim's work. At the time Durkheim began his study, suicide was largely treated as a nervous disorder and its causes were believed to derive from the psychological states of individuals. Many believed that suicide was the result of mental illness, depression, sudden tragedy, reversal of fortune and even personal setbacks and bankruptcy. In this light, suicide was seen by many as the result of a weak disposition and a psychological response to the burdens of life. Durkheim, however, called these views into question by shifting the focus from individual motives and psychological states to social causes in at least two distinct ways. First, by stating that the social causes of suicide precede individual causes, Durkheim eliminated the need to look at the various forms suicide assumed in individuals, including depression, personal setbacks, and psychiatric disorders. Second, in focusing his attention on the various social environments to which the individual was connected, including the family group, the religious group and the national group, Durkheim eliminated the necessity of looking at individual disposition or personality. He put this clearly when he pointed out that 'the causes of death are outside rather than within us, and are effective only if we venture into their sphere of activity.'[182] The suggested shift from a psychological to a social theory of suicide was stated by Durkheim in the following way:

> When suicide is considered as an individual action affecting the individual only, it must seemingly depend exclusively on individual factors, thus belonging to psychology alone. Is not the suicide's resolve explained by his temperament, character, antecedents and private history? If, instead of seeing in them separate occurrences, unrelated and to be separately studied, the suicides are taken as a whole, it appears that this total is not simply a sum of independent units, but is a new fact *sui generis,* with its own unity and consequently its own nature – a nature, furthermore, more dominantly social.[183]

After shifting the focus from a psychological to a social theory of suicide, Durkheim began to look for the causes of suicide within the social framework of society. In order to do this, he focused on the social attachment existing between

---

181 Durkheim, *Suicide: A Sociological Study*, New York: The Free Press, 1951, p. 39; Anthony A. Giddens, 'A Typology of Suicide,' *European Journal of Sociology,* 7, 1966, 276–295.

182 *Suicide*, p. 43.

183 *Suicide*, p. 46.

individuals and the wider society and the extent to which these attachments formed a system of social relations which serve to link individuals to social groups outside themselves. These attachments, he thought, not only serve to promote social activity outside the individual, but also they prevent social withdrawal to the individual ego and, overall, serve the purposes of situating individuals within in a system of social links and bonds. Durkheim took the view that social activity not only links individuals to groups outside themselves, but it serves the central social purposes of propelling individuals out into the wider society and he thought that when this process takes place it encourages social forms of attachment to three distinct social groups that include the religious group, the family group, and the national political group.[184]

Having outlined Durkheim's intention to look for the social causes of suicide, we can state the central thesis of Durkheim's study in the following way. People take their own lives not because of the psychological states of depression or mental illness, but rather because of the social forces acting on them which reduces their attachments to the wider society to the point that they become isolated, separate and autonomous from others. Durkheim thought that so much does the process of separation take place in industrial society that individual social attachments shrink down to the private ego, promoting excessive preoccupation with the self and constant and excessive self reflection. Durkheim then argued that if social activity serves to propel individuals out into the wider society by attaching them to the religious group, the family group, and the national group, then we should be able to:

> [D]etermine the productive causes of suicide directly, without concerning ourselves with the forms they can assume in individuals. Disregarding individuals as such, their motives and their ideas, we shall seek directly the states of the various social environments – religious confession, family, political society, occupational groups, etc. – in terms of which the variations of suicide occur.[185]

Opposition to Durkheim's Argument and the 'Corridor Incident'

By 1897, after Durkheim's study was published there were many in Europe and America who believed that suicide was a psychiatric disorder and, as a result, many were critical of Durkheim's assertion that suicide had social causes existing outside the individual. As the criticism mounted, several disagreements emerged[186] For one thing, Durkheim's theory of suicide was viewed as controversial because it overlooked the individual and focused outside the existing psychological framework within which suicide was understood. Second, in Europe and America there was a more formal turn to the study of

---

184 See Durkheim's discussion of how these social groups elicit different social forms of attachment begins in chapter 2 of *Suicide*, p. 152.

185 Ibid., p. 151.

186 For a discussion of the series of negative reviews Durkheim received just after the publication of *Suicide in* 1897 see Philippe Besnard, 'The Fortunes of Durkheim's Suicide: Reception and Legacy,' in W.S.F Pickering, and G. Walford (eds.), Durkheim's Suicide: A Century of Research and Debate, London: Routledge, 2000, pp. 97–125.

the individual factors of suicide which led to the ultimate rejection of theories that departed from an analysis of individual causes. Third, in America the stress on a psychological approach to suicide meant that the individual was the central subject of investigation, and as a result many believed that social factors had nothing to do with suicide. Fourth, at the University of Chicago during the 1890s, the social sciences were centered on an approach to suicide that focused on the individual and, accordingly, many tended to treat the search for social causes as unacceptable, and in some cases even absurd.[187] Since many thought that the concept of society was irrelevant to a theory of suicide, statements about the role society played in the cause of suicide began to disappear at Chicago and, as Philippe Besnard points out, even though Chicago was a center for the social sciences in America, they 'did not even mention Durkheim's suicide' in their review of sociological work.'[188]

In France, in addition to America, there were a series of critical attacks focusing on Durkheim's suggestion that the causes of suicide existed outside the individual. Since suicide was already the subject of intense debate at the time, and since the controversy concerning the causes of suicide began to focus on individual determinants, a contemporary of Durkheim's by the name of Gabriel Tarde began to call the validity of Durkheim's assertions into question. Tarde had argued that suicide was the result of a type of psychological contagion and that suicide proliferated in a medium he referred to as psychological imitation.[189] While there were several cases in the medical records that supported this view, one case in particular, known as the 'corridor incident' seemed to support Tarde's theory of psychological imitation. The case involved fifteen individuals who hung themselves in succession using the same hook in a dark passage in a hospital corridor.[190] However, as soon as the hook was removed from the corridor, the epidemic of suicides stopped. In light of the corridor incident, Tarde theorized that suicide appeared to be the result of psychological contagion transmitted from one individual to another, and though Durkheim had dealt with the corridor incident in chapter two of *Suicide*, many felt that the case supported Tarde's imitation theory. This led to a search for the biological basis of contagion and an imitation theory of suicide.[191]

---

187 For more on the American reception of Durkheim's work at Chicago and at Harvard see Ken Morrison, 'The Disavowal of the Social in the American Reception of Durkheim,' *Journal of Classical Sociology*, 1 (1), 2001, 95–126. For more recent discussion see Ken Morrison, review of J. Alexander & P. Smith (eds) *The Cambridge Companion to Durkheim, The Canadian Journal of Sociology*, www.cjsonline.ca/reviews, March 2006.

188 See Besnard, 'The Fortunes of Durkheim's Suicide,' p. 120. Besnard states that there was virtually 'no echo of Durkheim at Chicago.'

189 For how Tarde's nineteenth century theory of imitation was constructed around a series of statements about social behavior and contagion, see Gabriel de Tarde, *The laws of Imitation*. 2nd Ed., Gloucester, Mass.: Peter Smith, [1895] 1962.

190 Durkheim, *Suicide*, p. 97.

191 Criticism of Durkheim's study took a dramatic turn in 1897 when *Suicide* was reviewed by Gustavo Tosti in the *American Journal of Sociology*. Drawing on the authority of Tarde's argument, Tosti asserted that the 'social causes of suicide discovered by Durkheim appear to be nothing if not connected to the individual factor of nervous degeneration on the one hand and, on the other, with the general fact of the transmission of thought through imitative instinct which is at the very basis of suicide as shown by Tarde.' See Gustavo Tosti, 'Suicide in the Light of Recent Studies,' *American Journal of Sociology*, Vol. 3, 464–478, 1897.

The Concept of the Social Suicide Rate

In contrast to Tarde, who focused on the individual, Durkheim turned his attention to looking at what he thought were the social causes of suicide that existed outside the individual. To this extent, no complete understanding of Durkheim's assertion that suicide had social causes is possible without looking at the concept of the 'social suicide rate.' Durkheim arrived at the concept of the social suicide rate after a careful examination of the mortality data which had been obtained from public records of societies such as France, Germany, England, Denmark and Austria. These records contained information about cause of death, age, marital background, religion and the total number of deaths by suicide of the country from which they were gathered. The 'social suicide rate,' therefore, was a term used by Durkheim to refer to the number of suicidal deaths in a given society and the extent to which the 'suicide rates' themselves could be looked upon as establishing a pattern of suicide for a given society. But, what does this mean in relation to individual suicide? As we stated earlier, theories of suicide prevalent at the time had looked at individual motives and psychological causes. Suicide, many believed, was the desperate act of an individual who did not care to live or who could not face life's burdens. From this perspective, suicide was seen as an individual act dependent on factors which could only be explained psychologically.

Durkheim, however, took a completely different approach. Rather than looking at individual motives or psychological states, he began by looking at the 'social suicide rate' that existed in different countries. What he wanted to find out was whether individual suicides committed in a given society could be taken together as a whole and studied collectively. Durkheim's central question then was can the collective rates for a given society be studied independently of individual suicide? In order, therefore, to establish a theoretical footing, Durkheim began to look at the total number of suicidal deaths contained in public records of countries such as France, Germany, England and Denmark. The suicide rates for these countries had been collected between 1841 and 1872, and they contained a substantial amount of information related to social factors of suicide such as marital status, religion, occupation and military service.

After studying the rates, Durkheim made several key observations. First, he noticed that the rates varied from society to society. For example, they were higher in Germany in comparison with Italy; lower in Denmark in comparison to England and so on. Second, he observed that between 1841 and 1872, the number of suicidal deaths in each of the countries did not change dramatically and were considered to be stable. For example, between 1841–42 the number of suicidal deaths in France were 2814 and 2866 respectively; whereas in Germany for the same years they were 1630 and 1598.[192] As far as Durkheim was concerned, the stability of the rates within a given society was crucial since it meant that each society not only produced a

---

192 *Suicide*, p. 47.

'quota of suicidal deaths,' but that certain social forces were operating to produce what Durkheim saw as the 'yearly precision of rates.'[193] This turned out to be decisive because when considered collectively, the rates pointed in the direction of underlying social causes. This led Durkheim to reason that the predisposing cause of suicide lay not within the psychological motives of the individual but within the social framework of society. Third, the observed stability of the rates meant that each society was a distinct social environment with different social characteristics, different religions, different patterns of family life, different military obligations and thus different suicide characteristics. Under these circumstances, each produced rates of suicidal deaths distinct from the other. Fourth, when compared to the mortality rate, Durkheim noticed that the suicide rate demonstrated a far greater consistency than did the general mortality rate, which fluctuated randomly.

As a result, Durkheim drew three fundamental conclusions which turned on the question of the stability of the rates. First, he believed that the stability of the rates showed that, while individual motives for suicide vary from case to case, the regularity exhibited by the social suicide rate was consistently stable. Second, though the rates varied between societies, the stability of the rates within a particular society meant that each society produces a 'quota of suicidal deaths.'[194] Third, Durkheim took the position that the social suicide rate must represent a 'factual order' that is separate from individual disposition and, therefore, he thought it had a regularity which could be studied in its own right.[195] In that the 'social suicide rate' is independent of individual suicide and has a stability of its own, it should therefore be the subject of a special study whose purpose would be to discover the social causes leading to a definite number of people that take their own lives in a given society.

Durkheim believed that the social suicide rate was the clearest evidence he had for a social theory of suicide since what a study of the social suicide rate had established was that different societies had different suicide rates, and that these rates changed very little over time within any given society. For example, between 1841 and 1842 France had 2866 suicides while Germany had 1598 suicides. He went on to reason that if suicide were entirely the result of individual causes and individual psychology, it would be difficult to explain why the French would be almost twice as likely to commit suicide in comparison with the Germans. Durkheim then reasoned that once we shift the focus from the study of individual suicides to the study of the 'collective suicide rate' – France's suicide rate in relation to Germany's suicide rate – it became apparent that the collective rates pointed in the direction of underlying social causes, which in turn indicated fundamental differences in the social framework that caused France to have 2866 suicides each year, while Germany had only 1598.

---

193 *Suicide*, p. 51.

194 Ibid.

195 Ibid. Durkheim says 'the suicide rate is therefore a factual order, unified and definite as is shown by both its permanence and its variability.' The question, then, is can it be studied in its own right?

Taking the social suicide rate into consideration, the difference between the psychological and sociological study of suicide lies in the focus on the social suicide rate. This is in direct contrast with the 'psychologist' who, according to Durkheim, 'looks at individual cases isolated from one another and establishes that the victim is either nervous, bankrupt, or alcoholic.' Then, said Durkheim, the psychologist explains suicide by reference to one or another psychological states finding, thereby, a motive. But this motive does not cause people to kill themselves in each society in a definite period of time, and thus the productive causes of this phenomenon naturally escape the observer of individuals. To discover it, one must raise their point of view above the individual suicide and perceive what gives them unity.' [196]

Suicide and the Concept of Social Integration

One of the central concepts used by Durkheim in the study of suicide is social integration. Though he does not explicitly define the term, it plays a central role in the study of suicide and is therefore key to understanding the connection between individual suicide and society. Initially, Durkheim had used the term social integration in *The Division of Labor* to stress the nature of social links which attach individuals to social groups outside themselves.[197] In this sense, social integration can be defined as the extent to which individuals are linked to and feel allegiance for social groups to which they are attached. From this definition of social integration, it is clear that Durkheim believed that individuals do not exist by themselves autonomously and are therefore not separate from society.[198]

Durkheim went on to maintain that social integration serves several key functions. First, it creates social duties which operate to connect individuals to society by ensuring a high degree of social attachment to commonly held beliefs and collective purposes that act to focus individual interests outside the self and promote social bonds between individuals, institutions and groups. This, Durkheim thought, tends to reduce self-preoccupation, excessive self-reflection and withdrawal to the self. Second, social integration creates links of dependency and ties of social obligation. This performs connective functions because it propels individuals outside themselves and out into the wider society by creating links to social institutions and larger social groups and by promoting the perception that they are part of a collective whole. In turn, this tends to link them to common social purposes which give their life meaning by promoting the idea that they are part of a larger social group. Third, social integration serves as a check against excessive social isolation and individualism by imposing limits on how far individuals can withdraw into themselves. It therefore acts as a check against individualism by imposing restraints on internal needs and wants and by focusing interests outside the self. It does this by imposing social duties and

---

196 *Suicide*, p. 323–24.
197 Only a general discussion of social integration can be found in Durkheim's *Suicide*. See pp. 208–216.
198 *Suicide*, pp. 208–9.

obligations which propel individuals out into the wider society where they perform specific social roles within family, work and schooling institutions. This increases their degree of social linkage to groups outside themselves, promotes attachment to social things, and discourages personal isolation and social withdrawal. Durkheim went on to state that the three central groups in society possessing the quality of social integration are the religious group, the family group, and the political or national group to which a population belongs.[199]

In order to show how Durkheim justified the theoretical shift he took in looking for the causes of suicide in the social framework, it will be useful to look briefly at the steps he took in getting beyond the individual as the single solitary subject of suicide. In focusing on a theory of social integration, Durkheim's essential aim was to extend the investigative focus beyond the individual by looking at three distinct points of attachment related to the individual's connection to society. First, was the point of attachment existing between the individual and the social framework, which extended the focus from individual suicides to the objective structures of society. This showed that the causes of suicide lay not within the psychological motives of individuals alone, but within distinct social environments with different religions, different patterns of family life, different military obligations and thus different forms of attachment, and distinctly different suicide rates. Second was the point of attachment Durkheim established between a given population and the social suicide rate of a given society. This extended the focus from individual suicides to the collective suicide rate which varied from society to society, illustrating that each society produces a 'quota of suicidal deaths.' Along this axis, Durkheim was able to separate the social suicide rate from individual suicides, showing that, if suicide were entirely the result of individual psychology, it would be difficult to explain why the French were almost twice as likely to take their own lives as the Germans. Third was the point of attachment Durkheim established between what he called the integrative functions of society and the religious, political and family groups that existed outside the individual. He found that the integrative mechanisms attaching individuals to groups outside themselves reduced gaps between the individual and their attachments to the wider society. This extended the focus beyond the isolated individual who was thought to live separately from society, to the mechanisms of social integration which attached individuals to society at various points of social and institutional contact. This showed that the various points of attachment to religious and family institutions minimized the rise of egoistic suicide in industrial society where individuals tended to retreat to themselves and turn inward. The argument by Durkheim that individuals were attached to the wider society by mechanisms of social integration, meant that he was able to show that the 'gaps' which had formed in the integrative links in industrial society were the result of declining social and integrative functions. While the breakdown of these attachments served to make the individual more autonomous and separate, he thought that the

---

199 *Suicide*, p. 209.

social cohesion of these institutions served as a system of restraint on the development of individual egoism and on egoistic suicide. When this 'integration is weakened,' said Durkheim, 'individuals are less drawn together, and as a result spaces emerge between them where the cold winds of egoism blow.'[200]

It was Durkheim's argument that gaps in social integration only begin to appear in industrial societies when integrative functions decline. As a result, individuals withdraw to the private ego, neglect their social obligations and retreat to themselves and to their private life. This, he argued, not only led to the breakdown of the integrative mechanisms in society, but it also led to the appearance of different 'social forms' of suicide – egoistic in comparison with altruistic – and he thought this indicated the extent of the retreat that had taken place in the individual from the pre-existing attachments to the wider society to the private ego. In shifting the focus from individual suicide to what he called the 'social types of suicide,' Durkheim was able to conceptualize the existence of the social framework outside the individual and the role it played in the cause of suicide, and it is to this that we now turn.

Suicide and the Integrative Pole: Egoistic and Altruistic Suicide

Durkheim's theory of suicide is divided into two explanatory sections. In the first, Durkheim explains suicide by drawing on the concept of social integration, referring to the strength of the social bonds existing between the individual and society. In this case, egoistic and altruistic suicide form opposite poles of social integration. In the second part of the theory, Durkheim explained suicide by drawing on the concept of social regulation. Social regulation, in contrast to integration, refers to the restraints imposed by society on individual needs and wants and generally manifests itself through regulatory requirements that are imposed by society on individuals when their social needs and wants begin to exceed the means they have for attaining them. In the case of social regulation, anomic and fatalistic suicide form opposite poles in relation to the changes in the regulatory functions of industrial society that may lead to shifts in the suicide rate.

Durkheim began with the integrative pole and egoistic suicide. The term 'egoism' originates from the nineteenth century and was widely used by Durkheim and others to indicate the breakdown of social ties that came with the development of industrial society and the pursuit of private interest. Egoism can best be described as the process by which individuals detach themselves from the wider society by turning their activity inward and by retreating into themselves.[201] Egoism is characterized by excessive self-reflection on personal matters and a withdrawal from the outside world. In this state, said Durkheim, the 'springs of action' are relaxed and individuals

---

200 Durkheim, 'Suicide and the Birth Rate,' in Lester, David (ed.), *Emile Durkheim Le Suicide: One Hundred Years Later*, p. 132.
201 *Suicide*, p. 279.

turn inward toward themselves and away from society.[202] Egoism occurs, said Durkheim, when the ties binding 'the individual to others become slackened and are not sufficiently integrated at the points where the individual is in contact with the wider society.' Egoism therefore results from too much individualism and from the 'weakening of the social fabric.'[203] When the social bonds have broken down, individual ends are more important than the common ends of society and the individual's personality dominates over the collective personality. In such circumstances, 'the individual ego asserts itself in the face of the social ego and at its expense.'[204] In this context, egoism constitutes a threat to society because it undermines collective attachments, poses a danger to continued social maintenance and leads to gaps between individuals and the collective structure of society.

Religious Integration and Egoistic Suicide   The first point at which the individual is in contact with society is the religious group. Religion, said Durkheim, serves the function of social integration by linking individuals to persons and things outside themselves. Specifically, it integrates individuals into the different spheres of social life by placing restrictions on individual autonomy and self reflection, and by promoting bonds between the community, the church and the spiritual world. Taking religious integration into account, one of the first things Durkheim discovered in the social suicide rates was that Protestant countries had higher numbers of suicidal deaths than Roman Catholic countries. In fact, the statistical data showed that the social suicide rates were dramatically higher in Protestant countries, with the difference between Protestant and Catholic suicides varying from a minimum of 20 to 30 percent and a maximum of 300 percent.[205] Durkheim's question, then, was what social factors would lead to such differences? Durkheim noted that both religions condemn suicide with equal intensity and that each attaches religious sanctions prohibiting it. Still, Protestants kill themselves more frequently than Catholics, by as much as 300 percent in some countries. Durkheim reasoned that the most significant difference between Protestantism and Catholicism was the structure of their religious doctrine and teaching, and therefore the only way to explain the differences in suicide rates was to examine the differences that existed in the integrative hold which the doctrines had over their lives.[206]

To begin with, Durkheim observed that Protestantism and Catholicism differ fundamentally in the degree of authority that religious beliefs have over the individual. Catholics, for instance, tend to accept religious demands more readily than do Protestants. They rarely question religious doctrine and never openly criticize the demands which religious beliefs impose upon them. Similarly, in Catholic teaching, customs are fixed and unchanging and this places expectations on individuals which

---

202 Ibid.
203 *Suicide*, pp. 279–281.
204 Ibid.
205 *Suicide*, pp. 154–55.
206 *Suicide*, p. 153.

link them more closely to the church where they are more accepting of Catholic doctrine. Moreover, among Catholics, the system of traditional sacraments such as baptism, confession and communion play an important role in religious life and tend to increase the social integration which Catholics have to the church. This acts to create strong emotional bonds and attachments and it draws Catholics together so that the social spaces between them and the church remain intact. Catholics, therefore, accept their doctrine without question or criticism.

With Protestants, the situation is completely different. For one thing, Protestants encourage change and innovation at all levels of religious life and adopt a critical attitude toward formal doctrine. The freedom Protestants have to criticize their religious beliefs, according to Durkheim, is unprecedented and results in a breakdown of the social mechanism attaching individuals to the religious group and encourages social and religious withdrawal. Under such circumstances, Protestant doctrine differs from Catholic teaching in several respects. First, Protestants are free to supervise their own religious observances and have greater freedom in interpreting beliefs. Since this makes them responsible for maintaining their own faith, they have become immune to the influences which the doctrine exerts over their lives. This reduced their attachments to religious society and made them responsible for maintaining their own faith and their own integrative links to the church. Second, Protestants claim the right to critically evaluate religious doctrine and this led to an increase in self reflection and self consciousness. The greater the self reflection, the greater was the withdrawal from the religious community. Third, Protestants more than Catholics assert their autonomy from the hold that religious beliefs have over their lives, making it more difficult for the believer to accept the world as it is. Fourth, Protestants more than Catholics disrupt the pattern of routine which forms around religious beliefs and rituals and this makes their activity less subject to the constraints which religion imposes upon their lives and tends to undermine religious discipline.[207]

What stands out about Protestant teaching and religious doctrine is the degree of religious autonomy and individualism it creates in contrast to other religions. As this autonomy increases, individuals withdraw from religious society and reject the demands that religious beliefs impose upon their lives. In this case, the most important characteristic of Protestant doctrine is the development of what Durkheim called 'free inquiry.' This, he asserted, leads to the acceptance of a critical attitude toward religious beliefs and goes to the heart of Protestant religious teaching.[208] Essentially, the term 'free inquiry' was used by Durkheim to refer to the proclivity of Protestants to 'overthrow traditional beliefs' and to critically evaluate religious dogma by making it subject to criticism and reflection.[209] As religious beliefs are subject to critical scrutiny, said Durkheim, they lose their authority over the individual and the less binding is religious dogma on matters of faith. 'Free inquiry,' can therefore be

---

207 *Suicide*, pp. 158–59.
208 *Suicide*, p. 159.
209 Ibid.

defined as the overthrow of traditional beliefs inherent in religious doctrine and the disappearance of the emotional hold which the beliefs exert on the individual.[210] In comparison with Catholics who traditionally accept their doctrine on faith, Protestants developed 'free inquiry,' and this erodes the social integration they have to religious society, leading to a breakdown of the beliefs which ruled over their lives. This critical attitude, according to Durkheim, undermines religious integration and leads to religious individualism and a higher rate of suicide among Protestants in contrast to Catholics. But, if this is true, what is the connection between the breakdown of religious integration and suicide?

One of the central functions of religion is to create social integration by linking individuals to persons and things outside themselves and by creating a bond between the community of believers, the church and the spiritual world. To this extent, religion serves the function of integrating individuals among themselves by helping them accept life as it is. This social integration develops by linking individuals to a common doctrine whose bonds are as strong as the doctrine is strong. The stronger the system of beliefs, the greater is the bond between the individual and the religious community. When these bonds begin to erode, however, the less cohesive and unified is the religious group. As a result, the traditional practices lose their ability to maintain discipline and the emotional hold which the beliefs exert over the individual becomes weak. As faith in traditional practices is withdrawn from external doctrine, self reflection becomes more pronounced and individuals are obliged to supervise their own religious activity and thus withdraw to themselves.[211] This withdrawal to self-supervision accelerates egoism and the withdrawal from everything external. As soon as 'gaps' form between the integrative links of the doctrine and the individual believer, the greater is the retreat from religious society to the private ego.

As religious life becomes more dependent on self-definition and plays less of a role in the activity of the individual, the bonds connecting the individual to things that are greater than themselves become fewer and fewer, and the individual's attachment to the community of believers diminishes. This process of withdrawal from all externalities and from church institutions is evident in the Protestants' abandonment of religious confession. In that confession serves the function of drawing the individual into the center of religious life by creating a link between private thought and public faith, it places a claim on the individual to practice greater morality and, therefore, greater faith. But as Protestants become more individualized, confession was gradually replaced by self-reflection, encouraging more freedom from dogma and more freedom from religious authority. The same was true for religious ritual. Protestants reduce to a minimum the role ritual plays in religious life, thereby minimizing the obligation which ritual exerts over the individual.[212] This opens up a gap between the individual and the system

---

210 *Suicide*, p. 158.
211 *Suicide*, pp. 160–61.
212 *Suicide*, pp. 158–159.

of attachments which draw individuals together and which helped them deal with the difficulties of life, leading ultimately to a withdrawal to the private ego.

Where Protestants embrace change and encourage freedom in religious thinking, Catholics remain bound to traditional beliefs and reject change as unacceptable. The overthrow by Protestants of traditional beliefs is significant in two related respects. First, Protestantism loosened the tie linking the believer to religious doctrine by encouraging a critical attitude toward beliefs. Second, as free inquiry is substituted for doctrine, it increases individual autonomy by reducing the hold which the doctrine has over their lives. As soon as religious beliefs were called into question, individuals became more reliant on their own judgment and this served to break the bonds which religious beliefs create.[213] When beliefs 'have lost their hold' over the individual and when tradition has lost its ability to set boundaries and define the harsh realities of daily life, the more individuals turn inward and the more they become egoistic. As a consequence, they tend to bolster their own autonomy and privacy and this leads to greater self sufficiency, egoism and self reliance.[214]

As free inquiry reduces religious integration and increases egoism it brings about a loss of religious discipline. This, in turn, creates what Durkheim referred to as a reduction in the 'general immunity' from suicide which religious integration conferred. This immunity, he believed, is evident in the case of Catholic suicide rates which are significantly lower because the integrative bonds linking the individual to religious teaching are greater.

To support the contention that there is a relation between free inquiry and egoistic suicide, Durkheim looked at the suicide rate among other religious groups. For example, he pointed out that the suicide rate among Jews is low despite the fact that learning and free inquiry play a key role in Jewish life. In fact, Jewish religious life is associated with an intense focus on learning and in some cases even a critical attitude towards religion. Yet, the suicide rates for Jews are lower than for Protestants. What accounts for this difference, according to Durkheim, is the degree of religious solidarity and social integration. Jewish religious beliefs exert a strong hold over the individual and regulate every aspect of daily life, in some cases to an extreme degree. The social cohesion within the religious community is so well developed that integration between the individual and religious society is always high. In addition, religious solidarity among Jews is greater due to the intolerance shown toward Jews by the outside community.[215]

To provide further evidence showing that free inquiry breaks down religious integration and leads to egoistic suicide, Durkheim compared Protestant suicide rates in Germany with other Protestant countries such as England. He pointed out that suicide in Protestant localities in England is less developed, even though the English actually encourage individual autonomy and free inquiry.[216] Durkheim explained the

---

213 *Suicide*, p. 159.
214 *Suicide*, pp. 159, 162.
215 *Suicide*, p. 160
216 *Suicide*, pp. 160–1.

contradiction between Protestants in Europe and Protestants in England by noting that, in the case of England, the loss of integration brought about by the increase of religious autonomy is offset by the fact that many religious obligations have become instituted into secular law. In England, said Durkheim, a number of obligatory beliefs and religious practices have been legislated into civil law and thus have become part of everyday life.[217] This affects religious individualism in two distinct ways. First, it restricts daily activity and compels religious observance through secular vehicles which act to cut down on the autonomy created by religious individualism. Second, because England has a greater number of clergy in relation to the population of church goers, priests function as transmitters of tradition and doctrine and to this extent encourage the culture of self restraint. This, Durkheim believed, encourages religious attachments and increases social integration which in turn lowers the suicide rate within the religious group.

In this case, England serves to verify rather than weaken the theory that religious individualism tends to dilute common beliefs. In fact, as religious individualism increases, the religious community itself grows weaker since Protestantism is constituted differently than Catholicism. The case of England confirms this view since Protestants in England 'do not produce the same results' in terms of suicides and this is because their 'religious society is more strongly integrated and to this extent resembles the Catholic church.'[218]

Family Integration and Egoistic Suicide   The second point of attachment between the individual and society is the family group and domestic environment. Durkheim reasoned that if the social integration of religious society reduces egoistic suicide, then the social attachments to the family and the domestic environment would tend to have a similar effect.[219]

Durkheim began by looking at the commonly-held view about marriage and suicide. Many, he stated, tend to believe that suicide increased as the conditions of existence become more difficult, and since family life increased burdens and responsibilities it must also increase the risk of suicide. Common sense thus holds that because marriage increases difficulty, it therefore increases the suicide rate. Both these views are false, according to Durkheim, and cannot be substantiated by the evidence. In fact, the suicide rates show that when adjusted for age, unmarried persons take their own lives more frequently than do persons who are married.[220] In

---

217 Ibid.

218 *Suicide,* p. 161.

219 *Suicide*, pp. 171–202.

220 Initially, when looking at the number of suicides among the unmarried in relation to married persons, Durkheim found that married persons took their own lives more often than did the non-married. This 'disturbing result' was resolved when Durkheim found that children under sixteen were represented in the unmarried population. He reasoned that if adjusted for age, the appropriate result would be evident. For this detailed argument, see *Suicide*, pp. 171–177.

this case, marriage reduces suicide by about half. For example, in France between 1889–1891, of those between the ages of 30–40, there were 627 suicides for those who were unmarried in comparison with 226 who were married.[221] Similarly, of those between the ages of 40–50, there were 975 suicides who were unmarried in comparison with 340 who were married. Stated differently, not being married increases the potential for suicide by about 1.6 percent in the population.[222] But what social factors would account for the variation in the rates between married and unmarried individuals?

Durkheim believed that the answer to this question can be found by looking at the structure of the family group and the domestic environment. He asserted that there are features of the domestic environment which counteract egoism and reduce suicide and these are found within the family structure itself. According to Durkheim, the family is made up of two distinct groups or aggregates which together constitute the domestic environment. First is the conjugal group which is made up of husband and wife; and second, is the family group which is made up of the conjugal group including children.[223] He maintained that each of these groups within the family constitute different types of social bonds which contribute to integration in distinctly different ways. Chief among these are the primary ties of the conjugal group whose links are romantic in origin and whose roots are based on bonds of affinity. In and of itself, the conjugal group forms alliances based on generational similarities and forms bonds which are based on friendship and shared experiences. Conjugal links and integrative bonds not only supersede the family group itself, but tend to have priority over the family group. Conjugal links thus 'unite two members of the same generation' and form social bonds based on similarity and intimacy.[224] Second is the family group itself whose integrative bonds are distinct from those of the conjugal group. In this case, social integration arises from blood ties whose links connect members of one generation with members of another, creating loyalty and allegiance to family members that may supersede loyalties to the outside world. The difference between the conjugal and family group, according to Durkheim, is that the conjugal group historically precedes the family group and its links are based on ties of intimacy, whereas the family group is organized at a later date.

Durkheim maintains that the connection to the family group therefore constitutes membership in both conjugal and familial communities, and both these groups make up the domestic environment and the family system. The remaining question is, how does the domestic environment reduce egoism and protect against suicide? First and foremost, family life reduced egoism by ensuring that greater concentrations of commitment and integration were focused within the family group itself rather than

---

221 *Suicide*, p. 178.
222 *Suicide*, p. 173.
223 Ibid.
224 *Suicide*, p. 185.

on the individual privately, and this, in itself, acts to suppress the tendency to withdraw to the self.[225] Family society, like religious society, therefore acts to protect against suicide to the extent that it creates duties and obligations outside the self and in doing so attaches the individual to life and thwarts the development of egoism. As far as Durkheim was concerned, the family group performs this function because it creates two distinct kinds of integrative demands on individuals. One places demands and obligations on the individual which arise from the duties of the conjugal group itself. These may include duties and obligations which arise between spouses based on their history. The other exerts demands and expectations on the individual which originate from duties related to the family group, which arise from roles individuals perform as functionaries and as parental authorities within the family group itself where loyalties often create personal sacrifice based on social attachments.[226]

While the conjugal group and the family group contribute to social integration and link the individual to the group as a whole, they do so in an entirely different manner. To demonstrate the differences between conjugal and family bonds, Durkheim looked for an indication of which group was stronger and which group created greater social attachments. The strength of the conjugal bond, he said, can be observed if we look at families without children to see whether their members are more likely to take their own lives than those families with children.[227] If we compare married men with unmarried men of the same age, we find that married men take their own lives a third less than unmarried men. This changes dramatically when children are involved since the rates showed that the immunity to suicide doubles. This indicates that the integration of the family group is greater than that of the conjugal group and this is confirmed by the fact that the suicide rate is less in families where there are children. Durkheim went on to reason that one of the conclusions which can be drawn from the social suicide rate is that suicide is not due to life's burdens nor to an increase in the responsibilities which come with family life itself. In fact, the opposite seems to be true since suicide tends to diminish with marriage and family life, and therefore tends to diminish when burdens increase.[228]

Durkheim went on to argue that if suicide varies according to whether individuals are members of families, then it must also vary in relation to the size of family. He pointed out that the larger the family, the greater the sentiments and historical memories and therefore the greater the social cohesion. This is reflected in the lower suicide rates for larger families. Smaller families, by contrast, develop fewer sentiments and collective memories which lead to social cohesion and thus their shared experiences are not as intense. In addition, because the members are fewer, their contact is more intermittent and there are times when this contact may be 'suspended'

---

225 *Suicide*, p. 180.
226 Ibid., p. 198.
227 Ibid., p. 186.
228 Ibid., p. 201.

altogether.[229] Thus, the larger the family, the greater the social attachment to things and persons outside the self, and the greater the degree of protection against suicide. But how, in this case, does family integration diminish egoistic suicide? Like the religious group, the family group can be considered to be a society with its own social environment. As such, individuals are attached to it to a greater or lesser extent and their social integration connects them to each other and to the wider society. In the family environment, individuals have responsibilities and obligations lying outside themselves which act to reduce the inclination to focus exclusively on oneself alone and to retreat to the private ego. These obligations, in turn, function to create social attachments and loyalties which act to increase the individual's integration in the family group. Hence, the greater the obligations and social responsibilities beyond the self, the greater is the bond to social life and the greater the immunity to suicide.

Political Integration and Egoistic Suicide The third point of attachment between the individual and society is the political or national group.[230] This is a more obscure category of social integration than the religious or family group, and was less developed as a type of social attachment by Durkheim. Political society, according to Durkheim, refers to the type of social bonds which form between the individual and society at large, and encompasses the type of social links which develop between individuals and the national group to which they belong. Explicitly, the attachments to political society refer to the loyalty an individual has to their country or nation. Durkheim reasoned that to the extent these social links and attachments exist, it is possible to look at the extent to which they are manifested in the suicide rates during times of social crisis and political upheaval.

Durkheim began by drawing on historical cases of political unrest and suicide. For example, in Rome an epidemic of suicide erupted as the city states began to break down and become politically decadent.[231] Similar circumstances occurred in the Ottoman Empire where mass suicides were associated with political decline. Then again, there were suicides in France during the political turbulence of the revolution. Many, therefore, held the view that political upheaval and social crisis increase the number of suicides. But the facts, according to Durkheim, tend to contradict this view. They show that during the revolutions in France, the number of suicides actually fell at the time the revolution took place, in some cases by ten percent. Similarly, during the political crisis in Europe in 1848, suicide decreased. Again, in Bavaria and Prussia the suicide rate declined during the crisis of 1849.[232] In addition, large-scale wars tend to produce the same effect, bringing a dramatic decline in the suicide rate. During the revolution of Louis Bonaparte in 1851, suicide rates fell by 8 percent even

---

229 Ibid., p. 202.
230 Ibid., pp. 202–208.
231 *Suicide*, p. 203.
232 *Suicide*, p. 204.

though it marked a turbulent period in French political history.[233] In another context, the political struggles in France between 1848 and 1849 brought a decrease in the overall rates as well. Similarly, during the turmoil of 1848–49 in European countries other than France, the rates also declined. How can this decline in the suicide rates during political crisis be explained?

Durkheim argued that the decline in rates during political uncertainty can only be explained by one interpretation. Instead of breaking social ties, severe social disruption brought about by a political crisis actually increased the intensity of 'collective sentiments and stimulates patriotism' and therefore increased social attachments.[234] In fact, political crisis acts to stimulate partisan spirit and strong feelings of nationalism, and this focuses individual interests toward a single common end. This forces individuals to draw together under common conditions leading them to 'think less of themselves and more of common causes.' This, in effect, increases social attachments between the individual and the group and 'causes a greater integration in society.'[235]

In addition to inspiring national sentiment, political crisis creates what Durkheim called a 'moral effect,' which proliferates throughout society and, along with arousing public feelings and social attachments, places moral demands on individuals and increases their patriotic spirit. Often this 'moral effect' is restricted to the urban population who tend to be more involved and impassioned than the population in rural areas. In addition, the collective stimulation of public and national sentiment during political upheaval ignites national feeling and this has the effect of strengthening social integration in society. As this social integration increases, 'the individual thinks less of themselves and more of common social purposes.'[236]

Explanation of Egoism and Egoistic Suicide

We can now look more closely at the causes of egoism and egoistic suicide. Simply stated, egoistic suicide results from the absence of social integration and a weakening of the bonds which attach individuals to groups outside themselves. It occurs when the integrative mechanisms attaching individuals to the family, religious and political group form gaps in the links connecting individuals to society so that individuals retreat to themselves. In such circumstances, individuals rely more on themselves and less on society, and as a result, they withdraw their allegiance from collective life. As social integration declines the gaps emerging between the individual and the institutional points of contact become wider, and as a result individuals are less drawn together. In addition, between the spaces that emerge the 'cold winds of egoism blow.'[237] Durkheim gives the name 'egoism' to this state because it identifies a condition in industrial

---

233 Ibid.
234 *Suicide*, p. 208
235 Ibid.
236 Ibid.
237 Durkheim, 'Suicide and the Birth Rate,' p. 132.

society in which the individual ego prevails over the social ego due to the decline in social integration.[238]

Durkheim believed that the social attachment to the religious group, the family group and the national political group have a moderating effect on egoistic suicide because individuals share the common property of being strongly integrated into society, in contrast to being preoccupied with personal and private matters. The weaker the bonds attaching the individual to society, the less they depend upon them and the more they depend on themselves.[239] In this view, egoism is therefore the result of the weakening of the social bonds which tie the individual to society. But, if this is the case, what is the cause of egoism? Simply stated 'egoism' is the result of prolonged and unchecked individualism which, in turn, is a consequence of industrial society. In industrial society, Durkheim explained, the integrative links attaching the individual to social groups begin to diminish and, under such circumstances, 'the bond that unites the individual to life and prevents them from feeling personal troubles so deeply' begins to slacken and grows weak.[240]

Durkheim thought that individuals, by nature, cannot live without attachment to some social group which transcends them. Egoism thus attacks social bonds in at least two fundamental ways. First, by eroding the common bonds linking the individual to society, egoism makes private life a dominant aim and this acts to defeat collective purposes and attachments. Egoism is, in this sense, a state in which society is completely lacking in the individual.[241] Second, egoism promotes withdrawal from everything external to the individual and, when this occurs, 'society allows the individual to escape' its hold.[242] As a consequence, when individuals become detached from society they encounter less resistance to suicide. In egoistic suicide, therefore, the bond attaching individuals to life relaxes because the bond attaching them to society is slack.[243]

Altruistic Suicide and Social Integration   After discussing egoistic suicide and social integration, Durkheim turned his attention to altruistic suicide, the polar opposite of egoistic suicide. He began his discussion by citing the suicides of tribal societies where, rather than die of old age, individuals kill themselves to maintain their dignity. In other societies, by contrast, there are customs which dictate that dying a natural death leads to an after life which is intolerable and full of suffering. In still other societies, they believe that old men must throw themselves off a mountain when they are tired of life. In almost all these cases, those who take their own life are honoured and their families spared humiliation, while those who fail to do so are denied the honour

---

238 *Suicide*, p. 209.
239 Ibid.
240 *Suicide*, p. 210.
241 *Suicide*, pp. 210–16.
242 *Suicide*, p. 217.
243 *Suicide*, p. 219.

of a funeral, and a life of dishonor and pain is presumed to await them.[244] In almost all these instances 'the weight of society is brought to bear on the individual to destroy themselves' for purposes greater than them.[245] This type of suicide, in contrast to the type described earlier, is called altruistic suicide. It differs from egoistic suicide in that it results from too much social integration rather than too little. In order to understand what Durkheim meant by this assertion, we have to look more closely.

Durkheim first made his observations about altruistic suicide by looking at tribal societies. He observed that the social customs in these societies placed a high degree of social honor on individuals who take their own lives in the name of social purposes greater than themselves. In this category, Durkheim lists three specific types of suicides: (i) the suicide of older men threatened with severe illness; (ii) the suicide of women on the death bed of their husbands; and (iii) the suicide of followers on the death of their chiefs.[246] Under these circumstances, people take their own lives not because of their personal right to do so or because of their personal choice, but because a 'social duty' is imposed upon them by society.[247] So strong is this duty, that when individuals avoid their obligation to take their own life they risk being disgraced or religiously sanctioned. Yet, when these duties are carried out, society confers social honor upon them which is thought to extend to the after-life. In such circumstances, altruistic suicide is the clearest case of a 'social type' of suicide because suicide is imposed externally on the individual as a social duty and is the result of social rather than personal ends.

Since in these societies people take their own lives because their attachments to the group far exceed the loyalties they have to themselves, Durkheim thought that the cause of altruistic suicide is to be found in the levels of social integration attaching the individual to the group. The elevated levels of social integration occur, Durkheim reasoned, because the nature of group life in tribal societies is such that the individual tends to be over-absorbed in the web of society and over-absorbed in the web of social attachments. In tribal societies, social life is focused on the group and all social activity radiates from the center of tribal experience. Under these circumstances, the individual ego is overwhelmed by the social ego and is not permitted its own individual expression. In addition, because individuals live in such close proximity to one another, their social customs and beliefs tend to be unified to the point that their social attachments increase. As a result, collective supervision and social surveillance extend throughout society, leading to similarities in beliefs and social observances. Under such circumstances, the individual has no private life that is immune from collective surveillance. As a result, individuals are available to social claims upon their allegiance – allegiance which may otherwise be directed to developing individual tastes and private life. Under these circumstances, the

---

244 *Suicide*, p. 218
245 *Suicide*, p. 219.
246 Ibid.
247 Ibid.

individual has little independence from group life, and individual existence, by itself, has little meaning. In cases where society is able to produce such 'massive cohesion,' it almost always relied on social practices that elicit the highest possible degree of attachment and, accordingly, under these circumstances individualism is underdeveloped.[248]

Altruistic suicide is therefore at the opposite pole of social integration in relation to egoistic suicide. In egoistic suicide, there is an excess of individualism and autonomy from society, whereas in altruistic suicide little or no autonomy takes place since the private ego does not form. In egoistic suicide, the bonds between the individual and society grow weak and this takes its toll on individual life as the collective attachments decline. In altruistic suicide, by contrast, the bonds between the individual and society are developed to such an extent that the individual acquires an aptitude for the renunciation of life.[249] Thus, where 'egoistic suicide arises because society allows the individual to escape it, altruistic suicide occurs because society holds the individual in too strict a tutelage.'[250] 'Having given the name egoism to the state of the ego living its own life and obeying itself alone, that of altruism adequately expresses the opposite state, where the ego is not its own property and where the goal of conduct is exterior to the self in one of the groups in which it participates.'[251]

Durkheim maintained that altruistic suicide takes several different forms and went on to outline three distinct types. In every case of altruistic suicide, said Durkheim, the individual takes their own life by reason of a 'social duty' that is imposed upon them externally by society. He argued that this duty expresses itself in three distinct forms: (i) as obligatory altruistic suicide; (ii) as optional altruistic suicide; and (iii) as acute altruistic or mystical suicide. Each differs in the degree of explicitness and the severity of the obligation placed upon the individual to take their own life.[252]

(i) In the first category, obligatory altruistic suicide, society imposes an explicit duty on individuals to take their own life, but this duty may lack specific coercive pressure from the community. Obligatory suicide in some societies takes the form of a customary requirement which may be part of the beliefs of the community, or it may take the form of a less explicit expectation which is understood to be part of the customary practices of the group. To encourage suicide in instances where an individual is ill or aging, the group may attach social prestige to it – leaving those who resist to experience some stigma or religious sanction.[253] In such circumstances, an

---

248 *Suicide*, p. 221.
249 Ibid.
250 Ibid.
251 Ibid.
252 *Suicide*, pp. 222–3.
253 This may occur in cases of extreme altruistic suicide in a military environment where the individual is expected to sacrifice themselves for the higher aims of the group. In this case the honor flows to the individual. The ritualistic honors accorded to the kamikazi pilots of World War II mark out how social practices operate in cases where societies require individuals to prepare themselves to renounce their lives in the name of loyalties greater than themselves.

individual's life is assigned very little value over the group, and Durkheim made the point that, due to the social expectation put upon them, individuals are often willing to give up their lives at the 'least pretext.'[254]

Examples of obligatory suicide are found in India, where there is the practice of the Hindu 'sati' ritual. This consists of a social duty that falls on a woman on the death of her husband and involves the practice of a voluntary self immolation where the widow burns to death on the funeral fire of her husband's body. While the practice was banned in India in 1829 and then again in 1956, it returns from time to time and cannot be entirely extinguished by the authorities. In effect, the customary requirement of the sati ritual provides that the widow 'volunteers' to immolate herself as a result of the customary obligations that are imposed upon her. In such circumstances, the voluntary nature of the sati obligation acts to replace the private person with the ritual person so that the power of the social obligation acts to efface private individuality altogether. Other instances of obligatory altruistic suicide are found in Hindu society where the force of the social obligation obliterates the private self. For example, there are those who look upon suicide as a religious act, especially when it takes the form of self-immolation by widows; and when it consists in casting oneself under the wheels of the chariot of the god at Juggernaut, or as a self-sacrifice to the crocodiles in the Ganges, or drowning oneself in the holy tanks of the temples.'[255]

In all these instances, the act of self destruction is constituted by the force of the social obligation that is imposed on the individual from without, and which seems to override their personal loyalty to themselves in favor of intensifying the loyalties they have to the group. In all these case, what is clear is that the 'obligation' is imposed externally by religious society rather than by personal choice or private will.[256]

(ii) A second type referred to by Durkheim is optional altruistic suicide. In this category, the demand imposed on the individual by the community is less explicitly

---

254 Ibid.

255 Ibid.

256 The disappearance of the private ego in societies where excessive social claims on individuals takes place is evident in the case of cult suicides where groups form for the sole purpose of collective suicide. An example of this may be found in the case of the Jonestown Massacre in the 1970s, where a group headed by Jim Jones carried out a mass suicide of 365 people. This collective suicide demonstrates explicitly the degree of the emotional hold which collective beliefs had over individuals. At the moment the command was given at the Jonestown suicide, 365 people drank cyanide laced with Kool-Aid and fell dead on the spot. In this case, cults can be described as groups in which the collective attachments to the group far exceed the loyalties or attachments which individuals have to themselves. Under such circumstances, a surplus of attachment flows onto the aims and purposes of the group and away from the private ego. In addition, the social mechanisms of attachment in cults often works on individuals through religious ideas and beliefs, and cults often promise spiritual liberation and undreamed of spiritual connection in another world. So strong is the emotional hold, and so intense is the grasp which the beliefs have over the individual, that cults often erase the individual ego altogether and replace it with the social ego. Historical examples of attachments of this type leading to suicide is the case of the Heaven's Gate suicide and the Branch Davidian suicide. In these cases, social attachments and social integration worked to prohibit private life as much as possible, essentially by restricting activities to the public sphere of the cult where the individual was subject to as much public surveillance as possible. To this extent, the social controls of the group extended into private life to such a degree that it prevented the 'private self' from forming.

clarified or 'less expressly required' than in circumstances where suicide is strictly obligatory.[257] In some instances, the two types of obligatory suicide may be indistinguishable in terms of the degree of felt duty or the extent of explicitness inherent in the obligation. In either case, death may be held out as an expectation, where the duty to take one's own life is clear or whether there is honor assigned to the renunciation of life. In such circumstances, 'not clinging to life is seen as a virtue' and for those who renounce it, society attaches honors which produce the effect of actually lowering the importance of the life of the individual over the group, since the giving up of life is for the group itself.[258]

(iii) A third type of altruistic suicide is called 'acute altruistic suicide, This is the most extreme form of altruistic self-destruction. In this case, the individual's attachments to the group are so great that the individual renounces life for the actual felt 'joy of sacrifice.' [259] Examples of this can be found in Hindu society where suicide takes the form of religious hysteria and is looked upon with enthusiasm and great excitement. In some instances, members of a religious sect will climb to the top of a cliff which has sulfur flames below. Durkheim maintained that these individuals call out to their gods and wait for a flame to appear. As they utter the words which give their life as a sacrifice, the appearance of the flame is believed to be a sign to leap head first into it.[260] In these circumstances, Durkheim maintained that the individual actually seek to 'strip themselves of their personal being in order to be engulfed in something' which they regard as being of a higher order, or as having a truer form of existence. In this case, the believers violently 'strive to blend' themselves with a higher order which is believed to be greater than themselves.[261] Durkheim reasoned that to act in this way, the individual literally must have no life of their own, since only after death does the individual believe that his or her true being has been realized. Durkheim stated that to kill oneself so readily, they must not place too much value in their own life since 'altruism is acute.'[262]

In this case, altruistic suicide occurs because of an excess of social integration and attachment that develops within the confines of the group. In effect, the attachment is at the polar extreme of egoistic suicide. In egoistic suicide, individualism has advanced to the point where the aims of the individual were above the common purposes of society, resulting in the breakdown of social integration and the withdrawal of individual attachments to the private ego. In the case of altruistic suicide, by contrast, individualism hardly develops since the purposes of the group are valued over individual existence. The cause of altruistic suicide seems always to exist in the social duty that is imposed on the individual externally by society and by the

---

257 *Suicide*, p. 223.
258 *Suicide*, p. 222.
259 *Suicide*, p. 223.
260 *Suicide*, pp. 224–25.
261 Ibid.
262 Ibid. Durkheim refers to this as the 'euphoria of self obliteration.'

excessive social integration which leads to a lack of development of individualism. Under these circumstances acute altruistic suicide is the clearest case of suicide imposed by social ends and is thus a form of suicide induced by society.

Examples of acute altruistic suicide can be found in the case of the suicide bombings that occurred during the terrorist attacks in the United States on 9/11 and in Britain in 7/7. Here is a category of suicide that conforms to a 'social type' of suicide as distinct from a 'psychological type,' since the loyalties that develop between the suicide bomber and the terrorist groups to which they belong can only be understood by looking at the form of the social attachments which arises in these groups. Four provisional social characteristics seem to stand out. First is the religious element stirring the commitments to the highest point possible so that the 'initiate' literally feels outside themselves and already outside the world, on the way to a promised afterlife. So great is the emotional hold which the group has over them that, for all practical purposes, they have no individuality and their private ego has been replaced by a more powerful social ego that derives from the altruistic cause pursued by the group.

Like the sati ritual discussed earlier, their private name may be replaced by a symbolic name and they may rehearse through videos and other forms of representation how they will appear to themselves and their family members in the after life. In the case of the 9/11 and 7/7 terrorist attacks, all the individuals involved had become suicide bombers only as a result of replacing their private ego within the social ego of the group through a process of withdrawal from worldly acts. This served to reinforce the 'glorious religious link' to self sacrifice and martyrdom, and in these cases the withdrawal from worldly things and pleasures signify religious withdrawal from the world in preparation for the afterlife. Second is the religiously induced element of the 'glory' attained by the sacrifice itself, since this is a 'glory unto God' which acts to develop an attachment to the role that the initiate will play in the afterlife upon his or her 'glorious self obliteration.' Third is the process of the gradual stripping of the private ego and its replacement by the group ego, which can only occur in stages of initiation and the expression of commitment and self-sacrifice. Fourth is the moment before the bombing in which there is a staging of 'glorious sacrifice' that is about to come by a kind of ritualization of the sacrifice. This is the 'moment of glory' that occurs by means of an allusionist videotape made of the initiate against a religious backdrop, where the 'felt joy of sacrifice' and the glorious moment are portrayed with military-religious allusions to the afterlife which is about to come after the obliteration. In all these cases, suicide is induced by religious fervor and the attachments induced by the group are socially acute and overdeveloped.

Military vs Civilian Suicides   To support the contention that altruistic suicide is the result of excessive social attachments and social integration, Durkheim turned his attention to military suicide. He pointed out that, by far, suicide in the military exceeds suicidal death in the civilian population. For example, in countries such as

Austria and the United States, the suicide rate was six to ten times higher among the military. Durkheim finds these high rates surprising since military morale is thought to have a mitigating effect on suicide. What, then, are the causes of the high rate of suicide among the military?

Durkheim began by looking at popular opinion. Some believed that because many soldiers never marry, the high rate of suicide must relate to bachelorhood. Others, by contrast, take the view that military service itself is the cause since the hardship and discipline of military life creates a lack of freedom leading to more suicidal deaths than in the civilian population. Still others maintain that suicide is higher in the military because of the isolation of military life. Durkheim reasoned that none of these views are true. He pointed out that the effects of being unmarried on the soldier compared to the civilian should not be as great, since the soldier is 'anything but isolated.' In fact the soldier, in comparison with the civilian, is a member of a strongly unified group whose bonds are 'partially calculated to replace the family.'[263]

Durkheim maintained that these views are supported by comparative suicide data. For example, with respect to the hardships of military life, he pointed out that military discipline is less rigorous for officers than for non-career soldiers, yet officers in France and Italy are twice as likely to kill themselves as non-professional soldiers. Similarly, in comparison with the civilian population over a ten year period, suicide rates in the military tripled 'while for unmarried civilians during the same period it only rose by 20 percent.'[264] In addition, in the Prussian military there were 560 privates who took their own lives in contrast to 1140 who were officers.[265] Military suicide, therefore, is not only different from civilian suicide, it is in 'inverse proportion to the determining causes of civilian suicide.'[266] To what can these differences be attributed?

The military, asserted Durkheim, creates more suicides because first and foremost it is a society which is separate from the wider society. In this sense, it constitutes a sphere of thought and action distinct from the social group which surrounds it. He went on to maintain that this could only mean that the causes of military suicide are, in fact, different from the causes leading to suicide in the general population. In the civilian population, the prevailing cause of suicide stems from excessive individualism – a common characteristic of industrial societies in Europe and North America. Military suicide, by contrast, arises because of the very opposite condition of individualism and its cause, according to Durkheim, is underdeveloped individuation.[267] In fact, the traditions of military life, according to Durkheim, resemble those of traditional societies and, in the context of the military, traditionalism is thus the chief

263 *Suicide*, p. 229.
264 *Suicide*, p. 232.
265 *Suicide*, p. 233.
266 *Suicide*, p. 236.
267 Ibid.

opponent of individualism. Durkheim went on to suggest that military morality is an anthropological 'survival of primitive morality' and, in demanding too much allegiance from individuals, it leaves them little for the development of individual interests and private inclination.[268] He pointed out that this is reflected in the predisposition of soldiers who take their own life 'at the least disappointment, for the most futile reasons; for a refusal of leave, a reprimand, an unjust punishment, a delay in promotion, a question of honour, a flush of momentary jealousy.'[269]

Suicide and the Regulative Pole: Anomic and Fatalistic Suicide

To this point in our discussion, egoism and altruism have formed two polar extremes of social integration. At one end of the continuum is excessive individualism or egoism, while at the other is underdeveloped individualism or altruism. In contrast to the suicide of social integration, according to Durkheim, is the form of suicide that relates to the regulatory functions of society, and this has two polar extremes represented by anomic and fatalistic suicide. In order to understand what Durkheim meant by the regulatory function of society, however, it will be useful to define the term 'anomie.' Simply stated, anomie is a term used by Durkheim to refer to the decline that takes place in the regulatory functions of society and social institutions during industrial development when the capacity of society to set the necessary level of social restraint begins to weaken. But the question is how can social regulatory functions actually decline?

Generally, Durkheim thought that the regulatory functions of society served the purpose of imposing restraints and setting limits on individual needs and wants. To be clear on this point, Durkheim made the distinction between two different kinds of regulatory functions – between bodily needs and social needs. He thought that bodily needs and wants such as hunger or sleep were self regulating. In this context, the body's limit on needs and appetites is governed by biological limitations which cannot, as a rule, operate outside set boundaries. In the case of social needs and wants, however, the situation is completely different. He pointed out that social wants – such as the appetite for wealth, prestige and power – are essentially unlimited.[270] We seem to want as much as we can attain, and in some cases our needs have no natural limitation since the more we obtain the better.

Durkheim argued that whereas the limits for bodily needs and wants are imposed biologically, limitations for social needs and wants can only be regulated by society and are imposed externally by the system of social restraints. In this case, only the regulatory functions of society can act to set limits on social needs and wants and generally it does this by setting what Durkheim referred to as the level of social

---

268 *Suicide*, p. 238.

269 *Suicide*, p. 239.

270 Durkheim's discussion of the distinction between bodily needs and social wants in relation to anomie is excellent and can be found in *Suicide*, pp. 246–254.

restraint. Under these circumstances, social regulation serves to set limits on individual desires by placing restraints on social wants and by performing the important social function of balancing individual wants with the means individuals have at their disposal to obtain these wants. Only society can set limitations on social needs and wants – wealth, power, prestige – and only society can operate to set limits on individual wants of this type. Historically, social regulation was performed by society through specific social institutions, which operated to set social and moral restraints on individual appetites by linking social wants to the available means for attaining these wants and by imposing limitations based on moral and religious guidelines. After the development of industrial society, however, there was a general decline in restraints of this type as the economy became the dominant social institution, and limitations imposed on social needs and wants became incompatible with economic life and economic achievement. As the industrial economy developed, it removed the previous limitations that were imposed on individual wants, and this acted to reset the outer limit on social needs and wants in a way that altered the social framework of restraint.

Durkheim's discussion of anomic suicide begins by looking at the suicide rate of industrial society during periods of economic crisis created by financial recession and periods of economic decline. For instance, between 1845 and 1869 there were repeated economic crises in Europe, creating a dramatic decline in the business cycle and a rise in the number of bankruptcies.[271] During these crises there was a rapid rise in the suicide rate which increased as economic troubles worsened. As the crisis disappeared, the rates declined, but when the crisis returned it was followed by a rise in the rates once again. Durkheim reasoned that if we accept these facts at face value, we are led to believe that people take their own lives as social difficulties increase or as life becomes more difficult, especially during times of economic disaster.

According to this view, the cause of the fluctuation in the suicide rate is due to the fluctuation in prosperity and wealth. Durkheim, however, disagreed with this view on two specific fronts. First, he believed that it conforms too readily with popular opinion about suicide, and in this sense lacks science. Second, he stated that if this proposition were true, suicide rates would in fact decline as economic prosperity increased. But the suicide rates for other periods show that this decline never takes place. In fact, neither poverty, bankruptcy nor a sudden decline in the business cycle causes suicide and, therefore, the rise in the rates cannot be directly linked to economic disaster.

Durkheim went on to assert that if in an economic crisis there is an increase in the suicide rate, it is not because of the hardship associated with economic misfortune, since in times of prosperity the same rise occurs in the rates.[272] He reasoned that since the change in the rates takes place with equal intensity during times of economic collapse and prosperity, then it must be linked to some other event related to periodic

---

271 *Suicide*, p. 242.
272 Ibid.

adjustment in what he called the 'social equilibrium.'[273] In fact, Durkheim believed that whenever an abrupt shift in social stability occurs, it alters the mechanism which places restraint on individual desires and social wants. He therefore reasoned that the category of anomic suicide must be related to the shift in the regulatory mechanisms of society which occurs precisely during periods of economic hardship or prosperity, particularly in a society where the economy has become dominant over other institutions. This focus on the 'social equilibrium' allowed Durkheim to isolate the cause of suicide in the mechanisms of society which regulate social equilibrium rather than in causes which seem to attach suicide to fluctuations in the business cycle. Given this reasoning, the category of anomic suicide relates directly to the regulatory mechanisms of industrial society, since anomie refers to that state of affairs which results when there is an overall decline in the capacity of society to set the appropriate level of restraint.

Anomie, then, may be defined as the state that results from the weakening of the powers of society which regulate social equilibrium by setting the acceptable level of social restraint. In order to see how this process comes about, it will be useful to briefly review how Durkheim understood the connection between society and social regulation on the one hand, and setting the level of restraint on the other. In this regard, Durkheim stressed the importance of the regulatory mechanisms of society, and believed that a system of social regulation serves to set limits on individual desires by placing restraints on social wants and by serving the important purpose of balancing individual wants with the means for obtaining these wants.[274] When social wants exceed the possible means for attaining them, Durkheim thought that this leads to disappointment and feelings of individual failure and despair. In fact, Durkheim maintained that during the course of everyday life in industrial society there are constant internal demands on individuals to satisfy their immediate individual needs and wants, and these needs, Durkheim thought, are capable of becoming conscious desires which have the power to overwhelm them and to thus become outright material desires. It is, therefore, the direct function of society to set the level of restraint on individual needs and wants so that desires do not become conscious material wants for which individuals are prepared to break rules to obtain what they desire. In this respect, human social wants contrast sharply with the animal world. In nature, the needs and wants of animals are adjusted to bodily wants and thus are naturally regulated. With human beings, the case is otherwise. Since individual social wants are not related to the system of bodily needs or desires and can arise in the imagination relative to the material desires of industrial society, Durkheim believed that explicit limitations on social wants must be set by society. In fact, since nothing in human nature acts to 'set limits' on social desires, then society alone must act as a means of material restraint and external regulation.[275]

273 *Suicide*, p. 246.
274 Ibid, 'Needs,' says Durkheim, must be 'sufficiently proportioned to the means.'
275 *Suicide*, p. 247.

Durkheim maintained that human beings, in fact, have a greater feeling of well being when their needs are proportionate to their wants and when the means they have to satisfy these wants meet their own capacities. In a state of anomie, the regulatory limits usually imposed by society are absent and limits are not well defined. Under these circumstances, disappointment with life and the feeling of failure are quick to arise and readily blamed on the individual since externally defined limits are lacking.[276] When the majority of social wants cannot be attained, Durkheim thought that, at first, it leads to disappointment then, eventually, to chronic morbidity and finally to defeat. When social institutions fail to set limitations on social needs and wants, individuals continually exceed the means at their disposal, and their desires – by definition – become unattainable and out of reach. This can only happen, Durkheim maintained, when individuals constantly aspire to reach ends or goals which are beyond their capacity to obtain. In this respect, Durkheim thought that it is important to keep in mind that the 'motives' leading individuals to strive for goals which they cannot realistically obtain are due to the failure of the powers of society to set regulatory limits and impose restraints on social needs and wants. In fact, to pursue goals which are unattainable ensures repeated disappointment, and when goals are set which have no end or limit, individuals become despondent.

Durkheim believed that the inability of society to impose limitations on social needs and wants became more pronounced in industrial society. In traditional societies, religious institutions and the family system set limits on needs and wants by providing a framework of meaningful restraint on appetites and individual desires. In modern societies, by contrast, the limitations imposed by religion during earlier times have been replaced by the 'spirit of free pursuit' in economic and material matters, and this tends to raise the horizon of desirable goals beyond reach.[277] In addition, the system of restraint existing in institutions begins to disappear as a consequence of modern economic competition and the dominance of the economy as the major category of experience. As the economy replaced religion as the dominant social institution, all restraint was suspended since the economy taught that all desires were attainable with sufficient effort and hard work. Under these circumstances, restraint and limitation became incompatible with the pursuit of private gain, which is in itself unregulated, since the more one has the more one wants. As the economy removed natural limits, all desires became material wants and this led to an increasing scale of desire for material pleasures and possessions. The more individual desires increase the greater the need to obtain the means to satisfy these desires, and in the absence of restraint people are prepared to engage in rule breaking in order to obtain what they want. With the stress on commercial success and more wealth, all goals seem attainable and social limits imposed on needs and wants appear to be non-existent.

In comparison with industrial societies, traditional societies employ powerful social mechanisms in the family and religious system that act to set the framework

---

276 Ibid.
277 *Suicide*, pp. 247–249.

of restraint on social wants largely by means of customary practices and social rules that were consecrated by law. These customary social rules and practices impose an obligatory means of acting on individuals where important social rules are rarely broken, and where social wants are more readily integrated with the socially acceptable means for attaining them. Durkheim believed that 'the regulatory force of society must play the same role for moral needs as the body plays for physical needs,' and that when regulatory functions decline a state of anomie or deregulation ensues.[278] Since, according to Durkheim, human social wants at any given point in history 'are not automatically restrained by physiological mechanisms,' they can only be restrained and channeled by the regulatory force of society, and to this extent restraint must come from a source outside the individual and must be imposed by society.[279]

Durkheim took the position that abrupt changes in the suicide rates are a reflection of disturbances in the restraint setting mechanism of industrial society. He thought that so far as the major regulatory function of society was to set outside limits, then when these limits are absent or fail to be set, individuals feel unlimited want. Furthermore, when people have unlimited want in the absence of restraint, they begin to feel free to break important social rules to obtain want they want from the material world. This loss of social restraint, said Durkheim, can only set off a general decrease in the state of well being since people feel that social life has lost its central purpose. Durkheim maintained that in all societies it is necessary that a social framework exists which precisely regulates the degree of the ease of living that each social class feels to a different extent.[280]

This framework of restraint, he thought, varies with the shifting moral ideas of society and the collective authority that tends to be rooted in the moral ideas of the time. These socially imposed limitations on individual desires bring about what Durkheim called 'average contentment' and this creates feelings of well being and even happiness.[281] When these limits are set by society, individuals desire only what they can legitimately obtain with the means available to them. But as soon as these restraints are lifted, and as soon as change begins to occur in the moral framework of society, anomie and deregulation ensue. When disrupted by social crises, society is unable to exercise its regulatory function and to this extent it cannot act as a source of restraint on individual wants. In such circumstances, a state of deregulation ensues and this acts to increase rather than decrease social wants making individuals less disciplined.

Causes of Anomie and the Role Played by the Economy
Durkheim believed that one of the direct causes of anomie is the industrial and economic change of the

---

278 *Suicide*, p. 248.
279 *Suicide*, p. 248–49.
280 Ibid.
281 *Suicide*, p. 245.

nineteenth century. 'For a whole century,' he stated, 'economic progress had mainly consisted in freeing industrial societies from all regulation.'[282] Economic progress, he pointed out, can only advance at the expense of social regulation and moral discipline. This happens because the dominance of economic life acts to displace the regulatory functions of other social institutions. Religion is a case in point. Historically, the explicit function of religion was to impose regulatory limits on behavior by teaching tolerance in the face of hardship, and by counseling contentment with one's position in life. In addition, religion provided a framework of restraint by explaining the material differences between classes and promising that compensation for hardship comes in the next world.[283] In this respect, religion serves the function of placing life in perspective and teaching that worldly economic success and material pleasures are not the primary goal of life, and that material needs are to be subordinated to intangible goals. This tended to regulate economic life by setting into balance the relation between social and material life on the one hand, and between religious life and individual satisfaction on the other.

But with the development of advanced economies, technologies and world markets, individuals were capable of extending their grasp over natural limitations. As production and income began to accelerate and the division of labor began to develop more freely, the economy became dominant to an unprecedented degree. This meant that the old social threshold set by previous periods had been altered and this led to a new threshold of want and desire for material satisfaction, so that all the old limitations to progress were removed. As a result, needs and wants went sky high, and even entire perspectives were raised to what Durkheim called a 'feverish pitch.'[284] In addition to this, when the economy replaced religion as the major category of experience, it subordinated society to economic and industrial ends. The intense economic focus on material wants freed desires from previous social and moral limits, replacing them with utilitarian sanctions inherent in secular law and secular social rules. Eventually, the expansion of markets and world wide economic activity acted to increase material desires to such an extent that it became uncontrollable. At this point, said Durkheim, 'our capacity for social wants became so insatiable and such a bottomless abyss that the more one has the more one wants, since satisfactions only stimulate' further want. All this took place, he argued, 'irrespective of the old regulatory force of society.'[285] In a society that is expanding economically, ambition is widened to include world markets over and against the restricted locales of former times. This places stress on economic achievement and increases individual desires to such an extent that discomfort and restraint become less tolerable than they were in societies in which restraint was the norm. When the primary goal in life is to obtain material satisfaction through economic want and desire, there is an increased risk and a greater possibility for social crisis,

---

282 *Suicide*, p. 254.
283 *Suicide*, p. 255.
284 *Suicide*, p. 256.
285 *Suicide*, pp. 247–48.

especially at the level of the economy. Thus, it is the economically related functions, according to Durkheim, which create the largest category of suicide in contrast to other spheres of society in which the 'old regulatory forces' still prevail in practice more than does the new commercial spirit.[286]

History of the Term Anomie   Durkheim first used the concept of anomie in The Division of Labor in 1893, but it was not until 1897 that he began to use the term in a more narrow sense to describe the overall deterioration of the levels of restraint in society. Since he believed that the primary function of society was to set limits on social wants by providing a moral framework of restraint, then anomie refers to the state which results in industrial society when there is a decline of the social regulatory mechanisms related to levels of restraint. In that the regulative force of society plays the same role for moral needs as does the body for physical needs, the higher suicide rates of industrial society is an indication of pervasive anomie and deregulation. But what is the cause of this deregulation?

Durkheim believed that the causes of deregulation can be traced to two basic sources. First, the development of industrial society and private competition; and second, the dominance of the economy over other social institutions.[287] In the first instance, economic progress removes limits and frees social activity from regulation in three discernible ways. First, the replacement of religion by the economy as the dominant institution removed the regulatory mechanism by which religion governed the individual's relation to the material world and to the material satisfactions obtained in things. This led to the loss of restraint that, in earlier times, was applied to material want and this upset the traditional mechanisms for justifying one's place in the social order. As economic success replaced the efficacy of religious beliefs, it led to a loss of social contentment. Second, as industrial capitalism removed regulation in economic matters, it made economic life dominant over state and religious functions. Third, as needs and social wants became unregulated and social limits were removed, 'one's present existence seems valueless by comparison with the dreams of fevered imaginations.'[288] In Durkheim's view, therefore, industrial society sets desires at a level that only a few could attain. As material desire increases and as society loses its capacity to set the level of restraint, people feel free to break important social rules to obtain what they want.

Looked at in this way, anomie can be defined as the state which results from the decline in the regulatory mechanisms of society brought about by unchecked economic progress. There are two distinctly different forms of regulation that Durkheim refers to: first, the capacity of society to impose material limits and social restraints on wants; and second, the ability to impose restraints that act on individual perception. It

---

286 *Suicide*, p. 257.

287 Ibid., pp. 254–258. The weight Durkheim gives to the connection between anomie and economic progress is unmistakable.

288 *Suicide*, p. 245.

is this perception about the relative state of society which confer feelings of well being and directly affects the individual's relation to society with respect to meaning.

To this point in the discussion, Durkheim put forward three concepts making up a social theory of suicide: egoism, altruism and anomie. The first two concepts, egoism and altruism, explain suicide by looking at the framework of social attachments to society which Durkheim called social integration, and we have looked at the continuum of integration from egoism to altruism. The concept of anomic suicide, on the other hand, belongs to a framework which explains suicide by looking at the changes in the regulatory mechanism of society. Thus while egoistic suicide occurs because the individual is not well attached to society due to the absence of social integration, altruistic suicide takes place because the individual is over attached to society to the point that individualism is non-existent. While the first type is due to over developed individualism, the second is due to a lack of development at the level of the individual.[289] Anomic suicide, on the other hand, occurs because of the reduction of the regulatory mechanisms of society. In such circumstances, the limitations set by society are virtually absent or weakened.

Fatalistic suicide   Fatalistic suicide, the last category of suicide discussed by Durkheim, represents the opposite pole of suicide resulting from adjustments in the regulatory mechanisms of society. In the same way that altruism serves to pinpoint suicide which occurs because of an excess of social integration, fatalism signifies a form of suicide which Durkheim believed occurred because of an excess of social regulation. Durkheim stated that whereas anomie refers to the absence of regulation, fatalistic suicide occurs because of an excessive degree of regulation and an overly developed system of control over the individual. While Durkheim had little to say about the characteristics of fatalistic suicide, he cited as an example the suicide of slaves who, seeing no alternative to life except enslavement under a master, take their own life.[290]

The Elementary Forms of the Religious Life

The Historical Context of the Work

Durkheim wrote *The Elementary Forms of Religious Life* between 1902–1911, and first published it as a complete study in 1912. By the time it was published, Durkheim

---

289 *Suicide*, p. 221.

290 *Suicide*, p. 276. Durkheim's discussion of fatalism is brief. His interest in introducing the concept of fatalistic suicide is for purposes of conceptual symmetry. The idea is that each of the pairs of suicide types (egoistic-altruistic; anomic-fatalistic) demonstrate the polar opposites of both integration and regulation in a symmetrical manner. For discussion of how Durkheim arrived at the egoistic-altruistic pair, see Ken Morrison, 'Durkheim and Schopenhauer: New Textual Evidence on the Conceptual History of Durkheim's Formulation of the Egoistic-Altruistic types of Suicide,' *Durkheimian Studies*, 4, 1998, pp. 115–23.

was 54 years old and had become one of the leading thinkers in French social thought. While he had begun working on the problem of religion as early 1902, there were several reasons why he chose to study religion as a central subject of sociological interest at the time. First, religion had been one of the leading themes in Durkheim's sociological journal, the *Année Sociologique* where many of the issues had focused on the question of tribal religions as a result of Roberson Davies ethnographic research during the period. Second, as early as 1890, anthropologists and ethnographers had come to view religion and religious practices as the central subject matter of social and historical interest. Studies such as Spencer and Gillen's *The Native Tribes of Central Australia* published in 1899, and Benjamin Howitt's *Native Tribes of South Eastern Australia* were among the first to carry out ethnographic studies of the religious practices of tribal societies that had not been studied previously. Third, Durkheim's colleague Marcel Mauss was pursuing anthropological interests at the time and many of his articles were featured in the *Année Sociologique*, giving it a distinct anthropological focus.[291] By 1895, Durkheim was persuaded that religion would be a fitting subject of sociological study because it seemed to be at the center of the social framework of society.

Fundamental Aims of The Study

Generally speaking, *The Elementary Forms of Religious Life* had several key aims. First, was to study the structure of primitive religions in order to provide an explanation of their elementary organization. Durkheim thought he could do this only by looking at what he thought were the simplest of all religions, the totem tribes of Northern and Central Australia. He believed that an analysis of these simple religions would lead to the discovery of the most basic elements of religious life, and he referred to these elements as the 'elementary forms.' A second aim of the study was to go beyond the theory of social cohesion and social solidarity first outlined in *The Division of Labor* and in *Suicide* by pinpointing the physical and material effects that specific religious enactments had on collective social realities. In this case, Durkheim wanted to look at the role played by a type of religious ceremony he called 'effervescence assemblies' whose frenzied social and mental states had been first described by Spencer and Gillen in the form of the ritual known as a corroboree, whose periodic enactments took place among the totem tribes of central Australia.[292] Durkheim thought that these periodic ritual enactments indicated a point in the social

---

291 W.S.F Pickering traces the influence of Marcel Mauss' essays on Durkheim, particularly the essays related to Mauss' work on the two phases of Eskimo experience and on primitive classification. See Pickering, *Durkheim's Sociology of Religion: Themes and Theories*, London: Routledge, 1984, pp. 380–8.

292 While Durkheim used the expression 'effervescent social environment' and 'effervescent ceremonies' interchangeably, it was Bill Pickering who used the term 'effervescent assembly' and who preferred its usage to describe the point at which collective enactments become more intense. See W. S. F. Pickering, *Durkheim's Sociology of Religion: Themes and Theories*, London: Routledge, 1984, p. 385.

cycle of the group where the collective experience of society 'intensified' to the point where religion acted to consecrate their collective social acts and activities, making sacred their material objects and their ties to each other and to the religious order.

A third aim of the study was to undertake an examination of religious practices from the perspective of tracing the origins of what philosophers had called the 'categories of understanding.' These categories, he thought, were utilized by individuals in their perceptual relations with the external world not only during the exalted religious states created by their religious enactments, but also when they made spatial and temporal judgments and classifications about the external world. Durkheim's discussion of the categories of understanding is, therefore, key to the study of religion in two central respects. First is because Durkheim thought that the categories of understanding originate from material activity in society and therefore have a social origin rather than being innately given by human reason, as philosophers had believed.[293] In contrast to the philosophers, therefore, Durkheim put forward the argument that the categories of understanding have their origin in social experience and were the direct result of the tendency in all societies to create divisions and classifications in the material world. He reasoned that the human tendency to make divisions and to classify things in external nature was thus simply the extension of the religious principle onto nature and the natural world itself. Durkheim argued that religious experience must have been the first way of forming perceptual relations with the outside world and, as such, it must have functioned as a means of explaining the way the universe works to a tribal people, and of shaping their perceptions in relation to it.

A second reason why Durkheim's study of the categories of understanding is important is because it was the first theoretical argument to challenge the dominant philosophical view proposed by Kant and Hume who stated that the categories were an inherent part of the mental faculties, and that only through these faculties were human beings able perceptually to relate to the external world. According to this view, a logical order was thus conferred onto the world by mental categories and this meant that outer experience was itself actively shaped by the categories of understanding operating perceptually in relation to the world. Durkheim's argument sought therefore to reverse this view. Lastly, the fourth aim of *The Elementary Forms* was to demonstrate that, when reduced to its basic elements and its elementary forms, religion is nothing more than the expression of society in its consecrated form. Let us look more closely at this argument.

The Central Argument: Durkheim's Search for a Definition of Religion

Durkheim began by setting out a definition of religion that would be consistent with all forms of religious life and, in this case, he started from the perspective of looking for the basic elements and elementary forms of religious activity. He stated that whereas others have defined religion in terms of the supernatural or the mystical and tend to

---

293 *Elementary Forms*, p. 8.

conceive of it in the form of a mystical experience or in the form of the spiritual world, he turned his attention to a definition of religion that identified two central elementary forms of religious life. The first of these is the system of beliefs, practices and rites that are practiced toward sacred things.[294] These are defined simply as a set of ideas and attitudes which are held in relation to sacred things; whereas rites are defined more broadly to include a system of actions which are developed toward religious things and objects. A second elementary form referred to by Durkheim was the tendency in all religions to divide the world into two regions which he called the sacred and the profane. This is the principle that requires that 'sacred things be set apart from other things and forbidden.'[295] Durkheim believed that the division of the world 'into two regions, one containing all that is sacred, the other all that is profane, was the most distinctive trait of religious life.'[296]

Since no proper understanding of Durkheim's theory of religion is possible without elaborating on the distinction between the sacred and the profane, we turn to a brief discussion of these important concepts.[297] Durkheim believed that the division between the sacred and profane form the basis of religious life in several respects. First, he asserted that the sacred embodies not only gods, spirits and natural things, but also embraces beliefs, gestures and objects which represent the sacred as well. A belief, in this case, according to Durkheim is a practice or rite which can have a sacred character by virtue of the tendency to be viewed by others as a 'consecrated' thing. Second, words and expressions, and even combinations of words can be sacred. These can be uttered only by consecrated persons and involve gestures and movements which only certain people can perform.[298] In addition, a system of rites, beliefs and social practices emerge from sacred things and radiate around them.

In direct contrast to the sacred is the profane. This, according to Durkheim, is something subordinated in dignity to the sacred, and therefore is seen as radically opposite from the principle of the sacred. The profane, in contrast to the sacred, is the principle which has the capacity to defile or contaminate the sacred, and to this extent the sacred and profane are linked together since they appear within religious systems in the form of opposing powers. In addition to this, rules must exist in all religions which regulate the separation between the two regions, and in this case extraordinary precautions must always be taken when the sacred and profane come into contact with one another. Durkheim went on to outline several related characteristics of the sacred and profane. First, the sacred is always separated from all other objects and

---

294 *Elementary Forms,* p. 36. The term 'elementary forms' is misleading. Stated simply, the term refers to the fundamental elements of all religions. The two elementary forms of religion put forward by Durkheim are: (i) a system of beliefs and rites which specify attitudes taken up toward the world and (ii) the division of things into the sacred and profane.

295 *Elementary Forms,* p. 47; and Fields trans. p. 44.

296 *Elementary Forms* , pp. 37–47.

297 *Elementary Forms,* pp. 37–42.

298 *Elementary Forms,* p. 37.

therefore constitutes things set apart from profane things. Second, a system of rites and social practices arise which set out how the sacred is to be approached and how members of the group are to conduct themselves in the presence of the sacred object.[299] Third, sacred things are not only things set apart, but also they are protected by interdictions which have the force of prohibitions or taboos acting to protect and isolate the sacred from the profane. Fourth, sacred things are segregated from profane things and are thought to be superior in dignity and are therefore elevated from ordinary things. Fifth, the sacred and profane represent a principle of segregation which formally separates the natural from the spiritual world, the domestic world from the outside world and the inside of the tribal space from the outside. In this way, the sacred and the profane provide the group with a classificatory model of opposites such as good and evil, clean and dirty, pure and polluted, inside and outside, holy and defiled and so on.[300] Sixth, in the totem tribes studied by Durkheim, the passage from the profane to the sacred must be accompanied by rites which are thought to 'transform' one state into the other through rituals of initiation, rebirth or sacrifice.[301]

Search for the Most Elementary Religion: The Totem Tribes of Central Australia

Having outlined a definition of religion based on the elementary forms, Durkheim turned his attention to searching for what he called the most elementary religions. He began by reviewing some of the early claims regarding which religions were the most rudimentary and, generally speaking, he looked at two prevailing views. First, were those put forward by Edward Taylor who had claimed that 'animism' was the most elementary religion, and second, were the views put forward by Max Muller who had argued that 'naturism' was the most basic of all religions. Durkheim, however, rejected these views on several fronts. First, he stated that Taylor's view of religion relied on a spirit world that was vague and indeterminate rather than relying on a system of actions and practices found in reality. Taylor's 'spirits' and 'souls,' he went on, were not subject to observation, and are therefore not amenable to sociological study[302] Second was the view of Muller who believed that human beings create religion by themselves. This view, according to Durkheim, takes the position that religion originates from individuals and from human nature. But, said Durkheim, this is not possible since neither the individual or nature are sacred by themselves.[303] Third, Durkheim thought that since neither human beings nor nature are sacred on their own, religion must get its sacredness from some other source which can only be society. In this view, human beings have a religious nature not because of the spirit world or the natural world, but because they live

---

299 *Elementary Forms,* p. 41.
300 *Elementary Forms,* p. 40
301 *Elementary Forms,* pp. 39–41.
302 *Elementary Forms,* pp. 48–55.
303 *Elementary Forms,* pp. 81–2.

in society. On this account, Durkheim's aim was to show that religion had a social origin that can only be explained by looking at society.

Durkheim then went on to reason that in looking at religious life across distinct societies there must be a religion more fundamental than the ones discussed by Taylor and Muller. He went on to say that the earliest of all religions are the tribes of central and Northern Australia since these are the more elementary religions in comparison with others that have existed. There are several reasons for this. First, the beliefs and practices of the totem religions are relatively homogeneous across different societies and this leads more readily to finding a common principle underlying the practices and beliefs that unify them. Second, the anthropological and ethnographic evidence on totemic religions is generally more complete than it was on other religions. Among the most comprehensive descriptions of totemism, according to Durkheim, was the work by John McLennan who was one of the first to study totem religions in ancient societies. After him, Lewis Morgan studied the characteristics of totemism among North American Indian tribes and was among the first to look at religion as a unified system of beliefs and social practices. Then, in a series of ethnographic studies documenting the characteristics of totem religions, Spencer and Gillen provided key observations of totemic religions among the tribes of Central and Northern Australia. For these reasons, Durkheim believed that the totem tribes of Australia exemplified the most elementary religion and that the underlying system of beliefs and practices best exemplified the nature of religious life itself.

In addition to these reasons, Durkheim thought that the totem tribes of central Australia were interesting because they had a religious system that was linked to a definite 'social organization based on a specific set of religious ceremonies which developed in relation to the totem.'[304] Furthermore, not only were there a number of tribes that had a full blown religious system concentrated around very specific acts of religious worship of the totem, but they also formed into groups who occupied a region where the entire population was divided into clans who periodically came together for purposes of religious ceremonies that lasted for long periods of time. These were a people, according to Durkheim, whose religious beliefs and institutions were identical and when periodic religious feast and ceremonies arose they suspended their everyday economic activity and assembled in one place for a religious ceremony. By thus joining the people of the clan together with objects classified in it, as well as to their combined religious ceremonies, Durkheim thought that they formed a unified system with all the social and religious parts aligned systematically together. In this way, Durkheim believed that the circuit of religious enactments, together with their performance of specific rites, seemed to extend well beyond what at first appeared to be its boundaries.[305]

Having chosen totemism as the most elementary religion, Durkheim began to look more closely at the nature of totemic beliefs and into the structure of totemism more

---

304 Ibid., p.89 (Swain, trans); p. 85 (Fields, trans).
305 *Elementary Forms*, pp. 150–4.

generally. His discussion began with a simple but fundamental chain of observations.[306] First, he pointed out that all the members of the group refer to themselves by a tribal name, even though they are not blood relations. This binds them together as if they were blood relations, and identifies them as if they were family members. Second, the totem name they use designates them as a tribal people which compels them to recognize duties and obligations toward each other which are on the level of blood obligations. These include reciprocal aid, vengeance, mourning, and the obligation not to marry among themselves.[307] The totem thus binds them together collectively as if they were a family united by blood. Third, their beliefs involve a system of prohibitions and taboos which requires them to keep the totem apart from profane things and distinct as sacred things. This separation is enacted by a religious ritual which carries out the separation in a particular way and in accordance with a particular procedure that tolerates no error. Fourth, totemism is above all a tribal religion in so far as it represents the tribe as a whole descending from a mythical or ancestral being whose beliefs and practices are sufficiently strong enough to have survived over time. A fifth characteristic of totemism is its tendency to extend outward from the immediate affairs of the tribe to include a system of ideas representing all of human existence, specifically ideas representing causal forces in the universe and in the natural world. In this way, totemism extends outward into the world to encompass a total system of classification related to human existence, the creation of the universe and of the natural world itself.

The totem may therefore be described as an institution which leads to three distinct kinds of religious activities. First is a system of beliefs and rites which unifies and binds the social group together around a sacred object. Second is a system of special prohibitions and restrictions which sets out the obligations which the tribal members have toward the totem object. Third is a system of rites and religious ceremonies for drawing them together as a group and for worshipping the sacred totem. Fourth is a special class of religious rules referred to as interdictions which summons all the separate clans together for the purpose of a religious ceremony that lasts for several days. Given the basis character of the totem religions, said Durkheim, here is an elementary religious system that is linked to a definite form of social organization based on a division of society into clans and tribes which trace their descent from the single scared totem.

The Totem and the Social Classification of the Universe: The Fundamental Organizing Principle

Beyond their organization into clans, Durkheim believed that the totem religions were a complete system of religious ideas relating to the world and that, as such, it provided a total comprehension of the world and the universe in relation to itself. Durkheim reasoned that to the extent that this was the case, he thought at the heart

---

306 *Elementary Forms,* p. 102.
307 Ibid.

of the totemic religions lies a central principle whereby the tribes project their own sacredness onto the natural world and the universe and that from this arises the tendency to compare the divisions and classifications of the various clans and tribes, with the classifications and divisions of the natural world.[308]

While this may be difficult to understand, the principle by which the group projects its own sacredness onto nature is fundamental to understanding Durkheim's argument. Simply stated, Durkheim contends that as the totem makes the group sacred and classifies the tribal space into sacred and profane regions by specific separations and divisions, these divisions and classifications are projected onto external nature and onto the universe for purposes of further classification in the form of spatial divisions specifying north, south, east and west. In addition, the classifications are extended further into nature for purposes of dividing elements of time into seasonal variations such as summer, winter, fall and spring. Additionally, each of the divisions and separations are assigned causes and powers, such as when the region of the north is associated with coldness, or the south associated with heat. In this way, each one of the regions in space and each one of the segments in time are assigned powers which correspond to the divisions first formed within the clans. From this, said Durkheim, appears the tendency to apply further divisions and classifications to the external world in the form of classes, groups, and categories, and from this arises the tendency to project these classifications onto nature, then to the universe, and then to their cultural and domestic categories. Only in this way, Durkheim believed, are things in the natural world understood to belong to different groups and classes, and only then are they arranged by different classifications, different names and different groupings, each with their systematizations.[309] From these separtions and classifications, other separations follow such as the divisions and categories that emerge in their domestic practices related to food preparation where they divide the raw from the cooked and the spoiled from the rotten. Similarly, classifications emerge between the rooms where the food is prepared and the rooms where it is eaten. These divisions in the household in turn reflect the divisons where the sacred is separated from the profane, and the divisions they make between their different groups and classes as such. Durkheim then went on to reason that the principle of religious classification is thus the model of group organization, which in turn became the model for classifying things in the world and the universe. This, said Durkheim, tells us how 'the idea of class and category first took form in human groups,' and 'these classifications are the first we meet with in history.'[310] Durkheim then went on to say that since these are the first classifications:

---

308 The argument showing how the sacredness of the totem is connected to larger system of classification of the natural world is outlined in *The Elementary Forms*, pp. 141–49. Fields trans., pp. 141–9.

309 *Elementary Forms*, p. 142–44.

310 Ibid., p. 145.

[T]hey are modeled on the social organization, or rather they are taken from the framework of society as their own. It was the division into groups that served as genera and the clans as a species: All they did was make room for things in the groups they themselves formed. And if these various classes of things were not simply juxtaposed to one another, but arranged according to a unified plan, that is because the same social groups to which they are assimilated are themselves unified and, through that union form an organic whole: the tribe. The unity of these first logical systems merely reproduces that of society. Thus we have our first opportunity to test the propositions put forward at the beginning of the work: this is the assertion that the basic categories of thought are the product of social factors.[311]

From the central idea that a connection exists between religious beliefs, the sacredness of the totem and the organization of individuals into groups, classes and clans, Durkheim argued that that all the subsequent classification of the natural and social world thus derives from a religious system of ideas. Religion, in this view, must have been the first system for classifying the natural world by class and category, and this must have been extended to the social and domestic world as such. Why else, said Durkheim, would the Haida of North America classify the things of nature exactly like the divisions within their group, and why would these divisions parallel the system of totemic beliefs? Further, by 'joining the people of the clan and the things classified in it, they form a unified system with all the parts allied and vibrating sympathetically.'[312]

Durkheim went on to argue that along with all the material attachments and affinities which the totem provides among the members of the tribe, the totem principle also provides the group with a means of classifying and separating the natural world from the spiritual world. In this way, it creates a conceptual division in the cultural world of the tribe where the sacred is kept separate from the profane, where the pure is kept separate from the impure and where the interior of the tribal space is kept separate from the space that is exterior to it.[313] This means that as a people they come to see the world through the categories of these distinctions and classifications, and that they use these distinctions both in their everyday material world in their domestic practices, and in the religious world in their spiritual practices.

The Two Phases of Social Life: Effervescent Assemblies and the Birth of the Religious

After outlining the structure of totem religions and the principle of internal and external classification, Durkheim turned his attention to two sorts of issues. First was to isolate the social practices and ceremonies that put the group in motion so that they come together to carry out a religious enactment. Second was to pinpoint the practices and activities whereby persons, things, and spaces are set apart in the social

---

311 Ibid., pp. 145–6.
312 Ibid., p. 150.
313 *Elementary Forms*, p. 40.

world so that everything becomes sacred and is transformed into the spiritual world. These practices and activities, said Durkheim, manifest themselves in a process he referred to as the 'two alternating phases of social life' which take place as a religious ceremony approaches. The name he gives to this phase of social activity is the 'effervescent assembly' and on this he stated the following:

> Life in Australian societies alternates between two different phases. In one phase, the population is scattered in small groups that attend to their occupations independently. Each family lives to itself, hunting, fishing – in short, striving by all possible means to get the food it requires. In the other phase, by contrast, the population comes together, concentrating itself at specified places when a clan is summoned to come together and on that occasion they conduct a religious ceremony called a *corroboree*.

and

> These two phases stand in the sharpest possible contrast. The first phase, in which economic activity predominates, is generally of rather low intensity. Gathering seeds or plants necessary for food, hunting, and fishing are not occupations that can stir truly strong passions. The dispersed state in which the society finds itself makes life monotonous, slack, and humdrum. [But] everything changes when a corroboree takes place. The very act of congregating is an exceptionally powerful stimulant. Once the individuals are gathered together, a sort of electricity is generated from their closeness and quickly launches them into an extraordinary height of exaltation[314]

Then he went on to say:

> On ordinary days,[their acts are] utilitarian and everyone attends to [their] own personal business; and for most this primarily consists in satisfying the exigencies of material life where the principle incentive to economic activity has always been that of private interest. But on feast days, on the contrary, these preoccupations are necessarily eclipsed since, being profane, they are excluded from these sacred periods. At this time their thoughts are centered upon their common beliefs, their common traditions, the memory of their great ancestors, the collective ideals of which they are the incarnation. At this time, society is the foreground of their very consciousness and it dominates and directs all conduct; and they feel that there is something outside them which is born again, and that there are forces which are reanimated and reawakened and each individual participates in this collective renovation.[315]

There are, said Durkheim, two distinct phases which are reflected in the social life of the tribes which can be contrasted in the 'sharpest way' and which constitute what he called the 'two collective manifestations' of their social activity.[316] In one phase,

---

314 Durkheim, *The Elementary Forms of Religious Life* (Trans. by J. Swain), London: G. Allen & Unwin, [1915] 1964, pp. 214–15; and (Trans by K. Fields), New York: The Free Press, 1995, pp. 216–18.

315 Elementary Forms, pp. 348–49.

316 Durkheim, *The Elementary Forms*, pp. 214–18; 248–9/216–17; 352–3.

families go about their everyday activities of hunting and gathering which they perform out of necessity. In this phase, everyone is essentially 'scattered' and 'dispersed' for purposes of carrying out separate economic and domestic tasks which, under the circumstances, tends to 'awaken little passion' in them, and which tends to be 'under the control of their private wills.'[317] In direct contrast to this is the second phase of collective life, which begins with what Durkheim calls a periodic religious enactment in which each of the individuals is 'summoned to come together in one place to conduct a religious ceremony.' This, he said, immediately 'transports the individual into an entirely different world from the practical one they have before their eyes,' and under these circumstances the group suddenly assembles for purposes of a religious ceremony that puts them into motion in a new way.[318] By reason of assembling, said Durkheim, 'the individuals come together in a way that multiplies the relations existing between them' and this, he said, intensifies their relations and 'makes them more intimate with one another.'[319]

By the 'very act of congregating' there are several abrupt affects. First, it puts the group into action in a new way by propelling separate individuals together into a confined space, and this operates as a powerful stimulant that produces exaltation which seems to have no limit. All the families congregate together so that they become a unified group that moves in unison with synchronous cries and gestures so that all their acts are coordinated in gesture and in voice.[320] At this point everything becomes sacred: space, time, things and people; and consequently, this sacredness functions as a means of consecrating their acts and the collective space which they inhabit.[321] At this moment, they are removed from their ordinary activities and their ritual enactments function to put boundaries around their ceremonies in a way which formally designates them as separate from the outside world. These boundaries, in fact, act to separate certain aspects of reality and ignore others; and this serves to isolate certain properties of their enactments which explicitly draw on forms of representations that activate their sentiments and their perceptions, taking them further into an exalted state of mind.[322] It is here, said Durkheim, that the common sentiments can only express themselves collectively, rather than during the time that they are dispersed, and as these begin to be expressed by their enactments, their unity becomes stronger.

Furthermore, at the very point that they come together, certain social divisions are marked off and certain principles are enacted. A separation is made between

---

317 Ibid., p. 215.

318 Ibid., pp. 214–18; 248–9/216–17; 352–3.

319 Ibid., pp. 215, 226, 348.

320 Ibid.

321 For discussion of how effervescent assemblies consecrate things, spaces and times see William Ramp 'Effervescence, Differentiation and Representation in The Elementary Forms,' in N.J. Allen, W.S.F. Pickering and W. Watts Miller (eds.), *On Durkheim's Elementary Forms of Relgious Life*, pp. 136–148; and N. J. Allen, 'Effervescences and the Origins of Human Society,' pp. 149–161.

322 Ibid., p. 216. The theory of social representations proposed by Durkheim has become contentious in the last decade.

certain spaces and things. As spaces and things become subject to the rule of separation, they are demarcated from other things by virtue of the fact that they are sacred, whereas other things and spaces are removed from them and remain profane or impure.[323] At this point, their enactments consecrate spaces, things and people which before were impure and profane. This sets them apart, elevates them from their everyday activities and makes them sacred.[324] Also, the separations and divisions they make between the sacred and the profane, draws attention to the way religion is made manifest in the cultural world created by their acts. Not only do beliefs and practices have a sacred character at this point, but they also serve to consecrate things and consecrate acts.

A second broad effect of the religious enactments are the periodic rituals performed within the overall ceremonies themselves. These begin at certain times of the year and involve participants in deliberate enactments where they decorate their bodies and place masks and other paraphernalia upon themselves. Often these rituals are set apart from the overall effervescent assembly and are differentiated into specialized enactments that include rites related to grief and suffering called piacular rites. In the performance of these rites, they often mutilate their bodies and engage in collective enactments of dancing and shrieking. In this way, said Durkheim, a 'living reality exists outside the individual' and acts on the mind by what it does to the individual.[325] This underlines the fact that religious enactments come to be outside the assembled individuals as an object, and that their enactments come to consecrate the objective structures of society whose 'living reality unifies them in their body and their mind.'[326] Often these rituals are marked off in time and in space by processions, dances, singing, crying out and shrieking which lasts for several days in duration. At this point, said Durkheim, they are furthest from the individuality they experience on ordinary days.

In addition to the performance of the rite, other changes take place in the individual's perception of reality. The immediate suspension of their everyday activities, followed by their coming together in one place, marks off a new reality that is distinct from the reality of everyday life. Under these circumstances, masks and bodily decorations used in the rites come to figure materially in the inner transformation of their mental states, and those gathered together in the group feel themselves to be transformed in some way by it. Durkheim thought that it was out of this 'effervescent social environment that the religious idea was born.'[327]

---

323 The principle of dividing the world into two domains, one sacred the other profane, is 'the distinctive trait of religious thought' and this, says Durkheim, 'presupposes a classification of all things' into categories that involve the act of separation and segregation. For this discussion see Durkheim, *The Elementary Forms*, pp. 36–42/36–9.

324 Further discussion of the rule of separation and the purity rule can be found in Mary Douglas, *Purity and Danger: Analysis of Concepts of Pollution and Taboo*, Middlesex: Penguin Books, 1970, pp. 17–46.

325 Ibid., p. 227.

326 Ibid., p. 229.

327 Ibid., p. 218; and Fields trans. p. 220

A third effect that occurs during the performance of religious enactments is the appearance of a succession of religious interdicts. Interdicts, for Durkheim, denote a special class of religious regulation which has the power to place extraordinary restrictions on certain kinds of religious activity. Interdicts often apply to the performance of acts that are related to approaching or handling the totem in some way. In this context, interdicts set requirements about what must be observed in practicing different rites toward the totem that are mainly enacted during religious rituals and express themselves in the form of observances regarding the performance of acts related to sacred things. Durkheim identified two distinct kinds of interdicts, ones he called 'positive interdicts,' others 'negative interdicts.'[328] Both types of interdicts form themselves into two distinct classes of rites which are performed toward the totem. One governs the rites and duties associated with approaching the totem and maintaining it, while the other specifies what is forbidden in the realm of conduct while approaching the totem. Positive interdicts, according to Durkheim, set requirements which bring individuals into contact with the sacredness of the totem itself. The purpose of these rites is to secure bonds between the members of the group and to reinforce and reaffirm the efficacy and power of the totem. Negative rites and interdicts, on the other hand, concern themselves with how individuals approach the totem, whether in silence, under conditions of fast or whether by day or night. Sometimes interdicts will specify the precise ornamentation that is required and considered to be appropriate. Negative interdicts, therefore, ensure that individuals approach the totem with the highest possible feeling of 'religious gravity.'[329]

Positive and negative interdicts not only ensure that the totem is something that is kept apart from other things, but also it ensures that they protect the totem from impurities by laying out rules that are to be obeyed in worshipping the totem. Interdicts do this by designating the point at which religious obligations and duties are to be imposed. For instance, on a specified day the Arunta of Australia perform a rite called the Intichiuma that begins and ends with interdicts. At a precise point, the male members of the group are called together by an interdict and 'they are required to advance in profound silence without arms or ornaments.' Their attitude and their pace is marked with an extreme 'religious gravity,' and at a certain time specified by another interdict, the young men of the group are 'obligated to mix something of their bodies with the totem in order to make the rite more efficacious.' They do this by 'opening their veins to let streams of blood flow onto the rock' in the vicinity where the totem is located.[330] Further, the obligations carry with them the urgent need to be performed in the name of the religious order, and Durkheim pointed out that during the period when the interdicts are imposed, 'religious life remains intense' and this 'intensity is manifested by an aggravation of the system of interdicts.'[331] At this very moment, said Durkheim, 'the interdictions are strict and without exception' and

---

328 *Elementary Forms,* pp. 299 ff.
329 *Elementary Forms,* p. 328.
330 *Elementary Forms,* pp. 330–4.
331 Ibid., pp. 333–4.

they believe that 'any violation of the interdict would result in neutralizing the positive affects of the rite.'[332] Along with the performance of the rite, the interdictions tell them how they must act in relation to the totem, and it reinforces their relation to it since, while on 'ordinary days they may eat the animal or plant that serves as the totem,' 'they do not even dare to touch it' during religious days and the period of the interdicts.[333] Then, said Durkheim, a 'final ceremony terminates the period of extra-ordinary interdiction, and this closes the long series of rites.'[334]

The Material Effects of the Religious Enactments

So far, two essential characteristics of effervescent assemblies stand out: they foreground the power which the religious enactments have on the assembled group, and they highlight the material affects caused by the enactments. These are as follows. First, effervescent assemblies begin and end with interdictions which intensify social activities between individuals by inducing them to assemble from a state of being dispersed. This intensifies their relation to each other and to the collective structures of society. Second, effervescent assemblies perform the function of segregating and classifying the separate enactments by marking them off with boundaries and divisions that differentiate their ordinary activities from their religious activities.[335] This activates the collective memory and the tribal principle which is different from the memory of private life and their mundane activities.

Third, effervescent assemblies induce participation in activities referred to as 'piacular rites' involving collective displays of self mutilation, tribal initiation, violence and danger, which often involves the ritualistic use of weapons or blood that is drawn from their bodies in an effort to appease the totem animal or the totem substance.[336] At this point, said Durkheim, their private individuality is replaced by a collective identity that is manifested in their joint frenzy. As these rites are enacted, something comes over them so that they 'cooperate in unison, and their gestures tend to become rhythmic and regular.' At this point they 'release unheard of actions which act to remove the individual completely from their ordinary conditions of social activity.'[337] In this condition, they 'are to be seen running here and there like madmen, giving themselves up to all sorts of immoderate movements, crying, shrieking, rolling in the dust, throwing it in every direction, biting themselves, and brandishing their arms in a furious manner.'[338]

---

332 Ibid.

333 *Elementary Forms*, p. 328.

334 Ibid., p. 334.

335 Durkheim states that society not only consecrates human beings, but it also consecrates spaces and things. See Ibid., p. 213 (Swain trans.), p. 215 (Fields trans).

336 Durkheim discusses the violent nature of piacular rites in *The Elementary Forms*, pp. 390–3. Obviously, piacular rites are the most dramatic form of the material effects of religious enactments, and in this sense are key to the empirical efficacy of religious practices.

337 Ibid., p. 216.

338 Ibid., p. 215.

In direct contrast to the effects of the piacular rites, are the material affects of the interdiction that summons them to assemble in one place. While at one point they are dispersed, and yet at another 'society is able to rejuvenate the sentiments it has of itself only by assembling,' they cannot for practical reasons remain assembled all the time, 'so it scatters to assemble anew when it feels the need.'[339] From this perspective, everyday practical activity separates and individualizes them so that they cannot out of necessity remain in a congregated state indefinitely, yet neither can they remain in an individual state either and, out of another kind of necessity, they re-assemble by a religious interdiction. When this state of activity is reached, said Durkheim, individuals do not recognize themselves any longer since they occupy a new state of social being.[340] Only by periodic assembly, then, 'is society able to renew the sentiments it has of itself, and only by this assembly is the religious idea born and the collective memory enacted.'

Durkheim's Theory of the Social Origin of the Categories of Understanding

Having outlined Durkheim's argument for the elementary forms of religious life and having shown that the principle of classification and division into groups originates from the tribal organization, Durkheim turned his attention to a second line of argument. This has to do with the discussion of the 'categories of understanding' which appears in the introduction to *The Elementary Forms*. In this context, there are two immediate questions that arise. First, what does Durkheim mean by the categories of understanding; and second, what is the relation of the categories of understanding to the theory of religion? In order to answer these questions, we have to look at the introduction to *The Elementary Forms* where Durkheim initially tackled the question of the categories of understanding in connection with pursuing a theory of religion. He wrote:

> [O]ur study is not of interest merely for the science of religion. The study of religious phenomena gives us a means of renewing the problems which, up to the present, have only been discussed among philosophers. [Philosophers believe that] at the root of all our judgments there are a certain number of essential [categories] which dominate all our intellectual life; they are what philosophers since Aristotle have called the categories of the understanding: ideas of time, space, class, number, cause, substance, etc. Up to the present there have been only two doctrines in the field. For some, the categories cannot be derived from experience: they are logically prior to it and condition it. They are imminent in the human mind and are said to be a priori. Others, however, hold that they are constructed and made up of pieces and bits, and that the individual is the artisan of this construction.[341]

---

339 Ibid., p. 349.
340 Ibid., p. 218.
341 Durkheim, *The Elementary Forms*, p. 9; Fields trans. p. 8.

In this quotation, Durkheim stated that his interest in the 'categories of understandings' began with the observation that the sociological study of religion overlaps with the problems which have been discussed by philosophy concerning the categories of understanding. This overlap between the sociological study of religion and philosophy became apparent to Durkheim when he began to compare what philosophers have said about the categories of understanding with his own findings concerning the classification system in the totem tribes of Australia. What he found among these tribes was a system of classification in which the group divided themselves into clans corresponding to totems, and then they extended this classification to regions in space so that each division of the group was assigned an orientation with a region is space in which one clan belonged to the north, the other the south, etc. As far as Durkheim was concerned, this meant that the system of classification seemed to be modeled on the social organization, which he believed later became a model for the mental organization of the categories. It was this that led him to take the view that the categories of understanding must have had a social origin developed within society rather than arising from internal reason. In this view, the tendency to classify does not come from within, but is externally derived.

The discovery of this overlap between the study of religion and problems in philosophy caused Durkheim to turn his attention to a discussion of the philosophical categories of understanding that included a specific number of 'essential ideas' consisting of space, time, cause, force, category, substance, number, etc.'[342] He went on to say that in philosophy there were two formal positions that have attempted to explain the nature of the categories themselves. The first of these are the 'apriorists' who believed that the categories originate in the human mind and that they have 'a pre-eminent power to confer a logical quality to the world.' On this view, we only come to know the outside world by applying the categories of understanding to things and objects in it.[343] Second are the empiricists who take the position that the categories are constructed from the mind by individual sense perceptions, and that individuals alone construct the things of the world out of these sense perceptions. Thus, while the apriorists tend to believe that the categories of understanding are essentially 'given by nature' and are innate to human reason, the empiricists believe that 'the categories are constructed of bits and pieces' of sense data and that the individual is the agent of the construction.[344]

While the philosophers believed that the categories of space and time originate from internal reason and are innate to the mind, Durkheim began to re-define the problem of the categories in the context of the classification systems found in the Australian tribes. Based on this evidence, he established that it was their tendency to divide themselves into groups and marriage classes, and then to apply these divisions and classifications

---

342 Ibid., pp. 9–20.
343 Ibid., p. 13–14.
344 Ibid., p. 13.

to the external world in the form of regions in space and segments in time. In light of this, he reasoned that if the Australian system of classification into groups and classes correspond to the categories found in their cultural, spiritual and domestic practices, then their classification system served as a model for the mental organization with which they came to see the world. In putting this view forward, however, Durkheim came up against the philosophical view of the categories of understanding which held a completely different view of classification and a completely different view of the external world, setting Durkheim into opposition with philosophy.

Durkheim's Opposition to Philosophy

To see this, we need only look at the theory of the categories being put forward by philosophers and how this affected their view of the outside world. The classic statement regarding the philosophical view of the categories derives from the writings of Immanuel Kant whose *Critique of Pure Reason* was one of the first to put forward a philosophical view of categories.[345] Kant began by making two fundamental observations. First, he stated that the categories of understanding including time, space and cause are all supplied a priori by the reasoning faculties originating in the mind. In and of itself, this was key because Kant had formally separated into two realms what 'reason supplies for itself,' and what is in the outside world of experience already. Second, Kant asserted that the 'time in which these relations are set in the mind' seems to precede the 'moment we have consciousness of them in experience.'[346] What was so important about Kant's theory of the categories was that it introduced the fundamental separation between conscious reason in the mind and the existence of objects and things in the outer world, stating that we can only have understanding of the outer world through the operation of the categories, and that the categories come first before experience. This meant that without the a priori categories, the outer world cannot be perceived by itself, and that the categories act as condition of validity for judgments about external reality, since no judgment about external reality is possible without the a priori categories.

In direct contrast to Kant's position, Durkheim thought the existence of society came first before the reasoning faculties, and that the system for classifying space and time found in the totem tribes of Australia served as a model for the mental organization of the categories. Furthermore, he thought the system of classification existed in the outside social world independently of the a priori perceptions. In this case, Durkheim argued that the tendency to classify by the categories of space and time was therefore modeled on the tribal organization rather than the mental organization.

The second view of the categories was derived from classical empiricism and the work of David Hume. Hume's philosophy was key to Durkheim's argument because

---

345 Kant, *The Critique of Pure Reason*, 65–111.
346 Ibid., p. 43.

Hume had claimed that the categories of understanding were not derived from experience, but instead evolve from human mental dispositions and sense perceptions. Hume outlined his view on the basis of three key assumptions. First, he thought that our understanding of objects in the outer world was filtered through our sense perceptions, and that what we perceive in the objects outside of us is not the thing itself but only its 'sensible qualities' and its surface properties which we assimilate and bring together through the agency of the mind.[347] On this view, Hume asserted that our understanding of the outer world was thus limited to our mental contents and had little to do with a straightforward visual encounter with the world of experience. Hume thus believed that our experience of the outer world of things was nothing more than the product of our sense impressions which, in his view, acted to form the surface properties of objects, thereby making the outside world available to understanding.[348] Hume, therefore, denied that the material world and its objects exist independently of our sense perceptions, and it was this view that led him to take up what he called a 'skeptical' attitude to the existence of the material world and material things external to the mind.[349]

Second, Hume made the distinction between two different kinds of truths; the truths of science and the truths of observation.[350] The distinction between these two truths was applied by Hume in his famous argument about the observation of cause and effect relations in the external world. Hume asserted that we cannot ever attain knowledge of cause and effect relations because the causal affects we observe between two objects striking each other are not truths that are necessary, but rather truths of observation in which the 'necessary connection' between the cause and the effect is 'filled in' by the mind. In Hume's view, it is this 'filling in' that, in fact, supplies the 'necessary connection' between the two objects as it passes from one idea to another, from cause to effect.[351] At bottom, Hume reasoned that because the 'causal connection' is 'filled in' rather than observed, it is supplied by the mind and does not exist in the objective world of reality outside the mind. Hume went on to conclude that because we 'fill in' the causal connection with our minds by impressions and sensations, the observed causality between two objects in the outer world was only the 'feeling' of causality rather than the event of causality. Hume's skepticism about the reality of objects and causal events meant that we can never affirm our realist views of the world or the substance of objects that exist in it.

Third, Hume then took the extraordinary step of assuming that things and objects in the outer world were essentially inert, and that, in his view, they had no powers. He took this position essentially because he believed that since cause and effect

---

347 David Hume, *Enquiries Concerning Human Understanding*, pp. 25–8.
348 Ibid., pp. 18–21.
349 For an outline of this skeptical view in relation to the existence of external facts and Hume's dissolution of the factual, see Ibid., pp. 25–39.
350 Ibid., pp. 25–32.
351 Ibid., pp. 26–39, 63–79.

relations were 'filled in by the mind,' objects and things as such had no power and no affects, and were simply inert.[352] Based on this argument, Hume thought that all knowledge of the exterior world could therefore be reduced to sense impressions and that all facts and factual observations were made up of sense data, but did not exist in themselves independently of the thought operations and sense impressions. In this view, material facts were nothing more than psychological responses to the stimulus of the sense impressions rather than the appearance of the object itself. This meant that from the point of view of classical empiricism, valid judgments about reality and the outside world were not possible because the reality of objects did not exist in their own right. Lastly, in Hume's view all our own 'realist' inclinations to treat the exterior world as existing independently by itself could never be affirmed or justified.

The immediate consequence of this for Durkheim was that the apriorist and empiricist views of the categories had stripped the external world of all relations in reality, and all the relations that had formed in society which Durkheim believed had existed independently of the thought relations conceived of by philosophers. Since Kant and Hume had argued that there were no external material relations in reality apart from sense perceptions, philosophy had thus replaced exterior reality with a view that asserted that reality had no material powers since these were constituted by thought operations that did not exist in objective reality. Furthermore, since Kant and Hume had argued that no exterior relations exist in reality but are structured by the mind, their view was that outer experience did not exist in itself either. At bottom, therefore, Kant and Hume believed that the actual form of the outside world represented in experience did not exist independently of the thought operations, and in this sense judgments about 'substances' in reality, according to philosophy, could never be confirmed.

Durkheim's Theory of the Categories and his Opposition to Kant and Hume

Since Kant and Hume had called the existence of social realities and the effects of religious enactments into question, Durkheim had to demonstrate on the one hand that the categories originate from experience and were therefore social in nature and, on the other, that the material relations in reality affected individual actions and perceptions by the effects it brought about on the mind of individuals. In order to demonstrate that the categories of understanding originate from experience and were social in origin, Durkheim had to do two things. First, he had to show that the reality of society and the existence of material things came first over human perceptions and that then came the categories into which things were classified. Second, he had to show that the totemic systems for classifying space and time in societies like the totem tribes of Australia and the system for classifying time among the Zuni and the Sioux, were

---

352 Hume, *Enquiries Concerning Human Understanding*, p. 63.

modeled on their social organization. From this position he could then show that the categories of understanding were therefore modeled on the tribal categories.[353]

Some of these steps were in part taken by Durkheim and Mauss in 1903 when, in a work entitled *Primitive Classification,* they showed that the classification systems of the Australian tribes were similar to the classification systems of the Zuni and the Sioux. Based on the findings of the Australian classification, Durkheim and Mauss argued that the social origin of the categories of understanding could be looked for outside the mind in experience, arguing that the classification systems of the totem tribes was modeled on their social organization, and that this served as a model of the mental organization with which they saw the world. It was this that led them to examine the systems of classification in different societies by looking outside the confines of philosophy for a theory of the social origins of the categories of understanding.

Having stated that the categories of understanding were social in origin, Durkheim and Mauss proceeded to look at the principle of classification among the Zuni and the Sioux in North America and found that the principle of division into spatial regions within the tribal space corresponded to the divisions into groups classified by totems analogous to the Australian tribes. Then they found that in the Australian system the fundamental division into groups classified by totems led to other subdivisions into 'marriage classes' and then to groups organized into categories that were enclosed within each other.[354] In addition, they found that in the Zuni and Sioux classification certain restrictions and prohibitions were extended to the clans in ways that corresponded to their classifications into totems, and that many of these prohibitions specified what was forbidden, who must marry out, and which foods were permissible to consume. Further, they found that whereas in the Australian classifications prohibitions were extended to the clan divisions with respect to food, they found that in China the classifications extended the prohibitions to categories of marriage.

They then asserted that the divisions and classifications that emerged in society did not arise from human reasoning itself, but rather were derived from the principle whereby they were first divided into groups and classes arranged by totem and then into regions divided by space and seasons divided by time. This underlined the fact that in the societies Durkheim and Mauss looked at 'everything in the universe was assigned to one or another of these regions,' and that 'the classification of things reproduces the classification of people into groups.'[355] This brought with it several more observations including the fact that from the Pueblo to the Zuni, and from the Australian tribes to the systems of classification in China, the 'seasons are necessarily related to the cardinal points of latitude represented in their tribal space so that winter is associated with the north, summer with the south and so on,' showing that causes

---

353 Durkheim argued that the philosophical dualism of Descartes, Kant and Hume was problematic because it asserted that the outside world was a product of sense perception and that it did not exist in its own right. For this discussion see *The Elementary Forms*, p. 18.

354 Durkheim and Mauss, *Primitive Classification*, pp. 10–11.

355 Ibid, p. 11.

were assigned to these spatial points of latitude.[356] Under these circumstances, said Durkheim, 'the classifications and distinctions made about the seasons of the year are only a first step in the reckoning of time, and that this reckoning is derived from their social classifications which presuppose the social divisions into cycles, years, days, and hours which permit the measurement of any period of time, large or small.'[357] Durkheim and Mauss went on to argue that:

Far, then, from human beings classifying spontaneously by a sort of natural necessity, humanity in the beginning lacks the most indispensable conditions for the classificatory function. Further, it is not enough to examine the very idea of classification to understand that human beings could not have found its essential elements in themselves. A class is a group of things; and things do not present themselves to observation grouped in such a way. We may well perceive, more or less vaguely, their resemblances. But the simple fact of these resemblances is not enough to explain how we are led to group things which thus resemble each other, to bring them together in a sort of ideal sphere, enclosed by definite limits, which we call a class, species, etc. We have no justification for supposing that our mind bears within it at birth, completely formed, the prototype of this elementary framework of all classification.[358]

and

Far from being able to say that men classify quite naturally, by a sort of necessity of their individual understandings, we must on the contrary ask ourselves what could have led them to arrange their ideas in this way, and where they could have found the plan of this remarkable disposition. Having posed this question, we should like to adduce evidences which, we believe, may elucidate it.[359]

While Kant and Hume had assumed that our understanding of the outer world is always a product of the internal operations of the categories, and that the categories are innate to human reason and always precede classification, Durkheim and Mauss challenged this view by stating that the categories are first social in origin, are derived from experience and then subsequently become a part of human mental operations. In *The Elementary Forms*, then, Durkheim went beyond Kant and Hume to argue that the categories of understanding are material products of the system of division and classifications in terms of which totem tribes divide themselves into sections, and then extend this division to the outside world in the form of divisions in space and time. Once grouped in this way, said Durkheim, 'they then see the world in terms of fundamental divisions and classifications of these groupings,' rather than the other way around.[360] What Durkheim therefore tried to show in *The*

---

356 Ibid., p. 71.
357 Ibid.
358 Ibid., p. 8.
359 Ibid., p. 9.
360 Durkheim, *The Elementary Forms*, p. 82.

Elementary Forms was that the principle of division and subdivision in terms of which the totem tribes segment themselves, did not come from within but rather had a social origin. Durkheim's argument for the social origin of the categories thus stands as a serious first challenge to apriorism and empiricism, and Durkheim criticized Kant and Hume for not providing an account of the actual origins of the categories themselves.

Whereas Kant had thought that the mental operation of the categories preceded society and confer a logical quality on the world, Durkheim believed that society came first and then came the classification into things. According to this view, the material separations and division by clans corresponding to totems were the origin for the model of the mental organization of the category of class. From this came the view that 'because human beings were grouped and thought of themselves in the form of groups, that in their ideas they grouped other things, and in the beginning the two modes of grouping were merged to the point of being indistinct.'[361]

Durkheim's Evidence for the Social Origin of the Categories: Space as a Social Category

The next step in the argument was to provide evidence that the categories of space, time and cause had a social origin. While some of the evidence for spatial categories had in part been provided by Durkheim and Mauss in *Primitive Classification*, Durkheim looked further into the problem of spatial classification in *The Elementary Forms*. Working from ethnographic material provided by Howitt and others on how the totem tribes divide themselves into groups and clans according to their totems, Durkheim was able to show that the divisions into groups classified by totems were then extended to the division by 'regions' in space, illustrating that the principle of division into classes and clans corresponded with the divisions into regions. Then in addition to this, Durkheim found in the Sioux classification that the principle of spatial division by region was associated with the division into clans. In these circumstances, each division in the Sioux classification was assigned an orientation with a region in space so that one clan belonged to the north, the other the south, etc. The spatial division by clans was thus shown to be evident in the Australian tribes and the Zuni system of segmentation into groups, where they associated regions with divisions by clan. Also, in the Omaha tribes of the Sioux the system of classification by clans was used to divide the material world into regions.[362]

The division of space and spatial regions corresponding to divisions by clan showed two things: first, it showed that the division of the natural world into regions was connected to their tribal divisions into groups and clans associated with the divisions by totem. Second, it showed the division by clans was associated with the division of regions related to the north and the south, and that from this a given spatial

---

361 Durkheim and Mauss, *Primitive Classification*, Chicago: University of Chicago Press, 1963, pp. 82–3.
362 Ibid., pp. 54–5.

point was obtained as a means of understanding their own existence in space. Durkheim and Mauss therefore argued that the distribution of the tribal space into regions was simply a means of 'reducing exterior reality into the division between clans,' which in turn corresponded to the 'division of the world by quarters' which, in this case, was expressed in the form of north, south, east and west.[363] Durkheim therefore believed that the concept of space had its origin in the spatial divisions and separations of the totem tribes of Australia who tended to conceptualize their spatial separations in the form of a tribal circle, and when asked to draw a circle they drew the exact physical shape of the camp or village in which they lived. Durkheim stated:

> Since all the men of a single civilization represent space in the same way, it is clearly necessary that these methods of representation are social in origin. Their social form is made manifest when we look at the practices of early societies which conceive of space in the form an immense circle, but they do so because the camp has a circular form; and this spatial circle is divided up exactly like the tribal circle. Thus, the social organization is the model of the mental organization of the idea. The distinction between right and left which, far from being inherent in the nature of man in general, is very probably the product of representations which are religious and therefore collective.[364]

In the quotation above, Durkheim showed that so far as the spatial circle is divided up exactly like the tribal circle, the model of their social organization became the model for the mental organization for the idea of space and spatial relations. This means simply that the internalized concept of space and spatial relations mirrors the spatial division by regions of the tribal circle and this, Durkheim argued, became a model for the mental organization of the categories through which they come to see the world. In this view, the first framework for understanding the world and classifying other things in relation to spaces is the model of spatial relationships derived from the tribal principle of the disposition of their groups into regions designated by their totem.[365] In this case, the division of the tribe into totem groups and clans corresponds with their division into regions. As far as Durkheim was concerned, the concept of spatial direction, therefore, depends upon material relationships originating in the outside world rather than in internal reason. He went on to note that it is only possible to understand spatial relations by first conceptualizing a 'center' from which everything else 'is disposed in relation to the tribal space' and this focal point is the original space from which all other spaces and spatial relations radiate.[366] Further, to differentiate between these regions in line with the cardinal points of latitude allows them to understand which space they themselves belong to within the social framework. Since the concept of space is itself based on a 'fixed external point' and the

---

363 Ibid., pp. 13, 47–8.
364 *Elementary Forms,* pp. 11–12.
365 *Elementary Forms,* pp. 11, 441.
366 *Elementary Forms,* pp. 440–441.

segmentation into regions, the next step is to discover what point or place represents this in the social organization and tribal divisions.

Durkheim went on to reason that the space in which the group defines its existence becomes the first model of a given spatial point of direction. This spatial point, he argued, must be the village or camp which represents the fixed territory of the group. Without this, there can be no division into regions and no conceptualization of north or south, right or left, up or down, inside or outside. In fact it is impossible to conceptualize the world spatially without some common external standard in terms of which spatial relations can be judged. This was shown in the case of the Omaha Sioux who arranged their camp in a circular form so that each group had a fixed place corresponding to the division by clan. Durkheim and Mauss noted that, in particular, the two clans were assigned left and right spatial orientations and that these orientations were constructed with reference to the exit and entry points of the clans. Durkheim and Mauss reasoned that their place in space was thus assigned to them depending on their relationship to each other and on their relations to things and animals that were thought to be in their sphere of influence.[367]

In comparison to Omaha Sioux, the Osage classified not only by clans corresponding to left and right related to regions in the camp, but also by functions: one clan was assigned the function of war, the other peace.[368] Based on other evidence by Howitt, the tribes he studied divided the clans by spatial regions in a way that formed what Durkheim and Mauss called a 'compass card': that is, a map designating the configurations of the clan in relation to compass points each marked in relation to spatial regions.[369] In addition, their spatial regions were closely linked to structural elements in their social organization which explained how the classes and clans were related to each other.

From this, Durkheim went on to reason that the common spatial standard is the social organization of the tribal circle which provides a model for the mental organization of space, thus creating the original point of spatial direction. While he agreed with Kant that the perception of spatial relations was individual, he thought that the concept of space had its origins in group life and became the basis for the category of space and its classification into regions. Durkheim's theory of the categories is thus premised on the assumption that since human beings live in groups, the social organization of their groups became the model for the mental organization of their ideas. On this view, the system of spatial division first served as a basis for the system of classification in the external world, and then became internalized in the system of classification in thought. To the extent that 'individuals are grouped and think of themselves in the form of groups, they also group their ideas for understanding the external world.'[370]

---

367 Durkheim and Mauss, *Primitive Classification*, p. 57.
368 Ibid., p. 58.
369 Ibid, p. 60.
370 Ibid.

Durkheim's Evidence: Time as a Social Category   Just as the category of space had a social origin, so Durkheim believed that the category of time derives from society. Looking again at the Australian system of classification, Durkheim reasoned that the social organization of the totem tribes presented itself like a logic. First, they divided themselves into 'two fundamental sections' which are made up of a number of clans. Then the clans were divided into two 'marriage classes' where, depending on the totem group to which one belonged, certain classes were effected by prohibitions that corresponded to the totem group with which they had relations and in some cases these prohibitions were extended to certain foods and to certain activities related to marriage groups.[371] Here, said Durkheim and Mauss, were relations between divisions in the marriage classes and in classes affected by prohibitions, and these divisions were related to division by regions in the tribal space.

Durkheim and Mauss then went on to argue that time classifications, like spatial classifications, are the result of divisions of the seasons as opposed to divisions in respect to clans and regions. In order to demonstrate the relationship between time division and the seasons, Durkheim and Mauss looked at the Chinese system of classification where the year was divided into twenty four seasons, thus correlating time division with seasonal divisions.[372] The Chinese division of the year into twenty four seasons made it possible to link the classification of space by regions to the classification of time by seasons. As soon as this seasonal orientation was made, said Durkheim, the seasons were correlated with the cardinal points of latitude associating winter with the north, summer with the south and so on. This, they reasoned, is the 'first step in reckoning time' since it presupposes the division into other units of time graduated in smaller measurements such as months, weeks, days, minutes and hours.[373] All these units occur in classification systems which quantify time in order to grasp reality. This was the case in the Chinese system of classification where everything was arranged like a logic: regions, seasons, things, animals and periodic celebrations.

In the light of this, Durkheim argued that far from the concept of time being a universal a priori category inherent in the human mind, the idea of time emerged from the social activity of the group in the divisions it creates between work and periods of religious rituals and feasts. The divisions in time thus denoted by occasions such as feasts, rituals and harvests were then set into correspondence with periodic religious enactments arranged by seasons. Just as the concept of space originates from the classification extended to regions in space corresponding to the divisions of things and totems, so the activity of separating work from ritual according to seasons, gave rise to time classification whereby the group punctuates its daily economic routine with collective feasts and celebrations that consecrate in time the seasonal periods that mark the celebration of the totem with feast and rituals.[374]

---

371 Ibid., pp. 10–11; Claude Levi-Strauss, *The Elementary Structures of Kinship*, pp. 140–2.
372 Ibid., p. 71.
373 Ibid.
374 *Elementary Forms*, pp. 10–11, 440, 441.

The division of time based on seasonal variations can be illustrated in the case of the Sherente tribe of Africa who divide the year into two chronological parts that separate time by two periodic cycles: one signified by a period of dry weather, the other by a period of rain. During the period of rain, they anxiously watch the cluster of stars in the constellation Taurus for a signal that the period of rain is ending and, at the point that the signal occurs, they gather for the largest religious ceremony of the year.[375] In this case time classification is reckoned by an external principle in the movement from dry days to rainy days, so that time is marked by the beginning of the seasonal changes that are keyed to the celebration of religious days. According to Durkheim, this became the model for the mental category of time and is derived from it in so far as it is fixed externally and does not come from within. A second consideration for the social origin of the category of time, according to Durkheim, is the tendency of groups to organize their social experience on the bases of collective enactments marked by rituals and rites which establish periodic cycles, showing that the conception of time is rooted in religious enactments rather than internal mental reasoning. This can be seen in North American societies where the fixed occurrence of Christmas and Thanksgiving mark seasonal events that bring consecrated ceremonies together with consecrated times. These episodic and periodic enactments constitute religious rites and practices marking collective remembrances which return regularly at determined points or periods.[376] In this view, we are able to understand where the tendency to mark off one period of time from another arises, and how this 'marking off' becomes internalized as part of our mental dispositions as members of groups rather than as isolated individuals.

In this context, Durkheim thought that the social origin of the categories followed a certain order. First, the rhythm which religious life followed expressed itself separately from economic life, and when the two activities came together in the form of a religious enactment they became indistinguishable. Second, only by assembling to perform a religious enactment is 'society able to remake itself and its collective practices.'[377] Third, since the exigencies of life and the facts of economic survival do not allow the collective to remain in congregation indefinitely, it scatters to assemble anew when it again feels the need, thus giving rise to the next serial cycle marked by the time of the last assembly.[378] Fourth, the perception of time thus corresponds to the cycle of assembly between feasts, ceremonies and collective rites. The concept of time is thus not itself something that uniquely emerges from the human mind as Kant thought, but rather arises from the external activity of social life and the tendency of societies to divide experience into cycles marked off by ritual. Though every individual is conscious of living in a present which is distinct from the past, Durkheim

---

375 The Sherente practice of dividing the year into two parts is discussed by Claude Levi-Strauss, *The Raw and the Cooked*, New York: Harper Torchbooks, 1969, pp. 217–18.

376 *Elementary Forms*, p. 349.

377 Ibid.

378 Ibid.

maintained that the concept of time is not personalized or individualized, but involves a category shared by all members of the group. It is not that we naturally arrange our time in days, weeks, years, months or minutes, but rather that time in general first appears in the activity of the group whose tendency is to congregate in regular cycles that reappear on a yearly, weekly or daily basis.

Durkheim's Evidence: The Social Origin of the Concept of Cause   In addition to asserting that the concepts of space and time have a social origin, Durkheim thought that the concept of cause also had a social source originating in religious activity rather than being an a priori category of the mind. In tracing the origins of the concept of cause, Durkheim stated that the concept of cause as understood by science and philosophy must have had its origins in the observation of the material effects of religious enactments, since it was these enactments where the causal affects of religious rites were first observed. To the extent that the affects of religious enactments are the first expression of the concept of cause, Durkheim believed that philosophy and science are but rational derivatives of what was primarily a religious category.[379] He argued that the concept of cause begins first in religion and then comes to rest in science and philosophy. But, in what way is religion related to the concept of cause?

First, all religions began by offering explanations of the universe and by putting forward causal explanations of the apparent power of nature occurring in the change of seasons, the regularities of tides, phases of the moon and the orderliness of the universe. Among the ideas that individuals have, therefore, religion must have been the first system for classifying the powers of the natural world. Second, it follows that among the classes of ideas which individuals have held, the first conception of religious causation originates in the effects that religious rites have on the actions and attitudes of the individuals involved in the ceremony. It is these effects, Durkheim believed, which come to be the first exterior expression of causality.[380] If the concept of cause is derived from society, what then is its origin? Durkheim believed that the concept of cause could not have come from a priori reasoning alone because individuals have perceptual limitations which they can never really surpass. On this basis, he thought that society itself must have been of primary importance, since it encompasses all experience and other concepts and categories that extend beyond human perceptual limitations.

Not only are the categories of space, time and cause based on the existence of society, but their contents represent different aspects of society's social being. In regard to space, it was the separations and divisions within the tribal segment that first provided the material basis for the distribution into regions into which the clan and the world were classified, thus leading to the category of space. In regard to

---

379 *Elementary Forms*, pp. 367–8.
380 *Elementary Forms*, p. 368

time, it is the rhythm of the periodic enactments marking feasts and celebrations corresponding to the seasons that first provide the basis for the category of time and, in regard to causation, it is the effects of religious rites and the consecrated powers of the totem on the actions of individuals that provide the prototype for the concept of causality.[381] In each case, the categories are used to do the same things, namely to classify spatial separations and mark the cycle of periodic enactments which bring the group together and put it in motion in a new way. As far as Durkheim was concerned, the scientific conception of 'causation' in the natural world is only but a secondary extension of religious causation in the social world, and as such it has a social derivation in collective religious acts.

By reversing the way Kant had put a priori reasoning into dominance over the existing objective relations of society, Durkheim's account of the categories showed how 'experience' is always constituted within an already ongoing social framework, and that this framework is modeled on the religious organization of the tribe. Thus whereas Kant had assumed that the categories were logically prior to experience and always precede our apprehension of the outside world, Durkheim challenged this view by asserting that the categories originate from material activity in the world of experience and then subsequently become a part of our mental operations and individual dispositions, which in turn structures our reality.

Durkheim's Theory of the Categories of Understanding: Criticism and Debate

Warren Schmaus' View of Durkheim's Theory of the Categories Since it was first published in 1912, Durkheim's argument for the social origin of the categories has been the subject of criticism and debate among commentators as diverse as Gehlke, Parsons, Lukes and Godlove who have taken positions for and against Durkheim's view.[382] While much of this criticism appeared during an earlier period of debate, recent commentary from a number of writers has contributed to the discussion of Durkheim's theory of the categories. Included in this is a study entitled *Durkheim's Philosophy of Science and the Sociology of Knowledge* by Warren Schmaus which looked at the historical roots of Durkheim's interest in the categories of understanding. In addition to this, a paper by Anne Rawls entitled 'Durkheim's Epistemology: The Neglected Argument' looked at Durkheim's theory of the categories from the point of view of the effects of the religious enactments on individual minds.

---

381 *Elementary Forms*, pp. 440, 368, 11.

382 For a history of the debate on Durkheim's argument for the social origins of the categories see Charles Gehlke, *Emile Durkheim's Contribution to Sociological Theory*, New York: AMS Press, 1915; Talcott Parsons, *Structure of Social Action*, New York: The Free Press, 1968; Steven Lukes, *Emile Durkheim's Life and Works*, London: Penguin Books, 1973; and Terry Godlove, 'Epistemology in Durkheim's Elementary Forms of Religious Life,' *Journal of the History of Philosophy*, 24, 1986, pp. 385–401.

The discussion by Schmaus began by tracing the history of Durkheim's argument to the philosophic views held in France in the latter part of the nineteenth century. He noted that Durkheim first became interested in the social origins of the categories after an early paper by Marcel Mauss had argued that tribal societies conceptualize spatial relations in the form of the external geography of the camp, and that the tribal representation of space and spatial relations seemed to correspond to how groups classify the external world more generally in terms of specific spatial categories. Schmaus believed that it was at this point that Durkheim began to challenge Kant's philosophical account of the origin of the categories in an effort to put forward a social theory of the categories. Schmaus, however, takes a straightforward critical view of Durkheim's argument, stating that inconsistencies 'arise when Durkheim concluded that society is the cause of the categories.'[383]

While Schmaus believed that 'the cause of a particular way of measuring space and time can be found in society,' he stated that problems arise with Durkheim's reasoning when he tried to put the two positions together and concluded 'that society is the cause of categories like space and time in general.' Schmaus, then, argued that 'Durkheim simply confused a plausible empirical claim with a philosophical argument and drew an invalid sociological conclusion.'[384] Schmaus, therefore, believed that Durkheim's theory of the categories breaks down at the level of his philosophic argument because it can never show that the categories are both 'necessary and universal.' He then went on to claim that it would be more plausible to assume that Durkheim intended to argue for a 'functional explanation' of the categories rather than put forward a causal theory of the categories.[385] Schmaus reasoned that if this were the case, Durkheim would have been free to assume that the categories are both necessary and universal since they could be shown to be necessary conditions of social life found in all societies,' rather than simply the contingent effects of social causes.[386] On this account, Schmaus argued that a functional explanation of the categories solves three specific problems. First, it can be used to explain how the 'categories and their representations are transmitted culturally from generation to generation.'[387] Second, it can be used to explain how the 'categories are utilized in experience as tools for purposes of making judgments about space and time', and that this would explain the universality of categories and systems of classification in all societies. Third, Schmaus argued that if we accept a functional explanation of the categories, it is possible to show in this case how the categories explain the fact that periodic religious enactments create 'social feelings' of unity

---

383 Warren Schmaus, *Durkheim's Philosophy of Science and the Sociology of Knowledge*. Chicago: University of Chicago Press, 1994, p. 240.

384 Schmaus, *Durkheim's Philosophy of Science*, p. 176; pp. 239–40. While Schmaus states that Durkheim 'conflates causes with origins,' he frequently forces Durkheim's text.

385 Schmaus, 'Durkheim on the Causes and Functions of the Categories' in N.J. Allen, W.S.F. Pickering and W.Watts Miller (eds.), *On Durkheim's Elementary Forms of Religious Life*, London: Routledge, 1998, p. 178.

386 Ibid., p. 885.

387 Ibid., p. 884.

during the performance of religious rites, and 'how these feelings feed back to help preserve the society and the society's collective representation of the categories.'[388]

There are, however, several problems with this. First is the claim by Schmaus that Durkheim's theory of the categories lends itself to a functional explanation. To assume as Schmaus does that Durkheim's theory of the categories can be explained functionally overlooks Durkheim's realist argument for the existence of society, which is an error going as far back as Parsons' and Sorokin's functional and organicist interpretation of Durkheim. The functional-organicist view of society originated with Herbert Spencer who believed that society was a reflection of individual organic traits which served essential functions. While Spencer took the view that society was an organic whole with interrelated parts and functions that arise from individual traits, Durkheim's realist conception of society conceived of it as a set of objective relations existing outside the individual. Organicism thus treats society as a natural organism whose traits are selected for purposes of social functions related to the survival of the organism. In contrast to this view is the realist view which treats society as structures and mechanism – the religious structure, the marriage mechanism – whose system of obligations and duties place individuals under a necessity to act in relation to them. On this view, it would be an error to assume that Durkheim's conception of society was reducible to a functional explanation without taking into account the power that society has to impose external limits on individuals that are fixed by custom and do not come from within. In the former view, society does not exist by itself as an external reality since it is believed to originate from individual traits, whereas in the later view society exists as an external reality that has direct material affects on individual actions.[389]

Second is the problem of Schmaus' interpretation of Durkheim's view of outer experience. Since Descartes, philosophers have believed that outer experience has a logical and coherent quality only because it is conferred by the agency of the mind.[390] Philosophers thus hold the view that 'experience' in the form of the outside world does not exist independently by itself since they assume it is a product of sense perception. In this view, all material reality is a product of the internal preconstructions and sense perceptions of individual minds. This was the view of experience taken up by apriorism with respect to Kant, and it was the view taken up by classical empiricism with respect to Hume. Further, since Descartes, philosophers have tended to view experience as an extension of perception rather than existing on its own

---

388 Ibid.

389 The organicist view of society originated with Herbert Spencer and his assertion that society was a reflection of individual organic traits which served essential functions. But, unlike Durkheim, Spencer never viewed society as an independent reality that existed apart from the individual. In the structure of social action, Parsons erroneously equates Spencer's organicism view with Durkheim's realist view.

390 Descartes' dualist perspective marked the historical point at which philosophy broke off all relations with the material world after splitting subject from object and intension from cause. For Descartes, the inner mental idea of a material substance 'contained more formal reality than did the substance in objective reality.' See *Descartes Selections*, New York: Scribner's, 1955, p. 114. Later Hume and Kant perfected Descartes' dualist perspective.

outside the mind. This meant that the stark differences in the way philosophers conceived of experience and the way Durkheim conceived of it are critical to a social theory of the categories. What Schmaus overlooks is that Durkheim wished to treat experience as a freestanding independent structure whose obligations, duties and religious interdicts made up a total social framework that had specific material effects on individuals. Within a realist theory of knowledge, therefore, experience exists as a system that manifests itself in the form of a structured social framework.

Schmaus' philosophical view of experience thus differs from that of Durkheim's in several respects. Whereas philosophers tend to use the term 'experience' to refer to the unstructured space of the outer world that exists outside the mind, Durkheim believed that experience was constituted by the objective structures of society. In thus asserting that experience was a system organized within a social framework, Durkheim had to come up against the theory of experience that was put forward by philosophers. Whereas philosophers believed that experience was actively constituted by the mind, Durkheim opposed this view in order to show that 'experience is not sufficient unto itself, but presupposes certain conditions which are exterior to it.'[391] In this case, he wanted to show how experience depends 'upon its morphology or structure, and upon the ordering of its religious, juridical and economic elements.'[392] But even beyond this, Durkheim believed that philosophers had overlooked the key fact that if experience is structured like a system that exists in the form of the objective relations that structure individual acts, then this would show how the internalized dispositions of individual agents depend upon the way in which the 'exterior' is founded and organized.[393]

Along these lines, an additional problem for Durkheim was that if he were to claim that religious enactments had the power to bring about material effects, he would have had to show how the effects of the enactments would have originated from the material world of experience, rather than being a product of a priori sense impressions, as Hume and Kant argued. Since Hume and Kant held that the sense impressions and a priori categories structured experience, and that experience had no formal structure itself and imparted no powers, Durkheim knew that he had to come up against Kant's and Hume's argument. This meant that Durkheim had to challenge the concept of experience as held by philosophers who had argued that sense impressions and a priori categories structure experience rather than the other way around. Since Durkheim believed that experience was structured by society, and that this structure affected internal perceptions of the outer world, he had to show that the outside world and individual states of mind were not separate things, and that the altered states of mind created during religious enactments were 'material affects' of the religious interdictions, not 'social feelings of unity' created by the enactments or 'feelings which feed back to help preserve the society and its collective representations of the categories,' as suggested by Schmaus.'[394]

391 Durkheim, *The Elementary Forms*, p. 15.
392 Ibid., p. 16.
393 Ibid., p. 16.

A third problem in Schmaus' interpretation of Durkheim is his criticism of Durkheim's realist view of the social origin of the categories and his contention that the categories can best be explained by a functional interpretation. Schmaus argued that a realist theory of the categories could never show that the categories were both necessary and universal, and because of this he thought that a functional explanation was more plausible. Schmaus therefore argued that a functional interpretation of Durkheim's theory of the categories would explain how the 'categories and their representations are transmitted culturally from generation to generation,' and in this way serve necessary social functions. The claim by Schmaus that a functional interpretation of the categories has more explanatory power than Durkheim's realist theory overlooks three central considerations. First, it overlooks the critical question of how the categories become internalized dispositions over and against being culturally transmitted from generation to generation, as suggested by Schmaus.[395] Second, it overlooks Durkheim's realist argument for the existence of society as mechanisms and structures that exist outside the individual. In thus replacing Durkheim's realist argument with a functionalist explanation, Schmaus destroys the purpose Durkheim had in advancing a realist theory of society. For Durkheim, the purpose of *The Elementary Forms* was not to advance a functional theory of religion, but rather to put forward a realist view of society that showed how groups and classes advanced their understanding of each other by making the relations they have intelligible within a system of classification that aided their understanding of these relations. Furthermore, the aim of his theory was not only to advance how these groups and classes understood their relations to each other through the totem divisions, but also how it made intelligible their relations between their perceptions and the outside world by unifying their knowledge of these relations with their relations to things and regions in nature. Third, whereas Schmaus claimed that the religious enactments and practices exist because they make the members of the group 'feel good,' Durkheim believed that they exist in order to make the enactments and disposition coincide with the divisions and classifications in the cultural and spiritual world. In this case, Schmaus overlooks Durkheim's realist argument for the categories in favor of looking for the 'social functions that the categories perform' and 'how the categories become culturally transmitted.' In reality, Durkheim's question was how does the structure of experience become the internalized form of the objective relations, and how are the these relations reflected in the material dispositions of individuals during religious enactments?[396] As far as Durkheim was concerned, their religious enact-

---

394 Ibid., p. 884.

395 Ibid.

396 Pierre Bourdieu's re-working of the subjectivist and objectivist categories in writings such as *Distinctions* and *The Logic of Practice* shows that the discipline of sociology is still dependent on Durkheim's question about how the objective social relations realize themselves in the system of internal mental dispositions. Bourdieu's concept of 'habitus' thus envisages the programmatic outline provided by Durkheim in the conclusion of *The Elementary Forms*. For more discussion on this see R. Brubaker, 'Rethinking Classical Theory: The Sociological Vision of Pierre Bourdieu,' *Theory & Society*, 14, 1985, 745–75.

ments would not be possible unless the categories of space, time and cause had become the internalized form of the objective relations by which they demarcate consecrated acts and activities from ordinary acts and activities.

Anne Rawls' View of Durkheim's Theory of the Categories

In addition to Schmaus' criticism, is Anne Rawls' discussion of Durkheim's theory of the categories.[397] She explicitly turns her attention to Durkheim's theory of the categories, arguing that it should be treated as a free standing theory of epistemology equivalent to the classical epistemologies proposed by Kant and Hume. In her view, it was a fully developed epistemology because it provides an account of the origin of the framework of thought relations that comes to exist when individuals produce 'understanding' of the given objects to be known in the outside world. Where Rawls differs from others, however, is in her interpretation of Durkheim's account. In the main, she takes the view that Durkheim's theory of 'the genesis of the categories of understanding' is an account about how 'the enacted social practices become part of the individual's perceptual apparatus.'[398] In this view, the categories of understanding are the combined products of the physical and material interactions of individuals during religious enactments and, in this case, Rawls asserted that 'the enactments are their structures.'[399] Taking an interactionist approach, Rawls therefore believed that society is a product of individual interactions, and that consequently her interpretation of Durkheim does not include a theory of society which exists either as a reality outside the individual or as a system that structures individual perceptions. Rather for Rawls, it is the 'enacted practices' themselves which constitute the source of the categories of understanding.

It is therefore her contention that the material effects of the religious enactments and the psychological responses the individuals have to the performance of religious rites, are nothing more than the products of their face-to-face social interactions that take place during religious feasts and celebrations. Rawls therefore believed that the 'structures' of society are nothing but 'the enacted practices,' and that by her account the objective structures of society are actively preceded by or are coincidental with their material interactions. Durkheim, by contrast, believed that the objective structures of society exist outside the individual and, being structured like a system, contain structures and mechanisms which are exterior to the interactions that are made manifest in their material enactments.[400] Given that for Rawls society does not exist in any form outside the material interactions of individuals, the question then is not 'how are the enacted practices their structures' but rather 'how do the objective relations of society realize themselves in the system of dispositions that are their enacted practices'?

---

397 Anne Rawls, 'Durkheim's Epistemology: The Neglected Argument,' *American Journal of Sociology*, Vol. 102 (2), 430–482, 1996.

398 Ibid., p. 475.

399 Ibid.

400 Rawls, 'Durkheim's Epistemology: The Neglected Argument, p. 433.

The claim by Rawls that the 'structures are their enacted practices' thus produces a number of problems. First, the objectification of the structure of enacted practices by Rawls cannot be described in the language of interaction because the interaction itself owes its form to the objective structure of society, since this is what produces the dispositions of the interacting individuals and their relative positions in the interaction in the first place.[401] To this extent, Rawls neglects to take into account Durkheim's realist argument for the existence of the 'structure' as a reality outside the individual enactments, and therefore overlooks the objective relations of society which were key to Durkheim's theory of the categories. In her account, society does not exist outside the individual in the form of an independent objective structure. Second, along with Schmaus, Rawls accepts Hume's skeptical view of external reality and his rationalist epistemology which asserts that the external world can not be known independently of the mind. She thus takes for granted Hume's skeptical argument for a theory of knowledge that would take the form of a realist encounter with the material world. Third, Rawls fails to contextualize Durkheim's opposition to Kant and Hume by overlooking the fact that their epistemological outlooks put the existence of society as an external reality into question.

Fourth, Rawls aligns herself with the overall American acceptance of the rationalist critique of knowledge that goes back as far as Parsons, Sorokin, Lukes and Godlove, which states that society is not a reality that exists independently of the individual because it cannot be empirically verified, and therefore it does not play a role in structuring individual acts.[402] Rawls is therefore in disagreement with Durkheim's epistemological argument of the social origin of the categories, and for the existence of society as an objective structure lying outside the individual. Fifth, Rawls's refusal to accept the existence of external realities outside the individual fits perfectly with the overall American rejection of Durkheim's realist theory of society that goes back as far as Gabriel Tarde and the Chicago school, who asserted that society cannot exist independently of the individual. Sixth, Rawls agrees with Hume that objects and practices have no powers, and thus overlooks the fact that along with being a theory of religion, *The Elementary Forms* was a realist argument for the existence of society as an objective structure.[403] Rawls' interpretation of Durkheim's conception of society is thus consistent with the Chicago school's rejection of Durkheim, and Sorokin's and Parsons' erroneous conclusion that Durkheim was proposing the existence of a 'group mind' and a metaphysical reality that did not take the individual

---

401 Pierre Bourdieu's discussion of the subjectivist and objectivist categories in works such as *Distinctions* and *The Logic of Practice* shows that the discipline of sociology is still dependent on the Durkheim's question of how the objective social relations realize themselves in the system of internal mental dispositions. Bourdieu's concept of 'habitus' thus envisages the programmatic outline provided by Durkheim in the conclusion of *The Elementary Forms*.

402 This argument is classically expressed in Parsons' erroneous account of 'the objective realities of society' as an attempt by Durkheim to claim the existence of 'a group mind.' See Parsons, *The Structure of Social Action*, New York: The Free Press, 1968, pp. 378–447.

403 Rawls, Response to Schmaus, *American Journal of Sociology*, p. 446.

into account.[404] The fact that Durkheim's theory of society was never accepted in America and never withstood the test of empirical observation explains why Rawls collapsed the objective structures of society into the interactions of individuals. In this case, Rawls believed that the objective structures of society are thus the product of people's interactions, and that the interactions themselves are somehow to be seen as the coercive effects of the objective structures.

The Debate Between Schmaus and Rawls On the Origin of the Categories

In 1998, a disagreement between Schmaus' and Rawls' account of Durkheim's theory of the categories led to an open debate in the *American Journal of Sociology*. In a paper entitled 'Rawls, Durkheim, and Causality: A Critical Discussion,' Schmaus responded to Rawls' 1996 article entitled 'Durkheim's Epistemology' by stating that her 'empirical account of the social causes of religious enactments can no more account for the universality and necessity of the categories than traditional empiricism can.'[405] Schmaus asserted that Rawls neglected to take into account that Durkheim was unaware of Hume's argument that observable 'causal relations were unattainable,' and that unwittingly, Durkheim had pursued the implausible assumption that we can 'introspect causal powers and not merely their effects or causal relations.'[406]

Schmaus went on to criticize Rawls' views of Durkheim's theory of the categories by looking at the category of causality on two fronts. First, he believed that in relation to other categories, the category of causality is the most fundamental category in comparison with others such as space, time or class because it directly relates to the power of the religious enactments to bring about specific causal effects in reality. Second, the category of causality is singled out by Schmaus because he believed that Durkheim had erroneously stated that the powers which religious enactments have create the category of causality itself when, in fact, said Schmaus, if Durkheim had read Hume he would have known that 'objects have no powers.'[407] Before we look more closely at these issues, it is important to outline why 'causation' is a key category singled out by Schmaus.

Generally speaking, Schmaus' reasoning has to do with two assumptions. First, it has to do with the assumption by Durkheim that religious enactments are 'the original expression of the concept of force in the external world since they represent the first historical expression of causality.'[408] On this basis, Durkheim went on to conclude that the model of cause and effect in the external world during religious enactments became the model of causation in the mental organization, and in these terms Durkheim

---

404 For these arguments see Sorokin's *Contemporary Sociological Theories*, and Parsons' *Structure of Social Action*. For the Chicago School's rejection of Durkheim's realist theory of society for Tarde's imitation theory, see Gustavo Tosti, 'Suicide in the Light of Recent Studies.' *American Journal of Sociology*, 3, 1897, pp. 464–478.

405 Schmaus, 'Rawls, Durkheim, and Causality: A Critical Discussion,' *American Journal of Sociology*, 104, 1998, p. 874.

406 Ibid., pp. 875–78.

407 Ibid., pp. 873–75.

408 Durkheim, *The Elementary Forms*, p. 439.

reasoned that the category of causality was social in origin. Durkheim not only believed that effects of the religious enactments created the basis for the category of causality, but that the enactments were the exemplifications of the material powers of society and that these powers existed outside individual minds in the form of religious interdicts and sacrificial rites. Second, on the basis of Hume's argument, Schmaus called into question Durkheim's claim that religious enactments constitute the material powers of society and that the effects of the enactments can be observed during religious rituals by the powers the enactments have to bring about effects on peoples' actions and perceptions. Schmaus argued that because Durkheim believed that the causes of the actions were visible to the participants, he had staked everything on the claim that the causes and affects of religious enactments during effervescent assemblies – the shrieks, the moans, and the body mutilations – demonstrated that society existed as an external reality outside the individual and that it had powers to structure immediate experience in the form of the rituals and interdicts which structured their actions. Schmaus went on to argue that on the basis of this Durkheim incorrectly assumed that the religious enactments were therefore the first appearance of the category of causality in the external world and that this was later extended to nature and then to the universe.

According to Schmaus, however, if Durkheim claimed that religious enactments were the causes of their actions, he had to show how their causal efficacy would have originated from the material world of experience given that Hume had asserted that events in the world have no powers. Schmaus then went on to say that while Rawls wanted to claim that the causal force of religious enactments arises from experience as this was structured by their interactions, he believed that any argument that appeals to causality 'fares no better than any other argument which appeals to experience for a justification of causal affects.' This is the case, according to Schmaus, because it is 'open to the objections by Hume that we cannot ever perceive these forces or causes.'[409]

Schmaus then went on to argue that one of the reasons for this inconsistency in Rawls' account of Durkheim's theory of the categories is that Durkheim himself was not 'well versed in Hume's empirical argument' concerning causes and effects and that, according to Schmaus, Durkheim never came to terms with Hume's argument about causation when writing *The Elementary Forms*.[410] As far as Schmaus was concerned, it was Durkheim's lack of awareness of Hume's argument that invalidated his thesis about the categories and reversed any gains he might have made in putting forward a sociological epistemology over a rationalist one.

In order to understand this argument completely, it will be necessary to briefly review Hume's key assertions about causality. Essentially, two assertions are relevant here. First is the assertion that knowledge of causal relations in the exterior world is not possible because we can never actually observe the 'causal connection' since this is 'filled in' by the mind. Second is the assertion that causality and the causal

---

409 Ibid., pp. 873–5.
410 Ibid., p. 873.

connection do not exist in reality and therefore things in the world are inert and have no power in themselves.[411] Hume asserted that while this power is created by the sense impressions of the mind, it could never be observed in empirical reality. In this view, causality is only a 'feeling' in cognition, but never an event in the external world. From this, Hume went on to argue that while we assign this inner feeling to reality and assume that the causal connection exists, it is only the contiguous conjunction that exists, such that the feeling becomes a part of reality.[412]

In respect to Hume's key assertions, Rawls stated that Durkheim had dealt with Hume's problem in relation to causality by focusing on the internal perceptions of outside causal forces evident in people's responses to religious enactments, and that in her view religious enactments provide 'the experience of necessary force' and therefore the idea of causality.[413] According to Rawls, the responses created by the common feelings and reactions to the religious enactments showed that the participants must know the causes directly rather than indirectly 'because their feelings are manifested internally', which means that the causes of religious enactments can be known in the same way as causes in the external world.[414]

In response to this, Schmaus stated that 'if causes operate internally,' as Rawls claimed, then Hume's argument still applies, since in Schmaus' view it means that 'people can introspect only the effects of the social causes and not the causes themselves.'[415] This is the case because, as Hume stated, causality is always a feeling and never an event in the external world since objects have no powers. In this respect, Schmaus went on to assert that Durkheim's argument for the causal powers of religious enactments is therefore weak since we can never trace the concept of power or force back to the necessary connection discussed by Hume. Schmaus went on to argue that Durkheim only traced the causes to the internal relations, but never addressed the problem that direct social causes could never be observed within Hume's epistemological framework. Schmaus therefore went on to say that because Durkheim did not deal with Hume's argument about causality, it disqualifies his epistemological justification for the origins of the category of causality in experience.[416]

After dealing with Hume's argument in relation to causality, Schmaus turned his attention to Durkheim's knowledge of Hume. He stated that Durkheim was unaware of the subtleties of Hume's argument and that this is confirmed by evidence recently

---

411 Hume states that 'in reality there is no part of matter that does ever by its sensible qualities discover any power or energy or give us ground to imagine that it could produce anything or be followed by any other object. The power or force which actuates the whole machine (the outside world) is entirely concealed from us, and never discovers itself in any of the sensible qualities of the object.' See Hume's *Enquiries Concerning Human Understanding and Concerning the Principles of Morals*, Oxford: Clarendon Press, [1777] 1975, pp. 63–4.

412 Schmaus, 'Rawls, Durkheim, and Causality: A Critical Discussion,' *American Journal of Sociology*, Vol. 104, 1998, p. 875.

413 Rawls, Response to Schmaus, *American Journal of Sociology*, p. 446.

414 Ibid.

415 Schmaus, 'Rawls, Durkheim, and Causality,' p. 876.

416 Ibid., 877.

discovered in the 'Sens Lectures,' a series of talks given by Durkheim at the Lycée de Sens between 1883–4 where Durkheim's remarks were written down by the French philosopher Andre Lelande (1867–1964) who had attended the lectures. Since the Sens Lectures were first discovered in 1995, many believe they offer a unique glimpse into what Durkheim would have known philosophically during the period of the 1880s.[417] Schmaus argued that on the basis of the *Sens Lectures*, Durkheim's knowledge of Hume's philosophy during the period was limited, and he went on to make two assumptions about Durkheim's lack of familiarity with Hume's argument on causality. First, he stated that Durkheim overlooked Hume's argument on causality altogether, arguing that Durkheim was not 'well versed in Hume's argument regarding the origins of causality' and that he 'never came to grasp the full import of Hume's argument that forces and causes can be known no more by introspection than by external observation.'[418] On this basis Schmaus believed that Durkheim would have mistakenly assumed that we 'can introspect causal powers and not merely their effects or causal relations.'[419] Second, Schmaus assumes that even though Durkheim knew that 'the idea of causation cannot be found in external experience,' he would not have been aware of Hume's argument that it 'could not be found in our internal experience of the operation of the will.'[420] As a result, Schmaus argued that Durkheim 'did not take into account Hume's point that even our ideas of internal reflection are inert,' and as a result failed to consider the 'implications' this had for his 'theory of the origin of the idea of causal power.'[421]

There are, however, several problems with this. First, the *Sens Lectures* were given thirty years before Durkheim wrote *The Elementary Forms* where he came to terms with Hume's argument on causality in a section devoted explicitly to Hume. While Schmaus claimed that Durkheim failed to understand Hume on causality, it is clear that Schmaus failed to understand Durkheim's argument in relation to Hume in the context of Durkheim's overall opposition to classical rationalism and the skeptical view put forward by Kant and Hume about the existence of external reality. Second, because both Schmaus and Rawls overlook recent discussion of the realist theory of knowledge by Roy Bhaskar and Bhaskar's critical comments on Hume's theory of causation, neither Schmaus nor Rawls adequately represent Durkheim's realist view for the existence of society in *The Elementary Forms*.[422]

---

417 Robert Alun Jones discusses the importance of the Sens Lectures in *The Development of Durkheim's Social Realism,* Cambridge: Cambridge University Press, 1999. He makes the same error as Schmaus in assuming that the Sens Lectures constitute a superior source for making judgments about what Durkheim was thinking at the time that he was adopting a realist view of society. For discussion of the problem of using the Sens Lectures in this way, see my review of Jones' *The Development of Durkheim's Social Realism* at www.cjsonline.ca/reviews/ March–April 2000.

418 Schmaus, 'Rawls, Durkheim, and Causality,' p. 880.

419 Ibid.

420 Ibid., p. 881.

421 Ibid.

422 Roy Bhaskar, 'Philosophy and Scientific Realism,' in M. Archer et al. (eds.), *Critical Realism*, London: Routledge, 1998, pp. 16–47.

In direct opposition to Schmaus and Rawls who uncritically accept Hume's theory of causation and his skeptical view about the existence of the outer world, Bhaskar's criticism of Hume begins by opposing Hume's epistemological views in several respects. First, he asserted that Hume's theory of causation and skeptical outlook was a product of an outmoded philosophical standpoint that formed as a result of the direct opposition to the realist view of knowledge which had argued that knowledge of causal relations is obtained by a direct encounter with the material world. Second, Bhaskar argued that if science is to be possible then the sense perceptions asserted by Hume must occur in nature and therefore must belong to experience. Third, while Hume denied that we can ever philosophically establish the existence of material things outside the mind or their causes, Bhaskar disagrees with Hume's view by showing that causation is bound up with 'natural necessity' in which things have powers and dispositions to act in certain ways by virtue of their intrinsic structures and natures. In this view, therefore, objects and events have powers which may or may not be exercised.[423] Fourth, because reality for Hume was broken down into sense impressions and atomistic bits which were assembled by the agency of the mind, Hume argued that knowledge of the objective relations in experience was unattainable because we only perceive the impressions of things rather than the things themselves.[424] According to Bhaskar, however, Hume's claim that all experience is filled in by the mind and that the material world is simply a construction of sense impressions has been called into question. Bhaskar points out that the predispositions of the classical empiricism as proposed by Hume were problematic, and generally faulty. He argues that from the perspective of science, it makes no sense to assert, as Hume did, that gravity is a 'feeling' rather than an 'event.' Bhaskar therefore argues that if science is to be possible, then Hume's sense impressions and their conjunctions must occur in nature, and thus belong to experience.[425]

Durkheim's Battle with Classical Rationalism: The Critique of Philosophy

We can now return to the question posed earlier about why Durkheim would have opposed the philosophy of Kant and Hume at the same time that he put forward a sociological theory of religion. The answer to this question cannot be found in what Schmaus had claimed was Durkheim's limited knowledge of Hume's philosophy in the light of the Sens Lectures. Schmaus, in fact, might have asked the more central question concerning why Durkheim would have opposed Hume's assertion that causation cannot be found in the outside world of experience and that religious enactments would not themselves have been the cause of the categories of space, time and cause simply on the presumed material effects of the enactments. In this case, the

---

423 See Bhaskar, 'Philosophy and Scientific Realism,' pp. 16–47.
424 Ibid., p. 19.
425 See R. Bhaskar, 'Philosophy and Scientific Realism,' pp. 41–3; and R. Harre and E.H. Madden, 'Conceptual and Natural Necessity,' pp. 106–8.

question then becomes not what did Durkheim know about Hume's argument on causality in the 1880s, but rather what kinds of limitations did Hume and Kant place on knowledge of the exterior world of experience?

In order to answer this question, we have to look more closely at the history of classical rationalism and the limits which it placed on knowledge of society at the time, and then at Durkheim's battle with classical rationalism. To begin with, classical rationalism can be defined as a philosophic doctrine which came into being during the enlightenment and derived its underlying theoretical orientation from the works of Descartes, Hume and Kant. While it began as a distinct philosophic position in the seventeenth century with Descartes, it came into dominance in the eighteenth century after Hume and Kant extended Descartes' original argument by formalizing a new epistemological standpoint that imposed severe limits on knowledge of the exterior world.

At the center of classical rationalism are three fundamental assertions concerning knowledge of the outside world. First, was the assertion by Descartes that all external reality – all outness – was nothing more than an 'extension' of interior thought. In this view, all reality proceeds from thought and is nothing more than an 'extension' borrowed from thought itself. In using the concept of extension to define all external reality, Descartes argued that the outside world was not a material substance that existed on its own, and after differentiating the outside world of experience from the inner world of the mind, he asserted that everything outside the mind constituted what he called an 'extended' substance, or an object in extension. He then took the extraordinary step of referring to all material reality with the concept of 'extension' to the point that the concept of an 'object in extension' replaced the reality of the concept of an object as a material substance or solid.[426] As a result of this, new limits were imposed on knowledge of the exterior world since objects had no reality in themselves and could not exist independently of thought. Further, to the extent that the exterior world was defined by Descartes as all bodies and substances in 'extension,' it meant that the objective reality of society and history were outside the field of knowledge because they did not exist independently of the mind. Without an exterior, the contents of society and history were thus removed from philosophy as an object of knowledge.

Second, was Hume's assertion concerning knowledge of the outside world. Hume had argued that so far as all knowledge of the exterior world was reduced to sense impressions arising from the mind, all facts and factual observations were made up of sense data that created feelings and cognitions, but not factual events that existed in themselves independently of the perceptions. Hume had therefore argued that external realities did not exist by themselves independent of sense impression. He thought that

---

426 Descartes' extraordinary reductive step of reducing all external reality to 'objects in extension' was devised during his famous experiment with wax where he argued that the wax he was observing was an 'object in extension' rather than a material solid in the outside world. For this see Descartes, *Mediations* I–VI. For how this was a faulty argument see Gaston Bachelard, *The New Scientific Spirit*, Boston: Beacon Press, 1984, pp. 165–70.

they were made up of sensations and cognitions, but not external material events. This meant that in Hume's reasoning, the material world was nothing more than mental responses to the stimulus of impressions rather than the appearance of the 'truth' of material reality. From this point onward, statements related to knowledge of material reality never attained the conditions of the validity of objective reality existing outside the individual. In the light of the assertions by Hume, all Durkheim's 'realist' inclinations to treat the exterior world as an objective reality external to the individual could never be justified or realized since social and religious realities had no powers to affect the actions of individuals and were not real in themselves, according to Hume.

Third, was the assertion by Kant who argued that we cannot ever know the outside world without the operation of the a priori which he believed was innate to human reason and logically prior to experience. What was important about Kant's theory of the categories was that it introduced the fundamental philosophical separation between conscious reason in the mind, and the existence of objects or things in the outer world. Kant had stated that we can only know things in the outer world through the operations of a priori reasoning in the mind. Kant's discussion of how we come to have knowledge of the external world was thus historically important because it formally separated what 'reason supplies for itself' from what was in the world of experience.[427] Furthermore, in stating that the 'time in which these relations are set in the mind' seems to precede the moment we have consciousness of them in experience,' Kant fundamentally changed the terms under which the outer world could be known.[428] After Kant, valid knowledge of the material world could never be obtained because objects in the world could never be known 'as things in themselves.'

We can now answer the question posed earlier as to why Durkheim would have entered into a battle with classical rationalism while at the same time putting forward a theory of religion? Since essential to all rationalism is the opposition to the existence of the exterior world and the insistence that the outside world had no materiality in itself, the answer to the question is that Durkheim had to demonstrate that society was a structure that must first exist in external reality and secondly, he had to show how the structure of society exists in the mind of individuals in the form of dispositions taken toward objects during religious enactments. Further he had to show that the religious enactments in the form of the interdicts had power over the acts of individuals and that these powers were evident in the material effects that took place during the enactments that included shrieking and crying and the self-mutilation of their bodies. These powers, according to Durkheim, were evidence of society consecrated in the form of religious enactments.

Durkheim's opposition to classical rationalism in *The Elementary Forms* can thus be explained by the fact that classical rationalism had called the existence of the

---

427 Ibid., p. 43.

428 For the way Kant changed the 'rules of succession' for the appearance of the object in the mind in relation to the experience of it in the world see *The Critique of Pure Reason*, p. 87. Kant altered the relations of succession by stating that 'knowledge of the object in experience' is always after 'consciousness of them in experience.'

material world into question and this, as a result, led to a collapse in all the objective categories Durkheim had used for defining social realities external to the individual. Since it was Durkheim's aim in *The Elementary Forms* to establish a condition of validity for the reality of society as a structure outside the individual, he had to show that Kant's apriorism and Hume's empiricism respectively stripped objective reality of its material qualities, and that the material qualities of the religious enactments were powers in themselves and hence valid evidence of the external reality of society. Durkheim believed that once the material powers of religious enactments had been established, external social realities would 'acquire a reasonableness that the most militant rationalist cannot fail to recognize.'[429] This explains why in chapter VII, book II of *The Elementary Forms*, Durkheim explicitly criticizes Descartes' claim that all external reality is an 'extended substance' that does not constitute substantial realities outside the individual.[430] If this were to be accepted as true, it would mean that the material effects of the religious practices neither had reality or material efficacy.

Having completed our discussion of Durkheim's theoretical perspective, I now want to turn my attention to the next chapter and to the work of Max Weber.

---

429 Ibid.

430 Durkheim's opposition to classical rationalism has been overlooked by most commentators. New textual evidence showing Durkheim's response to Descartes assertion that 'extended substances' have no material reality has been provided by Karen Field's translation of *The Elementary Forms*, pp. 226–29. In so far as Durkheim's aim was to establish a condition of validity for the reality of society as a structure subsisting independently of the mind, he shows how apriorism (Kant) and empiricism (Hume) respectively stripped objective reality of its material qualities and created a collapse in the objective categories of knowledge. For more discussion on how Durkheim's opposition to classical rationalism has been overlooked by writers on Durkheim see Ken Morrison, 'Review Essay on The Elementary Forms,' *Social Forces*, 82, 2003, pp. 399–404.

4

Max Weber

The Historical Context of Max Weber's Work

Max Weber was born on April 21, 1864 in Erfurt, a small city located in the south-eastern part of Germany. His father was a well known lawyer and politician who played a minor role in his upbringing. Weber's mother, a far more dominant figure in his life, encouraged and supported him throughout his career. Weber grew up within the confines of a middle class family that was well situated in German society. He began his education in 1872 and established himself as an outstanding student early in his career. After finishing his secondary education he went to Berlin where he obtained a university degree in law and eventually a doctorate in political economy. After deciding to devote himself to scholarly interests, he received his first academic position in 1893 when he was twenty nine years old. In 1896, he was appointed to a professorship in economics at the University of Freiburg, and then to a more important position at the University of Heidelberg, where he taught political economy and economics. Only thirty two years old at the time, he was considered one of the youngest scholars to obtain a professorship at a major German university. However, a severe personal crisis the next year forced Weber to suspend his teaching activities and eventually resign his position at Heidelberg.[1] Between 1897 and 1903, Weber stopped all scholarly work and traveled throughout Europe while he waited for his nervous disorder to dissipate. In 1903, at the age of 39, Weber returned to academic work, but only slowly, starting research on two large essays, one related to capitalism and religion, the other to methodological problems in the social sciences.

While Weber did not resume his teaching duties for some time, he began to return to academic work in 1904, publishing the first part of his famous essay on capitalism and religion. In 1905, he published the second part of the essay which eventually became one of his best known works entitled *The Protestant Ethic and Spirit of Capitalism*. In 1909, he accepted the editorship of a sociological publication during which time he gradually increased his academic workload. By this time, a large circle of friends, including Georg Simmel, Robert Michels and others, met regularly at the Weber household to discuss the issues of the day.[2] By 1909, Weber

---

1 Marianne Weber, *Max Weber: A Biography,* New York: John Wiley & Sons, 1975.
2 M. Weber, *Max Weber: A Biography*, p. 65.

began writing a large two volume work entitled *Economy and Society* which was one of his most ambitious theoretical and historical works. Between 1905–1918, he carried out extensive research on the history of the world's religions, comparing the religions of the Occident with those of China and India. Then, between 1919 and 1920 Weber wrote his last academic work entitled *A General Economic History* which was a series of lectures he gave at the University of Freiburg on the history of capitalist development. In addition to his academic career, Weber participated in German political life and often gave public addresses and lectures on issues such as politics and science which were well received and eventually became famous in their own right.[3] In many of these talks, Weber tried to reconcile what he thought were conflicting value problems related to the role of the expert in political and scientific life. In June of 1920, Weber died leaving many of his works in unpublished state.

Weber's writings as a whole are best known for their historical grasp of modern Western societies and their economic, political, legal and religious development. The scope of his writings are extremely broad and wide ranging, and his contribution to theoretical problems such as the formation of modern social classes, the nature of political legitimacy, the development of modern law and the study of world religions, is extensive. In addition to these themes, his work has a distinct modernist emphasis, focusing on such issues as the rise of modern society, the formation of bureaucracy, the development of the modern political state and a comparative analysis of world economies and religions.[4]

A central feature of Weber's overall work is his approach to social theory. By and large, Weber was a modernist in his overall approach to social thought. He brought together various traditions of social theory and formed a unique theoretical perspective based on history, economics, philosophy, law, and comparative historical analysis. The theoretical influences in Weber's work derive from two broad schools of thought. First, was the influence of the German historical school of Carl Menger, Gustav Schmoller, Karl Knies and Heinrich Rickert.[5] As a result of his links to the historical school, Weber became involved in a methodological controversy which forced him to take a position critical to historical economics and the methods of the natural sciences. While Weber's involvement in the controversy shaped his work for the rest of his career, it eventually brought him into contact with Heinrich Rickert,

---

3 Weber's writings on the social issues of his time can be found in 'Politics as a Vocation' and 'Science as a Vocation,' in H.H. Gerth and C. Wright Mills, *From Max Weber: Essays in Sociology,* New York: Oxford University Press, 1967.

4 For studies of Weber, see Keith Tribe (ed.), *Reading Weber*, London: Routledge, 1989; S. Lash and S. Whimster (eds.), *Max Weber, Rationality and Modernity*, London: Allen & Unwin, 1987; Stephen Kalberg, 'On the Neglect of Weber's Protestant Ethic as a Theoretical Treatise: Demarcating the Parameters of Postwar American Sociological Theory, *Sociological Theory*, 14, 1, 1996, 49–69; and Stephen Kalberg, *Max Weber's Comparative-Historical Sociology*, Chicago: University of Chicago Press, 1994.

5 Thomas Burger, *Max Weber's Theory of Concept Formation*, Durham: Duke University Press, 1976; and Susan Hekman, *Weber, the Ideal Type, and Contemporary Social Theory* Indiana: University of Notre Dame Press, 1983.

whose participation in the debate led to a key distinction between the subject matter of the social and natural sciences, as we shall see later.[6] A second influence on Weber's theoretical perspective was the Marxist school of economics. At the time Weber was working, Marx's writings were pervasive in Europe and at the time there were many schools of thought which were critical to Marx's economic thinking.[7] As a result of this, Weber criticized Marx's perspective on several fronts and this led him to formulate a completely different view of the role played by history and economy in social development.

Weber's Theoretical Perspective and Fundamental Themes in his Work

Weber's most important works were written between 1903 and 1920, and include such writings as *The Protestant Ethic and Spirit of Capitalism*; *The Sociology of World Religions* and *Economy and Society*. By and large, most of his writings were written between periods of poor health and, as such, his work suffered from frequent interruptions. In addition, his health affected the way he approached his largest work entitled *Economy and Society*, and as a result a great deal of it was written in the form of sketches which Weber intended to elaborate on at some later date, but never did. Because only a few of his writings were complete studies, *The Protestant Ethic* constituted the first full length study published by Weber, and as a result it became the centerpiece of his major investigative work. Some of the shortcomings in Weber's overall body of works meant that his writings as a whole have generally not been viewed as a unified body of work organized as a complete thematic whole. Consequently, some commentators have taken the view that Weber's overall body of works can only be considered as a fragmented collection lacking in thematic organization, while others have stated that Weber's work was too obscure or incomplete to be dealt with in a systematic manner.[8]

Despite these limitations, there are a number of themes in his work which have led to a central body of social theory.[9] The key focus of this work can be grasped in the main by looking at a number of themes which form the focal point of his sociological

---

6 For an overall historical view of Weber and his work see Reinhard Bendix, *Max Weber: An Intellectual Portrait*, New York, 1960.

7 Stuart Hughes, *Consciousness and Society: The Re-orientation of European Social Thought 1890–1930*, New York: Vintage Books, 1958.

8 For a discussion of the question of the 'thematic organization' of Weber's work, see Friedrich H. Tenbruck, 'The Problem of Thematic Unity in the Works of Max Weber,' The *British Journal of Sociology*, 31, 1980, 316–25; Stephen Kalberg, 'The Search for Thematic Orientations in a Fragmented Oeuvre: The Discussion of Max Weber in Recent German Sociological Literature,' *Sociology*, 13, 1979, 127–39. Also, Benjamin Nelson's, 'Max Weber's Author's Introduction: A Master Clue to his Main Aims,' *Sociological Inquiry*, 44, 1974, 269–77; and Reinhard Bendix, 'Max Weber's Sociology Today,' *International Social Science Journal*, 17, 1965, 9–22. These authors state that the thematic organization of Weber's work provides an overall unity.

9 For a different perspective on the thematic continuity of Weber's writings see H.H. Gerth and C. Wright Mills, *From Max Weber: Essays in Sociology*, New York: Oxford University Press, 1946, p. 24.

writings. Generally these themes concentrate themselves around several repeated issues in his work which can be characterized as follows. First is his interest in civilization processes and the focus on how Western societies arose when and where they did. Second is his focus on the process he referred to as 'rationalization,' and the role it played in the development of Western society. In this regard, Weber was alone in believing that Western society reflected the process of rationalization in its system of law, science, politics, commerce and religion. Third are his comparative studies of religion and economic organization which focused on the effects of Protestant religious doctrine on the economic organization of the West.

Weber's Difference from Marx

Earlier we pointed out that Weber was influenced by Marx on issues related to the role played by the economy in historical development. Whether Weber applied Marx's historical methods or whether he exclusively criticized Marx is still a great deal in question, but what is clear is that Weber fundamentally disagreed with Marx on a number of key theoretical issues.[10] For all practical purposes, these disagreements converge on at least two distinct fronts: first, on the nature and purpose of social theory; and second, on the understanding of history and social and economic development.

To begin with, Weber rejected Marx's assertion that the central task of social theory was to change society. Marx believed that it was the historical obligation of all thought to change society and history rather than to simply observe it. As a result, he took the view that the sole purpose of theoretical work was to promote change and eliminate inequalities and hardship in society. Marx therefore believed that theoretical work must be linked to social and political change. Weber, by contrast, disagreed with this in several ways. First, he thought that the ultimate task of social theory was to search for historical truths and to gather historical facts about society and social development. Because of this, he believed that social theory itself was in principle a search for historical patterns and relationships in which knowledge of society and history could only be discovered by a comparison of different historical periods.

Second, Weber disagreed with the way Marx had used theoretical concepts. He thought that Marx used concepts mainly as critical instruments whose purpose was to point out the existing economic inequalities and hardships in society. This put Marx in the position of criticizing the underlying origins of social and historical inequality and the conditions leading to the divisions in the class system. Weber, however, was much less direct in his criticism of society and history, and believed that concepts in the social sciences should be neutral and not based on value judgments of the type that Marx had engaged in. In this respect, Weber felt that Marx had used concepts such as 'inequality' and 'class division' in a way that was value loaded and inconsistent with the search for historical truths.

---

10 For specific comments by Weber about Marx's theory of history see *The Protestant Ethic*, pp. 55–6, 61. In addition, Weber frequently refers to Marx in *Economy and Society* as 'that talented author,' p. 926.

Weber's View of History and the Continuity of Civilization Processes

In addition to differing on views about the nature of social theory, Weber and Marx differed in their understanding of history and historical development.[11] To begin with, Weber rejected the idea that all social life could be explained by recourse to underlying economic laws. While he agreed with Marx that the economic sphere was a central component of social life, he thought that economic history alone could not explain the development of modern societies and that other non-economic factors had to be taken into account in addition to economic ones. In contrast to Weber, Marx believed that history could be understood only in terms of underlying laws of economic development, and held that these laws shaped the material conditions of society and the structure of the class system.

It is along these lines that many authors took the view that Marx advocated a kind of economic determinism in his approach to history and social development. Economic determinism refers to the doctrine which holds that historical circumstances are determined by a sequence of economic events connected to the act of production. It includes the view that history can be understood only in terms of the laws of economic development, and that the economic foundation of society acts as determinants which place the economy at the center of social and historical development. Weber, by contrast, wanted to show that social and historical development could, in fact, be studied outside the realm of economic forces and took the view that there were other determinants of social life which derived from the political, religious and legal spheres of society. Weber believed that these social spheres, in fact, were fundamental to an understanding of social and historical development.

Weber's assumption concerning the interconnected nature of the 'social spheres' is one of the most important theoretical characteristics of his work. There are, according to Weber, four distinct spheres or realms which make up the structure of society: the political, legal, economic and religious spheres. While Weber thought that no one sphere was dominant in society at any given historical period, he did believe that the spheres largely overlapped in relation to each other, and that in this respect tended to exert influences affecting the development of adjacent spheres over time. Furthermore, he maintained that religion, law, economy and the political structure of society functioned only in relation to specific spheres, and that each of these spheres was a structure of objective relations that brought about necessary change and historical development. In particular, he thought that the 'religious sphere' and the 'law sphere' acted as causal forces affecting the development of the economic and political spheres in society. Marx, on the other hand, believed that all aspects of society including politics, law and religion were largely expressions of underlying economic forces and class interests and only these, he thought, were analytically important. Weber, by contrast, did not believe that economic

---

11 See Susan Hekman, 'Weber's Concept of Causality and the Modern Critique,' *Sociological Inquiry,* 49, 1979, 67–76.

forces were the only agents of social and historical change and he wanted to show that other causal factors were important in social and historical development. This was especially true of Weber's historical study of capitalism where he showed that the religious sphere placed its stamp on the formation of the economic sphere.

On a second front, Weber disagreed with Marx's claim that all social and historical processes could be reduced to economic laws of development and this led him to criticize Marx's materialist theory of history.[12] In this regard, Marx had claimed that historical processes are carried on in accordance with the laws of economic development and that the drama of history was played out on an economic front leading to the division of society into classes. Marx therefore reduced social and historical development to a set of economic laws, stating that political, legal and religious institutions existed on top of the underlying economic base of society. Weber, by contrast, thought that many of the important changes taking place in society and history occurred in spheres other than the economic realm of society.

The Theme of Rationalization in Weber's Work

At the center of Weber's writings is the study of social and historical processes he called rationalization. This is a concept used by Weber to denote a type of social development according to which modern industrial societies took the historical form that they did. In contrast to Marx, who thought that all the historical stages of social development were straightforward expressions of different economic epochs, Weber felt that a far more general principle was key to understanding the pattern of historical development, and he referred to this as the process of rationalization.[13] As far as Weber was concerned, all the spheres of society were subject to the process of rationalization and he believed that this process led to the progressive growth of modern Western society. Since no complete understanding of Weber's theoretical perspective is possible without focusing on the concept of rationalization, let us look more closely.

Weber used the term rationalization in several different contexts. While the earliest and perhaps most systematic treatment of the concept is found in the introduction to *The Protestant Ethic*, the term appeared somewhat later in his studies of the world religions and in *Economy and Society*.[14] In addition to this, one of the most extensive treatments of the term is found in an essay entitled 'The Social Psychology of the World Religions,' in which he stated:

---

12 For Weber's criticism of Marx's materialist theory see *The Protestant Ethic*, pp. 55–61.

13 See Weber's discussion in 'The Social Psychology of the World Religions' in *From Max Weber: Essays in Sociology*, H. Gerth and C.W Mills (eds.), New York: Oxford University Press, 1967, pp. 293–294.

14 For an additional discussion of the concept of rationalization see Weber, 'Author's Introduction,' in *The Protestant Ethic*, pp. 13–31; and *The Religion of China*, New York: The Free Press, 1951, pp. 33–52; 196–249. For other discussions of Weber's concept of rationality see Donald Levine, 'Rationality and Freedom: Weber and Beyond,' *Sociological Inquiry*, 51, 1981, 5–25; and Stephen Kalberg's 'Max Weber's Types of Rationality: Cornerstones for the Analysis of Rationalization Processes in his History,' *American Journal of Sociology*, 85, 1980, 1145–79.

We have to remind ourselves in advance that 'rationalism' may mean very different things. It means one thing if we think of the kind of rationalization that the systematic thinker performs on the image of the world: increasing theoretical mastery of reality by means of increasing precise and abstract concepts. Rationalization means another thing if we think of the methodological attainment of a definitely given and practical end by means of an increasingly precise calculation of adequate means. These types of rationalism are very different, in spite of the fact that ultimately they belong inseparably together. Similar types may be distinguished even within the intellectual comprehension of reality; for instance, the differences between English physics and Continental physics has been traced back to such a type difference within the comprehension of reality. The rationalization of life conduct with which we have to deal here can assume usually varied forms. The supreme ideal of the Renaissance was 'rational' in the sense of a belief in a valid canon, and the view of life of the Renaissance was rational in the sense of rejecting traditionalistic bonds and of having faith in the power of human reason. Rational may also mean a 'systematic arrangement.' In general, all kinds of practical ethics that are systematically and unambiguously oriented to fixed goals of salvation are 'rational,' partly in the same sense as formal method is rational, and partly in the sense that they distinguish between 'valid' norms and what is empirically given.[15]

Since in the above discussion Weber refers to the process of rationalization as a form of control imposed on the external world and as a 'mastery over reality,' we can begin to define the term by outlining several key principles that are linked to the overall process of historical development.[16] These include themes such as: (i) the principle of development in Western societies that is based on the rigorous control of external reality by the active mastery of the natural world; (ii) the growing stress on the rational containment of everyday life by methodical conduct and a consistent attitude of control; (iii) the widespread use of calculation as a strategy for social action and as a method of controlling the outcomes or ends of action; (iv) the freeing of all social action from magical thought and the pursuit of rational goals by means of strict calculation of ends and a consistent attitude of methodical action; (v) the emphasis on a practical orientation to empirical reality with the aim of the active mastery; and (vi) the widespread use of technical and procedural reasoning as a way of controlling everyday life circumstances.[17]

Rationalization Defined   To begin with, Weber used the term rationalization to describe the process by which nature, society and individual action are increasingly mastered by an orientation to planning, technical procedure and rational action. Weber believed that the rationalization process was not only evident in individual

---

15 *The Social Psychology of the World Religions*, in *From Max Weber*, H.H. Gerth and C.W. Mills, pp. 293–294.

16 Friedrich H. Tenbruck, 'The Problem of Thematic Unity in the Works of Max Weber,' The *British Journal of Sociology*, 31, 1980, 316–51. For Weber's own discussion of rationalization see his discussion in the introduction to the *Protestant Ethic and Spirit of Capitalism*, pp. 13–31; and in Gerth and Mills, *From Max Weber*, pp. 293–295.

17 Weber, *Protestant Ethic and the Spirit of Capitalism*, pp. 13–20.

action and in practical and technical orientations to reality, but also that it manifested itself in institutions and in the everyday orientation to empirical reality itself.[18] He believed that, more than other societies, modern Western societies reflected the tendency of rationalization in their system of law, politics, science and commercial life. He thought that all the spheres of society, including the economic, political and legal spheres underwent the process of rationalization during the modern period and it was this, he believed, which led to the rise of modern Western societies and the particular attitude they developed toward the world. In the economic sphere, for instance, rationalization involved the organization of commercial practices by means of technical rules calculated to produce profits by the use of rational accounting methods and by the control and regulation of the workday. In the sphere of the state, rationalization hastened the decline of absolute monarchies by creating forms of leadership and governance based on principles of legal legitimacy and the universal application of democratic law. In the sphere of law, rationalization altered the principle of legal judgments by creating a system of decision-making based on case precedent, universal legal principles and deductive reasoning based on facts related to the application of cases.

Weber's concept of rationalization therefore refers to two broad trends in historical development. First is the tendency of social and historical processes to become more and more reliant on calculation and technical knowledge in order to obtain rational control over the natural and social world. The development of science and engineering are examples of the control over nature and empirical reality. Second is the tendency of human social action to free itself from a dependence on magical thinking in order to rely on what is immediately given in empirical reality without regard for superstition. Rationalization therefore depends on two types of activities: (i) strategies of social action that are utilized in a direct encounter with empirical reality as a means of obtaining control over it; and (ii) adjustments of the means and ends of action in an effort to derive strategies for the attainment of necessary ends and selected goals.[19] In this case, an 'end' may be simply described as the goal of action, whereas the 'means' refer simply to the techniques or strategies used to obtain specific ends.

To illustrate how Weber used the concept of rationalization, let us turn to an example Weber drew on in his own work to illustrate how rationalization comes about. He stated that in certain kinds of economic activity we can generally make a distinction between two related forms of acquisition: forceful and capitalist. In forceful acquisition, wealth is obtained by means of force either inside or outside the law. Acquisition by this means, said Weber, is neither efficient nor 'oriented to obtaining

---

18 Weber's introduction to *The Protestant Ethic* provides a considerable historical dimension to the concept of rationalization and its principle of development in the West. See Weber, 'Author's Introduction,' *The Protestant Ethic*, pp. 13–31.

19 Both strategies of social action and adjustment of means and ends reappear throughout Weber's writings. See *Economy and Society*, pp. 3–30.

profits by systematic planning.'[20] In acquisition by capitalistic means, however, wealth is pursued rationally by utilizing peaceful means of exchange rather than forceful ones. As a consequence, 'action is adjusted on a frequent basis to calculate the means of success in terms of capital.'[21] This rational pursuit of profit, according to Weber, leads to a more general concern with efficiency in commercial activity and with greater control over empirical reality. This eventually leads in turn to new procedures for striking a 'balance' in accounting practices in comparison with the earlier technique of calculation by means of estimates.

Weber went on to say that historically the procedure for 'striking a balance' was itself born from the earlier practice of obtaining an estimate, since both share the same category of action having to do with calculation. However, the procedure of striking a balance is more rational than an estimate and thus achieves greater control over empirical reality. The difference between the two types of acquisition is that acquisition by peaceful means is rationalized on the basis of calculative activity in an effort to achieve control over economic outcomes. Weber went on to point out in this case that 'the important fact here is that the rational calculation of capital in terms of money is made more rational by modern book-keeping methods' which, he said, arise from earlier techniques related to the control over outcomes in economic matters.[22] What distinguishes these activities from the previous practice of obtaining estimates is that, in rational capitalism, 'everything is done in terms of balances. At the beginning of the enterprise an initial balance is taken, before every individual decision a calculation is made to ascertain its profitableness, and at the end a final balance is taken to ascertain how much profit has been made. To the extent that the transactions are rational, calculation underlies every single action' and this contrasts with the pure guess-work of traditional acquisition 'where circumstances do not demand strict accuracy' or control over empirical reality.[23]

Rationalization and Religious World Views   Another characteristic of the rationalization process, according to Weber, is the role it plays in bringing about a change in the regulation of economic conduct in the world. Nowhere is this more apparent, according to Weber, than in the appearance of a religious ethic in daily economic life. Weber first pursued the connection between religion and economic rationalization in *The Protestant Ethic*, and then in two later studies on religion entitled *The Religion of India* and *The Religion of China*.[24] In these works, Weber looked at the question

---

20 Weber, *The Protestant Ethic*, pp. 18–19.

21 Ibid.

22 Ibid.

23 Ibid.

24 Max Weber, *The Religion of India: The Sociology of Hinduism and Buddhism*, H. H. Gerth and D. Martindale (eds.), New York: The Free Press, [1919] 1958; *The Religion of China: Confucianism and Taoism* H. H. Gerth (ed.), New York: The Free Press, 1964. For further discussion of the theme of rationalization and religion see Weber's essay entitled 'Social Psychology of the World Religions' in H.H. Gerth and C.W. Mills (eds.), *From Max Weber: Essays in Sociology*, New York: Oxford University Press, 1967. The theme of religion and rationalization is discussed by Fredrich Tenbruck in 'The Problem of Thematic Unity in the works of Max Weber,' *British Journal of Sociology*, 31, 1980, pp. 316–348.

of how different religious world views tended either to advance the rationalization process or impede it by placing obstacles in its path. He believed that the specific point of intersection between a religious ethic and the rationalization of economic life occurred during the period after the Protestant reformation when religious doctrine placed a premium on inner self-control in relation to economic conduct in the world. It was at this point, said Weber, that a religious ethic placed its 'stamp' on 'life-regulation' as a means of rationalizing it and, in doing so, it created what he called 'methodic conduct' and self-control in relation to economic activity in the world.

In pursuing the theme of religion and rationalization in the *Collected Essays*, Weber looked at the problem of how the rationalization process was transferred from the sphere of religion to the economic sphere.[25] In this case, his aim was to show that the effects of rationalization in the world had the capacity to transform empirical reality by placing a premium on 'methodical life conduct.' This involved two separate but interrelated assumptions by Weber. First, was his belief that a religious world view produces a rational outlook toward the world, and that from this follows rational conduct. Second was his belief that historically the different religious orientations to the outside world lead to very different types of rational development in knowledge, science and art. This was especially true of societies in the East in comparison with societies in the West. As far as Weber was concerned, this meant that the orientation a society takes toward the outside world is always derived from its religious world view. He thought that the relationship between religion and the pattern of rational development could be demonstrated by looking at the path of rational progress of the sciences in China and India in comparison with the rational progress of science in the West.

He stated that in China, for instance, the rational progress of science was thwarted by specific obstacles whose origins were religious, and that religion interfered with the rationalization process by promoting magical thinking over the technical mastery of empirical reality. This happened in China, according to Weber, when the path leading to the development of astronomy was thrown off the track of rational refinement by a religious ethic that stressed a magical orientation to reality at the very point that astronomy would have become a science.[26] In the West on the other hand, Weber thought that there were rational refinements in astronomy which prevented it from becoming an astrology rooted in magic. For the same reason, he thought that the natural sciences in India failed to develop a method of experimentation because of religious obstacles, and that in India medicine lacked a biological and a biochemical basis that was most fully developed in the West.[27] Similar to this were the religious obstacles to the rational progress of the sciences in China, which acted to thwart their development.

---

25 This is discussed by Fredrich Tenbruck in his 'The Problem of Thematic Unity in the works of Max Weber,' *British Journal of Sociology*, 31, 1980, pp. 316–348.

26 Ibid.

27 I draw here on Weber's famous introduction to *The Protestant Ethic*. See pp. 13–16.

Weber went on to say that in the case of China what happened was that astronomy became astrology because it did not have a basis in empirical reality and calendrical science, and that as a result it became 'frozen' at the level of serving magical and religious functions that were based on tradition and traditional thinking. These magical functions included such things as making 'interpretations of earthquakes, predicting mountain slides and explaining the cycle of monstrous births,' while at the same time avoiding empirical reality.[28] He argued that it was these magical calculations that knocked astronomy off the path of rational development so that it did not form an empirical relation to reality. He thought that in China astrology maintained its connection to religious traditionalism and a magical view of reality, which prevented it from becoming a mathematically based science of astronomy. Under these circumstances, magicians in China became religious specialists who held a monopoly over legitimate claims about the frequency of the agricultural rain cycle and predictions about the likelihood of monstrous child birth, but were unable to make inroads leading to the control of the empirical world. This, Weber argued, led religion to form a magical relation to the world by confining the allocation of cosmic concepts of worldly events to predictions based on legends about the likely behavior of certain months of the year.[29] Weber believed that it was at this point that a religious ethic placed obstacles in the path of adopting practical conduct in the world while it was serving magical functions.

He went on to argue that notwithstanding the obstacles placed in the path of science in China, there were religious obstacles to the development of medicine. He believed that medicine in China failed to develop a rational pharmacology that promoted a science of bodily health based on biology and chemistry. For this reason he thought that medicine neglected to develop a science of anatomy which would have rationalized the conception of bodily 'health' more fully in the direction of practical functions of the body in relation to daily living. In direct contrast to this was the path of rational development of medicine in the West. He pointed out that by the eighteenth century Western medicine had adopted a rational anatomy and a rational biology after it had mastered the science of anatomical dissection and the concept of clinical pathology. In China, by contrast, medicine was thrown off the path of rational development at the very point that it served traditional medical functions such as acupuncture, which avoided surgical techniques to effect a cure because of religious beliefs about ancestor worship and the prohibition of surgical intrusion into the body. All this, said Weber, was cultivated during a religious ethic where 'breathing' was thought to be the sole carrier of life, and where a magical relation to the plant world was formed leading to a medicine that was in line with a cosmic view of health conceived of as a 'balance' brought about by efficient breathing.[30]

28 Weber, *The Religion of China*, pp. 196–7.
29 Ibid.
30 Ibid., pp. 197–8.

Weber believed that the existing differences between the two orders of world adjustment in the East and the West had to do with their religious world views. 'When the lines of rational development have been obstructed,' he pointed out, 'it usually means that spiritual obstacles have obstructed the development of rational economic conduct in the world and thus has met with serious inner resistance' and is therefore delayed.[31] For this resistance to take place, Weber reasoned, the 'techniques of living handed down by a religious ethic' had to be frozen in traditionalism so that, as a consequence, the religious ethic was simply not able to let 'rational regulation of life conduct develop,' and as a result religious obstacles were placed in their path.[32] The rational regulation of life explicitly happens, said Weber, only when a religious ethic tends to form linkages 'to technological and economic rationalism' which allows the ethic to make 'headway against traditions which, in the main, tend to be disposed towards magic.'[33]

Calculation and the Process of Rationalization In addition to the role played by religion, Weber thought that rationalization in the West was advanced by a process he called calculation. The term calculation and its relation to the rationalization process is found in Weber's discussion of the concept in *Economy and Society* and in other writings. In this context, Weber used the term to convey a key point in the historical development of the West where economic values began to penetrate the sphere of everyday life generally.[34] Weber believed that, initially, the introduction of 'money' in the sphere of commerce brought about a form of calculation in human activities which was far more precise than any traditional method of social action or measurement up until that time. Weber went on to use the term explicitly to describe the way a money rationality, with its stress on counting and quantitative reasoning, was the prime 'propagator' of calculation as a framework for ordering the world.[35] He believed that a counting rationality worked to eliminate all but quantitative considerations and as a consequence placed a value on controlling empirical reality by quantifying it. This, he believed, extended money rationality into the scope of thought and human social action so that it functioned in the world by making conduct more methodical and by aiding in the control of empirical reality.

In addition to this, Weber used the concept to describe the general process by which the system of money calculation penetrates other spheres of human action and social life. This came about, he said, only at a certain stage in historical development when monetary calculation began to become dominant over other forms of social action. At this stage, said Weber, the process of assigning money values to economic activities increased control over practical outcomes in the material world and became

---

31 Weber, *The Protestant Ethic*, pp. 26–7.
32 Weber, 'The Social Psychology of the World Religions,' p. 284.
33 Ibid.
34 *Economy and Society*, pp. 81–107.
35 *Economy and Society,* p. 107

a general orientation to reality. Because of the immense control it conferred on empirical reality and everyday life, calculative reasoning extended its scope to other realms in society. According to Weber, the practice of calculation begins with economic and monetary mechanisms and becomes fully established only when goods and services come to be manipulated by a standard of evaluation and accounting that is strictly outside the immediate sphere of function or utility.

On this basis, Weber reasoned that only when commodities are 'systematically compared' with a view to opportunities related to evaluation based on the possibility of gain and return, does the principle of calculation as a strategy of action begin to develop and enter into the various departments of life. Weber believed that calculation was thus evident at two specific levels of social action: first, at the level of everyday activity, in which quantitative reasoning and calculation began to be utilized to control practical outcomes in the material world; and second, at the level of thought in which the general practice of weighing up alternatives prior to action by evaluating means and ends in order to increase the chance of success became the norm.[36]

The Distinction Between Rationalization and Rationality

Another theme related to the rationalization process in Weber's writings is the concept of rationality. Weber refers to the term rationality repeatedly in his writings on economy, law, religion and social action and, generally speaking, he identifies at least four broad types. These are practical, theoretical, formal and substantive rationality.[37] It is important in this context to differentiate rationality from the overall process of rationalization. Rationalization, we argued, refers to the overall historical process by which reality is increasingly mastered by calculation, scientific knowledge and rational action. Rationality, by contrast, is a term Weber used to refer to the capacity of social action to be subject to calculation of the means and ends of action by taking up a methodical orientation to reality. While this may seem difficult to grasp, Weber argued that in modern society social action can vary depending on the 'orientation' of the actor, the sphere in which the action is carried out and the means and ends which the actor selects in a particular situation of action. For example, in carrying out professional duties, scientists and lawyers may be subject to different forms of rationality in carrying out their actions given the means and ends that are being considered. It is Weber's view that in situations of action the 'means' which individuals use to obtain their ends vary dramatically, depending on how specific orientations to reality impose adjustments on their actions. In and of itself, this can produce variations in rationality and rational action and lead to a strict means-ends calculation, depending on the desired outcome. In such circumstances the means of action explicitly refer to the procedures used for carrying out actions, whereas 'ends' refer to the goals, aims and end results of action.

---

36 Weber, 'The Social Psychology of the World Religions,' p. 284.
37 *Economy and Society*, pp. 63–90.

Having defined the concept of rationality, we can now look more closely at the different types. In a writing entitled 'The Psychology of the World Religions,' Weber outlined four possible forms of rationality. The first type referred to by Weber is practical rationality. This can be described as an orientation to reality that is based on what Weber called the 'methodical attainment of a particular end through increasingly precise calculation of adequate means.'[38] Practical rationality, in this respect, implies a specific orientation to the world based on a 'methodical attainment of ends by the precise calculation of adequate means.' To this extent, it therefore 'orders world content according to some plan.'[39] A second type of rationality discussed by Weber is theoretical or conceptual rationality. In contrast to practical rationality, which imposes order on the world by a straightforward orientation to what is empirically given in reality and by precise calculation, theoretical rationality imposes order on reality by conceptual reasoning. In this case, order is imposed on reality by conceptual mastery of the whole in terms of unified concepts or by patterns brought to light through the reasoning process. For example, science and mathematics apply theoretical rationality by producing an 'image of the world' by means of abstract concepts and conceptualizations.[40] The aim of theoretical rationality in this case is to penetrate the limits of everyday reality, by attempting to understand worldly processes with the aid of abstract concepts which view the world from the perspective of a unity that may be meaningful in terms of some valued standard. Theoretical rationality leads to a departure from the concrete world of everyday experience to the world of abstraction with the express aim of representing the whole in terms of some 'ordered system.' Theoretical rationality therefore undertakes an orientation to reality in the realm of theory.

A third type of rationality referred to by Weber is formal rationality. Weber used this term to designate the amount of quantitative calculation and accounting procedure that goes into an action or decision.[41] Rationality may be thought of as formal when there is a view to expressing a situation or conceptualizing an action by a straightforward application of numerical and calculable standards.[42] In this sense, 'formal rationality' refers to the amount of quantitative calculation and accounting procedure that goes into an act to ensure consistency of outcome and success in attaining desired ends or goals. Thus formal rationality imposes order on the world through calculation, economic accounting and practical efficacy. It therefore expresses itself by imposing order on reality in strict numerical and calculable terms. The

---

38 I draw here on the characteristics of rationality discussed by Weber in 'The Social Psychology of the World Religions,' in H.H. Gerth and C. Wright Mills, *From Max Weber*, pp. 293–4. Donald Levine's 'Rationality and Freedom: Weber and Beyond,' provides a useful classification of Weber's famous description by systematizing the four key types of rationality.

39 Ibid.

40 Kalberg, 'Max Weber's Types of Rationality,' pp. 1145–79; Levine, 'Rationality and Freedom,' pp. 5–25.

41 *Economy and Society*, p. 85.

42 Ibid.

formation of a 'budget of expenditure' as a means of planning business ventures is an example of how formal rationality imposes order on activity in the world in the economic sphere. In this case, formal rationality creates an orientation to action stressing strict adherence to 'cost effective' measures and a formal consideration of means and ends within calculable rules.

A fourth type of rationality discussed by Weber is substantive rationality. Weber used this term to refer to the degree to which action is shaped by an orientation to action in the sphere of values, regardless of the nature of the ends or outcome of action.[43] In contrast to formal rationality, substantive rationality is bound by criteria of ultimate values that are shaped by ethical norms of equality and justice over and against purely formal criteria of decision making based on calculation as strategies to obtain goals. Where formal rationality involves a practical orientation of action regarding outcomes, substantive rationality involves a commitment to values and to value scales in which the ends of action are ethical. In contrast to formal rationality, therefore, substantive rationality is at home in a number of different 'value scales' and thereby always involves considerations of social justice, ethical standards and a concern for social equity.[44] Whereas formal rationality is based on an orientation to decision-making with regard to norms of efficiency and practical costs, substantive rationality is based on the qualitative content of judgments which may be bound by ethical or aesthetic criteria. Weber believed that formal and substantive rationality are opposed in their orientations to reality, and that ultimately substantive rationality views formal rationality as contradictory to its own purposes.[45]

The Theme of Capitalism in Weber's Work

General Economic History

One of the central themes in Weber's work as a whole is his study of capitalism. Historically, Weber wrote two broad theories of capitalism in his lifetime. The first, published in 1904–5 and entitled *The Protestant Ethic and Spirit of Capitalism*, looked at the influences of Protestant religious doctrine on the development of capitalism. The second study, not as well known as the first, written in 1919 and given as a series of lectures at the University of Munich, was entitled 'Outlines of Universal Economic History,' and later published in 1922 as *General Economic History*. Because the text of the lectures represents one of the most systematic views of capitalism ever put forward by Weber, it is worthwhile to look more closely.[46]

---

43 *Economy and Society,* pp. 85–6.
44 Ibid.
45 Ibid.
46 Weber, *General Economic History*, New York: Collier Books, 1961. For a discussion of this work and its significance see Randall Collins, 'Weber's Last Theory of Capitalism: A Systematization,' *American Sociological Review,* 45, 1980, 925–42.

To begin with, there are several points of comparison between Marx's and Weber's view of capitalism. First, Marx restricted his discussion of capitalism to Western societies, primarily England. Weber, on the other hand, compared Western capitalism with the economies of the East and drew on the economic conditions of a number of countries including Germany, Russia, China, England and France. Second, Marx viewed capitalism as a necessary stage of economic development and believed that capitalism could only be understood by looking at how the productive forces in history led to class divisions in society. Weber, however, disagreed with Marx's view that economic forces were the single most important determinant of capitalist development. Weber, by contrast, looked at capitalism as a system of social action and based his analysis on a number of interconnections he saw between capitalist development and the influences of the religious, legal, and political spheres of society. Thus, while Marx believed that the development of capitalism was inevitable, Weber thought that capitalism was the result of a number of historical accidents and that many of the influences affecting its development derived from spheres other than the economy.

Economic Background   Like Marx, Weber began by looking at economic development. Focusing on comparative histories, Weber traced the economic development of early agrarian societies by looking at Germany, Russia, China, India, England and France. After some discussion of property relations and the formation of social groups, he traced the development of land systems outlining the differences that emerged in household economies, village organization and the development of towns.[47] After looking for patterns of economic development in the West in comparison with the East, Weber then turned his attention to the conditions of feudal economies which he thought had emerged principally in the West and rested generally on two decisive characteristics. First were the political and legal powers which landholders had over the land, and second were the political and legal class prerogatives which landholders had over others.[48] Weber went on to compare the characteristics of the feudal economies of Germany, Russia, England and France with those of China and India. After comparing the main features of feudal economies in these societies, he argued that the origins of the Western manorial system could be traced to three primary sources: (i) economic utility; (ii) military and political considerations; and (iii) social distinctions supporting prerogatives of a traditional aristocracy.[49]

Weber then turned his attention to the conditions leading to the decline of feudal economies and the rise of industrial production. While his discussion of these changes largely paralleled that of Marx, Weber pointed out that the process of decline began as landlords assumed rights of ownership over peasant holdings. Like Marx, Weber

---

47 *General Economic History,* pp. 21–53.
48 General Economic History, pp. 54–71.
49 *General Economic History,* pp. 63–80.

believed that capitalist development began as soon as landholders pushed peasants off the land and began to convert their holdings into sheep pastures. However, where Marx had argued that the transition to capitalism occurred in the main as the means of production became the private property of a capitalist class, Weber thought that other changes occurring in the political and religious spheres led to the development of capitalism. For Weber, the transition to industrial capitalism took place in the main because of the breakdown in the political authority of the landlords rather than because of their monopolization of the means of production. Weber thought that this shift took place in two distinct ways. First, as feudal land was freed from the system of rights and obligations, there was a breakdown in the traditional political authority of the landholder. This hastened the decline of the majority of political restrictions on land existing since feudal times and marked the transitional stage of development from the rural economy to the economy of cities. As the dissolution of the feudal economy took place, it freed peasants from their roles as agricultural producers and detached them from the legal obligations tying them to the landlords. Second were the internal and external forces leading to change. From within the manor the class system began to deteriorate as peasants left the land, and from outside the manor the development of markets and the growth of agricultural products jeopardized the feudal economy.[50]

On this account, Weber noted that the pace of industrial change varied from society to society. In England, the pace of decline was slow because peasant holdings were appropriated by legal procedures which created a gradual handover of lands from peasants to capitalists. In France, by contrast, the revolution brought an immediate end to the feudal economy and rapid change in the availability of land. In Russia, on the other hand, feudal restrictions on peasants were so harsh that Russian economies were slow to change. The widest discrepancy in terms of the pace of economic development, however, was between England and France.

In addition to looking at the economic changes leading to the development of capitalism in different societies, Weber gave the widest latitude to the role played by the different social spheres in society and the effects these spheres had on historical change and industrial development. Of key importance was the role played by the legal and political spheres. In the first case, Weber believed that the decline of the feudal economy made way for the modern system of law which brought about the elimination of feudal ties. In the second case, Weber argued that the abolition of feudal regulations led to the development of the concept of the 'citizen' which first made its appearance in France and then in England. Weber thought that as soon as the concept of the 'citizen' became a legal and political reality, it led to the collapse of the aristocracy and an aristocratic way of life.[51]

---

50 *General Economic History,* p. 82.
51 *General Economic History,* p. 233 ff.

The Role of the Guilds in Capitalist Development Like Marx, Weber believed that the trade guilds played a central role in capitalist development. In fact, up until the latter half of the nineteenth century, the guilds exercised almost complete authority over occupations which meant that work was impossible to obtain without guild supervision. Under these circumstances, guilds had almost complete authority because they were able to preserve the livelihoods of artisans. However, as the guild system began to break down, there were signs of capitalist development in England and Germany. In England, for instance, the textile trade became the main focus of capitalist industry and development, and by the early nineteenth century woolen goods had become the central focus of production. As the demand for these goods increased and the restrictive policies of the guilds were dissolved, the organization of the factory system geared itself to mass production based on specialization and the division of labor.[52] As a result, production accelerated and markets were created in the manufacturing of 'luxury requirements' such as soap, glass, silk, sugar, pottery and chinaware. As the demand for these types of 'consumptive requirements' grew, the modern household began to establish itself and this led to specialized demand in luxury goods and ultimately to the democratization of luxury.[53]

The Non-Economic Factors in Capitalist Development One of the key attributes of Weber's theory of capitalism is the role he allots to non-economic factors in capitalist development. In this, Weber differs from Marx in several ways. Whereas Marx believed that capitalism was inevitable and could only be understood from the perspective of the underlying productive forces in history, Weber doubted this and believed that other historical influences shaped capitalist development in their own right. Weber referred to these influences as the 'non-economic factors' of capitalism, and he thought there were four influences that were central and important. These are: (i) the emergence of a system of rationality; (ii) the development of a system of law; (iii) the emergence of new forms of citizenship; and (iv) the rise of the 'gain spirit' and the system of ethics corresponding to it.

The first non-economic factor Weber looked at was the emergence of a system of rationality which first took hold in commerce and in commercial activity at the beginning of the eighteenth century.[54] According to Weber, rational commerce is a form of economic activity whose principle elements are based on the development of what he called 'quantitative reckoning' and the dominance of quantitative reasoning in economic life.[55] Weber maintained that quantitative reckoning emerged only when there was a need for 'exactness' in commercial undertakings. He pointed out that in earlier periods commerce proceeded so slowly and informally that 'exactness' in calculation was not necessary. But as soon as the exchange of goods became more common and

---

52 *General Economic History*, p. 183
53 *General Economic History*, p. 107.
54 *General Economic History*, p. 170.
55 Ibid.

the quantity of materials and goods exchanged became more substantial, 'exact computation became necessary.'[56]As competitive markets were created there was greater fluctuation in prices and, Weber reasoned, this led to the necessity of book-keeping and the need to render exact accounts of transactions and trade. Furthermore, as the use of paper money became more widespread, the need for methods of exact-ness in commercial dealings could be satisfied only by rational means. This gave rise to the commercial ledger which acted to regularize bookkeeping and provide a uni-versal set of standardized commercial techniques for rendering a balance. As a result, the technical means of controlling commerce and commercial relations become more exact, which led to the acceleration of a quantitative tendency in economic matters and in other spheres of society, including the legal and political spheres.

Weber maintained that as soon as commercial activities became dependent on 'exact reckoning', it immediately lifted the irrational limitations on trade which had existed in the economies of the middle ages. This set into motion the buying and sell-ing of both commodities and labor that we see only in fully developed capitalist economies. As far as Weber was concerned, therefore, a key condition of this devel-opment was the dependence upon 'rational accounting as the norm of all large indus-trial and commercial undertakings.' Without it, capitalism would have been impossible, since it fundamentally reduced the management of commerce to calcu-lable rules which led, in turn, to 'calculable law.'[57]

According to Weber, 'calculable law' is a second non-economic factor related to the development capitalism. For commercial enterprises to operate rationally, 'they must be able to depend on calculable adjudication and administration,' and for this to occur there must be a link between the sphere of economy and the sphere of law.[58] As soon as the economic and legal spheres began to unify, commercial activity was freed from the restraint of inherited tradition which enabled industry and production to become rational. 'Without the stimulation of law,' said Weber, 'the development of capitalism would not have been possible.'[59] In fact, it was only with the emergence of rational law that a system of ethics governing commercial exchange became pos-sible and from this arose the legal concept of the citizen. According to Weber, the concept of the citizen emerges only in the West when the system of rational law began to ensure the free pursuit of individual gain.[60] In Weber's view, the introduc-tion of legal citizenship was key to the development of capitalism because it under-lined the fact that commerce was dependent on the political and legal sphere. But in what way was this the case?

Weber thought that there were several features which were unique to the idea of the citizen as it relates to capitalist development. First, in the economic sense, the rise

---

56 Ibid.
57 *General Economic History,* p. 228
58 Ibid.
59 *General Economic History,* p. 231.
60 Ibid.

of citizenship signified a class of persons having specific social and economic interests separate from those of the state. Second, in the political sense citizenship implied membership in a state economic community, where the individual was a holder of certain political and legal rights resting on the free pursuit of private gain. Third, in the social and historical sense citizenship signified a group of persons whose standard of life, rights of property, accumulation, and professional credentials conferred social prestige and privilege.[61] Weber, therefore, believed that the combination of economic, political and legal aspects of the citizen had never appeared before and were unique to Western capitalism. While the concept may be traced to earlier societies such as the Greek city states, its political, economic and legal expression are primarily modern in origin.

Another development related to the concept of the citizen was the emergence of the modern city, with its municipal organization and its bureaucratic administration. Weber pointed out that while the city creates struggles between various factions and political office seekers, it leads to a municipal environment which gives rise to art, science, mathematics and ultimately civil life and civil society. Weber thought that the city was a rational institution whose development can be traced to the decline of magic in all spheres of social life. The stress by Weber on the role played by the decline of magic in social life is completely unique. He believed that the city is an institution which arises from the concentration of inhabitants confined to a particular geographical space formed for reasons of common defense.[62] In the early stages of the capitalist development, city life led to the organization of autonomous groups whose competence consisted in their ability to bear arms and equip themselves to defend the city. As far as Weber was concerned, the main condition leading to a rational approach to city planning was the erosion of magic in Western societies. Magic in China and India, Weber reasoned, had led to monopolies by a priestly class who controlled spiritual and commercial resources. The rise of prophecy religions, however, brought about an end to magic because it situated the miraculous outside the collective camp rather than within it. 'Prophecy,' Weber wrote, 'destroyed magic because while magical procedure remained real, it was viewed as devilish rather than divine.'[63] In this view, it was the decline of magic which led the way to a town economy and a political life stressing markets, opportunity, labor, economic objectives and bureaucracy. All of this served to elevate capitalism to an economic system formed around a rational state and rational city life.

A third non-economic influence of capitalist development is the rise of the rational state itself. Weber thought that the rational state was defined generally by a set of social institutions based in law and officialdom which emerged only in modern

---

61 *General Economic History*, p. 233 ff.
62 *General Economic History*, p. 238.
63 Ibid.

society. This was not possible in feudal economies like those of Germany and England because there the dominant classes had too much power over commercial and industrial functions. Along with blocking the development of a centralized political authority, feudalism meant that economies and markets were under the control of aristocratic classes who functioned as autonomous officials. According to Weber, therefore, a feudal society with aristocratic officials is distinct from the modern state in several respects. First, in feudal societies everything was based on beliefs about how the dominant classes 'keep things in order.'[64] This tended to mean that power between landholders and peasants was always unequal and unbalanced. In the rational state, however, political and economic organization rests on 'expert officialdom and rational law' and decisions are based not on beliefs but on formal rules and procedures.'[65] Second, in the modern state in contrast to feudal society, a 'systematic legal doctrine' begins to emerge which gives rise to rational law independent of the powers of the aristocratic classes. This leads directly to the rationalization of procedure and decision making based on independent legal rules. The development of an independent system of law put the social classes on an equal political footing and created equality by universalizing legal process. Formal law, unlike its historical antecedents, was therefore calculable and predictable. 'Capitalism,' Weber pointed out, 'could not operate on the basis of belief and so what was required was a form of law which could be counted upon like a machine from which religious and magical considerations must be excluded.'[66]

Rational Capitalism and the Growth of the 'Gain Spirit' A fourth non-economic consideration of capitalist development discussed by Weber is the relationship between the economic and religious spheres. Weber began by making a distinction between societies of the East and the West. He believed that geographical distinctions can be made between the historical conditions leading to the development of Western capitalism and the obstacles that emerged to the development of capitalism in societies of the East. To illustrate, he pointed out that Eastern societies developed forms of commerce that were different from societies in the West. In the main, Eastern economies were mostly inland and their system of trade imposed religious restriction on the profit that could be gained by merchants. In Western societies, by contrast, the conditions leading to capitalist development were more favorable, and this gave rise to more intense commercial activity based on international markets and a form of commercial development which was unprecedented historically. While the major factors leading to capitalist development in the West were rational accounting and technology and law, these alone did not account for the full development of Western capitalism. In fact, Weber maintained that an additional element must have been

---

64 *General Economic History*, pp. 250–51.
65 *General Economic History*, p. 250.
66 *General Economic History*, p. 252.

present in the West which failed to develop in the East. This element, he believed, is the 'gain spirit' which was based on a rationalization of the conduct of everyday life in general and a rationalistic economic ethic in particular.[67] By 'gain spirit,' Weber meant a system of conduct based on ethical norms which govern commercial activity and which served to bring the economic and religious spheres together.[68]

In itself, Weber reasoned, the 'gain spirit' led to a system of ethics and norms of conduct which created rational action giving rise to commercial activities. Weber's assertion concerning the relation between the religious and economic spheres pinpoints his difference from Marx on capitalist development. While, for Marx, the capitalist stage of development was inevitable because underlying economic laws were always implicit in history, Weber believed that it was not a question of the inevitability of capitalism, but rather how it was possible given the religious restrictions and forces working against it.

According to Weber, there were several steps involved in the development of a system of action related to the growth of capitalism that implicate religion and religious influences. First, was the defeat of religious traditionalism which tended to hold back the rational development of trade and commerce. This was evident in societies of the East where incentives for economic gain were not in themselves sufficient to overcome traditional obstacles to trade and commerce. Second, in order for capitalism to develop, two obstacles had to be overcome: the system of internal barriers which maintained religious beliefs restraining the pursuit of gain for its own sake, and the elimination of the fear of trade which had its roots in the idea that any radical change in the 'conduct of everyday life' was inherently evil and therefore unacceptable.[69] Third, in order for the 'individual gain spirit' to develop in economic relations religious restrictions had to be removed.[70] At one level, unrestricted gain put individuals in competition with one another, but it also acted externally on society to erode the system of ethical restrictions on trade and commerce that stemmed from religious beliefs. Weber thought that the two systems of ethics, one internal, the other external, were completely distinct and operate in different ways. The dominance of one over the other, Weber noted, involved introducing calculation into the sphere of traditional beliefs and ethical norms, which acted to displace or rationalize the old religious beliefs and ethical doctrines. As soon as this development took place, two things happened. 'Naive piety' was brought to an end, and the ability of traditional ethics to restrain economic development based on the gain spirit diminished.[71] Weber believed that it was precisely this kind of development which took place in the West but not the East.

Weber held that the historical restrictions on the 'gain spirit' could occur only in societies where religion was dominant. In India, for instance, economic restrictions

---

67 *General Economic History,* pp. 260–1.
68 The link between these two spheres is more fully explored in *The Protestant Ethic.*
69 *General Economic History,* p. 261.
70 Ibid.
71 *General Economic History,* p. 262.

applied to certain religious castes who were prohibited from practicing commercial activity. In other circumstances, restrictions were placed on classes and castes who had hereditary economic rights, and in other cases there were legal limits placed on the amount of interest levied by groups in commercial transactions. Weber believed therefore that religious obstacles acted as a barrier to the development of capitalism in China and India. For instance, in China when groups attempted to change existing roads in order to improve commerce by introducing a rational means of transportation, many feared supernatural evils and placed obstacles in the path of the rational pursuit of gain.[72] In this respect, Weber's focus on the effects of the religious sphere on capitalist development lends authority to his view that a theory of capitalism must take into account the connection between the economic and religious dimension, as well as make distinctions between the development of capitalism in the East and the West. In this view, a theory of capitalism must be historical and comparative, since capitalism did not develop in the East due to religious restrictions and obstacles placed in the path of economic progress.

Weber's Theory of Social Classes and Status Groups

Having discussed the relationship between rationalization and the development of an economic ethic, I now want to turn my attention Weber's theory of social class and the emergence of status groups in society. Historically, Weber first developed his theory of social class between 1911 and 1920 while he was writing *Economy and Society*.[73] By this time, Weber had become interested in describing what he thought were key historical changes taking place in the class system that had indicated a much broader shift in the total class structure of society than had existed in previous periods. In looking at the modern class situation, Weber's aim was to describe the historical features of the shift taking place in the overall class situation by looking at the class inequality and class conflict that had existed at the outset of the nineteenth century. As a result of this, he began to call into question some of Marx's assertions concerning the class situation of the nineteenth century, and this led him to look into the history of class conflict during the modern period. Because no complete understanding of Weber's theory of social class is possible without first looking at what Marx had to say about the problem of class antagonism and class conflict, let us look briefly at what he had to say about the class struggle at this point in time. Marx writes:

> The history of all hitherto existing society is the history of class struggle. Freeman and slave, patrician and plebeian, lord and serf, capitalist and wage laborer stood in constant opposition to one another, and carried on an uninterrupted fight that each time ended either in a revolutionary reconstitution of society or in the common ruin of the contending classes.

---

72 Ibid.
73 For Weber's discussion of social class see *Economy and Society*, pp. 926–32.

The modern society that has sprouted from the ruins of feudal society has not done away with class antagonisms. It has but established new classes, new conditions of oppression, new forms of struggle in the place of old ones. Our epoch has simplified class antagonisms: Society as a whole is more and more splitting up into two great hostile camps, into two great classes directly facing each other: Bourgeoisie and Proletariat.[74]

Taking as our starting place Marx's assertion that the class struggle is an 'uninterrupted fight' in which the 'two great classes are more and more splitting up into hostile camps,' Weber's theory of social class begins by making three significant advances beyond Marx.[75] First, Weber made his observations about the class system sixty years after Marx's central claim that the new 'class antagonisms' and new 'forms of class struggle' had 'taken the place of the old ones.' This put Weber in the position of deciding whether what Marx had said was historically true and whether it fit the class situation of the modern period. Second, while Marx had argued that the 'antagonism' of the modern period was an inevitable result of the economic structure of society and of the splitting of society into two hostile camps, Weber thought that the economic sphere itself was not the major determinant of the class structure, and this led him to reject Marx's claim that class antagonism was an immediate outcome of economic forces in history.[76] Third, while Marx had claimed that the two classes were becoming more and more 'antagonistic,' and that the 'new form of the class struggle was in place of the old one,' Weber doubted this, stating that the changes taking place in the class structure of the modern period showed that there were three central adjustments that had taken place by that time. Weber referred to these adjustments as the shift taking place in 'class, status and party.'

Weber's Theory of Social Class: Class and the Market Situation   Weber began by looking at three distinct characteristics of social classes and class formations. First he looked at the formation of social classes in the context of what he called the modern market situation as opposed to the class situation of the early industrial period. Second he looked at the formation of the class structure in relation to different types of social action which he assumed flowed from class interests. Then third, he looked at the formation of the modern class system in relation to what he called the different historical types of class antagonism and class struggle, which he compared with previous class struggles of earlier periods. To begin, let us look first at Weber's definition of the concept of class. He wrote:

We may speak of a class when (1) a number of people have in common a specific causal component of their life chances insofar as (2) this component is represented exclusively by

---

74 Marx, *The Communist Manifesto,* F. L. Bender (ed.), New York: Norton, 1988, p. 55.

75 Ibid.

76 Weber refers directly to Marx's theory of class when he says that the link between class and class interests 'has been found in its most classic expression in the statement of a talented author.' See *Economy and Society*, p. 930.

economic interests in the possession of goods and opportunities for income and (3) is represented under the conditions of the commodity and labor markets. This is the class situation.[77]

In this context, two things stand out about Weber's definition of social class that contrasts with previous definitions. First is the idea that, for Weber, a class is to be defined as a group having the same 'causal component of life chances.' In this case, Weber uses the term 'life chances' to define the 'opportunities created when individuals sell their skills and their abilities on the market in exchange for incomes,' and the possibilities these incomes create for the pursuit of goods and services in the market. If we follow Weber on this point, class situation is determined by the life chances that a class has when individuals sell their skills and abilities on the market in exchange for salaries and incomes with which they obtain goods and services. In this case, what is decisive about Weber's definition of class is the stress on the 'life chances' individuals have in the market when they sell their skills, as opposed to the class positions they have as a direct result of their property ownership over the means of production.

A second thing that stands out about Weber's definition of class is the emphasis he placed on class situation and the market. Essentially, the term 'market' was used by Weber to refer to the sphere in society in which skills and services are produced and exchanged, and in these terms the market constitutes the field of exchange in society. The market, in this sense, is distinctly separate from the political and legal spheres of society to the extent that it imposes conditions on the realization of life chances and economic interests and incomes. In thus taking the step of restricting the class situation to the market situation, Weber changed the way the concept of class had been used historically. That is, whereas Marx had thought that the outright 'ownership of the means of production' was the sole determinant of the class situation, Weber challenged this view by claiming that as far as the modern class situation was concerned, life chances for income and wages can exist independently of the private ownership of the means of production.

Weber's theory of the modern class situation therefore differs from Marx's conception of class to the extent that it outlines the existence of two categories of the class situation. In the first category is the class situation determined by the outright ownership of property which creates returns on investments and incomes in the form of rents.[78] In this class situation, the ownership of property leads to the monopolization of the means of production by one group, and ultimately determines the class situation by creating economic monopolies over the means of production that favor one class. This, Weber believed, was largely the class situation of the industrial period where propertied classes confronted each other within the economic conditions of existence where life chances existed only for the propertied classes. A second class situation that arose in the modern period, according to Weber, is the category of class

---

77 Weber, *Economy and Society,* p. 927.
78 Ibid., p. 928.

that is determined by the kinds of skills and abilities obtained by education credentials that create life chances when sold in the market. These credentials, diplomas and certificates, Weber reasoned, are not only sold on the market in exchange for incomes and livelihoods, but they also have the distinct quality of creating life chances outside of the life chances of direct property ownership.

This category of class situation, according to Weber, is determined by the state of the market and its overall need for educated and trained personnel that would include 'technicians, civil servants, teachers and other white-collar workers.'[79] While these groups may lack the specific life chances of property, said Weber, what is new about this class situation is that they are able to obtain life chances in the form of incomes, salaries and wages that are the direct result of their education credentials which they sell in exchange for incomes.[80] Weber believed that the class situation of individuals who have life chances without directly owning property was a development of the modern class situation that did not exist when Marx was defining the concept of class in relation to property.

The two class situations described by Weber, the one determined by the life chances of property ownership, the other by the life chances created by education credentials, formally define the class situation of modern society. In the first instance, class situation is dependent on the outright ownership of usable property that includes 'dwellings, workshops, and agricultural lands' from which income in the form of rents is derived.[81] In this class situation, life chances exist in the form of holdings in capitalist ventures which put individuals into class positions for monopolizing opportunities that tend to increase their overall wealth and power in the market.[82] While this defines the class situation of the propertied, there is the class situation defined by those groups whose life chances are determined by opportunities created by skills and services derived from education credentials, while owning no property for themselves.

As far as Weber was concerned, this corresponds to the class situation of the modern period in that life chances exist by virtue of education credentials and opportunities in the market rather than by the outright ownership of property. While in such circumstances life chances are ultimately determined by whether or not the skills and services they have to offer may be sold under given market conditions, their life chances exist in relation to the kinds of services which they can offer independent of whether or not they own property. In so far as the second category of class defines the class situation of the non-propertied, Weber went on the argue that the emergence of the second category of class constitutes a major adjustment in the class situation of the industrial period, since life chances were restricted to the labor of fixed wages, over and against the life chances of the 'market situation' for trained workers.

Weber believed that the shift to a class situation where life chances exist independently of property ownership radically altered 'the effects of the naked possession'

---

79 *Economy and Society,* p. 305.
80 Ibid.
81 Ibid.
82 Ibid., p. 928.

of the means of production on the non-propertied classes. He argued that while the 'naked possession' of property must have been 'a fore-runner of class formation' of earlier periods when life chances were restricted only to those who owned property, the opportunity for life chances among the non-propertied classes did not exist in earlier periods.[83] In previous societies where this was the case, the class situation for the owners of property would have emerged as decisive over the life chances of the non-propertied, whereas in the modern class situation, the possession of property is no longer the sole determinant of life chances for the non-propertied.[84] The life chances created by education credentials in the modern class situation thus placed the outright 'naked' ownership of property and class privilege arising from it into the background.

Action Flowing from Class Interests

After discussing the changes taking place in the modern class situation, Weber turned his attention to issues of social class related to what he referred to as the different types of class conflict that emerge when 'economic interests' were expressed by classes who act on their interests at different stages of historical development. For instance, the dominant classes of antiquity and the middle ages acted on their 'naked class interests' to protect their monopolies over property. Similarly, capitalists acted on their interests in order to protect their property and their right to dispose of the means of production during the transition to industrial society. Then, too, workers acted on their interests during the industrial stage of development in order to protect the price paid to labor and to increase their wages.[85] In each of these separate instances, there are different types of social action flowing from different types of class interests. On this basis, Weber believed that Marx was in error when he assumed that a definite link existed between the concept of 'class' on the one hand, and the intensity of the 'class interest' that is being acted on, on the other.

Because Marx thought that class interests were economically determined by the division of society into unequal classes, he took the view that classes were 'carriers' of interests which were assigned to them historically, and that as such the classes acted on the basis of these interests all the time. As far as Marx was concerned, therefore, individuals were carriers of class interests because they always occupy class positions which are assigned to them by the class divisions in society. It was therefore Marx's view that class interests were assigned by structural determinants in society, and that interests were derived from the social relations of production rather than from individual motives. He went on to say that, at a certain stage of historical development, class interests would inevitably 'come into conflict with the existing class relations' and that eventually a period of 'social revolution' would ensue.[86]

---

83 *Economy and Society*, p. 928.

84 While Marx had defined a social class by denoting its property relation to the means of production, Weber's aim was to modify the definition of class by placing the emphasis on life chances over property relations.

85 Ibid., pp. 930–1.

86 See Marx, *A Contribution to the critique of Political Economy*, p. 21.

Weber disagreed with this view and criticized Marx's claim that class 'interests' were historically determined. He argued that the concept of class interest as proposed by Marx became 'ambiguous' as soon as one attempts to look beyond the simple 'factual direction of interests' emerging from the average class situation.[87] Weber thought that the actual direction of class interests could not be determined with any clarity, since the direction people are likely to pursue in their actions may vary according to their occupation and the size of the group affected by the class situation.[88] In this respect, the possibility of a mass social uprising where workers confront the propertied classes is, in Weber's view, impossible. The fact that a working class revolution never occurred confirmed for Weber that the adjustment in the modern class situation had taken effect because, in many instances, class interests were played out in the sphere of law by the end of the nineteenth century as opposed to the direct confrontations between classes with different economic interests at an earlier time.

In addition to this, Weber doubted that classes were equivalent to groups and thought that to conceive of them as if they were groups led to a distortion.[89] He thought that while it is possible that many people in the same class situation regularly act on their interest and engage in mass actions, classes as a whole do not act as groups. Instead, he believed that 'class situations emerge only on the basis of direct social action,' and that 'social action that brings forth the class situation' is usually 'an action among members of different classes.'[90] In this sense, there are different kinds of class actions. For instance, there were the actions of the classes of antiquity and the middle ages who sought to protect their monopolies over property; there are the actions of capitalists who mobilize to protect their right to the disposition over the means of employment; and there were the actions of workers who organize to increase wages and the price paid to labor.

As far as Weber was concerned, the action by a class against the class structure can occur in only one of two ways: either by 'irrational protest' and mass uprisings; or by 'rational associations' leading to the formation of trade unions. Class situations of the first type, said Weber, occur usually at an earlier period where differences in life chances were 'transparent' during times when power and wealth were the obvious monopoly of one class who owned the means of production.[91] In this category, Weber argued, class antagonism and class conflict were the direct outcome of mass action by a subordinate class against a propertied class which wanted to protect their monopoly over property. He went on to say that while this type of situation applied to the classes of antiquity, it did not apply to the class situation of modern times. In the modern class situation, mass action against a propertied class takes the form of rational associations that form as a result of trade unions where conflict over wage

---

87 *Economy and Society,* p. 929.
88 Ibid.
89 Ibid., p. 930.
90 Ibid.
91 Ibid.

disputes shifts to the level of law. Weber thus disagreed with Marx's assertion that class interests are assigned to individuals by their structural location in the economy since, in his view, life chances are no longer distributed only to those who own property or to those who have outright ownership over the means of production. He pointed out that in the modern class situation, interests vary among individuals who have different motives and inclinations in which the 'average class interests' cannot be determined. Hence, for Weber, there are no class interests *per se,* only 'average interests' of individuals in similar economic class situations.[92]

Under these circumstances, Weber saw class interests as the 'average interests' of different individuals sharing similar market situations and life chances, in contrast to Marx, who thought that individual class interests were determined only by an individual's relation to the means of production. In so far as this confers different motives to individuals which vary according to class situation, it differs explicitly from Marx. Whereas for Marx, class relationships were explained by reference to the concept of class location within the economy, Weber saw social action in terms of individual motives which arise from a class situation over which individuals have control in the choices they make about how to act. In light of this, the potential for the mass behavior of a class due to common conditions of subordination and inequality is diminished to the extent that grievances by individual workers are less likely to lead to mass action if their wage disputes are settled in the sphere of law. Weber reasoned that social action, in contrast to mass behavior, is more likely in the modern class situation since the class situation to which workers are linked does not place them in direct opposition to the 'naked' class interests which existed in the class situation of antiquity and the middle ages.

Whereas in previous periods, landless peasants were unable to defend themselves against landlords who owned the means of production, the class situation of modern times provides opportunities for individuals to react against a given class by acts of intermittent legal and political protest which lead to 'rational associations' and rational outcomes based on recourse to the sphere of law and legal judgment.[93] Class situations of the first type occur during the period of 'naked' ownership of property in which landlords monopolized products, industry, the means of production, trading and food stuffs. Class situations of the second type, however, occur only during the modern period where the class situation was altered by legal, political and social enfranchisement and the acquisition of political and legal rights.

Class Antagonism and Historical Types of Class Struggle

A third characteristic of Weber's treatment of the class situation of the modern period, was his discussion of class antagonism and the different types of class struggle. The

---

92 Ibid., p. 929.
93 Ibid.

context for Weber's discussion of the history of the class struggle derives directly from Marx's assertion that 'the history of all existing societies is the history of class struggle.' But beyond stating this, Marx asserted that the class struggle between 'freeman and slave, lord and serf, capitalist and wage laborer stood in constant opposition to one another, and carried on an uninterrupted fight that each time ended in a revolutionary reconstitution of society or in the common ruin of the contending classes.'[94] In addition to this, he went on to say that modern society had 'done nothing to do away with class antagonisms, and that it had established new classes, new conditions of oppression, and new forms of struggle in the place of old ones.' 'The modern period,' he went on, has done nothing but 'simplify class antagonisms and that society as a whole is more and more splitting up into two great hostile camps, into two great classes directly facing each other: workers and owners of the means of production.'[95]

While Weber largely agreed with Marx's view that the class struggles of antiquity and the middle ages were 'carried on as an uninterrupted fight' that often ended in revolution or in the 'ruins of the contending classes,' he believed that class antagonism existed because of the power of property ownership, and was carried on in a direct confrontation with the 'propertyless who acted against the monopolies of a propertied class.' These fights, Weber argued, took place on the economic front and were based on direct antagonisms that had to do with the outright control over the means of production by a dominant property owning class.[96] While these 'antagonisms' were acted out as direct confrontations between classes, Weber believed that the great shift that had taken place from the past up to the present time was the overall change that occurred in how these struggles were acted out. First, said Weber, were the open class struggles of antiquity and the feudal period where there were direct confrontations between landholders and serfs. Second, were the 'competitive struggles' over wages that existed between workers and owners of the means of production.[97] Third, were the struggles involving contested wage disputes at the level of the legal order which transferred the struggle from the direct confrontations between classes on the economic front to the reconciliation of wage disputes on the legal front. The great shift that takes place, according to Weber, is from the open class struggles between antagonistic groups to the progressive use of the legal order to resolve wages disputes between classes in the labor market that involves an overall decrease in the intensity of antagonism between classes.

On another front, Marx had argued that modern society 'had not done away with class antagonism,' and that it had 'established new classes and new forms of struggle that simplified class antagonisms.' He thought that modern society had therefore intensified the class struggle to the point where workers became a homogeneous

94 Marx, *The Communist Manifesto*, p. 55.
95 Ibid.
96 Ibid., p. 931.
97 *Economy and Society*, p. 930.

group whose class interests and cohesion were made more intense by the new conditions of oppression and poverty created by low wages and poor working conditions. This, according to Marx, transformed the class struggle to the point of conflict where the classes were directly facing each other. Weber, however, thought that 'to treat classes as conceptually equivalent to groups' who engage in class struggle by direct confrontation was a historical 'distortion' on Marx's part.[98] He reasoned that classes only form into homogeneous groups when the interests of workers were defined by a distinct economic opponent, a condition which would have existed between the classes of antiquity and between workers and capitalists during the early period of industrial transition.[99] For classes to be groups with common interests, according to Weber, there has to be an 'immediate economic opponent,' and this situation no longer exists or holds true in the class situation of the modern period.[100]

While Marx had argued that in modern society class antagonism would become more pronounced as differences in wealth, power and property ownership increased, he thought this would lead to further conflict, class struggle, and eventually social change and revolution. Weber, however, doubted this and disputed Marx's claim on several fronts. First, he argued that the working classes were not groups having common interests that made them act as a unified class against a dominant class. Rather, Weber believed that during the modern period classes were differentiated into individuals who acted on separate motives that made them autonomous from their class situations. He argued that when individuals compete alone in the market, they share only what he called 'a contemporaneous remnant' of their former class position, and as such they are unable to act as a class with unified interests which they mobilize against a dominant class.[101] Second, Weber believed that the earlier forms of class antagonism leading to historical class struggles only arose when the 'naked' ownership of property existed, as in the classes of antiquity and the middle ages. This, however, is no longer the case because 'the great change that has been going on continuously up to our time' shows that class antagonism has 'progressively shifted' from the direct confrontations of the classes of antiquity to the use of the legal order in the class situation of modern times.[102] Third, Weber thought that the class struggle of workers had progressed historically from the early conflicts and direct confrontations first defined by the 'labor bondage of the serf' to the later struggles over wages between bosses and workers, and then to the wage settlements of the current class situation where disputes over wages were mediated by trade unions on the labor market and by recourse to the conciliation of the legal order.[103]

---

98 Ibid. In this context, Weber calls Marx's historical precision into question.
99 *Economy and Society*, p. 931.
100 Ibid, p. 305
101 Ibid., pp. 929–30.
102 Ibid.
103 *Economy and Society*, pp. 930–31

While the class struggles of antiquity discussed by Marx were carried on by peasants directly against a land owning aristocracy and involved a fight over the means of production and the 'sovereign power of property,' Weber thought that competitive struggles of this type had their origins in property differences which lasted through antiquity and the middle ages, but eventually dissipated by the modern period. The disputes over property, he argued, were directly over the means of survival and were struggles of the propertyless against the propertied. The basis of this antagonism, according to Weber, had progressively weakened in modern societies not only because the direct confrontation between classes had shifted to the legal order, but because elements of the earlier class antagonism were absorbed within the political sphere, thus displacing the class struggle from the economic realm into the political realm.[104] Weber believed that the shift to the modern class situation had therefore changed the basic form of the class struggle in two fundamental ways. First, it altered the direct confrontation of the old class struggle that had taken place between property owners and workers by transferring the fight over wages to the legal sphere and to mediated wage disputes on the market.[105] Second, it altered the antagonism of the old class struggle by shifting the direct conflict between the classes to the legal rights of workers to form associations which acted on their interests by forming contacts settling wage disputes by legal means. Under these circumstances, the model of the class struggles of antiquity carried on by oppressed peasants who are rendered impoverished by a wealthy landholding class, no longer applied.

Weber's Concept of the Status Group: The Separation of Status from Class

The second form of adjustment in modern society, according to Weber, is the development of the 'status group.' Weber's reasoning here is twofold. First, he pointed out that as the direct confrontation between the class struggles of antiquity died down, new class struggles initiated the formation of new groups. Second, Weber thought that the formation of these groups took the form of 'status order' in which the old class struggles based on power and wealth shifted to a struggle between groups competing for prestige and social standing. While Weber's discussion of the status group tends to be obscure, it is possible to outline several themes that are relevant to the role of the status group in his theory of class and class stratification. To begin with, it is important to remember that Weber saw society in terms of various social spheres which he thought functioned autonomously and which led to different institutional orders of life activity and to different departments of life. In this view, family life, political life and economic life developed different dimensions of social action, different orientations to reality and were thus distinct in terms of their separate functions and their separate forms of social action. Weber thought that it was important to demonstrate

---

104 At this point, different 'class interests' were represented by different political parties.
105 Ibid.

how the different orders of life activity acted to form boundaries around distinct spheres of activity, and to exclude other realms of activity, and he thought that it would be relevant to outline types of social activities that were distinct from the class situation as determined by the market. The status group, according to Weber, constituted just such a sphere of activity.

To begin with, Weber defined a status situation in contrast to a class situation as 'every component of life fate that is determined by a specific positive or negative social estimation of honour.'[106] In order to completely understand Weber's meaning, it is important that we look at the distinction he makes between class and status. Earlier we saw that Weber defined a class situation as determined by opportunities for life chances in the market. In contrast to the class situation, however, the status situation is to be defined by its 'strict separation' from the economic order and the sphere of the market and, in this sense, it is functionally separate from class and the class situation.[107] Where class was restricted to the sphere of the market and characterized by life chances and by patterns of acquisition and income, status groups can be defined simply as a social grouping that forms outside the market and is characterized by patterns of consumption and the pursuit of specific life styles and the habits of taste that qualify members of a group for distinctions based on their standing or status.

While it may be difficult to separate class from status in conventional terms, Weber insisted on the distinction and believed that it is key to understanding the role played by the status groups as distinct from social classes. In direct contrast to the class situation, the status situation has to do with the specific choices and life style selections which individuals and groups make in 'surrounding themselves with furniture, cars, books, electronics, art, perfume, clothes and houses, as well as the status qualifications that are made in selecting types of entertainment,' sports equipment and leisure activities which they may become involved in.[108] Perhaps the best way to understand the distinction Weber makes between class and status is to view class and status simply as separate dimensions of the stratification system. Thus, whereas class is defined by the market situation and characterized by economic behavior related to the acquisition of incomes and opportunities, status operates outside the market order and is defined by the selections and choices individuals and groups make about the goods they consume and the activities and styles of life which organized their choices.[109] For example, Weber pointed out that, in the nineteenth century, Prussian army officers cultivated 'dueling qualifications' by obtaining facial scars for purposes of making claims to life styles that denoted status in terms of social honor and military rank.[110] Class and status

---

106 *Economy and Society*, p. 932.

107 Ibid, p. 937.

108 Pierre Bourdieu, *Distinctions: A Social Critique of the Judgment*, p. 173.

109 Ibid.

110 On the life stylizations of Prussian army officers, see Weber's 'National Character and the Junkers,' in H.H. Gerth and C.Wright Mills, *From Max Weber*, p. 392.

thus occupy different social spheres and different levels of activity and engage different segments of the stratification order. While social class, according to Weber, is thus stratified in relation to the pursuit of opportunities and incomes and the life chances of 'acquisition,' status activity is restricted to the selections and choices related to organizing life styles and putting forward a claim to social honor.[111]

The status situation, according to Weber, thus refers to activities involving individuals acting as members of groups who share life styles, habits of taste and the pursuit of social esteem which Weber referred to as 'social honor.' This restricts status groups to activities related to patterns of 'consumption' and to the status honor that flows to those who pursue specific life styles in order to be members of specific status groups.[112] Status distinctions are thus organized and expressed by the choices individuals make about how to decorate their homes, what 'vintage wine or cheese to select,' or the type of clothing they may choose to wear.[113] Thus in some communities, for instance, status distinctions may be reserved only for those having certain educational qualifications over those whose class distinction is based on wealth. Other communities may dictate that only those with similar occupations belong to society and see one another socially. Thus, while classes involve themselves in economic behavior related to income and accumulation in the market, status groups claim to distribute social honor by pursuing patterns of consumption and life style that bring them honorific rewards.[114]

The submission to the pursuit of certain patterns of consumption and taste qualifies an individual to be treated as a member of a status group and puts forward a claim to status honor. For example, opera goers constitute a status group whose cultivation and consumption of opera is realized through the status distinctions that are conferred upon them by others in the group who pursue specialized forms of musical experience. Similarly, those who own a piano put themselves forward to qualify for status distinctions and life stylizations associated with the pursuit of higher forms of musical taste over those who own accordions and whose claim to musical taste may be associated with ethnic dance.[115] In contrast to this are the status groups who expresses their preferences for golf and sailing, over status groups that express a preference for football or fishing. In addition to this, status groups in French society may exclusively associate themselves with groups who cultivate tastes for horse back riding and fencing, while those in the lower ranks may cultivate tastes associated with boxing and wrestling.[116]

Above all, the status order is expressed by the pursuit of specific styles of life for those who wish to be members of specific status groups, and by the choices and

---

111 Ibid.

112 Ibid.

113 Bourdieu, *Distinctions*, p. 56.

114 *Economy and Society*, p. 933.

115 The piano and accordion distinction is drawn from Pierre Bourdieu, *Practical Reason: On the Theory of Action*, Cambridge: Polity, pp. 1–13.

116 Pierre Bourdieu, *Distinctions*, p. 21; and *Practical Reason: On the Theory of Actions*, London: Polity, pp. 1–13.

selections that are made in reference to displays of luxury and habits of taste. Linked to these expectations are restrictions on social interaction which may arise for those who do not pursue the specific styles of life appropriate to the group. Golfers who purchase only badge name equipment of the very best quality place restrictions on those who have less than the best equipment and wish to gain admission to the group. These restrictions may confine outsiders from acquiring the necessary qualifications to be a member of the group simply because the qualifications necessary to enter the group cannot be met by outsiders.

The stratification of the status order is thus based on styles of life that evolve in a given community over long periods of time. For instance, in some communities only those who live on certain streets are considered to qualify for status considerations by virtue of the houses they own. Membership in these groups may require strict submission to the habits of taste that are dominant at the time, and the submission to these choices often decides the life fate of those who wish to be considered members of the group and the degree of status honor that is bestowed on their choices.[117] Examples of this are the submission to fashion that is reflected by the selection of distressed clothing among followers of the 'grunge' movement, and by the selection of the color black that constitutes status qualifications in styles of taste and fashion dictated by the 'Goth' movement. The submission to stylized choices and selections, said Weber, decides the life fate of those who wish to be insiders and the degree of status honor assigned to their choices. He went on to say that, whereas class differences are expressed in the form of different patterns of accumulation and acquisition, status differences are expressed by the boundaries and restrictions drawn to make separations between one group located at higher levels of the status order in relation to groups at lower levels of the status order. These boundaries and lines of demarcation are sometimes expressed by restrictions drawn around refinements and distinctions that exist for the consumption of luxury goods, such as certain vintages of wine or the selection of saké over beer. In the eighteenth century, for instance, sumptuary ordinances in England and France restricted groups outside a certain status order from consuming luxury goods such as caviar and foie gras used by groups higher in the status order for purposes of making status distinctions.[118]

The submission to fashion and forms of dress appropriate to the status requirements identifies a pattern by which certain groups form on the basis of the claim they put forward to qualify for social standing among 'esteemed families,' or for the status honor

---

117 *Economy and Society*, p. 933.

118 In the eighteenth century, sumptuary laws restricted the purchase of luxury commodities bearing status distinctions of groups high in the status order and prohibited the consumption of these commodities by groups occupying the bottom positions in the status order. In effect, the sumptuary restrictions on food and dress protected status groups high in the status order by restricting the status elevation of lower groups. At the same time it offered a regulatory mechanism protecting the class practices of the privileged strata in society. This is perhaps the most extreme expression of social regulation of one group by another because it restricts the sensations of 'joy' and 'elevation' that can be derived from the consumption of luxury goods.

that is usurped by those families who qualify as the 'first families' of a community.[119] It is Weber's argument that these groups set themselves apart by means of characteristic badges or objects of distinction and life stylization that qualify them for the claim of status honor. In some societies, status distinctions are protected by laws or by religious sanctions, rather than being left to mere convention. For example, the papal ring that is destroyed after the death of a pope signifies that there can only be one member of this status group. In some societies, status distinctions that identify members of status groups are protected by laws and sumptuary ordinances, while in others, such as India, laws banning the use of material commodities from religious castes considered to be below higher castes are strictly enforced. In some cases, religious marks signifying purity by those of a higher caste are restricted to those of a lower caste.

As far as Weber was concerned, this shows to what extent the status order was prepared to go to exclude whole communities or to assign marks of status distinction to outsiders which segregate them from all personal contact except that which is unavoidable. The untouchable caste in India exemplify a status group of this type. Under these circumstances, each community in the status order puts forward a claim to be regarded as the highest and most honorable. Some status groups on the other hand, produce extreme forms of status honor employing the highest forms of status elevation. Knights selected in previous societies because of their physical bravery and honor, and members of religious groups whose sacrifice and selflessness qualify them for status elevation to sainthood are exemplifications of this. In still other cases, honorific preferences and status honor may rest on preferences which consist of wearing special costumes, or eating special foods or carrying arms. Under these circumstances, certain goods may become objects of monopolization by status groups, such as the gold ring on the index finger of cardinals in the Catholic church or the fire arms displayed by law enforcement officers whose status qualifications exist in being licensed to possess and use such objects.

Whereas the market bears the stamp of the class situation and the 'naked power of property and wealth,' patterns of consumption and stylizations of life bear the stamp of the status order. To the extent that status is separable from class, status 'abhors' the market and the pretension of wealth which bear the stamp of acquisition over status accumulation. For instance, in some communities honorific reward may be given to those having certain educational titles that qualify them for status distinction beyond those whose titles of nobility qualify them for the class standing related to wealth or money. In circumstances such as these status can exist independently of wealth. In this sense, the status order is the reverse of the kinds of distinctions conferred by the market which may assign only wealth or class standing. Weber went on to say that the 'status order would be threatened to its roots if mere economic acquisition could bestow the same honor' as the status group claims for itself.[120] In this respect, the

---

119 Ibid.
120 *Economy and Society*, p. 936.

status order imposes restrictions against the pretensions of sheer economic acquisition determined by wealth, and in this sense the development of status over the pretensions of wealth constitutes the second form of adjustment in society, as far as Weber is concerned.

Characteristics of Status Groups

After the discussion of the status group, Weber turned his attention to outlining four distinct practices which status groups employ to mark themselves off from other groups. First, he pointed out that status groups employ certain criteria to evaluate their social worth and bestow honor based on the selections and choices individuals make in their life styles and habits of taste. Second, they segregate themselves from other status groups by placing boundaries around themselves that restrict access except to those who possess the necessary status qualifications that earn the esteem of the group. Third, they uphold patterns of consumption and stylizations of taste by promoting honorific distinctions for those who acquire certain badges and commodities to which honorific distinctions are assigned. Fourth, they tend to monopolize status privileges by prohibiting others from consuming and possessing commodities which confer status honor. Let us look more closely at some of these activities.

One of the central characteristics of status groups, according to Weber, is their capacity to bestow social honor and make judgments about what constitutes status distinctions. In contrast to social classes and the class situation, Weber believed that a status situation is determined by 'a positive or negative evaluation of honor.'[121] Status honor is thus typically expressed in the specific styles of life and patterns of taste which may act as an imposition on others who seek to enter the circle defined by the group. For example, in North America, status honor is bestowed on golfers who adhere to the standards of fashion and taste that are dominant within a given status group at a certain time. Within the status order defined by the game of golf, certain modes of dress may be designated by badge names such as 'Polo' or 'Lacoste' whose standards of submission may be strictly observed, as are the status considerations assigned to the 'correct' choices related to the best golf equipment.[122] Weber pointed out that an individual who puts forward a claim to qualify for status honor in a status group does so on the basis of their adoption of specific styles of dress and the strict submission to specific canons of taste that are assigned to their choices. In such circumstances, said Weber, they may be considered to belong only on the basis of a positive evaluation of a person's social worth by those in a position to confer status honor. Under these circumstances, where there is a positive evaluation of a person's social worth and conformity to the status considerations of the group, persons are

---

121 Ibid.

122 In this case, a distinction exists between the way the object 'serves' within the social logic of a 'fetish' in the economic universe, over and against the social logic of 'life styles' in the universe of status. For this see Pierre Bourdieu, *Distinctions: A Social Critique of the Judgment of Taste*, pp. xi–xii.

obligated to uphold the given styles and habits of taste which are deemed appropriate by the group; otherwise, they risk negative evaluation. For example, within the status order of those who wish to attain body fitness, slim bodies are assigned status honor, while persons with stout bodies are likely to be ranked lower than persons with appropriate status qualifications.

In connection with the kinds of expectations related to membership in a status group are the many 'restrictions' on social interaction that may accompany members of the group. This may include restrictions related not only to entry into the group, but also to 'marriage with those within the status circle,' creating what Weber calls 'complete endogamous closure' within the group itself. Weber stated that once these restrictions are laid out and satisfied by those who seek to gain admission to the group, it is obvious to everyone that status development in a particular life style is underway.'[123]

Because Weber believed that status groups share the same component of 'life fate,' two kinds of distinctions are central in understanding the logic of evaluation that takes place within the status order. First is the criteria applied to those inside the group; and second are the criteria applied to those situated outside the status group. In the first case, the criteria applied to those inside the group may include a system of evaluation employed by members to positively or negatively rank the activities and selections of others in regard to their social worth and status honor. These evaluations may depend on how well or how poorly insiders pursue the habits of taste and stylized choices considered appropriate by the status group. For example, those who pursue habits of taste consistent with grunge music may be compelled to pursue honorific qualifications relevant to choices of fashion that are dictated by the style of dress cultivated by Kurt Cobain. Similarly, within the status order defined by the Goth movement, the styles of life and habits of taste dictate that status qualifications are assigned to choices that cultivate multiple body piercings or strategically situated body tattoos. In the second case of status distinction referred to by Weber, there is a set of different criteria applied to those outside the group since when these criteria are applied they perform the function of maintaining closed boundaries to those whose qualifications do not meet the evaluative criteria of the group.

Weber went on to say that there are three criteria related to the evaluative activity of status groups. First are the criteria of status groups related to evaluations made on the basis of shared styles of taste and patterns of consumption which are held in common and used as criteria for evaluating others. Second are those evaluations related to how status honor obligates individuals to uphold specific life styles held in high esteem, and to be cognizant of the criteria according to which this esteem is awarded. Third are honorific preferences which would normally be opposed to pretensions of sheer property or wealth and the considerations by which these are ranked over status

---

123 Ibid.

qualifications.[124] In this case, because Weber believed that the pretensions of property are irrelevant to the status order, he separated prestige from wealth and, by implication, wealth from status honor.[125]

An additional characteristic of the status group, according to Weber, are the practices it employs to set itself apart from other groups, a practice he refers to as the logic of social segregation. He thought that the status group sets itself apart from other groups mainly by its life style choices and submission to fashion, and secondly by its social badges which act as status qualifications. He pointed out that where status groups have evolved practices of closing ranks to the fullest, they become closed castes from which there is no exit or entry.[126] In this sense, a caste may be defined as a status group whose boundaries have become rigid and backed up by legal or religious sanctions. Where this has taken place, status distinctions and considerations are supported by conventions of life style and habits of taste which have their foundation in a system of law or sumptuary restrictions that dictate what cannot be worn or eaten.

When this occurs, status distinctions which previously existed by convention find themselves being supported by law and religious sanctions. Under these circumstances, all social interactions between members of different groups or castes are regulated by rules which may carry some form of social stigma as a means of detecting ritualistic impurities in persons outside the group. The untouchable caste in India is a group in which ritual impurities are thought to exist. In this case, the status order concerns itself with regulatory constraints which control contact between different status groups. When impurities are obtained by unregulated contact, they must be religiously expiated.[127] The dominance of status considerations in caste communities often leads to legal and religiously entitled segregation.

As soon as status communities have been organized into separate status groups, their segregation may be driven by habits of taste, customary differences or even by mutual repulsion. This allows each group to see itself in relation to the others as more worthy of honor and social esteem. After some time, these hierarchies may become 'functional' in relation to the organization of society as a whole, since they are seen by others to be qualified to perform specialized functions and, by virtue of this, may be recruited to provide trained warriors, priests, artisans or leaders.[128] In this sense, the modern military functions as a status group from which certain kinds of specialists would be employed and recruited, and along these lines Weber went on to make two broad distinctions concerning the segregation of the status group. First is between 'positively' valued status groups, and second is between status groups which are 'negatively' valued. In the first case, status groups are positively valued when it

---

124 For this discussion see *Economy and Society,* p. 932.
125 *Economy and Society,* pp. 305–6.
126 *Economy and Society,* pp. 933–4.
127 Ibid.
128 Ibid.

is thought that traits of 'beauty or excellence' are in fact inherent to their social being, as in the Hollywood star system in the United States.[129] In the second case, a status group is negatively valued when they see their value as lying beyond this world. In the later case, religious beliefs in regard to claims of explicit difference from others are based on 'providential' ideas regarding the destiny of a pariah people.[130]

A third characteristic of the status group is the privileges associated with them. Weber asserted that status groups tend to create 'monopolization of material and ideal goods' for purposes of closing their ranks and setting up restrictions on outsiders.[131] The use of material and ideal monopolies on certain kinds of commodities refers to restrictions placed on special items of dress, certain social rituals and the possession of insignia or preferential titles that are restricted to one status group.[132] Material monopolies such as these provide the most explicit claims to social separateness and exclusivity. For example, the ring given to cardinals by the Catholic church designates the wearer's social separateness as a member of an elevated status order. In some cases, these status considerations and privileges become protected by laws or special offices and titles. Certain entitlements as well may become objects of monopolization: aristocratic titles, authoritative rights and in some cases even certain trades that have been classified as equivalent to extraordinary artistic merit. When this monopolization is positively expressed the status group may be empowered to manage scarce goods or titles. However, when it is negatively expressed the status group may be prohibited from owning or managing such socially coveted resources. In some cases, positively valued status groups become the sole purveyors of social conventions and traditions, as in the case of the British Royal family or the 'best and the brightest' during the Kennedy years. Other conventions which may operate to signify the separateness of status groups are the exemption from the performance of physical labor and the status honor that goes with it. In certain families this disqualification may become part of their accumulated status honor.

Political Parties

The development of political parties is the third dimension of social adjustment that takes place in conjunction with class and status. To this point, Weber has stated that social class was restricted to the sphere of the market, and that status groups were confined to the sphere of the status order. Political parties, according to Weber, are restricted to the realm of power and the political order. In contrast to the class and status situation which operate in the sphere of the market and status order respectively,

---

129 Ibid.

130 Ibid.

131 *Economy and Society,* p. 935.

132 The question of how a status group separates itself from the lower strata of society and protects its own social rank from encroachment by groups having a lower status by assigning official titles (lord and lady in England, chevalier in France) ensures that people of reputation are persons who by some legal rule are set above others by virtue of their official titles. On this see P. Bourdieu, *Distinctions*, p. 291.

the action of parties is oriented toward two kinds of activities. First is the acquisition of power, and second is influencing the action of others for political purposes.[133] In Weber's view, the primary purpose of political parties is to secure power and maintain separation from the economic and status spheres. Weber thought that the most important criterion of the 'party' is its voluntary solicitation and adherence to the rules of the group within the party itself. All association by persons of the party must be carried out in accord with rules of association which are prescribed by the political and legal spheres. Along with this is the tendency of political parties to take the electorate into account since their neglect of the electorate would tend to upset future election.[134] A key function of the modern political party, therefore, is its ability to absorb elements of the class struggle to within the party system itself. This occurs, Weber reasoned, as the stratification of political parties tends to align themselves with the representation of specific groups and social classes.

The Protestant Ethic and the Spirit of Capitalism

Weber's Central Thesis and Fundamental Aims of the Study

Weber wrote *The Protestant Ethic and the Spirit of Capitalism* between 1903 and 1904, and published it as two separate essays in 1905 and 1906. While *The Protestant Ethic* stands alone as an independent study, it established an immediate line of continuity with the themes of Weber's earlier essays on Protestantism and the spirit of capitalism, as well as his much larger work on world religions which he had begun at an earlier time.[135] There are essentially two overall themes which connect *The Protestant Ethic* to the themes of the early essays on religion. First was the overall historical link it established between the growth of Protestant religious doctrine and the development of modern capitalism. Second is the line of continuity it established between Protestant ethical maxims and the path of development taken by Western capitalism in its regulation of economic conduct by the imposition of restraint, time-thrift and the rejection of luxury in the pursuit of wealth.

Since its publication, *The Protestant Ethic* has been a controversial work that has been subject to harsh criticism by many writers for its central assertion that the ascetic regulation of economic life coupled with restraint, prudent saving and a stringent attitude toward work was religiously induced. While it was viewed as classic as soon as it was published, the criticism continued to the point that critical objections began to emerge from historians and theologians who claimed that Weber's argument

---

133 *Economy and Society*, p. 938.

134 *Economy and Society*, p. 287.

135 Three of Weber's essays relate to the study of Protestantism and capitalism, 'The Protestant Sects and the Spirit of Capitalism'; The Social Psychology of the World Religions; and 'Religious Rejections of the World and Their Directions,' in H.H. Gerth and C.Wright Mills, *From Max Weber: Essays in Sociology*.

had central weaknesses. Even today, criticism of Weber's study continues to generate controversy.[136]

Weber had a number of fundamental aims in writing *The Protestant Ethic,* and of these at least five stand out. First was to show that, beginning in the seventeenth century, the majority of commercial centers throughout Europe had demonstrated intense commercial activity at the same time that Protestantism was taking hold in Western Europe.[137] This, in Weber's view, led to a 'remarkable congruence between Protestantism and the development of modern capitalism' in countries where Protestantism had taken hold.[138] Second was to demonstrate how Protestant religious maxims had placed what he called an 'unambiguous stamp on the economic organization' of Western capitalism which was manifested in a clear set of attitudes toward work, punctuality and saving that had become incorporated into the spirit of capitalism and economic conduct in the world.[139] Third was to outline the impact of John Calvin's religious doctrine on what Weber believed to be specific forms of rational conduct leading to restraint, order and the rejection of luxury and excess in economic matters. This, he believed, led to a form of controlled rational conduct in the world based on the transmission of monastery asceticism and self denial to worldly economic activity. Fourth, Weber wanted to show that rational economic conduct in the form of restraint was not simply an inconsequential outcome of Calvin's religious doctrine, but was rather the result of a series of 'practical psychological motives' and ethical religious precepts that became incentives for life regulation in which religion fused itself to economic conduct in the world with the aim of controlling material reality and its temptations. Fifth Weber wanted to show that in response to Calvin's predestination doctrine, a certain type of Protestant religiosity produced what he called a 'psychological vehicle' that since the sixteenth century tended to create a form of conduct compatible with church doctrine, and even in some cases a very exaggerated form of it. Weber believed that this led to the introduction of a 'psychological premium' that created an adherence to 'methodic

---

136 For the early controversy over Weber's classic study see D. Chalcraft and A. Harrington, *The Protestant Ethic Debate: Max Weber's Replies to his Critics, 1907–1910,* Cambridge: Liverpool University Press, 2001. For a discussion of some of the later criticism of Weber's famous thesis see Kurt Samuelsson's *Religion and Economic Action: A Critique of Max Weber,* New York: Harper & Row, 1957. For discussion of some of the debates during this period see Robert W. Green, *Protestantism and Capitalism: The Weber Thesis and its Critics,* Boston: Heath & Co., 1959. Also, for the history of the 'neglect' of *The Protestant Ethic* by the American tradition, see S. Kalberg, 'On the Neglect of Weber's Protestant Ethic as a Theoretical Treatise: Demarcating the Parameters of Postwar American Sociological Theory,' *Sociological Theory,* 14, 1996, 49–69.

137 Weber states that 'a glance at the occupational statistics of any country of mixed religious composition brings to light with remarkable frequency a situation which has several times provoked discussion in the Catholic press; namely, the fact that business leaders and owners of capital and commercially trained personnel of modern enterprises, are overwhelmingly Protestant.' *Protestant Ethic,* p. 35.

138 Weber, 'Anti-Critical Last Word on The Spirit of Capitalism,' *American Journal of Sociology,* Vol. 83 (5), [1910] 1978, p. 1121.

139 For Weber's discussion of the 'unambiguous stamp' of a religious ethic on an economic ethic, see 'The Social Psychology of the World Religions' pp. 268–71.

forms of conduct' in the world toward work and the rejection of luxury which Weber thought contrasted sharply with the period of religiosity of the Middle Ages, which had not developed this attitude toward the world or life conduct.[140]

The Escape of Asceticism from the Religious Cage and the Impact on Economic Activity

After having outlined some of the central aims of Weber's thesis concerning the influences of Protestantism on the development of capitalism, it will be useful to briefly look at the concept of asceticism in the context of religious life and economic activity. In its most explicit sense, asceticism refers to rigorous self denial. Historically, the term originates from religious piety and is manifested by a systematic rejection of all material pleasure by the practice of self discipline in the world. As a religious doctrine of ethical conduct, asceticism had originated within the confines of the church and the monastery where it held that one can achieve a higher ethical state only by self-denial and a rejection of worldly pleasure. In monastic asceticism, the ascetic attitude was manifested in the form of the vows of poverty and the rejection of the world altogether. Asceticism, then, may be defined as an inner religious relation to the material world manifested in a form of a conscious self denial of worldly pleasure with the aim of achieving higher ethical states and of obtaining valued religious goals. In *The Protestant Ethic,* Weber used the concept of asceticism to pinpoint a way of living in the world based on the systematic self-denial of worldly pleasure for purposes of attaining future reward and achievement. He believed that in modern capitalism asceticism had become a category of social action regulating conduct in the world, since only in societies where capitalism flourished was self-denial linked to economic success and achievement.[141]

Having isolated ascetic conduct in economic activity, Weber went on to argue that religious asceticism had penetrated economic life only after the period of Protestant religious reforms of the seventeenth century. In this case, he set out to show that monastic asceticism had 'escaped from the religious cage' at a certain historical point and began to 'prowl around' everyday life 'like the ghost of dead religious beliefs making capitalism victorious.'[142] It was therefore Weber's central thesis that asceticism had escaped from the religious cage only after the introduction of Calvin's religious doctrine, and he went on to assert that on the basis of this asceticism took a huge leap into the economic sphere and other departments of life, so that by the

---

140 See Weber, 'Anti-Critical Last Word,' *American Journal of Sociology,* 83, [1910] 1978, pp. 1114–21.

141 The expression 'no pain, no gain' is a reflection of the ascetic attitude applied to accomplishment in the world and its relationship to the discipline of self denial and economic success. The religious idea conveyed here is that personal suffering imposed by self-denial and the delay of gratification is followed by personal gain in the world, whether material or economic. Thus, self-denial became the link between personal conduct in the world and opportunities for success.

142 Weber, *The Protestant Ethic,* p. 181.

eighteenth and nineteenth centuries the religious cage of asceticism had become the 'iron cage' of commercial activity. Weber wrote:

> Since asceticism undertook to remodel the world and to work out its ideals in the world, material goods have gained an increasing and finally an inexorable power over the lives of men as at no previous period in history. Today the spirit of religious asceticism has escaped from the cage. But, victorious capitalism, since it rests on mechanical foundations, needs support no longer. The idea of duty in one's calling prowls about in our lives like the ghost of dead religious beliefs.[143]

The 'Spirit' of Capitalism Defined

In order then to provide evidence for the claim that asceticism had escaped the religious cage and had taken a leap into everyday economic life, Weber set out to identify what he called the 'spirit of capitalism.' He began by noting that when compared to other systems of money making and other economies of wealth, Western capitalism was alone in developing a central philosophy or spirit which could be identified by three overriding imperatives or demands. First was the devotion to amassing wealth and profit beyond the personal needs and wants of the individual; second was the commitment to unrelieved toil and work coupled with self denial and the renunciation of luxury and excess; and third, was the use of personal restraint in the world and the avoidance of the use of wealth for purposes of private enjoyment. It was this ethical 'spirit,' Weber believed, that shaped Western capitalism as an economic way of life.[144]

To show how the 'spirit' manifested itself in economic life, Weber turned his attention to the works of Benjamin Franklin who he believed represented the characteristics of the 'spirit of capitalism' in its 'classical purity.' Franklin, in fact, was a successful entrepreneur who had written a self help guide in 1736 called *Necessary Hints To Those That Would Be Rich* and, in 1748, he followed it with another guide called *Advice to Young Tradesmen*. Franklin put forward a set of ethical maxims about how to be successful in business and stated the maxims in the following way:

> Remember, that time is money. He that can earn ten shillings a day by his labor and goes abroad, or sits idle, one half of the day, though he spends but sixpence during his idleness, ought not to reckon that the only expense; he has really spent, or rather thrown away, five shillings besides.

and

> Remember, that money is of the prolific, generating nature. Money can beget money, and its offspring can beget more, and so on. Five shillings turned is six, turned again is seven,

---

143 Ibid., pp. 181–2.

144 *Protestant Ethic*, pp. 27–8. As far as Weber is concerned, there were many capitalisms: adventurous capitalism, speculative capitalism, usurious capitalism and modern industrial or ascetic capitalism. By drawing our attention to the 'spirit,' Weber is saying that the religious forces shaping ascetic capitalism in the West are unique.

and three pence, and so on, till it becomes a hundred pounds. The more there is of it, the more it produces every turning, so that the profits rise quicker and quicker. He that murders a crown, destroys all that it might have produced, even scores of pounds.

and

Remember this saying, the good paymaster is lord of another man's purse. He that is known to pay punctually and exactly to the time he promises, may at any time, on any occasion, raise all the money his friends can spare. This is sometimes of great use. After industry and frugality, nothing contributes more to the raising of a young man in the world than punctuality and justice in his dealings; therefore never keep borrowed money an hour beyond the time you promised.

and

The most trifling actions that affect a man's credit are to be regarded. The sound of your hammer at five in the morning, or eight at night, heard by a creditor, makes him easy six months longer; but if he sees you at a billiard-table, or hears your voice at a tavern, when you should be at work, he sends for his money the next day. It shows, besides, that you are mindful of what you owe; it makes you appear a careful as well as an honest man, and that still increases your credit.[145]

What struck Weber about Franklin's language was not its practical outlook toward money making, nor its insistence that honest individuals pay their creditors promptly, but rather that the demand to promptness, prudence, honesty, and saving appears within the context of a proclaimed ethical duty to earn more and more capital. 'Truly, what is preached here,' said Weber, 'is not simply a means of making one's way in the world' on a practical basis, but rather 'a peculiar ethic,' and a particular way of regulating life conduct based on a set of ethical maxims which receive their force from the religious sphere. Weber went on to say that any 'infraction of these ethical maxims were treated not as foolishness but as a forgetfulness of duty.'[146] In Weber's view, therefore, Franklin's words go beyond the mere suggestion of prudent business advice. Rather, they refer to a specific ethic or 'spirit,' and 'take on the character of ethically colored religious maxims for shaping the conduct of life.'[147]

Weber went on to point out that while all of Franklin's recommendations to be punctual, save money, exhibit time thrift and work hard appeared to have practical significance, they contained what Weber thought was a 'surplus of religious

---

145 *Protestant Ethic*, p. 49–50.

146 *Protestant Ethic*, p. 51.

147 *Protestant Ethic*, p. 52. The religious maxims Weber refers to are reflected in the economic proverbs popular in the West in the eighteenth and nineteenth centuries and include 'a stitch in time saves nine,' 'penny wise and pound foolish,' 'early to bed, early to rise makes a man healthy, wealthy and wise,' 'idle hands are the devils plaything,' and 'cleanliness is next to Godliness.' Each of the proverbs urge the individual to action and each has the unmistakable stamp of a religious ethic embedded in an economic ethic.

virtue.'[148] In fact, Weber stated that Franklin believed that the practical advice he offered had virtues which were divine in origin, claiming that they 'were intended to lead the individual along the path of righteousness.' This led Weber to argue that 'something more than mere utility was involved,' and that all these 'psychological sanctions' related to restraint, time thrift, punctuality and prudent savings showed that religious beliefs and practices gave explicit 'direction to practical conduct in the world and held the individual to it.'[149]

Weber maintained that, from what Franklin had said, it was clear that the 'spirit of capitalism' had the effect of putting forward the expectation of hard work, restraint in life conduct, and the pursuit of wealth as a moral duty and, in doing so, it made the non-performance of work and the absence of restraint an 'infraction' of such duty.[150] Weber then went on to argue that the elevation of 'hard work' and 'prudent saving' to a moral duty was historically new and had not been seen before in other economies and other forms of capitalism. In this respect, the 'spirit' of capitalism can therefore be defined as the imposition of 'religious' maxims onto everyday economic activity which had not been seen before in previous systems of money making. In addition, Weber thought that coupled with the pattern of self denial in economic matters, the spirit of capitalism became a method for regulating life conduct in the world and of controlling one's relation to the material world through asceticism and conscious self denial.

Distinctiveness of the 'Spirit' in Modern Capitalism: Traditional vs Modern Capitalism

To this point, Weber had argued that the 'spirit' of capitalism was unique in two related respects. First, it developed only in modern Western capitalism and was lacking in other societies where capitalism and economies of wealth had existed. Second, it indicated that the appearance of ethical maxims in economic and commercial activity implied the presence of religious maxims. In order, then, to support the argument that the 'spirit' of capitalism developed only in the West, Weber went on to compare two forms of capitalism which he referred to as 'modern' and 'traditional.'[151] In modern capitalism employers used money saving techniques in pricing jobs according to different rates, and they did this, he argued, in order to obtain as much productivity from the worker as possible. In cases where high profits prevailed over heavy losses, or where employers sought to speed up production, piece rates in modern capitalism added incentives for workers to earn more money by working harder. This simultaneously benefited employers and workers at the same time since it maximized profits and

---

148 Ibid.

149 Ibid.

150 *Protestant Ethic*, p. 51. Weber puts it this way: 'Truly what is here preached is not simply a means of making ones way in the world, but a peculiar ethic. The infraction of its rules is treated not as foolishness but as forgetfulness of duty.'

151 *Protestant Ethic*, pp. 59–60.

wages. In the case of traditional capitalism, however, the attempt to raise piece rates had the effect of creating less rather than more incentive for workers to earn more money because workers were not prepared to work harder to increase their wages. According to Weber, 'the worker reacted to the increase by decreasing the amount of work.'[152] In traditional capitalism, therefore, 'the opportunity to earn more was less attractive than that of working less' since the traditional worker 'did not ask how much they could earn in a day if they do as much as possible? Instead, they asked: how much must I work in order to earn the wages which I earned before and which take care of my traditional needs?'[153] While traditionalism had existed previously in the economies of China and India, and briefly in Europe of the Middle Ages, in all these cases, said Weber, 'the particular ethical spirit' in money making and the pursuit of wealth 'was lacking.'[154]

Calvinism and Capitalism

After looking at the development of the 'religious spirit' of modern capitalism, Weber turned his attention to the religious reforms of John Calvin (1509–1564). He looked explicitly at the relationship between Protestant religious doctrine on the one hand, and the appearance of certain religious maxims in economic conduct on the other. Historically, Calvin was a Protestant reformer who came into prominence in the sixteenth century after studying theology and religion in France. In 1529 he developed an interest in ecclesiastical study and began to criticize Catholic theology for its failure to stress the rejection of worldly pleasure and for its permissive doctrine of salvation. Calvin believed that rooted in Catholic thought was the idea that the path to salvation was determined by a cycle of atonement, good works, confession and participation in the sacraments. This meant that in the light of Catholic theology salvation was conferred by God from above and that Catholics could obtain grace and salvation even if they had sinned. Calvin, however, believed that Catholic theology was much too tolerant in its salvation doctrine and, after joining the Protestant reform movement in France, he put forward a view of salvation which was much more restrictive.[155] In 1535, Calvin claimed that he had found a series of restrictive regulations related to worldly activity in the Old Testament and as a result began to stress a strict interpretation of Old Testament injunctions as they related to worldly conduct. Eventually, these took the form of a new salvation theology called the doctrine of predestination. After Calvin's doctrine began to proliferate

---

152 Ibid.
153 Ibid.
154 *Protestant Ethic*, pp. 52–3.
155 See Gordon Marshall, *Presbyteries and Profits: Calvinism and the Development of Capitalism in Scotland, 1560–1707*, Oxford: Clarendon Press, 1980.

more widely throughout Europe and have an impact on Protestant religious teaching, his views signaled a serious shift in religious thought and brought about a wave of reform unparalleled in its restriction on human action in the world. By 1536, Calvin published his theological writings on the doctrine of predestination in a work entitled *The Institutes of Christian Religion*.[156]

At the center of Calvin's religious reforms was a body of religious pronouncements known as the 'doctrine of predestination.' Calvin's doctrine was based on four essential decrees or dogmas which outlined his salvation theology. The first of these decrees stated that, before the world began, God had divided all humanity into two classes of persons; those whom he had elected to be saved, and those whom he elected to be damned. To those who had been elected to be saved, God gave everlasting life, salvation and eternal grace. To those who were condemned, however, God withheld salvation and gave them an after-life of everlasting damnation and dishonor.[157] Second, Calvin's doctrine stated that no Protestant could know whether they had been saved or damned until it was revealed to them upon their death. Since Calvin had argued that there were no physical signs or marks distinguishing the elect from the damned, no one could tell physically who was among 'the elect' or 'the damned'.[158] Third, was the decree which stated that nothing could be done to relieve, forgive or reverse the decrees; no priest, no prayer, no good works, no sacraments and no worldly forgiveness by confession or communion.[159]

Since Calvin believed that God had abandoned all but the elect and that Christ had endured suffering only for the elect, he introduced two uncompromising restrictions forbidding any reversal or exemption from the doctrine of predestination. First, he stated that however one's fate was decided by God, there would be no hope of appeal and no possibility of forgiveness through prayer, religious supplication, performance of good works or participation in the sacraments. Second, Calvin stated that God was transcendent and could not be called upon or approached, and thus was out of reach of personal prayer.[160]

As far as Weber was concerned, Calvin's doctrine constituted a radical reversal of Catholic theology and Catholic salvation. In Catholic theology, the believer was able to redeem themselves of sin and undo past error and transgression through penance and prayer in which forgiveness for one's sins led to religious grace and ultimately otherworldly salvation. Weber thought that the consequences of Calvin's predestination doctrine were unprecedented in three specific respects. First, it reversed Catholic salvation theology by asserting that salvation could not be won either by works,

156 John Calvin, *The Institutes of Christian Religion*, [1536], 1955; and Ernst Troeltsch, *The Social Teaching of the Christian Churches,* London: Allen & Unwin, 1956.

157 Calvin, *The Institutes of Christian Religion*, III, 21, p. 213.

158 *Protestant Ethic,* p. 110.

159 *Protestant Ethic,* p. 104.

160 *Protestant Ethic,* pp. 104–6.

sacraments, or God's forgiveness from above. Second, it created a 'feeling of unprecedented inner loneliness in Protestants and took away 'the most important thing in their life – the hope of eternal salvation.'[161] This, Weber maintained, put Protestants into a state of internal salvation anxiety, so that the first and most pressing question became: 'am I one of the elect?'[162] Since no direct answer was obtainable, the withdrawal of God's grace in this case had the effect of placing the individual totally on their own in religious matters. Third, in denying Protestants the opportunity to plead to God through prayer or sacraments for redemption, Weber thought that Calvin's doctrine had stripped Protestants of their control over their own salvation, and this created a crisis of faith so that the key question for Protestants became 'how can I interpret my relationship to God'?[163]

As Protestants adjusted to Calvin's decrees, Weber believed that as a result they became more isolated and individualized and this altered their relationship to the everyday world and to the social community. This took place in several respects. First, by eliminating the link to salvation provided by sacraments and confession, the decrees warned against trust in friendship and aid in the world.[164] Second, in proclaiming that God was out of reach, Protestants had no one to turn to in matters of faith and so they believed that all contact with God and with priests was withdrawn. In addition, feelings of isolation and abandonment were intensified by the requirement of worldly asceticism, since asceticism insisted that the world be renounced with inner resistance and that Protestants constantly be on the alert regarding temptation from the world. This tended to close off avenues of action with one exception: the obligation to combat self-doubt with labor and work. Weber maintained that the withdrawal of prayer, sacraments, and good works created a new form of self-isolation and self-examination by Protestants concerning why God had abandoned them. He believed that this led to a new form of action in the world in which Protestants had to proclaim self worthiness in the face of severe religious restrictions in regard to God's grace. In Weber's view, this led to feelings of separateness and isolation which were manifested in a lack of trust of others and in an attitude that cultivated detachment from the world. Protestants were thus forced to practice their faith in solitude and inner isolation, leading eventually to the development of the doctrine 'sola fide,' which meant 'faith alone.'[165]

Effects of Calvin's Doctrine on Conduct in the World: Psychological Sanctions and Inner Worldly Asceticism

After discussing Calvin's central doctrine, Weber turned his attention to outlining the affects of Calvin's decrees on worldly conduct. He began by comparing Calvin's

---

161 *Ibid.*
162 *Protestant Ethic*, p. 110.
163 Wolfgang Schluchter, 'Weber's Sociology of Rationalism and Typology of Religious Rejection of the World,' in S. Whimster and S. Lash, (eds.), *Max Weber, Rationality and Modernity*. London: Allen & Unwin, pp. 92–115, 1981.
164 Schluchter, 'Weber's Sociology of Rationalism,' p. 106.
165 *Protestant Ethic*, p. 80.

doctrine with three of the main branches of Protestantism that had emerged in Western Europe during the period of Protestant reform, including Pietism, Methodism, and the Baptist branches of the Protestant movement. Weber thought that Calvinism differed from the other branches of Protestantism in a number of key dogmatic principles related to the doctrine of predestination. In this case, Weber's principle argument was that Calvin's predestination doctrine gave birth to a form of conduct in the world that emerged only among adherents of Calvinism. He believed that it was because of the doctrine that certain ethical maxims of conduct in relation to life activity in the world began to emerge. He wrote:

> We are interested not in the influence of church discipline or in pastoral work, but rather in something entirely different. This is in the influence of those psychological sanctions which, originating in religious beliefs and the practices of religion, gave direction to practical conduct in the world and held the individual to it.'[166]

In the quotation above, Weber stated that Calvin's predestination doctrine placed a 'psychological sanction' on certain kinds of conduct in the world, and chief among these was the ascetic regulation of everyday life. Focusing then on the historical significance of Calvin's doctrine, Weber isolated four central effects on conduct in the world. First was the tendency among Protestants to distance themselves from the world. This occurred, according to Weber, immediately after Calvin's doctrine had transformed salvation into something that was given by God into something that was predestined and out of reach of Protestants. This forced Protestants to follow a path alone to meet their destiny where no one could help, not priests, not prayer, not sacraments.[167] This caused Protestants to take refuge to an inner world of self isolation and had the effect of placing individuals entirely on their own in religious matters.[168] As soon as this occurred, Weber noted, there was an immediate 'positive valuation' on conduct in the world that stressed inner diligence and the need to bring all action under constant self control.'[169] This, in Weber's view, gave birth to 'worldly asceticism'

---

166 Ibid., p. 97.

167 Ibid., p. 104. In a recent article entitled 'The Longevity of the Thesis: A Critique of the Critics,' Malcolm MacKinnon argued that Weber was in error in assuming that Calvin's doctrine brought about specific types of ascetic conduct in the world. He claimed that Weber failed to notice that the Protestant church in England revised Calvin's doctrine in a document called the Westminster Confessions of Faith in 1647. MacKinnon argued that because the Westminster revisions consigned Calvin's dogmas to 'the dustbin of history,' Weber's thesis was disproved. However, to claim that the Westminster revisions of Calvin's doctrine in 1647 would have expunged the historical record of Calvin's doctrine is not plausible because it overlooks the fact that Calvin's teachings would have proliferated in Europe from 1536 to 1647, a full 111 years before the Westminster Confessions of Faith altered the doctrine. This leaves a large block of historical time for the affects of the doctrine, thus giving credence to Weber's thesis. See H. Lehmann and G. Roth (eds.), *Weber's Protestant Ethic: Origins, Evidence, Contexts* Cambridge: Cambridge University Press, 1993, pp. 211–44.

168 Ibid., p. 106.

169 Ibid., p. 117.

which was in stark contrast to monastery or church asceticism.[170] As far as Weber was concerned, worldly asceticism differed from all other forms of religious asceticism by a straightforward attempt to bring action in the world under the ascetic ideal of regulation and rational control. Whereas all other forms of religious asceticism had been confined to the church and to the monastery, worldly asceticism was the singular product of Calvin's doctrine, because only Calvin's doctrine had put asceticism to work in the world to destroy all 'spontaneous enjoyment for purposes of bringing order into the conduct of daily living.'[171] If the most urgent task of all Protestant asceticism was the destruction of impulsive enjoyment, Weber believed that this introduced a 'methodical control over the whole of life' which came to rest solely on the regulation of action in the world.

Second, Weber thought that Calvin's doctrine had an impact on all other previous forms of religious asceticism and inner self regulation. He stated that in effect Calvin's doctrine had 'altered ascetic activity' because it created a worldly role for asceticism whereas all other forms of asceticism had been confined to the church and the monastery. This individualized religious life in personal conduct and gave birth to a new role for asceticism based on the transformation of religious activity into private activity in the world and consequently the transformation of the world itself.[172] As far as Weber was concerned, Calvin's doctrine constituted a key point of departure for asceticism because it marked the point at which asceticism undertook to transform conduct in the world, in contrast to other forms of asceticism which had been confined to the church. Thus, having escaped monastic life, church asceticism after Calvin became linked to methodical life conduct which served to reinforce how ascetic life penetrated everyday life. Calvin's doctrine therefore 'added something to asceticism' which provided an active faith in worldly activity that was unprecedented in Catholicism or in other Protestant sects, including Lutheranism and Methodism.

Weber therefore used the term 'this worldly asceticism' to refer to the fact that Calvin's doctrine was alone in putting asceticism to work in the world when all other forms of asceticism were 'otherworldly' in being confined to the sphere of the church and the monastery. Since Calvin's doctrine had provided a basis for church asceticism to penetrate the spheres of everyday life, it constituted a second point of departure in terms of the role played by religious asceticism itself. Weber stated that Calvin's doctrine thus substituted the worldly aristocracy of 'men of action' and worldly accomplishment, for 'the spiritual aristocracy of monks and saints.'[173] In this case, Calvin's dogmas had fused church asceticism onto everyday life conduct, thus leading to what Weber called the systematization of ethical conduct in the world. This marked the point at which a religious ethic placed its stamp on an economic ethic leading to 'a thoroughgoing Christianization of the whole of life' and, as a consequence, it

---

170 Ibid., p. 118–19.
171 Ibid., p. 119.
172 Ibid., p. 120.
173 Ibid., p. 121.

lent to ethical conduct a methodical quality which Calvinism forced on worldly behavior.[174]

Third was the effect of Calvin's doctrine on placing a psychological premium on a certain kind of economic conduct in the world and on the control of everyday life. According to Weber, Protestant asceticism had placed an incentive on the rational ordering of everyday life by placing a 'psychological premium' on the regulation of one's own life that influenced the development of capitalism as a form of economic conduct. Weber believed that Calvin's asceticism had turned its attention to the systematic suppression of the spontaneous enjoyment of life and this, Weber argued, created 'a powerful tendency toward the uniformity of life by the accumulation of capital through the ascetic compulsion to save,' and to place restraint on the consumption of one's own wealth and to re-model the world in terms of the ascetic ideal.[175]

In placing a 'psychological premium' on a certain kind of conduct – self restraint, prudent saving, time-thrift and rejection of luxury – Weber showed how Calvin's doctrine had created a 'psychological vehicle which stressed a type of conduct that was compatible with church doctrine, and in some cases even an exaggerated form of it.' The fact that Calvin's doctrine had put its psychological stamp on conduct in the world was, for Weber, decisive because no other religion had placed a psychological premium on methodic conduct in the world. He argued that 'Calvinism caused very specific psychological premiums to be placed on the ascetic regulation of life which Calvin demanded,' and this meant that Calvinism was first in placing a premium on the methodical adherence to restraint, prudent saving, time thrift and the rational pursuit of wealth in the economic sphere of life.[176]

Weber went on to say that the psychological premiums placed on ascetic conduct not only in life in general but also in a vocational choice in an occupational calling acted as a guarantee of the certainty of salvation. This, Weber thought, led to the inner life regulation of outer behavior in a way that became more pronounced as capitalism developed and exerted an influence in America. The development of life-conquering asceticism was, in Weber's view, in direct contrast to the absence of life regulation in monastic asceticism. He argued that while monastic asceticism demanded distance from the world and a rejection of luxury and excess, Protestant asceticism required a method for cultivating asceticism in the world, indicating a methodical adherence to a way of life. This led to an ascetic attitude to the regulation of life demanding the use of time, work and silence as a means of inducing a methodical way of life while suppressing instinctual urges'.[177]

According to Weber, Protestant asceticism differs from monastic asceticism in two broad ways. First, in rejecting the practices of monastic asceticism including poverty,

---

174 Ibid., pp. 123–4.
175 Ibid., pp.126, 166.
176 Weber, 'Anti-Critical Last Word,' p. 1114.
177 Ibid., p. 1121.

rejection of luxury and celibacy, Protestant asceticism placed an emphasis on rational ascetic practices which were applied methodically to economic activity in a calling. Second, in rejecting the routine of prayer and regularized habits of monastic asceticism, Protestant asceticism regulated action from within which gave birth to an asceticism of an inner-worldly way of life that involved self regulation. According to Weber, this gave Protestant asceticism a different internal structure than Catholic asceticism, and laid the foundation for what Weber called the inner-worldly turn of asceticism toward the self that was manifested in a methodic adherence to life conduct in work, time thrift, punctuality and inner self-control. Protestant asceticism thus only intensified the methodic way of life in the economic realm in so far as it placed its stamp on economic conduct in the world. Its great technical achievement, therefore, was the development of capitalism.

The Link between Salvation Theology and the Commercial Spirit

After looking at the effects of Calvin's doctrine on conduct in the world, Weber turned his attention to looking at the connection between Calvin's doctrine of salvation and commercial activity. He believed that there were two broad links between the two. First, Weber thought there was a link between Calvin's doctrine of salvation and the commercial spirit, and second, he believed there was a link between the Protestant withdrawal of salvation and the development of ascetic conduct. In the first instance, Weber thought that the emergence of worldly asceticism and rational conduct appeared only after Calvin's doctrine of salvation had deprived Protestants of any knowledge of whether they were among the elect or the damned. He demonstrated this by drawing a comparison with Catholicism which held that the path of salvation was clearly marked out in the cycle of atonement and confession, and this was reflected in the view that the cycle of sin, repentance and atonement is followed by God's forgiveness of one's sin.[178] In Catholicism, in addition, one can earn salvation through good works, whereas this is not possible in Protestantism. According to Calvin, salvation was not attainable because the decrees had proclaimed that it was predestined.

As far as Weber was concerned, the decisive difference between Catholicism and Protestantism was that Protestantism created a 'crisis of proof' in dogma because salvation 'was no longer by works' and Protestants could not know, nor were able to obtain proof that they were among the elect who would be saved.[179] The crisis, therefore, was how could election to salvation be proved? Weber thought that this constituted the key point of departure for Calvin's Protestantism over the other branches of Protestantism and sealed the fate of the doctrine in religious dogma. Weber argued that the withdrawal of 'works' as a means of obtaining salvation created two related responses in Protestants. First, was the 'crisis of proof in dogma' related to how

---

178 *Protestant Ethic*, p. 117.
179 Calvin, *The Institutes of Christian Religion* [1536], III, 21, p. 213; III, 22, p. 218.

Protestants could know whether they were among the elect. Second, Protestants developed the belief that intense worldly asceticism in life conduct was to be pursued as an end in itself and that this provided a worldly substitute for grace because, from the standpoint of monastic asceticism, self denial and labor always contained the power to confer grace upon the believer.[180] As a result, labor and hard work in a calling became associated with a method for eliminating doubt about whether one was among the elect, since in this context labor was used as a remedy against the feeling of damnation. Conduct in the world was thus given a positive valuation only if it was subjected to a consistent method for conduct as a whole, and this led to the systematization of ethical conduct in the world. Here, Weber thought that the 'crisis of proof' in dogma created the inducement to place a psychological premium on rational ascetic conduct in the world. In this view, it was thus Protestant asceticism that contained the incentive for a rational ordering of life conduct as a systematic whole.

In addition to finding a link between Calvin's doctrine of salvation and ascetic conduct in the world, Weber believed he had found a link between the doctrine of predestination and the appearance of asceticism in economic life. Since work and labor in the context of self denial had the effect of 'earning' temporary grace, religious self denial took on the economic meaning of 'earning interest' in the form of redemptive credit.[181] With asceticism came the view that self-discipline was attainable through strict self-denial and that, through this, Protestants could achieve a higher state by removing themselves from the world and by observing rigorous self denial in work. Since Protestant commercial activity was permeated with self-denying actions of restraint, prudence and thrift, Weber felt he had found a link between Protestant religious teaching and the work ethic. Further, since an ascetic attitude toward work increased the likelihood of amassing wealth, the attainment of wealth became a sign that one had been successful in worldly economic activity. The Protestant equation became one of believing that success in a commercial calling through hard work and self-denial was a way Protestants could interpret their relation to God and thus feel closer to salvation. Wealth, therefore, became the basis for interpreting one's relationship to God.

In addition, Weber believed he found the link between the Protestant commercial spirit and Protestant articles of secular religious faith. What was unique about Protestantism, according to Weber, was that whereas all other forms of religious

---

180 The religious logic that operates here is that the greater the self denial and the greater the resistance to worldly temptations, the greater is the feeling of spiritual elevation and grace.

181 Weber alluded to the fact that at some point 'religious faith' became the theological precursor to the concept of commercial credit. What is interesting is that when we compare the ascetic practices of the monastery – poverty, celibacy, restraint – with the ascetic practices in the realm of work – punctuality, frugality, industry and toil – their comparability shows that the practices seem to be carriers of interests from one sphere to another. Thus the logic of industry and punctuality in the sphere of work is comparable to the logic of grace, moral worth, election and salvation in the sphere of religion. It was here that Weber was able to find an interpretive link between religious prophecy on the one hand, and material economic activities on the other. That is to say that, if at some point 'time equals money,' then, at another point faith and self denial become synonymous with earned credit.

devotion were accompanied by a rejection of everyday life, Protestantism had introduced a thoroughgoing regulation of everyday life in an effort to bring worldly work under rational control. Weber believed that this only came about as a consequence of the Protestant conversion of monastic asceticism into worldly asceticism. While monastic asceticism required believers to isolate themselves from the world at large and reject the world because of its temptation, Protestant asceticism encouraged believers to practice self-denial in the world and to put asceticism to work in order to transform the world. This led to an unprecedented penetration of asceticism into worldly acts that were previously restricted to spiritual activity. Accordingly, Weber believed that he had identified two historical types of asceticism, one which he called other-worldly asceticism, the other inner-worldly asceticism.[182] While both rejected the world, they did so for different reasons. Other-worldly asceticism renounced the world because it presents temptation and because distance from it confers grace. In this case, salvation was sought along a path to the otherworldly through religious devotion, prayer, penitent living and self denial. Furthermore, otherworldly asceticism required a formal withdrawal 'from social and psychological ties with the family, from the possession of worldly goods, and from political, economic and erotic activities; in short, from all creaturely interests.'[183] Inner-worldly asceticism, by contrast, required distance from the world in all but selected categories of action, particularly those related to a rational ordering of life conduct so that time-wasting, relaxation, idleness and temptation became subject to an approved ascetic technique. In this view, certain activities in the world became the individual's 'responsibility so that they alone had to transform the world in accordance with an ascetic ideal.'[184] The inner-worldly ascetic thus sees the world in terms of a test devised by God of their ability to resist temptation in which each individual becomes an 'elect instrument of God' to toil in a life based on self-denial. On the basis of this reasoning, Weber argued, Protestants assumed that their personal worth comes from self-denial and that self-denial brings redemption. This hope, combined with worldly asceticism and the focusing of one's energies toward work, creates the inner asceticism necessary for capitalist activity.

Asceticism, Capitalism and the Transformation of the 'Calling'

After looking at the psychological premium which Protestant salvation doctrine placed on certain kinds of ascetic conduct in the world, Weber turned his attention to looking at the question of the 'calling' and its relation to a commercial vocation. In order to understand Weber's argument, it will be useful to describe the meaning of the concept of 'religious calling'. To begin with, the concept of the 'calling' can be traced

---

182 *Economy and Society*, pp. 541–544.
183 *Economy and Society*, p. 542.
184 Ibid.

to Catholic doctrine of the Middle Ages and essentially refers to being called to a 'life task' serving God in a religious vocation by performing ethical acts of devotion. By the seventeenth century, the concept of the 'calling' had taken on a major role in reformation theology due to Luther. In Catholic theology after Luther, the concept of the 'calling' denoted service to God in the form of religious duties which were above those of the everyday secular world. Later, the term took on the exclusive meaning of renouncing the temporal world for monastic purposes. This renunciation was based on the idea that the temporal world of experience was 'valueless' in relation to the spiritual world.

Weber pointed out that as soon as the concept of the 'calling' appeared within Protestant theology and Calvin's dogmas, it took on a new meaning. In contrast to Catholic theology, Protestants interpreted the 'calling' to signify service to worldly, rather than otherworldly duties. This had the effect of investing the temporal world with value. Weber pointed out that, while Luther was the first to develop the significance of the concept of the 'calling' for church life, it was with Calvin that the concept began to undergo significant transformation. This occurred, Weber reasoned, as soon as the concept of 'activity in the world' became subject to Protestant scrutiny. In early church history, activity in the world was viewed as degrading and secular. But, because it was considered necessary to life, the church tended to view it as morally neutral. The theological point of departure came with the introduction of the Protestant doctrine of *sola fide*.[185] *Sola fide,* which essentially meant practicing one's faith alone or in solitude separate from the church community, stood in sharp contrast to the Catholic concept of *consilia evangelica* whose equivalent was the church council. The difference between the two concepts of faith and church life was dramatic. On the one hand, the Catholic attitude of *consilia evangelica* was that religious faith took place collectively and was communal in nature in so far as it was related to others in the social and religious context of the church and solidarity together. On the other hand, the Protestant attitude was one of religious individualism, separateness and private conscience, or '*sola fide*.' With the introduction of *sola fide,* the renunciation of everyday life for monastic withdrawal not only lost its significance as a vehicle of faith and moral purpose among Protestants, but its personal justification as an act before God was diminished as well.[186] While Catholic theology defined faith as a withdrawal from the everyday world by emphasizing the otherworldly, Protestantism gave it a thoroughgoing worldly character. But what should be clear about Calvin's doctrine of *sola fide* is that it separated the Protestant believer from the community of the church, and as a consequence led to a 'feeling of unprecedented inner loneliness' and the perception that one was alone in the world and abandoned by God.[187]

---

185 *Protestant Ethic,* p. 80–1.
186 Ibid.
187 Ibid., p. 104.

Weber pointed out that the consequences of *sola fide* were clear. For the first time there was 'moral justification for worldly activity' both for spiritual purposes concerning one religious standing and for purposes of what Weber called 'a periodical discharge of the emotional sense of sin.'[188] This shift cannot be overestimated. Combined with worldly activity, Protestant asceticism provided an intense ethical focus to transforming the world through labor and self discipline. Combined with this, the Protestant concept of the 'calling' took on a second transformation in which there was a connection between worldly activity, asceticism and a religious justification to action. In Weber's view, this represented the first systematic attempt to separate the two ethical domains – worldly and otherworldly – and claim that one could be 'called' to worldly economic pursuits. He reasoned that the introduction of the 'calling' into everyday life and into commerce was completely novel. No religion up to that time had united the world of the spirit with the world of everyday life in this manner and, as a result, work became equivalent to virtue and to a religious calling. In Weber's view, this 'gave everyday worldly activity a religious significance, and created the conception of a calling to commercial activities.'[189]

Another related issue regarding the religious concept of 'calling' is the process whereby occupational pursuits such as business and commerce become transformed into an 'internal calling' which carries with it the strength of an inner conviction that one has been 'called to business.' The concept of the 'calling' thus indicates a transmission of ideas taking place between ethical and religious impulses in the outer world of daily life and impulses in the inner world of the conscience. The function of being 'called' to the commercial life must have been the psychological equivalent of being operated on by ethical and religious precepts in the form of an inner 'calling' which would serve as a substitute for righteousness and grace. In fact, the fulfillment of one's worldly duty became, in Weber's view, the only way Protestants could understand their actions as acceptable to God. The 'calling' of the individual to a worldly vocation was to fulfill their duty to God through the moral conduct of toil. In this scheme, toil becomes equivalent to a virtue. This brought dutiful pursuits and worldly activity to center stage, and was the link between asceticism in economic activity and the worldly pursuit of a commercial occupation. Good Protestants who wanted to supervise their own state of grace in the world through self-control and self-regulation were 'called' to commercial activity since work was seen as a secular method of attaining virtue and salvation. From this point of view, there could be no relaxation, no relief from toil because labor is an exercise in ascetic virtue and rational behavior in a calling is taken as a sign of grace. For Protestants, 'the most urgent task became the destruction of spontaneous, impulsive enjoyment.'[190]

---

188 *Protestant Ethic*, pp. 80, 106.
189 *Protestant Ethic*, p. 80.
190 *Protestant Ethic*, p. 119.

Weber's Methodology and the Theory of Knowledge in the Social Sciences

Between 1902 and 1903, Weber wrote a series of essays related to question of methodology in the social sciences. These writings have been generally referred to as Weber's methodological works and explicitly they deal with issues of investigation in the social sciences. Specifically, the term methodology refers to the procedures used in the social sciences to obtain valid knowledge of society and social history. While this may seem obvious and straightforward, in the social sciences the methods used to obtain knowledge of society are often not as clear as they are in the natural sciences. As a result, two works by Weber stand out in particular as being of central importance in the formation of Weber's methodological views. First is a work entitled *Roscher and Knies: The Logical Problems of Historical Economics*, written between 1902–3 and, second, a work called 'Objectivity in the Social Sciences and Social Policy,' written between 1903–4.[191] In order to look more closely at the themes of these writings, it will be useful to review some of the issues and questions raised during the period leading to Weber's involvement in the debates which shaped his methodological thinking. Key to the issue was the development of the social sciences. This, Weber thought, would not be possible unless a distinction was made between the methods of the natural sciences and the methods of the social sciences. In order to completely understand some of the reasoning behind Weber's views on these questions, we have to look more closely at the developments in philosophy and in the natural sciences taking place during the period.

Historical and Philosophic Background of Weber's Methodology

Between 1880 and 1900, there was dramatic growth in the natural sciences in Europe. Steady progress in experimental discoveries and technical advances led to an almost unrivaled dominance of the methodology of the natural sciences. Branches of knowledge such as physics, biology and chemistry had taken enormous strides forward, increasing their prestige in the scholarly community. As a result, the natural sciences had become preeminent in discovering certain truths about the natural world, and this gave the scientific method unparalleled authority over other more speculative methods of investigation. As these advances took place, the historical and philosophical sciences began to decline and, as a result, the authority which philosophy once had in refereeing knowledge debates between science and theory and in explaining the nature of reality, began to lose its foothold. As a result, an open clash developed between the natural sciences and social sciences on the question of knowledge and this drew attention to the distinction between the methodology of the natural

---

191 Max Weber, *Roscher and Knies: The Logical Problems of Historical Economics,* London: The Free Press, 1975; 'Objectivity in Social Science and Social Policy,' in E. S. Shils & H. Finch (eds), *Max Weber: The Methodology of the Social Sciences,* New York: Free Press, 1949, pp. 50–112.

sciences and the methodology of the social sciences. Many began to criticize the non-scientific nature of the historical and social sciences such as economics, sociology and political economy, seeing them as largely speculative and intuitive in nature. By 1885, a general crisis emerged in the legitimacy of historical and social sciences, and as a result many philosophers began to re-examine the relationship between the scientific method and philosophy.

By 1890, a movement based on a return to the work of Immanuel Kant emerged as a way of resolving the problem. Referred to as Neo-Kantianism, the movement was based on a re-examination of the relation between science and philosophy, and this called into question the validity of scientific knowledge itself.[192] The term Neo-Kantianism, then, is used in the social sciences to refer to a diverse group of thinkers who participated in a philosophical movement in Germany in order to secure the legitimacy of the social and historical sciences and to engage in debates about which methods where appropriate for the social sciences. Many of the participants in these debates, including thinkers such as Herman Hemholtz, F.A. Lange and Kuno Fischer, believed that a return to Kant would provide a solution to the problem of knowledge in the social and historical sciences.[193] Two of the central thinkers of the neo-Kantian movement – Wilhelm Windelband and Heinrich Rickert – believed that only two specific directions could be pursued to solve the problem. First, was the need to search for and develop a theory of knowledge that related to how history and society could be subject to investigation. Second, was the necessity of defining the differences in the subject matter of the natural and social sciences. One of the first solutions to the dilemma related to the methods of the natural and social sciences was devised by Wilhelm Windelband.[194]

Wilhelm Windelband's Criticism of the Natural Sciences

Wilhelm Windelband (1848–1915) was a German philosopher and historian who was a leading figure in the Neo-Kantian movement. He taught philosophy at Freiburg and is best known for applying Kantian philosophy to problems in the social sciences in a work that focused on the relationship between philosophy and history. In 1877, Windelband went to Freiburg where he began working on the problem of the connection between philosophy and culture. At the time, many believed the historical description of society was impossible because history was neither a scientific discipline nor a science of laws. Windelband set himself the task of outlining a philosophic framework in terms of which historical investigation could be scientific and, in this, he attempted to liberate the concept of method from the natural sciences.

---

192 L. W. Beck, 'Neo-Kantianism,' *The Encyclopedia of Philosophy,* Vol. 5, pp. 468–473.

193 See Thomas E. Willey, *Back to Kant: The Revival of Kantianism in German Social and Historical Thought 1860–1914*, Detroit: Wayne State University Press, 1978.

194 See H. S. Hughes, *Consciousness and Society: The Reorientation of European Social Thought 1890–1930,* New York: Vintage Books, 1958.

Windelband turned to Kant's writings to establish a philosophical justification for the social and historical sciences. The issue for Windelband was could historical investigation make a valid claim to obtaining objective knowledge? In reading Kant's works, Windelband found that while Kant had explicitly laid out the steps for the natural sciences to secure valid knowledge, he had excluded the historical and ethical dimension of human action from the sphere of legitimate knowledge. Windelband, however, believed that the historical and ethical dimension of human action should be the subject of social and historical investigation.[195]

Windelband reasoned that it would be of central significance to devise a theory of knowledge that was able to make valid claims about the existence of society and history that would, at the same time, withstand criticism from the natural sciences. Windelband had several issues to confront, however. First, by 1870, Hegel's idealist theory of history had been criticized and even discredited for its distinctly speculative theoretical stance. In addition, Hegel's method implied a split between the abstract sphere of the 'spirit' in history and the concrete factual world of historical observation. Windelband knew that in separating the sphere of the spirit from the world of concrete reality, idealist philosophy had abandoned any hope of explaining perceptible historical facts. This meant that the formulation of any causal laws of history would be impossible. In rejecting Hegel's historical methods as speculative and intuitive, Windelband returned to Kant to find a scientific justification for the historical sciences. But in returning to Kant, Windelband found that Kant had excluded history and human ethical pursuits from the sphere of valid knowledge, and that he had assigned historical fact to the realm of belief. Windelband argued that Kant had erred in excluding human action from the domain of factual knowledge and he reasoned that if Kant's exclusion of human action was valid, only the natural sciences would be the bearers of legitimate factual knowledge.

Windelband, then, went on to argue that the natural and social sciences were thus separate and distinct in terms of the type of knowledge which they sought to investigate. From this simple starting point, he set out to produce a synthesis between Kant's world of knowledge and the world of belief. In 1894, Windelband gave an address at the University of Strasburg where, for the first time, he outlined a viable methodological distinction between the methodology of the natural and social sciences. Some commentators viewed the speech as a key point of departure in the debate on knowledge because it amounted to 'a declaration of war against positivism' and scientific methodology.[196]

Windelband took the position that the natural and social sciences constitute, in fact, two different forms of knowledge and that both types of knowledge simply described different levels of reality. In the first type, Windelband argued, there is knowledge of facts and of the observable world in which causes and laws can be

---

195 Willey, *Back to Kant,* p. 26–28.
196 Stuart Hughes, *Consciousness and Society,* p. 47.

found in concrete reality. This level of reality belongs in the realm of the natural sciences. In the second type, Windelband reasoned, there is knowledge of human values and ethics, and this implies knowledge of an ethical realm consisting of the products of human culture, including the pursuits of actors and the judgments which they make in relation to the social world in which they live and act. This level of reality, according to Windelband, belonged to the domain of the historical and social sciences, not the domain natural sciences.

Windelband went on to reason that in the first domain of knowledge, judgments about the world are always in relation to factual states and to observation methods; whereas in the second sphere of knowledge, judgments are always about those objects which are not directly subject to observation such as human values, motives, purposes, morality and ethical pursuits etc.[197] History and the social sciences, argued Windelband, are therefore bodies of knowledge which concern themselves with the latter realm of objects that relate to the sphere of human values and that these values constitute the proper subject matter of the social and historical sciences and that they have universal validity in terms of the study of culture and civilization. In claiming this, Windelband made the leap from the methods of the natural sciences simply by stating that the social sciences study the realm of values, not the realm of facts and that the realm of values is concerned not with facts so much as with norms of conduct and with social and historical action.[198] While the natural sciences investigate concrete facts that are related to the physical world which are unchanging, the social sciences investigate norms or standards of conduct which may change from society to society depending on what ends are valued and pursued by historical actors.

Subsequently, Windelband focused his attention on the question of method. He thought that the scientific disciplines are distinct from the social and historical sciences, not because of their different subject matters, but because of their different methodologies. Essentially, he reasoned that there were two kinds of methodological approaches which were distinct from each other. First is the natural sciences which aims at the production of general laws and the explanation of events by observation and by deductive methods. Since in this case the aim is to show that empirical reality conforms to the assumptions which theory makes about the structure of the physical world, theory looks for confirmation in reality and thus believes that reality conforms to it. This, said Windelband, leads to what he called the generalizing tendency in the sciences where the search for commonalities in the concrete world tends to overlook what is individual and unique about particular events.[199]

Second is the methodology of the historical and social sciences, whose aim is to focus on individual events – the decline of feudalism, the development of capitalism – in order to determine their causes and their motivations by putting together a

---

197 Ibid.
198 Beck, 'Neo-Kantianism,' p. 470.
199 Willey, *Back to Kant,* p. 154.

picture of what took place historically. In this case, Windelband believed that the historical and social sciences must adopt methods which are inductive; that is, based on observation and information gathered about the event after which concepts and theories are formed to explain the event. Windelband thought that the natural sciences were thus 'nomothetic' or law-giving in their methods and orientations and that this, he thought, made them generalizing in the way they treat reality.[200] The historical sciences, by contrast, are 'ideographic' in their orientation; that is, they assemble information about events in order to arrive at a picture of the whole. The nomothetic sciences, Windelband went on to reason, aim at constructing general laws and explain events in the outer world by identifying these events as examples of laws; whereas the idiographic sciences look at the individual event to arrive at a general pattern. Windelband went on to argue that any given object could, in fact, be studied by either of these approaches and took the position that a truer picture of the world could be obtained by using both kinds of methods. 'Law and individual event,' he argued, 'remain together as the ultimate incommensurable limit of our representation of the world.'[201] This was equivalent to stating that both general and individual criteria constitute acceptable procedures for the social and historical sciences.

As a result of Windelband's work, two essential directions emerged from the Neo-Kantian tradition of reasoning. First, it presented a challenge to the authority of empirical observation in the sciences by showing that human perception of the world involved judgment rather than mere sensation of what was observable. On this view, knowledge was not the product of a straightforward observational encounter with the natural world, but was rather always preceded by human judgment which involved interpretation each time it encountered the world. Second, it rejected the scientific postulate that human social action could be reduced to mechanistic motives of utility by asserting that human judgments and evaluations always came before acts of human utility. This showed that human beings always act on their values and their judgments before they act on motives of utility.[202]

Heinrich Rickert and the Theory of Knowledge in the Social and Historical Sciences

A second major contribution to the debate between the natural and social sciences was the work of Heinrich Rickert, a student of Windelband and a contemporary of Max Weber. Rickert was born in Danzig in 1863, and taught at Freiburg where he developed a friendship with Weber. By 1896, Rickert replaced Windelband at Heidelberg, and it was there that Rickert made some of his most important contributions. He is best known for devising a method for making valid judgments about society and history in respect to social science knowledge. But, where Windelband

---

200 Beck, 'Neo-Kantianism,' p. 470.
201 Ibid.
202 Willey, *Back to Kant,* pp. 154–7.

had focused on the question of the different methodologies between the natural and social sciences, Rickert concentrated on subject matter and method. Rickert believed that the natural and social sciences differed on at least four separate and distinct fronts. First, he thought that they differed in terms of the theory of knowledge which they took up in relation to outside world. Second, he believed that there were differences in the way the natural and social sciences conceptualized specific events in the world and how they described these events. Third, he thought there were key differences in the way they formed concepts that were descriptive of reality; and fourth, he thought that they were different in the views they held about the role played by human values in social action, and to the acceptance of the 'sphere of values' as a viable subject matter for the social sciences.

In 1896 Rickert published a central work on the theory of knowledge in the social and historical sciences entitled *The Limits of Concept Formation in the Natural Sciences*. In it, he put forward a theory of knowledge that was valid on both logical and methodological grounds. He began initially by looking at how the natural sciences understood their relationship to empirical reality, and then looked at the theory of knowledge it had taken up in respect to the outer world. He assumed that the natural sciences generally took the view that knowledge was the result of a straightforward observational encounter with the natural world and that, from this perspective, knowledge was seen to be the accumulation of facts drawn from the physical world. Rickert, however, thought that this was incomplete in several respects. First, he believed that the natural sciences had an incorrect understanding of the procedures used to make sense of the empirical world. While it was widely held that the natural sciences obtained knowledge from the empirical world simply by forming opinions and drawing factual conclusions by observation, Rickert took the view that observation was a form of 'judgment' and this placed judgment before knowing and, therefore, before observation. In addition to this, it meant that observation could not take place independent of human judgment.[203]

In substance, Rickert had assumed that the act of judgment was, in effect, prior to the act of knowing, and this theoretically became central as far as Rickert's reasoning was concerned because he could claim that physical reality had substance only through the act of human judgment rather than through mere observation. This, of course, had the effect of diminishing the authority of observation in the acquisition of facts since, according to Rickert, observation was nothing more than human judgment operating in the visible world. Under these circumstances, observation was no longer the straightforward experience of the object in the outer world, but rather it was the simple operation of human judgment acting on the object. By making judgment prior to knowing, Rickert was able to claim that knowing itself was a kind of valuing, and this gave knowledge and judgment a basis in the empirical world.

203 Heinrich Rickert, *Science and History: A Critique of Positive Epistemology,* Princeton: D. Van Nostrand, 1962. pp. 18–19.

Rickert's formula was: first we judge, and then we know.[204] From this perspective, Rickert put forward a theory of knowledge which held that objects exist in the external world only through the human act of judging and valuing. This led to the view that facts themselves were things represented by judgment and thus involved interpretation of some kind.

Rickert went on to argue that the characteristics of history and reality were thus made up of human valuing and judging. He asserted that since the elements of reality comprising human judgment cannot ever be grasped by the generalizing law-giving perspective of the natural sciences, a new method had to be devised to capture how the human act of knowing was possible in relation to the social sciences. From this perspective, Rickert argued that history rather than physics was the true science of reality.[205]

After devising a theory of knowledge in terms of which the historical and social sciences could make valid claims about history and society, Rickert went on to look for a justification for the study of historical and social subject matter. In this context, he began to focus on the distinction between the natural and social sciences regarding their methodological approach to subject matter. He took the view that whereas the natural sciences dealt with subject matters whose events were recurring in nature and could be captured by laws, the social sciences tended to explain what he called 'individual non-recurring events.'[206] Rickert's distinction between 'lawfully recurring nature' and 'individualistic events,' identified something fundamental about the methods used to explain concrete reality by the natural and social sciences. Rickert stated that the natural sciences explain empirical world by what he called a 'generalizing' methodology in contrast to an 'individualizing' methodology of the historical and social sciences. To completely understand his distinction, it will be helpful if we look briefly at Rickert's conception of empirical reality.

Rickert thought that the natural sciences were 'generalizing' in their methodology because the nature of empirical reality was so inherently infinite and extensive in its scope that it could not be grasped or 'known' in its entirety by any science.[207] He went on to maintain that in order to overcome the problem related to the scale of the empirical world, the natural sciences had do two things: first, they had to generalize by essentially focusing away from the mass of particulars in order to concentrate on 'wholes,' and in doing so they looked for common properties among individual events. Second, they had to employ concepts in order to deal with large parts of the empirical world, and in doing so they essentially brought as many particulars and details as possible under one precise descriptive term. Empirical reality, according to Rickert, was thus dealt with by what he called the process of 'summary activity' in which traits common to objects were found and captured by procedures called concepts.[208]

204 Willey, *Back to Kant*, p. 143.
205 Robert Anchor, 'Heinrich Rickert' *The Encyclopedia of Philosophy*, Vol. 7, pp. 192–4.
206 Ibid.
207 H.H. Bruun, *Science, Values and Politics in Max Weber's Methodology*, Copenhagen: Munksgaard, 1972, p. 85.
208 Bruun, *Science, Values, and Politics*, p. 85.

This process, Rickert went on to say was essentially abstracting in that it classified individual objects under broad conceptual categories which tended to abstract all the separate properties of the objective world of nature. This meant that in the natural sciences only general features of the natural world are retrieved with the use of concepts and that as a consequence, individual events are eliminated altogether. Rickert then argued that these concepts are then related to a framework of regularities which yield only general laws of nature that are without reference to particulars.[209] In this respect, the natural sciences can therefore be characterized as an infinitely extended process of abstraction that tends to overlook the separate elements of individual events. From this perspective, therefore, one of the major limitations of the methodology of the natural sciences is that it tends to over generalize, and in doing so it overlooks the existence of individual elements which are part of concrete reality. In showing that the natural sciences depend on what he called a generalizing methodology, Rickert was able to draw attention to a central deficiency in the scientific method.

On another front, Rickert looked at the nature of concept formation in both the natural and social sciences. He maintained that each of the sciences employs concepts in different ways and this causes them to relate to reality differently.[210] In order to understand Rickert's meaning, it will be useful to look at the nature of concepts and concept formation in the sciences. Concepts, first and foremost, are the means by which all the sciences surmount the extensive all encompassing nature of material reality. Material reality cannot simply be dealt with except by organizing segments of it in terms of concepts which narrow down the subject matter in question. But in the natural sciences, concepts are fundamentally reductive of empirical reality and in the last instance completely disqualify 'the element of individuality and can in fact be said to lead away from empirical reality' itself.[211] Concepts do this to the extent that they search for common features among individual elements, and constantly relate individual events to a framework of generality. Thus, while concepts form material reality into coherent wholes so that they can be grasped by the mind, they also form conceptions of reality and in this sense represent or characterize it in some way.[212] In the social sciences, by contrast, concept formation attempts to relate as closely as possible to the reality being described and it does this, according to Rickert, by selecting individual events situated in a larger reality. The selection of these individual events are then linked to other elements of concrete reality and as this process takes place, it appropriates 'elements' of the event within the complex whole rather than representing reality as such. Eventually, this led to the fact vs value controversy in the natural and social sciences.

---

209 Bruun, *Science, Values and Politics,* p. 86.
210 Rickert, *The Limits of Concept Formation in the Natural Sciences,* pp. 23–9.
211 Ibid.
212 Burger, *Max Weber's Theory of Concept Formation,* p. 19.

Theories of Knowledge in the Natural and Social Sciences: Facts vs Values

After developing a theory of knowledge, Rickert turned his attention to showing that history qualifies as a science which can claim objective knowledge of reality. Up until that time, many believed that history had no claim to attaining valid knowledge of the material world because it provided no account of the laws of historical development. According to this view, if laws cannot be found by historical methods it can only mean that the foundations of its logic and methodological technique are unsettled, and that the historical sciences have no claim to reliable or valid knowledge.[213] Rickert, then, set out to solve the problem of objective knowledge in the social and historical sciences by looking at the question of what social science knowledge was and how it was structured. In the natural sciences, Rickert argued, knowledge seemed to be the result of a straightforward encounter with the external world in the search for facts and factual knowledge. Rickert, however, doubted this and argued that knowledge was not the direct grasp or apprehension of facts in the natural world, but was rather only developed by means of concepts which select and abstract individual features of things from the material world.[214] According to this view, the natural sciences form concepts by abstracting the larger totality and in doing so eliminate individual features of things under investigation. This method of abstraction, said Rickert, underlies the law-giving characteristics of the natural sciences.

In addition to this, Rickert went on to argue that in the natural sciences the use of concepts shape reality by selecting only certain elements of the empirical world. By selecting only some aspects of reality, Rickert believed that the work of scientific knowledge was not so much the 'grasp of external reality,' as much as it is making 'judgments' about the nature of the things and objects in the world. One of Rickert's insights was that scientific observation was in fact supplemented by 'judgment' and that the sciences were 'concept forming' in nature rather than being observational. According to Rickert's theory of knowledge, this meant that the natural sciences do not directly 'grasp' reality because they must conceptualize it by looking for common elements. On this view, the natural sciences thus produce a picture of reality which is made up of such simple elements that the empirical concreteness of the world disappears from experience. According to Rickert, the sciences have therefore oversimplified concrete reality, so much so that an experience of it is not included as part of the description. As far as he was concerned, human experience cannot be lived out in a generalized way, since everything about human history and society is specific and particular. Rickert therefore went on to reason that a scientific description of history and society would have no interest to human beings because it would contain no specific human experience. He reasoned, therefore, that what gives historical and social reality its

---

213 Ibid., p. 21.
214 Rickert, *Science and History*, pp. 27–31.

interest is individual particulars and individual experience, and he thought that our relation to this 'experience' was through what he called human 'values.'

Rickert's discussion of the role of values in the description of society drew attention to one of the key differences between the natural and historical sciences. He found that whereas the natural sciences do not take the sphere of human values into account as a subject matter, the human and historical sciences always reflect the sphere of 'values' since he claimed that in their actions human beings always act on what they value. Human action, said Rickert, is therefore guided by practical values and standards which are the product of history, and this points up the fact that an individual living in society during a historical time and place is always 'value oriented' in some way. This was decisive because it made it clear that whereas the natural sciences search for facts and factual knowledge, the social sciences concern themselves with knowledge of 'values.' Furthermore, this value orientation referred to by Rickert always leads to 'judgments and evaluations' with respect to society and the world within which individuals act. Human beings, according to this view, act in relation to ends which they value and so human action is always shaped by values, according to Rickert. Because Rickert thought that things in the natural world do not act on the basis of values, the distinction between the subject matter of 'facts' and the subject matter of 'values' became central to understanding the precise subject matter differences between the social and natural sciences.

Rickert went on to reason that objects studied in the natural sciences are things which act in reference to the laws of nature; whereas the objects of the historical and social sciences are things which act in reference to valued social ends. Examples of these values, according to Rickert, are expressed in the laws human beings make and in the customs and practices that constitute the cycles of social life that are evident in our language, our economic practices, our art and our religious beliefs. Rickert went on to reason that social institutions in society embody these values in a major way and human beings recognize them and act in relation to ends which they value. From this position emerged a fundamental distinction between the 'sciences of value' and the 'sciences of fact'. In sciences of fact, values are irrelevant because they do not enter into the laws of nature or to the way things act in nature. In the social and historical sciences, however, there must be a concern for values since human beings live in society and engage in activities which compel them to act in reference to principles and standards which are valued. Hence, the products of their actions always reflect their values.[215]

Here, then, is the point: human beings are value-conferring by nature because they live in societies where values and standards are a basis of social action. Rickert thought that the products of nature, however, were thus devoid of values, whereas the products of human society are value-relevant; which is to say that they always embody values. Products of society and history, according to this view, are always unique because they

---

215 Burger, *Max Weber's Theory of Concept Formation*, pp. 36–37.

have been valued by conscious knowing subjects, by living and acting human beings. 'The presence or absence of values,' Rickert reasoned, 'must serve as a reliable criterion for distinguishing between two kinds of scientific objects' and two kinds of sciences.[216] The first set of objects are those belonging to the natural world and these exist independently of human agency and have a life of their own. A second set of objects, however, are the objects of the social and cultural sciences. These are produced directly by human agents acting in relation to valued ends, standards and beliefs. In contrast to the objective sciences, these objects belong to social world so far as they are produced by human beings acting on the basis of what is valued.

Controversy Over Methods in the Natural and Social Sciences: The *Methodenstreit of the 1880's* During the period in which Rickert was working on the problem of concept formation and the methods of the social and historical sciences, Weber began to turn his attention to resolving theoretical disputes in the social sciences and to responding to arguments which challenged the validity of the social sciences in terms of method. In order to completely understand the direction which Weber took during this period, it will be useful to turn our attention to the historical context of the controversy over methods called the *Methodenstreit*.[217] Methodenstreit, is a German term referring to the methodological controversy which emerged out of the framework of German social thought in the last quarter of the nineteenth century.[218] The central issues in the controversy originated in the conflict over which methods were appropriate in the social sciences and this, as we stated earlier, involved three central points of disagreement. First, it involved questions of subject matter in relation to whether values would be dominant over facts; second, it involved a choice in the type of investigative methods to be pursued in the social sciences, and third, it involved decisions about what the main purpose and aim of the social sciences would be.[219]

First and foremost, the controversy over methods began over a dispute in economics. The dispute centered on whether historical economics could, in fact, be considered a valid science of society. The dispute reached its high point when Gustav Schmoller, the foremost proponent of the historical school of economics, reviewed a work by Carl Menger, the leading advocate of the classical school.[220] Menger had asserted that if economics was to be a science its purpose would have to be to discover laws of society, and to do this it

216 Heinrich Rickert, *Science and History: A Critique of Positive Epistemology,* Princeton: D. Van Nostrand, 1962, pp. 18–19.

217 For a discussion of the *Methodenstreit* of the 1880s see Thomas Burger, *Max Weber's Theory of Concept Formation: History, Laws and Ideal Types,* Durham: Duke University Press, 1987, pp. 140–153.

218 For a good general discussion of the *Methodenstreit* see Dirk Kasler, *Max Weber: An Introduction to his Life and Work,* Chicago: University Chicago Press, 1988, pp. 174–196; and Thomas Burger, *Max Weber's Theory of Concept Formation: History, Laws and Ideal Types,* Durham: Duke University, 1987, pp. 140–153.

219 Stuart Hughes, *Consciousness and Society: The Reorientation of European Social Thought 1890–1930,* New York: Vintage Books, 1958, pp. 296–314.

220 H. Stuart Hughes, *Consciousness and Society,* pp. 303–4; Toby E. Huff, *Max Weber and the Methodology of the Social Sciences,* London: Transaction, 1984, pp. 27–42.

must be generalizing in its methodology, since only a generalizing science is able to draw conclusions about the laws governing economic behavior. For economics to be a science, according to this view, social life must be subject to laws and this meant that they had to use the methods of the natural sciences. Menger found support for his contention in the work of John Stuart Mill whose utilitarian outlook took the position that all human economic acts could be reduced to motives of utility and self interest. According to Menger, this meant that all human action was reducible to the simple motives of economic utility.

In his review of Menger's argument, Schmoller criticized Menger for being short-sighted in his view of human action and proceeded to call into question the philosophical foundations of scientific methodology itself.[221] Schmoller believed that a new method had to be devised for the social sciences which would take into account the historical character of social science subject matter. Along with other members of the historical school, Schmoller took the position that, because societies tend to develop in historical stages and are fundamentally different from one another in their social structure, a generalizing methodology in search of causal laws would not be able to take individual differences between societies into account, let alone capture the complex nature of social action represented in economic behavior.

Taking these issues into consideration, there are five key points of disagreement between the classical and historical schools. First, the historical school believed that the generalizing methodology of the natural sciences could not explain the complex character of economic interchange since it made no distinction between the natural and social world or between natural and social acts.[222] Second, Schmoller and his colleagues took the view that causal statements about social and historical acts were out of the question because the scientific method had not yet recognized that societies were products of human social action. Third, so far as a generalizing methodology looks for laws, it overlooks specific individual events related to society, politics and social action. Schmoller thought that because each society is unique, concepts must accommodate the individualizing character of human social action and the different social values which act as motives of social action. On the view that societies were the result of historical development, social action and economic conduct could only be grasped by a theory which understood that societies develop in relation to human agents acting on the basis of what is valued.[223] This put values and ethics into the picture since values were seen to be a product of human social action. Fourth, was the issue centering on the question of human motives. Menger's law-giving natural science position asserted that all human behavior was the same and could be reduced to the pursuit of self interest and utility. Eventually, this led to the view that all individual acts have as their basis economic motives of utility which can be studied by science. In response to this the historical school disagreed, stating that no single

221 *Hughes*, p. 30.
222 Ibid.
223 Bruun, *Science, Values, and Politics*, p. 85.

rational motive underlies human social action since it is bound up with various political, religious and social beliefs, many of which are irrational in nature and which originate from society and social history. The fifth issue separating the historical school from the classical tradition of economics was the view that because economics was an 'objective' science, its purpose was to search for underlying laws that were subject to observation. In direct opposition to this, the historical school asserted that because social and economic life involve human beings acting on the basis of what they value, economics was a science which had to take into account the 'subjective' basis of human values and the relation of values to the realm of ethical conduct in society. This forced the classical school to abandon the concept of 'economic utility' as the principal motive of all social action.

Weber's Contribution to the Methodological Controversy

While the methodological controversy in economics eventually diminished, Weber took up some of the issues raised by Menger and Schmoller in order to develop his own methodological position. Between 1903 and 1906, Weber wrote a series of methodological essays underlining problems in the debate. In his discussion, Weber attempted to outline the methodological foundations of the social sciences by showing that the social sciences were different from other disciplines that formed a part of the natural sciences. In outlining these differences, Weber took several important steps beyond others who had focused on the methodological controversy. First, he demonstrated that the search for law like regularities was not possible in the social sciences. Second, he showed that the subject matter studied by the social sciences had different characteristics which marked them off from the subject matter of the natural sciences and that these difference ruled out the possibility of establishing a natural science of society. Third, since Rickert had accepted the idea that human beings always act on what they value, Weber wanted to demonstrate that the subject matter of the social sciences was made up of individuals whose social action was based on values, and he wanted to see if the social sciences could take account of the system of values related to social action in society. This led Weber to assert that the social sciences must begin the process of understanding how values act as a basis of social action and to what extent this could be described. Fourth, Weber sought to demonstrate that in all the disciplines including the natural sciences the facts never speak for themselves, which is to say that they do not identify themselves, nor do they offer information on how the facts fit into the scheme of description, since this requires interpretation.[224] In Weber's view no science can be fundamentally neutral, nor can its observation language ever be theoretically independent of the way individuals interpret the subject matter that is to be studied.[225] Fifth, Weber went on to show that the social sciences must arrive at a methodology which encompasses

---

224 Guy Oakes, 'Introductory Essay,' *Roscher and Knies*, pp. 19–37
225 Ibid.

both general and individual aspects of historical reality, a procedure he referred to as the 'ideal type.'

In his methodological essays, Weber began to turn his attention to issues of subject matter in the social sciences. But in order to completely understand how Weber began to resolve some of the problems in the methodological controversy, we have to go back to Rickert and the concept used by him called 'value relevance.'[226] Essentially, Weber drew on Rickert's discussion of value relevance and therefore our understanding of the term hinges on Rickert's theory of knowledge in the historical and social sciences.

In contrast to the view held by the natural sciences, Rickert had shown that knowledge of the empirical world does not derive from observation and sense perception because 'judgment' always occurs before the act of observation. Rickert therefore reasoned that because judgment comes before knowing, judgment itself is a form of selection and this meant that knowing itself was a kind of valuing. It followed from this that knowledge itself had its basis in human values. If, as Rickert reasoned, all knowing had a basis in values and values derive from the social historical context, then our interest in and knowledge of historical and political acts must derive from our relation to values and what we value. If this was true, what was the reasoning behind Rickert's assertion?

In his theory of knowledge, Rickert treated as a problem the idea that empirical reality presents itself as an 'infinite multiplicity' of events and objects.[227] If there is to be knowledge of the empirical world, he said, then the sheer scope and expanse of the outside world has to be overcome in some way. In the natural sciences, according to Rickert, the expanse of the natural world is surpassed by a process of selection which narrows empirical reality down to manageable elements. This process, Rickert thought, was carried out by means of concept formation, since concepts act in such as way as to frame empirical reality and 'reduce the mass of facts in the empirical world.'[228] 'Without concepts,' therefore, 'knowledge of the empirical world would not be possible'.[229] Rickert went on to reason that concept formation in the social and historical sciences was essential to descriptive activity since any judgment about reality was impossible without concepts.

Rickert went on to focus his attention on the process of selection and the criterion by which an historical event comes to the attention of the observer. He reasoned that when something is isolated for attention, this attention is not the property of the object, but must instead point to the observer's process of selection. Thus, according to Rickert, there are two main principles of selection.[230] The first concerns a criterion

---

226 Burger, *Max Weber's Theory of Concept Formation*, pp. 37–43.
227 Burger, Ibid., p. 21.
228 Ibid.
229 Rickert, quoted from Burger, *Max Weber's Theory of Concept Formation*, p. 21.
230 Burger, *Max Weber's Theory of Concept Formation*, p. 22.

of selection which searches for properties common to any subject matter. On this principle, what is essential are the common properties of the object, and subsequently what is individual is left out of analysis or set aside. The second principle of selection referred to by Rickert is a criterion which selects individual subject matter. This principle selects individual objects which are unique to the extent that they can be distinguished from other objects and have properties which are not common to other objects.

The first set of methods and principles of selection leads to 'general concepts' and is a practice common to the natural sciences. The second set of methods and principles leads to focus on 'individual events' which Weber thought was key to describing unique historical and social configurations such as capitalism, feudalism and the emergence of Protestant religious doctrine.[231] General concepts provide objective knowledge, whereas individual concepts provide knowledge of specific features of social and historical events. Since concept formation is a means by which objects are singled out from empirical reality, Rickert thought that the process of value relevance operates in both cases as the standard against which a selection is made. 'Every individual,' said Rickert, 'is guided by a conception of the world by which they separate everything existing into essential and inessential.'[232] Hence describing and observing is impossible without valuing what is of interest and, in this sense, selection always embodies values related to the act of selection.

Rickert went on to suggest that the objects of empirical reality must be of interest to us only because they are value relevant, not because they have intrinsic scientific merit. In fact, what interests us must be a part of the universal values of society, originating in society and the social context within which the individual lives with others in a social world. The point of Rickert's reasoning was that the means by which specific aspects of reality are brought to our attention has to do with the principle he called 'value relevance.' Rickert thought that the principle of value relevance comes into play when scientists use concepts, since it is by means of concepts that we are able to reduce the mass of facts in the empirical world to statements which describe it. Without concept formation, there is no understanding and thus concepts act as a means of separating the essential from the inessential and of describing aspects of reality. Hence the historical sciences are dependent upon the process of selection from empirical reality in order to arrive at valid historical subject matter.

As far as Rickert was concerned, the operation of selection was central to the investigative process. He thought that the criteria of selection in the natural and social sciences was essentially the same since each pursued aspects of empirical reality by separating out elements which were essential from those which were inessential. Considered in this light, an 'interest' always reflects its origin in the value framework of the society.

---

231 Ibid.
232 Rickert quoted from Burger, *Max Weber's Theory of Concept Formation*, p. 35.

As a result of his focus on values as a historical subject matter, Rickert's orientation to values became the center of his theory of history. Essentially, by the term 'value relation' Rickert was referring to the fact that individuals live their lives within the context of a historical age which is marked by an orientation to specific values. In the light of this, H.H. Bruun pointed out that 'a person who is really living is by definition value oriented in the sense that they are judging and evaluating the surrounding world. Thus defined, human beings cannot be interested solely in the general regularities of life, but must to a certain extent pay attention to things in their individual qualities and these individual qualities constitute reality as such.'[233] In this view, historians thus select material by means of a 'value relation'; that is, by means of a criteria of values which are in part based on their relation to a system of values in the wider society which they share in common with others. Simply stated, the 'value relation' refers to the idea that a certain subject matter is 'worthy of interest' on the basis of the scheme of values that are current in a society.[234] Using the criterion of value relevance, Rickert could claim that 'knowledge was not the grasp, so much as it was the construction of the object to be described.'[235] Viewed in these terms, the value relation became a form of constituting reality. This was important because it showed that the entire scope of the scientific method was governed by its relation to values.

Weber's Concept of the 'Ideal Type'

Weber first developed the concept of the 'ideal type' in a writing entitled 'Objectivity in the Social Sciences and Social Policy' which he published in 1905.[236] As a methodological concept the 'ideal type' was used by Weber as a technique to describe the comparative features of different societies by outlining their distinct social characteristics. He defined the ideal type as a 'conceptual pattern which brings together certain relationships and events of historical life into a complex' whole whose purpose is to describe historical societies by comparing their internal and external characteristics.[237]

While Weber identified different categories of ideal types, he thought that the principal form were those he called 'historical ideal types.' These can be described as ideal types that select general concepts that are common to a wide range of different social characteristics that exist among historical societies. In this case, historical ideal types begin by selecting features of different societies on the basis of their common characteristics, and employ a criterion of selection of general concepts 'which are precisely definable' and which may include concepts such as Protestantism, feudalism

---

233 H.H. Bruun, *Science, Values and Politics in Max Weber's Methodology*, pp. 88–89.
234 Ibid.
235 Willey, *Back To Kant*, p. 37.
236 Max Weber, 'Objectivity in Social Sciences and Social Policy,' in E.A. Shils and H.A. Finch (eds.) *The Methodology of the Social Sciences* New York: The Free Press, 1949, pp. 50–112.
237 "Objectivity," p. 90.

and capitalism.[238] In this case, the ideal type is designed to capture features of empirical reality by arriving at what Weber refers to as the 'analytical accentuation' of certain aspects of social historical reality. For example, when we attempt to understand the development of a city economy, said Weber, we compare it with a craft based economy, and when we engage in these sorts of ideal type comparisons we 'construct the concept of a city economy' and thus get closer to it.[239]

In this context, an ideal type is thus a 'picture of events' which approximates the reality of a given society under certain conditions of its organization.[240] For example, if once again we take the concept of a 'city economy' and construct a type, the general concept of 'city economy' lends itself to type construction by an extension of its traits and social characteristics. Under these circumstances, the essential traits of a city economy may include such elements as a rational market, a system of law based on statutes, the decline of magic and a system of private property. Other related traits may include the concept of a citizen, a municipal organization and a bureaucracy with political office holders. All this may presuppose a municipal environment with a civil life which is distinctive of a 'city economy' in Western society, and this stands in contrast to the city economy of the Greek city states.[241]

While in this case a 'city economy' has been abstracted from concrete reality, Weber thought that it is only possible to formulate the concept of a city economy by isolating what is essential from what is inessential. The ideal type, therefore, does not serve as a description of concrete historical reality, but simply as a construct used to elucidate the features of historical reality. This is carried out, Weber thought, by extracting essential 'traits' or characteristics which elaborate concepts by comparing them with the concrete features of the social structure. These traits are then compared to an ideal picture of social reality, and from this a workable type is formed. Finally, a type is created by providing a 'one sided accentuation of one or more points of view and by the synthesis of a great many diffuse, discrete, concrete individual characteristics arranged into a unified analytical construct.'[242] When applied to reality, said Weber, ideal types are useful in research and in social and historical description because they function by arranging what initially were indistinct traits into a consistent construct by an elucidation of their essential elements.

Another category of ideal types which Weber looked at are those which can be used to form what he called an 'ideal picture of the shift' that takes place in society by reason of certain historical factors.[243] This is carried out, said Weber, by introducing a 'developmental sequence' into an ideal type in order to capture the shift taking

---

238 Weber, 'Objectivity,' p. 92.
239 Weber, 'Objectivity,' p. 90.
240 Ibid.
241 *General Economic History,* p. 238.
242 'Objectivity,' p. 90.
243 'Objectivity,' p. 101.

place and the conditions leading to its development. Developmental ideal types, in Weber's view, lead in the direction of making theoretical conclusions about the prevailing conditions of society that lead to change. Examples of this can be found in Weber's comparison of the shift taking place in European societies from a system of administration by notables to a modern system of bureaucratic administration. This type of comparison is constructed, according to Weber, by forming the general concept of administration by notables, and by isolating common elements and characteristics of it such as the means of legitimacy, the degree of religious traditionalism and the characteristics of a system of traditional law. The shift from a system of decision making by notables to decision making based on bureaucracy, said Weber, may be conditioned by factors such as the development of legal authority, the dominance of formal rationality, the decline of magic, the development of a hierarchy of offices and decision makers, and the degree of reliance on written documentation and record keeping. All this presupposes the 'rationalization of the conduct of life,' and the adherence to patterns of social action oriented to administration based on bureaucracy. In this case, the ideal type offers a 'picture of the shift' from a patriarchal form of administration to a modern bureaucratic type of administration.[244]

A second criterion of ideal types is the tendency to build up a model of empirical reality in contrast to simply describing it. Along these lines, the most common ideal types are economic ideal types, according to Weber. These function to differentiate societies in terms of their economic organization by engaging in a comparison of the main characteristics associated with historical types of economies, such as a feudal economy in comparison with an industrial economy.[245] Weber argued that to illustrate the general concept of a capitalist economy, for instance, certain characteristics had to be included such as a market system, the form of rationality, the type of legal order and the concept of the citizen as a basis of social action. These different elements, according to Weber, are added progressively by selecting what is essential from what is inessential and by comparing these elements against other economies in different historical contexts.

According to Weber, the ideal type thus serves several distinct purposes. First, it can be used to make judgments about whether the type of society referred to in concrete reality actually exists and to what extent its characteristics can be made clear and understandable.[246] Second, it is an indispensable tool for the purpose of a comparative analysis of different societies and for developing an understanding of their social and historical characteristics, and how these may change over time. Third, while an ideal type is not a description of reality, it can be used to assist in reducing ambiguity about empirical reality by providing the means to foster adequate descriptions of it.[247] Fourth, as a methodology the ideal type leads to the formation of

---

244 Ibid.
245 Weber, 'Objectivity,' p. 101.
246 Ibid., p. 90.
247 Ibid.

new concepts about the social and economic organization of societies by inviting historical comparisons of given social types that are within the conceptual boundaries of history and reality.

Weber's Theory of Social Action

Weber's theory of social action follows directly from his discussion of the problem of methods in the social sciences. He first developed a theory of social action in *Economy and Society* between 1911 and 1920. Historically, the term 'social action' derives from the body of Weber's writings which were concerned with developing a theory of society that was consistent with making judgments about the decisions individuals make in their actions with others in a social environment. Because Weber's theory of social action was in part a product of the controversy over subject matter in the social sciences, it will be useful to summarize some of the views that led him to take the direction he did in pursuing what he called an 'interpretive theory of social action.' Following the disagreements which Weber had over issues of subject matter during the methodological controversy, he was persuaded that a theory of society had to take a new direction, and he began to pursue this in the opening pages of *Economy and Society* where he stated that 'sociology is a science concerning itself with the interpretive understanding of human social action'.[248]

Weber began to take a position on an interpretive theory of social action by 1903 after taking the view that the social sciences were different from the sciences which studied the objective world of outside nature. His discussion of these issues took several different directions. First, he maintained that the subject matters of the natural and social sciences were completely different. He thought that the natural sciences studied objects and events in the outer world, while the social sciences studied human social action within society. The distinction between the two sciences had the immediate effect of demarcating the existence of two different subject matters, one concerned with 'objective events' in the outside world, the other with 'subjective events' in the inner states of the actor. Second, he argued that by necessity each of the sciences sought to obtain different kinds of knowledge. In the natural sciences, knowledge is of the external world which can be explained in terms of general laws, while in the social sciences knowledge must be of the 'internal or subjective states of individuals' in that human beings have an 'inner nature' that must be understood in order to explain outward events that lead to their social actions in the world. Third, Weber thought that observation and investigation in the natural and social sciences take up completely different orientations and attitudes to their subject matter. In the natural sciences, it is sufficient to observe events in the natural world and to report factual relationships between things observed, whereas in the social sciences investigation must go beyond

---

248 Weber, *Economy and Society*, p. 4.

observation to look at how individuals act on their understanding and how this 'understanding' may be related to their social action in society.[249]

Between 1903 and 1907, Weber wrote several essays on methodological issues in which he discussed problems related to founding a theory of social action. While the essays were originally written as critical reviews of the ongoing debate between the natural and social sciences on the question of method, they became a theoretical justification for the pursuit of a theory of meaningful social action. In two of the essays entitled *Rocher and Knies* and *Critique of Stammler*, Weber argued that the objective sciences of the outer world of nature had failed to treat the problem of what he had referred to as 'human inner understanding' and, in the latter part of the argument, he claimed that the social sciences were concerned essentially with the 'inner states' of actors in contrast to the sciences of objective fact which were concerned with the 'outer states' of the natural world.[250] The distinction was central, according to Weber, because it meant that the social sciences 'have as their object those things which in principle are different from the objects of the sciences like physics, chemistry and biology.'[251] That is, whereas the subject matter of the natural sciences is devoid of 'understanding,' Weber believed that what sets the subject matter of social science apart, is that human beings have 'inner states' in terms of which they 'understand' the events of the outer world in which they come to act. Because of this 'understanding,' Weber reasoned, 'human conduct is in principle' distinct from 'physical events' in the outer world because the physical behavior of things in nature such as the action of the earth around the sun does not involve understanding, and is thus devoid of it.[252] The distinction referred specifically to the fact that human individuals 'understand' the actions of others by interpreting them, and that they depend on this understanding in order to act. Weber concluded that they therefore must interpret the actions of others before they can decide how to act. This, Weber thought, suggests that their actions involve 'meaningful interpretations' of the acts of others they are responding to, whereas the action of physical objects such as the movement of the earth around the sun is not based on an 'understanding' of the act of rotation. Weber thus used the term 'understanding' to identify the central subject matter of human social acts.

Second, after making the distinction between the subjective sciences which concern themselves with human conduct and the inner subjective states of individuals in contrast to the objective sciences that concern themselves with the outer world, Weber proceeded to draw on Rickert's distinction stating that the social sciences must take for their subject matter the world of meaningful values since human conduct is

---

249 The most developed discussion of Weber's theory of social action can be found in *Economy and Society*, pp. 3–26.

250 Weber, *Roscher and Knies: The Logical Problems of Historical Economics*, New York: The Free Press, 1975, pp. 125–143.

251 Ibid.

252 Weber, *Roscher and Kneis*, p. 125.

always value relevant, or relevant to values. Since Rickert had argued that the sciences are best distinguished from one another by reference to 'values' then, in this context, society is the product of what is produced by human beings acting according to values and valued ends. Thus whatever is produced in society by human action is the result of 'values attaching to it.'[253] According to Rickert, every product of society – history, language, art, religion – embodies some value recognized by human actors as having value attached to it. As far as the objective sciences are concerned, however, whatever is a product of nature is without regard to values or, as Rickert said, is devoid of values. As far as Rickert was concerned, then, the presence or absence of values served as a reliable criterion for distinguishing between the two kinds of objects: those objects that are without reference to values, and those objects that are recognized by the values attaching to them.

After showing that social acts were based on interpretive understanding and that human conduct is always the result of values being attached to it, Weber drew the conclusion that any form of investigation which reduces human action to its simple external characteristics would be meaningless since it would not capture the tendency of human interpretive understanding. He pointed out that 'if human conduct is interpreted by using the methods of the objective sciences, this conduct would be no different from the conduct of a boulder falling from a cliff,' since the boulder is devoid of any understanding.[254] Weber went on to point out that while in the objective sciences an account of an event is complete when the facts pertaining to the event in the outer world are linked to the laws or forces which determine it, in the social sciences an account of human conduct is only complete when 'we have knowledge of the nexus into which understandable human action fits, a nexus which is conceived as a determinant of the conduct in question.'[255]

While this may be difficult to grasp, Weber's meaning here is reasonably straightforward. What he means to point out is that, whereas in the natural world objects act without reference to interpretation or understanding, human beings can only act in the world after having interpreted the acts of others to whom they are responding. As far as Weber is concerned, this 'interpretation' and 'understanding' is a necessary condition of human conduct as opposed to the conduct of things in nature which do not act on their understanding or interpretation. In Weber's view, therefore, individual 'interpretation' and 'understanding' is thus the 'nexus' which acts as the determinant of the conduct in question.

Following this, Weber went on to introduce four concepts in order to elucidate the relationship between human conduct and subjective understanding. These were the concepts of understanding or *Verstehen*; the concept of interpretive understanding; the concept of subjective meaning; and the concept of social action. What followed was a theory of social action whose central thesis was that 'social action' takes place

253 Heinrich Rickert, *Science and History*, Toronto: D Van Nostrand, 1962, pp. 18–22.
254 Ibid.
255 Weber, *Roscher and Knies*, p. 142.

only 'when the acting individual attaches a subjective meaning to the act and when the act takes account of the behavior of others and is thereby oriented in its course.'[256]

Central to this discussion is the concept of *Verstehen*. The term *Verstehen* literally translates as 'human understanding,' and Weber used it to signify what he thought was unique about the subject matter of the social sciences. In contrast to the sciences of the objective world, the social sciences are concerned with the actions of human beings who make judgments and evaluations which lead them to understand and interpret their environments. According to Weber, this meant that human actors possess 'understanding' in contrast to the objects of the physical sciences which are devoid of understanding. Since the subject matter of the natural sciences do not possess 'understanding,' it therefore stands to reason that the methods of the natural sciences must be disqualified or ruled out as adequate to the study of human social action.[257] The basic presupposition being put forward here is that the objects of the physical sciences do not possess 'understanding'; only human beings make judgments and evaluations which lead them to act on their understanding. This led Weber to assert that social acts are identified not by their external characteristics like the objects of the physical sciences, but by their dependence on 'understanding' or *Verstehen*.

Rickert, like Weber, had distinguished between two kinds of scientific objects: those that are identified by the values attaching to it, and those that are identified as being devoid of values. As to the sciences that deal with manifestations of human activity and society, the presence of values serves as a reliable guide because it focuses on actions produced by individuals acting according to valued ends and the 'values attaching to objects such as religion, art, science, law, literature and language.'[258] In contrast to this, the objective sciences obtain knowledge related to facts in the outer world that are unrelated to values. Thus, according to Rickert, values always attach to cultural objects, whereas the objective sciences are devoid of values. Weber's theory of social action, therefore, may be defined as the body of social theory devised by him in order to make valid judgments about the 'inner subjective states' of individual actors in their social actions. By 'inner subjective states,' Weber is referring to the capacity of the actor to act on their interpretations and judgments, and to exercise 'rational' choice by carrying out their actions with a view to realizing their choices in the world. According to Weber, the decision to act in a certain way is always the product of the actors' values and interpretive judgments within a given society. This meant that 'interpretation and understanding' always necessarily precedes social action since individuals only act *after* they make their interpretations and judgments. Also, since Rickert had argued that values always attach to objects of culture, at the most fundamental level Weber believed that social action involved

---

256 Ibid.

257 Guy Oakes, 'The Verstehen Thesis and the Foundations of Max Weber's Methodology,' *History and Theory*, 16, 1977, 11–29.

258 Rickert, *Science and History*, p. 20.

actors in the process of attaching 'meanings' to the given factual states in the outer world. He reasoned that because these meanings and interpretive judgments do not already come 'attached' to the factual states in the outer world, they must be products of the meaning states of actors who assign meanings to things in the world.

Two Types of Understanding: Weber's Interpretive Theory of Action

A second concept in Weber's theory of social action is 'interpretive understanding.' In order to elucidate the meaning of this term, Weber made the distinction between two types of understanding that are possible in social action; one referred to as 'direct understanding,' the other as 'interpretive understanding.'[259] Weber defined direct understanding as the comprehension of a social action by virtue of the specific meaning that is attached to the act by focusing on what is going on in the sequence of events involved in the act. A home run, for instance, can be directly understood by the sequence of physical occurrences involved in hitting the ball, which is then followed by the tour of bases. In this instance, the meaning of an act is discernible from 'direct observation' of the physical characteristics of the act.[260] Weber often used the formula $2 \times 2 = 4$ to illustrate the meaning of direct understanding. This, said Weber, involves direct understanding 'when we hear or read it' since the meaning of the action follows directly from the sequences of steps enacted in a series.[261] Another example used by Weber is the example of chopping wood and an outburst of anger. These actions, said Weber, can be grasped by their visible characteristics which we come to understand through direct observation of the sequence of actions that occurred.

In contrast to this is explanatory understanding. This is distinct from direct understanding by the fact that the 'meaning' of an act is understood only by placing the action in a complex of meaning and by attaching a motive to the act. Explanatory understanding is thus characterized by the fact that it places an act within a context, and assigns a motive to it based on the context or situation in which it occurs. For example, inferring from a person's outer behavior that they are unhappy is an example of explanatory understanding because it 'adds' something to the physical act that provides a motive to the act by placing it in a context of meaning, e.g, a person is unhappy because of a prior disappointment. In this case, the interpretive addition that the actor attaches to what is visibly observed constitutes interpretive understanding. While explanatory understanding apprehends an action by its physical characteristics, what makes it different from direct understanding is the actor's attempt to lodge the action within a complex of meaning in order to provide a motive. This, Weber reasoned, involves interpretive activity which always adds something to the visible characteristics of the act. Thus, whereas direct understanding grasps the physical characteristics of an act occurring in the outer world, motive understanding constructs

---

259 *Economy and Society,* pp. 8–12.
260 Ibid.
261 Ibid.

reasons, assigns motives and engages in interpretive activity. According to Weber, motive understanding, in contrast to direct understanding, differs by virtue of the fact that the actor is able to 'place the act' within a context of motivation, and to assign a meaning to it on the basis of interpretation.[262]

In as much as explanatory understanding is a form of social action which engages in making judgments and assigning motives to acts, Weber believed that it takes place within the 'inner subjective state' of the actor and not, therefore, in the objective world. Weber called this 'subjective meaning' in order to denote that it occurs in the actor's 'cognitions' and is therefore out of range of the observation of others. While direct understanding is based on the comprehension of an act by a pattern of external events, interpretive understanding makes assumptions about the inner states of the actor by searching for a motive in order to give the act meaning. For Weber, this involved interpretative activity to the extent that the meaning of the act is obtainable only in the light of judgments about the possible motives that are sustainable with respect to a given act, e.g., the unhappiness of a person that is derived from disappointment. To discern a motive, Weber reasoned, the actor must exercise 'interpretive understanding' by attaching a meaning to the act, a meaning that is a product of their immediate judgment and evaluation. What is unique about the study of interpretive understanding, according to Weber, is that it accomplishes:

> [S]omething which is never attainable in the natural sciences, namely the subjective understanding of the action of the component individuals. The natural sciences on the other hand cannot do this, being limited to the formulation of causal uniformity in objects and events and the explanation of individual facts by applying them. The additional achievement of explanation by interpretive understanding, as distinguished from external observation, is of course attained only at a price – the more hypothetical and fragmentary character of results. Nevertheless, subjective understanding is the specific characteristic of sociological knowledge.[263]

In an essay entitled *Critique of Stammler*, Weber went on to make a second distinction between direct and interpretive understanding in his criticism of Rudolf Stammler's theory of society.[264] Stammler was a political economist who in 1896 published a controversial writing which had stated that every act of economic exchange was regulated by external social rules, and he thought that these rules were constituent features of society. Stammler went on to argue that the central characteristic setting the social sciences apart from the physical sciences had to do with the fact that social acts were rule-governed by nature. Stammler thought that all social activity could therefore be explained by reference to external social rules and, as far as he was concerned, the existence of external social rules were the only reliable evidence for observable regularities in society.

---

262 Ibid.
263 *Economy and Society*, p. 15.
264 Max Weber, *Critique of Stammler*, New York: The Free Press, 1977.

Weber's response to Stammler was key to understanding not only the central precept of his theory of social action, but also his central premise regarding the role of interpretive understanding. The argument revolved around one central point: how are 'social acts' to be identified? Stammler had argued that social acts are identified by their external physical properties and by their rule governed nature, whereas Weber believed that social acts were identified by their 'interpretive understanding.' In direct opposition to Stammler, therefore, Weber argued that interpretive understanding comes before the physical properties of the act, and that in fact the physical properties of the act are dependent on interpretive understanding. Weber's response to Stammler's assertion that an act is social by virtue of the external rules which regulate it, was based on the additional observation that 'interpretive understanding' comes before the observable behavior and the actual objective act which appears to be regulated by rules. Weber believed, therefore, that interpretive understanding comes first, not the objective physical properties of the actions themselves. This was captured by Weber when he stated:

> Let us suppose that two men who otherwise engage in no social relation – for example, two uncivilized men of different races, or a European who encounters a native in darkest Africa – meet and exchange objects. We are inclined to think that a mere description of what can be observed during this exchange – the muscular movements, the physical behaviors and the words that are spoken – would in no sense comprehend the 'essence' of what happens. The 'essence' of what happens is constituted by the meaning which the two parties ascribe to their observable behavior, a meaning which regulates the course of their future conduct. Without this meaning, we are inclined to say, an exchange is neither empirically possible nor conceptually imaginable.[265]

In this brief paragraph, Weber makes the point that the social nature of what takes place between the two actors consists in the meanings which they assign to each other's acts, rather than to their observable, physical compliance to external rules. These meanings, Weber went on to say, are the product of the inner interpretive activity of the actors, and the main feature that is important to note is that they reside in each of the actor's respective subjective viewpoints. Then, and only then, said Weber, comes the observable behavior in the form of the body movements that occur in relation to economic exchange. In fact, the physical component of the social behavior occurs only after interpretive understanding and is dependent upon it in this instance. According to this view, the subjective meaning and interpretive understanding make the exchange possible, since without it, the meaning which each of the actors assigns to each other's actions would not be possible. Without these meanings, Weber believed, no exchange, empirical or otherwise, could take place. As far as he was concerned, therefore, a social action only qualifies as an exchange when interpretive understanding takes place, which occurs only when the parties 'ascribe meaning to

---

265 Ibid., p. 109.

each other's observable behavior.'[266] The fact that meaning is attached to an act leading to understanding, Weber thought, constituted an acceptable basis to make distinctions between the natural and social sciences, since the objects studied by the physical sciences do not have 'understanding' attached to them.

Social Action and the Concept of Rationality

After putting forward a theory of social action, it was Weber's aim to make distinctions about the degree of rationality that was manifested in an action. Accordingly, it will be useful to briefly outline what Weber meant by the term rationality. Initially, we can define rationality as a term used by Weber to denote a standard of calculation that is introduced into action for purposes of the 'methodical attainment' of specific goals in the world. Weber believed, however, that a standard of 'calculation' was introduced into action only at a certain stage of social and historical development that corresponded with the appearance of rational action in modern Western societies as they began to bring the natural world under rational control. To this extent, rationality can be defined as a type of orientation to reality that is based on strategies for ordering the world for purposes of obtaining valued goals and ends.

Having briefly defined the term, we can now look more closely at the different types of rationality discussed by Weber. The first type of action referred to by Weber is called practical rationality. This can be described as an orientation to reality that is based on the 'methodical attainment of a particular end through increasingly precise calculation of adequate means.'[267] Practical rationality takes up an orientation to the world that employs methodical calculation for purposes of obtaining control over the circumstances of daily life through the mastery of everyday reality. To the extent that practical rationality is based on the control of daily life by the use of systematic strategies of action, it seeks to overcome all unforeseen eventualities by the 'ordering of world content according to some plan.'[268] Practical rationality therefore imposes order on the world for purposes of regulating life activity and for controlling a given way of life. In this respect it implies an orientation to the world based on methods that are repeated and handed down from the past and whose effectiveness consists in introducing 'regularities of action into the ways of living to varying degrees.'[269] In Weber's view, practical rationality follows explicit rules of experience and everyday practical conduct' in order to attain 'valued ends or goals which may be economic or religious' in nature.[270] In this case, it is identified by a 'mental outlook that is methodical so far

266 Oakes, 'The Verstehen Thesis,' pp. 21–2.

267 Max Weber, 'The Social Psychology of the World Religions,' in H.H. Gerth and C. Wright Mills, *From Max Weber*, pp. 293–4. For other treatments of the term see Donald Levine 'Rationality and Freedom: Weber and Beyond,' *Sociological Inquiry*, 51, 1981, 5–25; and Stephen Kalberg 'Max Weber's Types of Rationality: Cornerstones for the Analysis of Rationalization Processes in his History,' *American Journal of Sociology*, 85, 1980, 1145–79.

268 Ibid.

269 Kalberg, 'Max Weber's Types of Rationality', p. 1164.

270 Weber, *Economy and Society*, pp. 399–400.

as it uses the rules of experience and causation' to obtain concrete ends that are either economic, religious or political. Weber believed that it was important to show which sphere of life was being 'rationalized,' e.g., the economic, legal, religious or political spheres, and he thought it was important to know what type of activity was being subject to rationality in this case, e.g., economic, religious or legal activity.

A second type of rationality discussed by Weber is theoretical or conceptual rationality. This is a form of rationality that is distinct from the other types by virtue of the fact that it implies an orientation to the world based on the 'theoretical mastery of reality by means of increasingly precise and abstract concepts.'[271] The goal of this type of rationality is to master reality by devising a conceptual or theoretical picture of the world which conceives of it as an ordered totality, with the aim of providing a coherent meaning or explanation of the world or its patterns. Theoretical rationality seeks to master reality by a systematic orientation to concepts and to abstract theoretical principles in the domain of thought, in contrast to practical rationality which functions in the domain of practical action. Theoretical rationality takes up an orientation to the world in order to organize 'world content according to some theoretical plan' over and against employing practical action to control everyday life by a methodic application of some aspect of practical reality. Spain's dominance as a naval power in the sixteenth century was an application of conceptual rationality because it undertook the 'theoretical mastery of reality in the domain of thought by means of conceptualizing abstract concepts' of navigation, geography, the tactics of naval battles, the mathematical organization of men and material, and the perfection of military armaments for naval use.[272]

Formal rationality is a third type of rationality discussed by Weber. This may be defined as an orientation to the world which expresses itself by imposing order on reality in strict numerical, calculable terms. To this extent, Weber used the concept of 'formal rationality' to designate the amount of quantitative calculation and accounting procedure that goes into an action or decision.[273] Rationality, then, may be thought of as formal when there is a view to expressing a situation or conceptualizing action by a straightforward application of numerical and calculable standards.[274] Formal rationality thus creates an orientation to action that stresses strict adherence to 'cost effective' measures and the formal consideration of means and ends. In this respect, formal rationality formalizes action for the purposes of controlling the objective world from without. For instance, the use of fixed methods to obtain given practical outcomes in the economy by calculating appropriate inventory levels in the light of potential market sales constitutes formal rationality because it subjects levels of inventory to methodical calculation. This may require the manipulation of production

271 Weber, 'The Social Psychology of the World Religions,' pp. 293–4.
272 Ibid.
273 *Economy and Society,* p. 85.
274 Ibid.

techniques based on a formal ordering of the world by accounting procedure. Formal rationality can thus refer to the conscious orientation of action for the purpose of regulating different departments of life, and it can indicate circumstances where there is a consistent attitude toward methodical action in order to obtain mastery of the external world by ordering its content.

A fourth type of rationality discussed by Weber is substantive rationality. Weber used this term to refer to a type of rationality that takes up an orientation to the world based on ultimate values and value standards to which the actor is bound by principles of justice and ethics.[275] In contrast to formal rationality, substantive rationality is not bound by purely formal criteria of decision-making or by an orientation to reality geared to obtaining goals by strict calculable standards, but rather is bound by criteria of ultimate values which may be shaped by ethical norms or egalitarian standards as these are measured against a scale of values. Where formal rationality involves a practical orientation of action regarding outcomes, substantive rationality involves an orientation to values that guide action in the world along a path to which the actor may be formally and morally bound. In contrast to formal rationality, substantive rationality is at home in a number of different 'value scales' and thereby always involves considerations of social justice, ethical standards and a concern for social equity.[276] While formal rationality is based on norms of efficiency and practical cost procedures, substantive rationality is based on the qualitative content of judgments which may be bound by ethical or aesthetic criteria. Weber believed that formal and substantive rationality are opposed, and that ultimately substantive rationality views formal rationality as inimical to its own purpose.[277] Lastly, according to Weber, rationality can be applied in one of two ways. First it can be 'subjectively oriented,' in which case it refers to the degree of inner evaluation which the actor engages in cognitively before the act. Second it can be 'objectively oriented,' in which case it refers to the degree to which an action embodies rational principles by adhering to formal rules or to specific means-ends calculations and standards of conduct.[278]

Four Types of Social Action and their Forms of Rationality

After outlining the different forms of rationality, Weber went on to categorize social action in terms of four basic types: traditional, emotional, value rational and instrumental.

Traditional Action   The first type of social action discussed by Weber is called traditional action. This is a form of social action in which the individual reacts 'automatically' to problems in the outside world and to external circumstances in a

---

275 Economy and Society, pp. 85–6.
276 Ibid.
277 Ibid.
278 For further discussion of the distinction between subjective and objective rationality see Donald Levine, 'Rationality and Freedom: Weber and Beyond,' pp. 11–13.

habitual manner. Traditional action is based on a habitual response to the world that guides the behavior of the actor 'in a course of action which has been repeatedly followed in the past.'[279] To act in this way, Weber argued, the actor need not imagine a goal, picture an outcome or be conscious of a specific commitment to values or to value scales. Rather, action of this type is patterned by an orientation to a fixed body of traditional beliefs which act as imperatives upon the actor's judgment. According to Weber, the great bulk of everyday action corresponds to this type. In traditional action the ends and means of action are fixed by custom, there is no calculation in the attainment of ends, and there is little or no judgment. To the extent that traditional action lacks a specific orientation to rationality, it lies close to what Weber called the 'borderline of what can be justifiably called meaningfully oriented action.'[280] Traditional action is therefore devoid of a specific rational orientation to reality because it reflects the actor's habitual responses to the outside world and the degree to which these responses act as guides for future behavior. Traditional action thus lacks evaluative criteria and obeys no specific means-ends calculation and no weighing up of alternatives. A religious leader, for instance, may exhibit traditional action by a devotion to routine or to ways of living in the world that are frozen in tradition. In traditional action an individual may employ a 'practical rationalism' in their orientation to reality so far as their conduct is conditioned 'by the nature of their way of life' and upon a mastery of the outside world by the limited means at their disposal. Weber thought that traditional action constitutes a form of practical rationality so far as it orients to reality by the 'techniques of living frozen in traditionalism which are handed down from the past and which are repeated everywhere' in all departments of life. Its purpose is the 'regulation of life' by an adherence to maxims that act as guides to action.[281]

Traditional action is distinguished from the other types of action by the absence of a subjective meaning that is attached by the actor to the situation, and from this perspective Weber believed that traditional action forgoes a specific orientation to subjective meaning since the actor largely responds to situations based on a customary view of reality that is handed down from the past. To the extent that traditional action is determined by habit, the actor need not attach a subjective meaning to their own action since the aim of traditional action is to control external reality by maxims that confront reality through prophecy. In this respect, traditional action adopts a 'practical rationality' based on the control of all external reality by the will of the actor, the authority of tradition and the established ways of living handed down from the past. Traditional action thus systematizes the world by an application of formal maxims to external circumstances and means which put operative norms into play.

---

279 *Economy and Society*, p. 25
280 Ibid.
281 Weber, 'The Social Psychology of the World Religions,' p. 284.

Affectual (Emotional) Action   The second type of action referred to by Weber is affectual or emotional action. Action is emotional when it 'satisfies a need for revenge, sensual gratification, devotion, contemplative bliss, or the working off of emotional tensions.'[282] In this context, the actor is directly impelled to act on the basis of an emotional response to a situation or external circumstance that is determined by the state of mind of the actor. Like traditional action, emotional action lacks a specific orientation to a goal or to a set of ultimate values since its means of expression is based on the emotional state of the actor in a given circumstance. Under these conditions, emotional action lacks a specific rational orientation to the world and forgoes means and ends calculation since it is governed in the main by impulsive acts which often have no goal or aim. Like traditional action, emotional action is on the borderline of what is considered to be meaningful action and, in this sense, it is irrational in that it forgoes inner evaluation and subjective meaning.[283]

Value Rational Action   A third type of action discussed by Weber is value-rational action. This is a type of action in which ultimate values act as a guide to action. While the first two types of action were characterized by the absence of a specific meaning that is subjectively assigned by the actor, value rational action exemplifies a rational orientation to the extent that a specific meaning is applied to the action by the actor. Weber describes value rational action as a straightforward orientation to absolute values and considerations of action based on a value orientation to the world. Under these circumstances the actor seeks to 'put into practice their convictions of what seems to them to be required either by duty, honour, the pursuit of beauty, a religious call or the importance of some cause no matter in what it consists, regardless of possible cost to themselves.'[284]

In this case, the meaning of an action 'does not lie in the achievement of a result ulterior to it, but rather lies in carrying out the realization of the specific value considerations for its own sake,' and therefore the sole aim of value rational action is the realization of some specific value and the obligation placed on the actor by the value in question. While value rational action undertakes considerations with respect to the efficacy of the means of action, there is no weighing up of the ends against other ends, since the value pursued is paramount. The actor, in this respect, feels obligated to follow 'commands' or 'demands' which are 'binding' on the actor's commitment to specific values.[285] This may vary depending on how much 'value' the actor attaches to the action in question. For instance, the Dalai Lama acts on the basis of promoting peace in the world because of the meaning that attaches to the value of promoting human life and his commitment to the pursuit of such values. Since value rational

---

282 Ibid.
283 Ibid.
284 Ibid.
285 Ibid.

action holds out valued ends as paramount, it may be considered irrational from the point of view of the political sphere or the economic sphere to the extent that ends are pursued without 'possible costs' and hence without 'rational consideration' of other ends. Gandhi's campaign against the British, for instance, involved a specific orientation to the values of 'justice and equality' that were binding on him and others to pursue, without thought for themselves, the liberation of the people of India. Gandhi's commitment to specific value scales is an example of value rational action so far as it illustrates the degree to which values act as 'binding ends' or imperatives upon the actor and become paramount ethical obligations that adhere to 'standards of beauty and excellence.'

Instrumental Rational Action   The fourth type of action discussed by Weber is instrumental rational action. This type of action differs from value rational action by virtue of the fact that 'the ends, the means and the secondary results are all rationally taken into account and weighed' for the explicit purpose of maximizing successful outcomes and controlling unforeseen circumstances in reality.[286] To the extent that this type of action entails a systematic rational orientation to weighing up means and ends, in comparison with the other types of action instrumental action utilizes strategies in relation to the world based on the most effective procedures for attaining desired ends. Whereas practical rationality seeks to order the world according to some plan, instrumental action seeks to maximize personally beneficial outcomes whether they are political, economic or legal. Where practical rationality systematizes the world by ordering its content, instrumental action systematizes strategies in relation to outcomes by weighing up eventualities. In instrumental rational action, the actor is free to choose the means of action purely on the basis of its rational efficacy, and action of this type represents the greatest degree of rational orientation in as much as it systematically weighs up means and ends in relation to calculating possible outcomes. In addition to this, instrumental action utilizes an orientation to 'subjective rationality' in a manner that is distinct from the other types of action. That is, actors may choose to treat 'ends' as a given set of 'subjective wants and arrange them in a scale of consciously assessed urgency.'[287] To the extent that instrumental action orients itself to the 'rational achievement of ends,' it may, 'in limiting cases,' be without relation to values, and in this respect the actor may not be bound by specific values or value scales.

In addition to its rational orientation, instrumentally oriented action is broader in scope and in rationality than the other types of action. This is evident in the considerations it chooses to weigh up. For example, actors may systematically take into account the behavior of others and use this behavior as conditions to be considered in the 'attainment of the actor's rationally pursued ends.'[288] Under these circumstances, the most significant characteristic of instrumental rational action is the weighing up of

---

286 Weber, *Economy and Society,* p. 26.
287 Ibid.
288 *Economy and Society,* p. 25.

means and ends and the systematic taking into account of 'alternative means to the ends, of the relations of the end to the secondary consequences, and of the relative importance of different possible ends.'[289] In this view, the actor takes into account those conditions of knowledge that are based on an understanding of the circumstances as they may lead to alternate means, and the likely behavior of relevant others in their effect on secondary consequences and the extent to which these conditions affect particular ends.

In this regard, differences between instrumental and traditional action can exist when the actor is free to choose the means purely in terms of the efficiency or success that an action may bring about. For instance, traditional action is bound by a set of means which were often determined by regulatory rules existing outside the actors' evaluations. In instrumentally rational action, by contrast, the meaning of an act is based neither on fixed customs, duty or obligation, but on the technical use of means and ends as instruments to perfect the attainment of specific goals. In action of the instrumental type, the actor takes into account those conditions of knowledge calculated to produce the best possible outcomes. In comparison with this, value rational action is always undertaken for its own sake in the light of values that are meaningful to the actor independent of their chance of success, implying a commitment to the value that goes beyond successfully attaining the goals or ends of the action. Value rational action always involves 'value scales' to which the actor feels bound despite chances of failure. Instrumental rational action, on the other hand, differs from the other types by virtue of its stress on the amount of calculation that goes into the action by weighing up the available means with which the action is carried out, and the tendency to take into account the possible outcomes based on knowledge of the situation.

The Theory of Legitimate Domination:
Weber's Political Writings

Weber's political works were written between 1914 and 1920 and appeared in the first volume of *Economy and Society*. The body of Weber's political writings cover a wide range of themes relating to state development, the exercise of political power, the organization of political communities, the rise of the democratic state, and the historical comparison of different forms of political domination.[290] In the main, Weber concerned himself in these writings with two specific issues of social and historical development: first, he wanted to trace the pattern of historical development leading to the decline of empires and the rise of the modern state; second, he wanted to look at the changes taking place in the form of political authority as the modern state developed.

---

289 *Economy and Society,* p. 26.
290 *Economy and Society,* pp. 212–301.

Between 1914 and 1918, Weber's political writings reflected a number of key shifts that had taken place in society as whole. One of the major developments discussed by Weber in this context was the emergence of the modern nation state with its complex legal and political institutions. He believed that the dominance of the political and legal spheres in society only became a reality at the turn of the century, and that this signified major changes in the way the state was governed, the way it had exercised political power in society as a whole, and the way it regulated the overall population. Gone were the impoverished social classes of antiquity who were dominated by traditional land owning aristocracies. Gone were the empires with their absolute monarchies and dominant leaders who were not themselves subject to laws. Gone were the military conflicts which had for so long defined the dynasties and empires and their claims to territory and historical dominance. Replacing these were the democratic nation states with their parliamentary system, their bodies of rational law, their world markets and their enfranchised individuals. What was clear by the turn of the century was that the democratic nation state had completely replaced the old system of absolute monarchy, the dominance of aristocratic classes, the existence of economic monopolies, and the laws favoring one class over another. As the modern state formed around these considerations, its authority became centralized, markets and economies broadened, legal and political rights were allotted and the conduct of everyday life was rationalized. The rise of the new state system led to new forms of political authority, and it is to this that Weber turned his attention in developing a theory of legitimate domination.

The Concept of Political Authority, Legitimacy and Administrative Apparatus

At the center of Weber's political writings is his theory of legitimate domination, a broad based historical account outlining the different forms of political authority that have existed in distinct societies. Weber began his discussion essentially by focusing on what he thought were the key historical shifts that had taken place in the way power was exercised. At this point, he became interested in the way political power manifested itself in different historical contexts. This, he thought, called for a comparative analysis of the system of legitimate domination which had existed during specific historical periods. Generally, Weber used the term 'domination' and political 'authority' interchangeably in his discussion. Both terms derive from the German term *herrschaft*, which indicates leadership, political authority and domination at the same time. Technically speaking, the term *herrschaft* was used by Weber to refer to an entire system of dominance and subordination that was supported by a system of enforcement on the one hand, and a system of social regulation on the other.[291]

---

291 See Guenther Roth's introduction to *Economy and Society*, pp. xc. For further discussion of the term *herrschaft* and the debate related to its interpretation, see *Economy and Society*, p. 61, n. 31.

After defining domination and political authority, Weber turned his attention to making a distinction between power and domination. Power, according to Weber, is the ability of an individual to carry out their will in a given situation, despite resistance.[292] Domination, by contrast, refers to the right of a ruler within an 'established order' to issue commands to others and the expectation that they will be obeyed.[293] In a given historical situation, therefore, the ruler has the right to exercise commands and to expect compliance from others. In this case, Weber thought that the right of the ruler to issue commands on the expectation that they will be obeyed, forms a legitimate system of authority which applies to the political state, to large scale organizations, large families, large scale bureaucracies and state agencies.

In this context, Weber's primary aim was to concentrate on various systems of domination that had existed historically rather than on power itself, and in this case his focus is primarily on the structure of political domination. In the light of this, he began with the assumption that different systems of domination vary in the way commands are issued and in the expectation the ruler has of the obedience by individuals who are subject to their commands. Each system of domination, Weber reasoned, may be viewed as a total 'apparatus of authority' since each system reflects the relationship between the ruler, the administrative officials and the groups or persons existing within the 'established order.'[294]

In looking at the historical types of authority, Weber focused on two central elements which he thought were key to the system of domination. First, was the concern for the legitimacy of the ruler's power, and the perception by others that the ruler's authority was legitimate for those who were subject to it. Second, was the development of what Weber called an 'administrative apparatus' in which subordinates and various personnel carry out the commands of the ruler. Essentially, by the term legitimacy Weber was referring to the extent to which officials, groups and individuals actively acknowledge the validity of the ruler in an established order, and the right of the ruler to issue commands. Accompanying each established order, said Weber, are beliefs about the 'legitimacy' of a given system of domination. Accordingly, every system of domination is based on some corresponding belief by people in the legitimacy or right of the ruler to issue commands and rule over others. The second component, referred to by Weber as the formation of an administrative staff, is essential to any system of domination and its means of enforcement. For instance, in a feudal system of domination the administrative apparatus may include 'personal retainers, household officials, personal favorites and tributary lords.'[295] In modern societies with large populations, by contrast, those who lead require a large staff that can administer and enforce rules and commands. While the administrative staff serve as

---

292 *Economy and Society,* p. 53.
293 Ibid.
294 Reinhard Bendix, *Max Weber: An Intellectual Portrait,* New York: Anchor Books, 1962.
295 Ibid., p. 295.

a link between the leader and the people, Weber thought that the means of administration altered the nature of power.

Having established the importance of the concepts of 'legitimacy' and 'administrative apparatus,' Weber went on to point out that each system of domination varies in terms of four characteristics. First are the claims that a system of domination makes to legitimately rule over others; second is the type of obedience that a system of domination elicits in individuals; third is in the kind of administrative staff that forms around the ruler that is designed to carry out commands; and fourth is in the way in which a given system of domination exercises its authority and power over others.[296] Given the differences that may exist within any given system of domination along the lines of these characteristics, Weber then asked what form does a given system of domination tend to take in societies that have existed at previous periods in history? There are, for example, societies based on military dominance, others on the absolute power of the monarch; still others on a system of laws or on the power of a priestly class, and again others which are based on the direct use of physical force. The existing differences in all these forms of domination led Weber to look at the question of the social and historical conditions leading to long lasting systems of domination and the mechanisms by means of which these systems maintain themselves.

Given the historical differences in the system of domination, Weber put forward a theory of political authority based on three distinct types of legitimate domination: (i) charismatic domination; (ii) traditional domination; (iii) rational-legal domination. Weber believed that each of these types led to a corresponding form of legitimacy, type of obedience, administrative apparatus and a mode in which power was exercised. While Weber believed that generally modern societies incorporate elements of charisma, tradition and legality in their system of political domination, he proceeded to examine each of the types of domination as 'pure forms' or 'ideal types' of political authority.

Charismatic Domination

The first type of domination discussed by Weber is charismatic domination. In this case, the term charisma has its origins in religious history and essentially means the 'gift of grace.' Weber used the term to refer to 'a certain quality of an individual's personality which is considered extraordinary and treated as capable of having supernatural, superhuman, or exceptional powers and qualities' of some kind.[297] Charismatic leaders, according to Weber, are believed to have capabilities which are not accessible to ordinary individuals, and their powers 'are regarded as having a divine origin, and on this basis they come to hold power and are treated by others as leaders.'[298] These individuals, said Weber, can be prophets, persons with reputations, devout

---

296 *Economy and Society*, Vol. 1, pp. 212–216.
297 *Economy and Society*, p. 241.
298 Ibid.

religious believers or heroes in war. The powers manifested in these individuals are thought to transcend the routines of everyday life, are believed to rest on magical or oracular qualities, and are often based on their claim to see into the future. Leaders of this type may emerge from the ordinary population, they may announce themselves as saviors, or they may be persons with heroic reputations. What is of key importance, as far as Weber is concerned, is that the individual's power is regarded by others as valid and true. Proofs of validity may require demonstrations to believers that the leader's claims are legitimate by virtue of having undergone some extraordinary experience, of having had some revelation into the future, or of having special claims to inspiration or prophecy to a unique vision. Under certain circumstances, 'proofs' of the charismatic quality of the leader consist in the belief by followers that the leader's revelations constitute 'miracles.' Proofs of claims to charisma bring recognition by followers that the leader is in some way chosen and their devotion to the leader is unquestioned.[299]

In charismatic domination, Weber reasoned, the leader's claim to legitimacy originates from two related levels of belief: first is the level which derives legitimacy from people's belief that the leader is to be followed because of extraordinary capacities and powers of personal inspiration and unique ethical vision. Second is the level which derives legitimacy from what Weber calls the degree of 'felt duty' which the followers believe is put upon them to carry out the demands or commands of the leader. This 'recognition of duty' that is imposed upon the believer is key to the follower's felt belief that they undertake to put into practice the vision of the charismatic leader.[300] In such circumstances, believers adhere to the authority of the ruler on the basis of an inner conviction which they expect will resolve long-standing inner conflicts and suffering which as a people they hope to be emancipated from. This psychological connection to the leader increases the followers' inner commitment, and may induce the followers to suspend any critical judgments regarding the abilities of the leader.

Mahatma Gandhi's struggle against British domination in India is an explicit example of charismatic leadership based on the unique ethical vision of Gandhi who, with very little political power and no resources, mobilized a massive resistance that was fortified by Gandhi's charismatic connection to his followers. In this instance, the struggle of the Indian people took the form of a charismatic movement which was designed to break the hold which the British had over the Indian masses. Thus, with Gandhi's charismatic leadership the struggle was situated on the plane of a higher ethical order because it was based on the willed emancipation of the India people from their long suffering. Gandhi based his acts on principles he referred to as 'ideal truths' and on activities he called 'purification' which acted to create in the believer

---

299 *Economy and Society,* p. 242.
300 *Economy and Society,* p. 244.

the idea that Gandhi was the embodiment of a holy spirit. Similar to this, is the mobilization of the American civil rights movement in 1962 by Martin Luther King. Based on the political and legal emancipation of Afro-Americans for longstanding inequality and discrimination, this was a movement which made enormous gains on the political front by defining the struggle on the basis of a superior ethical plane to political equality in the form of a charismatic movement.

Weber went on to say that while the charismatic leader has extraordinary powers, charismatic leadership has the potential to become unstable if the 'proof' of the leader's claim to legitimacy should fail at any time. If success in the struggle for political change eludes the leader, or if the leader fails in their promises in some way, they may lose their power in the eyes of followers or they may suddenly be exposed as 'ordinary' or 'vulnerable.' For example, after Hitler lost the Second World War, his charismatic powers totality vanished. In circumstances where the charismatic leader appears to lose their power, or where they are defeated in their mission or appear to be thwarted by natural misfortunes, Weber stated that they may appear to their followers as 'deserted by God,' at which point their power evaporates.[301]

A second characteristic of charismatic authority is its ability to mobilize legitimacy by a process Weber referred to as the 'renunciation of the past.'[302] In this respect the charismatic movement may be associated with an emancipatory struggle or with revolutionary change. In Weber's view, this placed the leader squarely within the tradition of rejecting the past on the basis of some unacceptable inequality, longstanding suffering or some historical wrong or injustice that has been committed against the people. Thus, in its pure form charisma constitutes the legitimate authority to obtain the necessary compliance in persons by virtue of an authentic 'call' to a particular mission or to some 'spiritual duty' that may be defined as a struggle against an existing oppressive reality.[303] This led Weber to argue that one of the central features of charismatic domination is the tendency of the leader to reject the desires and needs of everyday life, and for the leader to elevate themselves from the everyday world by a renunciation of mundane reality on the basis of some higher religious duty or calling. He reasoned that the charismatic leader obtains legitimacy only by rejecting attachments to the routines of everyday life, and he thought that such a rejection created the necessity on the part of the ruler to transcend everyday activity by emotional indifference, renunciation of desire, and repudiation of worldly pleasure and material property.[304] The Dalai Lama's rejection of the material world of everyday life for higher religious duties is based on the religious rejection of the world as it is. This indicates that the leader must appear to others to create necessary distance from the world in order to confer 'religious grace.' This, Weber thought, served to create

301 *Economy and Society,* p. 242
302 *Economy and Society,* p. 244.
303 Ibid.
304 Ibid; and Bendix, *Max Weber,* p. 305.

the appearance that the leader was 'above' the everyday needs and routines of the masses, and that the leader is obligated to adopt an ascetic way of life.

Because of these characteristics, Weber believed that charismatic authority often emerges during periods of social crises. He argued that the charismatic leaders often come to power in a time of crisis either because the 'nation' or the 'people' are thought to be on the brink of a political or economic catastrophe or because the established ways of doing things are seen as inadequate. For example, Adolph Hitler came to power in the 1930s when Germany was in a severe economic crisis. In such circumstances, the charismatic leader often consolidates power by mobilizing national symbols of dominance based on claims to power that obtain an immediate emotional hold over the people, exempting them from the necessity of dealing with issues of historical or social substance. In this instance, charismatic authority presupposes the peoples' renunciation of the past in favor of pursuing a new direction founded on the leader's divine inspiration and extraordinary vision. Weber thought that because of these unpredictable and unstable qualities, charisma is thought to be incompatible with legal and traditional domination in several important respects. First, charisma is unable to accommodate demands which arise from the realities of everyday life and everyday routine, since these realities tend to undermine the leader's charismatic vision. Second, charisma, according to Weber, dislikes specified rules and procedures since this often interferes with or undermines their exercise of power. Third, charisma resists the development of a bureaucratic means of administration because bureaucracy tends, on the one hand, to dilute the power of the leader on the basis of bureaucratic procedure and, on the other, to delegate the leader's power to others in the chain of command.[305]

A third characteristic of a charismatic system of domination is the tendency to undergo a transformation in its orientation to power. This transformation may be forced on charisma by the necessity to change in some manner or become rationalized in ways which alter the administrative apparatus. When this occurs, it forces charisma to be constitutionally changed, and Weber referred to this transformation as the 'routinization of charisma.'[306] By the term 'routinization' of charisma Weber meant that the demands that are placed on a charismatic system of domination – including maintaining its form of legitimacy, its administrative apparatus, and the commands necessary to obtain obedience – may cause it to adjust to 'the normal, everyday needs and conditions of carrying on administration.'[307] Routinization can therefore be defined as any external demand imposed on the ruler which would cause charisma to adjust its means of administration to the practical routines and demands of everyday life and the practical economic conditions necessary for ruling the state. The necessity of routinizing charisma may in fact create a crisis for the charismatic leader, as was the case in the 1970s when Mao Tse Tung's charismatic leadership in China become routinized by the practical

---

305 *Economy and Society,* p. 245.
306 *Economy and Society,* p. 246.
307 *Economy and Society,* p. 252.

demands of feeding the people and of providing practical political administration to the state. Some of these practical political demands had the effect of diluting his charismatic power showing that it resisted routinization.

Weber largely believed that the problems of routinization were confined to two key areas of political adjustment. First was the adjustment which came with the replacement of the charismatic leader when the leader either dies, or is forced off the political stage because of age or illness. Weber believed that charismatic leadership was inherently vulnerable to the problem of succession because the new leader would be obliged to demonstrate that they possessed the same extraordinary charismatic qualifications as the previous leader. Second was the problem of necessary adjustment that occurs in the transition from charismatic administration to an administrative situation which is 'adapted to everyday conditions' and the demands of ruling related to the management of the political state.[308]

In charismatic domination, if the leader dies or becomes unable to lead there is always the potential of a crisis in belief and leadership. Weber thought that there are generally three ways of resolving the problem. First is to carry out a search for a new leader on the basis of matching the existing qualities of the original leader. In this case, the selection of a new leader is 'bound' to search for distinguishing marks or characteristics which most resemble the original leader. Second is to bring about the succession of the leader by what Weber calls 'revelation.' This relies on a method of selection based on 'oracles, lots, divine judgments or a combination of such techniques.' In this case the legitimacy of the newly selected leader hinges on the legitimacy of the 'techniques of selection.'[309] Third is to ensure the succession of the leader by the process of 'designation.' In this case, the original leader chooses a successor in which the personal endorsement of the leader functions as the means of transferring legitimacy. Under these circumstances, those in authority must ensure that the leader's doctrine is not compromised by the demands of the material world. This ensure that charismatic revelations attesting to the leader's powers and accomplishments are preserved and that the focus is on the words, utterances and commands of the leader's doctrine rather than on the personal qualities of the leader.[310] In other cases, such as the 'apostolic succession' of a pope in the Catholic church by Cardinals of the Roman Curia, selection may proceed by a search for the 'divine qualities' of the previous pope so that these qualities can be transferred to the successor. To outside observers, the process of selection may appear to be mystical because it draws on the highest and most consecrated level of church ceremony and procedure.

Charismatic Domination and Administration

After discussing the characteristics of charismatic domination, Weber turns his attention to the administrative organization of charismatic authority. First and foremost,

---

308 *Economy and Society*, p. 253.
309 *Economy and Society*, p. 247.
310 *Economy and Society*, pp. 246–8.

he points out that the administrative staff of the charismatic leader has no appointed officials or a hierarchy of offices, and its members are not technically trained.[311] Appointments to offices or positions are made by the leader who personally 'selects' disciples or followers who commit themselves to 'serve' the leader because of their beliefs in the leader's powers. Their service to the leader may function in the form of sacrifice based on the renunciation of their own interests for those of the leader's interests. Under these circumstances, the performance of administrative functions are carried out by trusted disciples rather than by appointed office holders.

For this reason, Weber believed that the decision making and other necessary judgments of the administration may be made by the leader personally on a case to case basis, generally at the leader's discretion. In such circumstances, decision making occurs in the form of an intervention by the leader.[312] Often the leader's judgments take on the quality of personal revelation or divine inspiration.[313] From this position, the leader obtains compliance in others by placing demands on followers and by exhorting them through personal revelation and the force of the leader's personal will. Because charismatic domination tends to reject specific rules of procedure and the development of an autonomous administrative apparatus, Weber believed that charismatic authority does not adhere to norms of rational decision making and therefore resists the tendency to bureaucratic administration.

Traditional Domination

The second type of legitimate domination discussed by Weber is traditional domination. Authority is traditional, according to Weber, when its legitimacy is based on tradition and custom and on the 'sanctity of age old rules and powers'.[314] Compliance to traditional authority is owed not to an objective system of legal rules but to the framework of obligations which bind individuals to the ruler by personal loyalties. Obligation to obey commands derives from the traditional status of the ruler and the ruler's power to command respect and honor based on tradition. In forms of domination of this type, leaders obtain their powers from inherited right and are seen as legitimate in the light of customary rights and traditional rules. Monarchies and the landholding aristocracies of the feudal period are historical examples of traditional systems of domination. In societies where traditional authority is dominant, duty and obedience is owed not to the enacted rules as such, but rather to the individual leader.

In such circumstances, the authority of the leader is obtained in two ways. First, by the prestige conferred by tradition, and by the belief that the ruler's commands are valid because of the authority inherent in the office, or the authority inherent in the

---

311 Weber says 'that the administrative staff of a charismatic leader does not consist of "officials," and least of all are its members technically trained', *Economy and Society,* p. 243.

312 Ibid.

313 Ibid.

314 *Economy and Society,* p. 226.

traditional right of the ruler. Second, rulers have authority by virtue of the discretionary powers which are conferred upon them by titles or hereditary claims to power.[315] In this case, power exists in the form of traditional prerogatives, privileges and rights which tend to confer almost unlimited authority to the leader. In as much as the ruler is considered to be a 'personal master' over those who are within the established order, followers are formally 'subject' to the ruler and 'obedience is owed not to enacted rules or traditions, but to the person who occupies the position of authority.'[316] Similarly, the relationship between the ruler and their followers is defined by the personal loyalty owed to the ruler by their subjects, rather than being defined by impersonal legal precepts, as is the case in systems where legitimacy is defined by legality. The relation between the ruler and their subjects is governed by traditional norms and customs which extend to the lifetime of the ruler, rather than by an agreement governed by contractual limitations.

A second characteristic of traditional domination has to do with compliance to the commands issued by the ruler. These are conceived to be legitimate within two overall spheres of action. In the first, a command is believed to be valid or legitimate in terms of the specific weight of customary rules which may apply in a situation. In the second sphere, however, the ruler's commands are perceived to be valid by virtue of the leader's inherited right to exercise personal discretion, in which case prerogatives are relied upon as a legitimating source of a command. In the latter case, the ruler is free of specific rules and obligations that would be binding on their conduct and, in such circumstances, the ruler is not bound by specific rules but rather acts on the basis of 'good will' even though it may not be legally binding on the ruler as such.[317]

Patrimonial and Patriarchal Forms of Administration

In addition to outlining the characteristics of traditional domination, Weber focused on the system of administration and the administrative apparatus that arises in a system governed by traditional domination. There are two formal types of traditional administrative authorities within traditional domination: patrimonial and patriarchal. In the first instance, patrimonial administration is common in feudal societies where traditional authority is prevalent, and where the landholder or lord exercises power entirely without administrative staff. In this system of domination, rulers may rely on family members, on subordinate dependents or slaves to perform specific functions for the master. Patrimonial forms of administration tend to be based on what Weber called a 'system of favourites' who perform functions for rulers out of loyalty or obligation.[318] Individuals who occupy official positions are invariably personal followers of

315 *Economy and Society*, p. 227.
316 Ibid.
317 *Economy and Society*, p. 229.
318 *Economy and Society*, pp. 231–6.

the master whose ties to the master are reinforced by loyalty and customary obligation. This form of administration, according to Weber, leads to arbitrary decision making which follows the personal discretion of the ruler, rather than to a strict set of administrative rules which apply equally to everyone.

A second type of administration identified in traditional systems of domination is patriarchalism. In this case, however, there is no clearly defined administrative staff. Typically, this form of administration is found in households in which the master obtains legitimacy and governs generally by rule of inherited title. The central characteristic of patriarchalism is the belief that authority is exercised by 'joint right' and in the interest of all members of the household.[319] In order for this system to maintain itself over time there should be no personal staff retained from family members, since this would create a conflict of interests. In such circumstances, the master's power remains tied to the 'consent' of the other members of the household, and compliance to authority is not dependent on a formal apparatus of enforced rules. Systems of administration of this type differ from others so far as they are entirely dependent on traditional norms and exist by force of obligatory entitlements rather than by formal enactments.[320] Under these conditions, obedience is owed directly to the master rather than to the enacted regulations of the law.[321] In this case, those tied to the master are more like be 'co-consenters' rather than political subjects.

Weber thought that traditional systems of domination tend to resist bureaucratic development and the differentiation of power into separate offices or office holders. In these circumstances, patrimonial forms of administration lacked rationally established hierarchies of offices, technical training and clearly delineated jurisdictions of power and responsibilities.[322] In this case, tasks are assigned on the basis of the discretion of the master, and roles are often performed by individuals who are tied to household positions to which they revert after performing their function. In such circumstances, masters may find themselves compromised between what their own interests dictate, and the pressure of outside interests which constantly seek favors, as well as the granting of privileges and grace.[323] As a result, decision making is always at the discretionary right of the master, and is based on the master's right to seek legal opinions in disputes, although these may not be binding on their decision making. For this reason, Weber believed patrimonial forms of authority do not develop fully-formed bureaucratic administrations.

Patriarchal Authority and the Power of the Edict

In traditional systems of domination, obedience is owed to the ruler rather than to objective legal rules. Traditional domination thus issues commands on the basis of

---

319 *Economy and Society,* p. 231.
320 Ibid.
321 *Economy and Society,* p. 232.
322 *Economy and Society,* p. 229.
323 *Economy and Society,* p. 232.

what Weber called the 'edict.' This may be defined as a personal decree issued by a ruler that tends to reflect the 'arbitrary' nature of traditional powers. Since the edict is simply a political decree based on the say-so of the ruler, the edict itself has no authority based in law. Because the power of the ruler is grounded in customary right rather than an explicit system of legal rules, there is no separation between the power of the ruler in this case and the political office. This aspect of traditional domination thus reflects patterns of social action that have been stable for long periods of time. Historically, in societies where the commands of the ruler are based on edicts, the power of the ruler operates outside the law.

Legal Domination

The third type of political authority discussed by Weber is legal domination. This is a system of domination characterized by legal authority where legitimacy rests on 'rational grounds' and on the belief in the inherent 'legality of enacted rules.' Modern democracies such as those found in Europe and the United States and Canada are examples of legal domination. In this case, those who have been elevated to political authority under the rule of law have the right to issue commands and form a system of legitimate authority.[324] In this system, said Weber, compliance is owed to those issuing commands on the basis of principles of law rather than the personal author-ity of the ruler, and individuals owe their obedience to an impersonal legal order rather than to the authority of the ruler. Authority in legal domination therefore rests in a system of rationally determined judicial rules and principles that are derived from a developed system of law and from a duly constituted legal order. In this system of domination, individuals pursue their interests within limits established by legal precepts and follow norms approved by the group governing them.

A key characteristic of legal domination is that officials in power are themselves subject to laws and must orient their action to an impersonal order of legal rules in their disposition of commands. In societies based on legal domination, individuals comply only in their capacity as members of society and the authority which they obey resides not in the person of the leader, but in the framework of legal rules them-selves. Claims to legitimacy in a system of legal domination rest solely on the belief in the inherent legality of the enacted rules and the rights of those in authority to issue commands.[325] Accordingly, a key characteristic of legal domination is that persons elevated to the office of leader are subject to the rules of law and must orient their action to these rules in the disposition of commands. Since the operation and organi-zation of this system of domination takes the form of legality, the total system of laws and judicial framework leads to a form of administrative organization which grows out of the principle of legality and the authority of law. Weber took the view that the administrative apparatus in legal domination tends to be bureaucratic in orientation

---

324 *Economy and Society*, p. 215.
325 *Economy and Society*, p. 219.

and this, Weber thought, is reflected in the organization of offices, the chain of command, an administrative staff of functionaries and the use of official files.

The connection between legal authority and a bureaucratically organized means of administration is central to Weber's reasoning in a number of ways. First, he believed that bureaucracy and a bureaucratic means of administration were technically the most rational means of exercising authority over people, and that its development was at the basis of the Western democratic state. Second, he thought that in a system essentially defined by legal precepts, the organization of offices necessarily followed a pattern of official hierarchy related to offices in terms of rank, and related to functions in terms of specified jurisdictions.[326] Each of these, in turn, would be governed by a system of supervision and control. This meant that the conduct of offices and officials would be regulated by technical rules and norms to such a degree that it would formally eliminate individual caprice or personal say-so typical of traditional authority. More than any other system of domination, legal authority reduces the uncertainty inherent in the administration of power by eliminating forms of authority and arbitrary judgment in which individuals wield power by virtue of status privilege or by the sheer appropriation of power through physical force.

In addition, the conduct of officials within the system of legality is guided by enacted rules, and officials act as functionaries only within the context of a given sphere of competence which is explicitly defined either by appointment or by a framework based on a division of labor and by law. Under these conditions, the means of obtaining the compliance of functionaries must be clearly set out and the use of any force is subject to definite conditions and procedures. Offices which are governed in this way function as administrative agencies with clearly defined limits imposed upon their powers and decision making. Members of the administrative staff are required to obtain certified technical training and act as functionaries within the administration. In this sense, officials occupy positions not as outright owners of the means of production nor as owners of their offices but as administrative official who are either 'appointed' or 'elected' to a term of office.[327] Notwithstanding the various structural features related to bureaucracy and legal domination, rational norms dictate that all administrative acts be put in writing. This not only made the written 'document' an official part of the legal order, but it also acted as a means of verifying procedural considerations since the retention of documents serves as a method to warrant that all procedural requirements have been met and are legitimate.

Statute vs the Edict

In contrast to charismatic and traditional systems of domination, Weber maintains that legal domination exists and creates legitimacy by virtue of what he calls the 'statute.' The statute, in contrast to the edict, is a formal regulation lawfully passed by

---

326 *Economy and Society,* p. 218.
327 Ibid.

a legislative body and is based on principles grounded in lawful decision making rather than on the arbitrary judgment of the ruler. The effectiveness of the statute resides in its lawfulness and adherence to objective legal rules. In Weber's view, legal authority thus implies a change in the way power is exercised, since it replaces the arbitrary judgment of the ruler with a system of rational law. Laws are seen as legitimate by persons only when they are seen to be enforced by reliance upon fair procedure and due process. In rational legal domination, both the ruler and the ruled are constrained by laws, and leaders who propagate laws are seen as having the right to act only when they have obtained their positions in accord with what is perceived as procedurally correct elections. These can be created and changed only by procedurally correct enactments, according to Weber.[328] Rational legal forms of domination are based on correct legal procedure and consequently require a large administrative apparatus.

Weber went on to say that the operation and organization of the system of legal rules was reflected in the form of administrative organization which he thought embodied the principle of legality itself. Weber argued that legal domination tended to form an administrative apparatus he called bureaucracy, which is ultimately reflected in its organization of officials and staff and the tendency to create a hierarchy of offices. The connection between legal authority and a bureaucratically organized means of administration is central to Weber's thinking in a number of ways. First, he believed that bureaucratic administration was technically the most efficient means of exercising authority over people, and that bureaucratic development was at the basis of the Western democratic state.[329] Second he thought that a system defined by legality led to an organization of offices based on an official hierarchy that related to offices in terms of their function and to specified jurisdictions in terms of authority. More than any other system of domination, Weber believed that legal authority eliminates arbitrariness in the exercise of power, and that it replaces forms of authority of the past where power was exercised by status privilege or by the sheer appropriation of physical force.

Weber's Study of Bureaucracy

Historical Context of Bureaucracy

Having discussed Weber's theory of political domination, I now want to turn my attention to Weber's discussion of bureaucracy which follows almost directly from his theory of legitimate authority. Weber first wrote on the subject of bureaucracy as early as 1908 in his study on the *Economies of Antiquity*.[330] Later, in *Economy and Society* he included a much larger section on bureaucracy in which he looked more extensively into the question of the development and growth of the modern

---

328 *Economy and Society,* p. 219.
329 *Economy and Society,* p. 223.
330 For references to this early work of Weber's see Guenther Roth's introduction in *Economy and Society,* p. L.

administrative apparatus. Formally, Weber's study of bureaucracy is a part of a much larger study of the theory of domination which appeared in *Economy and Society*.[331] Nevertheless, his discussion of bureaucracy stands alone as an independent investigation into the historical development of bureaucratic administration.

Weber began by tracing the development of the modern means of administration. He believed that a bureaucratic type of organization began in societies whose political organization tended toward an officialdom. Early examples of societies of this type are the Germanic and Mongolian empires and feudal estates of the twelfth and thirteenth centuries. Among these societies, Weber cites the case of emperors and feudal landholders who, when making known their decrees and pronouncements, would appoint commissioners whose powers were exercised within the lord's jurisdiction. Weber identifies six basic types of bureaucratic organizations in this respect: states which tend to control policy and policing functions; ecclesiastical communities which are required to administer to large population of believers; economies whose main function is to distribute goods and coordinate services and functions; the emergence of the modern agency or official bureaus; the military; and the judiciary.

Distinction Between Administratively Oriented Societies and Bureaucratic Societies

One of the chief interests Weber had in developing a historical understanding of bureaucratic administration was to show that it was mainly a development of modern society. In order to demonstrate this, he drew on several historical comparisons of administratively oriented societies. For instance, he looked at the administration of early Egypt and Rome, at the ecclesiastical administration of the Catholic church, at the administrations of Asiatic societies and at the feudal economies of central Europe.[332] While these societies developed administrative staff and trained decision makers they were, in Weber's view, formally pre-bureaucratic in their administrative organization. This meant that the bureaucratic means of administration was restricted to the development of industrial society. That bureaucracy was restricted to the development of modern society was confirmed by Weber in his discussion of the administration of early Egypt, where he made the point that while a large staff of 'scribes and officials' arose from the necessity to administer water resources, Egypt was not a bureaucratically organized society.'[333] Nor, said Weber, were the large households of the European feudal economies which had extensive administrations and a large staff of officials and assistants. Since these administratively oriented societies constituted the first rudiments of a bureaucratic means of administration, let us look at their characteristics.

Beginning with European feudal societies, Weber notes that the system of official organization in these societies was in the form of 'patrimonial administration' that

331 *Economy and Society,* pp. 956–1003.
332 *Economy and Society,* pp. 964–970.
333 *Economy and Society,* pp. 271–272.

included only the most general administrative characteristics. First, were the estate household which acted as the center of administrative activity, and at its head was the landholder who required a large administrative staff. In these circumstances, business and administrative dealings were conducted according to the discretion of the lord, and there was little or no official separation between the household and the office as such.[334]In addition, the administrative authority of the feudal household was concentrated in the patrimonial ruler. Powers, in this case, were defined by customary right rather than by written law, and few restrictions were placed on the leader's authority except those imposed by customary rules not written into law.[335] In this case, the head of the household observed customary restrictions and traditional norms, but generally speaking they were not bound by legal rules in the execution of administrative acts. This, of course, gave the widest latitude to the lord's discretionary powers.

Beyond this, all administrative acts were the private prerogative of the master and were carried out on the basis of the personal authority of the master. In this case, Weber believed the administrative rationality of the bureaucratic type was lacking. In addition, he thought that since relations between the head of the household and the official staff were based on personal loyalty, recruitment was carried out by the lord in terms of prerogatives associated with title and position. Officers performing administrative functions were often part of the lord's personal staff, and payment and supervision of functionaries were the personal responsibility of the lord. All offices and office holders, in this case, were considered 'part of the ruler's personal household and private property' and functioned as personal retainers who pledged loyalty through oaths.[336] In this case, all business and administration of the household was conducted by personal communication between functionaries or office holders rather than by written documentation, which is the opposite of the principle of modern bureaucracy.

In direct contrast to the administratively oriented feudal household of traditional societies, is the type of administration which developed under legal domination. Two important considerations occur in legal domination which favor the development of bureaucracy. First is that administrative activities are carried out under procedurally correct legal enactments and rulings, and the legitimacy of the rules rests on legal authority. Second, with modern society comes the 'quantitative extension' of administrative tasks, and these tend to increase to such an extent that there is a need for a large bureaucratic organization.[337] Under these circumstances, bureaucracy intensifies as the population grows and as the level of administrative tasks expand. A large population of citizens and an extensive political apparatus is thus the 'classical' starting place of bureaucratic development.[338]

---

334 *Economy and Society,* p. 1028.
335 For a discussion of these characteristics, see Bendix, *Max Weber,* p. 425.
336 *Economy and Society,* pp. 1028–9.
337 Ibid., p. 969.
338 Ibid.

A second factor leading to the development of bureaucracy is the emergence of a modern economy, the rise of civil politics, a rational political sphere and the need for police regulation.[339] In this case, the larger the population and the larger the state, the greater is the bureaucratic development. Weber then went on to say that modern industrial societies give rise to a bureaucratic means of administration on the basis of the following social and historical changes. First, as modern society develops the seat of administrative activity shifts from the household to the office, and as this shift takes place boundaries are demarcated and set aside. In contrast to feudal economies where administrative activity was centered in the household, the shift to the office subjects the 'means of administration' to new principles of office management and, at the same time, authority is distributed hierarchically in a chain of command according to offices. Second, in comparison with the feudal household of the middle ages, administrative authority is strictly bound by legal rules and the activity of the 'official' is governed by jurisdictional authority circumscribed by appointment and legal title. This serves to narrow the scope of discretionary powers that once belonged to the personal retainers and household officials of the feudal landholder. In this case, administrative acts are carried out on the basis of 'procedurally correct enactments' rather than the personal authority of the lord, or the lords personal retainers. Third, heads of offices observe legal limitations on their authority and are bound by rules which circumscribe their sphere of social action.[340] Fourth, the relation between heads of offices and subordinates is governed by procedural rules which regulate interaction between incumbents employed as administrators. In this case, staff is recruited on the basis of technical qualifications rather than personal loyalty. Officials are not obligated to those who are over them in authority, but owe their allegiance only to an impersonal legal order. In this case, the business of the bureaucracy is conducted in accordance with strict regard for official rules and rational procedure, and authority is strictly impersonal. Fifth, the implementation of rules in the bureaucracy is regulated by law and lawful enactments, and official rules govern the conduct of those within the bureaucracy. Offices are divided by jurisdictions which are organized into separate hierarchies of offices that function as spheres of authority linked by a chain of command. Sixth, consistent with the development of a bureaucratically organized means of administration, is the growth of what Weber calls an 'administrative rationality' which informs all decision making and maintains a rational orientation to problem solving. All business and communication of the bureau is conducted on the basis of written documentation and a system of file keeping based on the retention of records become a formal part of everyday bureaucratic activity.[341]

---

339 Ibid., p. 972.
340 *Economy and Society*, p. 957
341 Ibid.

Historical Factors Leading to Bureaucratization

Weber believed that several historical factors led to the development of the bureau-cratic means of administration. These, he thought, could be divided into two distinct categories of change. First, there were changes occurring in the conditions and organization of society; and second, were the changes occurring in the system of rationality and decision making. Among the first category was the process of indus-trialization itself in which machines were able to perform work previously performed by humans. This reduced repetitive labor and increased control over the environment by creating free time in order to plan activities. These changes motivated social inno-vation and the rational planning of activities, making know-how and ingenuity prominent. Second, as these changes took place there was a greater need for the use of rational accounting methods in industrial and commercial enterprises, leading to the rationalization of the conduct of everyday life and industrial production.[342] This promoted the decline of the old economic monopolies of the feudal period and their replacement by rational markets governed by universalistic legal norms. Third, was the development and gradual imposition of a system of 'calculable law' and legisla-tion.[343] This brought about the rationalization of commercial and business techniques through greater reliance upon written records, eventually giving rise to a system of accounting, file keeping and administration. Fourth, was the recognition of the util-ity of technical rules leading to greater efficiency in the means of administration itself. Eventually, this led to the separation of the home place from the work place and the emergence of a rational means for dealing with the work day. This gave rise to the sphere of the office whose concerns were official business and record keeping. With the rise of the technical means of administration and the appearance of the offi-cial, said Weber, the work day was subject to norms of efficiency and technical con-trol that far exceeded the control that could be exerted when work was not separate from the household.

Key Concepts in Weber's Study of Bureaucracy:
System of Rationality and Means and Ends

In order to completely understand how Weber used the term bureaucracy, we have to look at two additional questions. First, we have to look at how bureaucracy creates an 'administrative rationality'; and second, how bureaucracy constitutes a form of legal domination. To examine these questions we have to look at two additional con-cepts: means and ends, and formal and substantive rationality. Briefly, let us look at how Weber contextualizes the concepts of means and ends. Simply stated, the 'means' of action refer to the methods individuals use to obtain goals and reach desired ends or outcomes in the world. Means therefore refer to methods or techniques

---

342 Weber, *General Economic History,* p. 208.
343 Ibid.

used to realize goals and to organize action in the light of obtaining valued goals. 'Ends,' on the other hand, refers to the goals or results of action in the world and these 'ends' are often the desired objectives or aim of the means utilized to obtain them. Weber holds the view that, while all human action is governed by what he calls a 'means-ends rationality,' this rationality is subject to change from one historical period to another. For instance, during an earlier period of history, the means and ends of action were governed by a ethical standards which regulated the means and ends of action according to principles or values which were largely fixed. As societies became more modern, however, the ethical restrictions on the means and ends of action were replaced by a purely technical means for obtaining ends. As a consequences of this, Weber believed that the 'means and ends' of action became re-organized so that at some point the 'means' became 'increasingly more precise in calculating the methodical attainment of given practical ends.'[344] Weber's point here is that as the new 'practical rationality' become dominant by the end of the nineteenth century, its purpose was to eliminate all previous ethical restrictions on action by an orientation to the world based on an active mastery of reality. In the case of the bureaucratic means of administration and the sphere of the office, this tended to lead to the development of a system of rationality that was separate from everyday rationality.

In addition to the changes taking place in the means and ends of action, there were also additional changes occurring in the system of rationality that was key to the development of bureaucracy. Weber, in fact, saw bureaucracy as a triumph of one form of rationality over another. For Weber, this meant that 'practical rationality' became dominant over previous forms of rationality that had existed at an earlier period. According to Weber, practical rationality can be defined as 'the methodical attainment of a particular given practical end through the increasingly precise calculation of adequate means'.[345] The singular purpose of this rationality, Weber believed, was to obtain rational control over the outside world by a methodic regulation of every sphere of life. To the extent that bureaucracy undertakes an orientation to reality by adopting practical rationality as a means of controlling the empirical world by technical management and decision making, the means of action are always converted into 'techniques,' which act as tried and true procedures exercising mastery and control over reality by administrative means. This implies that the boundaries of decision making are fundamentally altered by practical bureaucratic rationality since a technical orientation to means and ends always rules out decision making in terms of ethical standards, even while adhering to the law. Weber thought that the distinctive feature of technical rationality was its systematic consideration of the adjustment in the means and ends of action for purposes of exercising control over material reality, in which case he thought that the ends are always treated as beyond doubt.

---

344 Weber, 'The Social Psychology of the World Religions', p. 293.
345 Ibid.

Weber went on to suggest that the development and success of bureaucratic administration was an indication of the triumph of 'formal rationality' over other types of rationality.[346] Weber used the term 'formal rationality' to refer to a form of rationality that had become dominant by the nineteenth century. It may be defined as a form of rationality that indicates the greatest amount of precise calculation and accounting procedure that goes into an action to maximize the attainment of practically given ends. Rationality is 'formal,' according to Weber, when there is a view to expressing a situation, solving problems or conceptualizing actions by a 'straightforward, unambiguous application of numerical, calculable standards.'[347] In this sense, formal rationality designates the amount of quantitative reasoning and accounting procedure which is technically possible and can be applied to an action or situation to ensure consistency of outcome and the assurance that goals will be obtained. For example, the administration of health care policy for large states is developed according to a formal rationality that calculates health care costs in accordance with the strict application of accounting procedure and calculable rules. This takes into account the segments of the population that are more likely to need health care services over other segments of the population.

The most important characteristic of formal rationality is that it imposes order on the world through a system of measurement and calculable activity. To the extent that formal rationality adheres to norms of accounting procedure, it conflicts with the criterion of values found in substantive rationality. Formal rationality therefore signifies the amount of calculation that goes into an action to increase its chance of success. Its decisive feature is its tendency to eliminate an orientation to values since values are not generally amenable to technical calculation. Rationality is formal, therefore, when there is a view to solving problems by a straight forward application of technical criteria.[348]

In contrast to formal rationality, substantive rationality is a term Weber used to refer to a type of rationality which is shaped by a criterion of values which involves an appeal to ethical norms independent of the actual outcomes of action.[349] Weber reasoned that the conduct of modern society was largely based on formal rationality which he thought was evident in the overall increased bureaucratization in the means of administration, in economic and business activity and in the activity of science and engineering. At the heart of bureaucratic development, therefore, is formal rationality with its technical guidelines, formalized decision making and methodical control over empirical reality by the 'increasingly precise calculation of adequate means' in the attainment of any given end without orientation to values.

---

346 *Economy and Society,* pp. 85–86; 225–6.
347 Ibid.
348 Ibid.
349 Ibid.

The Technical Superiority of Bureaucracy

One of the main concerns Weber had in looking at the historical roots of bureaucratic development was to examine its technical superiority over other forms of administration. A bureaucratic administration compares, said Weber, with other administratively organized societies exactly in the same way as does the development of the machine with a non-mechanical means of production.[350] The network of functions, coordinated offices, rules of procedure and the technical means of administration associated with bureaucracy forms an 'apparatus' of administration whose 'precision, speed, knowledge of files and cases,' leads to the subordination of everyday life to procedural rules and directives.[351] This reduction to formal norms and an emphasis on technical procedure plays a decisive role in promoting the superiority of bureaucracy over other means of administration, according to Weber.

To illustrate the technical superiority of bureaucracy, Weber compares it with two earlier types of decision making in previous societies which he refers to as the administration by notables, and administration by collegiate bodies.[352] Administration by notables and collegiate bodies, said Weber, is always less efficient because the interests of individuals inevitably conflict and bring about compromises between views. This creates inevitable delays which slow down progress and makes decision making less precise and less reliable. In a bureaucracy, by contrast, 'official business is discharged precisely and efficiently with as much speed as possible.' Accordingly, the degree of control afforded by the use of procedural rules in bureaucratic settings impose demands on the performance of individuals so that they are less likely to enter into conflict regarding personal interests.[353] In this way bureaucracy changes the nature of social cooperation and decision making between people because it requires the 'objective discharge of business according to calculable rules without regard for persons.'[354]

Another illustration of the technical superiority of bureaucracy is its tendency to promote the development of capitalism. Weber points out that bureaucracy develops only in a money economy and only where authority is under legal domination. According to Weber, the technical superiority of bureaucracy promotes capitalism in four broad ways. First, in so far as capitalism requires a market economy in which official business can be executed effectively in accordance with rules of procedure, bureaucracy enhances the speed of operations by promoting the regulation of work and a chain of command. Once in place, bureaucracy carries out administrative functions with maximum objective consideration and efficiency. Second, capitalism presupposes the rapid discharge of business activity by adherence to calculable rules. Stress on the 'calculability'

---

350 *Economy and Society*, p. 973.
351 Ibid.
352 *Economy and Society*, p. 974.
353 Ibid.
354 *Economy and Society*, p. 975.

of rules is decisive since the more bureaucracy develops calculation the more rational are its decisions and the more effective are its operations.[355] Third, the more perfectly bureaucracy develops, the more it tends to 'dehumanize,' and the more it does this the more it eliminates decision making based on 'love, hatred and personal considerations.' When fully developed, bureaucracy adheres to the principle of 'sine ira et studio' – without love or hatred.[356] Fourth, to the extent bureaucracy is associated with the emergence of rational law, the specialization of business and commerce tend to develop in relation to it. This acts to effectively replace the old patriarchal administrator of the middle ages with the trained expert of the modern period, leading to greater efficiency. 'The more complicated and specialized modern societies become, the more its external supporting apparatus demands the personally detached and strictly objective expert, in lieu of the landholder of feudal society who was moved to act on sympathy, grace and personal gratitude.'[357] Only bureaucracy has provided the foundation for the means of administration based on rational law 'systematized on the basis of statutes,' eliminating irrational considerations in the application of expediency.[358]

Characteristics of Bureaucracy

Weber went on to outline a number of key characteristics related to bureaucratic administration.[359] Among these are the following characteristics. First, a bureaucratic administration presupposes a chain of command that is hierarchically organized. This organization follows a clearly defined structure of offices and positions with duly assigned responsibilities. It is dependent on procedurally correct decision making based on consideration of levels of authority, jurisdiction, due process and correct rulings. Second, in a bureaucracy a system of impersonal rules govern the rights and duties of positional incumbents and the adherence to rules always prevails over sentiment or ethical considerations. Third, the rights and duties of officials are explicitly prescribed and proscribed in written regulations which have been properly 'enacted.' This results in the fact that staff members owe their allegiance to the system of impersonal legal rules rather than to the caprice of superiors.[360]

Fourth, bureaucratic officials receive contractually fixed salaries and do not own their offices or the means of production. This creates an official separation between the administrative sphere of responsibility and the private affairs of the official. Fifth, a bureaucracy presupposes a system of impersonal guidelines for dealing with and defining work responsibilities. Rules are designed for typical cases and officials deal with them effectively by applying uniform rules and procedures. Decision making is

---

355 Ibid.
356 *Economy and Society*, p. 225.
357 *Economy and Society*, p. 975.
358 Ibid.
359 *Economy and Society*, pp. 956–58.
360 Ibid.

carried out with regard to a reliance on technical knowledge and the concept of the expert prevails.

Sixth, a bureaucracy is predicated on a clearly defined division of labor based upon functional specialization of tasks and a well defined hierarchy of authority. Authority is strictly defined and officials take orders only from those immediately above them in rank. Seventh, within the bureaucracy norms of impersonality govern interpersonal relations. Employees act within their roles as incumbents of offices rather than in terms of personal ties. Eighth, bureaucratic officials are inclined to treat people in terms of 'cases' rather than as individuals and, under these circumstances, they remain impersonal in their contacts with the public. Officials interact with members of the public only in their capacity as incumbents of offices and roles. Ninth, in the bureaucratic office, written documentation and a rigid orientation to files is a precondition to legitimate decision making. Tenth, in a bureaucratic administration the discharge of responsibilities is based on calculable rules which are carried out 'without regard for persons.'[361]

Concept of the 'Office' in Bureaucratic Organization

One of the key characteristics of bureaucracy, according to Weber, is the concept of the office. By 'office' Weber means a sphere of legal authority that is granted to an area of work which is under the administrative jurisdiction of an official and their directives.[362] Bureaucratic office holders often obtain their position by appointment to public service which is in accord with the vocation of the office holder. Office holders are required to undergo 'prescribed courses of training which requires their total attention for a long period of time.'[363] They are required to take special examinations which function as preconditions to employment and service. In this context, officials perform their functions as 'duties' which are executed as administrative functions. Functions and duties of office holders are defined according to a set of legal precepts. In this sense, office holding stands formally outside the ownership over the means of production and access to gratuities which may be exchanged for services.[364] Officials exchanging services or granting favours for gratuities break legal rules which trigger removal from office and indictment. Loyalty to the office owes allegiance to the framework of legal rules which are contractually enforced. Weber points out that it is of key importance that the system of loyalty converges around the office and the system of legal rules rather than to persons or personal relationships within the bureau. Slippage in the direction of patrimonial authority or a widening of the sphere of personal discretion reduces stress on objective rules and is seen as an abuse of the office.

---

361 *Economy and Society*, p. 975.
362 *Economy and Society*, p. 958–9.
363 Ibid.
364 Ibid.

Weber went on to reason that so far as the bureaucratic official functions within a sphere of legal authority, a degree of social respectability is associated with the holding of offices.[365] Where this status is high, such as the officers corps of the German army, there is 'guild-like closure of officialdom' which carries with it the connotation of patrimonial authority.[366] On the other hand, where esteem is low, the demand for expertise is diminished and the authority of the official is weakened.

In addition to looking at the hierarchy of power in the bureaucratic office, Weber considered the difference between election and appointment of the office holder.[367] He stated that it is the norm for bureaucratic officials to be appointed to their positions by superiors. As soon as officials are elected by those they govern they immediately lose their bureaucratic characteristics. One obvious consequence of this is the procedure of elections which immediately alters the hierarchical structure of bureaucratic authority because elected officials tend to be autonomous in relation to their superiors, and are directly accountable to the people who elected them. In Weber's view, the procedure of election tends to impair the bureaucratic mechanism and weakens the hierarchy of authority and subordination. To illustrate this, Weber cites the example of the practices used in American municipal elections in which officials working with local bureaucrats use their power in what he calls a 'caesarist' manner.[368] The inclination to 'caesarism,' said Weber, grows out of the tendency of democracy to encourage the position of the 'caesar' as a freely elected trustee of the masses who, on the one hand is unfettered by tradition, and on the other is able to consolidate powers in the office in a monopolistic way. Weber believed that this type of rule by individuals works against formal democracy and the legal principle of officialdom.

Bureaucracy and Law

After looking at the structure of bureaucratic authority, Weber turned his attention to the relationship between bureaucratic decision making and the development of branches of law. He points out that the decision making apparatus of bureaucracy was preceded by earlier forms of authority based either on tradition, revelation, or informal judgments rendered in terms of ethical considerations. Other such decision making practices have rested on formal judgments rendered by drawing on analogies and even in some cases on assigning causal agency to forces outside individuals, such as those found in medieval legal judgments which were based on theological intervention by God.

In the discussion of bureaucracy and law, Weber makes the distinction between two different kinds of decision making. First, empirical decision making; and second,

---

365 *Economy and Society,* p. 959.
366 *Economy and Society*, p. 960
367 Ibid.
368 *Economy and Society,* p. 961.

rational adjudication by precedent.[369] Empirical decision making tends to rigorously exclude all considerations based on ethical or moral norms and looks instead for factual consistencies between cases. The primary principle of empirical decision making is its straightforward reduction to the facts and its ability to convert factual similarities into 'techniques' for rendering decisions within a system of rationality. Adjudication by precedent, on the other hand, tends to resist standards of equity and democratic fairness by working toward the principle of preserving the status position of elites and by controlling dominant interests. Adjudication by precedent is based on the aim of retaining closure on decision making practices, and in this sense it procedurally adheres to formal requirements and is 'bound to tradition.'[370]

For this reason, it is less rational and less universalistic. The use of Roman law, according to Weber, was far more rational. It introduced objective procedure into decision making and put an emphasis on procedural consideration by trained experts. Generally speaking English jurisprudence was, in fact, slow to accept Roman law because it emphasized universal procedure which tended to conflict with a decision making that favored elites. This led to a form of justice which was determined by notables, which was less rational and less bureaucratic in its development of legal decision making. Weber points out that the general tendency toward the principle of fact pleading in law, in contrast to the universal appeal to concepts, has made decision making more empirical.

This matter of factness in decision making and the tendency to develop a technical attitude toward trial procedure, made law more rational. Weber believed that rational law and bureaucratic decision making go hand in hand because it was important that arbitrary judgment and individual discretion be eliminated from decision making. It is always a bureaucratic ideal that a 'system of rationally debatable reasons' can be drawn on in bureaucratic administration to warrant decision making.[371] This places stress on legal guarantees against arbitrariness and ensures equality before the law. In addition it marks the transition from ethics to formalism and to rule-bound matters of factness in bureaucratic administration.

Leveling of Social Differences

After looking at decision making and bureaucratic administration, Weber's turned his attention to a process that takes place in the wider society as a result of bureaucratization, a process he refers to as the 'leveling effect' of bureaucracy. This 'leveling' effect, according to Weber, is a result of the dominant role played by bureaucracy in modern society. By 'leveling', then, Weber means the process of conforming to norms which emphasize standard procedure and the affects this standardization has on society and

---

369 *Economy and Society,* p. 978.
370 *Economy and Society,* p. 976.
371 *Economy and Society,* p. 979.

culture as a whole. He traces this leveling to the democratic process itself. This comes about, he believed, with the appearance of mass democracy which ultimately leads to the disappearance of elites and the social privileges of rank that go with elites. In so far as democracy requires complete equality before the law, it regularizes authority in its abstract form, and leads to what Weber calls the 'horror of privilege.'[372] Leveling in bureaucratic society, said Weber, is always to the lowest common denominator, the result being a disdain for rank, for honourific preferences and a removal of all social levels and distinctions.[373] He points out that the development of bureaucratization runs parallel to the development of state administration which he thinks arises in democratically inclined societies such as France, England and North America. In North American society, for instance, the norm of public opinion has replaced rank and privilege. In addition to this, there are two principles that go hand in hand with democracy: (i) intolerance for closed status groups in favour of universal accessibility; and (ii) the containment of the authority of officialdom so that 'public opinion' can be expressed to the widest extent and used to serve the public in establishing consensus. The social leveling that occurs as a result of bureaucracy brings with it a political and legal leveling as well.

Consequences of Bureaucracy

In the final section of Weber's discussion of bureaucracy, he examines the social consequences of bureaucratization by outlining two broad categories of affects: first, is the incompatibility of democracy with bureaucratic development. In this case, he states that as soon as bureaucracy develops the governed tend to accept the authority of bureaucratic decision making without question and in doing so they give up the right to accountable government.[374] Underlying this problem is the influence of moneyed elites who tend to wield power over bureaucratic agencies through political donations in exchange for patronage positions. This gives rise to economic interest groups who lobby state officials to advance their interests by manipulating the structure of power. A second consequence of bureaucracy is the tendency to develop secrecy, especially in regard to the knowledge they hold and to their intentions or their plans. This leads to the exclusion of the public from decision making and from participation in the production of consensus.[375] Bureaucratic institutions thus become closed, and this entails a loss of democracy.

---

372 *Economy and Society,* p. 983.
373 Ibid.
374 *Economy and Society,* p. 989.
375 *Economy and Society,* p. 1002.

Glossary of Concepts

Marx

Abstract Labor   A term used by Marx to describe the change that takes place in the system of social relations when human labor is treated only as an 'expenditure of energy' that is paid at the same hourly rate regardless of the differences in the skills and abilities of the worker. To illustrate how this process takes place, Marx makes the distinction between 'useful labor' and 'abstract labor.' Useful labor refers to the capacity of labor to confer use value to a commodity. A coat, for instance, has the use value to provide warmth only so far as the skill of the laborer confers a use value upon it and this value is capable of satisfying some distinct human need. Marx maintained that the capacity of labor to produce use or 'utility' in commodities is qualitatively different in each of the different types of labor, as is evident in the different skills that it takes to produce linen, coats, shoes, etc. 'Useful labor' is therefore qualitatively distinct and is a product of human skill. Abstract labor, by contrast, arises in industrial capitalism only when all useful labor is regarded as having an element in common so that it can be paid at the same hourly rate. When labor is conceived in this way it is 'abstract' because it is measured in the form of 'labor time' rather than as a skill conferring use value. Marx believed that this central shift from a 'qualitative' to a 'quantitative' framework for measuring the value of labor creates what he calls 'abstract labor.' From this point of view, all labor is simply the quantitative expression of what was once a qualitative social relation.

Abstraction   The concept of abstraction is central to Marx's thinking and generally describes a lapse or break that takes place in the system of social relations when individuals no longer see themselves as connected to society or to the productive power of their labor. Marx believed that human beings were once connected to society by a system of social relations which existed in the form of concrete ties to the land and the material means of production. At this stage, the individual appears as dependent and belongs to a greater social whole 'defined by the family extended to the clan.' As soon as modern capitalism began to develop, however, these links to the wider society were severed and replaced by abstract ties to the state in the form of political rights and legal freedoms. At this stage in history the 'isolated individual' thus appears as detached from their natural bonds which in an earlier period made them part of society. Marx believed that this period 'produces isolated individuals' who confront each other 'as a means towards their private purposes'. As the former ties to society became fragmented, the new system of ties only resembled the earlier ones in the abstract. The process is especially evident in alienation where the individual's connection to the larger system of social relations does not reflect their human qualities but only resembles it in the abstract.

Alienation   A central concept used by Marx to describe a state of disruption taking place in the laboring process when workers lose control over their labor and the self defining characteristics of their laboring activity. The concept was first used by Hegel in the nineteenth century to pinpoint the moment when human beings encounter obstacles and limitations in the world which act against them to block their progress and their self-realization. At this point, Hegel thought that they experience their own activity as something external to them and he described this as self-estrangement. Later, Ludwig Feuerbach developed the concept by arguing that, in making religion, human beings project their own humanity onto an image and make this image into God by assigning qualities to it that fit with the image of perfection to the point that it no longer resembles what is human. Alienation occurs, according to Feuerbach, at the moment when this image is re-imposed on the life of human beings in the form of unwanted rules and prescriptions requiring self-denial or self-estrangement. After Feuerbach, Marx expanded the concept by looking at the effects of the modern economy on the human labor process. Central to his reasoning is the role played by human labor in the process of self-definition and self-identity. Labor, for Marx, was central in that it served to connect individuals to themselves through the products of their labor and to the human community through the products they produced. For Marx, alienation takes place in four broad ways: first, when human beings lose control over the product of their labor as a result of the means of production falling into private hands. At this point, what they produce no longer belongs to them and as a result enters into the system of exchange where it is subject to buying and selling. In this case, alienation is experienced as a 'loss of the product.' Second, alienation occurs when individuals lose control over the self-defining aspects of their 'productive activity' because they are required to sell their labor in exchange for a wage, and because when they are at work, their laboring activity does not belong to them. At this point, their labor is owned by someone else during the workday. The loss of the control over productive activity leads to what Marx called a fundamental 'reversal' of what is 'human to what is animal.' This reversal takes place in the sense that workers are only free in those functions they share with animals, such as eating, sleeping and drinking, since it is only in these functions that workers are alone and unsupervised. Third, alienation takes place when human beings lose the connections they have to their own species since, in industrial capitalism, labor is turned into a physical act rather than a mental act. Like animals, human beings are required to perform their laboring functions only to fill their immediate physical needs and in doing this they relinquish their conscious mental being. Fourth, alienation occurs when human beings are estranged from their fellow humans as a result of the fact that their 'private labor' has turned them into individual beings who compete alone against each other in the pursuit of private gain. This disruption of the labor process estranges individuals from the human community since, at one time, labor was cooperative and collective, whereas now it is individual and private.

Ancient Mode of Production   This is a term used by Marx to refer to a stage of economic development existing in antiquity in which the ownership of the means of production are concentrated in the hands of a class of military rulers and all productive labor is carried out by a class of slaves. In an ancient mode of production, history begins with cities and an outlying rural economy in which the means of production are owned outright by a patrician class, and productive relations take the form of direct relationships of dominance and servitude in which the producer is an unfree slave. Growing directly from the productive system are relationships of domination and subjection in which economic compulsion appears in its most extreme form as slavery and as slave labor. In addition to relationships of dominance and servitude, relations of dependency emerge between the patrician and slave that take the form of bondage of the slave to the master. Greece and Rome constitute examples of societies with an ancient mode of production. In the early Roman empire slaves were utilized for purposes of forced labor service, agricultural production and for the maintenance of the Roman infrastructure. Private property was developed, there was rudimentary industry and trade and commerce existed in a developed form. Given the form of the social relations and the structure of the economic community, political power manifested itself in the form of direct subjection. In the feudal world, by contrast, political power appeared less as a direct confrontation between the landholder and the direct producer and economic and political relationships required less subjection.

Appearance–Reality   This term is used by Marx to draw attention to the distinction between the way things 'appear' on the surface in contrast to way things are in reality. The term was initially used in Greek philosophy to draw attention to the idea that the perceptible world can 'appear' to be different from or contradictory to some underlying pattern, truth or reality that lies beneath perception. While Marx thought that appearance and reality never really coincide, he argued that 'appearances' grow out of our system of social relations arising from economic production and class relationships. These relationships, Marx thought, come to constitute perceptual standpoints through which we see the world and form relations with reality. Under such circumstances, our material possessions often 'appear' to reflect our class standing and level of social prestige. This, Marx thought, constitutes the structure of appearances over and against an underlying reality in which we are human beings. In a key passage in his writings, Marx puts forward the idea that reality is shaped by how people use the means of production and their perceived position within a social class. In this sense, economic activity constitutes the structure of appearances since it shapes all our human social relations and relationships. At the center of the distinction is the idea that the material world is not a 'true' reflection of reality and that reality itself lies beneath the appearances. An example of this is found in feudal society where religious directives justify the serfs' unequal relation to the lord. It is Marx's contention that this inequality 'appears' to be acceptable only because it masks an underlying reality, making what is actual invisible. Marx thought that it was in the nature of the 'appearances' to present to the eye the exact opposite of the underlying reality. The question for Marx was as follows: to what extent do appearances dominate, what sustains these appearances in the light of an underlying reality, and what mechanisms can be used to reinstate reality over appearances?

Bonapartism　This is a term used in a writing by Marx entitled *The Eighteenth Brumaire of Louis Bonaparte* where he described the emergence of the modern state apparatus during the period of crisis which took place in France during the class struggle of 1848–51, when Louis Bonaparte ruled France and constitutional powers were suspended as France oscillated between a monarchy and a republic. By various political maneuvers Bonaparte was able to detach the controlling offices of the state from the parliament and convert them into organs of state executive power. At that moment, said Marx, the state became separate from society and its powers were independent and autonomous of the interests of the dominant classes. The term 'Bonapartism' is therefore used by Marx to identify the actual creation of the modern political state and the powers used to relieve the commercial classes of their claim to political dominance. By such maneuvers Bonaparte (i) weakened the political power of all the classes; (ii) claimed to represent the entire population of peasants, workers and shopkeepers equally independent of their class affiliation; and (iii) rendered the commercial classes incapable of realizing their own political interests. Though Marx felt that Bonaparte himself was unimportant historically, he thought that the Bonapartist period was significant in that it marked the development of the 'state' by pinpointing the political vacuum that was created at the moment when all classes lie 'prostrate' before the state machine.

Capitalism　Marx defined capitalism as a system of social relations and believed that neither money nor commodities alone were sufficient to make capitalism. For a society to be capitalistic, money and commodities had to be transformed into a system of social relations and this takes place only when (i) the worker is forcibly separated from the means of production, (ii) ownership is in private hands and (iii) a system of exchange emerges which governs the buying and selling of labor and commodities. Marx identified the advent of capitalism with a process called 'primitive accumulation' in which feudal land was coercively transformed into private property and the direct producer was divorced from the means of production. The process began in the fourteenth and fifteenth centuries, leading to world wide commerce, markets and trade by the eighteenth century. As capitalist production became established, it altered the labor process found in feudal society where laborers had direct access to the means of production, owned the product of labor and directly produced their livelihoods. In capitalism, by contrast, the laborer is separate from the means of production, work is directly under the control of the industrial capitalist and the product of labor belongs to the owners of the means of production. The basis of capitalist production is therefore exchange and the creation of private wealth.

Capitalist Mode of Production   Initially, Marx used the term 'mode of production' to show how economic production shapes the system of social relations and the class system arising from it. Since the way people produce governs the form of their social relations, a capitalist mode of production presupposes the development of the private ownership of the means of production, a class system of capitalists and wage laborers, and a system of exchange which governs the buying and selling of labor and commodities. Historically the capitalist mode of production arose during the decline of the feudal economy and the shift in production that took place from agriculture to industry. As the feudal economy began to dissolve, serf laborers were coercively separated from the land and turned into wage laborers, who were compelled to sell their labor on the market to satisfy their material needs of food, shelter and clothing. In a capitalist society, there is widespread emergence of private property, a developed class system of laborer and capitalist, and an advanced division of labor with trades and commercial activity. Capitalist classes draw their wealth from the class of wage laborers who perform 'surplus labor' and create more 'value' in the product they produce than they are compensated for in their wages. In this case, wages are always below the level of value that is created by the worker.

Civil Society   A central political concept used by Marx to identify the emergence of a new sphere of social action separate from the old political categories of the state and monarch. The term serves to describe the political changes taking place in society during the development of the modern state. It came into use with the work of Adam Smith and Georg Hegel, who first used the term to describe the birth of a civil realm which arose after the dissolution of the old political order and the demise of the monarchy as the center of the state. At that time, all society was political. With Marx, however, the term civil society was used to pinpoint the precise historical moment when there was the development of an independent economic realm separate from the political realm of the state, in which individuals compete privately and pursue their interests separately from political society. With the emergence of civil society, there is a shift in the center of gravity from the state to the economy as a sphere of free action separate from the state. At the end of the process of civil society stands the 'free individual' who is stripped of various ties to communal bodies and who is the possessor of political rights and freedoms based on the private pursuit of economic gain. According to Marx, the development of civil society presupposes three distinct but interrelated elements: (i) the emergence of a sphere of free action separate from the political sphere of society and immune to political intervention; (ii) the satisfaction of all wants through the pursuit of private economic gain; (iii) the protection of private property as a political right; and (iv) the replacement of direct ties with society by abstract political and legal links to the state.

Class   In classical Marxism, the term class is used to refer to a historical principle of development in which all societies divide themselves into two unequal groups, one of whom own the means of production as their private property, while the other class provides their physical labor in order to obtain their economic livelihoods. Marx isolated the principle of class formation at different stages of history and identified three distinct periods where classes formed. First, was the period of antiquity in which classes took the form of patrician and slave; second, was the feudal period in which classes took the form of landlord and serf; and third was the period of capitalist development in which classes took the form of capitalist and wage laborer. Marx then set out several characteristics for describing the concept of class. First, he thought that classes are structured according to what he called 'manifold and subordinate gradations of social rank.' This showed that classes always form in relation to a hierarchy of social and economic privilege which tends to concentrate power at the top of the class hierarchy, with little if any privilege or power at the bottom of the class hierarchy. Second, classes are historically structured so that they always 'stand in opposition to one another' and carry on what Marx called an 'uninterrupted fight now hidden, now open.' Third, at a certain point in history the classes engage in a 'historical struggle' which is carried out as an 'uninterrupted fight between the contending classes which often ends in the ruins of these classes.' Fourth, classes form 'interests' based on the conditions that form over time so that a class becomes a 'mass' mobilized in a struggle or a conflict which opposes itself to the interests of the dominant classes in a political struggle. The concept of class and class relations therefore identifies two immediate principles that refer to society and social history. First, it refers to the system of class relations that individuals enter into principally for purposes of production which are always the immediate result of economic necessity. These class relations always reflect a set of definite connections with other individuals with whom they must relate, and it is always within the system of class relations that social activity takes place. Second, the concept refers to the way in which the system of social relations entered into by individuals always structures the conditions under which the various social interchanges with society take place, and this structure often manifests itself in the form of dominant and subordinate class relations. The concept of class and class relations can therefore be defined as the name for a certain type of structured social relation that is formed within the field of the economy and the relations of subordination that arise from it. In feudal societies, for instance, class relations were formed when the landholder and the serf entered into relations of production that were clearly marked out in law and custom.

Class Consciousness A term used by Marx to designate the development of conscious awareness among the working classes that took place as a result of the increase in class antagonism during the rise of industrial capitalism. A full understanding of the term depends upon the distinction between the 'objective' conditions of a social class and the 'subjective' realization of these conditions. Marx believed that with the rise of capitalism the objective situation of the working classes worsened as ownership of the means of production fell into private hands and the growth of industry intensified the labor of the worker. The decline in the objective conditions of work and the existence of wages below subsistence led to the crystallization of a political and economic struggle which increased the overall unity of the working classes. Marx believed that the change in the objective conditions of existence created conscious awareness among the working classes in (i) their realization that the dominant class constitute a 'permanent opponent' whose interests conflict with their own; (ii) that this opposition promotes the cohesion of the working class, which in turn (iii) leads to an understanding that the situation in which they find themselves is a result of social inequalities inherent in the class system. As conscious awareness increases, workers are transformed from a 'class in itself' which is undefined and has no motivation, into a 'class for itself' with full awareness of their historical position and a motivation to obtain more from the production process.

Commodity A key concept in Marx's theory of capitalism which derives its significance from its early use by classical political economists to designate a category of production and a thing bearing value. Marx thought that the analysis of the commodity by classical political economists was incomplete and needed to be singled out for systematic treatment since it was so closely linked to capitalist production and the emergence of a capitalist economy. Marx thought that commodity production and the system of exchange was a central way of understanding capitalist society and he often compared it to feudal society, where there was no system of exchange and where everything produced was directly for use and therefore had only use value. Marx claimed that one of the distinguishing characteristics of commodity production in capitalism is that commodities are subject to buying and selling and, in this sense, enter into the medium of 'exchange' where they are sold for a price. It was this 'system of exchange' which had not been seen before and it had the effect of creating 'value in exchange' and reducing all social relations to economic transactions of buying and selling. According to Marx, commodities have two distinct properties: (i) use value which is capable of satisfying human needs; and (ii) exchange value in which quantities of one commodity can be expressed in the value of quantities of another commodity. Marx thought that exchange value is found only in capitalist society and his criticism of it centered on the dominance of the 'commodity' in social relations.

Consciousness A term used by Marx to differentiate human existence and experience from the existence and experience of animals. Marx believed that human beings are distinct from animals because they have conscious being, in contrast to animals who only have physical being. Marx reasoned that individuals distinguish themselves from animals to the extent that their existence requires them to produce their physical environment in order to satisfy their primary economic and material needs of food, shelter and clothing. In this respect, human beings are distinct because (i) they produce what they need to stay alive, whereas animals find what they need in nature; (ii) they enter into a conscious relation with nature in order to survive and produce; and (iii) they have consciousness and are capable of reflecting on their own situations, good or bad. This suggests that individuals reflect continually on their own circumstances, think about themselves in relation to others and society, and are impelled to act on behalf of their needs.

Contradiction A philosophical term initially used by Hegel to denote the presence of the principles of affirmation and negation existing at the same time. Hegel took the view that contradiction is rooted in reality and believed that it was reflected in the existence of opposing elements which bring about the process of change and development. Later, Marx used the term to identify contradictory elements in historical social relations which manifest themselves in the appearance of social classes and class conflict. Historically, capitalism entails two contradictory principles in its class relations of workers and capitalists. Both these principles are contradictory since each class does not have the same aim or interest and their activity develops along contradictory lines in so far as they oppose each other and cancel out each other's existence. For Marx, contradictions have their roots in class inequalities and always reflect the fact that social relations are based on unequal class divisions. It is the job of an economic ideology to manage the contradictions by (i) making them appear as legitimate; (ii) by resolving them in favor of the dominant classes; and (iii) by explaining the contradictions away by assigning their causes to sources other than the structural inequalities and class differences.

Corvée System The corvée system is a term used in Marx's writings to describe the labor obligations imposed on the serf by the landholder in feudal society. Originating from early Roman law, it defined the right of a Roman landholder to compel forced labor service from a slave and to specify the form and the amount of labor service to be provided. Later, the corvée right was essential to the feudal economy of France and England because it defined the legal privilege of the landholder to require free labor service in the form of corvée labor obligations on the lord's agricultural holdings. In addition, the corvée right crystallized the unequal class system in a legal form, by creating relations of dominance and subordination in productive roles that advantaged the landholder and disadvantaged the serf. The corvée right allowed the landholder to require (i) unpaid forced labor service in the form of corvée labor days on the lord's holdings and labor within the manor; (ii) to claim rights of ownership over half of the serf's agricultural production; and (iii) to impose economic levies on the serf in the form of taxes, dues and rents. The corvée system structured the class relations between the two different orders of society. The corvée right was abolished in France after the French revolution eliminated class distinctions embedded in the law.

Dialectic The term originates in Greek philosophy where it was used as a method to get at underlying truths which could not be obtained using the techniques of observation or sense perception. In the nineteenth century, dialectics reached its highest stage of development in the work of Georg Hegel, who employed the method to show the interconnections existing between various categories of experience such as history, human existence, and consciousness. Hegel's dialectic put forward a theory of development by stating that all things are in a continuous state of motion and change, and that the general laws of motion are intrinsic to the development of the individual and of history. The importance of Hegel's observation was that it viewed the world, existence and history in terms of 'interconnected' processes rather than seeing them as things separate in themselves. The doctrine that all things are interconnected later became the theoretical basis for the dialectical view of reality and history. Central to Hegel's theory of the dialectic is the principle of 'contradiction' which expresses itself in the wider struggle of existence, having three main stages: first, is the stage called 'affirmation' or thesis, referring to the capacity of an existing thing to affirm itself in the world actively rather than passively. In this stage, human beings strive to realize themselves in history by a process called 'self actualization' in which they affirm their 'potential' by expressing it in the world. Second is the stage Hegel called the 'negation' or antithesis, which refers to the principle in history and society which acts to thwart or block the capacity of an existing thing to realize itself and develop its own being. In this case, the negation acts against the individual by 'shutting out their existence' and by preventing them from obtaining self-realization. This can occur in the world when people are forced into servitude, experience poverty, have a sudden illness or suffer setbacks and losses that threaten to cancel out their existence. In this case, the principle of negation not only stands as the opposite of affirmation but it also implies the stronger connotation of that which shuts out existence along with denoting external limit or boundary. Third is the principle of 'negation of the negation' or synthesis. This refers to the capacity of an individual to 'negate' or cancel out the negating element in the context of a struggle against it so that the limit or obstacle is reconstituted and fundamentally transformed into something positive. Since negation itself stands for limit or boundary, then 'negation of the negation' is that principle of development which surpasses boundaries and reconstitutes limits. Negation of the negation can therefore be looked upon as a principle of development that sets up the tendency to resist the negative element, and this resistance as such acts as a means of affirmation. This is an act in the sequence of development completing the cycle, which then starts again. After Hegel, Marx took the dialectic in a different direction, developing it in relation to experience in the material world by looking at historical and economic development. Marx's doctrine of development is called the materialist dialectic to indicate the shift from the dominance of ideas in history emphasized by Hegel to the dominance of economic conditions in history. Marx took the view that the principle of change was manifest in economic production and, in taking this step, placed a decisive materialist emphasis on the process of development. He thought that the principle of contradiction manifested itself in the form of the coercive class structure of society and found the concept of social class and class inequality to be a material expression of the law of contradiction expressed at the level of economic relations. For Marx, the stages of development were related to economic production and the system of social classes arising from it. In the first stage, called primitive community, class relations are not crystallized, private ownership is not developed and class contradictions in the form of inequality do not exist. In the second stage, called ancient society, a system of ownership emerges leading to the crystallization of social classes and the structuring of historical social relations based on the dominance of one class over another. In the third stage, called feudal society, class relations are embedded in property relations from which emerge a class of producers subject to those who are dominant over them. In the fourth stage, called capitalism, classes are in direct opposition and conflict and this leads to the development of a revolutionary class who are conscious of the conditions which make them a subordinate class. In this sense, Marx's historical configuration of successive societies and class structures made the dialectic historically real.

Doctrine of Increasing Misery   This is a term used by Marx to convey the essential connection between the constant growth of capital, the accumulation of wealth and the growing social distress and poverty of the working classes. Marx believed that the connection between the growth of capital and the growing misery of the worker is fundamental to capitalism and can be seen to play itself out as the productivity of capitalism increases. He argued that, as the productive capacity of capitalism increases, it concentrates its resources on innovative techniques which result in a reduction in the amount of labor required for production. This acts to increase the population of unemployed, which in turn adds to the mass of the industrial reserve army of socially distressed workers. At the same time there is an increasing demand for labor. As the conditions of the worker become more impoverished the worker becomes part of the redundant population who, in being outside of the economy, is outside of society and dependent on the state. The greater the accumulation of wealth at one end of society, the greater the accumulation of misery at the other.

Dual Character of Labor   This is a term Marx used to refer to the capacity of human labor to add value to the commodity during the production process. Marx introduced the term in the context of the claim by political economists that the labor of the worker adds 'exchange value' to commodities and this is what makes the commodity valuable. Marx, however, insisted that there are two elements that labor puts into the commodity to make it valuable, and he called this the 'dual character of labor.' The two characteristics of labor identified by Marx are 'useful labor' and 'abstract labor.' Useful labor refers to the precise ability of the worker to add 'utility' to a commodity by conferring a use value upon it. A tailor, for instance, brings the utility of a coat into existence as a function of the labor that is put into it, so that in this case the coat provides warmth. Labor in its useful form is thus a condition of human existence since it serves a specific material purpose which is to sustain life. Marx goes on to state that the capacity of labor to produce 'use value' is qualitatively different in each of the different kinds of labor, as is expressed by the different skills that it takes to produce different commodities, e.g. shoes and coats. In these terms, labor is always qualitatively distinct since, if it were not, different commodities could not meet in the market with different use values. Thus, useful labor is the actual activity which adds exchange value to a commodity. Abstract labor, on the other hand, refers to the process of abstraction which human labor undergoes in industrial capitalism when all 'useful labor' is treated simply as an 'expenditure of energy' so it can be compensated for at the same hourly rate. When labor is conceived of in this way, it is abstract since it is measured in 'an amount of labor time' rather than as a qualitative skill conferring utility and use value to the commodity. While abstract labor adds value to the product, the hourly rate of wages pays the worker only for their expenditure of energy rather than the distinct skill that imparts utility to the commodity. Marx drew attention to the 'dual character' of labor in order to show the mechanism of exploitation that takes place in the production process in industrial society, which ensures that labor is never compensated for at a rate equivalent to the value it creates.

Economic Base   Marx used this term to demonstrate how the system of social relations in society is always derived from economic production. He reasoned that since human beings must produce to satisfy their material needs, the very first act of all societies is always economic and this leads to the formation of subsequent class relations based on economic production. The economic base may be thought of as the underlying historical process which makes it necessary for human beings to produce their material needs of food, shelter and clothing in order to live. Conceived of in this way, the very first act of all societies is always economic since human beings must at all costs satisfy their material needs. Marx thought that since all societies are founded on the need to produce the material means of survival, society itself tends to take the shape of the social forces of production in its class relationships. Marx believed that the evidence for this exists in the class structure of society which always reflects economic relations of production. In contrast to the base, the term 'superstructure' is used by Marx to refer to the social institutions which arise on top of the economic base. Chief among these are the legal and political institutions which, in Marx's view, are not separate from the economy and in this sense are determined by it. Using the concepts of base and superstructure, Marx was able to show that (i) economic production shapes all social relations and hence the structure of society; (ii) that economic production shapes the class structure and the corresponding relations of production which are the roles people play in the production process; and (iii) that the given relations of production determine the political configuration of the state.

Equivalent Form of Value   This is a term Marx used in conjunction with the concept of the 'relative form of value' to solve the problem posed by Smith and Ricardo concerning the value that is presumed to exist in the commodity as a substance. Political economists had asserted that commodities were bearers of value and because of this believed that 'value' was a substance found in the commodity. Marx disagreed with this view by showing that no commodity had value by itself and that 'value' could not be found to exist in a commodity as a substance. He argued that a commodity has value only in relation to other commodities, a phenomenon he referred to as relative value. This concept was central to his theory of value because Marx wished to show that 'exchange value' was in itself a product of a social framework and a set of social relations specific to capitalism rather than a 'substance' which actually exists in a commodity. Marx therefore introduced the term 'equivalent value' to complete his theory of the origin of value by putting forward the formula that a commodity only has value when the 'relative' and 'equivalent' forms of value confront each other. In his view, relative and equivalent forms of value therefore constitute 'two poles of the expression of value' and, in order for value to occur, commodities must confront each other in these two forms. For example, the value of wool cannot be determined until it is brought into comparison with the value of a wool coat. In this case, wool does not know its own value until it is reflected in the mirror provided by the value of the coat. 'The whole mystery of value,' said Marx, 'lies hidden in this simple form.'

Exchange Value   Marx used this concept to pinpoint the change taking place in the 'form of value' that occurred as a result of the development of capitalism and the emergence of a market which functioned as a medium of exchange. Marx believed that before capitalism value was in the form of 'use' or 'utility' which served directly as a means of existence. This was evident in feudal society where production was entirely for use, there was no separation between production and commerce and what was produced was consumed directly to satisfy human material needs. Under these circumstances, the products of labor did not become a commodity, use value was predominant, there were no markets and there was no buying and selling. Exchange value, by contrast, arises in capitalist society as a result of the development of a medium of exchange in which all commodities are subject to buying and selling. What is produced thus becomes a 'commodity' and its value is determined by its ability to enter into the system of exchange where it is sold for a money price. In this case, 'exchange value' becomes the dominant form of value over use value, and a separation emerges between production and commerce. It is important to note that the system of exchange and exchange value emerges only as a result of the development of capitalism and is a form of value not seen in other economies. Marx pointed out that under these circumstances, a new form of value appears called 'value in exchange.' He believed that because the system of exchange had become dominant in industrial society, all social relations between people are reduced to exchange relations between things and, accordingly, all their social relations take the form of exchange. Exchange value thus denotes the dominance of one form of value over the other and the resulting shift that occurs in the system of social relations. Marx's criticism of exchange value centers on how all social relations in society come to be determined by exchange so that human labor and commodities are only valuable when they can be exchanged for a price on the market. In this case, all value is determined by exchange.

False Consciousness   This term originates from Frederick Engels, who first used it in a letter to Franz Mehring in 1893 to describe a situation in which the working class was unable to grasp the 'true' nature of their class interests or their historical role as a subordinate class, because their view of reality was filtered through their class position. While this term was never used by Marx, Engels used it to describe how the working class as a whole attribute false motives to the causes of their hardship and suffering. Later the term was adopted by Georg Lukacs who took the view that false consciousness could be traced to structural relations in society. However, because of the ambiguity created by conceiving of consciousness as either 'true' or 'false,' the term became misleading and theoretically imprecise. When describing ideological relations, Marx preferred the more active term of the 'inverted' perceptual image in which reality appears upside down. By this he implied that, by reason of living in society, we see the world through a system of beliefs and economic standpoints that act as lenses with which we come to see the world and our relation to reality. Marx thought that there are no direct encounters with reality, since we always see the world and others through economic lenses that tend to turn reality 'upside down.' For example, because the homeless are outside the economy and outside of labor, they appear to us to have less 'value' than others who are employed. While in reality all human beings have 'value,' we nevertheless see the homeless through the ideological lenses which are products of a social framework and to this extent we see them upside down in reality as having less 'human value.'

Fetishism   A concept used by Marx to refer to the stage in the development of capitalism when commodities are assigned powers which they do not have in reality. Simply stated, a fetish can be defined as the display of unusual devotion toward a material thing or object in the belief that it has extraordinary abilities and powers. The term first emerged in the nineteenth century in the description of certain religious practices where objects were set aside from other objects because they were thought to have greater religious power. As a result, the objects became the focus of religious worship in the form of a fetish that was manifested by the devotion shown toward them. The concept of commodity fetishism was thus used by Marx to indicate the stage of economic development whereby individuals assign extraordinary value and power to commodities when they form relations with them that resemble a tribal fetish. Marx noted that this does not occur in feudal societies where the products of labor never become commodities and never obtain powers beyond their simple use values. As soon as commodities enter into a system of exchange, however, they appear to have values beyond their mere use. When this happens we form relations with the objects we possess – computers, jewelry, watches, cars, etc – that often surpass in intensity the relations we form with other human beings. Only at this stage do the objects we accumulate take on the fetish form. As a result, our social relations tend to be based on confronting each other in social life as possessors of these commodities, rather than as human beings. At this point, Marx believed, social relations between people are converted into object relations between things and this marks the point at which the commodity 'assumes a fantastic form different from its reality' as mere use value. In this sense fetishism can described as the stage in commodity production in which human beings are dominated by the products they possess, and are compelled by the powers these products have over them. As a direct consequence, we often relate to the objects we possess – BMWs, leather jackets, a Burberry scarf, an ipod – in a more 'sensuous' way than we do with other human beings. Marx thought that commodity fetishism established a new relation to material objects since, whereas in the past commodities had only use values and performed services for individuals by sustaining their existence, they now supplement their social relations in the world by the 'feeling' that is created when we imagine the effects that the possession of these commodities have on others who see us as owners of these commodities. Commodity fetishism, Marx believed, constitutes a reversal of 'value' in that people come to believe that they do not have value by themselves but only when they are possessors of commodities.

Feudal Mode of Production   This is a term used by Marx to refer to a stage of economic development in which the ownership of the means of production is concentrated in a class of landholders and all production is based on agriculture. In contrast to an ancient mode of production, a feudal mode of production begins in the countryside with agricultural and landholding and the absence of cities. The economic structure of the community takes the form of a feudal estate encompassing large bodies of agricultural land as a means of producing economic necessities, with social and political power residing in the landholder. From the system of production emerges class relationships centering on the landholder who presides over the production process and the serf cultivator who is the direct producer of physical labor. Superimposed on the class relationships are the productive relations which take the form of dominance and subordination in which the serf is bound to the landholder by labor obligations that take the form of the corvée right. In this case, relationships of dependency emerge in which the serf is personally dependent on the landholder for their economic livelihood and bound to the landholder by labor obligations that take the form of homage to the master. Landholders have corvée rights which require unpaid forced labor from the serf and corvée rights over the serf's agricultural production. Landholders in addition have rights to impose economic exactions upon the serf in the form of levies, dues and taxes. In contrast to an industrial mode of production, the feudal mode of production is based on rural agriculture in which the serf has direct access to the means of production and uses these to produce their economic livelihood. Historically, feudal modes of production have appeared in diverse forms in the West and in Asia and India, as well as in other regions of the East. In a feudal mode of production, the ownership of the means of production is concentrated in one class, relations of dominance and subordination emerge directly from the productive relationships and the productive relationships reflect the structure of the class relationships.

Feudal Society   This is a term used to refer to a type of society based on a system of land holding in which agriculture is the main form of economic production. In the early stages of feudal society the rural way of life was universal, there was an absence of towns and the production of a food supply dominated everyday life. Landholders drew their social and political powers from links to an aristocratic class which conferred rights centering upon land holding and economic and political prerogatives. At the center of feudal society was the relation between the landholder and the serf, a relation which formed the basis of the class system and determined how production was to be carried out. Serfs were attached to the land by labor obligations resting on customary rights rather than explicit legal rules, and serfs performed all physical and productive labor. Labor obligations existing in the form of the corvée right formed a system of privilege which defined the feudal way of life and its social distinctions. Serfs occupied agricultural holdings, cultivated land and produced their own economic livelihood. The system of customary rights linking the serf to the lord took the form of (i) economic obligations consisting of the right of the lord to compel unpaid labor service from the serf; (ii) social distinctions in which serfs were legitimately subordinated to the lord; and (iii) economic exactions that included taxes, dues, and fees which were levied by the lord upon the serf. Feudal societies as a whole began to decline during the sixteenth and seventeenth centuries after the development capitalism led to the dissolution of the feudal economy, giving way to a system of exchange, commodity production and wage labor.

Forces of Production   This is a term used by Marx to outline one of the major concepts of the materialist theory of history. The forces of production may be defined as capacities in material things and persons to be set into motion for purposes of production. Specifically, the forces of production refers to the available techniques existing in the means of production including the instruments, equipment, tools and the prevailing means of production themselves. According to Marx, societies always operate at the limits of the productive forces, so that new productive forces may effect a transition to a new mode of production. By themselves, the productive forces do not create class distinctions and social inequalities since they have to be put to use by the prevailing social relations of production that exist within a given stage of economic development. In themselves, the productive forces only create activities related to production rather than class inequalities or class relationships. New productive forces often lead to transition points creating the development of a new mode of production. The transition from the productive forces of feudalism – tools, ploughs and techniques of cultivation, etc – to the productive forces of capitalism – industrial production, science, machine technology – is an example of the shift in the prevailing forces of production. As far as Marx was concerned, the prevailing forces of production always correspond to the given relations of production of a given period. This is exemplified in his famous expression stating that 'the handmill gives you a society with a feudal lord; the steam mill, a society with an industrial capitalist.'

Free Labor   Marx used this term to describe the social and political conditions of the working classes existing after the dissolution of slavery and serfdom and during the development of capitalism. It is Marx's belief that in order for capitalism to develop, labor must be 'free' in order to be purchased as a commodity at a given price. In order for the owners of the means of production to find labor on the market as a commodity, certain essential conditions must be met: (i) the possessor of labor power – the worker – must be 'free'; that is, in a position to sell their labor as a commodity; and (ii) the laborer must be seen to be a 'free proprietor' of their own labor power and thus 'free' to dispose of it as they see fit. Marx, however, thought that this condition of 'freedom' was short lived since the laborer was always under the 'compulsion' of having to sell their labor in order to live. Therefore, the very precise condition of being able to dispose of one's own labor on the market is called 'free labor' and is fundamental to capitalism, since it makes the buying and selling of labor possible. Marx pointed out that while it appears as if buyers and sellers of labor meet in the market on an equal basis, it is obvious that the advantage is conferred to the buyer of labor power as opposed to those who sell it, and that this inequality is a direct manifestation of the division of society into classes and class relationships.

Guild system   The guild system can be defined as a professional association of craftsmen whose main function was to protect and regulate work relating to trades, crafts and skilled labor. Guilds were commonplace in Europe between the eleventh and eighteenth centuries and included all trades and all forms of craft labor produced by skilled workers. The guild system involved all aspects of economic life including the work of weavers, carpenters, bakers and wheelwrights, etc., and had the central function of regulating access to trades and controlling the price of goods and services produced by guild workers. During the seventeenth and eighteenth centuries, the guild system prohibited the expansion of workshops and restricted the development of capitalism by placing limitations on the number of workers a master could employ and by prohibiting the purchase of labor as a commodity. By the eighteenth century, the guild system began to decline, leading the way for capitalist development and the purchase of labor as a commodity.

History   While historians tend to conceive of history in the form of events unfolding in linear time and believe that it is the principle that belonged to the century – e.g., the feudal period belonged to the twelfth century – Marx believed that it was the 'principle that made history and not the history that made the principle.' In this view, it is not human beings who are the 'authors and actors in their own historical drama' but rather it is their productive acts which produces their history and, therefore, it is the period that belongs to the principle, which in this case is production. As far as Marx was concerned, instead of living in history, we live within the principle of production. Marx thus developed the idea that whereas the historian believes that 'it is the principle that belonged to the century,' he thought that the 'century belonged to the principle.' In this view, history is a succession of economic epochs of production rather than a succession of linear history. All the works of Marx reflect a conception of history that differs from the conception of history put forward by historians.

Hegel   Best known as the originator of German idealism, Hegel's (1770–1831) philosophy was key to the development of social and political thought and to the work of Marx and Engels. Initially, Hegel was influenced by Aristotle who believed that Plato's separation of the material and ideal realms was unnecessary and, instead of situating conceptual absolutes above human existence as Plato had, Aristotle thought that the material and ideal realms were fused together. This was a key philosophic step since it took the view that the principles of human and social development were implicit in all material activity. Hegel's contribution was in pioneering a system of thinking which attempted to explain history and existence as a process of development. One of Hegel's central concepts was that of 'human reason,' a term he used to refer to a 'unifying pattern' which confers order and meaning on the material and ethical world and in human existence across history. Marx criticized Hegel for (i) asserting that ideas were real and had purposes of their own and were actualized or manifested historically during specific periods rather than seeing that ideas in fact arise from economic material production and class relations; and (ii) for putting forward the view that ideas rather than economic production shapes the material world.

Human Essence   This is a term Marx used to describe a characteristic of human beings which he thought was realized through their human labor and productive activity. Distinct from Hegel's understanding of the human essence as 'contemplative,' Marx thought that human labor was the ultimate category of existence and self definition. He believed that, because laboring comes first, it is essential to human material well-being and self-realization. Marx thought that human beings are defined by their laboring activity in three specific senses: (i) by exerting control over nature they feel themselves to be active rather than passive in history; (ii) by producing material necessities of food, shelter and clothing they maintain their physical existence; (iii) by controlling their circumstances, they provide self-definition and feel confirmed in their activity. Alienation robs human beings of the self-definition created by their laboring activity since, in making the means of production the property of one class, labor is experienced outside the control of the individual.

Idealism   A philosophic term used to identify a tradition of social theory which takes the view that the fundamental task of philosophy is to investigate the existence of a realm of ideas thought to exist beyond the physical world. Plato was among the first to set out principles of thought asserting that the material world was constantly changing and that nothing can be known except concepts which are 'universal' or 'absolute,' such as existence, justice, equality, freedom, etc. This dimension gets its name from a set of ideas and absolutes which the Greeks believed were permanent and unchanging because they could be applied universally to all social and historical circumstances and to all humanity. Plato took the view that the ideal realm included concepts such as equality, justice and virtue which he thought could be considered to be 'absolutes' to the extent that they (i) were universally valid for all human societies, (ii) gave purpose and meaning to individual life and existence; and (iii) structured human action along the lines of ethical standards founded on the good of the political and social community. In the early nineteenth century, Georg Hegel pioneered a form of idealist philosophy which endeavored to explain history and existence as a process of development. Unlike Plato, who had believed the material and ideal spheres were separate, Hegel argued that they belonged together and were fundamentally rooted in the structure of reality and history. Hegel's theory put forward the idea that all history and humanity are in a continuous state of motion and change, and that the general laws of motion are intrinsic to the development of the individual and history. The importance of Hegel's observation was that it viewed the world, existence and being in terms of interrelated processes, rather than seeing individuals and history as separate by themselves. The doctrine that all things are interconnected later became the theoretical basis for the dialectical view of reality and history. The terms Hegel used to denote the interconnection between the material and ideal realms were existence, reason, history, consciousness, etc. Central to Hegel's philosophy was the focus on building a system that would show how our various experiences of the past, present and future are, in fact, linked together to form totalities and meaningful wholes which can be explained by theoretical analysis. Marx criticized idealist philosophy for its misrepresentation of reality and for its failure to come to terms with the basic material reality of satisfying everyday economic needs. Historically, idealism is opposed to a materialism which takes the view that economic production and the satisfaction of material needs is the primary reality.

Ideology   Marx and Engels first developed the theory of ideology in 1845–6 to show that, in contrast to Hegel, ideas have a material origin and arise from material activity rather than existing in a realm separate from the material world. In order to do this, Marx and Engels had to put forward three central premises which provided the framework for a theory of ideology. (i) First, they had to show that the ideas we have about the way the world works originate from material production and class relationships that arise from the production process. (ii) Second, they had to show that there are no direct encounters with reality because all our conceptions about the way the world works are filtered through the ideas, standpoints and attitudes through which we form relations to reality. (iii) Third, Marx and Engels had to show that all our ideas and conceptions come to represent our material relations with others in society and our own location within a class system. In this context, ideology can be defined as a system of ideas, attitudes and beliefs which are capable of affecting our perceptions about the way the world works and how we come to see the world and form material relations with it. Marx and Engels therefore believed that the ideas and beliefs we have are always products of a distinct social framework and function as lenses through which we see the world. According to this view, our perceptions of reality and the outside world are always filtered through the prevailing economic lenses in terms of which we see the world. In this view, we tend to see others in terms of the 'judgments of value' that are related to the dominant economic and material relationships in society. Under these circumstances, Marx and Engels wanted to know to what extent the ideas, conceptions and standpoints affected our perception of social relations, and whether the beliefs and ideas had the power to modify or 'invert' our perception of reality. For example, in a society where work, industry and productive activity are of paramount importance, we tend to see the world and others through the economic filters and lenses in which we tend to believe that work 'elevates,' and 'idleness' degrades and devalues. Consequently, those who do not work or who are outside of work are seen through the economic lenses of 'lower perceptions' and are believed to have less value. It is at this point, said Marx, that we see them 'upside down' or inverted in relation to reality, since in reality all human beings have equal value. From the perceptual standpoint of our economic lenses, therefore, we can see that in a society where the economy is the major category of perception and experience, we tend to believe that those such as the poor and the homeless who are outside of work and outside the economy, are valueless and without human worth since they are outside of the value-creating perceptual categories of work and labor.

Individual   Marx used the term individual to denote a social and political entity that makes its appearance in civil society at the end of the eighteenth century as a result of historical and economic changes taking place during the transition from feudalism to capitalism. For Marx, the individual was a legal construct denoting a social person who is the bearer of certain rights and freedoms, while at the same time being separate from society and subject to its conditions of existence. Marx argued that in all other periods of history the 'individual appears as dependent, and as belonging to a greater social whole defined by the family which was extended to clan.' Only in the eighteenth century 'does the individual appear as detached and isolated from the wider community.' Marx therefore put forward a theory of the development of the individual which begins with the break-up of the old political bodies of estate, caste and guild, resulting in the individual becoming a sphere of autonomous social and economic action. As action became a 'private affair' of the individual rather than part of the wider community, the satisfaction of all wants was through the pursuit of private economic gain. At the end of this process, said Marx, is the isolated individual, whose private autonomy is a political and social absurdity.

Industrial Revolution   Marx conceived of the industrial revolution as a shift which took place in the material conditions of society and in the social relations between persons as industrial development began to take place. So far as material relations were concerned, the industrial revolution began with a shift in property relations from landlords to capitalists, beginning with the dissolution of the feudal economy, the acceleration of the enclosure movement, the demographic transfer of agricultural workers to the centers of industry and the rise of town manufacturing and industrial production. This sparked an economic surplus leading to world markets, the development of trade and the production of commodities. In conjunction with this was the change which took place in the system of social relations, beginning with the break-up of all 'natural relationships' in favor of economic and class relationships, the creation of universal competition and the emergence of a capitalist class whose primary activity was material acquisition. As a consequence, a laboring class was created which 'bore all the burdens of society without enjoying any of the advantages.'

Labor   This is a term used in Marx's writings to describe the activity by which human beings produce the means of their existence and their economic livelihoods. Marx took the position that human labor was self-actualizing because it was through labor that human beings create use values, maintain their existence and define themselves in society and history. The term gained theoretical prominence when Marx called into question the way political economists used the term 'labor' as an economic category by describing labor as a commodity which the worker sells to the capitalist for a wage. Marx refused to think of labor in this way, arguing that labor was not a commodity but rather an activity which defines individuals in nature and history. Marx thought that there was a material and mental component that made human labor distinct from the labor of animals.

Labor Power   A key term in Marx's economic writings which enabled him to make a central distinction between 'labor' as a human activity and 'labor power' as a capacity to add value to commodities. Political economists believed that labor power was simply human 'labor' that was exchanged for a wage and purchased by the capitalist for the duration of the workday. Marx thought that political economists had been mistaken in their understanding of the term and went on to make the distinction between 'human labor' and 'labor power' in order to show that there existed an intervening category of labor. Therefore, human labor, in contrast to labor power, is the actual work and physical activity carried out when an individual works. Labor power, on the other hand, is what is sold to the capitalist at a value less than the value it creates. This distinction between 'labor' and 'labor power' allowed Marx to pinpoint the precise mechanism creating surplus value in capitalist society. As far as Marx was concerned, 'labor power' always creates more value for the capitalist than it does for the worker. In order for capitalists to profit, therefore, they must be able to find a commodity on the market which has the property of creating more value than it cost to purchase. The only commodity which answers to this demand is human labor. Marx points out that what the capitalist actually buys is not 'human labor' outright, since if it were slavery would still be in existence. Rather, the name Marx gave to the commodity which the capitalist buys is 'labor power.' Labor power has two essential attributes: (i) it is found on the market and purchased as if it were a commodity; (ii) it produces more value than the price at which it is purchased.

Labor Theory of Value　　Essentially derived from classical political economy, this theory holds that the value of any commodity is created by the labor that is put into it by the worker. While Marx adopted the rudiments of a labor theory of value from Smith and Ricardo, he took two additional steps beyond their view that labor was the sole source of value inherent in a commodity. First, he argued that political economy had completely overlooked the question of how 'use value' was transformed into 'exchange value' in different societies. Second, he rejected the view that value was a substance which can be found in a commodity by asserting that no commodity has 'value' embedded in it as a substance. Marx was able to demonstrate therefore that value does not reside in a commodity by showing that value is arrived at 'relatively' when one commodity is brought into comparison with another commodity. Marx's logic consists in the fact that the value of any commodity cannot be expressed in isolation by itself, but only in relation to other commodities. To illustrate: the value of linen, said Marx, cannot be expressed in linen: you can't say '20 yards of linen is worth 20 yards of linen.' But as soon as linen is brought into comparison with another commodity such as a linen coat, value emerges. This is called the 'relative form of value' and with this concept Marx was able to show that value is the product of a social framework rather than a substance which inheres in a commodity. This assertion immediately shifted the basis of value theory from the laws of economic exchange and market economies to a discussion of the historical origin of the differing 'value forms' existing between societies where use value and exchange value were dominant.

Law of Capitalist Accumulation　　This law states that the greater the accumulation of wealth by one class, the more there is an accumulation of poverty, misery and degradation of another class. Marx used the term to demonstrate the doctrine of internal relations by showing that accumulation of wealth was not an economic category by itself but that this accumulation took place at the expense of a class whose labor produced this wealth. 'Accumulation of wealth at one pole is at the same time an accumulation of misery and moral degradation at the opposite pole.'

Materialism　　This is a term used by Marx and Engels to refer to a theoretical perspective which holds that the satisfaction of everyday economic needs is the primary reality in every epoch of history. Opposed to German idealist philosophy, materialism takes the position that society and reality originate from a set of simple economic acts which human beings carry out in order to provide the material necessities of food, shelter and clothing. Materialism takes as its starting point the view that, before anything else, human beings must produce their everyday economic needs through their physical labor and practical productive activity. This single economic act, Marx believed, gives rise to a system of social relations which include the political, legal and religious structures of society. What is of central importance about this perspective is that it attempts to found a theory of society, history and existence from the starting point of human productive acts. It is therefore the most basic premise of materialism that society and history are created from a series of productive acts designed to fulfill human needs. The shift from German idealist philosophy to the materialist outlook marked the point in the history of thought in which theory turned its attention to the material conditions of human experience and the simple economic acts of production.

Materialist Theory of History   This is a term used to describe Marx's central theoretical perspective which explains the tendency of all societies to divide themselves into two unequal social and economic classes. The perspective holds that society and history develop in stages marked by distinct economic epochs in which social inequality is reproduced in existing class relations throughout all historical societies. It explains the origins of this process by looking for the laws of social and historical development that tend to concentrate the ownership of the means of production only in one class in society. The main precept of the theory states that history is governed by a process of economic development which is expressed in a series of productive acts. The guiding presupposition is that the very first act of all human societies is always economic since individuals must obtain the material necessities of food, shelter and clothing in order to live. From this simple act of production, one class seems always to possess a monopoly over the means of production, giving rise to a dominant class which has control over the means of production, and a subordinate class who provide their direct physical labor. Eventually a political, legal and religious superstructure arises on top of the productive relations forming the legal and political structure of society. Using the materialist theory of history, Marx was able to assert that (i) economic production shapes all social relations and hence the political structure of society; and (ii) that economic production gives rise to a legal and political superstructure which comes to represent the productive relations. This fundamental principle of development is expressed in all societies by the fact that they tend to divide themselves into unequal social classes in which the labor of one class is to the economic benefit and maintenance of another. Conceived of in this way, history can be divided into three economic epochs: ancient, feudal and capitalistic.

Means of Production   One of the three central concepts in Marx's materialist theory of history referring to any physical or material thing used to produce the main material needs of food, shelter and clothing. The means of production can be defined as anything in the external world that is put to use for purposes of producing material needs and sustaining existence. The way jobs are used to produce wages and land to produce food and fuel constitutes the means of production. It is important to note that material needs and economic necessities cannot be produced privately on one's own, but rather only when we employ the means of production. Marx believed that the private ownership of the means of production was the most fundamental historical fact leading to the division of society into unequal economic classes. Ancient and feudal societies are historical examples of this since the means of production are under the monopoly of a ruling class who compel slaves and serfs to perform unpaid forced physical labor. Marx traced the different historical periods that marked the transfer of the means of production into private hands and the point at which they became the special monopoly of one class. Marx reasoned that when the means of production fell into private hands during the transition from feudalism to capitalism, the worker was no longer able to employ the means of production freely on their own as they once did in feudal society. Marx thought that this constituted a reversal of what existed in the past, since instead of the worker employing the means of production on their own free will, the means of production now employed the worker. Marx reasoned, as a result of this, certain restrictions come into play that relate to how the means of production are to be used. First are the restrictions which appear in the form of hiring policies, the imposition of work schedules, and the limits imposed on wages and wage levels as far as workers are concerned. Second are the restrictions which penalize the worker in terms of infractions related to the hours of labor, the conditions of work and the rules regulating the conduct of the worker during the workday. These restrictions form a clear set of 'obstructions' to the means of production because, given restrictive hiring policies, some workers may never be hired, while other workers may be excluded on the basis of class, gender, race or age characteristics. Other restrictions may exist for untrained workers who may have limits imposed on their wages, or who may be required to work without wages until they are trained, or who may be required to work shifts with extended hours of labor. The means of production thus take on different technological identities in various periods of economic history. In ancient and feudal society, the means of production were concentrated in land and constituted the major productive resources. In industrial societies, on the other hand, the means of production became privately owned and became more diversified and concentrated in technologies, resources and the mechanical means of production.

Mode of Production   This is a term used by Marx to show that the overall growth of society takes place in a series of stages of economic development Marx called a mode of production. Each stage of development is defined by two key characteristics. First, it is defined by the 'way people produce' and enter into productive relationships with one another that make up the total way of life of society as this is determined by production. In this case, the form of the production determines the specific economic form of the community and the class relationship that arise directly from production. Second, a mode of production is defined by the specific productive relationships that arise at each stage of economic development and which are put into operation when people in society enter into the 'relations of production,' which are the roles allotted to them in the production process. Since in every mode of production ownership over the means of production is concentrated in one class, relations of dominance and subordination emerge directly from the productive relations that in turn reflect class relationships. Superimposed on the relations of production, therefore, are relations of dominance and subjection which manifest themselves in the form of labor obligations imposed on the direct producer by the landholder, as in the case of a feudal mode of production. In an ancient mode of production, the system of subordinate relations is structured as relations of dominance and servitude and appear in the form of slavery and slave labor. Marx identified three distinct modes of production: ancient, feudal and capitalistic, and each of these stages of economic development produced economic necessities that gave rise to (i) distinct class relations; (ii) different productive relationships and (iii) distinct relations of production which vary in the degree of political and economic subjection. In each mode of production there are class divisions arising from property relations which give rights to those who have a monopoly over the means of production to control both the product and the labor of the producer.

Natural Economy   This is a term used by Marx to refer to a type of economy which is found in traditional societies and which is distinct from the economies of industrial capitalism. Natural economies consist of economic communities in which land is owned in common, there is no system of exchange and all production is for the immediate personal needs of the community. Since no one class has a monopoly over the means of production, a class system does not develop, production is in common and everything produced is for the maintenance of life. Key to the structure of natural economies is the fact that 'value' is in the form of 'use or utility' and 'exchange relations' do not develop as they do in modern economies, where all production is for commerce. In such circumstances, use value predominates over exchange value, use is the only form of value and commodities do not enter into the medium of exchange. Natural economies are found in the village system of India, the peasant communities of central and south America and the ancient agricultural economies of Peru and China. A key characteristic of natural economies is that a 'system of exchange' does not form the basis of social relations. Marx observed that as soon as a system of exchange emerges, there is a formal separation between production and commerce and, as a result, all social relationships take the form of exchange relationships. Marx thought that as soon as the system of exchange stands on its feet, it shapes all social relations in the form of exchange and replaces all natural relationships with class relationships and all social relations with exchange relations. Marx thought that as capitalist economies develop they tend to destroy natural economies.

Objectification   This is a term used by Marx to refer to the capacity of human beings to positively 'duplicate' themselves in the world they create. According to Marx, this duplication in society takes place through human labor so far as it is the realization of human aims and goals. It is only through their labor, Marx reasoned, that human beings can 'contemplate themselves in the world they have created.' By producing things in this sense, an individual becomes an object for others within the structure of social relations and in this way creates civilization. For Marx, objectification is necessary if individuals are to humanize nature and transform it into something having human qualities. By making the distinction between alienation and objectification, Marx grasped the historical character of labor and argued that the end of alienation will emancipate human beings by rehumanizing labor.

Political economy   A term referring to the economic doctrine espoused by Adam Smith and David Ricardo, holding that the primary economic categories of production, exchange, value and labor can be studied as if they were independent economic categories that obey laws of their own and operate above human social and historical relations. Its central assumptions state that the laws of economic activity – production, exchange, consumption, labor, capital, value, etc. – are analogous to the laws of nature and apply to all societies irrespective of their historical and social development. Marx rejected these views by showing that the economic categories of capital and labor, and production and consumption were not universally valid for all societies but only have validity under certain historical circumstances. The theory of value became one of the most contentious battlegrounds between Marx and the political economists. While Smith asserted that exchange value was an attribute of a commodity, Marx rejected this view by stating that 'exchange value' was not a universal economic phenomenon, but emerged only under certain historical conditions, which came into play only in capitalist society where exchange value became the dominant form of value over use value. Marx was able to show that the concept of exchange value arises only in societies which develop a system of exchange called the market, and when commodity production is exclusively for exchange. Marx believed that the system of exchange comes into being only in capitalist society and he was able to link the concept of exchange value to a specific mode of production rather than it being a universal category of economic activity. Marx thought that classical political economy was incomplete because it did not look at the underlying system of social relations and because it mistook production, consumption and exchange as the reality of economic life when, as far as Marx was concerned, the essence of capitalism was the system of unequal class relations.

Primitive Accumulation   A term used by Marx to refer to the central process taking place during capitalist development when there was the coercive acquisition of feudal lands and a transformation of agricultural land into private property. Primitive accumulation began, according to Marx, at the precise historical moment when the serf laborer was divorced from the means of production and forcibly separated from the means of producing their own economic livelihood, as they once had done in feudal society. Marx thought that this accumulation was 'primitive' so far as it formed the historical basis of capitalism and the historical moment when serf laborers were transformed into wage-laborers in industrial capitalism. Marx argued that primitive accumulation is a process that takes place in two distinct historical stages. The first begins with the expropriation of the agricultural laborer from the land. This stage began during the seventeenth century when large populations of agricultural workers were 'forcibly' thrown from the land by eviction and foreclosure, leading to the dissolution of a whole way of life. The second stage was marked by the legal transfer of feudal lands into private hands by direct seizure and expropriation. This took place by means of the bills of enclosure and the enclosure movement, which by the middle of the nineteenth century, had created private property, the industrial worker, wage labor, the factory system and the private ownership of the means of production.

Reification   A term used to denote a stage of social and economic development when human beings experience society as if it were independent of their actions and indifferent to their existence. Marx used the concept to define the process by which society appears to have purposes of its own, while all along being a product of human labor. Though Marx believed that human beings create society in their economic and productive activity, the process of reification can be defined as the stage in the development when society no longer appears in a human form and no longer reflects human origins, but appears to have a life of its own disconnected from human aims. Reification takes place when the economy is perceived to have 'needs' of its own, e.g., the 'needs of capital' or the 'needs of production' and when human activity is perceived of as irrelevant to the needs of the market. Under such circumstances, human beings appear to be an 'accessory' of the real social functions and the real economic forces of the economy rather than active agents in history that make the economy. As 'accessories' of these functions, human beings appear in history as if 'they arose from them' and 'belong to them' in the first place. Reification thus reverses the process by which human beings create society by making it appear as if society gives birth to itself and then to human beings.

Relation   A term used by Marx to refer to the material link that exists between the major economic categories of production, exchange and consumption, and human social and historical activity. While the term relation derives from Hegel, Marx used the concept as a methodological tool in his criticism of Smith and Ricardo primarily as way of illustrating their tendency to treat economic concepts such as 'wealth' and 'profit' as if they were economic laws operating independently by themselves above human activity and social and political life. Marx showed that when political economists dealt with economic categories of 'labor and capital,' they did so from the standpoint of a one-sided theoretical perspective, in which they looked at economic questions only from the point of view of capital, rather than looking at capital in 'relation' to labor, or looking at production in relation to consumption. Marx believed that these concepts can only be understood in relation to each other, rather than independently by themselves. Drawing on the concept of the social relation, Marx argued that economic categories were not separate but interrelated and believed that there were always two sides in any 'relation.' Viewed from this perspective, money, capital and profit are not independent categories produced outside of a mode of production but rather are inherent in the activity of human labor. Using this technique, Marx was able to show that wealth was not an independent product of capital alone but a product of the 'relation' between capital and labor.

Relations of Production   This is a key concept in Marx's materialist theory of history which he used in connection with the concepts of the means of production, forces of production and mode of production to indicate the different social roles allotted to the production process in all historical societies. Essentially, Marx used the term to show that the roles individuals assume in the production process were directly related to the system of class relations that arise from the fact that ownership of the means of production tends to be concentrated only in one class in society. Marx thought that, from the class relationships, there arises two distinct social roles in production: those who preside over the production process, and those who provide their physical labor. Marx used the concept of the 'relations of production' to indicate how the productive roles were actually structured and he outlined two key characteristics. First, workers must enter into 'relations of production' in order to satisfy their material needs and, as soon as they do so, they become personally dependent on their superiors for their livelihoods. Second, as soon as the relations of production are entered into, relationships of dominance and subordination emerge from the productive relationships which are a reflection of the class relationships. Marx thought that the relations of production were key to the development of society because of their ability to be transformed into relations of domination, both politically and economically. Marx maintained that different relations of production manifest themselves at different stages of economic development and these always seem to coincide with the way societies produce. Patrician and slave, lord and serf, capitalist and wage laborer are the names given to the relations of production in ancient, feudal and capitalistic societies. Since different relations of production manifest themselves at different stages of economic development, productive relations vary in the degree of subjection that may exist within the productive relationships. In ancient society, for example, the productive relationships appear in the form of political and economic subjection by a dominant class over a class of slaves who are the direct producers. In this case, economic compulsion appears in its most extreme form as slavery and slave labor experienced directly as bondage to the master. In feudal societies, by contrast, the dominant and subordinate productive roles appear in the form of 'labor obligations' imposed by the landholder on the serf, in which case the serf is personally unfree. As a result of having a monopoly over the means of production, owners obtain rights in law to control both the product of labor and the labor of the producer. The relations of production therefore identify the coercive bond which exists between the owners of the means of production and those who provide their physical labor. Marx thought that the economic structure of society always determined the specific structure of the productive relations and that from this arises relationships of dominance and subordination.

Relations of Subordination   This concept is closely linked with the concept of class and the concept of the relations of production. Generally, it is used to pinpoint the different degrees of dominance and subordination that exist in a society as a result of a class hierarchy in which power is at the top, and little or no power at the bottom of the hierarchy. Traditionally, the relations of subordination have been the subject of special study in the context of class inequality, the structure of the caste system, the history of racism and the study of gender relations within social and political thought proper. Before these terms were used in contemporary social theory or in Women's Studies, the term 'relations of subordination' was used by Hegel, Marx and Weber in the nineteenth century to pinpoint a system of structured relations between individuals in which different forms of dominance and subordination manifested themselves at different stages in history. For all practical purposes, it was Hegel who first identified the existing relations of subordination by outlining the forms of dominance and dependency existing between the master and the slave in societies of antiquity. It is here, in fact, that we find the prototype for the social relations of authority and power, and the prototype for the class distinctions and oppositions which were so much a part of early feudal societies of the West, and previously ancient societies of Greece and Rome, whose economies presupposed the existence of slave labor. It is here, too, that we find the prototype of the form of dependency of an individual upon a superior who, through the power of their class position or the force of legal sanction, assumes a position in a social relation which is dominant over the subordinate position, which is unfree. The relations of subordination thus refer to a whole series of structured relations and oppositions which have existed historically between classes and castes, between bosses and workers and between landlords and tenants. Relations of subordination have existed in societies since classical antiquity and are evident historically up to the modern period. In ancient Greece there was the Athenian aristocrat and the slave laborer; in ancient Rome there was the *Civis Romanus* and the slave; in Russia there was the boyar and the peasants; and in India, there were the landlords (jagirdars) and the peasant cultivators. Much later in history, there was the American slave owner and then eventually the modern landlord and employer in industrial capitalism.

Relative Form of Value   Often used in conjunction with the concept of the 'equivalent form of value,' this concept plays a central role in Marx's theory of value and in his investigation into the question of what makes a commodity valuable. Simply stated, Smith and Ricardo had taken the view that value was a natural property of a commodity and could be found in it as a substance which exchanged for a price in the market. Marx broke with this tradition by stating that no commodity has 'value' in itself, except as use value. Using the concept 'relative value,' Marx was able to show that in an industrial economy a commodity has exchange value only in relation to some other commodity. For example, the value of linen cannot be determined until it is brought into comparison with another commodity such as a coat, in which the linen is worked up by the labor of the tailor who provides the utility of the coat to create warmth. In this case, said Marx, the value of linen is determined in 'relation to' the value of the coat. Marx believed that the value of a commodity emerges only in comparison with some other commodity, and the term he used to describe this phenomenon is 'relative value.' After demonstrating that 'exchange value' was not a substance that can be found in a commodity naturally but was established 'relatively,' Marx wanted to show that value was a product of a social framework rather than being a substance that exists in a commodity and exchanges for a price.

Relative Surplus Population   Marx used this term to challenge the theory of population proposed by Thomas Malthus in the nineteenth century who put forward a general law of population growth that applied to all societies. Malthus proposed that as the population increases it creates a 'surplus' population relative to the available food supply for sustaining this population. Malthus went on to draw several controversial conclusions about the relationship between a population surplus, the growing poverty rates and what he called the 'positive checks' on the surplus population, which he believed eliminated the poor and their 'drain on the food supply.' Malthus believed that poverty and starvation therefore acted as a 'natural check' on the poor population, and on this basis felt that charity from the state in the form of poor relief interfered with the elimination of the poor by natural processes. Marx, by contrast, argued that there are no general laws of population, only laws 'relative' to specific societies and given historical modes of production. He went on to show that the formation of a surplus population of unemployed poor was not a product of the general rate of population growth in the abstract, as argued by Malthus, but was the specific product of the operations of modern industry and capitalist development and its tendency to create high rates of unemployment and poverty. Marx believed that capitalism and modern industry set into motion processes which create a population surplus and that this population is always 'relative' to the cycle of labor requirements of capital and is thus a necessary condition of it.

Reserve Army   This is a term used by Marx to describe the tendency in industrial societies to create a population of unemployed workers who are held in reserve for purposes of acting as an army of laborers when the supply of labor runs short. Marx believed that the reserve army was created by two simultaneous demands on the capitalist system. On the one hand, there was the constant demand for refinements and productivity in the capitalist system producing labor-saving techniques which created a decrease in the demand for labor. This in turn created a decrease in the number of jobs and, consequently, an increase in the overall population of unemployed workers who become a permanent floating surplus collectivity and a burden to society. At the same time, however, there was an increase in the demand for labor as the requirements of capitalism become more refined and developed. This created an excess of jobs which could not be filled and a greater demand for labor, especially skilled labor. Marx believed that it was in the nature of the capitalist system to produce a reserve army of unemployed, since the more productive capitalism becomes, the greater the amount of 'workers it throws out into the streets.' Marx referred to the reserve army as the 'lazarus layers' of labor, to be brought back to life when the supply of labor was low. In addition, he thought that the population of poor, unemployed workers constituted what he called the 'hospital' of the reserve army of labor.

Serfdom   Since Marx believed that the structure of the economic community determines the productive relationships, serfdom is the name for the relation of servitude that emerges in a feudal society as a result of the labor obligations imposed on the serf by the landholder in relation to agricultural production. Technically, serf laborers are peasant cultivators who work on the land to produce their own economic livelihood and who enter into relations of production with the landholder that give the landholder rights over the labor of the serf and over the serf's agricultural production. Serfdom is thus an economic relation of production that individuals enter into as result of the economic necessity to produce their livelihoods. From the productive relations emerge relationships of dependency in which the serf is personally dependent on the landholder for their economic livelihood. Serfdom is historically significant for the reason that it economically 'binds' the serf to the landholder through compulsory labor obligations owed to the lord by the serf as defined by the corvée system. The landholder thus has legal jurisdiction over the serf's labor and the serf's agricultural product.

Slavery   This is a term used by Marx to denote an extreme form of economic compulsion existing in societies whose economy was based on slavery and slave labor. Confined mostly to the societies of antiquity, slavery is the name Marx gives to the relations of servitude that emerge in ancient societies as a result of the slave being the direct producer of physical labor. In ancient societies the productive relationships appear in the form of dominance and servitude which are direct reflections of the class relationships between patrician and slave. Slaves have neither control over their own labor or the means of production, and the product of their labor is forcibly appropriated by a class who are dominant over them. Slaves are outside of society, have no political or legal rights and are subject to the direct physical coercion by their masters. Slaves are the most dramatic expression of the labor and class relationship since, in the strict sense, they are defined as the property of others and are privately owned as a commodity. Greece and Rome exemplify the most dramatic expression of slave societies where the slave was at the center of the production process. Marx argued that the 'fact' of slavery was to be understood as a product of social relations rather than as an accident of nature. 'Society,' said Marx, 'is not merely an aggregate of individuals, but rather is the sum of the relations in which these individuals stand to one another.' Outside of society, a slave is but a human being; whereas inside society a slave is the result of socially determined relations, and thus only a slave in and through society.

Socially Necessary Labor   Marx used this term to identify the exact social mechanism whereby the worker becomes poorer as the owners of the means of production accumulate and acquire more wealth. Socially necessary labor can be defined as the part of the workday which it takes for workers to produce in wages the cost of their own maintenance in rent, food and clothing. Marx reasoned that if the workday is eight hours, it takes approximately four hours for workers to produce the cost of their own maintenance. However, during the remaining portion of the workday, which includes an additional four hours of labor, the labor of the worker is no longer necessary labor and does not furnish the maintenance of the worker at all. This part of the workday Marx called 'surplus labor'. In direct contrast to necessary labor, 'surplus labor' refers to the time during the working day where the labor of the worker creates value for the capitalist alone, not the worker. Marx believed that by dividing the workday into two parts he had discovered the origin of profit in the form of the surplus value that was created by the worker during the second part of the workday. In this reasoning, the worker obtains only four hours of pay for eight hours of labor. For Marx, 'socially necessary labor' identifies the mechanism by which workers create more value than they are compensated for in their wages and that the fact of 'surplus labor' is hidden in the wage form.

Socially Productive Power of Labor   This is a term Marx used to describe the economic benefit which goes to the capitalist by reason of making separate contracts with many individual workers during the rise of the factory system. Marx stated that in so far as the capitalist enters into contracts with one hundred unconnected individuals, he pays them the value of one hundred separate wages, but not for the combined labor power that is produced from their cooperative labor and productive activity. Marx thought that the 'combined' effect of labor is a 'free gift' to the capitalist as a result of the unification of the worker's labor power. Ultimately, he believed that this 'combined labor power' costs the capitalist nothing.

State   A key concept in Marx's political writings referring to the political apparatus which arises at a certain stage in the economic development of society. Marx's theory of the state departs from earlier political thinkers such as Aristotle, St. Augustine and Hegel who argued that the state was a political abstraction standing over and above society. Marx showed that the state arises only at a certain stage in the economic development of society and this allowed him to link state development with material activity and economic production. In his political writings, Marx set out to trace the development of the state by looking at the historical conditions leading to state formation in eighteenth century France. This process began with (i) the breakup of the old feudal economies and their separate political jurisdictions and (ii) the centralization of the political and economic spheres that took place during the transfer of power from landlords to capitalists. Marx's emphasis on the material nature of political functions led him to assert that the state arises out of the productive relations of society and is therefore linked to the economy, economic production and the subsequent class formation of industrial capitalism. In this sense, the state reflects the prevailing class structure of society and acts as an instrument of the ruling classes. This consolidation of the material and historical realms made Marx's theory of political society distinct from previous political thinking in its assertion that (i) economic production shapes social relations and hence the political structure of society; and (ii) that economic production gives rise to a legal and political structure which comes to represent the productive relations. Marx believed that the appearance of the state coincides with the development of 'civil society' which protects private property, promotes the individual pursuit of private interest and gives the illusion that private competition can be carried on in the context of equality even though the means of production have become the private property of one class.

Structural Theory   This is a term used to describe a family of perspectives in social theory which use certain techniques of interpretation for studying history, human nature and society. In the main, it is a perspective which gets its name from the tendency to conceptualize society as a group of structured social relations which are made up of various social fields existing outside the individual. These include the economy, the political structure, the law, the family system, schooling institutions and the religious realm. The central idea is that these structures first constitute themselves as diverse social fields which are thought to structure social activity and pattern social action by placing individuals under the necessity of acting in relation to social limits which override their personal discretions and individual choices. In this case, structural theory assigns agency to the objective structures of society such as class, history and economy over and against individual agency. The concept of structure as a reality existing outside the individual originates in the modernist logic of interpretation that was manifested in the structuralism of Marx, Hegel and Freud, and later in the structuralism of Durkheim and Levi-Strauss. While the structuralist logic of analysis assumed that history, economy and society are 'real' and place individuals under the necessity of acting in relation to external limits, the critique of structuralism by postmodern theories led to a suspension of the key structuralist concepts of history, economy, class, society, etc. Also suspended was the presupposition of a linear development of history that had been used up until that time in structuralism to identify and define a fixed system of relations and historical patterns. As a result of the critique, structural concepts emphasizing unities and structural regularities were replaced by poststructuralist concepts such as grids, sectors, nodes, planes and vectors, which in theory had moments of intersection, but no real or actual structure in and of themselves. Since the 1970s, structuralist theories have been set into opposition with postmodern theories which are based on a critique of structuralism by a theory of discourse which argues that unities such as society, economy, class, history, etc., are products of discourse and do not exist in themselves. Critiques of this view, however, have been recently advanced by Pierre Bourdieu.

Surplus Labor   Surplus labor can be defined as the form of overwork or excess labor that is extracted from the worker as a result of the inequalities embedded in class relationships and the relations of production. This overwork appears in ancient, feudal and industrial societies and falls as an obligation imposed on the worker rather than on the owner of the means of production. Marx points out that 'surplus labor' has a historical basis that reaches its highest stage of development in capitalist societies. This can be made clear if we contrast capitalism with feudal societies where surplus labor was carried out by the serf for the lord and was demarcated very clearly in space and time. In the corvée right, the lord was able to extract unpaid free labor service – surplus labor – from the serf during the corvée labor days, and then again by the corvée right which required the serf to expend surplus labor by producing agricultural products for the lord. Both instances of surplus labor performed by the serf are clearly marked off in space and time, and both these instances are clearly unpaid labor as required by the corvée and which constitutes a distinct advantage to the landholder. In addition, the labor which the serf carried out for purposes of his own maintenance was marked off from the surplus labor which the serf performed for the maintenance of the landholder, which was unpaid. In slavery, by contrast, the unpaid nature of surplus labor was also clearly marked off in that all labor by the slave appears as labor for the master. In these two instances – feudalism and slavery – unpaid labor forms the basis of surplus labor. Only in capitalism, however, does unpaid labor appear as 'paid' since work is compensated for at an hourly rate, giving the appearance that all hours worked are paid according to the clock. Marx, however, identified a portion of the working day in which the labor of the worker is over and above the labor which the worker needs to produce the cost of his or her own maintenance in food, rent and clothing, and is therefore surplus labor. Marx called this added labor 'surplus labor.' He reasoned that the labor expended by the worker during this part of the workday provides no benefit for the worker in extra wages, but instead adds value to the product that goes to the capitalist in the form of wealth and profit. The value which the worker creates during this part of the workday benefits the capitalist alone and constitutes unpaid surplus labor. While Marx believed that industrial capitalism 'did not invent surplus labor,' he thought that whenever one part of society possesses a monopoly over the means of production, workers must add to the labor time necessary for their own maintenance an extra quantity of labor time in order to produce the means of subsistence for the owner of the means of production.

Surplus Value   This is a concept Marx used to identify the form of value that was created by the surplus labor of the worker. In all societies, said Marx, productive relations are structured to extract excess surplus labor from the worker. In ancient societies, slaves were compelled to perform surplus labor in exchange for bare necessities, and in feudal societies serfs were obligated to perform free unpaid labor service as a result of the corvée obligations. In both these cases, surplus labor confers an advantage to the class who own the means of production and identifies the specific mechanism that creates value and wealth which benefits one class but not another. 'Surplus value' is the name Marx gave to the specific form of value that is created in capitalist society as a result of the surplus labor extracted from the worker. To show how the mechanism of surplus labor operates, Marx made the distinction between necessary and surplus labor. Necessary labor refers to the part of the work day it takes for the worker to produce in wages the cost of his or her own maintenance. Marx reasoned that if the workday is 8 hours, it takes approximately 4 hours of labor to produce the cost of maintaining the worker in food, rent and clothing. Surplus labor, by contrast, refers to the part of the working day in which laborers expend labor power but creates no value for themselves. The labor expended by the worker adds value to the product and the value the worker creates during this part of the day benefits the capitalist alone. Marx stated that the laborer is paid only for one part of the workday and that the unpaid part constitutes the 'surplus' which is the part of the workday which produces the 'value' for the capitalist in the form of profit and wealth. Surplus value has four central attributes: (i) it is the value created by the surplus labor of the worker; (ii) it is unpaid and therefore creates value for the capitalist but not the worker; (iii) it presents a deception since it claims to be paid labor; and (iv) it is the recognized form of overwork in industrial capitalism since the worker is not paid for the value that is created by their surplus labor.

System of Social Relations   This is a term used by Marx to refer to the social relations which exist between individuals as a result of their productive acts in society. According to Marx, the system of social relations eventually forms a total social framework that constitutes the social conditions of existence. As far as Marx was concerned, the system of social relations is always the product of the existing connections people have with one another in production and without these relations, bosses and workers, landlords and tenants, producers and consumers would not exist. The concept of social relations thus covers two principle meanings in classical Marxism: first is its reference to the system of social relations individuals enter into in production which are always the immediate result of the economic necessity to satisfy their material needs. Second is the reference to how the system of relations entered into by people is structured by the existing class relations in society. Marx believed that the system of social relations structures an individual's participation in society so that an individual's relation to their employer or to their landlord, is an example of how the system of social relations structures social interchanges between individuals within class relations. In these terms we enter into relations with society only by enacting the social positions we assume in the system of social relations as workers, bosses, landlords and tenants, etc. It is important to note that these relations are always structured along class lines.

Theory of Value   This refers to a central argument in Marx's economic writings which relate to the problem of the 'value of a commodity' and the larger question of what makes a commodity valuable. Marx developed his theory of value in *Capital* Volume I in response to Smith and Ricardo, who had asserted that 'value' was a substance found in a commodity which is created by human labor during the production process. Marx began by noting that commodities come into the world in the form of use values – the value of corn, the value of linen, the value of iron, etc – and in this sense he thought 'value' was in the form of 'use' or 'utility' because it served to maintain human existence. In capitalist economies, however, commodities are the bearers of exchange value, e.g. the price of corn, the price of linen, the price of iron, etc., and in this sense, value is in the form of 'exchange.' For Marx, the mystery was how do commodities that exchange for a price in the market become bearers of exchange value? In comparison with Smith and Ricardo who had asserted that the 'exchange value' of a commodity was a substance that exists in the body of the commodity, Marx began by noting that exchange value does not exist in the form of a substance since this is, according to Marx, impossible. He stated that 'we may twist and turn these simple commodities as we wish, but it is impossible to find the substance which represents its value. No chemist has ever found this substance in the commodity as such and, under these circumstances, 'not one atom of matter enters into the commodity as value.' Marx believed that value originates in the system of social relations in which the existing 'value form' arises directly out of the productive relations. He went on to reason that since the value of a commodity does not exist in the form of a substance, then value must be an expression of something else in relation to which it has a value. This form of value Marx called 'relative value' and it refers to the fact that no commodity has value in isolation by itself and that the value of any commodity is always expressed relatively in relation to some other commodity. To illustrate, he uses the example of linen and coats. The value of linen, said Marx, cannot be expressed in linen itself since we can't say 20 yards of linen has the value of 20 yards of linen. However, as soon as linen is brought into comparison with another commodity such as a coat, value can be established 'relatively.' Marx asserted that since no commodity is valuable by itself, then it stands to reason that 'exchange value' does not belong to a commodity naturally, since there are only use values. Instead, he reasoned that 'exchange value' must belong to the social framework rather than existing in a commodity as a substance. His proof for this was that exchange value only came into existence during the development of economies based on exchange and did not exist in natural economies, such as those found in the village system of India or the traditional economies of Peru and China. In this case, Marx showed that exchange value must be a product of a system of social relations which exists within the ongoing framework of society. Hence 'exchange value' emerges only at a historically given economic epoch, precisely at the moment when the value of one commodity is brought into a relation of exchange with another, and exchange emerges as the dominant form of value over use.

Use Value   A central term used by Marx to denote the capacity a commodity has to satisfy distinct human needs and sustain existence. Marx used the term to differentiate 'use value' from the 'exchange value' and feudal economies from industrial economies. Understood in this sense, use value is a term that refers to the ability of a commodity to render a particular service to an individual by satisfying a need which sustains life. A coat, for instance, provides warmth and food diminishes hunger which serves directly as a means of existence. Marx believed that in feudal societies all production was predominantly for use and that all production was immediately consumed to satisfy human needs and sustain life. In this case, Marx thought that value was in the form of 'use' or 'utility' which served directly as a means of existence. In feudal societies, therefore, the prevailing form of value was 'use value' and exchange value did not exist because all production was for consumption rather than commerce. In capitalist economies, by contrast, all production enters into the medium of exchange called the market where it is subject to buying and selling. In such circumstances value is in the form of 'exchange,' there is no direct consumption and commodities and human labor must enter into the medium of exchange where they are sold for a money price. Marx thought that it was during this period that exchange value became dominant over use value and that this brought about a change in the 'value form.' In use value, commodities differ in 'quality' – the quality of bread to diminish hunger, the quality of a coat to provide warmth, etc. In exchange value, however, commodities differ in terms of quantities – 'a quarter of wheat, a hundred weight of coffee,' a bolt of linen, a dozen knives. In these cases, the unit is the quantity or measure, not the use or utility rendered by the commodity to the individual.

Durkheim

Abnormal Forms   A term used by Durkheim to identify a type of disturbance taking place in the division of labor resulting from its failure to produce social solidarity linking individuals to each other in society. Durkheim thought that the normal function of the division of labor was to produce social solidarity tying individuals together in a manner that served the overall social cohesion of society. As industrial society develops, however, there is a rapid rise in economic specialization and the occupational division of labor expands. As a result, integrative functions 'are not adjusted' to each other as they once were so that 'conflict' becomes more prevalent over solidarity. Durkheim identified three abnormal forms which resulted in the lack of adjustment in the division of labor. These are: (i) the anomic division of labor where there was a breakdown in the body of social rules regulating relations between individuals so that the social restraints preventing disputes gave way to conflict; (ii) the forced division of labor in which people were placed in occupational roles by necessity instead of by aptitude, leading to a situation where individuals were linked to their social functions as a result of one class taking control of the division of labor; and (iii) the insufficient coordination of the division of labor resulting in the mis-allotment of social and occupational roles.

Altruistic Suicide   This is a term used by Durkheim to describe a 'social type' of suicide which occurs when the individual's attachments to society far exceed the loyalty they have to themselves. Altruistic suicide is best understood in the context of social integration, a term used by Durkheim to describe the extent to which individuals are linked to social groups outside themselves by various degrees of attachment and social cohesion. In relation to egoistic suicide, Durkheim claimed that individuals take their own lives when social integration to the religious group and the family group is either absent or not well developed. In this case, their attachments shrink down to the private ego, and the individual withdraws to themselves and engages in excessive self reflection. At the opposite end of the integrative pole, however, is altruistic suicide which occurs when social attachments to the group far exceed the loyalties which individuals have to themselves. This usually occurs when social integration is excessive and over developed, as in the case of tribal societies or cults where religious law prevails and where the emotional hold over the individual is intense. Altruistic suicide is thus the clearest case in which suicide is imposed as a 'social duty' upon the individual who takes their own life in the name of social purposes greater than themselves. In almost all these instances 'the weight of society is brought to bear on the individual to destroy themselves' for purposes greater than them. The Jonestown suicides of the 1970s and the 9/11 terrorist attack constitute altruistic forms of suicide since the social allegiance to the group was greater than the loyalty individuals had to themselves. Under these circumstances, people take their own lives, not because they assume the personal right to do so or because of their psychological state of mind, but rather because of the intense 'social obligation' that is imposed upon them by the group which glorifies their honor and guarantees them a place in the after life. In these circumstances, people look upon suicide as a religious duty and as an act that glorifies their past existence. There are three forms of altruistic suicide identified by Durkheim: (i) obligatory altruistic suicide; (ii) optional altruistic suicide; (iii) acute altruistic or mystical suicide. Each differs in terms of the degree of social obligation placed upon the individual to take their own life.

Anomic Division of Labor   A term used by Durkheim to describe a type of disturbance taking place in the division of labor when there is a loss of social solidarity due to excessive occupational specialization. Under normal circumstances, the division of labor produces social solidarity among groups by creating links and bonds between individuals that connect them to each other and to the wider society. This serves the purpose of adjusting social relations between groups so that there is a sufficient level of cooperativeness. However, during the rapid development of the occupational division of labor in industrial society, a lack of adjustment occurs between groups which leads to more frequent disputes and conflict. In traditional societies where social cohesion is greater and the division of labor is not well developed, social relations between members of groups show more solidarity and, as a result, conflicts and disputes rarely arise. Where organic solidarity develops, however, work is divided, employers and workers exist apart, and the social links between individuals in society diminish and break down. As the links and bonds between employers and workers become weak, there are more frequent conflicts and disputes that undermine the spirit of cooperativeness. As a consequence, individuals form links with their occupations and pursue their private interests more readily. Thus the more separate and specialized labor becomes, the less social solidarity there is. In addition, as social relations are governed by contracts as opposed to bonds of obligation, the existing obligation between groups tends to diminish and groups treat one another as adversaries rather than as 'cooperators.' As a result, an industrial crisis is more likely because discipline breaks down and the ties binding groups become dispersed, giving way to a decline in consensus and social cohesion.

Anomic Suicide   A term used by Durkheim to describe a social type of suicide resulting from the overall decline in the regulatory powers of society and its inability to set the level of external restraint and impose limits on the individual. Durkheim believed that one of the most important functions of society was to set restraints and limitations on individuals so that social wants such as wealth, power and prestige would not become conscious material desires that could override restraint. Durkheim thought that, in comparison with other types of needs, human social wants of wealth and power were unlimited and therefore restraint and external limitation must be imposed by the regulatory institutions of society. In industrial society, the limitations that were once imposed by social institutions in the past were replaced by a 'spirit of free pursuit' of individual goals and, accordingly, the system of restraint began to break down. As a result, material desires began to increase and social wants exceeded the available means for attaining these wants. The tendency in industrial society for people to break rules in order to obtain what they want is thus a result of the absence of regulatory mechanisms in society. Durkheim thought that when social restraint is absent it leads to disappointment and feelings of individual failure and even to despair. When social wants exceed limitations imposed by society, disappointment with life and the feeling of failure increases. Durkheim thought that this circumstance was compounded in modern society at the point that the economy became the dominant social institution and social restraints and limitations on individual wants became incompatible with economic competition. When society fails to set limits on social wants, individuals continually exceed the means at their disposal and their desires, by definition, become frustrated and out of reach. This can only happen, Durkheim maintained, when individuals constantly aspire to reach ends or goals which are beyond their capacity to obtain. To pursue goals which are unattainable ensures repeated disappointment, and when goals are set which have no end or limit, individuals become despondent, and anomie ensues indicating the absence of social restraint. Anomic suicide therefore occurs when society is unable to set the level of restraint and impose limits on individual needs and wants. In this case, social regulation is either weak or absent.

Anomie   A term first used by Durkheim in 1893 in *The Division of Labor* to describe the decline that takes place in the regulatory mechanisms of social institutions and in the capacity of society to set the level of social restraint. In such circumstances, anomie refers to a decline in the capacity of regulatory institutions to impose limits on individuals during the development of industrial society. Durkheim thought that anomie originated from unlimited economic progress in industrial society, which tended to free social activity from the regulation imposed by social institutions such as the family and religion. This happened when religious institutions were replaced by economic institutions and the traditional mechanisms of restraint imposed by religion were lifted. At the same time, economic institutions backed away from social regulation to the extent that it encouraged the attainment of goals that were out of reach. This led to a deterioration of moral restraint that was unique to industrial society. At the same time, the division of labor was unable to produce social solidarity and regulatory restraints were unable to set limits on social wants so that needs began to exceed the means to attain them. Later in 1897, Durkheim used the term to put forward a theory of anomie in relation to suicide by pinpointing the decline of the regulatory mechanism of society which took place during the time that the economy became dominant and social restraint was lifted. As the economy developed, markets were extended and social wants were freed from previous limitation. As a result, the 'capacity for social wants became insatiable so that the more one has the more one wants.' The stress on economic success increased individual desires to such an extent that the discomfort and restraint that were tolerable in the past became less acceptable. Durkheim believed that it is in the economically related functions of society where anomie creates the largest category of suicide, in contrast to other spheres of society in which the 'old regulatory forces' still prevail. Looked at in this way, anomie can be defined as the decline which takes place in the regulatory mechanisms of society brought about by unchecked economic progress. This decline occurs as society is unable to regulate social wants which develop as the economy becomes dominant over other institutions.

Categories of Understanding   This is a term used by Durkheim in *The Elementary Forms* to identify a key set of ideas which since Aristotle have been called the 'categories of understanding' by philosophers and which includes ideas such as space, time, cause, class, category and number. These categories are believed to be fundamental to human thought to the extent that they are used in perceptual relations with the external world when space and time references are employed to understand reality. Historically, there are two formal positions in philosophy that have attempted to explain the origin of the categories. First are the 'apriorists' who believe that the categories originate in the human mind and that they have 'the pre-eminent power to confer a logical order to the world.' On this view, we only come to know the outside world by applying the categories of understanding to things and objects in the world. Second are the empiricists who argue that the categories are constructed from the mind by individual sense perceptions, and that individuals alone construct the things of the world out of these perceptions. While the apriorists believe that the categories of understanding are 'given by nature' and are innate to human reason, the empiricists believe that 'the categories are constructed of bits and pieces' of sense data and that the individual is the agent of the construction. In *The Elementary Forms* Durkheim challenged these views by re-defining the problem of the categories, comparing what philosophers have said with the ethnographic findings concerning the classification systems of the totem tribes of Australia. What Durkheim found was that the Australian tribes divided themselves into distinct classes and clans corresponding to logical divisions by religious totem. He went on to note that once they had done this, there emerged logical classes and categories for classifying external nature and these served as a distinct framework for the classification of other things such as classes of plants and animals, thus giving rise to the category of class as a group of things set apart from other things. In addition, he found that the classifications of the world of the religious totem went with classifications in the natural world regarding divisions into regions in space so that one clan was assigned the region of the north, the other the south, etc., and that this led to the logical classification of the cardinal points of latitude, thus giving rise to the category of space. Durkheim reasoned that the categories of understanding were therefore modeled on the social organization and that this served as a framework for the mental organization with which they saw the world. In Durkheim's view the categories of understanding emerged outside the mind in experience and were therefore a derivative of society, as opposed to originating in internal reason.

Clan   A term use by Durkheim in *The Rules of Sociological Method* for classifying different types of society according to their structural complexity and level of development. According to Durkheim, the totem tribes of Australia were organized by clans in contrast to other societies that had different organizing principles. Initially, a clan refers to a social segment within a larger society that is made up of many members and groups divided into different clans. A clan denotes a type of society which is at the earliest stage of development and may be defined as a group which has no additional social elements and no clear political divisions. Clans develop from simple societies called 'hordes' which are the least complex form of social organization. Durkheim reasoned that the horde must be the social species from which all other social types develop. Clans were once hordes and therefore possessed the morphology of hordes. However, as they progressed their structural characteristics took the form of a clan formation. As they become more complex, they become compounded into segments and these segments combine to give a more complex group structure. Initially, the concept of the clan was used by Durkheim to show that societies are made up of structures that extend beyond the individual.

Classification, System of   Durkheim used this term in a work entitled *Primitive Classification* to show that our system for classifying things in the world by class and by category is not a product of internal reason as argued by philosophers. Working from ethnographic evidence derived from the totem tribes of Australia, Durkheim noted that they tended to divide themselves into different marriage classes and clans which correspond to their divisions by totem. He found that once they divided themselves into different groups and classes arranged by totem, there emerged logical classes and categories for classifying external nature which served as a direct framework for the classification of other things, such as classes of plants and animals as distinguished from classes of vegetables, and that a class was a collection of things set apart from other things. Moreover, he found that the classifications of the totem world went with classifications in the natural world regarding divisions into regions in space so that one clan was assigned the region of the north, the other the south, etc., and that this led to the logical classification of the cardinal points of latitude. From these classifications there emerged many associations and distinctions as to what goes together according to classifications related to resemblances or pairs, or associations between classes of food and classes of plants. In addition, Durkheim found that the classifications in the totem world were extended to classifications in the natural world for purposes of dividing elements of time into seasonal variations such as summer, winter, fall and spring, and that these divisions corresponded with periodic religious feasts held during certain seasons. This meant that, for Durkheim, the system of classification did not arise internally as a function of human reason, but was rather based on the way societies divide themselves into groups and classes which indicated that the principle of classification was socially derived. Thus, rather than being a spontaneous product of the mind, the classification scheme arises from the tendency of societies to arrange their ideas in ways that correspond to their division into groups. Durkheim argued that the division into logical class and categories and the framework for classifying things in external nature corresponds to the totem divisions first formed within the clans. He believed that only in this way are things in the natural world understood to belong to different groups and classes. This, said Durkheim, tells us how 'the idea of class and category first took form in human groups,' and how 'these classifications are the first we meet with in history.'

Classification of Social Types   This is a term used by Durkheim in *The Rules of Sociological Method* to establish a system for classifying different types of societies. Generally, the system for classifying different types of society is referred to by Durkheim as a 'social morphology,' which denotes the relationship between the complexity of a society and its structural characteristics such as the size of the group, its institutional components and its divisions into classes and clans. Durkheim identifies three types of societies, each of which has a distinct social form and a distinct type of social cohesion and dynamic density. These are: (i) a horde, which is the most elementary social form characterized by an absence of different parts; (ii) a clan, which is formed by the combination of various groups leading to a more complex social structure; and (iii) polysegmentals, which are societies made up the combination of various aggregates which together form a confederated group or common tribe.

Collective Representations   This concept is used by Durkheim in *The Rules* to identify the existence of external social realities and common social practices that form rules of conduct that have the authority of the group. They can be defined as any subject matter into which the collective practices of society have been condensed so that they come to 'represent' the common social and customary rules that are prevalent within a society. Examples of the collective representations into which social subject matter is concentrated are religious doctrine, legal rules, social obligations, customary practices, and social traditions. These customary rules and practices – such as the patriotic respect shown to one's national flag – have the power of external coercion and the ability to impose limits on individual behavior that is fixed in custom. Durkheim believed that collective representations reflect social subject matter in four distinct ways: (i) they reflect an external reality different from that of the individual; (ii) they have characteristics of their own which are autonomous from individuals and which make up the external reality of society; (iii) they can be investigated in their own right without being subsumed under psychological or biological laws; and (iv) they arise from the collective activity of society and group life.

Common Conscience   A central concept used by Durkheim in *The Division of Labor* to refer to a body of collective beliefs and social practices formed by society which are held in common by all members of society to the extent that it determines the relations they have to one another and to society itself. The common conscience is diffused throughout the society, functions as a basis of collective action and generally structures the pattern of social life. It may be thought of as a determinate system of practices, attitudes and beliefs which create social likenesses among individuals in society. Durkheim took the view that the common conscience develops according to its own laws, forms the structure of society and its institutions and has an independent existence that can be studied according to the methods of observation. Durkheim outlined four broad characteristics of the common conscience: (i) volume, which refers to the extent of the reach of collective beliefs and related social practices to all parts of society; (ii) intensity, referring to the degree of emotional hold which the collective practices and beliefs exercise over individual attitudes and behavior; (iii) determinateness, referring to how well the collective beliefs and social practices are defined and the extent of resistance the beliefs have to change, transgression or violation; (iv) content of the common conscience, which refers to the dominant characteristics of the society and to its collective nature. Content can be religious, in which case the primary form of collective sentiments originates from religious law and exert a hold over individuals through religious expiation; or it can be secular, in which case the primary form of the collective sentiments are divested of their religious content and concentrated in a system of law and scientific knowledge.

Consecrate   A term used by Durkheim in *The Elementary Forms* to refer to the power of religious acts performed in relation to the 'totem' in the tribes of Australia to make people, things and spaces sacred through religious enactments and periodic religious rites. For example, among the Arunta of Australia Durkheim pointed out that an object called a 'churinga,' consisting of a polished piece of stone, was among the most 'preeminently sacred things' in society having the power to 'consecrate' spaces, things and people by foregrounding the sacred while at the same time keeping the profane at a distance. Durkheim's argument in *The Elementary Forms* was that 'religion' was simply society manifested in its consecrated form.

Constraint, Social   A term used by Durkheim in *The Rules of Sociological Method* to refer to the coercive power of social facts and external social rules to impose limits on individual conduct which is fixed in custom and which has the power to override personal choices and private considerations. Social constraints are made manifest in social duties and obligations, in customary requirements and religious interdicts, which Durkheim believed are capable of structuring social activity by compelling individuals to act in ways which often override their personal dispositions. Technically speaking, Durkheim thought that 'constraint' was the property of external social rules to place individuals under the necessity of acting in relation to these rules in ways that made the objective structure of society more visible. Social constraints are always external to the individual, originate from society and precede the individual historically. Constraints are properties of social facts and collective representations and denote the power of social rules to impose limits on individuals by securing their compliance.

Contract Law   Sometimes called 'written law' by Durkheim, this term is used in *The Division of Labor* to refer to a system of judicial rules and legal sanctions which arise in industrial societies as a result of the development of the division of labor. Contract law is a derivative of industrial society and has two central characteristics: (i) it prescribes obligations and expectations by binding contracting parties; and (ii) it defines sanctions as they relate to offenses and breaches against contracts. In contrast to segmental societies whose law is based on religion and penal sanctions, industrial society leads to the development of new social institutions which become increasingly specialized. In this context, the law emerges as an autonomous social institution which functions on the basis of specialized agencies such as the courts, arbitration councils, tribunals and administrative bodies. In this case, the authority of legal rules is thus exercised through specific functionaries such as judges, magistrates and lawyers who possess specialized credentials and specialized authority. In contrast to penal law or religious law, the function of contract law is to regulate relations between particular individuals rather than acting in the name of the sacred rules consecrated by the group. The purpose of contract law is to develop rules which bind individuals to each other by regulating contractual obligations. Durkheim took the view that this system of law did little for social solidarity since it did not regulate the bond between the individual and society by obligation and social duties, but restricted itself to regulating only contractual links between individuals.

Division of Labor, Social   This is a central concept used by Durkheim in *The Division of Labor* to describe the social process by which labor is divided up among individuals in a group so that the main economic and domestic tasks are performed by different individuals for the purpose of the collective maintenance of society. The process of the division of labor begins as soon as individuals form into groups and begin to cooperate collectively by dividing their labor and by coordinating their economic and domestic tasks for purposes of survival. Durkheim believed that the division of labor was therefore the result of a social process taking place within the structure of society rather than the result of the private choices of individuals or the result of organic traits that emerged during evolution. Durkheim used the term 'social division of labor' to distinguish it from the process Adam Smith called the 'economic division of labor.' Smith had used the term to refer to the process of dividing up labor in manufacturing for purposes of increasing the rate of production. Durkheim, however, thought that the social division of labor was distinct from the economic division of labor because it referred to the principle of social cohesion that developed in societies when social links and bonds between individuals emerge when their labor was divided along economic and domestic tasks. What Durkheim observed beyond Smith was that (i) the social division of labor led to the formation of what he called social 'links and bonds' between individuals in the same society, and that these links and bonds actually formed a structured network of activities which shaped their social attachments and structured their overall social cohesion. In this case, he found that (ii) the social division of labor formed attachments between individuals by linking actual 'cooperators together' in a way that formed a society. In addition, he found that within the social division of labor links and bonds manifest themselves in two distinct ways: first is in the form of links of dependency which determine social relations between individuals who carry out economic and domestic tasks jointly and collectively; and second is in the form of bonds of social obligation which regulate expectations and interchanges between individuals in the same society. While links of dependency often emerge between those who perform economic and domestic tasks, bonds of obligation emerge between members of the same society because of the network of duties and obligations that arise in relation to religious and family institutions. Durkheim's central point was that within the system of activities which the social division of labor coordinates, social links and bonds arise which affect the various attachments between individuals by generating a system of obligations and dependencies which would never have developed if individuals lived separately or in isolation. Each of these points of attachment to the wider society intensifies the 'emotional hold' which society has over the individual. Lastly, the term division of labor is used by Durkheim to describe the effects on social cohesion which result when work is divided into minutely specialized occupational functions which arise as a result of the development of industrial society. In this case, social solidarity is no longer by direct social links and bonds which form during the activity of common economic and domestic tasks within segmental societies, but by the role individuals play in the occupational structure that develops as a result of the increased division of labor. This is followed by an increase in the density of society due to the expansion of the population, the growth of cities and the development of means of transportation and communication.

Dynamic Density   A term used by Durkheim to describe the degree of social activity created by populations interacting with one another. Durkheim employed the term to look at the relationship between different types of society and the extent of interaction created among the population. The dynamic density of society determines the degree of 'concentration of aggregates' and the ways in which the concentration of aggregates lead to increased economic and social interchange. Two kinds of facts act on the dynamic density of society: (i) those related to the differences in the structural organization of the group that are found in segmental and industrial societies; and (ii) those related to the proximity of individuals to each other and the intensity of their interactions and interchanges. Measurements of dynamic density may determine how intense social life is and the 'horizon of thought and action of the individual.'

Effervescent Assemblies   This is a concept used by Durkheim in *The Elementary Forms* to refer to a phase in the social life of societies where the immediate focus is on assembling for the purpose of a religious ceremony. There are two distinct phases of social life which are reflected in Durkheim's discussion of effervescent assemblies. In one phase, families go about their everyday activities of hunting and gathering which they perform out of necessity. In this phase, everyone is essentially 'scattered' and 'dispersed' for purposes of carrying out separate economic and domestic tasks. In the second phase, however, each individual is 'summoned to come together in one place to conduct a religious ceremony.' This, said Durkheim, immediately 'transports the individual into an entirely different world from the practical one they have before their eyes,' and under these circumstances, the group suddenly assembles for purposes of a religious enactment that puts them into motion in a new way. By reason of assembling, they intensify the relations existing between them, and this 'makes them more intimate with one another.' At this point everything becomes sacred: space, time, things and people; and consequently, this sacredness functions as a means of consecrating their acts in the collective space of society. At this moment, according to Durkheim, they are removed from their ordinary activities and their ritual enactments function to put boundaries around their ceremonies in a way which formally designates them as separate from the outside world in ways that alter their perceptions and creates an exalted religious state of mind. There are two broad effects as a result: (i) social divisions are marked off and certain principles are enacted which separate spaces and things. As spaces and things become subject to the rule of separation, they become consecrated things by virtue of the fact that they are sacred. In this way, said Durkheim, a 'living reality exists outside the individual' and acts on the mind by what it does to the individual. (ii) As soon as they come together for the performance of ceremonial rites the religious experience is born, and this experience is eminently social in that it consecrates society.

Egoism   The term 'egoism' originated in the nineteenth century and was widely used by Durkheim and others to indicate a breakdown in the social links tying individuals to society as a result of the development of industrial society. Egoism can be described as the process by which individuals detach themselves from the wider society by turning their activity inward and by retreating to themselves. Egoism is characterized by excessive self reflection on personal matters and a withdrawal from the outside world. In this state, the 'springs of action' are relaxed and individuals turn inward and away from society. Egoism occurs when the integrative links binding the individual to the family and religious group begin to deteriorate and are not sufficiently integrated at the points where the individual is in contact with society. It results from an excess of individualism and from the 'weakening of the social fabric' that occurs as gaps form in industrial society between the individual and the institutional points of contact that attach individuals to society. In a state of egoism, social bonds break down and individual purposes are more important than the common ends of society. Under these circumstances, egoism constitutes a threat to society, to aggregate social maintenance and to collective authority. Durkheim believed that there was a direct connection between suicide and the decline of social integration that attached individuals to social groups outside themselves. Egoism is the result of prolonged and unchecked individualism which is a consequence of industrial society.

Egoistic Suicide   This is a term used by Durkheim in his study of *Suicide* to identify a type of suicide which occurs in industrial society as the mechanisms of social integration break down during the period of advanced individualism. Durkheim believed the individual does not live separately from society and that mechanisms of social integration attach individuals to society at different points of social and institutional contact which include the family and the religious group. In addition to this, Durkheim showed that these points of social attachment had different 'intensities,' so that family and religious attachments form the greatest and most intense relations. In industrial society, however, 'gaps' form between individuals and the points of social contact to religious, familial and national groups and as a result egoistic suicide increases as social integration declines and individuals retreat to themselves. Durkheim found that the integrative mechanisms attaching individuals to groups outside themselves reduced gaps between the individual and their attachments to the wider society. When 'gaps' form, individuals retreat to themselves and became more self-preoccupied. Durkheim found that the suicide rates increased as social integration declined and the links binding individuals to religious groups deteriorated. In one case he demonstrated that because Protestants tended to be more autonomous than Catholics in matters of religious integration, this led to greater self sufficiency and egoistic withdrawal, and ultimately higher suicide rates among Protestants.

Epistemological Argument   This is a term used to refer to Durkheim's formal argument in *The Elementary Forms* which explains how relations between thought and reality work so that reliable assumptions can be made about the outside world. Since Aristotle, philosophers have believed that relations between thought and reality can be explained only by a limited number of central ideas, called the 'categories of understanding,' which include concepts such as space, time, class, category, number, cause, etc. Philosophers believe that the categories of understanding are imposed on the external world by human reason and that they act as conditions of validity for judgments about external reality. Kant, for instance, thought that we cannot know the outer world directly, but rather come to grasp it only as a result of the a priori categories which are always a function of human internal reason that confers logical order on the world. Since formal philosophy conceived of thought and reality as separate, the term epistemology can be defined as a branch of reasoning that concerns itself with how thought relations work between the mind and reality to make reliable assumptions about the external world. Whereas philosophers believed that thought relations always proceed from the mind outward into reality, Durkheim's epistemological argument reversed this view, stating that thought relations are first modeled on the social organization and later became a model for the mental organization with which we come to perceive the world. In this view, the categories of understanding derive from external experience and are internalized in the mind as thought relations in the form of the categories. Durkheim's argument was based on ethnographic evidence related to the classification system of the totem tribes of Australia. What Durkheim found in the ethnographic evidence was that the Australian tribes divided themselves into distinct classes corresponding to logical divisions by religious totem. He noted that once they divided themselves into different groups and classes arranged by totem, there emerged logical classes and categories for classifying external nature and these served as a distinct framework for the classification of other things, and that this gave rise to the category of class as a collection of things separate from other things. Durkheim went on to argue that since all societies divide themselves into groups and classes, their divisions serve as a framework for the classification of other things in external nature into logical classes and categories. Durkheim's epistemological argument asserted that the origin of the framework for thought relations between the mind and reality derived first from the social organization and was later internalized within the mental organization, which in turn corresponded to the disposition of the outer world in terms of regions in space and segments in time. The argument is historically important because Durkheim was the first to put forward a sociologically based epistemology that opposed formal philosophy.

Experience   This is a concept used by philosophers to refer to the process by which the mind shapes outer experience and confers a logical order on the world. Since Descartes, philosophers have believed that outer experience has a logical and coherent quality only because it is conferred by the agency of the mind. Philosophers therefore take the view that experience does not exist independently of the mind but is instead constructed by it. Hume, for instance, thought that objects and substances in the outer world were products of sense perceptions and thus had no powers in themselves and did not affect the actions of individuals. In *The Elementary Forms*, Durkheim wished to show that experience was a freestanding independent structure made up of a total social framework that had specific material effects on individual acts and that these effects were evident in the religious enactments seen in the performance of certain rites, where the participants mutilated their bodies in the name of religious beliefs. In contrast to Hume, therefore, Durkheim argued that religious enactments and their effects proved that experience was not only structured like a system but that religious interdicts had powers to affect the acts of individuals, thus confirming the existence of external social realities. Durkheim therefore used the concept of experience to describe the impact of social reality on the mind of the individual which is the reverse of the philosophical view. Durkheim therefore believed that experience was constituted by the objective structures of society and to this extent disagreed with Hume and Kant.

Fatalistic Suicide   This is a term used by Durkheim to refer to a category of suicide which is the polar opposite of anomic suicide and which results from an excess of social regulation as opposed to the absence of regulatory restraint. Fatalistic suicide occurs when the prospects, goals and aspirations of individuals become blocked due to an excess of social regulation imposed by others or by society. Durkheim cites the example of slaves who, because of severe restraint and deprivation, take their own life due to restrictions and limitations in their social horizons.

Forced Division of Labor   This is a term used by Durkheim to refer to the changes taking place in the division of labor of industrial societies when dominant classes gain strategic control over the division of labor. Under these circumstances, occupational roles and tasks are not divided either by the skill, merit or personal ability of the worker but are forcibly assigned on the basis of the interests of one class in society. In order for the division of labor to produce solidarity it had to work as a process which assigned tasks to individuals in ways that 'fit their aptitude.' When this process is managed by a dominant class in society, individuals are allotted their social and occupational functions solely on the basis of 'force' and at the advantage of their employers. Under these circumstances, disputes occur more readily, social cohesion is diminished, and individuals have little stake in the production process and in the economy. The forced division of labor is manifest (i) when there is hereditary transmission of occupations, (ii) when inequalities arise in contracts and (iii) when groups monopolize opportunities and close off avenues for the pursuit of specialized occupations and the performance of prestige bearing work roles.

Individual   A term used by Durkheim to draw attention to the fact that the proper subject matter of sociological investigation are the collective social realities external to the individual. In so far as social realities exist in the form of rules of conduct manifested in the form of social duties and obligations, Durkheim thought that the existence of social rules identified a distinct subject matter outside the individual which could be studied in its own right separate from individual psychology. Durkheim's view of the individual was evident in his assertion that 'society cannot exist if there are only individuals.' Durkheim's anti-individualist stance led to his criticism of thinkers such as Hobbes and Rousseau who believed that society derived from individuals, and of psychologists such as Gabriel Tarde who argued that the individual was the preeminent focus of a theory of society based solely on imitation and imitated acts. Tarde opposed Durkheim's assertion that collective realities exist outside the individual and argued that anything social, whether a religious rite, a legal statute or a moral maxim was transmitted and passed on from one individual to another by imitation. In response to this Durkheim argued that if there is nothing in society except individuals, how can there be anything external to them? Durkheim believed that to focus on the individual alone is to ignore the larger social framework and rules of conduct which form the basis of society.

Individualism   A term first used by Durkheim to describe the shift which takes place when the individual becomes the social and political center of society. It identifies a period which formally began after the French revolution when political and legal freedoms were assigned to individuals as a function of their new social statuses and freedoms. Later, with the work of Durkheim and Tonnies, the term referred to the glorification of the individual, which came about as a result of industrial development and the emergence of the economy as the dominant institution. In early societies, individuals were thought to participate in social life only as members of larger social groups. Under these circumstances, individuals were absorbed into collective life, their links to society were direct, and social control was repressive. As integrative links and social ties began to weaken due to the division of labor and the emergence of industrial society, individuals became the recipients of rights and freedoms in which their ties to society were expressed indirectly through the system of legal rights. This led to adjustments in social solidarity that freed individuals from the claims which society exerted upon them and, as a result, they retreated to themselves. Durkheim used the term individualism largely to designate the themes of egoism and autonomy which were thought to have been brought about as the links connecting individuals to larger groups began to dissolve. Many believed that the focus on the individual jeopardized the greater collective interests of society and, for some, the progress of individualism meant the collapse of social unity and the dissolution of society into autonomous isolated individuals. In nineteenth century France, individualism was seen as a crisis which threatened to atomize society and destroy collective unity.

Integration, Social   A major concept in Durkheim's study of suicide used to stress the nature of social links attaching individuals to social groups in the wider society. Initially the term social integration can be defined as the extent to which individuals are linked to and feel allegiance for social groups outside themselves. To this extent, social integration serves several key functions: (i) it operates to connect individuals to society by ensuring a high degree of attachment to commonly held values and beliefs which promote bonds between the individual and the group that reduces self-preoccupation and excessive self-reflection; (ii) it acts as a check against excessive individualism by imposing restraints on private needs and wants and by focusing interests outside the self; and (iii) integration serves connective functions so far as it propels individuals out into the wider society by creating links to larger social groups and institutions promoting the perception that individuals are part of a larger social whole. Durkheim used the concept in his study of suicide to extend the investigative focus beyond the psychology of the individual by looking at three institutional points of attachment related to the individual's connection to society. First, was the point of attachment existing between the individual and the social framework, which extended the focus from individual suicides to the objective structures of society. This showed that the causes of suicide lay not within the psychological motives of individuals alone, but within distinct social environments with different religions, different patterns of family life, different military obligations and different forms of attachment leading to different suicide rates. Second, was the point of attachment Durkheim established between a given population and the social suicide rate of a given society. This extended the focus from individual suicides to the collective suicide rate which varied from society to society, illustrating that each society produces a 'quota of suicidal deaths.' Along this axis, Durkheim was able to separate the social suicide rate from individual suicides showing that, if suicide were entirely the result of individual psychology, it would be difficult to explain why the French were twice as likely to take their own lives as the Germans. Third was the point of attachment Durkheim established between what he called the integrative functions of society and the religious, political and family groups that existed outside the individual. He found that the integrative mechanisms attaching individuals to groups outside themselves reduced gaps between the individual and their attachments to the wider society. This extended the focus beyond the isolated individual who was thought to live separately from society, to the mechanisms of social integration which attached individuals to society at various points of social and institutional contact. The argument by Durkheim that individuals are attached to the wider society by mechanisms of social integration, meant that he was able to show that the 'gaps' which had formed in the integrative links in industrial society were the result of declining social and integrative functions. In addition, he was able to show that the different points of social attachment had different 'intensities,' so that the family and religious attachments form the greatest and most intense relations. When this 'integration was weakened,' said Durkheim, 'individuals are less drawn together, and as a result spaces emerge between them where the cold winds of egoism blow.'

Interdicts, Religious   This is a term used in *The Elementary Forms of Religious Life* to refer to a type of religious restriction imposed on individuals during religious activities in the totem tribes of Australia. Specifically, interdicts are used to enforce adherence to what is forbidden in regard to religious ceremonies and what is forbidden during religious feasts where certain restrictions are imposed on religious acts related to the totem. Religious interdicts therefore designate what is forbidden across the entire range of society and generally regulate individual acts and activities by laying out the precise consequences that may occur if interdicts are not adhered to. Used synonymously with 'taboo' and 'religious prohibition' in maintaining the sacred quality of the totem, interdictions may arise during religious days when ceremonial enactments are put in motion by collective celebrations and ritual feasts. In this case, religious interdicts govern the rules that relate to bodily contact with the totem including the rules related to eye contact, the method of approaching the totem and the food prohibitions that apply during the enactment of a religious rite. Durkheim identified two distinct kinds of interdicts: 'positive interdicts' and 'negative interdicts.' Positive interdicts govern the rites and duties associated with approaching the totem and maintaining it, while negative interdicts specify what is forbidden in the realm of conduct when approaching the totem. Interdicts ensure that individuals approach the totem with the highest possible feeling of 'religious gravity.' During the period when the interdicts are imposed, 'religious life remains intense' and this 'intensity is manifested by an aggravation of the system of interdicts.' The religious restriction imposed on Catholics related to the consumption of meat during Lent is an example of a religious interdict that forbids certain foods from being eaten during religious days.

Mechanical Solidarity   This is a term used by Durkheim to describe a society whose social solidarity originates from a type of social structure that is made up of many homogeneous groups that form a society based on the organization of clans. These societies are disposed over a confined territory, live in close proximity and are united together as a confederated people similar to the Indian tribes of North America. Their social solidarity originates from the fact that they are united by a central religion, have a coordinated division of labor and perform collective family, political and religious functions which act to intensify their social relations by links and bonds of obligation. This a society made up of small groups called segments who live together and cooperate collectively on the basis of joint economic and domestic tasks. There is little private life, little or no separation between individuals and families, and they have a rudimentary economy based on hunting and gathering with some agriculture. Societies of this type constitute typical examples of mechanical solidarity because their structural characteristics derive from a form of social solidarity that ties them directly to society. They have a simple division of labor which patterns their activity so that links of cooperation emerge between the segments along religious and political lines. Distinct social bonds develop between the segments and between individuals, forming a system of social obligations that are based on common religious practices which have their roots in religious law and which acts to consecrate the group as a sacred people. Their social cohesion is created by a system of social attachments that emerge as a result of carrying out joint economic, domestic and religious activities that form direct links of dependency and bonds of obligation. Links of dependency emerge between those who perform tasks related to economic and domestic production, while bonds of obligation form from the network of social duties that arise in relation to common religious enactments and ceremonies. The force of their social links and bonds intensifies their social solidarity and forms a structured network of activities which exercise an emotional hold over them which makes their social attachments more intense and cohesive. Their social links and bonds are such as to discourage individual autonomy, and society as a whole envelops the individual so completely that all individual differences are subordinated to the group. Collective observances and common social rules are predominantly religious in nature and a strong common conscience pervades all aspects of social life. Customary practices are based on penal law and offenses against society are penalized by repressive sanctions which act to re-affirm sacred rules and beliefs by severe punishment causing bodily harm.

Moral Rules   Durkheim used this term throughout his writings to refer to rules of conduct that are consecrated by the group and which can be studied as realities existing external to the individual. Moral rules impose 'obligatory ways of acting' which ultimately have the power of external coercion to impose duties and obligations on individuals which place them under the necessity of acting in relation to social limits which are fixed in custom. The term 'moral' is used by Durkheim to denote the power of a social 'obligation' that is imposed on the individual. Durkheim was interested in the way these rules were capable of overriding individual discretion and he believed that social rules of this type were moral in that they originate from collective norms and sentiments that impose 'moral imperatives' on individual actions.

Organic Solidarity   This is a term used by Durkheim in *The Division of Labor* to denote a type of society whose social solidarity derives from a structure that is distinct from societies whose solidarity is mechanical. Societies of this type have (i) large populations spread out over a broad geographic territory; (ii) an economy that is industrial and (iii) a complex division of labor in which people perform separate and specialized occupational functions where they work separately from each other, in contrast to working collectively, as in mechanical solidarity. In societies of this type, individuals are grouped not by their relation to the tribal lineage or to the clan segment, but according to the specific type of occupational activities which they carry out. In this case, different groups and classes arise from the organization of society according to occupations, as opposed to a society organized by clan lineage. As a result, the natural work environment is no longer the domestic space of the clan, but the occupational environment, which is separate from the family environment. Social life is concentrated in cities which become the center of industry and political and economic organization. Rather than being organized by clans or segments, societies of this type become territories concentrated with inhabitants, commerce, transportation and industries necessary for supplying the country. At the same time, the division of labor must accommodate the concentrations of industry, and to this extent give rise to the organization of the inhabitants by occupation. A network of occupational and economic functions are thus created where individuals no longer cooperate directly, but rather their cooperation is indirect and patterned through the division of labor as this compels them to carry out economic tasks by performing separate occupation. Their solidarity is organic because the social links individuals have to the wider society emerge from their occupations and form as a result of the increase in the division of labor. Because the occupational environment in which they carry out economic roles is distinct from the existing family environment and the overall structure of the population, a new system of links and social attachments based on the performance of occupational functions begin to form the basis of their social cohesion. Consequently, people begin to lead their own lives separate from others and this leads to private life and separation from the extended family and the religious system of the tribal segment. As the new framework of occupations is substituted for the old framework of segments, society expands beyond the focal point of the family and tribal segment. Common social links based on similarities begin to disappear, and the links and bonds to society created by religious solidarity begin to deteriorate and re-emerge in the form of social links based on the separate and specialized occupational roles performed within the economy. As private life emerges, cooperation and social obligation begin to decline, and social cohesion takes place through the division of labor rather than directly through the immediate social cooperation of the tribal segment. As result 'personal bonds become rare and weak, and individuals more easily lose sight of one another.' Their solidarity is 'organic' to the extent that their social links develop from the dependency individuals have on others performing occupational functions, rather than on direct links of cooperation that emerge in mechanical solidarity. Under these circumstances, bonds of obligation are replaced by bonds of contract and social links grow weak. The system of law is based on restitutive sanctions in which judicial rules redress social wrongs by restoring things to their original state.

Penal Law   Prevalent in segmental and traditional societies, penal law can be distinguished from other forms of law by its repressive sanctions, its basis in religious law and its straightforward intention of imposing bodily harm on the offender for the damage created to the collective beliefs and common social rules. It does this either by reducing the social honor of the offender or by depriving offenders of their freedom or their life. In a system of penal law punishment is severe, and sanctions against offenders are 'repressive' in nature. It is the function of repressive sanctions to maintain social cohesion by setting examples which act to re-consecrate the collective rules of the group that may have been damaged in the act of wrongdoing. In this case, penal law is motivated to 'destroy' the offender and their acts. Penal law and repressive sanctions are found in societies whose solidarity is mechanical. It is a form of law that is distinct from contract law in that no criterion of justice operates to ensure that the 'punishment' fits the crime.

Profane   This is a concept used by Durkheim in *The Elementary Forms* to pinpoint the tendency in the religious life of tribal societies to separate the world into two distinct domains, the sacred and profane. The division between these two realms forms one of the central principles of a sociological theory of religion and is the most distinctive element of religious life since it defines one of its elementary forms. The profane may be defined as anything which is subordinated in dignity to the sacred and radically opposite to it. In this sense, the profane is the principle which has the capacity to contaminate or defile the sacred. In all religions, rules exist which regulate the separation between the two realms and outline the precautions that must be followed during religious enactments to maintain their separation. The profane, therefore, often carries with it the potential to defile, contaminate or inspire disgust or horror. Profane things are thus set apart from sacred things and are regulated by a special class of religious prohibitions called 'interdictions.' It was Durkheim's view that the division of the world into the sacred and profane led to the first system of classification regarding physical boundaries in societies and in external nature. Durkheim reasoned that since the profane is always kept separate from the sacred, social boundaries are formed which separate the two regions in space. Whereas the principle of the sacred has the capacity to consecrate things, spaces and persons, the principle of the profane has the capacity to pollute, defile and contaminate things, spaces and objects.

Realist Perspective   This is a term used to refer to the theoretical perspective adopted by Durkheim in the 1890s to demonstrate that society is an objective reality existing outside the individual. First and foremost, realism can be defined as a perspective which takes as its starting point the view that external social realities exist in the outer world and that these realities are independent of individual sense perceptions. In this context, the realist perspective takes the view that our awareness of and knowledge about the outside world is a straightforward encounter with the visual perception of external reality. This view, however, was opposed by David Hume, a classical empiricist who held that objects and things in the outer world were products of human sense perceptions and did not exist independently of these perceptions. Second, realists believe that the external framework of society can be treated as if it were made up of structures and mechanisms that constitute 'realities as substantial and definite as those of the psychologist or biologist.' On this view, realists argue that the structures and mechanisms of society have powers and dispositions which affect people's actions by the limitations and restrictions they place on them, and that these powers are intrinsic to the structures and mechanisms of society. Third, in contrast to the empiricists, realists accept the view that the external realities of society have powers that are capable of exerting restraint, and that these restraints create effects that are visible in people's actions. To this extent, realists assert that social realities act as direct causes that are defined 'externally to the individual' and which are made manifest by social duties and obligations whose external limits are fixed by custom. Historically, Durkheim used the realist perspective in *The Rules of Sociological Method* and in *Suicide* to study what he called the objective structures of society which he thought had a direct material effect on individual acts. Gabriel Tarde, Durkheim's rival at the College de France, actively opposed this view and argued that there were no external social realities, only individuals.

Religion   Durkheim defined religion in *The Elementary Forms of Religious Life* as a set of beliefs, rites and practices relative to sacred things and he adopted the view that all religions could be identified by three elementary forms: (i) the tendency to divide the world into sacred and profane spheres; (ii) the formation of beliefs relative to sacred things; and (iii) the development of a system of rites specifying the duties and obligations owed to sacred objects. Durkheim's point of departure in the study of religion was his assertion that religion originates from the social activities of groups and the tendency of groups to form a system of beliefs relative to sacred objects and to express these beliefs through periodic religious enactments that consecrate society. In this respect, he differed from those who believed that religion was derived from nature, from the universe, or from the experience of the divine. Religion exists, said Durkheim, because it serves to consecrate the collective realities of society by making space, time, things and people sacred. Durkheim's interest in studying religion was based on the power religious enactments had to intensify collective life and to place boundaries around acts whose reality was separate from the reality of the outside world.

Repressive Sanctions   This term is used by Durkheim to refer to a form of punishment found in segmental and traditional societies where solidarity is mechanical and law is penal in nature. The central characteristic of repressive sanctions is their tendency to punish individual transgressions swiftly and violently, serving the purpose of repairing the damage done to the collective social rules. The rules which these wrongdoings offend are so central to the well being of the group that they are endowed with a sacred authority which has been consecrated by the group. Punishment therefore has a religious character and takes the form of expiation, which refers to the process of making things right through atonement and by the destruction of the offender. Repressive sanctions are social responses to wrong doings and transgressions which are perceived to be an offense against society and the collective social rules and laws. The purpose of repressive sanctions in this case is to punish the offender rather than to determine the nature of the offense or arrive at a just punishment. Durkheim believed that penal law always seeks public vindication and therefore acts without fully weighing the circumstances of the crime.

Restitutive Sanctions   This is a term used by Durkheim in *The Division of Labor* to describe a system for redressing social wrongs in industrial societies by means of restoring things to their normal state that existed prior to the offense. Restitutive sanctions originate from a system of judicial rules in which solidarity is organic and law is contractual as a result of the emergence of specialized institutions that arise in industrial society. Within this system of law, sanctions are restitutive rather than repressive and the application of legal rules becomes a specialized function of an advanced division of labor with a developed judiciary and a system of contract law that is distinct from religious law. A central characteristic of restitutive sanctions is their ability to establish a criterion of justice by ensuring that the punishment adequately fits the crime. In contrast to repressive sanctions, restitutive sanctions have the job of restoring things to the way they were prior to the offense and of reconciling interests between special parties in order to restore the damage that may have been caused by the offense. These restorations may be exercised through various agents or agencies such as lawyers, magistrates and quasi-legal officials. Unlike repressive sanctions, restitutive sanctions do not directly involve the major institutions of society but only specialized parts or segments.

Sacred   A term used by Durkheim in *The Elementary Forms* to refer to the tendency in all religious life to divide the world into two distinct regions, one designated as sacred, the other as profane. Durkheim noted that the capacity of religious acts to designate things as 'sacred' by consecrating things, people and spaces becomes the basis of all religions and all religious experience. This was especially the case with the totem tribes of Australia, who drew boundaries between scared and profane things by setting sacred objects such as the totem apart from other objects in order to render special duties and observances toward them. Durkheim argued that sacred things embody gods, spirits, totems and natural objects and embrace beliefs and social practices. A belief, practice or rite can have a sacred character and carry with it the tendency to be viewed by others as a 'consecrated' thing. Durkheim thought that the religious activities performed in relation to the sacred object such as the totem involved an intensification of gestures and enactments that created a different reality from the reality of everyday experience. In this respect, the sacred refers to a system of rites, beliefs and social practices performed in relation to the tribal totem which creates the experience of religion. Under these circumstances, the sacred (i) is separate from all other objects and therefore constitutes things set apart; (ii) constitutes a system of rites and social practices which set out how the sacred is to be approached and how members of the group are to conduct themselves in regard to it; (iii) is protected by interdictions which have the force of prohibitions which specify what is forbidden; (iv) is segregated from profane things and is thought to be superior in dignity; (v) represents a unifying principle which separates the natural world from the spiritual world and provides society with a model of opposites such as good and evil, clean and dirty, holy and defiled, etc.; (vi) must be accompanied by rites of initiation or rebirth when a profane state is transformed into a sacred state.

Segmental Societies   A term used by Durkheim in *The Division of Labor* to describe a type of society that is organized on the basis of separate clans who are united together as a common people into a single social body similar to the Indian tribes of North America. Societies of this type are made up of groups called 'segments' consisting of many homogeneous clans who are unified together to form a confederated tribe, such as the Iroquois Nation. Groups of this type are disposed over a confined territory, live in close proximity and are united together as a sacred people who trace their descent to a single ancestor. Segmental societies have a structural organization that is like the 'rings of an earthworm,' an image Durkheim used to signify the separate segments or rings which form the structure of the group into one integrated social organization. In some cases the separate segments of the clan form a linear series of groups, and in others they form unions of several clans 'each with a special name' descended from one tradition and from the same ancestor. Societies of this type have a division of labor which patterns their activity so that links of cooperation develop between the segments along religious and political lines, where they coordinate their activities and cooperate together in the joint performance of economic and domestic tasks. Distinct social bonds develop between the segments and between individuals, forming a system of social obligation that is based on common religious practices which have their roots in religious law and which act to consecrate people, spaces and things by periodic religious ceremonies. Because their religious system is the most active social component, it forms a common set of beliefs and practices that pervade the entire social group and are made up of a series of rites by which they all assemble for the purpose of religious enactments that intensity their social relations. All members of the group are considered to be unified by a family name, creating affinities and bonds of obligation which unite them. In some cases, societies of this type are made up of several thousand people who share domestic and economic relations with members from each segment acting as the central religious and political authorities. Eventually, the segments begin to break down as the division of labor accelerates, giving way to specialized occupational functions and the development of industrial society. As soon as these interrelated functions emerge, segments are replaced by new organs creating attitudes and beliefs which give rise to a central authority, a system of administrative and judicial functions, contract law and a modern economy.

Social Facts   This is a term used by Durkheim in *The Rules of Sociological Method* to describe the existence of social realities outside the individual. In order to establish the existence of social subject matter, Durkheim thought it was important to know which 'facts' were commonly called social in contrast to individual psychological facts. He pointed out that when 'I fulfill my obligations as a brother or a citizen, I perform duties which are defined externally to myself and my acts in law and custom and I feel their reality objectively.' These rules of conduct often manifest themselves in the form of social duties and obligations that are distinct from individual facts and 'constitute a new subject matter' that is 'external to the individual', and it is to these things that the term 'social' ought to be applied. Social facts, therefore, constitute rules of conduct and ways of acting that present the noteworthy property of existing outside the individual' and are distinct from psychological facts to the extent that they do not come from within. Social facts can be defined as (i) any rule of conduct that is external to the individual and (ii) is manifested by the 'power of external coercion exercised over the individual or by the existence of some sanction that is imposed on individuals who attempt to violate them.' Social facts manifest themselves in the form of social duties and obligations which place individuals under the necessity of acting in relation to social limits which override their personal considerations. According to Durkheim, the material form a social fact assumes constitutes the active expression of the reality of society that exists outside the individual. For instance, the rule of conduct that forbids the consumption of certain prohibited foods during religious days such as Lent, is an example of the power of a social fact to impose an external limit on individuals that is fixed by custom, and does not come from within the individual.

Social Links and Bonds   These are terms used by Durkheim in *The Division of Labor* to refer to the social attachments that develop between individuals and society when their labor is divided for purposes of carrying out joint economic and domestic tasks for the maintenance of society. What Durkheim observed was that the social division of labor led to the formation of social 'links and bonds' that attach individuals to the wider society by links of dependency and by bonds of obligation. These social links form a system of attachments which lead to a unified form of social cohesion Durkheim referred to as social solidarity. He took the view that it was from these links and bonds that whole societies formed and a whole set of social relations and attachments were created. Durkheim believed that two kinds of links and bonds existed during the social division of labor. First were those that involved links of dependency which determine social relations between individuals who carry out economic and domestic tasks jointly and collectively. Dependency links refer to those ties formed between individuals in the division of labor who carry out functions that others are dependent upon, such as the provision of food and the performance of domestic tasks. Second are the bonds of obligation which exist between individuals which function to regulate the distribution of duties and the performance of tasks between individuals from the same society. While links of dependency often emerge between those who perform tasks related to economic and domestic production, bonds of obligation between members of the same society arise from the network of duties and obligations that form in relation to religious and family institutions. Durkheim's central point was that the system of attachments would never have developed if individuals lived separately or in isolation. During the transition to industrial society, the social links and bonds are transformed into bonds between individuals regulated by contracts rather than by immediate social cooperation or by the force of obligation. What Durkheim found in contrast to thinkers such as Adam Smith was that the social division of labor leads to social links and bonds between individuals that form a structured network of activities which shape their social attachments and structure their overall pattern of social cohesion.

Social Morphology   This is a term used by Durkheim in *The Rules* to describe a system for classifying societies according to the principles of organization by which groups, classes and clans form within society. For Durkheim, social morphology was the first step in devising a system for classifying different types of societies by examining the elementary parts which constitute their structure. According to Durkheim there are two broad groupings: (i) classifications of societies organized by clans, some of which form in a linear series of groups organized by segments, others which form unions of several clans into confederated tribes; and (ii) classification of complex societies which have greater concentrations of groups, classes and overall inhabitants. Durkheim believed that the procedures for classifying societies began with the step of understanding how simple societies 'form compounds,' and how these compound societies become more complex in their structure. In beginning with simple societies and progressing to complex ones, Durkheim believed that it was possible to examine the structural and morphological changes taking place from one form of society to another.

Social Suicide Rate   A central concept in Durkheim's study of suicide arrived at after studying the mortality data of different societies. Durkheim inferred from the mortality data that each society had a 'suicide rate' and that the 'rate' could be studied independently of individual suicides motivated by psychological states. In this case, Durkheim found that each society was a distinct social environment with different social characteristics, difference religions, different patterns of family life, different military obligations and thus different suicide characteristics. Using the suicide rates for different societies rather than looking at individual cases of suicide, Durkheim found that the French were almost twice as likely to take their own lives as the Germans. He went on to reason that if suicide were entirely the result of individual causes and individual psychology, it would be difficult to explain why the French would be almost twice as likely to commit suicide in comparison with the Germans. This established a basis for looking at the 'social causes' of suicide independent of individual motives and psychological states. After studying the rates, Durkheim observed that they varied from society to society and that the number of suicidal deaths in each of the countries he studied did not change dramatically and were considered to be stable. The stability of the rates within a given society indicated that the social framework operated in such a way as to produce what he called the 'yearly precision of rates.' This led him to reason that the predisposing cause of suicide lay not within the psychological motives of the individual, but within the existing social framework of the society. He took the position that the suicide rate must represent a 'factual order' that is separate from individual disposition and therefore presents a regularity which can be studied in its own right. Durkheim thought that because the 'social suicide rate' is independent of individual suicide, it should be the subject of a special study, the purpose of which would be to discover the social causes leading to the conditions in which a definite number of people take their own lives in a given society.

Solidarity   This is a concept used by Durkheim in *The Division of Labor* to look at the overall unity of a given society and the mechanisms of social cohesion which create this unity. Initially, solidarity can be defined as the system of social relations linking individuals to each other and to society as a whole. 'Without these social links,' said Durkheim, 'individuals would be independent and develop separately, but instead they pool their efforts' and live collectively. Durkheim used the term in several different ways. In one context he used the term to describe the degree to which individuals are connected to social groups existing outside themselves. In another, he used it to refer to the system of social interchanges which go beyond the brief transactions that occur between individuals during economic exchange in society. He thought that the system of social interchanges between individuals eventually forms a vast network of social solidarity which extends to the whole range of social relations and acts to link individuals together to form a social unity based on common religious beliefs, shared social practices and a network of social obligations and duties that bind them together as a group. In yet another context he asserted that social solidarity takes two principle forms: mechanical and organic. Each provides a system of links in which the social bonds between individuals and social groups vary according to the division of labor in society and the extent of the 'emotional hold' which the beliefs exert over individuals. In drawing attention to the solidarity existing in society, Durkheim was able to focus on the system of social rules and related social practices which develop as individuals form social groups.

Tarde, Gabriel   A nineteenth century French social theorist well-known for his criticism of Durkheim's definition of society and for his opposition to Durkheim's conception of social facts and his theory of suicide. Tarde believed that anything social, whether a religious rite, a legal statute or a moral maxim was transmitted and passed on from one individual to another by a process called 'imitation.' On this basis, Tarde opposed Durkheim's theory of society as an external reality by insisting that 'imitation was the process through which society alone exists.' Durkheim disagreed with Tarde, stating that if we accept Tarde's view that 'there can be nothing external to the individual,' then sociology would have no distinct subject matter of its own. In response to Tarde's opposition to his claim that social facts constituted a reality in their own right, Durkheim argued that the material form that a social facts assumes is the active expression of the reality that exists externally to the individual. Tarde criticized Durkheim for excluding the individual in his theory of society and mounted a critique of Durkheim's view of society by opposing his definition of the sociological domain as a reality existing outside the individual. Durkheim, on the other hand, criticized Tarde for his imitation theory of society in which Tarde had argued that society was nothing more than the transmission of imitated acts from one individual to another.

Theory of Knowledge   Durkheim first outlined his theory of knowledge in 1903 in an essay entitled *Primitive Classification* when he began to look at the system of classification found in the totem tribes of Australia. In putting forward a theory of knowledge, Durkheim was looking at the question first posed by philosophy concerning the tendency of human reason to divide things in nature into logical classifications and into categories and classes. According to philosophy, the answer to this question was that human beings tend to classify things into groups naturally and that the scheme of classification is the product of internal reason which necessarily separates and groups things into logical classes and categories. In putting forward a theory of knowledge Durkheim took two important steps beyond the prevailing philosophical view. First, he claimed that the categories leading to complex systems of thought such as science, logic and philosophy ultimately derive their classificatory frameworks from the fact that human beings live in groups and thereby tend to group their ideas and the things which they find in external nature. Second, he took the view that mental categories are originally derivatives of group categories, which is contrary to Kant's contention that internal mental categories are the primary means by which human beings understand and apprehend the world. Working from ethnographic evidence gathered on the totem tribes of Australia, Durkheim found that the totem tribes divide themselves into two fundamental sections comprised of classes and clans, and that each group is classified by a totem into subsections of marriage classes and groups. Durkheim then went on to show that the divisions into groups classified by totem were then extended to divisions in the outer world by 'regions' in space in which one clan belonged to the north, the other the south, etc. This illustrated that the principle of division by totem into classes and clans corresponded with the divisions into regions in space. This, he believed, showed two things: (i) first, that the division of the natural world into regions in space corresponded with the tribal divisions into groups and classes associated with the divisions by totem; (ii) second, it showed the division by clans stood in a fixed relationship to the division by regions related to the north and the south, and that from this a given spatial point was obtained as a means of having 'knowledge' of their own existence in space. Durkheim showed that far from being based on internal reason, the first framework for understanding spatial relations in the physical world derived from the principle of division by which the totem tribes of Australia divided their groups into segments and assigned regions in space to each of them, thereby giving rise to the cardinal points of latitude. Durkheim extended this reasoning to the concept of time, arguing that time was not an internal category related to internal reason but rather had its origins in the classification of the seasons – winter, summer, fall, etc., – which also corresponded to divisions in the totem tribes concerning periodic religious enactments in time that coincided with a particular season. According to this view, knowledge of the outside world does not spring from internal reason, but rather arises from the classification of clans and classes by totem and that this becomes a model with which they come to see the external world and form knowledge of it by grouping things into logical classifications. Durkheim reasoned that the classification for grouping things in the external world later put its stamp on the mental system and, because it paralleled the classification of totem groups, it was social in origin. According to Durkheim, the divisions into classes and clans was then internalized in the form of mental dispositions with which they ordered the world. Far from arising from internal reason, therefore, the categories for classifying external nature had their origin in the classification by totem.

Theory of Suicide   Durkheim's central thesis in his study of suicide was that people take their own lives not because of psychological states of depression or mental illness, but rather because of the social changes taking place in industrial society which reduces the social attachments individuals have to the wider society to the point that they become isolated, separate and autonomous from others. Durkheim thought that the process of social separation took place in industrial society to the point that the individual's social attachments shrank down to the private ego, promoting an excessive preoccupation with the self and constant and excessive self awareness. Durkheim argued that if social activity serves to propel individuals out into the wider society by attaching them to the religious group, the family group, and the national group, it is possible to argue that the reduction in the intensity of their attachments to groups outside themselves shows up in the collective suicide rates. Durkheim, therefore, shifted the attention from individual suicides to the collective 'suicide rate' which he thought could be studied independently of the psychology of the individual, which many believed led people to take their own lives. By focusing attention on the 'social suicide rate' within a given society, Durkheim found that the rates varied according to social factors such as religion, marital status, occupation and military obligations. Durkheim's theory explains suicide by drawing on the concept of social integration which refers to the intensity of the 'social attachments' which individuals form to social groups outside themselves, including the religious group, the family group, and the political or national group. So far as social integration serves connective functions by propelling individuals out into the wider society and by promoting the perception that they are part of a larger social whole, Durkheim thought that when gaps form between the individual and the institutional points of contact, individuals withdraw to themselves to the point where they become excessively preoccupied with themselves and retreat to the private ego. The argument by Durkheim that individuals are attached to the wider society by mechanisms of social integration meant that he was able to show that the gaps which had formed in the integrative links of industrial society were the result of declining social and integrative functions that showed up in the higher rates for egoistic suicide. Conversely, when integrative links are over developed, as is the case in tribal society where social attachments are intense, suicide is imposed on the individual as a social 'duty,' leading to a social type of suicide Durkheim called altruistic suicide. The Hindu sati ritual, where women volunteer to end their life by self immolation on the death of their husbands and the suicide bombers, who take their own lives for religious purposes greater than themselves, are examples of altruistic suicide. In this case, suicide is imposed as a 'social obligation' and a religious duty rather than a private choice. Durkheim believed that he had identified 'social types' of suicide that were distinct from 'individual types' of suicide motivated by personal or private ends.

Totem Religions   This is a term Durkheim used in *The Elementary Forms of Religious Life* to refer to the tribal religions existing among the totem tribes of Australia studied by Benjamin Howitt and Spencer and Gillen. Durkheim utilized their studies to put forward a sociological theory of religion and to identify the central characteristics of religious life. Totemism may be defined as a tribal religion that represents the group as descending from a mythical being called a totem, which could be a plant or an animal that is treated as a sacred thing and set apart from other things so that religious duties could be rendered toward them. Durkheim thought that the totem unites all members of the clan together as if they were a sacred people who originate from the same ancestor and whose system of obligations requires them (i) to refer to themselves by a common tribal name with a common ancestry; (ii) to recognize duties and obligations toward each other that are on the level of blood obligations; (iii) to treat as sacred all prohibitions and interdictions which keep the totem apart as a sacred thing and which maintains it as an object of ritual and ceremonial worship; and (iv) to engage in the performance of religious ceremonies which periodically draw them together as a group for purposes of consecrating people, spaces and things. Here, said Durkheim, is an elementary religious system that is linked to a definite form of social organization based on a division of society into clans and tribes which trace their descent to a single sacred totem. Durkheim thought that in this way totemism linked the natural world to religious experience and ultimately religion to society.

Weber

Action, Effectual (Emotional)   One of the four types of social action discussed by Weber in *Economy and Society* to demonstrate the degree of rationality and inner evaluation that may be contained in a social act. Action is effectual or emotional, according to Weber, if it 'satisfies a need for revenge, sensual gratification or the working off of emotional tensions.' In this type of action, the actor is motivated by an emotional response to a situation largely dictated by the state of mind of the actor. Under these circumstances, emotional action lacks a specific rational orientation to the world and forgoes calculation based on means and ends since it is governed by an impulse which often has no goal or aim. Like traditional action, emotional action does not take up an orientation to specific goals or choose among possible means and, to this extent, does not consider the outcome of action in advance. Showing anger in public as a result of a minor annoyance is an example of an action that is motivated by the emotional state of the actor. Like traditional action, 'purely emotional behavior is on the borderline of what is considered meaningful' action, and is irrational because it does not undergo inner evaluation and involves little or no judgment on the part of the actor.

Action, Social   The term 'social action' derives from Weber's methodological writings in which he put forward a theory of social action. This was concerned with developing a theory for making valid judgments about the decisions and evaluations individuals make in their actions with others in a social environment. In contrast to physical behavior, action is the name Weber gives to a form of activity in which the actor (i) attaches a subjective meaning to an act; (ii) interprets the actions and acts of others in a social environment in order to determine how to respond; and (iii) acts only after having 'understood' the actions and acts of others. Weber used the term 'social action' to denote a central distinction in the subject matter of the natural and social sciences. While in the exact sciences it is sufficient to observe events in the natural world and to report relationships between things observed, in the social sciences investigation must go beyond the observation of physical behavior to look at how individuals 'act' on their 'understanding,' assign meaning to the acts of others and explain how this understanding may be related to their social action. Because human actors 'interpret' the acts of others, Weber thought that the natural and social sciences obtain different kinds of knowledge. In the natural sciences, knowledge is of the external world which can be explained only in terms of valid laws, whereas in the social sciences knowledge must be 'internal' or 'subjective' in the sense that human beings have 'inner' subjective states that must be understood in order to explain outward behavior. Since social action is the product of the 'inner states' of the actor, Weber sought to devise methods to show how these 'inner states' enter into the social acts of individuals as action considerations. The primary assumption of social action theory is that individuals act on their understanding (Verstehen), and that this understanding reflects their judgments and evaluations. Weber's main aim was to develop a way of elucidating how these judgments were evident in the social acts of individuals without taking recourse to a 'psychology' of the act.

Action, Instrumental Rational   Weber used this term to refer to a type of social action in which the actor is free to choose the means of action purely in terms of rational efficacy, essentially by taking into account and weighing up the means and ends of action prior to the act so that the chances of success will be maximized. In this case, the actor takes into account and weighs up 'the ends, the means and the possible secondary results' for purposes of forming strategies in advance of action with the ultimate aim of successful outcomes, even at the cost of forgoing value considerations. To this extent, the actor systematically takes into account the behavior of others, the conditions of reality that exist, the possible likely obstacles and the alternative strategies that are possible in order to ensure that their primary aims and goals are achieved. All these considerations are used as a basis for knowledge to be considered and weighed up in the 'attainment of the actor's rationally pursued ends.' According to Weber, the most significant characteristic of instrumental action is its persistent 'instrumental rationality.' This calculates means and ends and systematically takes into account the conditions of action, the 'alternative means to the ends and the secondary consequences.' In comparison with other types of action, instrumental action takes up an orientation to the world and material reality by forming strategies that are based on arriving at the most effective procedures for attaining desired ends. While practical rationality 'orders' the world according to some plan, instrumental rationality seeks to maximize personally beneficial outcomes whether they are political, economic or legal. In this case, the actor takes into account those conditions of knowledge that are (i) based on an understanding of the circumstances as they may lead to alternate means and (ii) the likely behavior of relevant others in the situation and their effect on secondary consequences, as well as the extent to which the prevailing conditions of reality affect the attainment of particular ends.

Action, Traditional   A term used by Weber to refer to a type of social action which is based on a fixed body of traditional beliefs that act as moral imperatives on the actor's judgment. Traditional action is distinguished from the other types of action by the absence of a subjective meaning that is attached by the actor to the situation, and by responses to situations based on a customary view of reality that is handed down from the past. Traditional action is based on a habitual response to the world that guides the behavior of the actor in a course of action which has been repeatedly followed in the past. To act according to tradition, the actor need not imagine a goal, picture an outcome or be conscious of specific commitments to values. Weber believed that the great bulk of everyday action conforms to this type so far as both the ends and means of action are fixed by custom. To the extent that traditional action lacks a specific orientation to rationality, it lies close to the 'borderline of what can be justifiably called meaningfully oriented action.' The lack of rational orientation in traditional action exists because of the actor's habitual response to the outside world and the degree to which these responses act as guides for future behavior. Traditional action lacks evaluative criteria and is not rationally oriented to the calculation of means and ends, and does not weigh up means in relation to ends prior to action. Clergy adhering to church doctrine to solve practical problems of everyday life is an example of this type of action.

Action, Value Rational This is a term used by Weber to describe a type of social action that is based on an orientation to the world that is governed by ultimate values, which seek to bring into practice standards of equality and justice no matter what the cost to the actor. Value rational action is characterized by a specific meaning that is subjectively assigned to the action by the actor for purposes of bringing about some greater good, and to this extent pursues only ethical means for bringing about the desired ends or goals of action. Weber describes value rational action as a straightforward orientation to absolute values with the ultimate purpose of 'putting into practice the actors' convictions of what seems to them to be required by duty, honor, standards of beauty, a religious call or the importance of some cause no matter in what it consists.' In this case, the meaning of an action 'does not lie in the achievement of a result ulterior to it, but rather lies in carrying out the realization of the specific value considerations for its own sake.' To this extent, the aims of value rational action are (i) the realization of some specific value or higher good that is selected as meaningful to the actor and (ii) the obligation placed on the actor by the value in question. Under these circumstances, there is no weighing up of ends against other ends, since the values pursued are paramount. In this respect, the actor feels obligated to follow 'commands' or 'demands' which are 'binding' on the actor's judgment and commitment to specific values. In this case, actors pursue values regardless of the possible cost to themselves and act to put into practice their convictions of what seems to them to be required by principles of justice and equality. For example, the Dalai Lama's pursuit of 'peace in the world' is based on the meaning that attaches to the value of promoting human life and his commitment to the pursuit of such values as a motivation for action. Action of this type may select values such as 'equality and justice' as a way of orientating to the world and to others.

Asceticism A term used by Weber in *The Protestant Ethic and the Spirit of Capitalism* to denote a form of self-denial which arises in everyday life to prohibit spontaneous enjoyment and worldly pleasure. Historically, the term originates from religious piety when self-denial was expressed through renunciation of all worldly enjoyment with the purpose of diminishing sin and obtaining salvation. In monastic asceticism, the ascetic attitude was manifested in the form of the vows of poverty and the rejection of the world altogether. As a religious doctrine, asceticism holds that one can achieve a higher state through self-discipline and self-denial, and that the postponement of enjoyment brings reward and the feeling of moral elevation. Weber used the concept to establish a connection between modern capitalism and self-denial by showing how self-control and rational conduct becomes a category of social action in societies where capitalism flourished and where self denial was linked to the regulation of the material world and to achievement in everyday life. It was Weber's thesis that at the end of the eighteenth century asceticism escaped from the religious sphere and penetrated everyday life by shaping certain kinds of economic conduct that manifested themselves in the form of work discipline, prudent saving, punctuality, self restraint and time thrift. Weber identified two types of asceticism: (i) world-rejecting and (ii) inner-worldly. While both seek the path of salvation by involving the believer in a formal withdrawal from the world, the first requires the believer to renounce the world because it is corrupt and its material pleasures offer temptation; whereas the second requires the individual to focus their activities in the world undertaking the responsibility to 'transform' it in some way. The ascetic attitude operates in different departments of life and demonstrates how religion tends to regulate the individual's relation to material reality by inducing caution and fear about our material satisfactions and the appetites and desires generated by material culture.

Authority, Political This term is used by Weber in his theory of political domination to refer to the overall legitimacy that a political leader has to issue commands, exercise power and obtain compliance from others within a total system of political authority. Technically speaking, the term political authority refers to the entire apparatus of political authority that exists between the ruler and the ruled, and that is supported by a system of enforcement and a system of social regulation. While there are many kinds of authority, Weber focuses primarily on political authority and its various historical expressions across different societies. Included in his description are (i) legal authority, in which the ruler's right to issue commands and obtain compliance from others rests solely on the authority of 'legality' and the system of laws and legal rules; (ii) traditional authority, in which the right of the ruler to issue commands and obtain compliance rests solely on the sanctity of age-old rules and the authority inherent in tradition; and (iii) charismatic authority, in which the right of the ruler to issue commands and obtain compliance rests on the exceptional powers of revelation the leader is perceived to have by followers.

Bureaucracy   Weber used this term to denote the development of the modern means of administration that arises in industrial societies with the formation of the democratic nation state. Weber believed that bureaucracy was an outcome of historical and social development that advanced the principle of legality as a means of administering social policy and of regulating a population. Beyond the formal characteristics of bureaucracy, Weber put forward a theory of bureaucratic development in which he linked the rise of bureaucracy to the emergence of legal domination. In a system of legal domination, authority is derived from rules which are legally and rationally enacted. It was Weber's contention that legal domination develops only in Western society, and only within this context does a full-blown bureaucratic system of administration arise. A bureaucratic means of administration includes (i) the principle of office hierarchy; (ii) a chain of command based on the belief in the authority of the office; (iii) a reliance on procedurally correct decision-making which presupposes 'correct rulings;' (iv) a reliance on due process; (v) the regulation of offices by impersonal rules; (vi) a form of decision-making that is reliant on technical correctness, calculative reasoning, and the ethics of factual consistency; (vii) the tendency to produce the 'leveling' of differences in society and to appeal to the broadest possible interpretation of the 'common interest' and (viii) a strict orientation to practical rationality as a way of obtaining control over material reality. Bureaucratic society represents the dominance of formalistic rationality over substantive rationality.

Calculation   A term used by Weber in *Economy and Society* to refer to the general process by which the system of money calculation and accounting procedure penetrates other spheres of social action to the point that it becomes a method for controlling the empirical world. It was Weber's contention that, at a certain stage of historical development, monetary calculation began to dominate over other forms of social action, and he saw this as part of the overall process of assigning an accounting technique to a system of calculative reasoning that deals with the world by controlling circumstances and by devising 'strategies of action' that are based on numerical sorting as a means of controlling material reality. The most developed form of calculative reasoning of this type is the science of statistical analysis. Calculation in this sense functioned in the world by making conduct more methodical and by aiding in the control of empirical reality. Because precise calculation tended to increase efficiency and led to control of the outside world, calculative reasoning extended its scope to other activities in social life. According to Weber, the practice of calculation begins with monetary mechanisms and became fully established when goods and services came to be manipulated by a standard of evaluation and accounting procedure. Ultimately, accounting rationality extends itself into all departments of life including economic, political and religious conduct.

Calvinism   A branch of Protestantism which began with the theological teachings of John Calvin, a sixteenth century Swiss cleric, who in 1534 severed his ties with the Catholic church because it refused to stress the rejection of worldly pleasures. Calvin is best known for his restrictive regulations on worldly enjoyment and for his salvation theology referred to as the 'doctrine of predestination.' The doctrine of predestination took the view that God had divided all humanity into two classes of persons: the saved and the damned. To those whom God had elected to be saved, He gave everlasting life, salvation and eternal grace. To those from whom He had withheld salvation, He gave a life of everlasting death and dishonor. Calvin decreed that no believer could have knowledge of their fate until it was revealed upon their death. In addition, he insisted that nothing could be done to relieve, forgive or reverse the decision, neither prayer, good works, confession or sacraments. In *The Protestant Ethic*, Weber argued that this created a 'feeling of unprecedented inner loneliness' among Protestants since, according to Weber, it placed into jeopardy their hope of eternal salvation. It was Weber's contention that, as a substitute, Protestants threw themselves into commercial activity and eventually viewed their 'success' in business as a 'sign' that they had been 'elected' to be saved. Weber believed that Calvin's predestination doctrine led to a 'psychological vehicle' creating 'methodic forms of conduct' compatible with the development of capitalism including a stringent attitude toward work, prudent saving, punctuality, time-thrift and the rejection of luxury.

Capitalism, Ascetic   This is a term used by Weber in *The Protestant Ethic* to denote the point at which Protestant religious doctrine transformed economic practices and money-making in Western capitalism by promoting the regulation of life on the basis of ascetic conduct and by fostering an attitude toward the world based on self denial and the rejection of worldly pleasure. Since the aim of asceticism is to reject the material world and the pleasures of everyday life, Weber wanted to show that a religious ethic had placed its stamp on economic conduct at a certain historical point and that this had affected the development of capitalism by promoting self-denial. Weber believed that this was manifested in a clear set of attitudes toward work, punctuality, prudent saving, restraint, the rejection of luxury and the spontaneous avoidance of the use of money for personal enjoyment. Weber wanted to show that in response to Calvin's predestination doctrine, a certain type of Protestant religiosity produced what he called a 'psychological vehicle' that since the sixteenth century tended to create a form of ascetic conduct compatible with monastery asceticism. He argued that ascetic conduct in the form of restraint was not simply an outcome of Calvin's religious doctrine, but was the result of a series of 'practical psychological motives' that became incentives for life regulation in the world with the aim of controlling material reality and its temptations.

Capitalism, Modern   Weber defined modern capitalism in two distinct ways. First, he defined it as a type of money economy that was historically distinct from other economies by its straightforward introduction of rational methods of accounting and accounting procedure in 'industrial undertakings.' Such procedures, he thought, were capable of coordinating and mobilizing physical resources such as land, machinery and tools that may be required to be placed at the disposal of private operations for purposes of production and the creation of wealth. In Weber's view, this led to the emergence of rational markets which replaced the 'irrational limitations' once placed on commerce and trade by religious restrictions. The 'rationalization' of industry and trade eventually led to the development of 'calculable law' which ensured the rational operation of economic life by universally applied legal rules and the elimination of all privilege and privileged classes. Second, Weber defined capitalism as a type of economic organization whose development was equated with Protestant religious doctrine which he believed affected the growth of a certain kind of economic conduct that led to the emergence of work discipline, prudent saving, time-thrift and the rejection of luxury in the pursuit of wealth. Weber believed that Protestant religious maxims had placed what he called an 'unambiguous stamp on the economic organization' of Western capitalism that defined the spirit of capitalism and its form of economic conduct in the world. Weber showed that the religious maxims affecting economic conduct were the result of John Calvin's predestination doctrine that eventually became incentives for life regulation and the control of material reality by asceticism.

Capitalism, Traditional   Distinct from ascetic capitalism, traditional capitalism may be defined as a form of economic activity which rejects opportunities for economic gain in favor of enforcing traditional norms of work and satisfying minimum needs. In traditional capitalism the motive for gain is absent, there is no economic incentive for gain and individuals reject the opportunity to earn more in favor of working less. Weber believed that 'ascetic capitalism' replaced traditional capitalism as soon as the Protestant religious reforms of the seventeenth century began to equate the pursuit of economic gain with religious virtue and moral duty leading to stringency in work and an ethical attitude toward prudent saving, punctuality, rejection of luxury and time-thrift. Weber argued that the elevation of economic gain to a 'moral duty' was historically new and had not been seen in traditional forms of capitalism.

Charismatic Domination   One of the three types of legitimate domination discussed by Weber in his theory of political authority. Charismatic domination refers to a form of political authority whose claim to legitimacy, leadership and the exercise of power lies in the people's belief that the charismatic leader has divine powers to see into the future and is able to galvanize followers by virtue of resolving long-standing historical hardship or longstanding suffering. Often based on the promise of the leader to emancipate oppressed peoples by fusing their purposes to the realization of a 'true' social destiny or rightful national place, charismatic domination is seen as legitimate only so far as the powers possessed by the leader are not accessible to the ordinary person and are therefore perceived as extraordinary. Weber believed that charismatic domination was inherently unstable, not amenable to the development of an administrative apparatus and had the potential to lose legitimacy when discredited by the failure of the leader to realize goals or promises. Mahatma Gandhi's struggle against British domination in India is an example of charismatic domination based on the unique ethical vision of Gandhi who, with very little political power and no resources, mobilized a massive resistance that was fortified by Gandhi's charismatic connection to his followers. In this instance, the struggle of the Indian people took the form of a charismatic movement which was designed to break the hold which the British had over the Indian masses and the Indian economy. Thus, with Gandhi's charismatic leadership the struggle was situated on the plane of a higher ethical order because it was based on the willed emancipation of the Indian people from longstanding suffering. The ability of the charismatic leader to see into the future and refer to the realm of 'ideal truths' created a connection to the religious sphere and to religious legitimacy. Similar to this is the mobilization of the American civil rights movement in 1962 by Martin Luther King. Based on the political and legal emancipation of Afro-Americans from longstanding inequality and discrimination, this was a charismatic movement which made enormous gains on the political front by defining the 'struggle' on the basis of a superior ethical claim to political equality that had been denied up until that time.

Class   This is a concept used by Weber in *Economy and Society* to refer to the formation of groups who 'share the same casual component of life chances' in the market, independent of their ownership of property. Differentiating himself from Marx, who had defined class as the historical tendency of societies to divide themselves into two unequal economic classes due to the ownership by one class of the means of production, Weber defined the concept of class according to what he called the class situation of modern times. In contrast to the old industrial classes discussed by Marx, Weber claimed that the classes of modern times formed in relation to 'life chances' that were created when they sold their skills and training on the market in return for salaries and wages. Weber's theory of social class is therefore as follows: (i) Weber thought that 'life chances' were made possible when workers obtained education credentials and diplomas which they used to sell on the market in exchange for incomes; (ii) Weber believed that groups of this type constituted class formations because their life chances and economic opportunities were not dependent on the ownership of private property or the ownership of the means of production, but rather on the life chances of education credentials; (iii) Weber claimed that in contrast to the two unequal classes existing during the early period of industrial production, the class situation of modern times was determined by the market existing for trained workers such as 'technicians, civil servants, teachers and various levels of white-collar employees' whose education credentials constitute their life chances; (iv) while these classes lack the specific life chances of property, they are able to obtain income in the form of salaries and wages as a result of selling their skills and abilities on the market and therefore take up class positions independent of their outright ownership of the means of production; (v) according to Weber, this leads to the formation of the middle classes whose education and training is a source of class mobility. As far as Weber was concerned, therefore, Marx considered only the class situation of those who had property. This shift in the class composition described by Weber changed 'the effects of the naked possession' of property, suggesting that the possession of property itself must have been only a 'fore-runner' of the class situation. The transition to the class situation of modern times expanded the political rights of workers and led to a reduction of class antagonism. In Weber's view, the class struggle was altered in the later stages of capitalism, and the possibility of revolution resulting from the class struggle was minimized because many workers had been absorbed into the class structure.

Formal Rationality   Weber used this term to designate the amount of quantitative calculation and accounting procedure that goes into an action or decision in order to obtain control over the outcomes of action and over material reality. Rationality may be thought of as formal when there is a view to expressing a situation or conceptualizing an action by a straightforward application of numerical and calculable standards. Formal rationality therefore imposes order on reality by the use of strict numerical and calculable terms. The formation of a 'budget of expenditure' as a means of planning a business venture is an example of how formal rationality imposes order on the world in the economic sphere. This may entail an orientation to action stressing strict adherence to 'cost effective' measures and a formal consideration of means and ends within calculable rules. In this case, formal rationality designates the amount of quantitative reasoning which is technically possible in a situation to ensure that goals will be obtained. To the extent that formal rationality adheres to norms of accounting procedure and imposes order on the world by calculation, it conflicts with the criterion of values found in substantive rationality and, in this case, formal rationality does not take the consideration of values into account.

Historical Explanation   This term in used in Weber's methodological studies to make a distinction between explanation in the exact sciences and explanation in the social sciences. Weber believed that explanation in the social sciences had to be historical in so far as it (i) attempts to explain concrete historical reality rather than search for general laws; (ii) takes recourse to 'interpretive understanding' rather than relying on methods of observation; (iii) focuses on human social action rather than on events in the natural world; and (iv) seeks to obtain knowledge of the inner 'subjective states' of the actor that must be understood in order to explain outward behavior.

History   Instead of conceiving of history in the form of linear development in time, Weber thought that historical progress and development were expressed in the form of a process he called 'rationalization.' This, rather than history, imposed 'order' on the world by the rational containment of everyday life and by the regulation of conduct in the control of empirical reality. In his studies of the religions of China and India, Weber showed that the process of rationalization occurred at a point historically when the religious and economic spheres intersected and, as a result, imposed order on the world by shaping reality and by making conduct more rational. Weber's conception of history, therefore, involves two separate but interrelated assumptions. First, was his belief that a religious world view produces a rational outlook toward the world and that from this follows rational conduct. Second, was his belief that different religious orientations to the outside world led to different types of rational development in knowledge, science and art. Weber thought that societies of the East and the West had different developmental histories because the process of rationalization involved different points of convergence between a religious world view and an economic world view. For instance, in China the path leading to the development of astronomy was thrown off the path of rational development by a religious ethic that stressed a magical orientation to reality at the point that astronomy would have become a science. Weber thought that this put religious obstacles in the path of rational progress. In the West, by contrast, rational developments in scientific technique freed astronomy from magic and prevented it from becoming an astrology at the point that it stopped serving a religious ethic. In this case, the religious and the economic spheres were the two major agents promoting historical change and rational development. Many of Weber's studies emphasize a view of history that focuses on the shift from one period to another only as the result of the convergence between the religious and economic spheres, as exemplified by the development of capitalism. He argued that the specific point of convergence between a religious ethic and the rationalization of economic life occurred during the period after the Protestant reformation when religious doctrine placed a premium on inner self-control in relation to economic conduct in the world. It was at this point, said Weber, that a religious ethic placed its 'stamp' on 'life-regulation' as a means of rationalizing it and, in doing so, it created what he called 'methodic conduct' and self-control in relation to economic activity in the world.

Ideal Type   This is a term used by Weber to refer to a methodological technique he utilized to study the subject matter of the social sciences which he believed was different from the subject matter of the natural sciences. As a result of the differences in subject matter, Weber believed that the social sciences had to devise a method that was different from the methods of observation used by the natural sciences. Because social and historical subject matter cannot be directly observed or reduced to law-like regularities, Weber thought that the 'ideal type' could be used as a means of describing common characteristics of societies that included their path of historical development and social change. In this view, societies can be studied 'comparatively' by outlining and describing their distinct social characteristics. For example, a feudal society will include such 'ideal type' characteristics as an agricultural economy without city life, a form of political authority based on traditional domination and rule by notables, a system of ecclesiastical law with de facto powers, and a religious system in which the church possesses a monopoly over religious revelation. These ideal type characteristics may then be brought into comparison with feudal societies in different historical contexts such as France, England and Germany, or they may be brought into contrast with feudal societies of the East. In this case, the ideal type is designed to capture the aspects of empirical reality of feudal societies through a comparison of their characteristics at different stages of social and historical development and by arriving at what Weber called an 'analytical accentuation' of the characteristics of the society in question. He therefore defined the ideal type as a 'conceptual pattern which brings together certain relationships and events of historical life into a complex' whole whose purpose is to describe historical societies by comparing their internal and external characteristics. For Weber, the main category of type formation was the historical ideal type. It functions to elucidate the features of historical reality by extracting essential 'traits' which form an ideal picture of social reality and from this a workable type is formed. For example, to understand the development of a city economy, a comparison can be made between aspects of a modern industrial economy and the city economies found in Florence in the fourteenth century. The traits of a city economy may include such elements as a system of law based on statutes, the concept of the citizen, a municipal organization governed by notables, a bureaucratic means of administration and political office holders. In this case, an ideal type functions to form a picture of events which approximates the reality of a given society under certain conditions of its organization and this can be compared with city economies of the modern type found in the West.

Interpretive Sociology   This term is used by Weber in *Economy and Society* to define a body of social theory designed to make valid judgments about the 'inner states' of actors in their actions with others in a social environment. Because Weber believed that the subject matter of the social sciences was distinct from the subject matter of the natural sciences, he took the view that individuals act in and come to understand the social world only through interpretive acts, in comparison with physical objects in nature which do not act on the basis of interpretation. At the most fundamental level, therefore, human social action involves the process of assigning meanings to the given factual states in the outer world, and since these meanings do not already come 'attached' to the socio-cultural facts of the world, Weber took the position that they must be products of the meaning states of actors. Weber believed, therefore, that all social action was 'interpretive' in that the actor could not decide how to respond to the acts of others without interpreting their acts by first assigning a meaning and then deciding how to respond. He then took the view that the process of assigning meanings to the acts of others and the factual states of the outer world constituted evidence of the 'inner states' of actors who rely on their inner judgment and evaluation – their understanding or *Verstehen* – to interpret the acts of others.

Legitimacy, Political   This is a term used by Weber in his theory of legitimate domination to indicate the extent to which individuals, officials and groups within an established order actively acknowledge the validity of a ruler to have the right to issue commands and exercise power. Accompanying each established order, according to Weber, are beliefs about the 'legitimacy' of a given system of domination. Every system of domination, including the charismatic, traditional and rational-legal, is therefore based on some corresponding belief by the population in the legitimacy and right of the ruler to issue commands and rule over others. In modern society, for example, the rule of law is the basis of political legitimacy, whereas in traditional societies the ruler's political legitimacy is based on inherited right and the authority of tradition in contrast to the authority of law.

Legitimate Domination   Weber used this term in his theory of political authority to refer to the right of the ruler in an 'established order' to issue commands and to expect that these commands will be obeyed and adhered to. Weber thought that the right of a ruler to exercise power and expect compliance from others forms an established system of authority. According to Weber, the two central elements necessary for the development of a system of domination are (i) the perception by those who are ruled that the political authority of a ruler is legitimate for those who are subject to it; and (ii) the development of an administrative apparatus that acts as a barrier between the ruler and the people. Weber identified three types of legitimate domination: (i) charismatic; (ii) traditional; (iii) rational-legal. Each system encompasses a total 'apparatus of authority' reflecting the existing relation between the ruler, administrative officials and the groups and persons existing within the 'established order' who act as a means of enforcement. In his theory political domination, Weber looked at the social and historical conditions leading to long standing systems of domination and the mechanisms which maintain them.

Magic, Emancipation from   Weber used this term in his study of religion to identify the historical point at which a religious world view frees itself from a connection to magic so that there can be rational development in law, the growth of cities and the rationalization of economies. Weber took the view that, in early societies such as China, magic created priestly classes which developed monopolies over bodies of knowledge and control over spiritual and commercial resources. To this extent they actively controled the perception of empirical reality. Under these circumstances, the hold created by magic over everyday life leads to an absence of social change and the dominance of religion in the interpretation of experience. This, Weber thought, places religious obstacles in the path of the development of science, medicine, learning and commerce. In his view, therefore, the development of modern civilization proceeds directly in relation to the decline of magic in social life. This is evident in his discussion of the growth of the city as a rational institution and the development of a prophecy religion. Weber thought that prophecy brought about an end to magic because it situated the miraculous outside the collective camp and this 'destroyed magical procedure to the extent that it was viewed as devilish rather than divine.' It is the decline of magic, Weber believed, that led to the development of world markets, rational commerce and science.

Means and Ends of Action   These are terms used by Weber throughout his writings to indicate the different degrees of rationality that go into a social action and the extent to which these rationalities serve as guides toward the realization of ends or goals. Weber took the view that all social action could be understood from the point of view of a 'means-ends' rationality. This is the case because in all situations of action, the 'means' which individuals use to obtain their ends vary dramatically depending on their orientation to reality. Under these circumstances, the means of action may be defined as the methods or procedures used for carrying out an action, whereas 'ends' refer to the goals, aims and end results of action. At one time, the 'means' used to obtain particular goals or ends were governed by moral and ethical principles that imposed obligations on actors to pursue goals in the light of means and ends that were acceptable to religion. During the development of modern society, however, the means and ends of action were freed from ethical guidelines, and as a result 'ends' or goals were pursued strictly in terms of their practical and technical attainment. As a result, 'means' were chosen on the basis of their ability to deliver results, and to this extent became separate from ethical choices. To this extent, the 'means and ends' of action were no longer governed by ethical standards but rather by standards of practical utility, and this made them more technical as goals became more desirable. As societies became more modern, action was regulated less by ethical standards, and the means and ends of action were subject to rational calculation. The development of modern society therefore brought with it a change in the means-ends scheme.

Methodological Controversy (Methodenstreit)   This term is used by Weber to refer to the debate carried on in Germany in the latter half of the nineteenth century concerning which methods were to be used in the social sciences for the study of society. The focus of the debate was on two distinct fronts: first were the differences in subject matter that existed between the natural and social sciences; second, were the differences that existed in the types of knowledge sought after by the natural and social sciences. With respect to subject matter, Weber argued that the natural sciences had failed to treat the problem of 'human inner understanding' simply because these sciences were concerned with the 'outer states' of the natural world and with law-like regularities. Weber believed that what sets the subject matter of social science apart from the natural sciences is that human beings have 'inner states' in terms of which they 'understand' the events of the outer world in which they come to act. In Weber's view, the subject matter of the natural sciences is therefore simply devoid of such 'understanding.' Because of this, Weber reasoned that 'human conduct is in principle' distinct from 'physical events' in the outer world because the physical behavior of things in nature does not involve understanding. After showing that social acts were based on interpretive understanding and that human conduct is always the result of values being attached to it, Weber drew the conclusion that any form of investigation which reduces human action to its simple external characteristics would be meaningless since it would not capture the tendency of human interpretive understanding. This distinction between the two sciences had the immediate effect of demarcating the existence of two different subject matters, one concerned with 'objective events' in the outside world, the other with 'subjective events' in the inner states of the actor. On a second front, the social sciences were different from the natural sciences on issues related to the type of knowledge they wished to obtain. Weber argued that by necessity, each of the sciences sought to obtain different kinds of knowledge. In the natural sciences, knowledge is of the objective facts of the external world which can then be explained in terms of general laws. In the social sciences, however, knowledge must be of the 'inner subjective states of individuals' in that human beings have an 'inner nature' that must be understood in order to explain outward events that lead to their social actions. Weber thought that observation and investigation in the natural and social sciences take up completely different orientations and attitudes to their subject matter. In the natural sciences, it is sufficient to observe events in the natural world and to report factual relationships between things observed, whereas in the social sciences investigation must go beyond observation to look at how individuals act on their understanding and how this 'understanding' may be related to their social action in society.

Party   This is a term used by Weber in the context of his theory of political domination to refer to the sphere of activities appropriate to political parties after the formation of the modern nation state. For Weber, the development of political parties forms the third dimension of social adjustment, along with class and status which takes place in the later stages of modern society. In contrast to class and status, the place of political parties is in the sphere of political power, which is separate from the sphere of the economy and separate from the sphere of law. Political parties are thus oriented to the acquisition of power and to the influence of the actions of others for political purposes and for acquiring the right to rule over others in a system of political domination. In Weber's view, parties must maintain their separation from the economic and status spheres of society and take the electorate into account, since their neglect would upset future election. Weber believed that modern political parties alter the class structure of society by absorbing elements of the class struggle within the party system by their tendency to represent all groups and classes in society.

Power   A term used by Weber in his theory of legitimate domination to describe the state of affairs in which individuals are in a position to carry out their own will over others 'despite resistance' and to have their commands followed or adhered to in the exercise of power. According to Weber, power is defined as the likelihood that an individual will realize their will in a situation of social action. By contrast, domination refers to the 'probability' that a specific command will be 'obeyed by a given group of persons' by virtue of the legitimate right of a ruler to issue commands.

Practical Rationality   This is a term used by Weber to describe an orientation to reality that is based on what Weber called the 'methodical attainment of a particular end through increasingly precise calculation of adequate means.' Practical rationality, in this respect, implies a specific orientation to the world based on a 'methodical attainment of ends by the precise calculation of adequate means.' To this extent, it 'orders world content according to some plan' and imposes order on the world by a straightforward orientation to what is empirically given in reality and by precise calculation. Practical rationality thus employs methodical calculation for purposes of obtaining control over the circumstances of daily life through the mastery of everyday reality. To this extent it is based on the control of daily life by the use of systematic strategies of action, and seeks to overcome all unforeseen eventualities by the 'ordering of world content.' Practical rationality therefore imposes order on the world for purposes of controlling a given way of life. In this respect it implies an orientation to the world based on methods that are repeated and handed down from the past and whose effectiveness consists in introducing 'regularities of action into the ways of living to varying degrees'. In Weber's view, practical rationality follows explicit rules of experience and everyday practical conduct in order to attain 'valued ends or goals which may be economic or religious' in nature. In this case, it is identified by a 'mental outlook that is methodical so far as it uses the rules of experience and causation' to obtain concrete ends that are either economic, religious or political.

Predestination, Doctrine of   This term is used by Weber in *The Protestant Ethic* to denote a doctrine of salvation introduced by John Calvin in the sixteenth century. Calvin's salvation theology was based on four distinct decrees or dogmas. First, was that before the world began God had divided all humanity into two groups or classes of persons, the saved and the damned, and each was assigned an eternal fate which they were powerless to change. To those who had been elected to be saved, God gave everlasting salvation and grace, whereas those who were condemned were given everlasting death and dishonor. Second, according to Calvin's doctrine Protestants could not know their fate or which group they belonged to since this was revealed only after their death. Third, nothing could be done to forgive the decrees since, according to Calvin, no priest, no prayer, no sacrament and no worldly works could reverse them. Fourth, Calvin maintained that God had abandoned all but the elect since, in his view, Christ had endured suffering only for the elect. In *The Protestant Ethic and Spirit of Capitalism* Weber argued that Calvin's doctrine created 'salvation anxiety' among Protestants and, in order to overcome it, they threw themselves into worldly work and sought to re-interpret their relationship to God by practicing self-discipline and self-denial in the world. In Weber's view, Calvin's doctrine brought about a convergence between religion and commercial activity after the Protestant reformation when religious doctrine placed a psychological premium on inner self-regulation in relation to economic conduct, leading to self restraint, the rejection of luxury, work discipline and prudent saving. It was at this point, said Weber, that a religious ethic placed its 'stamp' on 'life-regulation' as a means of rationalizing it and, in doing so, it created what he called 'methodic conduct' and self-control in relation to economic activity in the world.

Protestantism   A sixteenth century religious doctrine espoused by Martin Luther and John Calvin. Protestantism was of interest to Weber because he thought that Calvin's teachings penetrated everyday life and commercial activity with Protestant religious maxims that induced self-regulation, distance from the world, a rejection of luxury and excess and self-denial in economic conduct. Three key elements of Calvin's doctrine were definitive as far as Weber was concerned: (i) the introduction of asceticism, methodic conduct and self denial in all departments of life; (ii) the doctrine of predestination stating that God had divided all humanity into two classes of persons, the saved and the damned;

(iii) the doctrine of 'sola fide,' which made religious faith a private matter and placed the individual on their own in spiritual life by removing prayer, confession and sacraments as a means of obtaining closeness to God, forgiveness and salvation.

Puritanism   Weber used this term to identify a type of conduct in the world common among Baptists and Quakers that was largely based on a pattern of self-denial, distance from the world and an antagonism toward sensuous pleasure by extreme forms of self regulation and restraint focusing on labor and commercial activity. Puritanism presupposed individual autonomy in spiritual matters and a commitment to purge the church of Catholic influences.

Rational   Weber used this term to refer to (i) types of societies, (ii) types of conduct and (iii) types of orientations taken up toward the world in the context of social action. In the first instance, rational societies demonstrate the development of calculable law, rational commerce, and a practical orientation to reality by the control over and mastery of external nature. With respect to an orientation to social action, rational refers to the 'methodical attainment of ends by the precise calculation of adequate means' and by various means-ends calculation which increase the attainment of practical outcomes and social goals by ordering world content according to some plan. Concerning a rational orientation taken up toward the world, rational refers to a form of social action that is freed from the influences of magic or of a religious world view.

Rationality   This is a key concept in Weber's work used to refer to a form of action that takes up an orientation to reality based on the rational attainment of given ends or goals by means of precise calculation. In contrast to rationalization, which is a term Weber used to refer to the overall historical process by which reality is increasingly mastered by procedural technique, rationality refers to the capacity of social action to be subject to calculation of the 'means and ends' in order to take up a methodical orientation to reality. Weber believed that different types of rationality became dominant at different stages of social and historical development. This, he thought, tends to eliminate other orientations to reality based on magic, prayer, fate or oracles. Rational orientations to reality, therefore, replaced earlier orientations by a straightforward attempt at controlling the empirical world and its circumstances. Weber identifies four distinct types of rationality: (i) practical; (ii) theoretical; (iii) formal; and (iv) substantive. Practical rationality can be described as an orientation to reality that is based on the 'methodical attainment of a particular end through increasingly precise calculation of adequate means.' Practical rationality imposes order on the world by a straightforward orientation to what is empirically given in reality and by precise calculation. It therefore 'orders world content according to some plan.' Theoretical rationality on the other hand, imposes order on reality by conceptual mastery of the whole in terms of unified concepts brought to light through the reasoning process. Science and mathematics are examples of this in that they produce an 'image of the world' by means of abstract concepts that undertake an orientation to reality in the realm of theory. Formal rationality, by contrast, designates the amount of quantitative calculation and accounting procedure that goes into an action or decision to ensure success in the attainment of goals. Formal rationality imposes order on the world through calculation, economic accounting and practical efficacy. A fourth type of rationality discussed by Weber is substantive rationality. Weber used this term to refer to the degree to which action is shaped by an orientation to action in the sphere of values, regardless of the nature of the ends or outcome of action. In contrast to formal rationality, substantive rationality is bound by criteria of ultimate values that are shaped by ethical norms of equality or justice over and against purely formal criteria of decision making based on calculation. The four types of rationality differ in the stress placed on the degree of consideration given to the means and ends, and the degree of calculation in the attainment of ends and the amount of control that is obtained over the empirical world.

Rationalization   A central theme in Weber's work encompassing his general theory of history and social development. It refers to the overall historical process by which reality is increasingly mastered by calculation, scientific knowledge and rational action. Weber used the term rationalization to describe the process by which nature, society and individual action is increasingly mastered in Western societies by an orientation to planning, technical procedure and rational calculation of means and ends. Weber thought that Western societies, in contrast to societies of the East, reflect a tendency in their system of law, science, medicine, and commercial practices to obtain mastery over empirical reality. In this context, several fundamental principles of rationalization link it to themes in Weber's overall approach to historical development. These include: (i) the principle of development inherent in the process of civilization and Western society; (ii) the stress placed on the rational containment of everyday life through regulation and self control; (iii) the widespread use of calculation as a strategy of social action; (iv) the freeing of social action from all magical thought; (v) the emphasis on a practical orientation to empirical reality; and (v) the reliance on technical procedure as a way of controlling practical outcomes and mastering everyday life. Rationalization depends on strategies of social action and adjustments to the means and ends of action in the attainment of goals over time.

Rational-legal Domination   Weber used this term in his theory of political domination to refer to the type of political authority whose legitimacy rests on a system of legally enacted rules to confer a right on those elevated to political office to issue commands and exercise power over others in an established system. The overriding characteristic of legal authority is its basis in a system of rational law. The nation states of Europe and North American are examples of political domination by legal authority. In this case, leaders and their officials are subject to the rule of law and must orient their action to the law in their disposition of power and authority. In addition, those obeying rules owe their allegiance not to the individuals who have power, but to an impersonal legal order. Rational legal authority thus arises in societies with a developed system of industrial production, democratic procedure, rational markets and a bureaucratic means of administration. Legal domination is based on the authority of the 'statute' as opposed to the 'edict,' since statutory laws and regulations are developed through legislative acts rather than by the personal authority or say-so of the ruler.

Religion and Rationalization   In pursuing the theme of religion and rationalization, Weber looked at the problem of how the rationalization process was related to the religious sphere and to the sphere of the economy. In this case, his aim was to show that the rational control over world activity had the capacity to transform empirical reality by placing a premium on 'methodical life conduct.' This involved two separate but interrelated assumptions by Weber. First was his belief that a religious world view produces a rational outlook toward the world, and that from this follows rational conduct. Second was his belief that historically the different religious orientations to the outside world lead to different types of rational development in knowledge, science and art. This was especially true of societies in the East in comparison with societies in the West. Weber found that the specific orientation a society takes up toward the outside world is always derived from its religious world view. He thought that this could be demonstrated by looking at the path of rational progress of science in China and India in comparison with the rational progress of science in the West. He stated that in China, the rational progress of science was thwarted by specific obstacles whose origins were religious, and that religion interfered with the rationalization process by promoting magical thinking over the technical mastery of empirical reality. This happened in China, according to Weber, when the path leading to the development of astronomy was thrown off the track of rational refinement by a religious ethic that stressed a magical orientation to reality at the very point that astronomy would have become a science. In the West on the other hand, Weber thought that there were rational refinements in astronomy which prevented it from becoming an astrology rooted in magic. For the same reason, he thought that the natural sciences in India failed to develop a method of experimentation because of religious obstacles, and that in India medicine lacked a biological and a biochemical basis that was most fully developed in the West.

Sola Fide   This is a term used by Weber to describe the particular features of Protestant religious doctrine which tended to promote private solitude and withdrawal from the world in the practice of religious faith. Weber took the view that the principle of 'sola fide' put forward a new doctrine of religious action since it diverged sharply from the Catholic concept of 'consilia evangelica,' in which religious faith took place collectively, was based on sacraments and was communal in nature. Weber believed that sola fide was an outcome of John Calvin's doctrine of salvation called predestination and was a practice that led to inner calculation, distance from the world and self-conscious planning in relation to conduct in the world.

Social Spheres   Weber used the term social sphere to indicate different realms in society whose existence, conduct, activities, and level of rationalization (i) create orientations in respect to social action and (ii) impart influences and patterns of development to other social spheres. Chief among these spheres are the legal, political, religious, and economic realms of society. These may be thought of as analogous to social institutions whose combined structure is made up of actions, activities and techniques which influence other spheres in society. Many of Weber's writings have explored the influence of the religious sphere on the economic sphere by looking for the changes in economic conduct that occurred after the Protestant reformation beginning in the sixteenth century. Weber's conceptualization of the different social spheres is important for the connections he makes between diverse realms of society and the role these realms played in the patterning of social change, the emancipation from magic, degree of rational control over empirical reality and the overall structure of social action. Weber showed that no single sphere was dominant historically, but that the spheres overlap and intersect one another to bring about change and development. Examples of the interconnection between social spheres is found in Weber's study of capitalism where he found a link between the economic and religious spheres, and in his theory of political domination where he found links between the legal, religious and political spheres of society.

Spirit of Capitalism   A term used in *The Protestant Ethic* to identify the unique characteristics of economic conduct in Western capitalism that developed after Calvin's doctrine of salvation placed a premium on inner self-control in relation to conduct in the world. It was at this point, said Weber, that a religious ethic placed its 'stamp' on 'life-regulation' and created what he called 'methodic conduct' and self-control in relation to economic activity. This illustrated a point of convergence between Protestant ethical maxims and the regulation of economic conduct by the imposition of work discipline, prudent saving, restraint, punctuality, time-thrift and the rejection of luxury in the pursuit of wealth. Weber believed that, when compared to other systems of money making, Western capitalism was alone in developing a central philosophy or 'spirit.' He thought that the spirit of capitalism was unique in two respects: (i) it developed only in modern Western capitalism and was lacking in other societies where capitalism had existed; (ii) it brought about the appearance of ethical demands in economic activity and implied the presence of religious doctrine based on the transmission of monastery asceticism and self denial to worldly economic activity. He reasoned that the spirit of capitalism can be identified by four overriding imperatives: (i) distance from the world and a rejection of luxury and excess; (ii) the devotion to amassing wealth and profit beyond the personal needs of the individual; (iii) methodical adherence to a way of life involving a commitment to unrelieved toil and work coupled with self denial; and (iv) the avoidance of the use of wealth for purposes of personal enjoyment.

State   Weber defined the state as a rational institution characterized by a system of law, a rational economy and a bureaucratic means of administration. The modern state is distinct from other political formations by (i) its monopoly of the legitimate use of violence; (ii) its system of domination based on the legitimacy of legal authority; and (iii) the right of the ruler to exercise power and issue commands based on duly enacted legal principles. At the center of Weber's theory of the state is the connection between legal authority and a bureaucratic means of administration. Bureaucratic organization affects the state in two ways. First, it ensures that the legal and political spheres are separate from the economic realm and that the economy is governed by rational legal norms. Second, it ensures that all groups are enfranchised by political rights and legal freedoms advocating universalism and equality. As a bureaucratic norm, universalism offsets the power of those who rule by creating the need to mobilize consensus within society and by promoting equitable social policy. In contrast to Marx, who reduced state activities to sheer economic domination by one class and to judicial and police functions, Weber believed that the state was concerned with the practical and technical exercise of power and the active construction of consensus.

Status Group   This is a term used by Weber in conjunction with his theory of social class to refer to the form of social adjustment taking place in the formation of social groups during the late modern period. Weber drew the distinction between 'class and status' in order to look into the question of whether groups formed on the basis of 'status considerations' and whether these were distinct from the formation of social classes in the economic sphere. A status group may be defined as a social grouping that forms in society based on patterns of consumption and the pursuit of specific life styles and habits of taste that qualify members of a group for distinctions based on their standing or status. In contrast to class, status groups involve (i) the activities by means of which groups set themselves apart from other groups; and (ii) the badges and insignia employed in defining the status group in relation to other groups and the prestige of those within the group. Whereas classes are engaged in the activity of 'acquisition' as related to income and wealth, status groups are formed in part on the basis of the badges they 'accumulate' for purposes of status considerations. Members of status groups share a common perspective based on life style and a common criterion of evaluation. Status groups uphold patterns of consumption and stylizations of taste by promoting honorific distinctions for those who acquire certain badges and commodities to which honorific distinctions are assigned. Social differentiation by 'strata' involve 'strict submission' to codes of dress, habits of taste and monopolies over certain goods and professions. Submission to these codes are indications that individuals put forward a claim to qualify as members of a status group. Weber sees class and status as separate dimensions of the stratification system. While class is defined by the market situation related to the 'acquisition' of incomes and opportunities, status operates outside the market order and is defined by patterns of 'consumption.' In North America status honor is bestowed on golfers who adhere to the standards of fashion and taste that are dominant within a given status group at a certain time. Within the status order defined by the game of golf certain modes of dress may be designated by badge names such as 'Polo' or 'Lacoste' whose standards of submission may be strictly observed, as are the status considerations assigned to the 'correct' choices related to the best golf equipment. Weber pointed out that an individual who puts forward a claim to qualify for status honor in a status group does so on the basis of their adoption of specific styles of dress and the strict submission to specific canons of taste that are assigned to their choices. Class and status thus occupy different social spheres and engage different levels of the stratification system.

Subjective Dimension   Weber used this term to identify an order of events related to human social action that involves the judgments and evaluations that occur in the 'inner states' of the actor before the act takes place. Technically speaking, the term 'subjective' refers to the inner state of conscious evaluation of the actor and is intended to demarcate itself from the purely outward states of physical behavior that occurs during action. Weber believed that the social sciences were distinct from the natural sciences because (i) they study human social action which involves reference to the 'evaluative' states of actors and (ii) because human beings, unlike the objects of nature, attach meaning to their acts and engage in subjective judgment in the effort to evaluate their social environments. In addition to this, they must also assign meaning to the acts of others before they can decide how to respond. This makes all social action interpretive. Weber thought that the actors' judgments and evaluations occur in the subjective dimension of human awareness as opposed to the objective dimension of the outside physical world. For Weber, a theory of social action had to be based on human subjective processes in order to devise a complete theory of society and a theory of social action.

Substantive Rationality   Weber used this term to refer to the degree to which social action is shaped by an orientation to ultimate values, in contrast to action which is shaped by purely formal or practical ends and calculations. In contrast to formal rationality, substantive rationality is bound by a criteria of values that are shaped by ethical norms of equality and justice over and against purely formal criteria of decision making based on the calculation of means and ends. Where formal rationality involves a practical orientation to the calculation of outcomes, substantive rationality involves a commitment to values in which the ends of action are governed by ethical standards. Weber contrasted 'substantive rationality' with 'formal rationality' and believed that the operation of modern Western society was largely based on formal rationality evident in the increased bureaucratization and the practical orientation to the means and ends of action. Whereas formal rationality entails an orientation to decisions which rely on norms of efficiency, substantive rationality relies on qualitative judgments which may be bound by ethical or aesthetic criteria. Weber believed that formal and substantive rationality are opposed, and that ultimately, formal rationality views substantive rationality as inimical to its own purpose.

Technical Rationality   Weber used the term to indicate an orientation to reality stressing a systematic evaluation and consideration of the means and ends of action for specific outcomes. In technical rationality the means are converted into 'techniques' which act as tried and true procedures in attaining goals whether administrative, economic or political. The distinctive feature of technical rationality is its systematic consideration of means, in which case the ends are treated as beyond doubt. The highest form of technical rationality is the scientific experiment which leads to a calculated stress on the means in order to achieve specific anticipated ends or outcomes. To the extent that action is technical, it is functionally oriented to the selection of means.

Theoretical Rationality   This is a term Weber used to describe a type of rationality that takes up an orientation to reality by conceiving of it from a conceptual point of view. Theoretical rationality, therefore, imposes order on the world by conceptual reasoning and abstract thought. In this case, order is imposed on reality by conceptual mastery of the whole in terms of unified concepts or by patterns brought to light through the reasoning process. For example, science, engineering and mathematics apply theoretical rationality by producing an 'image of the world' by means of abstract concepts and conceptualizations. The aim of theoretical rationality in this case is to penetrate the limits of everyday reality by attempting to understand worldly processes with the aid of abstract concepts which view the world from the perspective of a unity that may be meaningful in terms of some valued standard. Theoretical rationality leads to a departure from the concrete world of everyday experience to the world of abstraction with the express aim of representing the whole in terms of some 'ordered system.' Theoretical rationality therefore undertakes an orientation to reality in the realm of theory.

Traditional Domination   A term used by Weber to denote a system of domination in which the ruler's claim to legitimacy is based on the 'sanctity of age-old rules,' inherited right and customary practices and traditions. In societies in which traditional forms of domination prevail, leaders obtain their positions and justify their power in the light of custom and customary right. Power resides in the ability of the ruler to issue commands by virtue of the authority inherent in the person. Sovereigns, monarchs and lords of feudal estates are examples of traditional systems of domination based on hereditary right. In this case, obedience is owed to those in power by virtue of the recognition of the ruler's inherited right to the position and the authority engendered by it. Obligations to the leader in the form of loyalty are owed to the 'person' rather than to objective legal rules. In addition, the apparatus of power relies on a rudimentary administrative staff whose loyalty is based on patrimonial allegiance to the ruler. Traditional authority thus issues commands on the basis of what Weber called the 'edict' as opposed to the statute. An edict is a personal decree issued by a ruler or by heads of state which must be obeyed, thus reflecting the arbitrary nature of traditional powers. Because the power of the leader is based on custom rather than an explicit system of legal norms, there is no separation between the power of the leader and the political office. The elements of traditional authority thus reflect patterns of social action that have been stable for long periods of time.

Value Orientation   Weber used this term to pinpoint one of the key differences between the subject matter of the social sciences and the subject matter of the natural sciences. Weber believed that one of the major characteristics setting the subject matter of the social sciences apart from the exact sciences was that human social action always reflects an orientation to 'values.' Human beings, according to this view, always act in relation to ends which they value whereas the objects studied by the exact sciences act only in reference to the laws of nature, and are thus devoid of values. In this view, society is the product of what is produced by human beings acting according to values and valued ends. Thus, whatever is produced in society by human action is the result of 'values attaching to it.' According to Weber, every product of society – history, language, art, religion – embodies some value recognized by human actors as having value attached to it. As far as the objective sciences were concerned, however, whatever is a product of nature is without regard to values or, as Rickert said, is devoid of values. From this standpoint there emerged a fundamental distinction between the sciences of value and the sciences of fact. In the sciences of fact, values are irrelevant because they do not enter into the laws of nature, whereas in the social sciences such as history and sociology values are central because they concern themselves with human individuals whose actions reflect the judgments and evaluations of a surrounding social world. In this sense the products of their actions always reflect an orientation to values and, accordingly, the social sciences must undertake the study of these values.

Value Neutrality   Weber used this term in his methodological writings to indicate (i) the degree of objectivity necessary for researchers to make judgments and solve problems in the social sciences, and (ii) to refer to the caution social scientists should exercise in making 'value judgments' when those judgments coincide with the beliefs or motives of the researcher. What is important to note is that while Weber believed that value neutrality was the aim of research, he thought that the social sciences must engage in the interpretation of values and attempt to understand the value orientation of social actors.

Value Relevance   This is a term used initially by Heindrich Rickert and then by Weber to refer to the means by which specific aspects of reality are brought to the attention of observers and isolated as a matter of investigative interest. Weber used the term in relation to Rickert who believed that the principle of value relevance comes into play when researchers use concepts, since it is by means of concepts that observers are able to reduce the mass of facts in the empirical world. The principle of value relevance is a way of dealing with the claim that the natural sciences select what is of research interest solely on the basis of its objective scientific merit. It was Rickert who suggested that the objects of empirical reality must be of interest to us only because they are 'value relevant,' not because they have intrinsic scientific merit. According to this view, what interests human beings must be related to the universal values of society.

Verstehen   Literally translated as 'human understanding,' this term is used by Weber in the context of a theory of social action. Weber employed the term to convey what he thought was unique about the subject matter of the social sciences in contrast to the natural sciences. Weber believed that, however precise the natural sciences were, their subject matter confined them to the study of the external characteristics of the natural world and the outer state of things. By contrast, he thought that the social sciences were 'subjectifying' in that they concern themselves with the 'inner states' of actors who act on their 'understanding' (*Verstehen*) of the acts of others and on their interpretation of their social environments. Since the subject matter of the natural sciences do not possess 'understanding' (*Verstehen*), it stands to reason that the methods of the natural sciences should be disqualified or ruled out as adequate to the study of human social action. It is this dependence on 'understanding' which made the study of human 'social acts' distinct from the study of the physical and natural world.

Bibliography

Primary Texts

Marx, Marx and Engels

Marx, Karl. *Critique of Hegel's Philosophy of Right*, J. O'Malley (ed.), Cambridge: Cambridge University Press, [1843] 1970.

Marx, Karl. 'On the Jewish Question,' R.C. Tucker (ed.), *Marx-Engels Reader.* New York: W.W. Norton, [1843] 1978.

Marx, Karl. *The Economic and Philosophic Manuscripts of 1844*. New York: International Publishers, [1932] 1964.

Marx, Karl and Engels, Frederick. *The Holy Family, or Critique of Critical Criticism*. Moscow: Progress Publishers, [1845] 1956.

Marx, Karl and Engels, Frederick. *The German Ideology*. New York: International Publishers, [1845] 1947.

Engels, Frederick. *The Condition of the Working Class in England*. Oxford: Basil Blackwell, [1845] 1958.

Marx, Karl. *The Poverty of Philosophy*. New York: International Publishers, [1847] 1982.

Marx, K. and Engels, F. *The Communist Manifesto*, F.L. Bender (ed.), New York: Norton, [1848] 1988.

Marx, Karl. 'Wage Labor and Capital,' in R. C. Tucker (ed.), *The Marx-Engels Reader*, 2nd Ed., New York: W.W. Norton & Company, [1849] 1978, pp. 203–17.

Marx, Karl. *The Eighteenth Brumaire of Louis Bonaparte*. Moscow: Progress, 1977 [1852], pp. 104–105.

Marx, Karl. 'British Rule in India,' in Marx, Karl, and Engels, Frederick, *On Colonialism*. New York: International Publishers, [1853] 1972.

Marx, Karl. *Pre-Capitalist Economic Formations*, E. J. Hobsbawm (ed.), New York: International Publishers, [1857–58] 1965.

Marx, Karl. *A Contribution to the Critique of Political Economy*. Moscow: Progress Publishers, [1859] 1977.

Marx, Karl. *Grundrisse: Foundations of the Critique of Political Economy*. Middlesex, England: Penguin, [1953] 1973.

Marx, Karl. 'Value, Price and Profit,' *Collected Works,* Vol. 20. London: Lawrence & Wishart, [1865] 1985.

Marx, Karl. *The Civil War in France*. Peking: Foreign Languages Press, [1870] 1970.

Marx, Karl. *Capital: A Critique of Political Economy,* Vol. 1. Middlesex, England: Penguin, [1867] 1976.

Marx, Karl. *Capital: A Critique of Political Economy,* Vol. 2. Moscow: Progress, [1876] 1971.

Marx, Karl. *Capital: A Critique of Political Economy,* Vol 3. London: Penguin, [1894] 1981.

Marx, Karl. *Theories of Surplus-Value*. Moscow: Progress, [1871] 1971.

Engels, Frederick. *Anti-Duhring*. Peking: Foreign Languages Press, [1878] 1976.

Hegel

Hegel, G.W.F. *The Phenomenology of Mind*. New York: Harper Touchbooks, [1812] 1967.
——. *Phenomenology of Spirit*. Oxford: Oxford University Press, [1813] 1977.
——. *The Philosophy of Right*. Oxford: Clarendon Press, [1820] 1952.
——. *The Science of Logic*. Oxford: Clarendon Press, [1820] 1929.
——. *The Philosophy of History*, New York: Dover, [1830] 1956.

Durkheim, Mauss, and Related

Durkheim, Emile. 'Inaugural Lecture at Bordeaux,' *Sociological Inquiry*, 44 (3):189–204, [1887–88] 1974.
Durkheim, Emile. 'Suicide and the Birth Rate,' in Lester, David (ed.), *Emile Durkheim Le Suicide: One Hundred Years Later*. Philadelphia: Charles Press, [1888] 1994, 115–132.
Durkheim, Emile. *The Division of Labor in Society*. New York: The Free Press, [1893] 1933.
Durkheim, Emile. *Suicide: A Sociological Study*. New York: The Free Press, [1897] 1951.
Durkheim, Emile. 'Minor Editorials: Durkheim's Response to Tosti,' *American Journal of Sociology*, Vol. 3, 848–9, 1898.
Durkheim, Emile. *The Rules of Sociological Method*. New York: The Free Press, [1895] 1938.
Durkheim, Emile. *The Elementary Forms of Religious Life*. London: (Swain trans.) Allen & Unwin, [1912] 1915.
——. *The Elementary Forms of Religious Life* (K. Fields trans.), New York: The Free Press, 1995.
Durkheim, Emile and Mauss, Marcel. *Primitive Classification*. Chicago: University of Chicago Press, [1903] 1963.
Durkheim, Emile. 'On Totemism,' *The History of Sociology*, 5, [1902] (Spring) 1985, 91–122.
Durkheim, Emile. 'The Dualism of Human Nature and Its Social Conditions,' [1914] in Kurt H. Wolff (ed.), *Essays on Sociology and Philosophy*. New York: Harper, 1960, 325–340.
Durkheim, Emile. 'Individualism and the Intellectuals' (trans. S. and J. Lukes), *Political Studies*, 17, [1898] 1969, 14–30.
Mauss, Marcel. *The Gift: Forms and Functions of Exchange in Archaic Societies*. London: Routledge & Kegan Paul, [1906] 1969.
Mauss, Marcel. *Seasonal Variations of the Eskimo: A Study in Social Morphology*. London: Routledge & Kegan Paul, [1905] 1979.
Tarde, Gabriel. *The laws of Imitation*, 2nd Ed. Gloucester, Mass.: Peter Smith, [1895] 1962.

Weber

Weber, Max. *The Protestant Ethic and The Spirit of Capitalism*. New York: Scribner's, [1904–05] 1958.
Weber, Max. 'Anti-critical Last Word on The Spirit of Capitalism,' *American Journal of Sociology*, Vol. 83 (5), [1910] 1978, 1105–113.
Weber, Max. *From Max Weber: Essays in Sociology*, H. Gerth and C.W Mills (eds.), New York: Oxford University Press, 1967.
Weber, Max. *Economy and Society: Volumes 1 & 2*, G. Roth and C. Wittich (eds.), Berkeley: University of California Press, 1978.
Weber, Max. 'Objectivity in Social Sciences and Social Policy,' in E.A. Shils and H.A. Finch (eds.), *The Methodology of the Social Sciences*. New York: The Free Press, 1949.
Weber, Max. *Critique of Stammler* (trans. Guy Oake). New York: The Free Press, 1977.
Weber, Max. *Roscher and Knies: The Logical Problems of Historical Economics* (trans. Guy Oakes). New York: The Free Press, 1975.
Weber, Max. *General Economic History*. New York: Collier Books, 1961 [1918–1920].
Weber, Max. 'The Social Psychology of the World Religions,' in H. Gerth and C.W Mills (eds.), *From Max Weber: Essays in Sociology*. New York: Oxford University Press, [1919] 1967, 267–301.

Weber, Max. 'Religious Rejection of the World and Their Directions,' in H. Gerth and C.W Mills (eds.), *From Max Weber: Essays in Sociology*. New York: Oxford University Press, 1967, 323–359.

Weber, Max. 'The Protestant Sects and the Spirit of Capitalism,' in H. Gerth and C.W Mills (eds.), *From Max Weber: Essays in Sociology*. New York: Oxford University Press, [1919] 1967, pp. 302–322.

Weber, Max. *Ancient Judaism*, H. H. Gerth and D. Martindale (eds.), New York: The Free Press, [1917–19] 1952.

Weber, Max. *The Religion of India: The Sociology of Hinduism and Buddhism*. H. H. Gerth and D. Martindale (eds.), New York: The Free Press, [1919] 1958.

Weber, Max. *The Religion of China: Confucianism and Taoism*. H. H. Gerth (ed.), New York: The Free Press, 1964.

Secondary texts

Acton, H.B. 'The Materialist Conception of History,' *Proceedings of the Aristotelian Society*, 1951–52, 205–224.

Allen, N.J., Pickering W.S.F. and Miller, W.Watts. *On Durkheim's Elementary Forms of Religious Life*. London: Routledge, 1998.

——. 'Mauss and the Categories,' *Durkheimian Studies*, 4, 39–50, 1998.

——. 'Effervescences and the Origins of Human Society,' in N.J. Allen, W.S.F. Pickering and W. Watts Miller (eds.), *On Durkheim's Elementary Forms of Religious Life*. London: Routledge, 1998. pp. 149–161.

Althusser, Louis. *Reading Capital*. London: Verso NLB, 1970.

——. *Lenin and Philosophy*. New York: Monthly Review Press, 1971.

——. 'Ideology and Ideological State Apparatuses,' in *Lenin and Philosophy*. New York: Monthly Review Press, pp. 127–186.

Anchor, Robert. 'Heinrich Rickert,' *The Encyclopedia of Philosophy*, Vol. 7, pp. 192–4, 1975.

Anderson, Perry. *Lineages of the Absolutist State*. London: Verso, 1979.

——. *Passages from Antiquity to Feudalism*. London: Verso, 1978.

Arendt, Hannah. *On Revolution*. New York: Viking, 1963.

Aron, Raymond. *Main Currents in Sociological Thought* (2 Vol.) New York: Doubleday, 1970.

Bachelard, Gaston. *The New Scientific Spirit*, Boston: Beacon Press, 1984.

Balibar, Etienne. 'On the Basic Concepts of Historical Materialism,' L. Althusser and E. Balibar, *Reading Capital*. London: Verso, 1979.

Barbalet, J.M. *Marx's Construction of Social Theory*. London: Routledge, 1983.

Barrett, Michele. 'Ideology, Politics, Hegemony: From Gramsci to Laclau and Mouffe,' in S. Zizek, *Mapping Ideology*. New York: Verso, 1994

Beck, L.W. 'Neo-Kantianism,' *The Encyclopedia of Philosophy*, Vol. 5, pp. 468–473.

Bendix, Reinhard. *Max Weber: An Intellectual Portrait*. New York: Doubleday, 1962.

Bendix, Reinhard. 'Max Weber's Sociology Today,' *International Social Science Journal*, 17, 1965, 9–22.

Berger, Thomas. *Max Weber's Theory of Concept Formation*, Durham: Duke University Press, 1976.

Berger, Peter and Pullberg, S. 'Reification and the Sociological Critique of Consciousness,' *New Left Review*, 35, 1966, 56–71.

Besnard, Philippe (ed.). *The Sociological Domain: The Durkheimians and the Founding of French Sociology*. Cambridge: Cambridge University Press, 1983.

——. 'The Fortunes of Durkheim's Suicide: Reception and Legacy,' in Pickering, W.S.F. and G. Walford (eds.), *Durkheim's Suicide: A Century of Research and Debate*. London: Routledge, 2000, pp. 97–125.

Bhaskar, Roy. *A Realist Theory of Science*. London: Leeds Books, 1975.

——. 'Philosophy and Scientific Realism,' in M. Archer, R. Bhaskar, A. Collier (eds.), *Critical Realism*. London: Routledge, 1998, pp. 16–47.

——. 'Dialectical Critical Realism and Ethics,' in M. Archer, R. Bhaskar et al. (eds.), *Critical Realism*. London: Routledge, 1998, pp. 641–687.

——. *Reclaiming Reality*. London: Verso, 1989.

Black, Antony. *Guilds and Civil Society in European Political Thought from the Twelfth Century to the Present*. London: Methuen and Co., 1984.

Blackburn, Robin (ed.). *Ideology in Social Science: Readings in Critical Social Theory*. New York: Pantheon, 1972.

Bland, A.E., Brown, P.A., and Tawney, R.H. (eds.), *English Economic History: Select Documents*. London: Bell & Sons, 1925.

Blum, Jerome, 'The Rise of Serfdom in Eastern Europe,' *The American Historical Review,* 62, 1957, 807–836.

Bourdieu, Pierre. *Distinctions: A Social Critique of the Judgement of Taste*. Cambridge, Mass.: Harvard University Press, 1984.

——. 'The Social Space and the Genesis of Groups,' *Theory & Society,* 14: 723–744, 1985.

——. 'Structuralism and the Theory of Knowledge,' *Social Research*, 35, 681–706, 1969.

——. *The Logic of Practice*. Stanford, California: University Press, 1990.

——. *Outline of a Theory of Practice*. Cambridge: University Press, 1977.

——. 'Symbolic Power,' in Denis Gleeson (ed.), *Identity and Structure: Issues in the Sociology of Education*. Driffield, England: Nafferton Books, 1977.

——. *Practical Reason: On the Theory of Action*. London: Polity, 1998.

——. 'Legitimation and Structured Interests in Weber's Sociology of Religion,' in S. Lash and S. Whimster (eds.), *Max Weber, Rationality and Modernity*. London: Allen & Unwin, 1987, pp. 119–136.

——. 'The Three Forms of Theoretical Knowledge,' *Soc. Sci. inform*. 12, 1973, 53–80.

Bourdieu, P., Chamboredon, J-C., and Passeron, J-C. *The Craft of Sociology: Epistemological Preliminaries*. Berlin: Walter de Gruyter, 1991.

Bourdieu, Pierre, and Wacquant, Loic. An Invitation to Reflexive Sociology. Chicago: University of Chicago Press, 1992.

Bottomore,Tom (ed.), *A Dictionary of Marxist Thought*. Cambridge, Mass.: Harvard University Press, 1983.

Bottomore, Tom and Nisbet, R. (eds.), *A History of Sociological Analysis*. New York: Basic Books, 1978.

Bradby, Barbara. 'The Destruction of Natural Economies,' in Wolpe, Harold (ed.), *The Articulation of Modes of Production*. London: Routledge, 1980, pp. 93–127.

Brubaker, Rogers. *The Limits of Rationality: An Essay on the Social and Moral Thought of Max Weber.* London: George Allen & Unwin, 1984.

——. 'Rethinking Classical Theory: The Sociological Vision of Pierre Bourdieu,' *Theory & Society*, 14, 745–75, 1985.

Brunt, P.A. 'Free Labor and Public Works at Rome,' *Journal of Roman Studies*, 70, 1980, 81–99.

Bruun, H. H. *Science, Values and Politics in Max Weber's Methodology*. Copenhagen: Munksgaard, 1972.

Burger, Thomas. *Max Weber's Theory of Concept Formation: History, Laws, and Ideal Types*. Durham: Duke University Press, 1976.

Calvin, John. *The Institutes of Christian Religion*, T. Lane & H. Osborne (eds.), London: Hodder and Stoughton, [1559] 1986.

——. Calvin's Ecclesiastical Advice, M. Beaty and B.W. Farley (trans.), Louisville, Kentucky: Westminster/John Knox Press, 1991.

Carling, Alan. 'Forms of Value and the Logic of Capital,' *Science and Society*, 50, 1986, 52–80.

Chalcraft, D.J., and Harrington, A. (eds). *The Protestant Ethic Debate: Max Weber's Replies to his Critics, 1907–1910*. Liverpool: University Press, 2001.

Chambers, J.D., and Mingay, Gordon E. *The Agricultural Revolution, 1750–1850*. London: Batsford, 1966.

Chambers, J.D. 'Enclosure and the Labor Supply in the Industrial Revolution,' *Economic History Review 2nd Series,* Vol. V, 1953, 319–343.

Chambliss, William. 'A Sociological Analysis of the Law of Vagrancy,' *Social Problems*, 12, 1964, 67–77.

Charlton, D.G. *Secular Religions in France 1815–1870.* London: Oxford University Press, 1963.

——. *Positivist Thought in France.* Oxford: Clarendon Press, 1959.

Claeys, Gregory. 'Individualism, Socialism and Social Science: Further Notes on a Process of Conceptual Formation 1800–1850,' *Journal of the History of Ideas*, 33, 1986, 81–93.

Clark, Terry N. *Gabriel Tarde on Communication and Social Influence.* Chicago: University Press, 1969.

Cohen, G.A. *Karl Marx's Theory of History.* New Jersey: Princeton University Press, 1978.

Colletti, Lucio. *Marxism and Hegel.* London: Verso, 1979.

Collins, Randall. 'Weber's Last Theory of Capitalism: A Systematization,' *American Sociological Review,* 45, 1980, 925–42.

Cornforth, Maurice. *Dialectical Materialism: An Introduction.* London: Lawrence & Wishart, 1953.

Cropsey, Joseph. 'Karl Marx,' in Leo Strauss and Joseph Cropsey (eds.), *History of Political Philosophy.* Chicago: Rand McNally & Co., 1963, pp. 697–723.

Dawe, Alan. 'The Relevance of Values in Weber's Sociology,' in A. Sahay (ed.), *Max Weber and Modern Sociology.* London: Routledge & Kegan Paul, 1971, 37–66.

Descartes, Rene. *Descartes Selections.* New York: Scribner's, 1955.

Di Quattro, Arthur. 'Verstehen as an Empirical Concept,' *Sociology and Social Research*, 57, 1972, 32–42.

Dobb, Maurice. *Studies in the Development of Capitalism.* New York: International Pub, 1947.

Dohrenwend, B.P. 'Egoism, Altruism, Anomie and Fatalism: A Conceptual Analysis of Durkheim's Types,' *American Sociological Review*, 24, 1959, 466–472.

Douglas, Jack. 'The Sociological Analysis of Social Meanings of Suicide,' *European Journal of Sociology*, 7, 1966, 249–275.

Douglas, Mary. *Purity and Danger: Analysis of Concepts of Pollution and Taboo.* Middlesex: Penguin Books, 1970.

Duby, Georges. *Rural Economy and Country Life in the Medieval West.* Columbia, S.C.: University of South Carolina Press, 1968.

Dumont, Louis. 'The Modern Conception of the Individual,' *Contributions to Indian Sociology,* 8, 1965, 13–61.

——. 'The 'Village Community' From Munro to Maine,' *Contributions to Indian Sociology*, 9, 67–89, 1986.

Dunayevskaya, Raya. *Marxism and Freedom.* London: Pluto Press, 1971.

Eagleton, Terry. 'Ideology and its Vicissitudes in Western Marxism,' in S. Zizek (ed.), *Mapping Ideology.* London: Verso, 1994, pp. 179–226.

——. *Ideology: An Introduction.* London, Verso, 1991.

Eisenstadt, S.N. (ed.). *The Protestant Ethic and Modernization.* New York: Basic Books, 1968.

Feuerbach, L. *The Essence of Christianity.* Buffalo, N.Y.: Prometheus, 1989.

Findlay, J.N. *Hegel: A Re-Examination.* London: George Allen & Unwin, 1958.

Finley, M.I. *Slavery in Classical Antiquity.* Cambridge: Heffer, 1968.

——. *The Ancient Economy.* London: Ghatto & Windus, 1973.

Fielden, John. *The Curse of the Factory System.* New York: Augustus Kelley, [1836] 1969.

Fields, Karen. *The Elementary Forms of Religious Life.* By Emile Durkheim. New York: Free Press, 1995.

Feyerabend, Paul K. *Problems of Empiricism.* London: Cambridge University Press, 1981.

Foucault, Michel. *Madness and Civilization.* New York: Vintage Books, 1988.

——. 'About the Concept of the 'Dangerous Individual,' in Nineteenth Century Legal Psychiatry,' *International Journal of Law and Psychiatry*, 1, 1978, 1–18.

——. *Discipline and Punish: The Birth of the Prison.* New York: Vintage Books, 1979.

——. 'The Politics of Health in the Eighteenth Century,' in *Power/Knowledge.* New York: Pantheon Books, 1972.

Fukazawa, H. 'A Note on the Corvée System in the Eighteenth Century Maratha Kingdom,'*Science and Human Progress.* Bombay, 1974, pp. 117–30.

Gehlke, Charles. *Emile Durkheim's Contribution to Sociological Theory.* New York: AMS Press, 1915.

Geras, Norman. 'Essence and Appearance: Aspects of Fetishism in Marx's Capital,' *New Left Review,* 65, 1971, 69–85.

——. 'Fetishism in Marx's Capital,' *New Left Review*, 65, 1971.

——. 'Post-Marxism,' *New Left Review*, 163, 1987, pp. 40–82.

Gerth, H.H. and Wright Mills, C. *From Max Weber: Essays in Sociology.* New York: University Press, 1946, p. 24.

Giddens, Anthony. *Capitalism and Modern Social Theory.* Cambridge: Cambridge University Press, 1971.

——. 'The 'Individual' in the Writings of Emile Durkheim,' *European Journal of Sociology*, 12, 1971, 210–228.

——. 'A Typology of Suicide,' *European Journal of Sociology,* 7, 1966, 276–295.

——.'Four Theses on Ideology,' *The Canadian Journal of Political and Social Theory*, 7, 1 & 2, 1983, pp. 18–21.

Godelier, Maurice. 'Politics as 'Infrastructure': An Anthropologist's thoughts on the Example of Classical Greece and the Notions of Relations of Production and Economic Determination,' in J. Freidman and M.J. Rowlands (eds.), *The Evolution of Social Systems.* London: Duckworth, 1977, pp. 13–28.

Godlove, Terry F. 'Epistemology in Durkheim's Elementary Forms of Religious Life,' *Journal of the History of Philosophy*, Vol. 24 (3), 385–401, 1986.

Gordon, Marshall. *In Search of the Spirit of Capitalism.* New York: Columbia University Press, 1982.

——. *Presbyteries and Profits: Calvinism and the Development of Capitalism in Scotland, 1560–1707.* Oxford: Clarendon Press, 1980.

Green, R.W. (ed.). *Protestantism, Capitalism, and Social Science: The Weber Thesis Controversy.* Lexington, Mass.: D.C. Heath and Co., 1973.

Green, Robert W. Protestantism and Capitalism: The Weber Thesis and its Critics, Boston: Health & co, 1959.

Habib, Irfan. 'Economic History of the Delhi Sultanate: An Essay in Interpretation,' *Indian Historical Review*, 4, 2, 1978, 287–303.

——. 'Classifying Pre-Colonial India,' *Journal of Peasant Studies*, 12, 1985, 44–53.

Halbwachs, Maurice. *The Causes of Suicide.* New York: The Free Press, [1930] 1978.

Halevy, Elie. *The Growth of Philosophic Radicalism.* Boston: Beacon Press, 1955.

Hekman, Susan. *Weber, the Ideal Type, and Contemporary Social Theory.* Notre Dame, Indiana: University of Notre Dame Press, 1983.

——. 'Weber's Concept of Causality and the Modern Critique,' *Sociological Inquiry,* 49, 1979, 67–76.

Henderson, W.O. *The Industrial Revolution on the Continent 1800–1914.* London: Frank Cass, 1947.

Hertz, Robert. 'The Pre-eminence of the Right Hand: A Study in Religious Polarity,' in R. Needham (ed.), *Right & Left: Essays on Dual Symbolic Classification.* Chicago: University of Chicago Press, 1973.

Hibbert, A.B. 'The Origins of the Medieval Town Patriciate,' *Past and Present,* 3, Feb. 1953, 15–27.

Hilton, Rodney. *The Transition from Feudalism to Capitalism.* London: NLB Humanities Press, 1976.

——. 'Introduction,' The *Transition from Feudalism to Capitalism,'* London: NLB Humanities Press, 1976.

——. 'Capitalism: What's in a Name?', *Past and Present,* 1, Feb. 1952, 32–43.

——. *The Decline of Serfdom in Medieval England.* London: St. Martin's Press, 1969.

——. The English Peasantry in the Later Middle ages. Oxford: Clarendon, 1975.

Hobbes, T. *Leviathan*. Middlesex, England: Penguin, 1968 [1651], p. 186.

Hobsbawm, E.J. *The Age of Revolution*. New York: Dover, 1938.

Hook, Sidney. *From Hegel to Marx*. London: Victor Gollancz, 1936.

Hughes, H. Stuart. *Consciousness and Society: The Reorientation of European Social Thought 1890–1930*. New York: Vintage Books, 1958.

Hume, David. *Enquiries Concerning Human Understanding and Concerning the Principles of Morals*. Oxford: Clarendon Press, [1748] 1975.

Huff, Toby E. *Max Weber and the Methodology of the Social Sciences*. London: Transaction, 1984.

Jones, G.S. 'History: The Poverty of Empiricism,' in Robin Blackburn (ed.), *Ideology in Social Science: Readings in Critical Social Theory*. New York: Pantheon, 1972, 96–118.

Jones, Robert Alun. 'Durkheim, Totemism and the Intichiuma,' *History of Sociology*, 5, 2, 1985, 79–89.

——. *The Development of Durkheim's Social Realism*. Cambridge: Cambridge University Press, 1999.

——. *The Development of Durkheim's Social Realism*. Cambridge: The University Press, 1999.

Jordan, Z.A. *The Evolution of Dialectical Materialism*. New York: St. Martin's Press, 1967.

Kalberg, Stephen. 'The Search for Thematic Orientations in a Fragmented Oeuvre: The Discussion of Max Weber in Recent Sociological Literature,' *Sociology*, 13, 1979, 127–39.

——. 'Max Weber's Types of Rationality: Cornerstones for the Analysis of Rationalization Processes in his History,' *American Journal of Sociology*, 85, 1980, 1145–79.

——. 'On the Neglect of Weber's Protestant Ethic as a Theoretical Treatise: Demarcating the Parameters of Postwar American Sociological Theory,' *Sociological Theory*, 14 (1), 1996, 49–69.

——. 'The Rationalization of Action in Marx Weber's Sociology of Religion,' *Sociological Theory*, 8, 1990, 58–84.

——. *Max Weber's Comparative Historical Sociology*, Chicago: University of Chicago Press.

Kant, Immanuel. *The Critique of Pure Reason*. New York: St. Martin's Press, 1965.

Kasler, Dirk. *Max Weber: An Introduction to his Life and Work*. Chicago: University Chicago Press, 1988.

Keane, John. 'Democracy and the Theory of Ideology,' *Canadian Journal of Political and Social Theory*, 7, 1983, 5–17.

Kerridge, Eric. *The Agricultural Revolution*. New York: Augustus Kelly, 1968.

——. 'The Movement of Rent, 1540–1640,' *Economic History Review 2nd Series,* Vol. VI, 1953, pp. 17–34.

Konvitz, Milton R. and Murphy, R.E. (eds.), *Essays in Political Theory*. New York: Kennikat Press, 1972, pp. 130–152.

Korner, S. *Kant*. Harmondsworth: Penguin, 1955.

Korsch, Karl. *Karl Marx*. New York: Russell & Russell, 1963.

Laclau, Ernesto. 'The Impossibility of Society,' *Canadian Journal of Political and Social Theory*, 7, 1 & 2, 1983, 21–24.

—— and Mouffe, Chantal. *Hegemony and Socialist Strategy*. London: Verso, 1985.

Laibman, David. 'Modes of Production and Theories of Transition,' *Science and Society*, XLVIII, 1984, 257–294.

Larrain, Jorge. *Marxism and Ideology*. London: MacMillan Press, 1983.

——. *The Concept of Ideology*. Athens, Georgia: University of Georgia Press, 1979.

Lash, S. and Whimster, S. *Max Weber, Rationality and Modernity*. London: Allen & Unwin, 1987.

Lasonick, William. 'Karl Marx and Enclosures in England,' *Review of Radical Political Economics*, Vol. 6, 2, 1974, 1–32.

Lefebvre, Georges. *The French Revolution From its Origins to 1793*. London: Routledge, 1962.

Lehmann, H. and Roth, G. (eds.), *Weber's Protestant Ethic: Origins, Evidence, Contexts*. Cambridge: Cambridge University Press, 1993.

Lester, D. *Emile Durkheim Le Suicide: One Hundred Later*. Philadelphia: Charles Press, [1888] 1994, pp. 115–132.

Levine, Donald N. 'Rationality and Freedom: Weber and Beyond,' *Sociological Inquiry*, 51, 1981, 5–25.

Lévi-Strauss, Claude. *The Elementary Structures of Kinship*. Boston: Beacon Press, 1969.

——. *The Raw and the Cooked*. New York: Harper Torchbooks, 1969.

——. *The Origin of Table Manners*. New York: Harper & Row, 1978.

Lindsay, A.D. 'Individualism,' *Encyclopedia of the Social Sciences*, 7, 1930–33, 674–80.

Lukacs, Georg. *History of Class Consciousness*. London: Merlin Press, 1968.

Lukes, Steven. *Emile Durkheim: His Life and Work*. Stanford: Stanford University Press, 1973.

——. 'Prolegomena to the Interpretation of Durkheim,' *European Journal of Sociology*, 12, 1971, 183–209.

——. *Individualism*. Oxford: Basil Blackwell, 1973.

Luxemburg, Rosa. *The Accumulation of Capital*. London: Routledge and Kegan Paul, 1951.

Malthus, Thomas. *An Essay on the Principle of Population*. London: Ward Lock, 1890.

MacKinnon, Malcolm H. 'The Longevity of the Thesis: A Critique of the Critics,' H. Lehmann and G. Roth (eds.), *Weber's Protestant Ethic: Origins, Evidence, Contexts*. Cambridge: University Press, 1993, pp. 211–44.

Macpherson, C.B. *The Political Theory of Possessive Individualism*. London: Oxford University Press, 1962.

Mauss, M. *The Gift: Forms and Functions of Exchange in Archaic Societies*. London: Routledge, 1970, pp. 1–210.

McLellan, David. *Karl Marx His Life and Thought*. New York: Harper & Row, 1973.

Mantoux, Paul. *The Industrial Revolution in the Eighteenth Century*. London: Methuen, 1907.

Marcuse, Herbert. *Reason and Revolution: Hegel and the Rise of Social Theory*. New York: Humanities Press, 1954.

Marglin, Stephen. 'What Do Bosses Do? The Origins and Functions of Hierarchy in Capitalist Production,' *Review of Radical Political Economy*, 6, 2, 1974, 33–60.

Marshall, Gordon. *Presbyteries and Profits: Calvinism and the Development of Capitalism in Scotland, 1560–1707*. Oxford: Clarendon Press, 1980.

Meek, Ronald L. *Economics and Ideology and Other Essays*. London: Chapman and Hall, 1967.

—— . *Studies in the Labor Theory of Value*. London: Lawrence & Wishart, 1973.

—— (ed.), *Marx and Engels on Malthus*. New York: International Publishers, 1954.

Mill, John Stuart. *Utilitarianism, Liberty, Representative Government*. London: Dent & Sons, 1910.

Morrison, Ken. 'Durkheim and Schopenhauer: New Textual Evidence on the Conceptual History of Durkheim's Formulation of the Egoistic-Altruistic Types of Suicide,' *Durkheimian Studies*, 4, 115–124, 1998.

——. 'The Disavowal of the Social in the American Reception of Durkheim,' *Journal of Classical Sociology*, 1 (1), 2001, 95–126.

——. 'Review Essay: The Elementary Forms of Religious Life,' *Social Forces*, vol. 82, 2003, pp. 399–404.

——. 'Review of Robert Alun Jones,' *The Development of Durkheim's Social Realism, The Canadian Journal of Sociology*. ww.cjson/line.cu/reviews/ March–April 2000.

Morrison, Ken, Review of J. Alexander & P. Smith (eds.) *The Cambridge Comparsion to Durkheim, The Candaian Journal of Sociology*, www.cjsonline,ca/reviews/March 2006.

Nelson, Benjamin. 'Max Weber's 'Author's Introduction' (1920): A Master Clue to his Main Aims,' *Sociological Inquiry*, 44, 1974, 269–78.

Oakes, Guy. 'The Verstehen Thesis and the Foundations of Max Weber's Methodology,' *History and Theory*, 16, 1977, 11–29.

Ollman, Bertell. *Alienation: Marx's Conception of Man in Capitalist Society*. London: Cambridge University Press, 1971.

Padgug, Robert A. 'Problems in the Theory of Slavery and Slave Society,' *Science and Society*, 40, 1976, 3–27.

Palmer, R. R. 'Man and Citizen: Applications of Individualism in the French Revolution,' in Park, Robert E. and Burgess, Ernest W., 1921, *Introduction to the Science of Sociology*. Chicago: University of Chicago Press.

Parsons, Talcott. *The Structure of Social Action,* Vol. I. New York: The Free Press [1937] 1968.

Patterson, Orlando. *Slavery and Social Death: A Comparative Study*. Cambridge, Mass.: Harvard University Press, 1982.

——. 'On Slavery and Slave Formations', *New Left Review,* 117 (Sept.–Oct.) 1979, 31–67.

Pickering, W.S.F. *Durkheim's Sociology of Religion*: *Themes and Theories*. London: Routledge & Kegan Paul, 1984.

Pickering, W.S.F. and G. Walford (eds), *Durkheim's Suicide: A Century of Research and Debate*. London: Routledge, 2000.

Plummer, Alfred. *The London Weavers' Company 1600–1970*. London: Routledge & Kegan Paul, 1972.

Poggi, Gianfranco. 'The Place of Religion in Durkheim's Theory of Institutions,' *European Journal of Sociology,* 12, 1971, 229–260.

——. *Calvinism and the Capitalist Spirit: Max Weber's Protestant Ethic*. London: Macmillian Press, 1983.

Polanyi, Karl. *The Great Transformation*. Boston: Beacon, 1957.

Pollard, Sidney, 'Factory Discipline in the Industrial Revolution,' *Economic Historical Review,* 2nd Series, 16, 1963–64, 254–271.

Poulantzas, N. *State, Power and Socialism*. London: NLB, 1978.

——. *Political Power and Social Classes*. London: Sheed and Ward, 1973.

Ramp, William. 'Effervescence, Differentiation and Representation in the Elementary Forms,' in Allen, N. J., Pickering W.S.F. and Miller, W. Watts, *On Durkheim's Elementary Forms of Religious Life*. London: Routledge, 1998.

Rathbone, D.W. 'Review Articles: The Slave Mode of Production in Italy,' *Journal of Roman Studies*, 73, 1983, 160–68.

Rawls, Anne Warfield. 'Durkheim's Epistemology: The Neglected Argument,' *American Journal of Sociology*', Vol. 102 (2), 1996, 430–482.

——. 'Durkheim's Challenge to Philosophy: Human Reason Explained as a Product of Enacted Social Practice,' *American Journal of Sociology*, Vol. 104 (3), 1998, 887–901.

Ricardo, David. *On the Principles of Political Economy and Taxation*. London, [1817] 1821.

Rickert, Heinrich. *Science and History: A Critique of Positivist Epistemology*. New York: Van Nostrand, 1962.

Richardson, Ruth. *Death Dissection and the Destitute*. London: Routledge & Kegan Paul, 1987.

Ricoeur, Paul. *Lectures on Ideology and Utopia*. New York: Columbia University Press, 1986.

Rousseau, Jean-Jacques. *The Social Contract and Discourse on the Origin of Inequality*. New York: Simon & Schuster, 1967.

Rubin, Isaak Illich. *Essays on Marx's Theory of Value*. Montreal: Black Rose, [1928] 1973.

Samuelsson, Kurt. *Religion and Economic Action: A Critique of Max Weber*. New York: Harper & Row, 1957.

Schluchter, Wolfgang. *The Rise of Western Rationalism*. Berkeley: University of California Press, 1981.

——. 'Weber's Sociology of Rationalism and Typology of Religious Rejection of the World,' in S. Whimster and S. Lash (eds.), *Max Weber, Rationality and Modernity*. London: Allen & Unwin, pp. 92–115.

Schmaus, Warren. *Durkheim's Philosophy of Science and the Sociology of Knowledge*. Chicago: University of Chicago Press, 1994.

—— (ed.). 'Durkheimian Sociology,' *Journal of the History of Behavioral Sciences* (Special Issue), 32, 1996.

——. 'Durkheim on the Causes and Functions of the Categories,' in Allen, N.J., Pickering W.S.F. and Miller, W. Watts. *On Durkheim's Elementary Forms of Religious Life*. London: Routledge, 1998.

——. 'Rawls, Durkheim, and Causality: A Critical Discussion,' *American Journal of Sociology*,' Vol. 104, (3), 872–886, 1998.

Sharma, R.S. *Indian Feudalism*: c 300–1200. Calcutta: University of Calcutta, 1965.

Simon, W. *European Positivism in the Nineteenth Century*. New York: Cornell University Press, 1963.

Smith, A. *The Wealth of Nations.* London: Dent & Sons, [1776] 1910.

Smith, Dorothy. 'The Ideological Practice of Sociology,' *Catalyst,* 8, 1974, 39–54.

——. The Conceptual Practices of Power: A Feminists Sociology of Knowledge. Toronto: University of Toronto Press, 1990.

Soboul, Albert. *The French Revolution 1787–1799,* Vol. 1. London: NLB, 1974.

Sohn-Rethel, Alfred. *Intellectual and Manual Labor.* London: Macmillan, 1978.

Sorokin, Pitirim. *Contemporary Sociological Theories.* New York: Harper & Row, 1928.

Steven Spitzer. 'The Production of Deviance in Capitalist Society,' *Social Problems*, 22, 5, 1975, 641–646.

Stepelevich, L.S. *The Young Hegelians: An Anthology.* Cambridge: University Press, 1983.

Strauss, Leo and Cropsey, Joseph (eds.). *History of Political Philosophy.* Chicago: Rand McNally & Co., 1963.

Swart, K.W. 'Individualism in the Mid-Nineteenth Century (1826–1860),' *Journal of the History of Ideas,* 23, 1962, 77–90.

Swingewood, Alan. *Marx and Modern Social Theory.* London: Macmillan, 1975.

Tarde, Gabriel. *The laws of Imitation*, 2nd Ed. Gloucester, Mass.: Peter Smith [1895] 1962.

Tawney, R.H. *The Agrarian Problem in the Sixteenth Century,* New York: Harper & Row, 1967.

——. *Religion and the Rise of Capitalism.* Harmondsworth, England: Peguin, 1984.

Tenbruck, Fredrich. 'The Problem of Thematic Unity in the works of Max Weber,' *The British Journal of Sociology*, 31, 1980, 316–348.

Thompson, E.P. *The Making of the English Working Class.* Harmondsworth: Penguin, 1968.

——. 'Time, Work-Discipline, and Industrial Capitalism,' *Past and Present*, 38, 1967, 56–97.

Tosti, Gustavo. 'Suicide in the Light of Recent Studies,' *American Journal of Sociology*, Vol. 3, 1987, 464–478.

——. 'The Delusions of Durkheim's Sociological Objectivism,' *American Journal of Sociology,* Vol. 4, 1988, 171–7.

Toynbee, Arnold. *The Industrial Revolution.* Boston: Beacon Press, [1844] 1956.

Tribe, K. (ed.) *Reading Weber*. London: Routledge, 1989.

Troeltsch, Ernst. *The Social Teaching of the Christian Churches.* London: Allen & Unwin, 1956.

Tucker, R.T. *The Marx–Engels Reader* (2nd Ed.). New York, Norton.

Viner, Jacob. *Religious Thought and Economic Society.* Durham, North Carolina, Duke University Press, 1978.

——. 'Adam Smith and Laissez Faire,' in J.M. Clark and P.H. Douglas et. al., Adam Smith 1776–1926. New York: Augustus Kelly, 1966.

Ward, J.T. *The Factory Movement 1830–1855.* London: MacMillan, 1962.

Weber, Marianne. *Max Weber: A Biography.* New York: John Wiley & Sons, 1975.

Weidemann, Thomas. *Greek and Roman Slavery.* London: John Hopkins, 1981.

Whimster, S., and Lash, S. (eds). *Max Weber, Rationality and Modernity.* London: Allen & Unwin, 1987.

Willey, Thomas E. *Back to Kant: The Revival of Kantianism in German Social and Historical Thought, 1860–1914.* Detroit: Wayne State University Press, 1978.

Wood, Ellen Meiksins. *The Retreat From Class: A New 'True' Socialism.* London: Verso, 1998.

Zizek, Slavoj. *The Sublime Object of Ideology.* London: Verso, 1992.

——. *Mapping Ideology.* New York: Verso, 1994.

Index

DATE DUE
